FROM NEW PEOPLES TO NEW NATIONS

Aspects of Métis History and Identity from the Eighteenth to the Twenty-First Centuries

From New Peoples to New Nations is a broad historical account of the emergence of the Métis as distinct peoples in North America over the last three hundred years. Examining the cultural, economic, and political strategies through which communities define their boundaries, Gerhard J. Ens and Joe Sawchuk trace the invention and reinvention of Métis identity from the late eighteenth century to the present day. Their work updates, rethinks, and integrates the many disparate aspects of Métis historiography, providing the first comprehensive narrative of the Métis in more than fifty years.

Based on extensive archival materials, interviews, oral histories, ethnographic research, and first-hand working knowledge of Métis political organizations, *From New Peoples to New Nations* follows the history of Métis identity from the Battle of Seven Oaks to today's legal and political debates.

GERHARD J. ENS is a professor in the Department of History at the University of Alberta.

JOE SAWCHUK is a professor emeritus in the Department of Anthropology at Brandon University.

The cover illustration is taken from a lithograph of a painting by Arthur Fitzwilliam Tait, *Life on the Prairie – Buffalo Hunt* (1862), published by Currier and Ives. The image appears courtesy of the Yale Collection of Western Americana, Beinecke Rare Book and Manuscript Library. It is doubtful that Tait ever saw a Métis and he certainly never witnessed a plains buffalo hunt, given that he never travelled farther west than the Adirondacks. It is likely, however, that this scene and the figures in it are an embellishment and artistic rendering of images of the Red River Métis and their buffalo hunts that appeared in a series of articles by Manton Marble entitled "To Red River and Beyond," published in *Harper's New Monthly Magazine* between August 1860 and February 1861. This image thus has some relevance to the themes of perception and representation of Métis identities that are of some consequence to our analyses.

From New Peoples to New Nations

Aspects of Métis History and Identity from the Eighteenth to the Twenty-First Centuries

GERHARD J. ENS AND JOE SAWCHUK

UNIVERSITY OF TORONTO PRESS
Toronto Buffalo London

Toronto Buffalo London
www.utppublishing.com

ISBN 978-1-4426-4778-1 (cloth) ISBN 978-1-4426-2711-6 (paper)

Library and Archives Canada Cataloguing in Publication

Ens, Gerhard J. (Gerhard John), 1954–, author
From new peoples to new nations : aspects of Métis history and identity from the eighteenth to the twenty-first centuries / Gerhard J. Ens and Joe Sawchuk.

Includes bibliographical references and index.
ISBN 978-1-4426-4978-1 (bound) ISBN 978-1-4426-2711-6 (paperback)

1. Métis. 2. Métis – History. 3. Métis – Ethnic identity. 4. Métis – Social life and customs. 5. Métis – Government relations. 6. Métis – Legal status, laws, etc. 7. Métis – Social conditions. I. Sawchuk, Joe, 1942–, author. II. Title.

FC109.E66 2015 971.004'97 C2015-905561-X

This book has been published with the help of a grant from the Federation for the Humanities and Social Sciences, through the Awards to Scholarly Publications Program, using funds provided by the Social Sciences and Humanities Research Council of Canada.

University of Toronto Press acknowledges the financial assistance to its publishing program of the Canada Council for the Arts and the Ontario Arts Council, an agency of the Government of Ontario.

Canada Council for the Arts Conseil des Arts du Canada

Funded by the Government of Canada Financé par le gouvernement du Canada

Contents

Part III: Government Policy and the Invention of Métis Status in the Nineteenth Century

Part IV: Economic Marginalization and the Métis Political Response, 1896 to the 1960s

Part V: Politics, the Courts, and the Constitution: Reformulating Métis Identities since the 1960s

Figures and Tables

Figures

Tables

Acknowledgments

The research for this book was initiated by a research grant from the Social Sciences and Humanities Research Council of Canada, and we would like to acknowledge its assistance. This grant, as well as one from the Brandon University Research Committee, allowed us to hire researchers to conduct interviews across the country. In this light, we would like to thank Doug Racine, Robin Cavanaugh, and Allan Bork for the interviews they conducted on our behalf in Manitoba, Saskatchewan, Ontario, and the NWT. Joe Sawchuk would also like to take this opportunity to thank the many members, workers, and leaders of the Manitoba Métis Federation, the Association of Métis and Non-Status Indians of Saskatchewan, the Métis Association of Alberta, the Métis Nation of Alberta, the Federation of Métis Settlements, the Congress of Aboriginal Peoples, and the Native Council of Canada for the opportunity to work with, study, and learn from them over the years. While there are too many people to thank individually, he would like to single out Stan Daniels, Jim Sinclair, and Angus Spence as leaders who not only left an indelible impression on him, but made a lasting impression on Métis political organization and identity as we know it today. While these people, through either example or direct discourse, helped us to form our understanding of Métisness as we have discussed it in this book, they are in no way to be held responsible for any misunderstandings or distortions on our part. The interpretations and analyses are our own.

Our appreciation is extended to the anonymous reviewers for their insightful comments. As well, we would like to thank Len Husband, acquisitions editor in Canadian history at the University of Toronto Press, for his encouragement and support, and to Catherine Frost, copy editor at the University of Toronto Press, for her careful reading of the text and the numerous corrections she made to it.

The cover illustration is taken from a lithograph of a painting by Arthur Fitzwilliam Tait, *Life on the Prairie – Buffalo Hunt* (1862), published by Currier & Ives. The image appears courtesy of the Yale Collection of Western Americana, Beinecke Rare Book & Manuscript Library.

Last but not least we dedicate this book to the memory of John E. Foster, who was one of the initiators of the project, and whose work still inspires us.

Abbreviations

AANDC	Aboriginal Affairs and Northern Development Canada (formerly DIAND)
ACS	Aboriginal Council of Saskatchewan
AFN	Assembly of First Nations
AM	Archives of Manitoba
AMMSA	Aboriginal Multi-Media Society Association
AMNSIS	Association of Métis and Non-Status Indians of Saskatchewan
AO	Archives of Ontario
APS	Aboriginal Peoples of Saskatchewan
ASHSB	Archives de la Société historique de Saint-Boniface
ATC	Athabasca Tribal Council
CAP	Congress of Aboriginal Peoples
CASNP	Canadian Association in Support of Native Peoples (formerly IEA)
CCF	Co-operative Commonwealth Federation
CMS	Church Missionary Society
COPE	Committee for Original Peoples Entitlement
CPR	Canadian Pacific Railway
CYC	Company of Young Canadians
DIAND	Department of Indian Affairs and Northern Development (now AANDC)
DNR	Department of Natural Resources
FCA	Federal Court of Appeal
FMSA	Federation of Métis Settlement Associations

FSIN	Federation of Saskatchewan Indian Nations
GA	Glenbow Archives
GNWT	Government of the Northwest Territories
HBC	Hudson's Bay Company
IAA	Indian Association of Alberta
IBNWT	Indian Brotherhood of the Northwest Territories (now the Dene Nation)
I.D.	Improvement District
IEA	Indian-Eskimo Association (now CASNP)
ITK	Inuit Tapiriit Kanatami
LAC	Library and Archives Canada
MAA	Métis Association of Alberta (now MNA)
MANWT	Métis Association of the Northwest Territories (1972–91)
MMF	Manitoba Métis Federation
MNA	Métis Nation of Alberta (formerly MAA)
MNBC	Métis Nation British Columbia
MNC	Métis National Council
MNNWT	Metis Nation of the Northwest Territories (1991–2000, formerly MANWT)
MNO	Métis Nation of Ontario
MN-S	Métis Nation-Saskatchewan
NARA	National Archives and Records Administration (USA)
NCC	Native Council of Canada
NDP	New Democratic Party
NRTA	Natural Resources Transfer Agreement
NSMA	North Slave Métis Alliance
NWAC	Native Women's Association of Canada
NWC	North West Company
NWMP	North-West Mounted Police
NWTMN	Northwest Territory Métis Nation (formerly SSMC)
OIC	Order in Council
OTM	Outer Two Miles
PAA	Provincial Archives of Alberta
RCAP	Royal Commission on Aboriginal Peoples
SFMB	Saskatchewan Fish Marketing Board
SFMS	Saskatchewan Fur Marketing Service
SSMC	South Slave Métis Council (since 2002, NWTMN)
SCC	Supreme Court of Canada

FROM NEW PEOPLES TO NEW NATIONS

Aspects of Métis History and Identity from the Eighteenth to the Twenty-First Centuries

Introduction

On 8 January 2013, a federal court ruled that both Métis and non-status Indians could now be considered "Indians" under subsection 91(24) of the Constitution Act, 1867.[1] Although this ruling might have been expected to be welcomed by Métis spokespersons and their political organizations (it affirmed a legal responsibility of the federal government for Métis and non-status Indians, a recognition long pursued by leaders of both groups), it was met with consternation and anger by some Métis leaders and spokespersons.[2] At the heart of this dismay was the way the court had defined Métis, trivializing it in the eyes of many by reducing it to nothing more than a mixed ancestry that stressed the Indian part of a person's heritage.[3] No mention was made of a political, geographic, or cultural heritage that would serve to identify a person as a member of *la nation métisse*, the Métis Nation of the Northwest, or "Louis Riel's people." To the Métis, this apparent lack of concern regarding the core of their identity was merely another example of the resistance they have faced in their long struggle to be recognized as a separate and distinct Aboriginal people in Canadian society.

However, as disconcerting as *Daniels v. Canada* may have been for some, the issues it raised regarding Métis identity are hardly new. Who or what constitutes a Métis has been a hotly debated issue in Canada ever since the Constitution Act, 1982 recognized the Métis as one of Canada's Aboriginal peoples, but without defining exactly what the term "Métis" meant. As a result, it is currently found and used in all parts of Canada, certainly beyond the prairie provinces, and can refer to groups with little or no historical or cultural links to Red River. Métis identity, of course, also has a longer lineage stretching back to the early nineteenth century and encompassing numerous struggles for recognition and rights.

This book is an attempt to place these struggles in a historical and political context. It is also an attempt to update, rethink, and tie together three centuries of Métis history, providing both a thematic and a chronological account of a people's histories that are ongoing. It takes as its unifying theme the historical emergence of the Métis as distinct peoples in North America and their attempts to create and recreate enduring identities from the eighteenth to the twenty-first centuries. This concept of "ethnogenesis" has been used by historians and anthropologists as a tool for developing critical historical approaches to culture and identity as an ongoing process of conflict and struggle over a people's existence. Ethnogenesis is thus not merely a label for the historical emergence of culturally distinct people but a concept encompassing a people's cultural and political struggles to create enduring identities in general contexts of radical change and discontinuity. In this view, self and group identity built on ethnicity are constantly shifting as people, in this case the Métis, seek to establish a sense of life's meaning and to secure tenable positions within the wider society. Ethnogenesis involves individuals and groups creating symbols, language, and social constructs with which to interpret and shape their environment. In our view, ethnicity is culturally constructed over historical time: ethnic groups in modern settings are constantly recreating themselves and ethnicity is continuously reinvented in response to changing realities within both the group and the larger society. This concept thus allows for the appearance, metamorphosis, disappearance, and reappearance of ethnicities.

This was no simple or straightforward process. People of mixed Indian and European ancestry could adopt very different identities. Some were raised as Indians and never knew another identity; others were raised as French Canadians or Acadians and did not consider themselves Métis. Thus, racial or cultural "mixedness" is, by itself, no guarantee of a group or an individual becoming Métis. As well, cultural elements expressed by a people may appear or disappear with little consequence for a people's distinctiveness. Even more confusing, some cultural practices considered Métis can be mirrored in the lives of others who are viewed as separate entities. As well, each of two geographically separated groups of mixed Indian and white ancestry who share few cultural traits can see themselves as Métis. Thus a focus on cultural elements without reference to *ethnos* tends to produce seemingly endless cultural inventories that are not particularly useful.

Our approach has been to put the focus on the ethnic group rather than on a way of life and shift the analysis to those cultural, economic, and political strategies that serve to define a people's boundaries. This approach takes seriously the importance of ascription (self-definition) in dealing with questions about who is and who is not a member of a particular people. Ethnicity, in this view, is a function of the beliefs of historical actors who are both "insiders" and "outsiders." Thus, among the factors responsible for the origins of the Métis are those associated with a time and place when a particular population saw itself as Métis and when outsiders shared this view. These factors underline the fact that it is impossible to describe the Métis in isolation; they can be studied only in contrast to and interaction with other groups. It is generally an act of political assertion that delineates the group. According to this framework it is quite possible for an ethnic group to spring up, to recede, and then to reformulate at a later date, all due to external political and economic pressures. Likewise, ethnic boundaries and the criteria by which members are included or excluded also can change, even though the name of the group remains constant. This is indeed the case with the Métis; the term "Métis" means something quite different today than it did 150 years ago, and the meaning is still changing. Indeed, no one definition is monolithic, and different concepts of Métis identity can coexist in different regions. Finally, not only does this approach allow a focus on group maintenance of cultural and political identities, but it also explains how and why individuals at different times in their life course could cross ethnic boundaries.

In carrying out our analyses we shift back and forth from outsider views of Métis ethnicity to those of self-identification (insider views) because of our belief that Métis ethnicity and identity are a dialogic process between the two. Indeed, our book begins with a chapter on the changing ethnological and historical constructions of hybridity, as they make explicit the colonial context and racial terminology within which Métis peoples emerged at particular times and in particular places. Further, we argue not only that outsider views conditioned government policy towards the Métis and the creation of Métis statuses and categories, but that these views conditioned the ways in which the Métis viewed themselves in relation to other groups. Having outlined the various historical constructions of hybridity and the economic patterns of ethnogenesis in various parts of North America, we then consider how Métis self-perceptions coalesced around various ideas of Métis nationhood between 1816 and 1885. After establishing these parameters of group coalescence, we next look at how changing government policy in the last third of the nineteenth century created "Métis" as a status category and the repercussions of this recognition on Aboriginal identity politics. Then, moving into the twentieth century, we examine how the economic marginalization of the Métis led to the rebirth of Métis political organizations in Canada. Finally, we discuss the ways the courts and constitutional change since the 1980s have again affected the ground rules of Métis ethnicity and identity.

From our title it should also be obvious that our discussion of Métis history intersects with a more general debate about the relationship between ethnicity and nation/nationality. As such, our terminology and position require some explanation. By "new peoples" we are simply referring to various ethnic communities who through time came to view themselves as Métis. According to Anthony Smith and John Hutchinson "ethnic communities" are "named human populations with myths of common ancestry, shared historical memories, one or more elements of shared culture, a link with a homeland, and a measure of solidarity, at least among elites."[4] By this standard the fur trade in North America spawned numerous "new peoples," who later came to see themselves as Métis. The transition from Métis as "ethnic community" to Métis as "nation," however, is a much rarer phenomenon. If one takes the definition of "nation" as "a named human population occupying a historic territory or homeland and sharing common myths and memories; a mass, public culture; a single economy; and common rights and duties for all members,"[5] then "Métis as Nation" is much more problematic. This "problem," however, did not stop observers from labelling the Métis as a "new nation" in the early nineteenth century, or the Métis from appropriating the term from the late nineteenth century onward (most notably from the 1980s).

Our analyses of these phenomena differ from almost all other works of Métis historiography. From the early twentieth century until the very recent past, most historians have adopted a view of Métis ethnicity and nationality that can best be described as "primordialist" – that is, the view that these formations (ethnicity and nation) are determined by prior "givens" such as kinship, descent, language, religion, race, and custom and are "largely immune to 'rational' interest and political calculation."[6] This book is, to a significant degree, a debate with this kind of Métis primordialism, which we feel is unable to account for historical changes in Métis ethnicity and the variability of religious, linguistic, and cultural attributes within Métis communities. In this debate we take an "instrumentalist" and "social constructionist" position.

By "instrumentalist" we mean an approach that sees ethnicity and the rise of nationalism as situational and strategic: a product of politics and the manipulation of resources by individuals and elites.[7] By "social constructionist" we mean an approach that sees the Métis Nation as a social construct rather than as something natural or primordial. It is the view that all nations are forged by elites "who design symbols, mythologies, rituals, and histories specifically to meet modern mass needs."[8] This "invention of tradition" approach also takes the view that nations are narrated and cultural artefacts or texts and are to be deconstructed or decoded.

In taking these interpretive positions we are well aware of their potential pitfalls. Inherent in the instrumentalist approach is a tendency to overemphasize the material base of interests and the role of elites in manipulating mass behaviour. While we hold that the role of material interests and elites is crucial, even paramount, to Métis ethnicity and nationalism, we also acknowledge the cultural dimensions of these formulations. In particular we pay attention to, and take seriously, the symbolic aspects of ethnicity and nationalism such as religion, shared memories and myths, rituals, and traditions in instilling a sense of belonging and permanence in Métis communities.[9] However, we have not attempted to provide any detailed analysis of the kinship bases of Métis identity and communities. That approach would have been well beyond the scope of this already large book and would have worked at cross-purposes to our instrumentalist focus.[10]

As well, we are aware that the use of the term "invented traditions" can easily be interpreted as "fabrication" or "falsehood." Though we try to deconstruct these traditions to emphasize how they were not "natural" formulations, we stand with Benedict Anderson in seeing these inventions as an "imagining" and a "creation," which undergird all nations.[11] Lastly, we acknowledge that Métis elites and individuals have not been entirely free agents in determining the shape of their traditions and identities. Métis ethnogenesis and the articulation of a national tradition took place within the context of colonialism. British, American, and Canadian racial and status categories constrained, and indeed shaped, the choices the Métis had in defining their identities.[12]

It is no accident that we open this Introduction with reference to the *Daniels v. Canada* court case. The writing of Métis history has always paralleled the economic and political fortunes of the Métis themselves. The first scholarly histories of the Métis peoples were researched and published in the 1930s and 1940s at a time when Métis communities were in crisis and at a time when many social scientists and historians believed that these peoples would disappear.[13] The political resurgence of the Métis after the 1960s had its historiographical counterpart as scholars began investigating past Métis political leaders in greater detail[14] and anthropologists began paying more attention to the role of contemporary political organizations in maintaining and reconstituting Métis ethnicity.[15] The political and legal struggles of the Métis for both recognition and rights produced a number of detailed studies of Métis land rights.[16] This political and cultural renaissance also saw the publication of detailed monographs of regional Métis populations.[17] These activities paralleled the regional patterning of Métis identities and regional political organizations.

However, since the recognition of the Métis as an Aboriginal people in the repatriated Canadian Constitution in 1982 and the formation of the National Métis Council, no synthetic history of the Métis peoples has been attempted. The last general histories were those published by Marcel Giraud[18] and Joseph Kinsey Howard[19] in the 1940s and 1950s, which, though still valuable today, are rife with ethnocentric judgments and assumptions that the days of the Métis People were in the past. Neither of these two works attempted any sustained account of Métis history in the twentieth century.

Given this is a co-authored book, some explanation of the background of the authors and authorship is in order. The idea for this book had its origin almost fifteen years ago when John Foster (historian), Gerhard Ens (historian), and Joe Sawchuk (anthropologist) decided to try to write a general history of the Métis peoples of North America. Shortly after the inception of the project, however, John Foster, the main guiding force, died. Much of the momentum for the project slowed and, when the remaining co-authors came back to the project, it was decided to narrow its scope. While we held on to the idea of examining Métis history over three centuries, we abandoned the idea of providing a comprehensive and complete history. Instead we focused on the thematic issues of origins, changing identities, politics, and the growth of the "Nation" concept. We make no apologies for our narrowed emphases, but we acknowledge that numerous communities and groups have been left out. This is perhaps most apparent in the section related to the history of Métis developments since the 1960s, as we provide no treatment of the Métis of British Columbia and Quebec. We do believe, however, that the dynamics we analyse and discuss in the other chapters has a general relevance to all parts of the northern United States and all parts of Canada.

The book as it now exists is informed by the disciplines of both history and anthropology. It is based on extensive archival research and interviews of Métis politicians and leaders, and although the two authors come from different disciplinary backgrounds, both participated in the archival research and fieldwork. In the process of this research we have come to very similar views about the nature of Métis history and politics and conceptualized the monograph as a unified whole. However, given our different disciplinary contexts and different areas of expertise (history in the eighteenth and nineteenth centuries versus anthropology and twentieth-century Métis politics), no attempt has been made to homogenize our writing styles or approaches. Most of the first ten chapters were written by Gerhard Ens and most of chapters eleven through eighteen were written by Joe Sawchuk. Despite the stylistic and thematic differences found in these sections, both authors participated in the research process of the entire book and endorse all the findings.

Finally, the authors would like to alert the reader to the fact that historically there was a good deal of imprecision and confusion associated with the terms "Métis" and "half-breed."[20] At various times and places these terms have referred to racial categories (the offspring of miscegenation), at others as a quasi-legal status (who was entitled to Métis scrip?), and, most important, to denote cultural or ethnic communities. The term "Métis," originally a French word (*métis*) meaning "mixed," is used by scholars to designate individuals and communities who identify their antecedents with historical communities connected to the fur trade and refers to people who possess a distinctive sociocultural heritage and sense of self-identification. These peoples or communities were distinct from indigenous Indian bands and from the European world of the trading posts. Some of these communities used "Métis" to identify themselves, though other terms were used, including "Michif," "bois brûlé," "chicot," "half-breed," "country-born," and "mixed-blood," among others.[21]

PART ONE

Hybridity and Patterns of Ethnogenesis

1 Race and Nation: Changing Ethnological and Historical Constructions of Hybridity

Métis ethnogenesis cannot easily be disentangled from the views held of them by governments, missionaries, ethnologists, and historians of the day. As such, this chapter attempts to outline some of the changing views that formed the backdrop against which the Métis struggled to define themselves over the last two centuries. The ethnological categories and historical constructions of hybridity that we deal with in this chapter were the contexts within which Métis ethnogenesis occurred. That is, not only did outsider views condition government policy towards the Métis and the creation of Métis categories or statuses, but these views affected the ways in which the Métis viewed themselves in relation to other groups. These views are outlined at the outset because they affected the central dynamic around which our analysis revolves: the interplay and conflict of those discourses that constructed the Métis in racial terms and those that constructed them in national terms.

These themes of race versus nation were present from the early nineteenth century and continue into the twenty-first century; however, another argument of this chapter is that by the 1930s historical writing about the Métis (at least in Canada) witnessed a shift from racial to ethno-national conceptions of identity. This is not to say that there was any linear progression from racialized to national views, or that race stopped being a factor in outsider perceptions of the Métis,[1] but only to say that the historiography of the Métis in Canada by the 1930s had begun to emphasize national conceptions of Métis identity, and that this shift opened the way to re-imagine Métis history.

From the eighteenth century onwards various outsiders noticed and commented on individuals of mixed ancestry (Indian and European) whom they considered distinct from Indian bands and colonial populations. Although fur trade sources in different historical periods refer to "mixed-blood" households who assimilated into Indian or European communities, it is also true that many other individuals and households remained distinct from both Indian bands and the white community. While individuals could and did cross ethnic boundaries during their lives, the Métis communities themselves sustained distinct boundaries and were recognized as such by fur traders. As early as 1768 Hudson's Bay Company employees were noting attitudinal differences between the "half-caste" children around their posts and the surrounding Indian Bands. Andrew Graham, writing in 1768, noted that the children of Englishmen on Hudson Bay regarded themselves as "above the true born Indians."[2] By the nineteenth century these "mixed-blood" offspring had become so numerous that their fur trade fathers worried about their future, since they neither fit in with Indian society nor could be brought back to Britain. As a consequence, ninety Hudson's Bay Company servants petitioned Lord Bathurst, the colonial secretary, to found a colony for them and their children.[3]

In the Great Lakes and the Missouri basin economic and kinship ties in the French fur trade also produced distinctive bicultural and biracial peoples groups who by the mid-eighteenth century acted as brokers or cultural and occupational intermediaries between tribal nations and the French fur traders. These proto-Métis populations were neither adjunct members of tribal villages nor agents of European civilization. From the Great Lakes to St Louis on the Mississippi River, French, British, and Spanish fur traders recognized these in-between peoples as distinct.[4]

By the early nineteenth century both the British and the Americans recognized the Métis as a new ethnological phenomenon, using terms such as "half-breed," "métifs," and "bois-brulés" to refer to these children of the fur trade. This era also corresponded with the early efforts by members of the group to assert their social and political rights in the Red River region in the period 1811–1818, when Lord Selkirk was trying to establish a colony there. Their assertion of political rights arose first in relation to the fur trade wars between the North West Company (NWC) and the Hudson's Bay Company (HBC) following the establishment of the Red River Settlement in 1811. The founding of this colony by Lord Selkirk was seen by the North West Company as a direct threat to their trade and territorial interests. Having failed to induce the Indians to destroy Selkirk's budding settlement, the partners of the North West Company next turned to the Plains Métis. Closely tied to the various bourgeois of the North West Company by consanguinity and employment, the Métis were encouraged to oppose the Hudson's Bay Company's efforts to found a colony in Assiniboia and to resist any attempts to impose government over them.

In 1815 the leaders of the Plains Métis – Cuthbert Grant, William Shaw, Bostonais Pangman, and Bonhomme Montour (all in the employ of the NWC)[5] – presented the leaders of the Selkirk Colony with an ultimatum: the settlers must abandon the colony or face annihilation. Peter Fidler's[6] peace proposal and the Métis response make it clear that the HBC regarded the Métis as distinct from both European and Indian. As well, these documents show that the Plains Métis identified themselves with a unique lifestyle and with values emphasizing the freedom to claim the benefits and privileges of their maternal or paternal heritage, whichever they should choose.

This escalating conflict between the Hudson's Bay Company, the North West Company, and the Plains Métis allied to the North West Company, eventually led to a climactic battle at Seven Oaks, in the Red River Settlement, in which Cuthbert Grant and his Métis followers defeated a contingent of Red River settlers and HBC men led by Robert Semple, the governor of the colony. In this battle of 19 June 1816 Semple and twenty of his men were killed, and the colony was abandoned. This extreme violence was considered by both Canadian and colonial officials in England as an affront to British control over the region, and a commission of inquiry was convened to determine the causes of the conflict and to apportion blame.[7] The records of this investigation provide a useful glimpse at how both fur trade companies and British colonial officials regarded the Métis at a period when their collective socio-political consciousness was only beginning to emerge. Three different views of the Métis can be seen in the testimony and correspondence of this investigation. The officers of the Hudson's Bay Company, anxious to have all the blame for the twenty-one deaths placed on the heads of the partners of the North West Company, described the Métis as merely the offspring of North West Company officers who had been duped into doing the dirty work of the company. The partners of the North West Company, on the other hand, anxious to deflect blame from themselves and their immediate employees, portrayed the Métis as an independent band of Indians protecting their ancestral lands and rights. Most commentators and witnesses, however, portrayed the Métis as a group distinct from both trading companies and Indians. Most witnesses identified this group as "bois-brulés," "métifs," or "half-breeds," who made their livelihoods as buffalo hunters and provisioners, clerks, interpreters, and boatmen.[8]

The officers of the Hudson's Bay Company, while they recognized the Métis as a new social grouping, did not accord them any distinct political independence. Choosing to blame all the troubles and violence on the machinations of the North West Company, they saw the Métis merely as the "mixed-blood" children of NWC servants who had been manipulated by that company's officers to do their dirty work.[9] As already mentioned, the officers of the North West Company, wishing to deflect blame from themselves for the killing of Semple and his men, put forth the argument that the Métis represented a new and independent tribe of Indians over whom the North West Company had little control.[10] W.B. Coltman, the officer who headed the inquiry, noted that the Métis had been tutored by NWC officers to call themselves a nation of Indians.

The correspondence and reports of the British colonial officials related to the Red River problems explicitly acknowledge the Métis as a separate social and political entity in the west, who claimed some ancestral rights to western lands. In the immediate aftermath of the Battle of Seven Oaks, Lieutenant General Sir John C. Sherbrooke noted that the Métis represented an independent group of some consequence who were willing to appeal to the American government for their independence.[11] Coltman, the officer in charge of the investigation, noted that this had been the first occasion when the "half-breeds" had taken any part in the disputes of the Indian country and had done so, not only at the urging of the North West Company but also out of apprehension that the Hudson's Bay Company and the colony were infringing on their rights to hunt the buffalo freely.

This recognition by fur traders, and to a lesser extent by colonial officials, that the Métis were a distinct group provided the ethnological space to create a new identity. Yet if there was some recognition that the Métis constituted a separate ethnological category, this did not necessarily translate into separate legal or status rights. A people claiming the rights of both Indians and Europeans was hard for a European to conceptualize.[12] While this ambiguity never completely disappeared from the minds of European fur traders, nevertheless by the 1830s they had accepted the Métis as a separate ethnic grouping distinct from the Indians. What remained in dispute were the rights of the Métis in relation to the Hudson's Bay Company's monopoly of trade. The HBC regarded the Métis as British subjects and thus precluded from trading in competition with them. The Métis, while seeing themselves as distinct from the Indians, argued that their Native-born status and their Native ancestry gave them special rights above other British subjects.[13] This debate was carried to England in 1847, when A.K. Isbister[14] presented a petition from the Métis of Red River to the British Colonial Office to grant them relief from the strictures of the HBC monopoly and its tyrannical rule.[15] The petitioners, who described themselves as loyal British subjects objected to the harsh administration of the HBC, which kept the "Natives" in a state of dependency and misery, inhibited trade, and ignored the claims of the Indians and Métis as the original owners of the soil. In making this case to the Colonial Office, Isbister conflated both the identity and the rights of the Métis and Indians to which the Hudson's Bay Company immediately objected, noting that the Indians and Métis were quite distinct, with different rights and privileges. J.H. Pelly, for the HBC, noted that the fact that the Métis were born in the country entitled them to call themselves Native, but it neither conveyed to them any privileges belonging, or supposed to belong, to the Aboriginal inhabitants, nor divested them of the character of British subjects. As such, the Métis (unlike the Indians) were precluded by the HBC's charter from trafficking in furs.[16]

From the HBC's perspective the petition and memorial to the Colonial Office had been inspired by the illegal traders of the Red River Colony who employed the Métis of the settlement and who were trying to attack the monopoly of the HBC through the instrumentality of Métis rights.[17] In responding to Pelly, Isbister acknowledged that there was a distinction between the Métis and Indians, but that this distinction could not divest the Métis of their Aboriginal rights. At this time the Colonial Office did not directly comment on the distinction between Métis and Indians, but after some investigation Earl Grey, the Secretary of State for the Colonies, ruled that the petition and memorial were without foundation and no further action would be taken.[18] An examination of the records of the Council of Assiniboia and of the General Quarterly Court of Assiniboia bears out the argument that the Métis and Indians were regarded as separate and distinct in law; that is, the Hudson's Bay Company and the Council of Assiniboia regarded the Métis of the Red River Settlement not as Indians but as British subjects. Alexander Christie, the governor of Assiniboia, noted in 1845 that "as British subjects, the halfbreeds have clearly the same rights in Scotland or in England as any person born in Great Britain."[19]

The Views of Travellers, Explorers, and Ethnologists

Travellers and explorers in the western interior provide another perspective on the ways in which the Métis were viewed or conceptualized.

While these published accounts are a literary genre that often reflected more the reading tastes of the Canadian, American, and European public than an accurate portrayal of the regions and peoples encountered on their travels,[20] nevertheless, at the very least they provide a glimpse of the popular conception of the Métis at different times in the nineteenth century. Hybridity, or the mixing of species or races, was a topic of immense interest in the nineteenth century as the emerging disciplines of ethnology, archaeology, and anthropology were trying to come to terms with the origins and progress of the human species. Travellers' accounts of the Métis were therefore filled with observations and speculation regarding which of the traits of the Métis could be traced to Europeans and which to Indians. Concerned about whether the mixing of European and Indian races represented progress or degeneration of man, these accounts are filled with racial imagery; they represent an amateur attempt to discern whether the Métis represented a retreat to "savagism" or a step in the evolution of the Indian race towards "civilization." Canadian and British observers, as well, attributed different behavioural traits to the English as opposed to the French Métis.[21]

Ross Cox, a fur trader who conducted general exploration of the Columbia River and travelled across much of the western interior in the period 1811–17,[22] provided an early description of the western Métis in a book published in 1831.[23] Cox's observations occurred largely within the context of North West Company, for whom many of the Métis worked, and consequently his description emphasizes the European or "civilized" aspects of their character. The "half-breeds," which he considered a race, were by this time numerous throughout the Indian country, particularly on the east side of the Rocky Mountains.[24]

William H. Keating, an American,[25] encountered the Métis a few years after Cox's stay in the west (1823) at their settlement at Pembina. His impressions of this independent band of Plains Métis buffalo hunters are far more negative than Cox's and emphasize their propensity to "savagery." In the account of his travels published in 1824[26] he noted that most of the residents at Pembina, consisting of 350 souls, were "half-breeds" who were free of the Hudson's Bay Company. "These men receive here the name of *Gens libre* or Freemen, to distinguish them from the servants of the Hudson's Bay Company, who are called *Engagés*. Those that are partly of Indian extraction, are nicked-named Bois brulé, (Burnt wood,) from their dark complexion."[27] For Keating these "half-breeds" represented a racial category between Indian and white, but this racial mixture was viewed as an unfavourable development, as they had acquired mainly the vices of each "stock." Though superior to Indians, on the scale of civilization they rated very low and reflected the negative stereotyping of mixed races that was becoming predominant in the United States at this time.[28]

The views of Canadian and British explorers were somewhat more positive. By the 1860s two separate scientific explorations produced the most detailed descriptions of the land and peoples of western Canada.[29] Both Henry Yule Hind, one of the leaders of a Canadian expedition, and John Palliser, the leader of the British expedition, noted the existence and separate identity of the western Métis and made attempts to describe these people. Hind, a professor at the University of Toronto, was much interested in the effects of racial mixing and saw it as a salutary effect, though he noted that with the passage of time the Métis had a tendency to revert to their Native roots.

His observations on this last issue were indicative more of continuing scientific discussion than of his own observations. In the 1860s there was an important ongoing debate among ethnologists between degenerationists and amalgamationists.[30] Amalgamationists claimed that all humans could interbreed in unlimited ways and that the mixing of peoples produced a new mixed race, with merged but distinct physical and moral characteristics. The opposite view, held by degenerationists, argued that miscegenation produced a mongrel group that corrupted both of the original groups – degenerate and degraded, threatening to subvert the vigour and virtue of the pure races with which they came into contact.[31] Within this debate Hind was somewhere in the middle, admitting the amalgamation of different peoples, but holding that any "mixed breeds" either die out quickly or revert to one or another of the permanent parent types. In this he very closely mirrored the thinking of A.P. Reid of the Halifax Medical College, who had spent two years observing the Red River Métis in 1860–61. Reid classified the Métis or "Halfbreeds" by distance from their European ancestors. At the top of the pyramid were those Métis who had Euro-Canadian fathers and Indian or Métis mothers. At the bottom were those who were at least once removed from European forebears.[32] Hind's views were very close to this perspective, seeing the Métis as a new ethnological element distinct from the Indian, but one that was in danger of subsiding to the condition of the Indian without the influx of European or Canadian "blood."[33]

There was a certain circularity in the respective views of travellers and ethnologists regarding the Métis. The writing of Canadian ethnologists, in many ways, reflected the writing of explorers and travellers, as they used these writings as evidence for their various theories regarding the origins of Indians and the status of "mixed-bloods" in the Canadian population. In turn, the observations of travellers, as we have seen, were much shaped by both popular and scientific attitudes towards Indians and Métis.[34] These views are important, however, in that they shaped the policy towards the Métis in both Canada and the United States.

The widespread intermarriage and mixing of Indian and European populations in North America was recognized at a very early date and became the subject of considerable debate within the scientific community in both the United States and British North America from the late eighteenth century onwards. This discussion was framed both by the policies of various governments and philanthropists seeking new approaches for "civilizing" the Indian and by the larger debate over the origins of man and the question of the racial origins of North American Indians. As Robert E. Bieder has noted, the debate over "mixed-blood" turned on changing whites' assumptions about the Indian and his future, and was "polarized over the issue of whether the mixed-blood was a new race, a 'mongrel' more Indian than White, or the hybrid offspring of two separate species."[35]

In general, the various views of Indians' origins were subsumed under two broad schools of thought: monogenism and polygenism. The monogenists saw mankind as one species derived from a single pair and argued that Indians had originally come from the Middle East or Asia. This theory produced a positive evaluation of the capabilities and potential of Indians for civilization. On the other side were polygenists, who maintained that each of the major human races had been created separately and differed radically not only in appearance but also intellectually and emotionally. This theory was used to oppose the emancipation of blacks and to provide a scientific gloss for the widespread conviction that Indians were incapable of adopting a European style of life.

From the American Revolution to the late 1820s the monogenists dominated the ethnological scene in North America and their views were shared by the government and the public. The optimistic belief in mankind's progressive nature was a product of the Enlightenment belief, which seemed to be confirmed by the success of the American Revolution. This belief led to the view that Indians could be incorporated into the New Order not on a "separate but equal" basis, but rather on the basis of the ideal of genetic unification – the genetic blending of races that would result in a unified American people.

While miscegenation never became official government policy in the United States, Thomas Jefferson advocated it in regard to the Indians.[36] It was a view that mirrored early French practice in North America.[37]

To government officials, missionaries, and philanthropists the physical characteristics resulting from such unions were less important than the effect of intermarriage on "civilizing" the Indian. Observers noted that wherever there were "half-breeds" there was a faction within Indian communities that espoused the interests of civilization and Christianity. Thus, education, Christianization, and miscegenation became the means by which philanthropists in the early nineteenth century sought a solution to the problem of how best to "civilize" Indians and incorporate them into American society.[38]

By the late 1820s, however, American attitudes towards Indians and the "mixed-bloods" shifted from a positive belief in their capabilities and potential for civilization to one of reservation and finally to discouragement over their lack of progress. Mixed marriages or unions acceptable in Sault Ste Marie and Mackinac in the 1820s were by the 1830s no longer viewed favourably, and, as more "genteel" society moved west into frontier areas, such alliances were no longer economically advantageous and were socially condemned. These changing attitudes mirrored the ascendancy of the polygenists' assumptions, at least in the United States, and ethnologists increasingly demonstrated a growing preoccupation with questions of race. By the 1850s the principle tenets of polygenism, and the concomitant rejection of the unity of the human species, had captured the allegiance of almost all American anthropologists and naturalists.[39] These views were then popularized by the publication of *Types of Mankind* by Josiah Nott and George Glidden[40] in 1854, which became something of a best-seller. While it might be assumed that the slavery question was driving this debate in the United States, William Stanton has shown that most scientists adopted polygenist views not so much because of their sympathy with southern institutions, but out of their anti-clericalism, anti-biblicism, and "the characteristic American situation of three races in uneasy conjunction." The doctrine of diverse origins, or polygenism, was soothing to the cultural nationalism of the times.[41]

The turn to polygenism in scientific circles affected government policy towards Indians. The decline of Indian populations and Indian intransigence in the face of change, despite the efforts of missionaries to "civilize" them, convinced many members of the public, the government, and the scientific community of the inferiority of the Indian race – an inferiority now deemed innate rather than due to the lack of education. This view was reflected in the United States by the government policy to remove Indians to west of the Mississippi.[42]

The new attitude had ominous implications for the public perception of the Métis. If Indians and European were separate species, the offspring of the union of the two were hybrids and were "faulty stock" that resulted from a violation of nature's laws. Métissage, in this view, became not a part of the progress of man, but a degeneracy that portended the demise of civilization. In the minds of some, métissage entailed a "pollution" of America, the end result of which would be the death of Anglo-Saxon civilization.[43] By mid-nineteenth century the views of the polygenists were ascendant in the United States, and "mixed-bloods" were no longer looked to as the agents of civilization. Robert Bieder has argued that the prevailing belief among most Americans by the 1850s was: "If a person possessed some Indian blood, he was an Indian. Blood not only gave a person his identity but served to shape the public's expectations of his destiny ... Not only were mixed-bloods considered 'faulty stock,' but they were believed to prefer Indian life and to have cast their lot with the Indian. Like the Indian, the mixed-blood was viewed as headed for extinction."[44]

However, the polygenist argument did not convince everyone, and in the United States its success was due, in part, to the fact that it closely reflected the fears of the time. Its ascendancy over monogenism did not derive from good evidence; indeed, very little data supported it.[45] Monogenists continued to believe that "mixed-bloods" were not only catalysts for the civilization of the Indians, but also offered proof, through their fertility, that Indians and Euro-Americans were one species. There is ample evidence that in Canada monogenism held sway and was crucial to the formation of Indian policy in British North America. The policy of Indian removal, a policy in force in the United States and advocated in Canada by Francis Bond Head in 1836, was in fact rejected by both missionaries and British colonial administrators.

The most influential proponent of monogenism and the salutary effects of métissage in Canada in the period from the 1850s through the 1860s was Daniel Wilson.[46] Prior to his arrival in Canada in 1853, Wilson's research in Scotland had already aroused his interest in a variety of anthropological issues, but his residence in Canada stimulated his interest in North American archaeology. Wilson came to believe that a study of contemporary changes in the New World would result in a more general understanding of the nature of cultural contact, racial mixing, and adaptation to the environment. The publication of *Prehistoric Man: Researches into the Origin of Civilization in the Old and the New World* in 1862 represented the culmination of not only his past European training, but eight years of research in Canada.[47]

His views on métissage were much coloured by what he observed in and around Native communities and reserves in Canada. The "extinction" of the Indian in North America was for him inextricably tied to the absorption of Indian races into the Anglo-American population by way of intermarriage and racial mixing – a process he regarded as "progress."[48] Wilson's approach to these subjects, as Bruce Trigger has pointed out, was grounded in the philosophy of the French Enlightenment, which had become deeply rooted in Scotland in the eighteenth century, and he held that cultural progress typified human history. It was accepted that all groups of human beings shared a common origin, had a similar nature, and were equally capable of benefiting from intellectual progress. Human groups in different parts of the world developed along generally similar lines independently of one another, although it was recognized that knowledge could also spread from more developed nations to their less advanced neighbours. Progress might be retarded by unfavourable environmental settings. The main force bringing about cultural evolution was believed to be rational thought. This not only enabled human beings to control nature, but also perfected human nature by eliminating ignorance, superstitions, and antisocial violence.[49]

In reaction to the growing polygenist trend among American ethnologists, which held that Indians were incapable of adopting a European way of life, Wilson began researching and writing on the subject of prehistoric man and the results of racial mixing. In *Prehistoric Man*, shaped in large measure by his opposition to polygenism, he set out to refute the claim that the Amerindians represented a uniform and separately created species. He did this by demonstrating craniometrically that there was considerable variation both between and within American Native populations. In accordance with Enlightenment beliefs, Wilson maintained that human nature was God-given and could not be permanently altered by the influences of the natural environment or by changing levels of cultural development. He did believe, however, that human potential could be enhanced by cultivation or diminished by abuse. As well, he allowed that intellectual development and brain function could be influenced for better or for worse by factors such as climate, social class, diet, education, and state of health. This potential for human development was most completely realized in a civilized society. When peoples at radically different levels of development encounter one another, Wilson observed, the result was frequently the rapid degeneration and collapse of the less evolved society and the integration of its surviving members into the more advanced one. He believed that this process of contact and cultural and biological mixing was one of the most important ways of bringing about cultural progress.

Wilson viewed all human races as temporary and believed that new races came into existence as a result of interbreeding among existing ones. He looked forward to the creation of a new North American people, in whom the "blood" and cultural achievements of Natives and blacks, as well as Europeans, would be represented. Wilson also insisted on the normality, and probable superiority, of "half-breeds" such as the Métis of western Canada and maintained that interbreeding between Natives and Europeans had gone on in eastern North America to a much greater extent than was generally acknowledged. He reminded readers that, in the course of British history, progress had resulted from new peoples invading Britain and mingling with its previous inhabitants.[50]

These ideas, fully worked out and published by 1862, form the backdrop for Wilson's most detailed analysis of the Canadian Métis in his article "Hybridity and Absorption in Relation to the Red Indian Race" published in 1875.[51] For Wilson, the Métis were a transitory and intermediate race portending progress and the eventual absorption of the Indian races within the Anglo-Canadian nation. While the numbers of Indians were increasing in numbers by the 1860s, bespeaking any extinction of their race, Wilson argued that at the same time the "pure race" was being largely replaced by younger generations of "mixed blood," and that "at best the results point rather to such a process of absorption as appears to be the inevitable result wherever a race, alike inferior in numbers and in progressive energy, escapes extirpation at the hands of the intruders."[52] Wilson observed that "half-breeds" could be members of various tribes; a separate ethnological, ethnic, or racial category; or fully merged with the Anglo-Canadian population. The trend, however, was towards absorption. Those who were still affiliated with various tribal entities did so to share in the Indian funds granted by the government; otherwise they "would long since have merged in the common stock."[53] He noted, "But the condition of men and women of mixed blood, admitted to all the privileges of citizenship, and mingling in perfect equality with all other members of the community, is in striking contrast to that of the occupants of the Indian reserves, where they are settled, for the most part in isolated bands, in the midst of a progressive white population. Such a condition is manifestly an unfavourable one, and one, moreover, which cannot be regarded as other than transitional. They are confessedly dealt with as wards, in a state of pupilage."[54]

In the frontier areas, where the mingling of European and Indians races was the natural result of the shortage of European women, a distinct "half-breed" population arose and was maintained in this border land. Some of these offspring, Wilson argued, "cling to the fortunes of the mother's race, and are involved in its fate; but more adhere to those of the white father, share with him the vicissitudes of border life, and cast in their lot with the first nucleus of a settled community."[55]

The history of the Canadian northwest, Wilson argued, offered proof of this progression and the salutary result of métissage. Here intermarriage between fur traders and Indian women produced a Métis population greatly outnumbering the whites. This "race of Half-breeds" was divided into two classes according to their Scottish or French paternity, who had kept themselves distinct in manners, habits, and allegiance from both whites and Indians. He noted: "This rise of an independent Half-breed tribe is one of the most remarkable results of the great, though undesigned, ethnological experiment which has been in progress ever since the meeting of the diverse races of the Old and New World on the continent of America; and now that the peculiar circumstances which favoured this result have come to an end, it is important to note the most striking phases presented by it, before they are modified or effaced by the influx of European emigration."[56]

To glean evidence from this laboratory of racial mixing and human evolution, Wilson sent a questionnaire to Hudson's Bay Company officers, missionaries, and others in the country to determine the interactions between and dynamics of the Indian and Métis populations. Metissage, he noted, had produced a superior human specimen. The "half-breed" was a large and robust race superior in every respect to Indians both mentally and physically. The Métis were also healthier and physically more powerful than Europeans. Though they exhibited some Indian traits, they were nearer the European, and within the Red River Settlement were accepted with perfect equality by the European settlers.[57]

Within the larger "hybrid" population in the west, Wilson noted several categories. He acknowledged that racial "hybridity" did not preclude an Indian identity, but that the general trend was towards an intermediate identity that would eventually merge with the European population. Wilson not only clearly distinguished the Métis from the Indian, but argued that métissage was associated with the progress of mankind.[58] He noted that it could not but excite regret that any race with unmistakable aptitudes for civilization should utterly perish, but that the progress of colonization entailed expatriation, extermination, or the absorption of the races as an ethnical element of the young nation that was supplanting them. For Wilson, the Métis were a transitional race in every way superior to the Indians, not requiring the protection and tutelage required for the "civilization" of the Indians.

Canadian Indian Policy and the Métis

The general trend of Canadian Indian policy after the inauguration of the "civilization" policy in the 1830s was in keeping with contemporary ethnological thinking, adopting as it did the incorporation (absorption) of the Indian within the Canadian population. Daniel Wilson's ideas regarding métissage and the intermediary role that the Métis played in this absorption, fit in well with the policy of the day. As a rule Canadian legislators did not accord the Métis any separate legal status or recognition. While they used the term "half-breed," this was purely a biological distinction. Persons of "mixed-blood" could under certain circumstance be recognized as Indians or whites – "half-breeds" and "Métis" carried no separate legal or constitutional rights.

A new rationale for a coherent Indian policy and the maintenance of the Indian Department began to emerge by the late 1820s. The increase of missionary activity among the Indians and the rise of the evangelical movement in Britain put pressure on the British Colonial Office to treat its Native peoples better throughout the empire. With these new forces at work, the motive behind Indian policy in Canada shifted from military alliances to the more "humane" goal of "civilizing" the Native. This involved congregating Indians in villages and providing sufficient funds for their support, instruction in agriculture and husbandry, assistance in building houses, and instruction in the Christian faith. These objectives became official Indian policy in 1830, and were paralleled by the transfer of control of Indian policy to civilian control in Upper Canada.[59]

This new "civilization" policy was conceived to facilitate the full incorporation of Indians into Canadian society, and reserves were to be the instrument to achieve it – they were to be halfway houses on the route to civilization, as the ideal of full citizenship was not seen as immediately possible or desirable.[60] Within this conceptual and policy framework of incorporation and assimilation there was no room for a separate "Métis" category.

As settlement increased rapidly in the Canadas, however, Indian reserves were increasingly encroached upon by squatters, and resources such as timber and game were taken at will. Such intrusions threatened the integrity of the Indian reserves, which had been intended to insulate Indians as they adapted to Euro-Canadian society. This situation, along with the perception that Indians were not progressing along the path to "civilization" quickly enough, led to the appointment of numerous commissions of inquiry between 1828 and 1858.[61] These commissions (particularly the Bagot Commission of 1844[62] and the Pennefather Commission of 1858[63]) clarify to some extent the government's view and lack of recognition of the Métis as a separate legal entity. The commissioners also noted, however, that in those instances where the difference between Métis and Indians were clearly marked the Métis were not to be considered "Indians." Their views were eventually adopted in legislation intended to define "Indian."

One of the major policy questions that the Bagot Commission dealt with was the issue of annual presents to Indians. This was pressing concern to imperial authorities, as it entailed considerable expense, and there had been moves as early as the 1820s to curtail or end this practice. The government, however, felt constrained in acting precipitously on this matter, as the Indians held a special regard for the gifts. As John Leslie has noted, "in the 1840s presents were the only concrete affirmation of Indian Status."[64] Bagot recommended that presents be limited in the immediate future and eventually abolished. To limit them Bagot recommended that censuses be prepared of all resident Indians, that band lists be drawn up and maintained, and that only Indians on band lists would receive presents. In his proposal Bagot dealt with the question of "half-breeds" and their status:

> 4th That no half breeds, or descendants of half breeds where the difference is clearly marked, receive Presents unless they be adopted by the Tribe with which they are connected, and live, as Indians among them.
>
> This rule would apply particularly to the uncivilized Indians of Upper Canada among whom frequent intermarriages with the Canadians take place, and the line of distinction can be clearly drawn. It is according to the former practice at Drummond's Island, subsequently abandoned at Manitoulin, it is strongly recommended by the resident Superintendent

> at the latter place, by whom it was successfully carried out at the last distribution: it has been formerly acted upon in Lower Canada and its maintenance has been recommended by one of the oldest officers of the Indian Department in that part of the Province, Superintendent Hughes. Its principle also has been lately sanctioned by the Governor General who has directed that no Indian woman living, married, or otherwise, with a white man, shall receive Presents.[65]

Thus, "half-breeds" were to be regarded as Indians if adopted by a tribe and living as an Indian, but, where the difference was "clearly marked" and they were not a member of a "tribe," they had no separate status. With these considerations in mind, that part of Bagot's report that dealt with "past and present conditions" of the various Indian groups in Canada specified those tribes that had "mixed-blood" members.

Some of Bagot's recommendations were eventually adopted and legislation in 1850 marked the first time that "Indian" was defined in legislation to protect Indian lands. However, this legislation, passed in two separate bills (one for Upper Canada – Canada West and one for Lower Canada – Canada East), defined "Indian" only in the Lower Canadian bill.[66] It is probable that the difference in the two pieces of legislation arose because of the different circumstances in Lower Canada. In that province Native land and property were most threatened by individuals who had a plausible claim to "Indian" rights because the question of who was an "Indian" was not easily answered. By 1850, after several hundred years of interaction, the population of Lower Canada was, biologically speaking, largely of mixed European and Indian heritage. Under these circumstances people often claimed rights to reserve land and property, even though many members of the reserve communities might consider them outsiders. This often became an issue of internal conflict. The definition of "Indian" in this context was designed to protect Indian reserve lands. In defining "Indian" legislators directly addressed the issue of "half-breed" as Indian. Section 5 of the Lower Canadian legislation stated that all "half-breeds" who lived with an Indian band were accepted as members and were considered Indians.[67]

Protests from some Indian bands led to amendment of the act in 1851 and it was made somewhat more restrictive in its wording, but the general provisions relating to "half-breed" eligibility remained.[68] This situation would not change until 1869, when "An Act for the gradual enfranchisement of Indians, the better management of Indian Affairs, and to extend the provisions of the Act 31st Victoria, Chapter 42"[69] amended the definition of "Indian" so that "any Indian woman marrying any other than an Indian, shall cease to be an Indian within the meaning of this Act, nor shall the children issue of such marriage be considered as Indians within the meaning of this Act."[70] As well, the act prescribed that in the division of annuity monies or rents no person of less than one-fourth Indian blood should receive a share if the chief or chiefs of the band testified to this fact by certificate and it was sanctioned by the superintendent general.[71] This blood quantum definition, however, does not appear in subsequent statutory definitions of Indians.

In Upper Canada there was no statutory definition of "Indian" until 1868, but there is some evidence that, at least initially, a similar practice prevailed. In negotiating the treaties on Lakes Superior and Huron in 1850, W.B. Robinson allowed numerous "half-breeds" into treaty as long as they were accepted as tribal members.[72] Indian demands that "half-breeds" receive some special treatment, however, were rejected out of hand by Robinson: "I was then ready to receive their signatures; the two chiefs, Shinguacouse and Nebennigoeing, repeated their demand of ten dollars a head by way of annuity, and also insisted that I should insert in the treaty a condition securing to some sixty half-breeds a free grant of one hundred acres of land each. I told them they already had my answer as to a larger annuity, and that I had no power to give them free grants of land."[73] By 1858, however, this practice appears to have changed somewhat in the province. Special Commissioner Pennefather in his report on Indian Affairs in Canada noted: "The word 'Indian' in Western Canada [Canada West], is held, more perhaps from usage than from any legal authority, to comprise not only all persons of pure Indian blood, but also those of mixed race, who are recognized members of a tribe or band resident in Canada, and who claim Indian descent on the father's side. An Indian woman marrying a white loses her rights as a member of the tribe and her children have no claim on the lands or moneys belonging to their mother's nation."[74] By this interpretation only "half-breeds" who claimed Indian descent on the father's side were to have any claims on Indian land and moneys, and in his detailed descriptions of the various bands in the province, particularly those who had signed the Huron-Superior Treaties of 1850, Pennefather noted those band members who could claim Indian ancestry only on the mother's side.

From the foregoing it should be clear that, while the colonial government of Canada did admit persons of mixed ancestry into treaty and defined them as "Indian," they did so only when these "half-breeds" lived with the Indians and were considered members of the tribe or band. Those Métis who assumed an identity distinct from Indian or Euro-Canadian and who lived separately from Indian bands were considered ordinary citizens with no special privileges.

American Indian Policy and the Métis

American policy with respect to "half-breeds" was as constitutionally restrictive as the Canadian approach, but in some respects the American government was more generous in providing land and cash to the Métis through the treaty process. Like the British and Canadians, the Americans had problems with intermediate racial categories and ambiguity and had trouble fitting the Métis into a racial framework.[75] As was true in Canada, the United States government gave no official distinct status to Métis individuals or groups, and the Métis were never made official parties to any Indian treaties. For example, in 1851 when the United States negotiated a treaty with the Pembina Ojibwa (Chippewa), the Métis claimed that they should be dealt with as well. The Métis were not signatories to the treaty, however, as the government negotiator, Alexander Ramsey, did not believe he should treat with people whom he regarded as "our *quasi* citizens."[76]

Yet the Métis did become important in the treaty process in the United States, as they tended to reside close to Indian communities and at treaty time were usually present in fairly large numbers. Their attendance and influence on tribal leaders at the treaty negotiations complicated the process. As a consequence, Métis individuals were often included in these final agreements from 1817 onwards. Tribal leaders argued strenuously to obtain concessions for the Métis, who were often close relatives. For government negotiators it was seen as part of the game to get treaties signed.[77] As in Canada, many of these treaties allowed those "half-breeds" who elected to reside among their tribal kin the same rights and privileges of "full-bloods." However, many Métis rejected a tribal identity and assignment to a tribe, and the government agreed, at the insistence of tribal leaders, to insert various clauses to include a separate land grant (tracts), scrip, or cash payments to these non-tribal "half-breeds."[78] While not official parties to these treaties, they were granted some concessions. One such clause in the Ponca Treaty of 1858 read:

> The Poncas being desirous of making provision for their half-breed relatives, it is agreed that those who prefer and elect to reside among them shall be permitted to do so, and be entitled to enjoy all the rights and privileges of

> members of the tribe; but those who have chosen and left the tribe to reside among the whites and follow the pursuits of civilized life ... there shall be issued scrip for one hundred and sixty acres of land each, which shall be receivable at the United States land-offices in the same manner, and be subject to the same rules and regulations as military bounty-land warrants.[79]

Most of the treaties west of the Great Lakes and north of the Missouri River contained these types of provision. "Half-Breed tracts," however, never became Métis enclaves, as the pressure of Anglo-American settlement in the late 1840s and 1850s impelled the Métis to sell their allotments or scrip and to either assimilate into American society or join tribal groups on their reservations and accept tribal benefits.[80]

When the Red River Métis heard that the American government was planning to negotiate a treaty with the Pembina and Red Lake Ojibwa (Chippewa), many decided to relocate to the American side of the border to take advantage of the benefits of this treaty.[81] During the negotiations the Métis claimed that "it was they who possessed the country really, and who had long defended and maintained it against the encroachments of enemies."[82] However, the treaty that was signed between the United States and the Pembina Chippewa on 20 September 1851 did not include the Métis as signatories, as the government believed, as noted earlier, that it should not treat with people whom it regarded as "our *quasi* citizens." The government negotiator did stipulate that he would not object "to any just or reasonable arrangement or treaty stipulation the Indians might choose to make for their benefit." As a result the Chippewa inserted a clause into the treaty that $30,000 be given to their Métis relatives.[83] The treaty, however, was not ratified by Congress and many of those who had claimed United States residence returned to the Red River Settlement in British Territory.[84] When a treaty with the Red Lake and Pembina bands was finally ratified by Congress in 1863, the Métis were not included in the deliberations, as Governor Ramsay insisted that only Indians could cede land. There was, however, a "half-breed" clause inserted at the insistence of tribal leaders that provided some compensation for "mixed-blood" relatives who were not considered a part of the band, but were considered citizens of the United States. Article 8 noted:

> In further consideration of the foregoing cession, it is hereby agreed that the United States shall grant to each male adult half-breed or mixed-blood who is related by blood to the said Chippewas of the said Red

> Lake or Pembina bands who has adopted the habits and customs of civilized life, and who is a citizen of the United States, a homestead of one hundred and sixty acres of land, to be selected at his option, within the limits of the tract of country hereby ceded to the United States, on any land not previously occupied by actual settlers or covered by prior grants, the boundaries thereof to be adjusted in conformity with the lines of the official surveys when the same shall be made, and with the laws and regulations of the United States affecting the location and entry of the same: *Provided,* That no scrip shall be issued under the provisions of this article, and no assignments shall be made of any right, title, or interest at law or in equity until a patent shall issue, and no patent shall be issued until due proof of five years' actual residence and cultivation, as required by the act entitled "An act to secure homesteads on the public domain."[85]

The Manitoba Act and "Métis Status"

This somewhat more liberal treatment of the Métis in the United States did not provide any legal or constitutional room to create or carve out a separate status in which Métis identities could flourish. As in Canada, the Métis in the United States were classed as either "Indians" with status or ordinary citizens. Canadian and American policies towards the Métis began to diverge only in the period after 1870, when Canada's acquisition of Rupert's Land and the Manitoba Act[86] invented a new Métis status. In the aftermath of the Riel Resistance of 1869–70, the Government of Canada negotiated with the delegates of Red River in regard to its terms of entry into Confederation. In these negotiations, discussed at greater length later in the book, it became clear that the federal government would not surrender control of lands and resources to the newly created province, and at that point discussion shifted to compensation for the loss of control over public lands. These discussions quickly focused on the putative rights of the Métis as descendants of Indians.

In particular, it was section 31 of the Manitoba Act that would provide the Métis of Red River and, by extension, other western Canadian Métis with the recognition necessary to redefine themselves on legal and constitutional grounds. This type of separate status, achieved almost by accident, would never be realized in the United States. Section 31 of the Manitoba Act provided for 1.4 million acres to be allocated among the children of half-breed heads of families residing in Manitoba on 15 July 1870 and was justified as being expedient towards the extinguishment of Indian title to the lands of the province. The issue of extinguishment arose during the negotiations in Ottawa that resulted in the drafting of the Manitoba Act. The three Red River delegates, Father N.J. Ritchot, John Black, and Alfred Scott, began serious negotiations in Ottawa on 25 April 1870. When it became clear that the federal government would not surrender control of lands and resources to the newly created province, discussion shifted to compensation for the loss of control over public lands.[87] From this point on, discussion shifted to a land grant for the Métis population to extinguish their alleged title. As Father Ritchot, the chief negotiator for Riel's provisional government, would later admit, because of Métis Indian blood, their title was not quite certain, but that in order to find a satisfactory solution, it was deemed best to regard it as certain. It was, Macdonald and Cartier told Ritchot, the only way to get a Métis land grant through Parliament.[88] The legitimacy of this concern was more than justified by the Liberal opposition to the Manitoba Act in the House of Commons. Alexander Mackenzie, the opposition leader, noted, in relation to what would become section 31 of the Manitoba Act (Métis Land Grant), that he could find no reasonable explanation for this reservation. It was unasked for by the people of Manitoba and no one in the Commons had "vouchsafed an explanation as to who this demand for reservations came from."[89] Mackenzie regarded the entire bill one of the "most preposterous schemes" ever submitted to the Legislature. In relation to the Métis land clause he noted that the Métis were either Indians or not. And as they did not consider themselves Indians, they should not receive any more special considerations than other settlers.[90] Although the Conservative Macdonald government agreed that the Métis were not Indians unless they chose a tribal identity, they felt it expedient to justify the 1.4 million acre grant by stipulating that the Métis had claims in addition to their settler claims by virtue of their Native "extraction."[91] As Adams Archibald, the first lieutenant governor of Manitoba, and as such the official in charge of implementing the grant, noted in late 1870, "I presume the intention was not so much to create the extinguishment of any hereditary claims (as the language of the Act would seem to imply) as to confer a boon upon the mixed race inhabiting this province."[92] Despite strenuous Liberal opposition, the Manitoba Act passed final reading in the Commons on 10 May 1870 and received royal assent on 12 May.

Born of the political exigencies of the Riel Resistance of 1869–70 and the difficulties of getting a Métis land grant through Parliament, the 1.4 million-acre grant, in extinguishment of Indian title, opened the door to Métis special status. In 1885, under the pressure of a Métis rebellion, again led by Louis Riel, the government of Canada extended the Manitoba precedent and granted the Métis of the North-West Territories land and money scrip in extinguishment of their rights – a process and recognition that would extend into the twentieth century.

Métis scrip, literally provisional certificates entitling the bearer to a certain amount of federally owned and surveyed land in Manitoba and the North-West Territories was issued to those adults and children who could document that they were of Indian-European ancestry and who had been born in British or Canadian territory. The program was designed to provide the Métis of the North-West Territories with access to land and was granted in extinguishment of Métis claims to Indian title. This massive administrative program constituted the governmental roots of a modern Métis ethnicity at a time when the occupational bases of Métis ethnicity were disappearing on the plains. The various scrip commissions that held hearings in the North-West Territories from the 1880s to the 1920s not only created a massive administrative, statistical, and genealogical archive, but named and defined an ethnicity or identity to which the Métis ascribed to in order to receive the benefits of scrip.

While Métis communities and individuals in the nineteenth century had a wide variety of cultural and economic affiliations with vague ethnic boundaries that did not admit of discrete either/or divisions, the scrip program demanded distinct and absolute boundaries. By the time scrip and treaty commissioners had travelled to northern Alberta to negotiate Treaty 8 in 1899, they found few differences between the Indian and Métis populations, who were much intermarried. They offered the Métis of the region the choice of extinguishment of their Aboriginal title either by entering treaty or taking scrip. Once they chose, however, they were bound by their decision. It was possible, and indeed the reality in a few cases, that some members of one family became treaty Indians while others were granted scrip and were enumerated as Métis. In a sense, a type of person came into being at the same time as the "Métis scrip" category was being invented. Scrip and treaty administrative practices that defined and counted collective identities in an all or nothing manner enabled/forced people to see or organize themselves in light of these categories.[93]

Historians and the Métis

These governmental policies and their administrative regimes kept the Métis in the Canadian public consciousness from the 1880s until the 1920s. In the process, Canadian perceptions of the Métis also began to change. The predominant discourse regarding the Métis in the nineteenth century had been racial, but by the third decade of the twentieth century, the discourse of nationalism and "Nation" began to supplant it in Canadian historiography. This narration of the Métis Nation was very much the product of twentieth-century historical writing, which served to naturalize and essentialize the Métis Nation as an unproblematic idea of national progress providing the Métis with a story of national origins and the myth of a founding father. As this discourse became more and more accepted, it opened a new stage in the ethnogenesis of the Métis in Canada – one that remained closed in the United States until the very recent past.

Throughout the nineteenth century the view of the Métis as an unstable racial group rather than a national or political grouping was dominant, owing, as noted earlier, to the racialized ethnographic and scientific thought common throughout Europe and North America until well into the twentieth century. This view governed the historical writing about the Métis until at least the 1930s. In the latter half of the nineteenth century and early twentieth century, the chief chroniclers of Métis history were the Roman Catholic priests who worked among them, and their portrayals mirrored the more positive views of the scientific community. Culturally, they saw them as a conflicting mixture of "primitivism" and "civilization" – a people torn between two different heritages. For the Catholics priests, the conversion and "civilization" of the Métis not only would achieve religious objectives, but represented their best chance to establish institutional Roman Catholicism in the Canadian west. While the Métis were regarded as a separate or hybrid race, distinct from both Indians and Europeans, they were French and Catholic and, as such, natural candidates for citizenship in the French-Canadian Catholic Nation.[94] An indication of the strength of this racial discourse of the Métis can be seen in the reaction to Auguste-Henri de Trémaudan's *Histoire de la nation métisse dans l'Ouest canadien*,[95] the first full-blown history of the Métis as Nation published in 1935. Within three years of the publication of this book, the Catholic priest Adrien Gabriel Morice, a prolific writer on the Métis and the Catholic Church in the northwest, published a book-length critique of Trémaudan's work.

In addition to defending his own credentials as the great champion of the Métis and pointing out the factual and other errors Trémaudan had made, Morice was adamant that the title of the book, indeed the whole focus of the book, was erroneous. There never was nor would there ever be a Métis Nation, Morice thundered. A nation, he argued, was a collectivity of men, women, and children who had the same language, culture, common laws, and lived in a clearly bounded territory that was theirs from time immemorial. The Métis, he wrote, had none of these characteristics, and Métis history was not the history of collective action but of a race of individuals acting separately. They were a race, not a nation.[96] By 1935 Morice was on the wrong side of an emerging historiographical tradition, but his published diatribe against Trémaudan was also a clear indication of the strength of the racial discourse of Métis hybridity.

Trémaudan's book, in fact, was commissioned by L'Union national métisse Saint-Joseph to defend and rehabilitate the reputation of Riel, promote the idea of the Métis Nation, and create a narrative of identity.[97] Though it was popular with French Canadians and Métis from the outset, the idea and acceptance of the Métis Nation in the English-Canadian historical tradition was achieved along a different trajectory. The key figures in the birth of this tradition were G.F.G. Stanley and A.S. Morton, who approached the history of western Canada, from an imperial rather than a Canadian perspective.[98] Stanley's *The Birth of Western Canada*, published one year after Trémaudan's *Histoire*, set the history of the Riel uprisings of 1869 and 1885 in the imperial context of the clashes between Native peoples and an expanding "progressive" British civilization. Though largely unconcerned with the origins of the Métis peoples and Nation, Stanley implicitly accepted the idea that the foundation of the Métis resistance to this new civilization was a strong racial and national feeling. He wrote:

> The half-breeds as a race never considered themselves as humble hangers-on to the white populations, but were proud of their blood and their deeds ... They developed a resolute feeling of independence and a keen sense of their own identity which led them to regard themselves as a separate racial and national unity, which found its expression in their name "The New Nation" ... This consciousness of community and strong racial feeling dominated the half-breed "nation" for almost a century: it was a basic factor in the frontier problem of Western Canadian History.[99]

Stanley never examined the evidence for these assumptions, but they had a far-reaching impact and became the jumping-off point for another Canadian historian with an imperial mindset, A.S. Morton, who for the first time established detailed chronology of the emergence of the Métis Nation.[100]

Morton, who published his magisterial *A History of the Canadian West to 1870–71*[101] in 1939, treated western Canada as a regional unit, defined by the fur trade and having separate origins and a different dynamic from the story of Canadian Nationality. Western Canadian history, for Arthur Morton, was part of the story of the Great Frontier of the British Empire,[102] and the evolution of a separate Métis Nation in this region served his purposes of developing a separate regional identity. He argued that Métis national consciousness was born in the conflict between the NWC and HBC over the establishment of the Selkirk Colony at Red River. Convinced by the NWC that the land belonged to them, the Métis were incited to attack and destroy the colony in 1816.[103] For Morton, the Battle of Seven Oaks and the dispersal of the colony in 1816 became the central event in the birth of the Métis Nation, and the conception of "the new nation," instilled in the Métis during this struggle, never died. Without providing any evidence, but stating the argument in bold relief, Morton's framing of the origins and development of the Métis Nation have endured until today: "Nationalism born of racial feeling, nurtured by common language and community interests, is an undying flame."[104] Though quiescent in times of calm, this national feeling would always resurface in times of conflict. The dates and events that Morton identified as crucial – the Battle of Seven Oaks in 1816 and the initiation of national feeling, the fight over free trade in the period 1844–49 and the flexing of the Nation's muscles, and the Riel Resistance of 1869 as the apex of Métis Nationalism – have over the years become almost a catechism of Métis nationalism.[105]

If Morton established the chronology of the Métis Nation, Marcel Giraud provided the factual details. His massive 1945 *Le Métis canadien*[106] itself is a curious mixture of race and nation approaches. Although Giraud described the origins of the Métis in largely racial terms, he also included an almost book-length section devoted to the context and events surrounding the Battle of Seven Oaks, which he called "L'ÉVEIL D'UNE CONSCIENCE NATIONALE" (The Awakening of a National Consciousness). Though he acknowledged that this national consciousness had been awakened by the urgings of the North West Company in opposing the Selkirk Colony and the HBC, still it had captivated the Métis. Led by Cuthbert Grant, their hero, they asserted their collective right to the Red River region: "Henceforward, convinced of their sovereign rights over the immense plains of the West where by virtue of their origins they represented the indigenous element, they were not slow to think of themselves as a group coherent enough to demand the standing of an independent nation and to claim the restitution of a territory which it was proposed against all legality to take away from them."[107] Although Giraud acknowledged that this nationalism was built on a slender foundation, and that it would flicker and fade in subsequent years, he argued, like A.S. Morton, that it would always resurface in times of crisis. Giraud's argumentation has major logical and evidentiary gaps, but the sheer volume of factual detail piled on to his reasoning has convinced most historians who have come after him, few of whom have revisited the question with any detailed examination of the sources. While few in Canada read this French tome, an indication that Giraud's arguments and massive compendium of evidence had won the day in the scholarly community can be seen in the long and positive reviews his work received from English-Canadian and imperial historians.[108]

A historian who gave Giraud a very positive review was W.L. Morton, one of the pre-eminent scholars in Canada at the time. Morton, who himself was imaginatively inventing the west's place in the Canadian Nation, found Giraud's and A.S. Morton's arguments related to the Métis Nation useful in documenting the bias of prairie politics and evidence for his compact theory of Confederation. While Morton's endorsement of the concept of the Métis Nation was more muted than Trémaudan's, A.S. Morton's, and Marcel Giraud's, his acknowledgment of the Métis as a Nation still gave the notion credibility among mainstream historians. Echoing both A.S. Morton and Marcel Giraud, W.L. Morton would write that the Métis were convinced by the NWC that they were a new nation possessed through their Indian mothers an unextinguished title to land in the northwest. For them the Selkirk Colony seemed an unwarranted interference with their accustomed mode of life.[109] He noted that the triangle of land from Pembina to the Red River and along the Assiniboine River was regarded by the Métis as the corporate possession of their race.[110] "Their devotion to the buffalo hunt and their role as a shield to the settlement served to perpetuate in the *métis* their strong sense of identity, their belief that they were a 'new nation.'"[111] Morton did not characterize the 1869–70 Resistance as a national uprising, but he did argue that Riel and the Métis resisted in defence of corporate group rights (land, language, faith) in the face of Canadian offers of individual rights. "Language and faith gave them a sense of unity; they cherished the old belief that they were a 'new nation' and a peculiar people";[112] While the last assertions are more myth than established fact, Morton gave them a credibility by both his force of argument and his reputation. In later years, he would back away somewhat from these assertions as he studied the early years of the Red River Settlement in more detail, but by that time the die had been cast.[113]

The Métis Nation as accepted fact and orthodoxy was signalled by Gerald Friesen's *The Canadian Prairies: A History*. Published in 1984, following the inclusion of the Métis as an Aboriginal group in the amended Canadian Constitution of 1982, it constituted an unambiguous embrace of the idea of a Métis Nation. Friesen states that this "new nation" constituted one of the new factors introduced into western Canadian history in the first half of the nineteenth century.[114] Instead of trying to explain away NWC manipulation of Métis sentiments in the 1814–16 period, Friesen makes a virtue of it by arguing that the Métis were happy to oblige the NWC bourgeois in dispersing the Selkirk Colony for their own purposes. The Métis commitment to the NWC cause, the violence of the fur trade wars, and plains warfare were expected parts of the seasonal round. The tragedy of the Battle of Seven Oaks was not an unexpected aberration, but a predictable flare-up. The Métis were not ruthless and thoughtless renegades but soldiers in a just cause, and Cuthbert Grant was not only the loyal son of an NWC bourgeois, but also the leader of an organized movement to drive colonists out of the country.[115] By these small steps Friesen turned manipulation into justice. The significance of the Battle of Seven Oaks, he argued, lay in its impact on the Métis, who had been moulded into a community and were now a collective force – a new nation. Seven Oaks was their ordeal by fire and gave them a sense of nationhood, later reinforced by Louis Riel and Gabriel Dumont.[116]

In discussing the Riel Resistance of 1869–70, Friesen was at first more circumspect, given the lack of evidence, and closely followed the lead of W.L. Morton. He began by stating that Riel and the Métis action in 1869 had their roots in the French fear of English-Canadian rule in Red River. However, as in his treatment of the Battle of Seven Oaks, Friesen here moved step by step from arguments that can be supported by evidence to an article of faith. The slow progression makes the leap almost imperceptible:

> Behind their suspicion of the boastful Canadian expansionists, the French-speaking metis were groping for a sharper definition of their own aspirations. This was not the retention of the hunt alone, but a defence of their rights as full citizens in the new order: ... In addition to these demands for recognition of individual rights that were part of the British heritage and modern industrial capitalism, the metis were expressing vaguer and more difficult concerns. These included language, faith, kinship networks, and schools ... and have been described as corporate rights, the rights of the metis 'new nation' as a community within the community. This concern for their collectivity, for their culture in the broadest sense, not for 'frontier' and not for language and religion alone, underlay the metis struggles of 1869–70.[117]

Friesen's book, which derives much of its authority from his apparent even-handed analysis of contending views, here essentializes the Métis Nation as a natural event rather than a contested invention. To be sure, Nation rhetoric had been widely accepted before Friesen wrote *Canadian Prairies*, but his treatment enshrined it as the new orthodoxy in Canadian historiography.

This embrace of the "Métis Nation" by Canadian historians does not imply that their understanding of "Nation" was the same as Riel's or that of the various Métis organizations that emerged in the twentieth century. As Albert Braz has shown, Canadian writers appropriated Riel, and Canadianized him, for their own purposes.[118] Métis nationalism for historians such as Morton and Friesen is situated firmly within the Canadian nation state, the Métis being another ethnic group fighting for their place in the ethnocultural mosaic of Canada. It is not the same kind of nationalism of the later Riel, who wanted some form of separation from post-Confederation Canada.[119] The argument made here, however, is that the articulation of a "historic Métis Nation" by Canadian historians in the period after the 1930s has provided the imaginative space wherein Métis identities could be rearticulated in national as opposed to racial terms. It was a space not present in American historiography until late in the twentieth century.

This brief overview has shown how Métis ethnogenesis and identity has been constrained and shaped by the policies and discourses of fur traders, scientists, governments, and historians. In the period prior to the 1870s, fur trade practices and government policies in Canada and the United States were similar and allowed for the development of similar patterns of Métis group formation whether in the Great Lakes region, the Missouri River basin, or at Red River. With the spread of settlement and the demise of the fur trade on the plains, these occupationally based identities were harder to maintain and in many cases Métis communities were overwhelmed. In Canada, however, the Riel Resistance of 1869–70 and subsequent government scrip programs created a new constitutional space wherein Métis identities could be reformulated along political lines. This was an avenue not open to the Métis in the United States, where the government recognized no intermediate status between Indian and white. Consequently, Métis identity would remain closeted in family and kin networks in the United States and there was little room for a political articulation of Métis peoplehood.

These divergent developments in Canada and the United States after 1870 also affected the respective national historiographies. While Canadian historians increasingly articulated a limited notion of Métis nationalism within the Canadian state, American historians largely ignored the Métis until the 1970s. This acceptance of the concept of "Métis Nation" in Canada, however limited it was, allowed Métis organizations to articulate new definitions and ways of being Métis.

2 Economic Ethnogenesis: The Fur Trade and Métissage in the Eighteenth and Nineteenth Centuries

In the following chapter we have attempted to outline a common pattern of economic ethnogenesis that the fur trade made possible in various parts of North America in the eighteenth and early nineteenth centuries. As the chapter title makes clear, we place a premium on the economic aspects of European colonialism and capitalism in the emergence of Métis peoples.[1] In emphasizing this creative aspect of the expansion of the European fur trade we do not mean to downplay the destructive and violent aspects of colonialism that were also part of Métis ethnogenesis. As Pekka Hämäläinen reminds us, ethnogenesis took place in the context of a "shatter belt of dispossession, repression and population collapse."[2] Indeed, the Métis of the plains and Upper Missouri emerged in the shadow of smallpox epidemics, shifting patterns of indigenous occupation, and inter-ethnic warfare.[3] As James Sweet has noted, "cultural mixture and ethnogenesis were rarely neutral exchanges among peoples of equal power, and it was through these hierarchies of power that collective identities emerged and evolved."[4] Some of these themes of violence, repression, and resistance will be addressed in subsequent chapters, but here the focus is on economic patterns of ethnogenesis.

In biological terms racial mixing in North America occurred from the earliest contact. This racial mixing or "métissage," however, did not automatically determine a person's social, ethnic, or political identity, and many children of mixed ancestry were raised with no identity other than Ottawa, Fox, Osage, Ojibwa, Cree, Dene, British, or French. In those instances where fur trade marriages or sexual liaisons were temporary or short term the resulting children were usually raised in the mother's community and were enculturated as "Indian." In other instances, where the children of more prominent fur traders were sent back to Euro-American centres for an education and raised by the father's family, these children were enculturated as European. For example, in Acadia and New France mixed-blood or biracial populations were identified as early as the 1600s, but these populations did not produce an identifiable sociocultural or politically distinct population. The communities remained either Indian or French.[5] Cornelius Jaenen, examining miscegenation in New France, has found that until the fall of New France in 1760 most "mixed-bloods" were accounted part of the Amerindian "nations" without distinction. The proper nouns *Métis* and *Métisse* do not appear in historical documents or come into common usage until after the Conquest.[6]

Likewise, the experience of the offspring of European fishermen and Innu/Inuit women in Labrador demonstrates the contingency of Métis ethnogenesis. Documented contact between European fishermen and the Innu and Inuit women occurred sometime in the 1770–80 period, when amicable trade ties were established. However, the children that resulted from these unions were absorbed by the Innu bands.[7] In the subsequent century and a half, southeastern Labrador was visited by many American, French, and Newfoundland fishermen during the summer. This seasonal fishery eventually fostered permanent settlement, as men would leave the employ of merchant fishing companies and attempt to fish and net seals on their own in the period after 1830. Such settlement was made possible by an indigenous (Inuit) source of wives. Their adaptation to the Labradorian life included both indigenous practices and practices imported from English and Irish homelands in an economy that included trapping, sealing, and fishing, The identity of these peoples and communities remained European and Labradorian, however, despite intermarriage and hybridity.[8] The social and economic conditions that would eventually produce a "Métis" identity did not emerge until the second half of the twentieth century.[9]

The process of Métis ethnogenesis or the development of distinct Métis communities had to await specific political and economic conditions. Recent studies have emphasized that, rather than being a widespread and natural phenomenon, the Métis as community was an infrequent, if not unique, sociocultural product of particular events and circumstances.[10] The dynamics of this community formation are best seen through an examination of the different patterns of fur trade contact; children born in the fur trade country experienced family and community relationships that varied according to the time, place, and fur trade company setting in which they matured. Identifiable Métis communities emerged first in the Great Lakes region, but also arose on the Great Plains, on the Missouri River, and in the Canadian North.[11] The Great Lakes Métis appeared in the region of the Upper Great Lakes in the first quarter of the eighteenth century. A century later, with their dispersal in the face of American settlement, individuals and families journeyed westward to the Missouri River and the Red River of the north and beyond. By 1800 Plains Métis were emerging in the valleys of the Athabasca, North Saskatchewan, Assiniboine, and Red Rivers. Over the next half-century they would extend their presence southward towards the Missouri River and westward to the foothills of the Rocky Mountains. These communities and groups varied considerably, depending on the region they arose in, the Indian bands they were allied with, the ethnicity and nationality of their fur-trader fathers and the particular roles they fulfilled within the fur-trade economy. What they all had in common was that they were bicultural communities that functioned and specialized as intermediaries or brokers between Euro-American fur traders on the one hand and hunting and trapping Indians bands on the other. It was in these interstitial spaces that unique Métis identities were forged. Being Métis had many advantages in these fur-trade worlds. It was an ethnic positioning that allowed individuals to cross boundaries separating indigenous and European societies. It allowed for flexibility in self-definition whereby an individual could accentuate those personality and kinship aspects that would allow entrée into both worlds.[12]

Throughout North America intermarriage between Indians and Europeans accompanied the fur trade. It was virtually assured by both the presence of adult European males isolated from European women and the hospitality of many Indian bands. However, intermarriage was not only a result of the scarcity of European women, but also an integral part of the fur trade. Based, as the trade was, on a commodity exchange between two culturally distinct groups of people, it engendered a mutually dependent economic relationship. Many fur trade practices took place within the structure of Indian social and political customs. Kinship was a major determinant in the trade and alliance structure of indigenous societies. Fur traders wintering in the Indian country found that marriage to an Indian woman not only cemented trade ties, but also provided the trader with a much-needed source of labour. The Indian woman familiarized the fur trader with the customs and language of her tribe and performed important domestic tasks, such as providing him with moccasins, snowshoes, canoes, dressed furs, and food. In return, the Indian woman increased her prestige, as she became a source of technology and goods for her band.[13] It was a pattern initiated by the French on the St Lawrence River and in the Maritimes and repeated by the English when they established themselves on Hudson Bay in the seventeenth century.

This accommodation of fur traders was not necessarily regarded as permanent by either the fur trader or the Indian bands, and the same individual could and sometimes did repeat these types of ritualized kinship attachments with other bands. The norm was not casual, promiscuous contact, however, and over time marital unions did emerge that gave rise to distinct family units – marriage "à la façon du pays." According to the custom of the country, this type of union closely followed traditional Native marriage rites. A trader who wished to take an Indian wife first had to get the consent of her parents and then pay a bride price determined by the woman's relations. The bride price usually entailed some combination of trade goods. This type of marriage did not involve the exchange of marriage vows, but was solemnized by other Native rituals. The trader usually visited the Indian camp to claim his wife and the couple would then be escorted to the fort. Thereafter, they were considered husband and wife. Given that polygyny[14] was common among many North American Indian groups, having a Native wife did not preclude further marriages "à la façon du pays." These country marriages, as has already been noted, did not lead inevitably to separate, identifiable Métis communities. Some "mixed-blood" progeny were raised among their mother's people and assumed an Indian lifestyle, while others were taken to European or American metropolitan centres by their fathers to be educated and assimilated into European society. The emergence of distinct Métis groups had to await specific historical circumstances.

The Great Lakes Métis

During its first decades, New France contained a high proportion of young men, many of whom were engaged in the fur trade and entered into alliances with Indian women. While these traders sought both short-term personal gratification and trade advantages, they expected neither that their familial obligations would be permanent nor that their alliances would lead naturally to independent Métis communities. The children born of these alliances were readily absorbed into the mothers' Huron matrilineage and raised in Huron villages.[15] Conditions conducive to the formation of Métis communities emerged with the destruction of the Huron Confederacy after 1650. To replace their Huron trading partners, the French moved inland, where they wintered and traded with the various Indian bands. In time, these French clerks (*commis*) and voyageurs took over the role of the Indian trader in acquiring furs from the hunting bands and transporting them to Montreal.

Peace between the French and the Iroquois after 1695 encouraged Algonquian Indians to form permanent villages near the shores of Lakes Michigan and Superior and pulled the locus of the fur trade and its personnel away from Montreal and towards the Great Lakes. These traders loosened their ties with New France and formed more lasting bonds with each other and their Indian associates. They did not give themselves up to Indian society, but carved out a role as brokers among the Indian bands to the northwest and European society to the east. Establishing positions of influence at Michilimackinac, Sault Ste Marie, Green Bay, Prairie du Chien, and elsewhere, they worked primarily as traders, voyageurs, and clerks who journeyed to and lived among the Indian people. Through their monopolization of the middle occupational rungs of the fur trade system, these traders and their Native families constructed a separate identity.

The crystallization of a Métis identity in the various communities along the Great Lakes probably occurred after the British conquest of New France and the fall of Michilimackinac to the British in 1763. The British takeover encouraged a pronounced exodus of Canadians and Métis from Michilimackinac and its environs to smaller communities along the shores of the Great Lakes. In these communities, the traders and their Métis families were left to follow their own social and economic customs. The establishment of permanent villages that were geographically separate from adjacent band villages was a hallmark of Métis development in the Great Lakes area.

During the eighteenth century, the Métis of the Great Lakes became brokers between Indian hunters and Euro-Canadian merchants. Successive engagements with a fur trade entrepreneur (often an older kinsman) enabled the voyageur to establish an enduring marriage, because he returned regularly to his wife and children and the Métis village. His children could then retrace the cycle by entering the fur trade, thereby producing a new generation of Métis mediators.[16]

Within the Métis communities of the Great Lakes region the husbands headed the patriarchal households and linked their children to the outside European/American worlds, but their Native wives exerted considerable influence over how and where the family actually lived. Traders, clerks, and voyageurs travelled far from home procuring provisions and trading in furs. The family lived, therefore, in a localized, kin-oriented world closely related to the wife's people. However, these fur trade or Métis families were differentiated by their Catholicism or folk-Catholicism. Indian women who married French traders did not become French, but many converted to Catholicism and used the forms of this religion (baptism, marriage, godparenting) to construct alternative kin networks. By the eighteenth century an identifiable Catholic kin network had evolved compatible with and often parallel to that of indigenous society. Over time these Catholic kin networks, along with other factors, contributed to the development of distinctive Métis communities closely meshed with the surrounding Indian bands.[17] In these circumstances children were enculturated into the fur trade world. Boys learned from their fathers the various fur trade rituals and skills necessary to operate in both Native and European spheres as they prepared to be traders, clerks, runners, and boatmen. This training would have been significantly different than the enculturation of their maternal cousins raised as Ojibwa and Ottawa. Métis girls would be trained in the skills needed to be a wife in fur trade society.[18] Growing up in these occupationally homogeneous trading hamlets (residents were almost exclusively dependent on the fur trade), fur traders increasingly married among their own group (fur trade endogamy).[19] As Jacqueline Peterson has pointed out, "These people were neither adjunct relative-members of tribal villages nor the standard bearers of European civilization in the wilderness. Increasingly, they stood apart or, more precisely, in between. By the end of the last struggle for empire in 1815, their towns, which were visibly, ethnically, and culturally distinct from neighbouring Indian villages and 'white towns' along the eastern seaboard, stretched from Detroit and Michilimackinac at the east to the Red River in the northwest."[20]

However, these Métis communities did not have an overt political consciousness of themselves as a "new people" or behave in collective action, as would the Plains Métis further west. It is difficult, in fact, to find evidence in the historical record of clear self-identification as "Métis," or recognition of such by outsiders. Terms used by missionaries, fur traders, and government officials included "French," "French Canadian," and "Canadian" and were used to refer to all French speakers with only occasional reference to an individual's ancestry. It is not until the after the 1760s that the term "Métis" is used[21] and not until the

1820s that reference to "half-breeds" begins to appear in the writings of outsiders.[22]

Harriet Gorham has argued that, as individuals, most "mixed-bloods" in the Great Lakes region demonstrated a greater awareness of the uniqueness of their way of life as fur traders and their attachment to their homeland than of any clear sense of distinctiveness created by their mixed ancestry. She opines that the mixed-blood trading population may well have formed an occupational class rather than an ethnic group.[23] These qualifications are useful in pointing out the contingent aspects of the Métis identity in the Great Lakes, but they overlook the degree to which occupational specialization could be a marker of ethnic identity and the way in which the lack of a stable, self-declared Métis ethnicity could be strategic in the fur trade world of the Great Lakes. That is, the dual, bicultural aspects of Métisness allowed individuals to strategically represent their personal identity depending on the context (Indian or European) they needed to operate in.

Another caution against naturalizing the "mixed" populations of the Great Lakes as "Métis" is the work of Chris Andersen, who, noting the lack of extensive documentation of historical self-ascription, has argued that ethnohistorians have "retrofitted" or "imagined" these settlements as Métis. By presenting separateness as the basis for Métis identity, ethnohistorians have marginalized a hallmark of Métis groupness: political self-consciousness and attachment to a self-ascribed people.[24] While we acknowledge these caveats, our approach to Métis ethnogenesis in the Great Lakes does not focus solely on "mixedness," nor does it naturalize the Métis; rather it tries to contextualize a "process" of ethnogenesis through a fur trade instrumentality.

The British conquest of New France did more than provide a catalyst for Métis group identity in the Great Lakes; it also opened a new phase in the Canadian fur trade and in fur trade family history. Between 1760 and 1780, political and economic control of the Montreal trade passed to anglophone leaders, among whom Highland Scots predominated. French Canadians were still employed as *engagés* for the canoe brigades and labour at the inland posts, but they now seldom rose in the company ranks to become partners or officers. When the British Nor'Westers (agents or traders working for the North West Company) travelled into Indian country, they, like the French, allied themselves with Indian women for the same personal and trade reasons. As fur trade officers, they also carried with them their loyalties, connections, and familial attitudes. Unlike the French, however, they infrequently developed permanent attachments in the Indian country. Nonetheless, some did establish longer-term relationships with Indian women and ensured that the household – women and children – accompanied them as they moved from post to post. On occasion, these marriages lasted a lifetime.[25] The British traders, however, came to rely on the Métis who resided in and occupied key strategic and occupational positions in the fur trade society of the Great Lakes. British traders wintering in the interior continued to employ the Métis to trade British goods with their Native kin. Consequently, the British did not disrupt the social order of the Great Lakes and the Métis continued in their role as a people "in between."

The increasing presence of American traders and military authorities in the Great Lakes region after the War of 1812 did not bring an immediate change, as the American Fur Company adapted many of the institutions of the this "middle ground" in order to combat the British trade. The introduction of American laws, institutions, increasing settlement, and racism, however, eventually led to the demise of Métis society in the southern Great Lakes.[26] Several factors encouraged the departure from the region of those Métis who wished to continue in the trade. Among these was the depletion of fur-bearing animals in the Great Lakes area, Indian cessions and removals, and American land speculation and settlement in the early nineteenth century. For example, as early as 1800 the Grignons, a Métis family that originated in the Great Lakes area, in their search for furs wintered as far west as the headwaters of the Mississippi River and the Pembina River. Many of the Great Lakes Métis pulled up stakes and moved to trading stations and new town sites further west.

The Métis of the Lower Missouri

As both the French and the British fur trades spread into the interior, fur trade domesticity followed. St Louis, founded in 1764 and dominated early on by French-speaking fur traders and their Native families, became a new epicentre of Métis ethnogenesis in the trans-Mississippi west. Here, as in the Great Lakes, mixed-blood offspring comprised up to 80 per cent of the fur trade labour force and acted as the intermediaries between the Ponca, Omaha, Kansas, Osage, Otes, Missouri, and Ioway nations on the one hand and European traders on the other. Their cultural orientation, political loyalties, and ethnic identities formed the milieu for the creation of Métis peoples in this region.[27] As Tanis Thorne has noted, although the terms "*métis*" or "*méetif*" rarely appear in contemporary documents, the bicultural and biracial French of the Mississippi clearly acted as a people "in between."[28]

In the eighteenth century St Louis was located in a free-trade zone, where neither the Spanish nor the English could enforce their laws or control the fur trade, and as a consequence the region became a mecca for a large transient population of young males working in the Indian trade. Many of these men were emigrants from the Illinois and Great Lakes regions and were second- or third-generation descendants of French-Indian intermarriage.[29] Spending much of their time in Indian country working as trappers, traders and *engagés*, these men frequently married Indian women of various tribal affiliations and used these kin connections to expand the trading networks of French firms such as that of the Chouteau Family of St Louis.[30] During the period up to the 1780s these biracial and bicultural families enjoyed a high degree of autonomy and prospered in the St Louis area as go-betweens and buffers between Native groups hostile to each other. In the process they carved out distinct occupational and economic roles as middlemen in the trade. The cultural hallmarks of this emerging identity and the aspects that set them apart from tribal groups included French Catholicism, patrilineal and patrilocal family forms, residential stability, a shared occupational niche, and fur trade endogamy.[31]

The increased competition in the trade after 1790 and American domination after the War of 1812 worked to erode the position of the independent trader and his biracial and bicultural intermediaries. Fur trade employees could no longer supplement their wages with independent trapping and trading, and this fact, along with the influx of Anglo-American settlers into St Louis, led to an outmigration of these families westward to smaller fur-trading sites on the Missouri River and its tributaries. Both pushed and pulled up-river, they continued their intermediary roles further into the interior, settling in more homogeneous fur-trading sites along the Missouri in close proximity to their Native kin.[32]

This diaspora from St Louis after 1812 inaugurated another phase in the evolution of a Métis identity in the Lower Missouri. Fur-trading centres such as Cote sans Dessein (at the mouth of the Osage River on the Missouri), Kawsmouth (where the Kansas River empties into the Missouri), and Council Bluffs (higher up the Missouri) became the nuclei of new Métis communities. Located near trading posts that often included mission stations, military posts, and Indian agencies, these villages became the sites of Métis acculturation and employment. Here tightly knit Métis families farmed, trapped, traded, and intermarried, and successive generations of males followed their fathers' footsteps as middlemen in the fur trade of the trans-Mississippi west. Indeed, Council Bluffs was seen by some observers as the equivalent of the Red River Settlement in the British territory to the north. As such, it mirrored the centripetal forces of the fur trade in the Great Lakes region and that of the northern plains (discussed later).[33]

However, the fur trade would not last much longer in this region. By the 1840s and 1850s the decline of game and fur-bearing animals and the inrush of Anglo-American settlers caused the replacement of the fur trade with agriculture and transformed fur trade sites into bustling cities.[34] As the fur trade waned, so too did the utility of the Métis as intermediaries in a disappearing dual economy. Given the short duration of these fur trade enclaves, there was little chance to develop a clear sense of Métis ethnicity in socio-political terms, and the American government was not willing to foster such aspirations, even though there were often "Half-breed Tracts" included in various Indian treaties. As a result, the choice for most Métis involved either assimilation or re-tribalization.[35]

The Métis of the Northern Plains

The origins of the Plains Métis can be found in the advent of the *"les gens libres"* (freemen) in the Great Lakes trading systems and their extension westward in the eighteenth century. As political and economic control of the Montreal trade passed to anglophone leaders after 1760, these British Nor'Westers, as well as their French-Canadian *engagés*, frequently allied themselves with Indian women. Their marriages by the custom of the country engendered a large "mixed-blood" population in the northwest, complementing those Great Lakes Métis who had migrated further west. While the Scottish Nor'Westers often retired to Canada without their fur trade families, this was not the case with their French-Canadian *engagés* and others on the lower end of the scale in the company. Often having spent most of their lives in the west, they had few ties pulling them back to Canada. By the 1780s and increasingly by 1800 some older *engagés*, or voyageurs, who had taken country wives from bands with whom they had wintered, chose to become free on the plains and live out their lives as buffalo-hunting provisioners, trappers, or traders. As these men frequently were past their physical prime, and as they tended to have large families who were provisioned at or attached to some post, the "bourgeois" at these posts would see this as a positive cost-saving step.[36]

The usual practice of the North West Company (NWC) and other fur-trading companies from Montreal was to give *engagés* their freedom at Montreal, far from where some might be tempted to initiate a competing trade. On the Upper Saskatchewan River, however, the vast distances from the northwest to Montreal precluded all but the best-financed and best-organized from adopting such a course of action, so that many older *engagés* on the Upper Saskatchewan took their release from the companies in the west. These "freemen," as they were called, usually had some kinship ties to Indian bands in the area, which helped to assure their safety as they carved out a niche as suppliers of furs and provisions to fur-trading companies.

The northwestern fur trade, which was expanding into the Athabasca country, could not secure sufficient provisions from the plains Indians, and consequently the trading companies turned to these recently released servants and their Native families. The "freemen" – "*les gens libre*" – with their greater interest in European goods remained in relatively close contact with their former fur-trading bourgeois and posts. Their importance to the NWC was reflected in the higher prices they received for these provisions and in the services extended to them, which were not given to the Indian trade. In time, the Hudson's Bay Company (HBC) posts looked to these bands of freemen to provision their posts as well. Mutual dependence tied the trader to these freemen and their mixed-blood families; thus, the households of the freemen proved to be admirably suited to fill the provisioning niche in the western fur trade.

From their first appearance in the late 1780s, their behaviour distinguished them from Indians. They pursued the buffalo and beaver with a dedication that Indians would have found unnecessary. Meanwhile, the Cree of the region were tolerant of these newcomers, with whom they had ties of kinship. They came to identify the freemen as "*O-tee-paym-soo-wuk*," or their own boss. It is from this group of freemen that the Plains Métis would emerge. Forming relationships with other freemen in the trade, they established enduring households and communities in the interior much as they had done on the Great Lakes.[37]

Those *gens libres* who established enduring households that were succeeded by a later generation of buffalo hunters became the Métis. By the early 1800s the families of these freeman bands whose economic rationale and role were to provide both fur-trading companies with provisions – largely pemmican – were recognized as a distinct Métis group. Like the Great Lakes Métis, these provisioners and trappers depended upon their recognized hunter bourgeois to negotiate the necessary social and political relationship with the trading post that would maximize their interests, and, as it was for the Great Lakes Métis, the image of cultural broker was central to the way of life that emerged.

This ethnogenesis, according to John Foster, occurred in a two-stage process: wintering and "going free." According to him, a critically important relationship in the emergence of the Metis involved two or three outsider males who, along with their Native partners and children, wintered together in Indian country for extended periods, hunting, fishing, trapping, and trading together. Over time these types of grouping came to constitute a social milieu from which the succeeding generation would choose marriage partners. While some individuals did marry into indigenous Indian bands, the majority of children born in this milieu chose spouses from other freeman families and bands. John Foster has noted that the families of freemen who failed to form these workmate partnerships tended to become part of the indigenous Indian tradition. Without the relationship with other outsider males, a winterer and his household could enjoy hunting and trading success, but his generational legacy "would be overwhelmingly in an Indian, not a Métis, tradition."[38]

The second stage of Metis ethnogenesis on the northern plains emerged with the decision of the experienced *engagé* to become a freeman. On quitting his job with a fur trade company, the freeman would claim his family from the band or fort and begin an independent pursuit of provisions and furs in surplus amounts, which he traded to the various fur-trading companies in the region. His single-minded pursuit of furs and provisions for trade purposes made him and his family distinct from the indigenous Indians. The formation of freeman bands with other like-minded outsider men ensured the protection of the group, and the marriage of his children to the children of other freeman families ensured generational continuity. By this process, Métis ethnogenesis on the western plains was complete by the first quarter of the nineteenth century.[39]

This ethnogenesis occurred from the Upper Missouri River in the south to the Peace/Athabasca country in the north. In the early nineteenth century HBC journals and district reports noted significant freeman populations as far north as Lesser Slave Lake consisting of

Canadians and Iroquois of Lower Canada and their descendants. All these Canadians were old servants of the North West Company "who have Indian women and children by them and thus get Completely attached to the Country and Indian way of living."[40] By the time Treaty 8 was signed at Lesser Slave Lake in 1899, there were hundreds of Métis families camped at the lake waiting to apply for the Métis scrip being offered by the Canadian government.[41] Charles Mair, one of the scrip commissioners, in commenting on this population noted their indigenous roots in the region, their distinction from Indian populations, their reliance on the fur trade, and Métis endogamy:

> They were unquestionably half-breeds, and had received Christian names, and most of them had houses of their own, and, though hunters, fishermen, and trippers, their families lived comparatively settled lives ... In speaking of the "Lakers" I refer, of course, to the primitive people of the region, and not to the half-breed incomers from Manitoba or elsewhere. There were a few patriarchal families into which all the others seemed to dovetail in some shape or form. The Noóskeyah family was one of these, also the Gladu, the Cowitoreille, and the Calahaisen ... The place, in fact, surprised one – no end of buggies, buckboards and saddles, and brightly dressed women, after a not altogether antique fashion ... How this could all be supported by fur it was difficult to see, but it must have been so, for there was, as yet, little or no farming amongst the old "Lakers."[42]

By the 1840s the buffalo robe trade complemented the summer provisioning hunt with family bands of Métis joining with others to establish sizeable winter villages in wooded oases on the prairie. They became known as "*hivernants*" (winterers). In time the Métis found their economic interests tied to commercial capitalist interests outside the region and witnessed the resurgence of a Métis trading class. These Métis traders were invariably the patriarchal heads of wintering villages on the prairies. It was this new commercial and trading interest that was at the root of the free-trade controversy, culminating in the Sayer Trial in 1849. The trial saw the Red River Métis successfully challenge the Hudson's Bay Company's use of its royal charter to protect its commercial interests from competition.

On both the summer hunts and the robe hunts violent incidents could occur, involving the Dakota/Lakota southwest of the Red River Settlement and, further west, the members of the Blackfoot Confederacy. The most famous incident was the Battle of the Grand Coteau in June of 1851.

Métis from the White Horse Plains, a community on the Assiniboine River on the western extremity of the Red River Settlement, came under sustained attack from the Yankton Dakota near Dog Den Butte, close to the Missouri River. Circling their two-wheeled Red River carts to corral their oxen and horses and shelter the women and children, the men charged forth the distance of a gunshot to scrape gun pits in the prairie sod. From these vantage points they inflicted casualties that the Dakota found unacceptable and they retreated. Although conflict would continue into the 1870s, the Métis saw themselves as paramount on the northern plains. They had become not only a unique and discernible community, but also a military force to be reckoned with.

Although these Métis bands were found across the northern plains from the Missouri to the Athabasca, Métis political identity in the early nineteenth century was focused on the Red River Settlement. It was here that the Métis became conspicuous as a socio-political entity. Their assertion of rights arose first in relation to the fur trade wars between the North West Company and the Hudson's Bay Company following the establishment of the Red River Settlement in 1811. The founding of this colony by Lord Selkirk was seen by the NWC as a direct threat to their trade and territorial interests. The Plains Métis, closely tied to the various bourgeois of the NWC by consanguinity and employment, were encouraged to oppose the HBC's efforts to found a colony in Assiniboia and resist any attempts to impose government over them. While it is not clear to what extent the Métis needed any encouragement, it is certainly true that this conflict, which ended in violence and the deaths of twenty-one colonists at the Battle of Seven Oaks in 1816, came to be seen by the Métis as the assertion of their political rights and the initiation of a "new nation." Following the merger of the Hudson's Bay Company and North West Company in 1821, the Plains Métis accepted the Red River Settlement as their own and began colonizing it in large numbers. They, along with the Hudson Bay or English Métis, would dominate the population of the settlement and it was considered, until the 1870s, their homeland.

The English Métis of the Red River Settlement and Saskatchewan

The biracial descendants of the Hudson's Bay Company servants, some of whom would assume a Métis identity, followed a slightly different pattern of ethnogenesis. Through most of the eighteenth century these "natives of the Hudson's Bay," as Jennifer Brown has remarked, did not become classed as a separate ethnic/racial entity, as the Hudson's Bay Company actively suppressed the growth of dependent post communities, and most offspring were assimilated among the Home Guard Cree[43] – those Indian bands that had taken up year-round residence on the shores of Hudson Bay to supply the various HBC posts with provisions.

At an early date, posts on Hudson Bay were fortified residential enclaves organized by military and semi-monastic ideals. The official policy of the company dictated non-fraternization between Indian women and British-born officers and servants. The realities of life on the Bay, however, led to a more practical, unofficial policy that saw frequent intermarriage between the two groups.[44]

The Home Guard Cree worked out an arrangement with the British-born employees. Adult males of an Indian band permitted British-born males to consort with Indian women only in the context of a marital relationship. Such a relationship benefited Indian women, who thus secured access to the warehouse of the trading post. In return, Indian wives served as a conduit for small furs and goods such as toboggans, snowshoes, and canoes. In spite of the many acculturative forces that influenced the Home Guard Cree, their ways were firmly tied to Indian traditions. Usually the children of these marriages became enculturated in the ways of the band. While Home Guard Cree bands were a biologically "mixed" people by the eighteenth century, they remained culturally within the Cree context.[45]

The emergence of a distinct Métis community demanded a sequence of events that directed the Home Guard Cree along divergent paths, beginning with the removal of HBC trade operations to inland posts after 1790. This move resulted from intense competition with Montreal traders and caused a labour crisis in the Hudson's Bay Company. Not only did the company need servants to staff these new posts, it also needed a large workforce on the boats bringing trade goods inland and furs back out. To obtain this labour the Hudson's Bay Company turned to the Home Guard Cree, particularly to the Native sons of servants and officers whose kinship ties drew them close to the trading post and made them at least partially amenable to the ways of command in the company's service. However, these Cree demanded the traditional privilege of having their families live within the confines of the trading post during the length of their contract. In desperation the company agreed. As some young men renewed their contracts, over the years their families became better acquainted with life in the trading post.

Beginning in the 1790s the Hudson's Bay Company registers listing the names of the young men employed in the HBC boats going inland noted that they were born on the Hudson Bay. With this step the Home Guard Cree males became full-fledged members of the trading posts. The first two decades of the nineteenth century witnessed the increasing tempo of the competition of the fur trade, and in this period of chaos the "mixed-blood" children of the Hudson's Bay Company posts acquired some interesting skills. Although Cree continued to be spoken, a knowledge of basic English became common. A few could read and write the language of their British-born fathers. Perhaps the most crucial skill acquired by these children, however, was an understanding of the social structure, not of one post, but of all the posts in the HBC network. In learning the intricacies of this social system, the "mixed-blood" children of the trading post also familiarized themselves with the other social systems that were intertwined with the formal social structure and influenced its operation. Among these was the camaraderie of the various adult male groupings and the various kinship links between "mixed-blood" families, British-born officers and servants, and the members of the surrounding bands of Home Guard Cree. The complex interplay of these various social systems within a cohesive whole created a unique social world.[46]

The first generation of Native sons who were raised in the fur-trading posts evolved a system of values that were different from the values and attitudes of the British-born servant. For those who enlisted in the company's service in Britain the remunerative aspects of work were of cardinal importance. For the Native-born servants the social aspects of work (status and rights) were of greater importance. Thus, as a punishment, the fine was an effective tool for dealing with the delinquent British-born servant, while physical coercion worked best with Native-born servants.

By the early nineteenth century, British-born traders and Native-born traders possessed distinct values and attitudes. The British-born valued monetary gain above all, while the Native-born considered the social aspects of work most important. The "mixed-blood" servants of the Hudson's Bay Company developed an ethos epitomized by the lifestyle of the Indian trader. They had internalized the values of the British patriarchal household that had been transferred to the Hudson Bay trading posts. Day-to-day relations among men at a trading post were governed by an authoritarian social hierarchy, presided over by a patriarchal Indian trader. Native-born employees saw him as a man without peer, a man of immeasurable wealth and power. For many young sons of the fur trade, born and raised in or around a trading post, the Indian trader was the ideal whom they strove to emulate. Having kin ties to previous Indian traders and an education equal or superior to that of their British forefathers, they believed themselves destined to occupy this lofty position after they had worked their way up the ranks. However, there were too many "mixed-bloods" vying for the available positions.

The amalgamation of the Hudson's Bay and North West Companies in 1821 marked the final step in the historical and cultural process that moved some "mixed bloods" to adopt a Métis identity. This union initiated the migration of hundreds of laid-off employees from the posts of the Hudson Bay trading system to the Red River Settlement. In Red River these "mixed-bloods" continued their pursuit of the good life as their years in the Hudson's Bay Company trading posts had defined it. Although many became farmers, they did not share the attachment to the land of their Kildonan Scots neighbours, whom Lord Selkirk had brought to Red River. Some tried to become merchants, but few enjoyed success as businessmen. Frustrated, many turned to trading in furs in contravention of the HBC monopoly and in the process generated the free-trade movement in the 1840s. In the role of free traders based in Red River and further westward they assumed an intermediary position between the Native fur trade on one hand and the European trade on the other. In this social and economic space they forged a distinctive identity.

Under the influences of the institutions of a British and Protestant community the Native-born of the Hudson Bay tradition completed the cultural transformation that had begun a century earlier. Speaking English and professing an Anglican religion, they pursued in greater numbers than previously the goal of the good life epitomized in the lifestyle of the Indian trader. This aspect of their lives at Red River was uniquely their own. More than anything else in the settlement, it set them apart from the other communities, including the Plains Métis, and identified them as culturally distinct people. Obviously related to both the British and the Cree traditions, they were more than a simple mixture of these traditions; the English Métis were a sociocultural creation of the fur trade in the Hudson Bay trading system. It is interesting to note that those "mixed-bloods" who remained at the posts on Hudson Bay and James Bay, such as Moose Factory, did not develop a separate group consciousness. While they were distinguishable from the Home

Guard Cree, there was little evidence of a Métis identity before the twentieth century. The absence of any independent settlement and the relatively small numbers apparently prevented ethnogenesis.[47]

The Northern Métis

While elements of the foregoing processes were evident in the north (from the English River to the Mackenzie River) there were some crucial variations that both delayed the emergence of a Métis community and identity in the region and were important factors in the eventual Métis ethnogenesis there. Although fur-trading posts were established in this region from the late eighteenth century onward and both French- and English-speaking traders set up networks of economic and familial alliances with Cree and Dene groups,[48] Métis ethnogenesis did not occur until much later in the nineteenth century. Children of fur trader-Cree/Dene unions were either absorbed into the mother's band or raised in the European world of the fur trade post. As well, the isolation from the south and even other fur trade posts made any regional coalescence more difficult. Political developments such as the Battle of Seven Oaks and the Riel uprisings had little resonance in the north during the nineteenth century and slowed the development of a regional Métis identity.[49]

As in other fur trade localities, unions between fur traders and Native women in this region resulted in significant numbers of children of mixed ancestry. Until the mid-nineteenth century, however, there is little evidence that there existed Métis communities either self-ascribed or recognized by outside observers. Instead, these children were either raised in Cree and Dene bands or were members of trading-post communities. A search of HBC records,[50] Church Missionary Society (CMS) Records,[51] and selected Oblate sources[52] shows that, while both fur traders and missionaries noted persons of mixed ancestry, they neither acknowledged nor mentioned specific Métis communities outside the trading-post context prior to the mid-nineteenth century. When terms such as "half-breed" or "*métis*" were used prior to this time, they were almost always used in a strictly biological as opposed to a cultural or ethnic context. For example, in 1837 the post journal at Île-à-la-Crosse noted, "A Chipewyan called Janvier arrived ... this Chipewyan is a half breed."[53] Even as late as the 1890s, the Île-à-la-Crosse journals described Magloire Maurice as the leader of a Cree band at the Narrows.[54] Robert Hunt, the Anglican missionary at Lac la Ronge, noted in 1852 that Mahnsuk, the chief of the Fishing Lake Cree (in the extreme southwest of the English River District), "did not appear to be a pure Indian, as indeed many of them did not – and the mixture of blood is easily accounted for."[55] The Catholic Oblates noted similar dynamics. Father Petitot, on an 1873 trip that encompassed Lac La Biche, Green Lake, and Île-à-la-Crosse, noted that in the region of Cold Lake there were families named Montgrand, Jolibois, Janvier, Buisson, and Gladu living among and like the Chipewyans. They were raised in the woods, he said, thinking, speaking, and acting as Indians: "Tous noms français comme leur origine; mais ces bonnes gens n'en sont pas moins de vrais sauvages élevés dans les bois, pensant, parlant et agissont en sauvages, à la réserve de leur foi, qui est bien vive et qui m'a beaucoup édifié."[56]

To the extent that a Métis consciousness emerged in the nineteenth century it was focused on fur trade families localized around posts on the various river basins. These Métis identities were very fluid and associated more with specific trading-post localities and occupational roles in the fur trade than with abstract cultural or genealogical precepts, since family and kin networks were often loosely defined.[57] Métis populations emerged in the north and assumed a regional framework, in the context of the labour requirements of the NWC/HBC transport systems. Métis participation in these networks enabled fur trade kin groups to remain in contact and resulted in a web of fur-trade communities along river trade routes.[58] The families of fur trade employees, raised in the sphere of trading posts often hired themselves out as seasonal workers on summer boat brigades ranging from Fort Good Hope and Fort Simpson on the Mackenzie River, Hay River and Fort Resolution on Great Slave Lake, Fort Chipewyan on Lake Athabasca to Lesser Slave Lake and Île-a-la-Crosse further south. These transport roles along with roles as independent trappers, traders, and middlemen associated with specific fur trade posts became the fulcrum of Métis identity in the north. The point made here is that emergence of distinct and recognizable Métis communities in the north was a late, and not a generalized, development.

This late emergence in the context of the northern fur trade requires some explanation. In particular, it seems that an indigenous *gens libre* or freeman tradition was slow to develop. While there are sporadic reports of freemen passing through the district in the early nineteenth century, few seemed to stay or establish any separate hunting or trading community in the area. Until at least the 1870s furs brought into the posts in the northern districts were directly transported by Indians in the region.[59] Thus, little scope was left for an independent freeman or Métis niche or tradition to develop in this trade, separate from the activities of the Cree or Dene bands. There were a few exceptions, but for the most part the exceptions tended to confirm the rule. For example, in the Portage La Loche locality a small number of freemen were employed to take care of the horses and oxen used in transport across the portage. Further north the Beaulieu family had begun to develop independent trading activities by the late 1850s, and indeed in 1857 Antoine Beaulieu made a trip to Red River to sell the furs he had trapped and traded in the Fort Resolution region. Yet the development of an independent trading role by the Beaulieu family seems to have been an exception, given that the Hudson's Bay Company made special provisions to counter and contain their operations.[60]

However, these dynamics began to change in the 1870s, as outside trading interests from the Saskatchewan and Red River regions began to penetrate the district and supply goods to an increasing number of freemen in the area. In 1872 Samuel McKenzie, the postmaster at Île-à-la-Crosse, noted that the number of servants in the district was reduced to thirty-eight and that ten servants had "gone free" that spring.[61] By 1874 the company felt it necessary to establish outposts to watch the movements of an increasing number of free traders in the district,[62] and by the late 1880s and early 1890s post reports from Green Lake were listing the private traders in the area, including Solomon Venne from Batoche, Baptiste Boyer supplied from Winnipeg, Paul Laronde supplied from merchants on the Saskatchewan River, James Sinclair, Frederick Kennedy, and Cyprien Morin (former HBC servants and clerks in the area).[63] Similar dynamics began to arise in the Mackenzie Basin by the 1890s.[64] By 1892 very few Indians were bringing their furs to the Green Lake post, and instead trade was conducted by the HBC and free traders sending runners to the various Indian camps, forcing the company to directly supply free traders and freemen, who then traded their furs back to the HBC. This practice probably started earlier, as the district accounts at Île-à-la-Crosse, as noted earlier, began keeping "Freemen's Accounts" in the period 1885–88.[65] These new practices and the development of an indigenous freeman tradition after the 1870s provided the economic conditions whereby a Métis tradition, neither Indian nor European, could develop. By 1900 the district report for the Green Lake HBC post noted that Paul Laronde with his sons and relatives reached almost every Indian camp tributary to Green Lake.[66]

This argument for the emergence of a Métis tradition in the area in the period after the 1870s is supported by the changing dynamics of the HBC transport/brigade system, which provided the employment opportunities for another aspect of Métis identity in the region. The expansion of the Canadian fur trade into the Athabasca and Mackenzie Districts in the late eighteenth century necessitated new routes and travel logistics that would bring the Lac La Loche, Île-à-la-Crosse, and Green Lake areas into new prominence and would eventually provide new economic opportunities for freemen in the region.

Not only was the Athabasca country separated from Montreal and Hudson Bay by thousands of miles, but it lay in the Arctic watershed. In order for the canoes (later York Boats) of the North West Company and the Hudson's Bay Company to reach the Athabasca they had to portage across the height of land between the rivers of the Hudson Bay watershed and the Arctic watershed.[67] From the 1770s until the 1880s the most convenient and efficient route lay through Lac La Loche and across the twelve-mile portage to the Clearwater River. From Lake Winnipeg the Athabasca fur brigades used the Saskatchewan River until they reached Cumberland House, where they turned north following the Sturgeonweir (Maligne) River through a series of lakes to Frog Portage, which put the brigade on the banks of the Churchill (English) River. Although the Churchill from Hudson Bay to Frog Portage was too big and fast for navigation, above Frog Portage the river was a series of lakes linked by short rapids that offered only minimal navigational hazards. This route would then pass through Lac Île-à-la-Crosse, Buffalo Lake, and via the Methye River to Lac La Loche. From here, via the twelve-mile Methye Portage (Portage La Loche), the brigade would reach the Clearwater River, a tributary of the Athabasca River.[68] In the spring the returns from all the posts from the Athabasca District were collected at Fort Chipewyan and in May, as soon as the rivers had broken up, the brigade would start south. As far as Île-à-la-Crosse they would subsist on fish taken at Fort Chipewyan in the winter. There they would obtain pemmican for the 500-mile leg of the trip to Cumberland house, where they would again replenish their provisions for the trip either to Lake Winnipeg and on to Fort William (NWC) or to York Factory (HBC).[69]

After the union of the North West Company and the Hudson's Bay Company in 1821, the new HBC increasingly used York Boats for their transport system, and to carry goods and furs in and out of the Athabasca District it instituted a two-stage brigade system. One operated from the Mackenzie and Athabasca Districts to Portage La Loche and the other from Portage La Loche to York Factory. In this way only, the cargo had to be portaged across the twelve-mile carrying place.

Goods were brought from York Factory to Norway House and dispatched to the Athabasca and Mackenzie Rivers about the middle of June in the following year by the Portage La Loche brigade, consisting of Métis and Indians recruited in the Red River Settlement.[70] This brigade arrived at Portage La Loche, discharged its trading goods and provisions, loaded the furs brought to this point by the Athabasca/ Mackenzie brigade (recruited in those regions), and then retraced its route. The Mackenzie River brigade usually began at Fort Simpson at the end of May, went downstream to Fort Good Hope, and collected the furs at that post as well as those of Fort Norman. This northern brigade arrived at Portage La Loche about the end of July. The trade goods were loaded and the brigade returned in early August and distributed supplies to the various northern posts. Furs from Portage La Loche were taken to York Factory and sent to England. The Portage La Loche brigade then returned to the Red River Settlement from York Factory in late autumn. While this transport system provided employment for sons of the fur trade in the Mackenzie and Athabasca Districts, the Portage La Loche brigade hired few local Natives, as these brigades were recruited almost exclusively in the Red River Settlement until the late 1860s. The only employment opportunities outside the fur trade post in the English River District were the small number of jobs keeping horses and oxen used at the portage.

However, by the 1860s changing transportation technology and routes had begun to affect and alter the Portage La Loche transport network. The arrival of the railway at St Paul (Minnesota) made the shipment of goods from the United States cheaper than by way of England via York Factory. The placement of river steamboats on the Red River, Lake Winnipeg, and the Saskatchewan River only accentuated the competitive advantage of this new route from the United States.[71] By the early 1870s some Athabasca freight[72] was being sent overland from the Red River Settlement by cart to Fort Carlton (between Fort Pitt and Prince Albert) on the Saskatchewan River and from there by road to Green Lake.[73] At Green Lake "batteaux"[74] were built to ferry these pieces to Portage La Loche. By 1875 half of the Mackenzie District and all of the Athabasca District freight was shipped this way,[75] and by 1877 nearly all freight bound for either the Athabasca District or the Mackenzie District was shipped by way of Green Lake to Portage La Loche.[76]

The point of the foregoing description of the changing HBC transport system using the Portage La Loche route has been to emphasize its role in the creation of communities of freemen, who had found work in the transport business as tripmen on the brigades and as freighters between Fort Carlton and Green Lake by the 1870s. It also brought Métis from the Red River Settlement through these communities as members of the Portage La Loche brigade. Some of these Métis, as well as Métis from the Saskatchewan River, would settle in the English River region to take advantage of work on the transport route. As such, work on transport brigades, as well as trading roles in the fur trade, provided a niche in which Métis identities could evolve.

This type of process is illustrated in the career of Pierre Laliberte, a long-time employee of the HBC.[77] As early as the 1830 Chipewyans had begun to collect around Portage La Loche to offer assistance to passing brigades. The HBC, however, found that the hiring of Indians not only was expensive but disrupted the trade of the English River District, as it distracted them from hunting and trapping. As a result, the company encouraged freemen to settle at the portage to work with the horses on transport. By 1843 the HBC was persuading Saskatchewan River freemen to settle at Lac la Loche to prevent the Cree and Chipewyan from abandoning their hunts, and in 1848 the horses at the portage were put in the charge of Antoine Desjarlais, a Lesser Slave Lake freeman.[78] The HBC by the 1850s had stationed oxen and cattle at Lac La Loche, where they erected a trading post to coordinate the business of transport across the portage and the employment of freemen. For most of the late 1850s and 1860s the man in charge of the Portage La Loche post and the transport business was Pierre Laliberte. By the early 1870s the postmaster at Île-à-la-Crosse noted that several families had built houses or huts at certain points on Lac la Loche and were cultivating small patches of potatoes. Some families also settled at Bull's House, located at the north end of Buffalo Lake, where oxen were being wintered for summer transport across Portage La Loche.[79]

When the overland route from Fort Carlton to Green Lake became the primary route to Portage La Loche in the 1870s, the Green Lake area became a settlement site for freeman trippers. Pierre Laliberte, earlier in charge of the transport business of Portage la Loche, was transferred to Green Lake in the late 1860s, where he took over similar duties. When Laliberte retired from HBC service in 1874, he did not take up a hunting and trapping lifestyle but instead opted to go into the independent transport business. William McMurray, the postmaster at Île-à-la-Crosse noted in 1874 that Pierre Laliberte was leaving the service and intended to go to Manitoba to dispose of some property and afterwards to come back to Green Lake to settle. Laliberte did not intend to become a free trader. Rather, he wished to acquire oxen and haul freight from Fort Garry to Carlton or Green Lake and thereafter to be employed as a freighter on the Carlton/Green Lake Road. McMurray further noted that Laliberte had several sons and was connected with the Morins and others in the district. If he could get the freighting contract from the HBC, he would employ these friends and relatives and they would be prevented from joining the employment of competing trading interests.[80] It is interesting to note that Pierre Laliberte and all his extended family would take Métis scrip in the period from the 1880s to the early twentieth century. In other words, employment in the transport business was another route to Métis ethnogenesis in the Green Lake region.

Conclusion: Patterns of Ethnogenesis

Although there are divergences in the process of Métis ethnogenesis in different regions (Great Lakes, Lower Missouri, Northern Plains, and the north) there are also common patterns related to the fur-trading economy. Occupational and economic aspects of ethnogenesis have been emphasized not because the cultural or kinship aspects of Métis identity are unimportant, but because it was the fur trade economy that created the social and economic space wherein a distinct culture and identity could develop. Common to all the processes outlined above are a number of specific stages or steps. The first necessary step was the decision of European fur traders to winter in Indian country. Here they not only became acclimatized to the environment and Native groups, but also formed relationships with Native women and kin connections with her band. It was this stage that produced a large number of offspring of mixed ancestry. They second step was the process of "going free" or leaving the employ of fur-trading companies to become an independent trapper, trader, or tripper. This step led almost inevitably to a third stage, where various freemen families would join together in bands (northern plains) or trading villages (Great Lakes and Lower Missouri), usually in close proximity to a trading post and Native kin. It was in these residential enclaves, separate from both European trading post and Indian group, that a new identity was forged emphasizing the middleman-broker skills crucial to operating as an independent factor in the fur trade. Here successive generations of Métis children would marry among themselves (endogamy) and sons and daughters would follow the occupational and cultural patterns of their parents. The biracial and bicultural skills of these Métis families and individuals made them the pre-eminent and predominant middlemen and labourers in the dual economy that was the fur trade. Without a catalyst like the fur trade economy, which put a premium on biracial and bicultural skills and offered relative isolation from the assimilating forces of large Anglo-American or Euro-Canadian populations, Métis ethnogenesis would have been very challenging.

PART TWO

The Genesis and Development of the Idea of the Métis Nation to the 1930s

Nations are not inscribed into the nature of things, they do not constitute a political version of the doctrine of natural kinds. Nor were national states the manifest ultimate destiny of ethnic and cultural groups. What do exist are cultures, often subtly grouped, shading into each other, overlapping, intertwined; and there exist, usually but not always, political units of all shapes and sizes. In the past the two did not generally converge ... But nationalism is not the awakening and assertion of these mythical, supposedly natural and given units. It is, on the contrary, the crystallization of new units, suitable for the conditions now prevailing, though admittedly using as their raw material the cultural, historical and other inheritances from the pre-nationalist world.

Ernest Gellner, *Nations and Nationalism*
(Ithaca: Cornell University Press, 1983), 49

In 1991, the Canadian historian Lyle Dick published an article in which he deconstructed the historical discourse that had arisen in English-Canadian historical writing regarding the Battle of Seven Oaks in 1816.[1] This battle, arising out of the violent competition between the North West Company (NWC) and the Hudson's Bay Company (HBC) for fur trade dominance in the British northwest, involved an attack on the Red River Settlement by the North West Company using their Métis kinsmen as the shock troops to disperse the settlement. In this battle the colony's governor, Robert Semple, was killed along with twenty of his men (one Métis died in the battle), and the colony was dispersed until Lord Selkirk re-established it by force. In an interesting analysis of the literature that sprang up about this battle, Dick tried to demonstrate how, after 1870, Anglo-Canadian historians used partisan accounts of the battle along with romantic plot structures to reinterpret the Métis action in this incident as a savage slaughter. According to Dick, this alleged Métis "savagism" at Seven Oaks functioned allegorically to justify the dispossession of Métis land by the incoming settlers and discredit the legitimacy of the Riel Resistance to Confederation and by extension all Métis rights.[2]

As interesting as Dick's analysis is in its particulars, his larger arguments and conclusions seem to us to miss an important point. Despite the claim that Dick is deconstructing a significant English-Canadian historical tradition, he examines the Battle of Seven Oaks in a narrow fashion. "Who fired the first shot?" "Did the Métis mutilate the bodies of Semple's men?" "Who should bear most of the blame for two dozen or so deaths?" While these questions did engage the minds of historians in the late nineteenth and early twentieth centuries, they began to be displaced by another discourse in the 1930s – the Battle of Seven Oaks as the genesis of the Métis Nation.

While racial discourse regarding the Métis was dominant in the nineteenth century, by the third decade of the twentieth century "Nation" discourse was beginning to supplant it in Canadian historiography. That is not to say that race and nation were incompatible formulations, and indeed racial thinking continued to permeate the ideas of Marcel Giraud and W.L. Morton even as they began to speak of the inauguration of the Métis Nation at the Battle of Seven Oaks, but this new discourse was of a different order. In this narration of the Métis Nation, the Battle of Seven Oaks was given pride of place as the political and military midwife in the birth of a new nation. Very much the product of twentieth-century historical writing, these events and interpretations have not been used, for the most part, to justify Métis dispossession or discredit Métis rights, as Dick argued. Rather, since the 1930s, the crediting of the Battle of Seven Oaks as both the time and the place of the political emergence of the Métis has served to naturalize and essentialize the Métis Nation as an unproblematic idea of national progress, providing them with a story of national origins and the myth of a founding father. This story, once established as unproblematic and natural, becomes the story of martyrdom at the hands of the Canadian state with the annexation of Rupert's Land.

The purpose of this section of the book is to present a brief analysis of how the idea of the Métis Nation became the dominant narrative of Métis history in the twentieth century and to explain the place of the Battle of Seven Oaks in that history. We will argue that the Battle of Seven

Oaks as the origin story is both old and modern. There were, indeed, competing narratives of nation, not the least of which was Riel's messianic vision, which had to be jettisoned for the Battle of Seven Oaks to become the ideological form of the present Métis Nation. It is this process that will be narrated in the following chapters.

3 Fur Trade Wars, the Battle of Seven Oaks, and the Idea of the Métis Nation, 1811–1849

The fur-trade dynamics and events leading up to the Battle of Seven Oaks have been recounted many times, but a brief retelling is necessary here to show how the Métis Nation became a part of this discourse and how it was further articulated in the three decades after 1816. This retelling denaturalizes the simple narrative of "Birth of a Nation" and argues that different and competing interpretations emerged from the battle. These narratives, articulated by the competing fur-trading companies, paid scant attention to the views and actual claims of the Métis themselves. Only in the succeeding thirty years did they begin to articulate a series of claims as national rights that made the Battle of Seven Oaks the usable history it has become.

The Context and the Battle of Seven Oaks

The immediate context of the Battle of Seven Oaks was the decision in 1811 by Lord Selkirk and the London Committee of the Hudson's Bay Company (HBC) to establish a settler colony in the heart of Rupert's Land at the forks of the Red and Assiniboine Rivers, and the increasingly violent competition for fur trade supremacy in the northwest, particularly in the Athabasca region, between the HBC and the North West Company (NWC). Even before its establishment in 1812 the Nor'Westers believed that the Selkirk Colony would disrupt their supply and communications routes between the Athabasca and Fort William. Its projected site would sit astride their crucial provisioning route. The Nor'Westers rightly suspected that the colony was part of the Hudson's Bay Company plans to compete more effectively in the Athabasca. Until 1811, through intimidation, violence, and advantages in manpower and provisioning, the North West Company had been able to monopolize the Athabasca fur trade, the last fur eldorado of the northwest. If the Selkirk Colony provided the Hudson's Bay Company with better provisioning and manpower, and if the colony infringed at all on the North West Company's provisioning system, the Nor'Westers believed that their advantage in the Athabasca would be lost, and with it their chance of victory in the "Fur Trade Wars."[3] For all of these reasons the NWC tried to prevent Selkirk from acquiring land from the HBC; it disrupted Selkirk's recruiting of Scottish settlers and, after the colony was established, it attempted to destroy the fledgling settlement by turning the Indians, freemen, and Métis against it.

The environmental and ecological context of the Battle of Seven Oaks is also important for understanding both the timing of the conflict and the motivations of the North West Company in instigating the battle. The first of these climatic/ecological factors was the onset of the shorter summers and longer and harsher winters in 1810–11, lasting until 1818, which were accompanied by severe droughts from 1815 to 1819.[4] By far the most important aspect of these weather disruptions was the effect they would have on the plains provision trade.[5]

From at least 1809 through 1814 there are reports from Edmonton, Carlton, and Brandon that weather patterns were erratic and that provisioning levels were at crisis levels. On the North Saskatchewan, the winter of 1810–11 was particularly bad, with very deep snow and extremely cold temperatures, killing both horses and buffalo and producing a provisioning crisis.[6] Spring came late that year and freeze-up early[7] and provisions were again short the next winter though for different reasons. The winter was mild and with almost no snow, with the result that the buffalo stayed too far out on the plains and thus out of reach of the fort hunters. Provisions continued to be scarce through the summer and fall of 1812, as drought and large prairie fires kept the buffalo south of the South Saskatchewan River.[8] The drought and prairie fires were again a problem through the spring, summer, and early winter of 1813. The buffalo could be found only below the South Saskatchewan, and Indians in the vicinity of Edmonton house were starving and the fur trading companies had few provisions other than fish.[9] At Carlton House provisions were almost as scarce during this period. In the winter of 1811–12 the want of snow and the mild weather kept the buffalo out on the plains far from the post.[10] By June of 1812 Carlton was out of dry provisions.[11] The supply of provisions had increased slightly by the spring of 1814,[12] and by the winter of 1814–15 provisions were again abundant, and the buffalo moved towards Carlton House very quickly and in large numbers.[13]

At Brandon House provisions were at crisis levels in the winter of 1811–12.[14] Deep snow and a cold winter made it difficult to find buffalo and Indians brought in very few provisions as the Cree and Assiniboine themselves were starving.[15] There are indications that the winter of 1814–15 was very difficult in the Red River District as well,[16] but by the late summer of 1815 provisions were again abundant in this district.

Thus, at the very time that the Selkirk Colony was being planted, the northwestern plains were undergoing some of the worst provisioning years in more than a decade. Feeding the Selkirk settlers in the winter during this period was a tenuous proposition when relations between the freemen and Métis and the North West Company were not overtly hostile and impossible when they were.

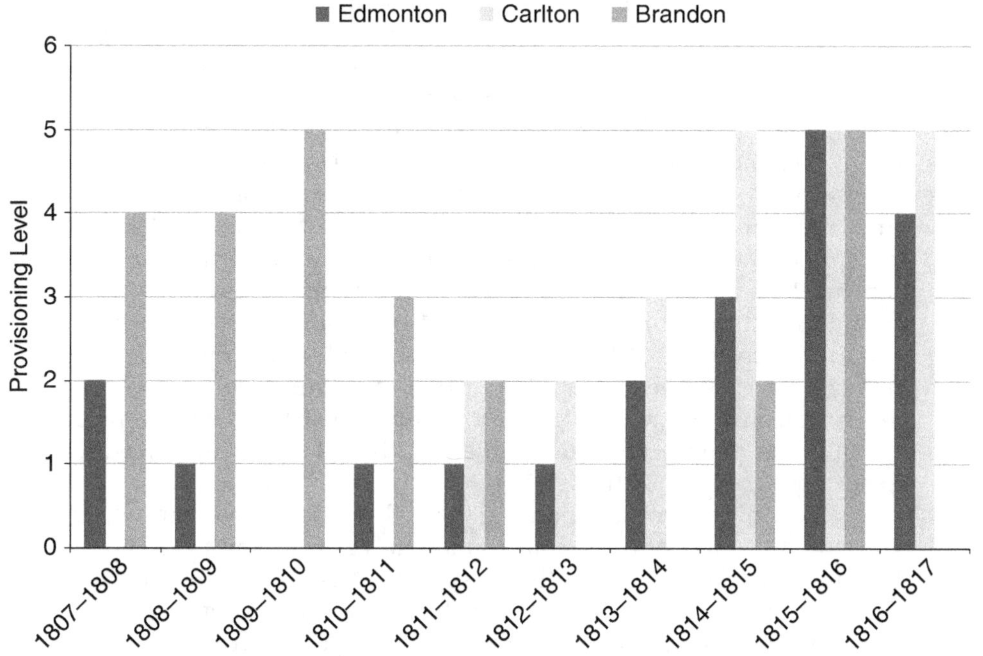

3.1 Plains provision by year, 1807-1817. Hudson's Bay Company Archives, post journals.

On 12 June 1811 the HBC had conveyed 116,000 square miles of territory (Assiniboia), centring on the forks of the Red and Assiniboine Rivers, to Lord Selkirk for colonization purposes. The first settlers from Scotland arrived in the fall of 1812, too late to plant crops and unprepared to feed themselves through the winter; consequently, they were forced to relocate to Pembina for the winter, where they were provisioned by freemen and Métis buffalo hunters and aided by the NWC traders. In the spring of 1813 the settlers returned to the forks, where they began building their houses on lots surveyed by Peter Fidler in close proximity to the HBC's Fort Douglas. The next winter saw some colonists winter at Fort Douglas, but the majority again retreated to Pembina with their governor, Miles Macdonell, where they could be supported by the provisions provided by the buffalo-hunting freemen and Métis wintering there. By this time, however, the NWC partners in Montreal had informed their wintering counterparts that the Selkirk Colony posed a grave risk to the fortunes of their company, and from this point on the Nor'Westers used their considerable powers of suasion to separate Métis and freemen interests from the struggling colony.

Struggling to feed even his small contingent of settlers in the winter of 1813–14 and expecting a significant increase in colonists in the summer of 1814, Governor Macdonell issued his infamous "Pemmican Proclamation" in early January 1814. While Miles Macdonell's Pemmican Proclamation would have been ill advised during normal times, in January 1814 it was probably an act of desperation. James Bird, writing from Edmonton House in response to Macdonell's request for pemmican for the spring of 1814, replied that he could send none, as he had none to send.[17] While the supply of provisions improved very slightly at Carlton in the late spring of 1814, Macdonell had few prospects of collecting pemmican in the winter of 1813–14 sufficient to feed an expected increase of settlers in 1814.

The Pemmican Proclamation, legal or otherwise, stated that no persons trading in furs or provisions could remove provisions from Assiniboia for the next twelve months except what traders required to carry them to their destinations. To take such necessary provisions out of the territory, however, traders had to apply for permission from the governor. Those provisions needed to feed the settlers would be paid for at the customary rate, but failure to abide by the proclamation would lead to the seizure of goods and prosecution.[18] Meeting with little cooperation from the North West Company, Governor Macdonell sent Sherriff John Spencer to seize provisions from the Nor'Westers at White Horse

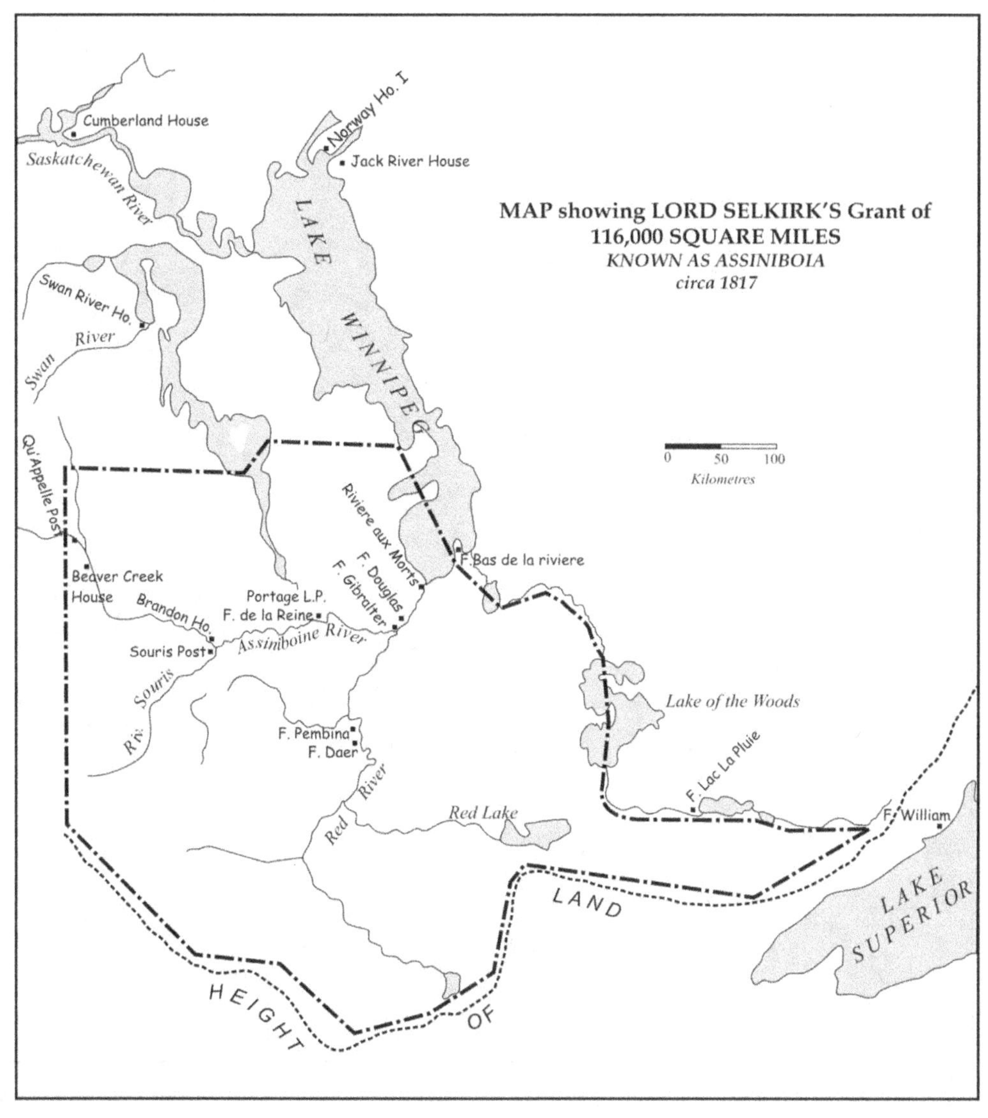

3.2 Lord Selkirk's Grant, 1811. Adapted from George Bryce, *The Five Forts of Winnipeg* (Winnipeg: Royal Society of Canada, 1885), plate III.

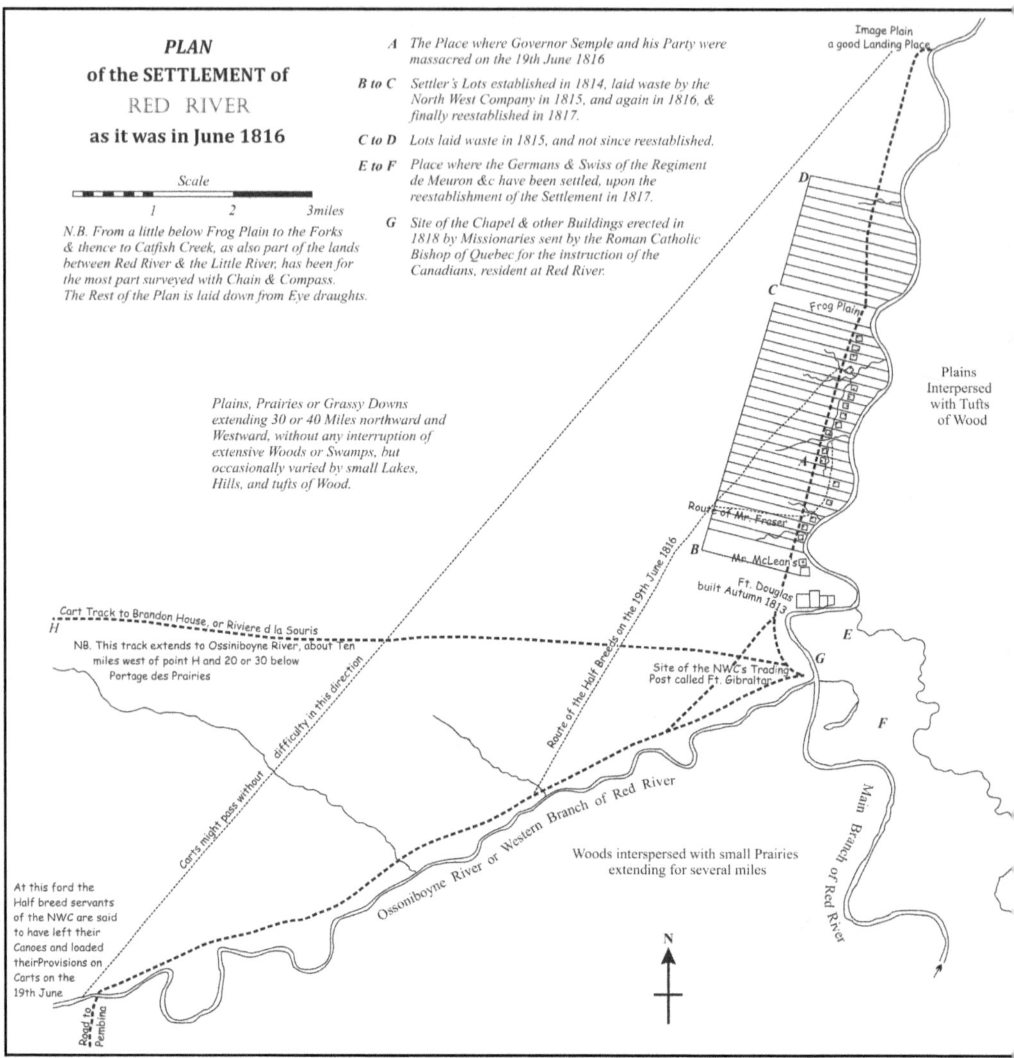

3.3 Métis movements at Red River, 19 June 1816. Adapted from Aaron Arrowsmith's Map in *Report of Trials in the Courts of Canada, Relative to the Destruction of the Earl of Selkirk's Settlement on the Red River with Observations* (London: J. Murray, 1820).

Plains on 25 May 1814.[19] Facing this threat to their supply system, an NWC bourgeois stopped at the Selkirk Colony in June of 1814, on his way to Fort William, and negotiated a release of enough pemmican to supply the NWC northern brigades. As well, the company was given permission to export more fat and pemmican in return for a commitment to help feed the colonists over the coming winter.[20] With this agreement, trouble seemed to have been averted. Evidence from the annual NWC meetings at Fort William, however, indicates that the company had little intention of holding to this agreement, and by the summer of 1814 the Nor'Westers were committed to defending their property at all costs as well as to the destruction of the colony.[21]

With more settlers in the colony and expecting a hard winter, Governor Macdonell issued another precipitous proclamation in July 1814 prohibiting the hunting of buffalo on horseback for the remainder of the year for fear this type of hunting would drive the buffalo too far onto the plains and out of range of the settlement hunters. If Macdonell's Pemmican Proclamation of January 1814 was understandable in the context of a provisioning crisis and NWC hostilities, his proclamation forbidding the hunting of buffalo on horseback was ill advised. Given there were few buffalo within range of the colony or HBC trading posts that winter, this proclamation had little effect other than to raise the ire of the Métis, who in any case did not heed it.

These two proclamations, coming one after the other, did much to turn many freemen, Métis, and Indians against the governor, if not the settlement. Commenting on the Pemmican Proclamation, Grandes Oreilles, a chief of the Ojibwa, is reported to have asked[22] how the "Landworkers" (his term for the colonists) dared to deprive the NWC of the provisions they (the Indians) had traded. This was not an issue just for the trading companies but for the trading Indians as well. They were accustomed to encamp around the forts of their traders in spring (a typical time of scarcity), when the companies would feed their children with pounded meat and grease. Grandes Oreilles wished to see the settlers and the North West Company at peace, but if the "Landworkers" did not allow the company to trade as usual, he noted, "they shall be destroyed."[23] The prohibition against running the buffalo was also an interference with the practices of the freemen and Métis, and when the NWC traders saw the ill will the proclamation had stirred up, they fed this resentment and refused to supply the colony with any meat.

The winter of 1814–15 was a very difficult one, as the Métis buffalo hunters at Pembina were now increasingly hostile to the colony. Most of the settlers who wintered at the forks (Miles Macdonell and another group returned to Pembina for a third winter) became discouraged and were convinced by Duncan Cameron, the NWC bourgeois at Fort Gibraltar, to accept his offer of passage to Canada. Consequently, in June of 1815, 133 settlers departed Red River in NWC canoes. For the remaining colonists the situation only got worse. Later in June of that summer a group of NWC servants and Métis headed by Cuthbert Grant laid siege to the settlement, burning their crops, killing their cattle, and eventually forcing Governor Macdonell to surrender. The remaining settlers and HBC personnel, headed by Peter Fidler, were forced to sign a capitulation to abandon the colony.[24]

Colin Robertson, en route from Montreal to spearhead a northern trading expedition for the Hudson's Bay Company, met these settlers at Norway House and convinced them to return under his protection. They reached the forks in the fall of 1815, where they re-established their homes and harvested what crops had not been destroyed. At that point the NWC post, Fort Gibraltar, was captured and later dismantled by Robert Semple, the incoming governor of the colony. Then, in November of 1815, 120 new colonists arrived at the re-established colony.

The North West Company, infuriated that the colony had not disappeared and their own Fort Gibraltar had been destroyed, resolved to crush the settlement for good, to which purpose they began to gather freemen and Métis associated with the Nor'Westers from across the northwestern plains at Fort Qu'Appelle in the late winter of 1816.[25] In May of that year HBC boats loaded with furs and pemmican departed Qu'Appelle for Red River. Within a few miles they were captured by NWC servants and Métis, and the HBC and colony men manning the boats were imprisoned in the NWC post at Qu'Appelle. From there the Métis, again led by Cuthbert Grant, moved on to Brandon House, capturing this HBC post in early June, from whence they embarked for the forks, both on horseback and in boats, arriving at Portage La Prairie by mid-June. By this time Governor Semple and the Selkirk colonists had been warned by friendly freemen and Saulteaux that Alexander Macdonell of the NWC and a group of Métis were travelling down the Assiniboine to destroy the settlement.

Semple kept a close watch from Fort Douglas, and in the early evening of 19 June 1816 the sentry spotted approximately sixty men on horseback with two carts crossing the prairie about one or two miles from the fort and headed north to the settlers' houses. With few alternatives available to him, Semple gathered slightly more than twenty men and marched out on foot to intercept the Métis. On seeing Semple and his men, the mounted Métis split into two flanking columns and quickly surrounded them. A short parlay took place during which Semple grabbed the gunstock of François Boucher and a shot was fired (in all probability by the Semple party), beginning a fire fight in which Semple and all but two of his party were killed. The next day the Métis under the leadership of Grant demanded that the settlers leave and the HBC surrender the fort or meet with the same fate as Semple and his men. With this demand, the Selkirk Settlement was dispersed for the second time in two years.

From eyewitness testimony collected by W.B. Coltman in 1817 and various trials in Upper Canada in 1818, it is clear that the violence that occurred on 19 June was unplanned. The Métis led by Cuthbert Grant were intending to circumvent the Fort Douglas to avoid an immediate confrontation. It was Semple's action in marching out to confront the Métis party that led to the battle. Just as clearly, however, this was no peaceful pemmican run to resupply NWC boats coming from Fort William and heading north. Grant's intention was to avoid Fort Douglas, occupy the settler houses, and cut off any retreat of colonists from Fort Douglas and then to lay siege to Fort Douglas until it surrendered. In other words, the strategy was to duplicate the strategy of 1815: avoid a full-blown battle but still manage to disperse and destroy the colony.

The Métis and the North West Company did not destroy the Selkirk Colony in 1815 and again in 1816 because it threatened their provisioning system or because the buffalo-hunting economy of the Métis was being threatened by the Pemmican Proclamation and the strictures against the mounted buffalo hunt. By the summer of 1815 there were no restrictions on the Métis Buffalo hunts or on the movement of pemmican out of Assiniboia. The provisioning crisis was over. In the Red River District there were large quantities of dried meat and pemmican in all the district posts by the early summer of 1815;[26] by the fall of that year buffalo were plentiful even near the Red River Settlement.[27] There was an excess of pemmican everywhere and the buffalo were numerous from Pembina to Brandon House to Edmonton through 1817 (see figure 3.1).[28] Indeed, all posts in the northwest were flush with dried meat, fat, and pemmican. While one might make the case for residual Métis resentment of the attempt to control their buffalo hunting in the Red River District in 1814, the NWC actions in gathering Métis from across the west to attack the colony (they came from as far away as Fort Augustus on the North Saskatchewan River) in 1816 belies this point.

James Bird's explanation for the violence is more plausible. He noted that the North West Company encouraged Métis aggression against the colony in 1816 because of the abundance of provisions throughout the northwest by the summer of 1815. Travelling from Edmonton House to York Factory in the spring of 1816, he became aware of the NWC and Métis actions against the HBC posts in the Qu'Appelle region and at Brandon House and the planned actions against the Red River Settlement. On reaching Cumberland House, he noted that in the present state of affairs Cumberland House should prepare to defend itself from NWC aggression. If it was not defended, he feared that the NWC would seize the post, destroy the pemmican there, and thereby crush any attempt the HBC could make on expanding their Athabasca campaign that year.[29] A few days later he was even more explicit and noted that, with the uncommonly large amounts of dry provisions available at all provisioning posts, NWC hopes of being able to shut the HBC out of the Athabasca District were being defeated. It was this dynamic that Bird believed was behind the NWC seizures at Qu'Appelle and Brandon House in May of 1816 and the root of the NWC campaign against the Red River Settlement.[30] While the provisioning crisis was over by the summer of 1815, the battle for the Athabasca fur lands was still red hot. If the HBC were able to easily provision their brigades and posts in Athabasca, the NWC dominance in the region would be threatened. The seizure of the HBC posts at Qu'Appelle and Brandon (both provisioning posts) and the destruction of the Selkirk Colony (a strategic settlement in the reorganization plans of the HBC) all were, according to Bird, part of the NWC campaign to defend their interests in the Athabasca District.

The NWC versus the HBC and the Competing Discourses of Race and Nationalism

The meaning of, and the blame for, the Battle of Seven Oaks began to be disputed almost as soon as peace had been restored. The extreme violence that had marked the competition between the two fur-trading companies, especially the twenty-two deaths in the battle, was regarded by Canadian and colonial officials in England as an affront to British control over the region and a commission of inquiry was convened to determine the causes of the conflict and to apportion blame.[31] In this investigation the officials of the North West Company tried to deflect any blame for the violence from their company. According to William McGillivray, Lord

Selkirk's and the Hudson's Bay Company's colonizing efforts at Red River had been aimed from the start at destroying the NWC. The North West Company, he testified to the Coltman Commission, had acted only in self-defence and had scrupulously followed the law. It was Selkirk and the HBC who were the aggressors.[32] To explain the twenty-one deaths of the colonists at Seven Oaks, and to deflect blame from the NWC and its employees, McGillivray noted that the actions of the Métis were separate from those of the company. He portrayed the Métis as an independent band of Indians who, in protecting their ancestral lands and rights, had attacked the colony on its own volition. The North West Company had no control over this new nation:[33]

> The assemblage of half-breeds requires a little further comment; we need not dwell here upon the organization of that class of men. You are yourself, Sir personally aware, that although many of them, from the ties of consanguinity and interest, are more or less connected with the North-West company's people, and either as clerks or servants, or as free hunters, are dependent on them; yet they one and all look upon themselves as members of an independent tribe of natives, entitled to a property in the soil, to a flag of their own, and to protection from the British Government.
>
> It is absurd to consider them legally in any other light than as Indians; the British law admits no filiation of illegitimate children but that of the mother; and as these persons cannot in law claim any advantage by paternal right, it follows, that they ought not to be subjected to any disadvantages which might be supposed to arise from the fortuitous circumstances of their parentage.
>
> Being therefore Indians, they, as is frequently the case among the tribes of this vast continent, as *young men* (the technical term for warrior) have a right to form a new tribe on any unoccupied, or (according to Indian law) any conquered territory. That the half-breeds under the denomination of *bois brulés* and *metifs* have formed a separate and distinct tribe of Indians for a considerable time back, has been proved to you by various depositions.[34]

It was in the interests of the North West Company that the Métis should be considered a new nation of Indians, for if the Métis were regarded as an independent tribe of Indians who had attacked the Red River Settlement for their own reasons, the NWC could not be blamed for the bloodshed in 1816.

Lord Selkirk and the Hudson's Bay Company officials took a diametrically opposite view of both events and the role and affiliation of the Métis. According to Selkirk, the North West Company had from the first resolved to destroy the colony on the Red River. Having failed to induce the Indians to destroy Selkirk's budding settlement, the partners of the North West Company next turned to the Plains Métis. Closely tied to the various bourgeois of the North West Company by consanguinity and employment, Selkirk argued that the Métis were encouraged to oppose HBC efforts to found a colony in Assiniboia and resist any attempts to impose government over them. From correspondence intercepted by Selkirk's agents at Red River it was clear to Selkirk and his supporters that the NWC partners were encouraging the Métis to destroy the Red River Settlement.[35] Far from being a new nation, these Métis, according to Selkirk, were little more than "lawless banditti, technically termed, in that country, *Métifs, Bois Brulés*, or *Half-breeds*." As the illegitimate progeny chiefly of the Canadian traders and others in the service of the North West Company, by Indian women, Selkirk further argued that they had "always been much under the control of that Company, by whom they are frequently employed as hunters, chiefly for provisions, an occupation in which they are very expert, hunting and shooting the buffalo on horseback."[36] Selkirk argued that in order to destroy the colony the NWC collected and organized the Métis tied to the company from all parts of the northwest to descend on the colony. Though encouraged to consider themselves a separate tribe of men, a "Nation of Independent Indians," these "*Bois Brulés*" were, Selkirk argued, with few exceptions, in the employ of the NWC and their dupes.[37]

The "half-breeds" in the Hudson's Bay Company system were also beginning to emerge as a separate collectivity, though with a decidedly anti-Métis bias. James Bird, the chief factor of Edmonton House in this period, and the HBC officer who took over control of the company's operations in the northwest when Semple was killed in 1816, noted from Jack River:

> All the Half Breeds (sons of servants of the Company) that are here have expressed a wish to embody themselves under affairs of their own choosing and to come forward to arrest the alarming influences which the Canadian Half Breeds may now acquire by their achievements in Red River; they are perhaps rather inferior in point of numbers to their Enemies yet if collected from all parts of the Country and regularly organized they cannot fail to be a powerful check … I have thanked our young men for their offer & given them every encouragement in my power to take every measure that may enable them to come forward hereafter with Effect.[38]

Here then are the two dominant discourses that would dominate the discussion of the Métis to the present, and both arose in the aftermath of the killings and violence at Seven Oaks. The one authored by Selkirk and the HBC saw the Métis largely in racial terms – the hybrid offspring of fur traders and Native women. Those in the employ of the NWC were also controlled by them. To be sure, the HBC did regard them as a new social grouping, as noted by both Selkirk's comments and Bird's observations of "half-breeds," emerging in the HBC system. Neither of these social groupings, however, was accorded any distinct political independence. Choosing to blame all the troubles and violence on the machinations of the North West Company, the Hudson's Bay Company saw the Métis merely as the "mixed-blood" children of North West Company servants who had been manipulated by NWC officers to do their dirty work. The other discourse, authored primarily by the officers of the North West Company, wishing to deflect blame from themselves for the killing of Semple and his men, portrayed the Métis primarily in political terms as a "new nation," with a sovereign claim to the soil, a political consciousness, and a flag.

The Invention of a Tradition

From the 1930s on, Canadian historians have increasingly accepted the latter discourse as more accurate because it fits more conveniently with subsequent events, especially the Riel-led uprisings of 1869 and 1885. An examination of the developments after 1816, however, makes these assertions problematic. While the Battle of Seven Oaks would spur the emergence of cultural, historical, and symbolic aspects of group consciousness that, when tied to a claim to the soil, would become the hallmarks of Métis nationalism, this process was anything but straightforward.

The first of these symbolic markers was the flag that the Métis carried into battle in 1815, described by Peter Fidler as a blue cloth about four feet square with a large, white figure 8 horizontal (the infinity symbol) in the middle.[39] This flag had become, by the latter part of the twentieth century, the universal symbol of the Métis Nation, but any attempt to read this meaning back to 1815 or even the mid-nineteenth century meets with some serious roadblocks. We now know that the flag was designed and given to the Métis by the North West Company to try to instil patriotic fervour.[40] As well, between 1816 and the twentieth century this flag was nowhere to be seen. Indeed, during the Riel Resistance of 1869–70 Riel chose a very different flag to symbolize his new nation, one that featured the fleur-de-lis and a shamrock. This obvious association with Quebec and Irish Catholicism, however, became a stumbling block to a more inclusive Métis nationalism in the latter part of the twentieth century and hence the Métis reverted to the horizontal 8 as their national flag.

In order for it to make the case that the Métis / *Bois Brulés* were an independent nation/tribe of Indians with claims to the soil,[41] in 1816 the North West Company had encouraged them to paint themselves as Indians and put feathers on their heads. According to the testimony of Antoine Houle, this had never been the practice of the Métis or freemen before this point.[42] To this end, after the first dispersion of the Selkirk Colony in the summer of 1815, when the Métis forced Peter Fidler to sign a capitulation in June of that year, Cuthbert Grant, Bostonais Pangman, William Shaw, and Bonhomme Montour signed the document for the Métis as "The four chiefs of the Half-breeds,"[43] though in fact all four were employees of the North West Company and sons of NWC partners. That such posing as a "separate and distinct tribe of Indians" was at least partly a fiction was obvious in 1816 when Cuthbert assumed control of Fort Douglas after the Battle of Seven Oaks and signed a nine-page inventory of goods seized at Fort Douglas as "Received on Account of the North West Company, by one Cuthbert Grant Clerk to the North West Company." As J.M. Bumsted has noted, by signing as a clerk of the North West Company rather than as chief of the "new nation," Grant was suggesting "that he himself did not believe he was acting principally as an autonomous leader of his people."[44]

That the Métis were not regarded by Indians as an independent band/tribe/nation having claims to the soil or territory is also clear from the treaty negotiations of 1817. From at least 1812, Miles Macdonell was under instructions to investigate the possibility of making a treaty or purchasing land from the Indian groups of Assiniboia so as to legitimate the colony at the forks.[45] To this end Macdonell treated liberally with the Cree, Assiniboine, and Saulteaux of the region, and by 1813 he was able to tell Selkirk that, regardless of the fears the North West Company had stirred up against the colony, all the Saulteaux, who occupied the region around the settlement, were favourably disposed to it and were open to making a sale or signing a treaty. They referred to Macdonell as the "Master of the Soil" and their father who had come for their good. From that point on the various Saulteaux chiefs of the region, including Peguis, supported, even defended, the colony.[46] When Lord Selkirk's men recaptured Fort Douglas in January 1817 they were accompanied by Peguis and his warriors, who thereafter helped defend the colony from counter-attack and helped provision it as well.[47]

When Selkirk arrived at Red River later that summer, he quickly made arrangements to sign a formal treaty with the Indians of the region. The various Indian chiefs who had an interest in the territory were sounded out on this matter by William Coltman, and on 18 July an agreement was signed by Le Sonnant (Cree chief), Le Robe Noir (Ojibwa or Saulteaux chief), Le Homme Noir (an Assiniboine chief), Peguis (an Ojibwa or Saulteaux chief) and Premier (Ojibwa or Saulteaux chief) by affixing their totems to the agreement (see figure 3.4). The terms of this treaty included a payment of 100 pounds of tobacco to be paid annually to the Saulteaux and Cree bands in exchange for which Selkirk was granted land "extending in breadth to the distance of 2 English statute miles" along the banks of the Red River from Lake Winnipeg to Grand Forks, and a similar strip of land along the Assiniboine River from its junction with the Red River to Musk Rat Creek near Portage La Prairie. In addition, three circles, each with a radius of six miles, were granted around Fort Douglas, Fort Daer, and Grand Forks.[48]

Throughout this process no one – not Coltman, not Selkirk, not the Métis interpreters – believed it necessary to consult the Métis, and during the speeches made at the various meetings Chief Peguis was quoted as having said that the *Bois Brulés* were not acknowledged as an independent tribe.[49] Indeed, for a group so small and so young (barely one generation), it is not surprising that they were accorded no claims to territory. According to Peter Fidler's survey of the freeman and Métis population in the Red River / Qu'Appelle region in 1814, this group amounted to only fifty-five families (sixty-five families if the Swan River District is included). Compare this figure to Fidler's count of 480 tents and 1,300 warriors of the Saulteaux, Cree, and Assiniboine bands in the region.[50] But if Métis claims went unacknowledged in 1817, even by the Métis themselves, the upheavals of 1814–17, including the Battle of Seven Oaks, did set in motion a nationalist dynamic that would ripple through the rest of the nineteenth and twentieth centuries.

The Articulation of a National Tradition, 1816–1849

Although the Métis military actions in dispersing the Selkirk Colony in 1815 and 1816 were largely the product of the North West Company's organization and goading of their Métis kinsmen, the performance of these military actions acted as a powerful spur for the Métis to re-imagine

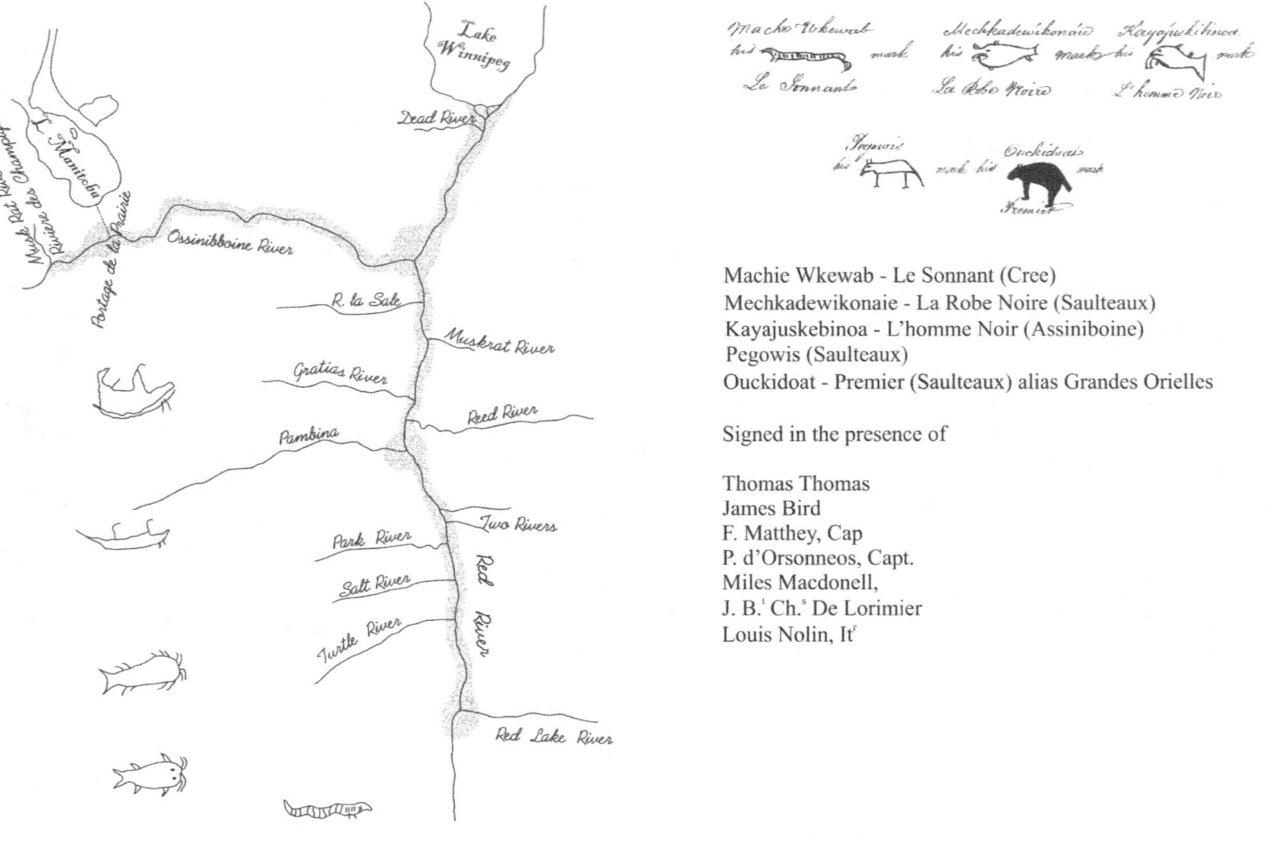

3.4 The limits of the Selkirk Treaty, 18 July 1817, and Native signatories. Adapted from Aaron Arrowsmith's Map in *Report of Trials in the Courts of Canada, Relative to the Destruction of the Earl of Selkirk's Settlement on the Red River With Observations* (London: J. Murray, 1820).

who they were. Over the next three decades they would come to regard themselves both as British subjects, with the rights this status entailed, and as Natives, with Aboriginal claims to the soil. Though the term "Nation" was seldom if ever used in the thirty years after 1816, the Métis actively defended and began to articulate a series of claims as national rights.

The first Métis expression of this new-found confidence was probably Pierre Falcon's[51] *Chanson de la Grenouillère,* written to commemorate or celebrate the Métis victory at Seven Oaks.[52] Composed very shortly after the battle, probably as the Métis camped at Frog Plain that night, the song directly appealed to Métis pride and sensitivity. While hardly a national anthem, it does portray the Métis as a brave and honourable group prevailing over an assembly of outsiders with an overconfident and overreaching leader (Semple). The song defines the Métis by name (*Bois Brûlés*), makes a claim to territory that needs defending from incursion by Orcadians and Englishmen, and celebrates the military feats of the group.[53] As Kathy Durnin has noted, whether Falcon intended to write a Métis anthem or merely to commemorate the feat of a particular group of men, his song was destined to become both.[54] However, there is a case to be made that *Chanson de la Grenuouillère,* like the Métis flag, was a product of North West Company propaganda. The earliest version of the song we have found appears in the Selkirk Papers and, from the marginal notes on the song and the contextual positioning in the Selkirk Papers, it seems likely that this version was among the NWC documents captured by Selkirk at Fort William in late 1816. If this was the case, then no sooner had Falcon composed the song than it would have to have been written down and rushed by canoe to Fort William, which could have happened only if the North West Company had seen a political reason to have the song in Canada when the news of the Battle of Seven Oaks broke.[55]

Whatever the case, the song struck a nerve with the Métis, capturing a quality they recognized in themselves. Easily remembered and repeated, the song took on a life of its own. Travelling through the Red River Valley in 1864 in the brigade of Antoine Gingras, the Reverend J.A. Gilfillan complained that Gingras sang the song so often that he became heartily sick of it.[56] Isaac Cowie, a Hudson's Bay Company trader in the Qu'Appelle District, noted that in 1869, during the Riel Resistance, the song that generated the most fire and fervour among the Métis was *Chanson de la Grenouillère.*[57] Even when the voyageur brigades and buffalo hunts were on the wane, Henri de Lamothe, travelling through western Canada in the mid-1870s noted that the song was still popular.[58]

Other observers also remarked on the new-found Métis confidence and belligerence after 1816. The officers of the Hudson's Bay Company noted that the Métis had become harder to control and deal with. James Bird, the chief factor of the Saskatchewan District and appointed acting inland governor after Semple was killed at Seven Oaks, noted in September of 1816 that the Métis were unlikely to confine their depredations to Red River. Given their success there and realizing their new strength, they might well conceive of themselves as sovereigns of the country and try to dictate laws to the trading companies.[59]

These fears did not come to pass and after the merger of the Hudson's Bay and North West companies in 1821 even Cuthbert Grant was brought into the new HBC as "Warden of the Plains" and was convinced to remain in the Red River Settlement at White Horse Plains, where he helped George Simpson manage and control the Plains Métis.[60] But even as Grant abdicated his role as the leader of an independent group of Métis for a paying position with the Hudson's Bay Company, Métis claims to land and rights continued to evolve.

The catalyst of this new campaign for Métis rights arose in response not to the Battle of Seven Oaks, but to the merger of the two companies that had brought peace to Rupert's Land. Indeed, the early leadership in this new campaign for Métis rights would come from the English Métis who in 1816 had offered to battle the French Métis in defence of the HBC. As more English Métis gravitated to the Red River Settlement in the 1820s, after the merger of the fur-trading companies had reduced employment opportunities, they joined the French Métis in agitating for freer trade. Given the HBC attempts to prevent their participation in the fur trade, they now adopted a new Aboriginal rights position. The writer of the Winnipeg post journal in 1827 noted that he had received information "that the English halfbreeds have taken much umbrage at the late search for furs, which they consider an infringement upon their liberty and independence as natives. They affirm that by birth they are sovereign lords and Masters of the Soil, and consequently not subordinate to the laws and regulations of the place, like the White; whereas on the other hand, when occasion requires; they claim as settlers the same privilege as the European part of the community."[61] For the Hudson's Bay Company officials, as for the Colonial Office later, this demand for both Aboriginal and settler rights seemed inconsistent. As the journal writer went on to note, when the Métis incorporated themselves as citizens of the colony, surely they became subject to its laws and forfeited their rights to birthright privilege if such rights had ever been recognized as belonging to them.[62]

A few years later, George Simpson, the governor of the Hudson's Bay Company in North America, also reported an upsurge in Métis activity in the Swan River District. Simpson complained that he was at a loss of how to respond, as these people were "native": "were they whites we should insist on their settling in no other part of the country than Red River, but as natives of the country they conceive they have a right to settle where they please and to deal with the natives as they think proper, and this feeling and opinion I am sorry to say is beginning to obtain among the Red River half-breeds particularly those of European parentage."[63] In these battles with the company, the Métis were aided by their fathers, now retired from the HBC at Red River, who urged their sons to petition Britain for the right of free trade and, if refused, to gain it by force.[64] Indeed, the concept of Métis/half-breeds as "natives of the country" was according to Simpson, first broached by James Bird, an erstwhile chief factor of the HBC and the father of at least three "mixed-blood" sons.[65] Simpson would later also warn the governors of the HBC that the Métis/half-breeds were planning to establish a village in the Swan River District in 1831. If this were allowed, Simpson argued, the village would attract other Métis and in no distant future the Métis population in Swan River would become a threat to the trading interests of the Hudson's Bay Company, as this group could not support themselves on agriculture, there being no markets, and must enter into the illegal trade of furs with the Indians and thereby "revive the question of rights and privileges as natives of the soil." This assertion, he went on to add would then be backed by strength and numbers.[66] Because of this threat, Simpson argued that the HBC should lose no time in breaking up the infant colony and removing it to the Red River Settlement.[67]

This nascent feeling of Métis rights became articulated in the free trade controversy of the 1840s and the petition campaign to secure the rights to trade freely. The Métis, while seeing themselves as distinct from the Indians, argued that their native-born status and their Native ancestry gave them special rights above other British subjects. That is, they had both the rights of citizens and Aboriginal rights. In an exchange with Alexander Christie, the governor of the Red River Settlement, the Métis clearly articulated a position that "Halfbreeds, or natives of European origin" had rights both as Natives of the country and as British subjects.[68] Christie's response reflected the perplexity of the Europeans regarding these dual rights: "Now as British subjects, the halfbreeds have clearly the same rights in Scotland or in England as any person born in Great Britain: and your own sense of natural justice will at once see, how unreasonable it would be to wish to place Englishmen and Scotchmen on a less favourable footing in Rupert's Land than yourselves. – Your supposition further seems to draw a distinction between halfbreeds and persons born in the Country of European parentage: and to men of our intelligence I need not say that this distinction is still less reasonable than the other."[69]

Receiving no satisfaction from the HBC, the Métis carried the debate to England. In 1846–47 A.K. Isbister[70] presented a petition from the Métis of Red River to the British Colonial Office to grant them relief from the strictures of the HBC monopoly and its tyrannical rule.[71] The petitioners, who described themselves as both Native and loyal British subjects, objected to the harsh administration of the HBC, which kept them in a state of dependency, inhibited trade, and ignored the claims of the Indians and Métis as the original owners of the soil. As Natives they wanted the right to trade freely, and as British subjects they wanted representative government and the right to import goods. If they were deprived of these rights, they warned, discontent and violence would follow.[72] J.H. Pelly, responding for the Hudson's Bay Company, noted that the fact that the Métis were born in the country entitled them to call themselves Native, but it neither conveyed to them any privileges belonging or supposed to belong to the Aboriginal inhabitants nor divested them of the character of British subjects. As such, the Métis (unlike the Indians) were precluded by the HBC charter from trafficking in furs.[73] From the HBC's perspective the petition and memorial to the Colonial Office had been inspired by the illegal traders of the Red River Colony who employed the Métis of the settlement and who were trying to attack the monopoly of the HBC through the instrument of Métis rights.[74] In responding to Pelly, Isbister acknowledged that there was a distinction between the Métis and Indians, but that this distinction could not divest the Métis of their aboriginal rights.[75]

After some investigation Earl Grey, at the time the secretary of state for the colonies, ruled that the petition and memorial were without foundation and no further action would be taken on the matter.[76] Emboldened by this ruling, the Hudson's Bay Company continued to harass the Métis to prevent them from trading in furs. The company regularly searched for and seized furs from the Métis, culminating in the 1849 trial of Pierre-Guillaume Sayer and two other Métis for contravening the HBC monopoly in trading furs from Indians and smuggling them to American merchants. It was only after this trial, which found the three guilty, that the Hudson's Bay Company realized they had no way of enforcing the court decision, given that hundreds of armed Métis had surrounded the courtroom and would accept no punishment for the three. It was only after that point that the company stopped their policy of seizing illegally traded furs and initiating legal action against Métis traders in the Red River Settlement.

Thus, by the 1850s the Métis in the Red River District had developed a view of themselves as holding both the rights of British subjects and Aboriginal claims to the soil. They seldom if ever used the term "Métis Nation" to articulate their rights, but it was a position that might easily be construed as "national." However, it was not a position or sentiment that was present in1816 when Cuthbert Grant and the Métis destroyed the Red River Settlement. This articulation of nationalism was spurred by the merger of the two fur-trading companies and the attempt by the new HBC to curtail the trading rights of the Métis in the two succeeding decades. The Battle of Seven Oaks certainly became a source of pride for the Métis, and it would later become an important part of the narrative of the Métis Nation, but only in the sense of an "invented tradition." Not until thirty years after Seven Oaks did events produce a coherent view of what the national rights of the Métis were.

4 Louis Riel and the Religion of Métis Nationalism, 1869–1885

Sitting in a jail cell in Regina in 1885 during the last months of his life, Louis Riel penned an essay in which he not only set out the Métis grievances against the Canadian state as a justification of the Rebellion of 1885, but he also articulated a claim for Métis Nationhood and the right to self-rule in the northwest. Entitled "Les Métis du Nord-Ouest,"[1] this essay argued that the Métis constituted a new nation distinct from the Indians of the northwest. Their claims to land were based not only on descent from their Indian mothers, but also on their military prowess in defending their territory from hostile Indian groups,[2] and the existence of their own political organization and traditions.[3] This articulation of the "Métis Nation," striking as inclusive a tone as Riel ever was able to manage, does not seem that different from the one worked out by the Métis between 1816 and 1849, except that Riel drops any mention of the rights of the Métis inherited from their British status as subjects or citizens, the main contribution of the English Métis in the 1840s. In this essay, and in other writings, Riel's version/vision of the Métis Nation substitutes any notion of British rights with an emphasis on French-Canadian nationalism and natural rights. For Riel, Aboriginal ancestry did not constitute the only, or even the main, claim to nationhood and a homeland. In "Les Métis du Nord-Ouest," he states categorically that the Métis homeland is a gift from God:[4] the Métis are a Nation created by God[5] and God's plan is to be revealed to the Métis by his prophet Louis "David" Riel.

From this very brief exposition, it should be clear that there existed, as Albert Braz has pointed out, several conflicting nationalisms within the writings and thoughts of Riel.[6] The purpose of this chapter is to trace some of these strands in his thinking about the Métis Nation from

1869 to 1885. In the process I hope to show why twentieth-century Métis leaders have jettisoned a good part of Riel's vision while retaining Riel as a symbol and martyr of their Nation.

Riel and French-Canadian/Catholic Nationalism, 1869–1870

That Riel emerged at the leader of the Métis in 1869 is in one sense surprising.[7] His father, also Louis Riel, was a farmer and miller in the Red River Settlement and had been one of the leaders of the free trade movement in 1849, but the younger Louis Riel had no natural constituency among the Métis. He had left the Red River Settlement at the age of thirteen in 1858 to study in Montreal and returned to the colony only in the summer of 1868, after his dream of a career in the priesthood had ended. He did not farm, he did not participate in the buffalo hunt, he did not trade, and on his return to Red River he spurned the invitation of his friend Louis Schmidt to enter the freighting business. Indeed, from 1868 until he assumed the leadership of the Resistance in late 1869, it is not clear that Riel did much of anything. Those historians who even bother to question why Riel rose to the leadership of the Métis at such a young age usually point to his education as putting him naturally in the forefront. While this reasoning is plausible, it would not have carried much weight with the Métis buffalo hunters, merchant traders, or councillors of Assiniboia.[8] Whatever notions Riel had at this time about his Métis identity or the Métis Nation, they were inextricably connected to his sense of belonging to a French-Canadian Nation.[9] Indeed, when the Métis first responded to the news of the planned Canadian annexation, they did so on the basis of the Aboriginal rights paradigm they had developed prior to 1849. In this they were opposed by Riel, who proposed a defence of their rights based on religion and language. It was only after Riel had defeated the first plan and its Métis leaders that he assumed leadership of the movement against annexation.

The news that Canada planned to annex Rupert's Land arrived in Red River in the summer of 1869 and caused a good deal of consternation. In response to the vitriolic demonstrations of the Canadians in the colony,[10] and in order to protect their land rights, a number of Métis called a large public meeting. This group included some of the traditional Métis leaders in the settlement such as William Dease, Pascal Breland, and William Hallet. Dease was the son of John W. Dease and Jenny Beignet, and had been born in 1827 at Calling Lake. He had settled in Red River and married Maguerite Genthon. The couple and

4.1 Louis Riel in 1870. Archives of Manitoba, Riel, Louis 19 (N5771).

their large family lived and farmed in both St Vital and St Norbert. By 1869 Dease was a prominent French Métis trader and member of the Council of Assiniboia. An indication of Dease's close connection to the various Native communities around Red River was his fluency in French, English, Ojibwa, and Sioux.[11] Pascal Breland, a son-in-law of Cuthbert Grant, was a hunt and trading chief of numerous hivernant villages on the plains, the patriarch of the parish of St François Xavier on the Assiniboine River, and a member of the Council of Assiniboia in 1869. William Hallet was the most prominent English-Métis chief of the annual buffalo hunts, and he had close family ties to numerous French-Métis families.[12]

These men placed an advertisement in the *Nor'Wester* inviting all Métis to meet at the courthouse on 29 July 1869 to discuss what the Métis response should be to the proposed transfer of Rupert's Land to Canada.[13] At this meeting, William Dease quickly took the initiative and proposed that the Métis response should be based on their Aboriginal ancestry, which gave them claim to the Red River Settlement.[14] Dease called on the Métis to defend their rights to land in the settlement, and he disputed the validity of the Earl of Selkirk's purchase of the same from the Indians. The Métis, he said, should demand the £300,000 that Canada was about to pay to the Hudson's Bay Company. To this end the Métis should form a new government in the colony to displace the HBC and make their case to the Canadian government. While the first proposal elicited considerable support, the call to form a new government did not, and the meeting broke up with no clear plan of action decided.

This was a position that had already been developed in the decades prior to 1849 and had been elaborated on in 1860 when it appeared that Red River might become a Crown colony, as this change in status had raised questions about Indian title, Hudson's Bay Company jurisdiction, and individual land rights in Red River. Debate over who had title began in 1860 when Peguis, the Saulteaux chief who had signed Selkirk's treaty, challenged the HBC claim to the land in the Red River Settlement with the argument that the Indians had never sold it to Lord Selkirk and the Hudson's Bay Company.[15] That prompted the Métis, under the chairmanship of Pascal Breland, to hold a large meeting at the Royal Hotel near Fort Garry to discuss their position. All the most eminent Métis traders and hunters – William Dease, Urbain Delorme, Pierre Falcon, William Hallet, George Flett, and William McGillis – spoke, and all agreed that, the treaty being one of friendship, not sale,

4.2 Pascal Breland, 1880s. Archives of Manitoba, Macleod, Margaret A. 23 (N9337).

the HBC had not received title to the Red River Settlement by treaty with Peguis in 1817. Indeed, it was their view that the Métis had legitimate claim to the land and, moreover, that their claim should have priority; they were the descendants of the Cree, the first residents of the area, while the Saulteaux had not arrived in Red River Region until shortly before 1817. Accordingly, the meeting concluded with an agreement by all present that, since no proper arrangements had been made with the Native tribes of the region and since the Métis were now on the land and were the immediate representatives of the first tribes in the region, the Métis should use every legitimate means to advance their claim for consideration in any arrangement that the imperial government might see fit to make. When it became clear that the proposal for Crown colony status was not forthcoming, the Métis agitation died away. However, in 1861 when the HBC tried to extract payment for all lands occupied in the Red River Settlement, the Métis again restated their claims that the HBC had no claim to the settlement, and that it was the Métis who had a very palpable right to it, being the "descendants of the original lords of the soil."[16] The "indignation meetings" called to protest the HBC's actions in 1861 illustrate that the traditional Métis leadership had worked out a theory of Métis rights and were ready to use it to defend their land claims in Red River. It was this theory that Dease reiterated in July 1869.

What is most surprising about the developments that followed the July meeting of 1869 was that both Riel and the Catholic clergy in the settlement opposed this articulation of Métis nationality and rights. Indeed, in the months that followed it became clear that Riel's true constituency was the Catholic Church, and it was through the Church that most of his influence would come. With Archbishop Taché out of the colony, Father Dugast (the main teacher at St Boniface College) and Father Ritchot (the parish priest of St Norbert) took the lead in guiding their Métis flock and were close partners in deciding Riel's strategy.[17] Both men were secular priests who had been born in Quebec and shared a French-Canadian nationalism that saw the French Métis sharing a common history, language, and culture with the *Canadiens*. Ritchot, in particular, felt very threatened by the recent arrivals from Canada and feared for the religious rights of the Métis.[18] Furthermore, both men condemned the traditional buffalo-hunting economy of the Métis, hoping to win them over to a settled agricultural way of life.[19] It is therefore not surprising that the two men distrusted the traditional Métis leadership and their Aboriginal-rights justification for resistance in 1869. For his

4.3 Father Dugast. Archives of Manitoba, Dugast, George I.

part, Ritchot personally disliked William Dease (though Dease was a Catholic) and regarded him as a man "sans princippe et aussi hignorant qu'orgueilleux."[20] Father Dugast, meanwhile, criticized Dease's Aboriginal-rights justification in a report to Taché, calling Dease a fool and adding that if the details of the assembly of 29 July were heard in Canada, all the Métis would be taken for a band of lunatics.[21]

For Dugast and Ritchot, then, Riel most closely represented their ideal for the Métis of Red River. As a student at the College of Montreal, he had been educated by the Sulpician fathers (who trained their students "as a Catholic and French-Canadian élite, proud of their difference from the English majority of North America"[22]) and so was steeped in the twin tenets of patriotism and religion. As Riel wrote in 1874, "The French-Canadian Métis of the North (West) are a branch of the French-Canadian tree. They want to grow like that tree, with that tree; they never want to be separated from it, they want to suffer and rejoice with."[23] Accordingly, it is easy to understand why Ritchot viewed Riel as a "jeune homme du pays (et de talent)."[24]

Following Dease's speech of 29 July calling for the Métis to defend their aboriginal rights, John Bruce took the floor and castigated him for advocating revolt. Bruce, who would later become the first president

4.4 Father Ritchot. Archives of Manitoba, Ritchot, Joseph-Noël 3 (N12782).

of Riel's "National Committee," noted that Dease was a magistrate and member of the Council of Assiniboia, and should be the first to defend the government of the country and all such intrigues should be opposed. Apparently, Bruce's arguments found their mark and the assembly broke up without endorsing Dease's plan of action. Father Dugast's lengthy report of this meeting makes it clear that Bruce had been carefully coached in his address.[25] Most of the evidence suggests that Ritchot, Dugast, and possibly Riel, had done the coaching and, indeed, Ritchot later admitted that he had advised his parishioners to be on their guard, and that he considered the object of the meeting to be of a dangerous character.[26] As well, both Ritchot and Dugast went out of their way to paint the Dease initiative as being inspired by John Christian Schultz.

Further meetings followed in August as the Métis continued to debate the position they should take to protect their rights considering the proposed transfer to Canada.[27] The Dease initiative, however, had collapsed by early October and with it the Aboriginal-rights paradigm of Métis resistance. Crucial in its collapse was the determined opposition of Riel, Ritchot, and Dugast and their elaboration of another paradigm of Métis nationality that carried more emotional weight with the French Métis.

By the end of August, the French Métis had increasingly come to see Confederation as the annexation of Red River by Protestant Orange Ontario and, consequently, as a threat to their religious rights.[28] News that William McDougall would be the new governor of the territory only raised the fears of the French-Catholic clergy and the many French Métis who viewed him as one with the other Canadians in the colony (John Schultz, Charles Mair, John Snow, and J.S. Dennis), all of whom were widely distrusted.[29] Moreover, by this time there were also rumours circulating that McDougall was a "priest murderer."[30]

How these sentiments and rumours were spread remains unclear, but the feelings were undoubtedly shared by the Catholic clergy, who, by October 1869, increasingly justified resistance to Canada in terms of protecting French and Catholic rights in Red River and who closely supported Riel, clearly the ascendant Métis leader. Thirty-five years later Dugast would write: "In reality he [Ritchot] was the soul of the movement. It was he who launched it and without him the movement would not have taken place … It was M. Ritchot and I who not only guided but who drove on that opposition to the Canadian government – this is the real truth. I did not say it in my book because all truth is not suitable for publication. I say it to you. The ignorant *métis* would never have thought of vindicating their constitutional rights if M. Ritchot and I had not made them aware of them. *Without M. Ritchot and me the movement remains inexplicable.*"[31]

With Dease's initiative in disarray and with the active support and encouragement of Ritchot and Dugast, Riel moved to take the lead. Along with Baptiste Tourond and a few other Métis, he stopped the Canadian survey on 11 October as it approached the river lots of the Parish of St Vital, an action that, given the increasing fears and paranoia of the French Métis, won him considerable support. Then, when news arrived of the imminent arrival of McDougall in Pembina, Riel and his faction – which by this time included many of the younger and more militant boatmen of the colony – took steps that would breach the established order and initiate a period of crisis in the Red River Settlement. On 20 October Riel and his men met in the home of John Bruce, where they organized a "National Committee" and made plans to stop McDougall from entering the colony. All was planned with the approval and knowledge of Ritchot.[32] The next day "la barrière" was erected across the Pembina trail at St Norbert, and all incoming and outgoing traffic was stopped and searched.

This act overturned the status quo, directly challenged the Council of Assiniboia's legitimacy, and threw the colony into an uproar. Already humiliated by the combined efforts of Riel, Ritchot, and Dugast, and aware that most Métis still did not agree with the precipitous and resolute action Riel and his men had taken, William Dease now took an uncompromising stand against Riel, arguing that McDougall should be permitted to enter the territory and hear the Métis complaints. Sensing that support for Riel's course of action was slipping, Ritchot called for an assembly of Métis to meet in St Norbert on 24 October to resolve the divisions among the people. At this meeting, Dease and his supporters threatened to dismantle the barricade across the Pembina trail, and only the intercession of Ritchot quieted the following uproar. Ritchot calmed the assembly by asking if they did not agree that Canada had treated the colony with a lack of respect and if it was not proper that some resistance be made. Even Dease's men could not disagree with this approach, and Ritchot eventually persuaded the majority of the Métis at the assembly to agree to back the path taken by Riel. Most of the rest agreed to stay neutral.[33] Riel had won. Dease, however, was not satisfied and continued his opposition to Riel throughout the winter and spring of 1869–70. While other prominent French Métis would slide back and forth between neutrality and opposition, Riel never again lost the support of most of the French Métis.

Usually treated as a minor and almost inconsequential interlude, the Dease/Riel conflict played a major role in defining the nature of the Métis Resistance in 1869–70 and how the Métis Nation would be defined. On a symbolic level, it was a battle over whether the Métis Nation and Resistance would be grounded broadly on a concept of Métis Aboriginal rights and headed by the traditional Métis leadership, or whether the Resistance would be more narrowly a defence of French and Catholic rights in the settlement led by the young Riel. To be sure, the Resistance had many facets not touched upon here, and there were other reasons (class, economic, familial, and generational) why many French Métis opposed Riel;[34] however, unless one understands the symbolic nature of the Dease/Riel conflict, one cannot understand how key participants understood the events in which they were involved. Those Métis leaders who had been upstaged by Riel, and sometimes badly treated,[35] were never able to accept his leadership.

Riel tried to broaden the scope of the Resistance after October 1869 to win over the support of the English Métis, but it never lost the French and Catholic tinge it had acquired in the period from July through September. This made it extremely difficult for him to build any settlement-wide consensus. After Riel and his men seized Upper Fort Garry in November of 1869, they raised a flag adorned with the fleur-de-lis and the Irish shamrock. This ceremony was carried out by a Catholic priest who was attended by sixty of the scholars of the Roman Catholic seminary in St Boniface.[36] This symbolism was not lost on the English Métis. By allying himself so clearly with the Catholic clergy to defeat the Dease faction, Riel would never be acceptable as a leader to anyone other than a small minority of English-Protestant Métis.

The Riel/Dease conflict has significant implications for evaluating the nature of Riel's Métis Nationalism and its relationship to those ideas of Métis rights that had developed prior to Riel's return to Red River in 1868. Thomas Flanagan, in a useful study of the political thought of Louis Riel, has argued that the question of aboriginal rights played no role in the public debates of the 1869–70 Resistance. Riel's strategy in 1869 was to present the Métis as civilized men with rights equal to those of any British subject.[37] "Riel wanted the colony to enter Confederation as a province with institutions modelled on those of Quebec: local control of land and natural resources, responsible government, a bilingual Governor, bilingualism in the legislature and courts, and a tax-supported system of Protestant and Catholic schools."[38] It is difficult to find any notion of Métis Nationality in Riel's official writing of this period in which he puts any emphasis on its aboriginal foundations. During the debates in the Convention of Forty in early February of 1870 Riel stated explicitly: "The Half-breeds have certain rights which they claim by conquest. They are not to be confounded with Indian rights."[39] Given his opposition to Dease's aboriginal paradigm of Métis rights, this belief is not surprising. Even in his more private writing – his poetry – Riel put more emphasis on God's creation of the Métis Nation or People and Catholicism and Quebec Nationalism as the font of Métis identity.

In "La Métisse," written in 1870,[40] the Métis are named as a nation, its members proud of its military prowess in defending their country from Schultz and the Canadians in the settlement, but they are a people/nation created by God and their victory is the fulfilment of a religious mission. It is this connection to religion that gives the nation its legitimacy. Indeed, in Ottawa, the Métis are represented by their Catholic priest (Ritchot), who returns having achieved provincial status, not a homeland for the Métis.

La Métisse

Je suis métisse et je suis orgueilleuse	I'm Métis and I am proud
D'appartenir à cette nation	To belong to this nation
Je sais que Dieu de sa main généreuse	I know that God's generous hand
Fait chaque peuple avec attention	Makes each people with care
Les métis sont un petit peuple encore	The Métis are still a little people
Mais vous pouvez voir déjà leurs destins	But you can already see their destinies
Etre haïs comme ils sont les honore.	To be hated as they are honours them
Ils ont déjà rempli de grands desseins	They are already full of grand plans

Refrain:

Ah! si jamais je devais être aimée	Ah! If I am ever to be loved,
Je choisirais pour mon fidèle amant	I will choose for my faithful lover
Un des soldats de la petite armée	One of the soldiers of the small army
Que commandait notre fier adjudant	Commanded by our proud adjutant
Je choisirais un des soldats	I will choose one of the soldiers
Que commandait notre fier adjudant.	Commanded by our proud adjutant.

Quand ils ont pris Schultz avec sa phalange	When they captured Schultz with his band
Le sept Décembre au soir il fit bien beau	The evening of December seventh was fine
Notre soleil couchant, beau comme un ange	Our setting sun, beautiful as an angel
Veillant sur nous, retira son flambeau	Watching over us, quenched his torch
Seulement quand Schultz eut rendu les armes	Only when Schultz and his men had surrendered their arms
Le lendemain fut splendide pour nous.	The next day was beautiful for us.
Le huit Décembre, entouré de ses charmes	The eighth of December, surrounded by his charms

Vit les Métis triompher à genoux.	Saw the Métis celebrate victory on their knees.
N'ai-je pas vu, moi qui suis jeune fille,	Have I not seen, I who am a young girl,
Le Fort Garry plein de soldats métis?	Fort Garry full of Métis soldiers?
Huit cents métis dans le fort et la ville	Eight hundred Métis in the fort and town
Je les ai vus, défendre le pays	I saw them defending the country
Avec autant d'amour que de vaillance.	With a mixture of love and valour.
Que c'était beau de voir ces hommes fiers	How splendid it was to see these proud men
Courbant le front, prier la Providence	Bowing their heads, praying for Providence
De leur aider à garder leurs foyers.	To help them protect their homes.
Un saint pasteur, un prêtre inébranlable	A saintly pastor, an unwavering priest
Partit un jour du côté d'Ottawa	Left one day for Ottawa
On l'entoura d'un bruit épouvantable	Surrounded by frightful mayhem
Mais pour passer le Bon Dieu l'appuia.	But he went with the Good Lord's support.
Il s'en revint avec notre Province	He returned with our province
Heureusement faite en six mois de temps,	His task successfully completed in six months' time,
Et McDougall, un moment notre prince	And McDougall, at one time our prince
Resta confus de tous ses mauvais plans!	Remains confused in all his evil plans!

In "O Québec!"[41] the roots of Métis identity are even more closely linked to Catholicism and Quebec nationalism. It is Quebec from whom the Métis inherit their distinctive ways ('the heirs of your heart"), and Quebec that is the mother colony of the "Métis-Canadiens."

O Québec!

Québec! Mère Colonie!	Quebec! Mother Colony!
Tu fus de nos aïeux sans cesse les amours!	You were ever our ancestors' true love!

Et durant toute ma vie,
J'aimerai ton doux nom, le prononçant toujours.
Québec! Province chérie!
Oublieras-tu jamais tes Métis-Canadiens!
De Manitoba trahie
Tes enfants, O Québec, sont poutant soutiens!
Des ennemis fort à craindre
Menaçant le berceau de tes enfants chéris.

Mais ils ne pourront atteindre,
O Québec! Malgré toi, jamais notre pays!

Que la sainte Providence
Inspire à notre égard tes hommes d'ottawa.
Souviens-toi combien la France
Te fit mal! O Québec! Lorsqu'Elle t'oublia!

Noble pays! ton courage
Te rend superbe après un siècle de combats!
Accepte le beau présage
De l'Immortel Pie-Neuf bénissant tes soldats!
Toi qui fournis des zouaves
A l'Eglise, jamais aurais-tu la douleur

de voir écraser tes braves
Tes fiers enfants du Nord, héritiers de ton Coeur!

Québec! Tu le sais, Ta gloire
Consistera toujours dans la religion.
Qu'ontario dans l'histoire
Vante sa politique et son ambition!

And throughout my life,
I would love your sweet name repeated forever.
Quebec! Dear Province!
Never forget your Canadian Métis!
By Manitoba betrayed
Your children, O Quebec, nevertheless supports!
Enemies to be greatly feared
Threatening the cradle of your beloved children.
But they will be unable to reach,
O Quebec! Despite yourself, never our country!
May Holy Providence
Inspire your men in Ottawa to respect us.
Remember how France
Did you wrong! O Quebec! When It forgot you!

Noble country! Your courage
Makes you superb after a century of fighting!
Accept the good omen
Of the Immortal Pius IX blessing your soldiers!
You who provided the Zouaves
To the church, never will you feel the pain
Of seeing your brave men crushed
Your proud children of the North, heirs of your heart!

Quebec! You know your glory
Will always be in religion.
Historically, Ontario
Boasts of its politics and ambition!

Pour toi, tes missionnaires Iront dans tout l'ouest, Et jusqu'au Pôle Nord Du Christ portant les lumières, De mortels par milliers adoucissant le sort.	For you, your missionaries Will go throughout the west and as far as the North Pole And Christ, bearing light To thousands of souls, will ease their fate.

Riel and Messianic Nationalism, 1875–1885

The arrival of British and Canadian troops at Red River in the fall of 1870, following Manitoba's entry into Confederation, forced Riel to flee from Fort Garry and eventually leave Manitoba and Canada. Faced with arrest, imprisonment, and even murder for the execution of Thomas Scott during the Resistance, Riel would have to stay in hiding and eventually take refuge in the United States. Although he would run for, and win, election to Canadian Parliament in 1874, he was never allowed to take his seat and was expelled from the House of Commons.[42] In 1875 Riel was granted amnesty for his role in the Red River Resistance of 1869–70, but the price was banishment from Canada for five years. Yet elimination of Riel from Manitoba and Canadian politics did not stop Riel from obsessing about the Métis and their place in the "New World." His view of both the Métis Nation and his role in bringing about their destiny, however, changed dramatically in the years after 1875.

Explaining the chronology of his thoughts and beliefs at the end of his life, Riel noted three events in 1875 that altered the course of his career and his views of the Métis Nation. The first of these was a letter dated 15 July 1875 from Bishop Bourget, who, in Riel's words, announced to him in writing: "God has directed you and has always assisted you up to the present, will not abandon you when your trial is greatest, for he has given you [a] mission which you must accomplish."[43] The other two events were visions Riel had in Washington, DC, in December of the same year. He records in his "autobiographical notes" that, on 8 December 1875, while receiving the Holy Ghost during High Mass in St Patrick's Church, in Washington, DC, "God anointed him with his divine gifts and fruits of his Spirit, as prophet of the new world."[44] Six days later on 14 December Riel notes that the "Spirit of God" again came upon him and filled "his body and soul of his divine light and essence; transport[ed] him to the fourth heaven and

4.5 Louis Riel circa 1875. LAC, Jean Riel fonds, PA-139073.

instructed him about the nations of the earth."[45] These events, taken together, completely transformed Riel's image of himself from a failed political leader living in exile to the "Prophet of the New World."[46] Then in early January of 1876 Bishop Bourget again wrote to Riel advising him never to depart "from the path which divine Providence had laid out for you." He told Riel that a "time of mercy" would come for the Métis, when religion would arise from the present state of oppression to crown Riel's people with honour and glory.[47] As Thomas Flanagan has noted, "in Riel's agitated state, this promise seemed like the divine seal of approval upon his mission,"[48] and shortly afterward Riel began signing his name Louis "David" Riel.

At this point Riel's friends became concerned about his state of mind and had him committed to an asylum in Quebec,[49] where he would remain for the next two years. Though he was released on 23 January 1878 as "cured," Riel never gave up his views of his mission. Indeed, his Catholic friends' turning a deaf ear to his message only convinced him that he must break with the Church in Rome and establish another Church in the New World.[50]

4.6 Louis Riel in 1878. LAC (credit: Baldwin), Louis Tardival Collection, C-086500.

After his release from the Beauport Asylum in January 1878 he slipped over the border into New York State, somewhat chastened, but maintaining faith in his mission. He travelled west to St Joseph in the Dakota Territory and began dreaming of a great confederacy that would unite the Métis and Indians of the northern plains and, using Montana as base, invade western Canada to establish an independent Native Republic. This plan foundered in 1879 when Riel could not win the support of either the various Indian bands or the Plains Métis.[51] Staying in Montana, Riel settled down to a life of trading and ranching, eventually becoming a schoolteacher at the Jesuit Mission at St Peter's on the Sun River. In the meantime he had also become a U.S. citizen and married a local Métis woman by the name of Marguerite Monet dit Bellehumeur, with whom he had two children.

Throughout this period, Riel continued to develop the ideas of his mission for the religious and political renewal of the "New World" and the place of the Métis people in this renewal. The head of the Church would move from Rome to the New World, first to Montreal and then eventually to St Vital. With Riel's personal transformation into the "Prophet of the New World" the Métis were also transformed into God's "Chosen People." They would continue to perfect the evangelical mission of New France in America that the Métis had inherited from their French-Canadian fathers.[52] The Aboriginal ancestry of the Métis was also important to Riel, but less so to confirm their claims to the soil than to connect the Métis, the new "Chosen People," to the first "Chosen People," the Hebrews; according to Riel, American Indians were descendants of the lost tribe of Israel.[53] In Riel's view the Métis Nation had been created by God and had a right to the Northwest as their country both through their Indian ancestry[54] and from natural law. God was the father of all nations and tribes and he did not create them without their own country.[55] As Albert Braz has commented: "In short, by virtue of its existence alone, a people has a divine right to a territory of its own, a homeland."[56] At his trial, Riel remonstrated with the judge and jury: "Who starts nations? The very one who creates them, God. God is the master of the universe, our planet is his land, and the nations, the tribes, are members of his family, and as a good Father, he gives a portion of his lands to that nation, to that tribe, to everyone, that is his heritage, that is his share of the inheritance, of the people, or nation, or tribe."[57]

These ideas had found little resonance in Montana, so it is little wonder that Riel quickly accepted the invitation of the South Branch Métis to return to the Canadian northwest to help his people defend their rights. This invitation and his decision to travel north on 10 June 1884 reinforced Riel's sense of mission. As Albert Braz has noted: "Riel became convinced that his call to Batoche was part of God's larger providential plan for him. He was not just to counsel the local populace on federal-territorial relations but was a divine emissary sent by God 'to establish a new code of laws in the North West.' More specifically, he was the 'second David' chosen to redress all the wrongs done to his suffering nation and to 'lead my people, Israel, out of tyranny.'"[58] Riel's return to the Canadian northwest in 1884 also illustrated a change in his views towards Quebec. In 1869–70 Quebec had very much been the "mother colony," and his Métis Nationalism was a variant of Quebec Nationalism. In 1884, as Riel was to state at his trial, he decided to return to Batoche because the northwest was his "Mother Country."[59]

While Riel immediately set to work to alleviate the specific claims of the South Branch Métis (their river-lot claims as squatters and scrip claims in extinguishment of their Aboriginal title), he added to these his own agenda of Métis collective Aboriginal title and sovereign control over the soil of the northwest. According to his views, the Hudson's Bay Company had no claim to Rupert's Land and the true owners were the Indian tribes and the Métis. As well, the Manitoba Act had to be seen as a treaty and the Métis were entitled to the same proportion of land in the North-West Territories (one-seventh of the land) as they had received in Manitoba.[60] His prophetic religious views also began to come to the forefront. He revealed to his closest Métis followers that a great war was coming in which Britain would be defeated and that Canadian territory would be divided among various ethnic groups and nations. The northwest would be divided among the European immigrants and the Métis, including the English Métis, who would control one-seventh of the territory. Interestingly, although Orangism would be eradicated, Protestants would have claims to territory[61] and no territory was to be allocated to Indian groups, as, according to Riel, they were destined to disappear in the global metissage that would be the Aboriginal-European melting pot.[62] Finally, his new religion would include Catholics and Protestants alike in a unified Church of the New World. This new idea of unification was part of a growing ecumenical spirit in Riel's thinking by 1885 as he broke with the Catholic Church,[63] but it was also prompted by his need for the help of the Protestant Métis in the coming conflict that seemed imminent by the spring of 1885.

Riel's nationalism, or rather his views of the Métis Nation, was less universal than his proposed new Church. For Riel the Métis Nation was still tied together by Catholicism and the French language. Prior to breaking with the Church in the spring of 1885, he articulated a Métis genealogy in which the Métis were the offspring of New France just as the *Canadiens* were the offspring of France. In a poem written in 1883, Riel set out this genealogy clearly in the title: "Le peuple Métis-Canadien-français."[64] The Métis were a tripartite amalgam in which the virtues of each race compensated for their individual weaknesses. At the end of the poem Riel uses the image of the three-leafed trillium to represent the happy combination of three groups united in the Métis, and forged into a Nation by the Catholic clergy.[65]

Le peuple Métis-Canadien-français

Métis et Canadiens ensemble Français, si nos trois éléments S'amalgament bien, il me semble Que nous serons un jour plus grands.	Métis and Canadians with the French, if our three elements Blend well, it seems to me That one day we will be greater.
Les trois feuilles du trèffle peuvent Exister sur le même pied. Toutes les trois, jolies, se meuvent A l'unisson, comme il leur sied.	The three leaves of the trillium can Exist on the same footing. All three nicely move In unison, as suits them.
Le clergé qui nous édifie Nous unira bien sûrement, Comme le trèffle identifie Ses trois fleurs admirablement.	The clergy who enlighten us Will certainly unite us Just as the trillium wonderfully Displays its three petals.
Son grand coeur prend beaucoup de peine A consolider, je le sais, La nation manitobaine Des Métis-canadiens-français.	His big heart takes great pains To consolidate, I know, The Manitoba nation Of French-Canadian-Métis.

In September of 1884, during a visit by Bishop Vital Grandin to Batoche to perform the sacrament of confirmation, Riel pressed Grandin to recognize Métis nationality by granting them a patron saint and a special national festival. According to Riel, this saint and festival should symbolize the kinship and unity of the Métis, the French Canadians, and the French as children of France. When Grandin agreed, Riel proposed St Joseph as the patron saint of the Métis and it was decided that 24 July should be their national holiday.[66]

In the spring of 1885 Riel and his new council, the "Exovedate," took up arms, in their words, to save the country from a wicked government and to transfer a revitalized Catholic Church to the New World. Riel saw himself as the second "David" redressing all the wrongs done to his Métis Nation and leading his people out of tyranny. On 18 March 1885 Riel pronounced that Rome had fallen (his struggle was as much religious as it was political) and initiated open rebellion against the Canadian state.[67] In this he had the support of the South Saskatchewan Métis communities and, in particular, Gabriel Dumont, who followed him implicitly even when he disagreed with Riel's strategic choices. The rebellion itself was comparatively brief, and the Métis were overrun by

Canadian troops at Batoche on 12 May 1885. Gabriel Dumont would escape to the United States, but Riel chose to surrender to General Middleton on 15 May 1885. While in prison and during his trial for treason in Regina, Riel would further articulate the views summarized above.[68] Even when his lawyers tried to defend him, using an "insanity" plea, Riel spurned this defence to argue the legitimacy of both his complaints against the state and his religious views. On 1 August 1885, Riel was convicted of treason and was hanged on 16 November 1885. Riel became a martyr of the Métis Nation.

Since his execution in 1885, Riel has come to be seen as the Father of Manitoba and Martyr of the Métis Nation. For the Métis he is an indispensable aspect of their history and national heritage. Riel's religious conceptualization of the Métis Nation, however, was a major barrier to any pan-Métis identity or organization. Both his extreme Catholicism and Franco-centric definitions of Métis Nationalism would be jettisoned in favour of earlier definitions more clearly based on Aboriginal rights and ties to the soil. In choosing a Métis flag, the Métis National Council (and almost every other Métis organization in North America) chose the one used during the Battle of Seven Oaks (horizontal figure eight), ignoring the symbolism Riel had favoured (the fleur-de-lis, the three-leafed clover, the trillium, and Our Lady of Lourdes). In the 1990s, the Royal Commission on Aboriginal Peoples (RCAP) provided a brief synopsis of the "historic Métis Nation," based on their consultations with various Métis organizations in western Canada. In this account of the history of the Métis Nation there is no mention of Catholicism, the French language, Quebec, or France as defining elements. Instead, the RCAP *Report* noted that the Métis claim to nationhood was based on a distinct culture "derived from the lifestyles of the Aboriginal and non-Aboriginal peoples from whom the modern Métis trace their beginnings." The right to pursue this distinct lifestyle and their own homeland was demonstrated by their military prowess during the Battle of Seven Oaks in 1816, the Sayer Trial in 1849, the Riel Resistance of 1869–70, and the 1885 Rebellion.[69]

Although Riel remains fully in the forefront of Métis consciousness as a martyr and father figure to the Métis Nation, his religious and linguistic definitions of Métis Nationalism have vanished.

5 L'Union nationale métisse Saint-Joseph, A.-H. de Trémaudan, and the Re-imagining of the Métis Nation, 1910 to the 1930s

In the years following the execution of Riel and as the growing immigrant population of the Canadian and American west increasingly marginalized both Métis communities and their land base, the concept of a "Métis Nation" became problematic. While recent historical scholarship has shown that the Métis continued to "know who they were,"[1] prejudice against all things Native and increasing poverty pushed many Métis to give up notions of Métis nationality and instead to identify as "Franco-Manitoban," American, or in many cases join treaty and identify as First Nations. The concept of a "historic Métis Nation" that is so ubiquitous today, was rehabilitated in the early decades of the twentieth century in Manitoba as a particular strategy to reinvigorate an ethnic identity that was waning and to provide support for the French language, which was under attack in western Canada.

This re-imagining of the Métis Nation is not meant to imply a lack of authenticity, but merely to demonstrate that "nation," like any other discursive subject, is constructed. As Benedict Anderson has noted, "all communities larger than primordial villages or face to face contact (and perhaps even these) are imagined. Communities are to be distinguished, not by their falsity/genuineness but by the style in which they are imagined."[2] In many other contexts traditions that are claimed to be ancient frequently turn out to have been recent inventions intended to provide continuity with a real or imagined past. They establish group membership in communities, legitimize institutions, and serve to socialize and inculcate beliefs, value systems, and behaviour. These "neo-traditions" are often suitably tailored discourses intended to promote a unitary sense of nation. Some even argue that "getting history wrong is crucial to the creation of a nation."[3]

Our approach to this topic – and we do not claim that it encompasses all aspects of this question – is to examine the discursive formation of the Métis Nation promoted by L'Union nationale métisse Saint-Joseph du Manitoba through their goals and activities in the first decades of the twentieth century. In particular, we examine the writing, editing, and revision of the book they commissioned in the 1920s and published in 1935: A.-H. Trémaudan's *Histoire de la nation métisse dans l'Ouest canadien*.

From its reorganization in 1909–10, L'Union nationale métisse very consciously set out, not so much to preserve the past, but to rehabilitate a concept of the Métis Nation that would serve the conceptual needs of their day. As a part of this project they commissioned a history of the Métis Nation in which they set out not only to correct the factual errors of the English-Canadian historiography, but to disseminate a history that would create a narrative of identity. In the process, they not only selected the topics to be covered, forced revisions in the portrayal of key events, significantly influenced the emplotment and rhetorical strategy of the book, but also excised large portions of the manuscript they received. In doing so they fashioned an effective and embraceable past that provided almost a catechism of the Métis Nation and group identity.[4] These events or processes are crucial to an understanding of the conception of the "historic Métis Nation" that holds sway today (although there are also significant discontinuities), and as such we would argue that Trémaudan's book, which is usually ignored by academic historians, deserves closer attention.

L'Union nationale métisse Saint-Joseph du Manitoba

The first activities of L'Union nationale métisse Saint-Joseph du Manitoba[5] date back to 17 July 1887 when a group of Métis, most of them close relatives or former associates of Louis Riel,[6] met in the residence of Joseph St Germain in St Vital. The purpose of the meeting was to find some way to restore pride and meaning to being Métis and to rehabilitate the reputation of Riel. At this meeting it was decided to form a society, which was duly incorporated as "L'Union nationale métisse Saint-Joseph du Manitoba" (National Métis Union) on 1 March 1888.

The stated purpose of the society was to organize an annual national holiday, hold meetings and discussions to further the life and history of the Métis Nation, and make the Métis more influential in public affairs and politics. Little is known of the early activities of the organization outside of its efforts to erect a monument on the grave of Riel in 1891 (a gift from friends in Montreal), and to commemorate "la barrière" (1906) where the Métis stopped Lieutenant Governor designate William McDougall from entering the Red River Settlement in 1869.[7]

This early incarnation of L'Union nationale métisse seems to have lost some of its impetus by the early twentieth century (not surprising, given the advancing age of many of its founding members), as by 1909 it was decided to reorganize it on a broader basis. Meeting in the home of Joseph Riel on 13 June 1909, the reformed union seems to have brought a new generation into leadership positions. While a number of the older members remained active in the new society (Joseph Riel, Elzéar Lagimodière, Martin Jérôme, André Nault, and Ambroise Lépine), by the second decade of the twentieth century it was given direction by a new generation of Métis leaders (sons and nephews of the 1870 generation). These men, such as Roger Goulet (inspector of schools in St Boniface), Guillaume Charette (lawyer), Camille Teillet (civil servant), Samuel Nault (estates officer), Diedomme Delorme, Alex Nault, William Beauchemin, Joseph Lavallée and Maxime Carrière (farmers) were middle-class professionals or farmers.[8] Like its earlier incarnation, the stated purpose of the new society was to find some way to instil pride in the Métis, who had become silent and withdrawn since 1885, "their heads bowed low under an avalanche of calumny."[9] One of the first acts of this new group of Métis leaders was to form a historical committee to respond to all slights on the past of the Métis in the newspapers of the day and to forcefully restate their history – "the true story" of what had happened in 1869–70 and 1885.[10]

The new constitution of the National Métis Union clearly indicates the historical context in which the organization arose, and it succinctly outlines its goals. Established at time when the French language was still under attack in the west, the union clearly aligned itself with all other French-Canadian associations in the west, but insisted on preserving its autonomy.[11] Correspondence of the officers of the union and letters to the editors of various Manitoba newspapers indicate that, while the Métis appreciated the support they had received from Franco-Manitoban organizations and from the writings of ecclesiastical authorities, these opinions were not fully in accord with their own views of their history and interests.[12] It is also clear from their first constitution that the Métis of Manitoba were trying to repair the breach that had opened between them and the Catholic Church during and in the aftermath of the Riel Rebellion of 1885 and the disputes over Riel's religious views. The National Métis Union was placed under the patronage of the Archbishop of St Boniface, and the stated purpose of the society was the union of French-Métis Catholics to protect their common interests and preserve their national traditions. The priorities in the constitution, listed in order, were as follows:

I. Submission to ecclesiastical authority
II. Loyalty to the British Crown
III. Inalterable attachment to our language
IV. Demonstration of these feelings in all public occasions
V. Preservation of the cult of our ancestors and national traditions
VI. A profession of independence in their exercise of the duties of citizenship for the intellectual and moral progress of the Métis people.
VII. Constant consideration of the material advancement of the Métis Nation without injuring the interests of a higher authority.[13]

Given this orientation, it is not surprising that membership requirements narrowed the definition of who belonged to the Métis Nation. To be an active member one had to be a practising Roman Catholic, to be a French-Canadian Métis or allied to the Métis by links of family, to speak the French language, and to have a good reputation and be of good morals. French Canadians who arrived in the west before 1870 and their descendants would also be admitted as members.[14] While the requirements of language and religion would loosen somewhat over the years, they are indicative of the time period when the organization was formed and the legacy of Riel's emphasis on Catholicism, the French language, and the Métis ties to Quebec. Also significant are the western orientation of the National Union and its use of 1870 as a benchmark boundary.

Over the next twenty-five years the main activities of this National Union, in addition to the more mundane organizational work at the national and local levels, included the rehabilitation of the reputation of Louis Riel, the celebration of an annual National Métis Day, and the writing and publication of a history of the Métis Nation that would not only set the record straight, but that could be used to instil pride in the heritage of the Métis Nation and change public opinion.

The Historical Committee of L'Union nationale métisse

The Historical Committee of the union was charged with the task of collecting historical materials and responding to every slur on the reputation of Riel in all newspapers in Manitoba and Quebec. Given that the twenty-fifth anniversary of the 1885 Rebellion was fast approaching and newspapers were printing numerous reminiscences of aging veterans of the conflict, this task proved an almost full-time job for some members. The archives of the Historical Committee are filled with press clippings of their letters to the editors.[15] In particular, the letters defended the Provisional Government of 1869 as a legitimate government and the execution of Thomas Scott as a legal execution, and they argued that the population of Red River generally supported Riel in 1869–70. The most vehement of these exchanges occurred between the members of the Historical Committee and Franco-Manitoban journalists who questioned Riel's stability, fidelity, and obedience to the Catholic Church in 1885.[16]

One of the main goals of members of the Historical Committee was to restore the reputation of Riel, who, according to their view, had done no wrong. Riel was not only a saint and martyr of the Métis people, but had saved the west for Canada. As such, both he and the Métis Nation deserved recognition within the Canadian Dominion. The major disagreement that the Métis National Union and its Historical Committee had with their French-Canadian and Catholic clerical allies was the imputation that Riel had been unstable in 1884–85 and had strayed from the Catholic faith. Riel not only was a good Catholic in their eyes, but should be accorded martyr status. This martyrdom project is evident in the writing and correspondence of the Historical Committee almost from its inception. At an early date the committee had erected a monument to Riel, and by the 1920s there were plans to refurbish the monument and erect a new, larger one incorporating at least one visage of Riel.[17] To keep the face of Riel before the public a pilgrimage to the Riel monument was planned for 16 November 1925, the fortieth anniversary of his death.[18] Both the new statue and the pilgrimage were intended to convince the public of Riel's martyr status: "Cela montrera au public que nous n'avons pas perdu la chose de vue, bien au contraire. Je n'y attendais. Seulement, nous avons tout de même atteint un certain but qui est de répondre notre idée et de faire connaître le Grand Martyr."[19]

By the early 1930s the union had leased land from the Rural Municipality of St Vital and had created a park named after Riel, where they subsequently held their annual "Fête nationale." These annual national celebrations were usually held on 16 July in conjunction with the annual General Assembly of the National Union. In all likelihood the date was chosen so as not to interfere with the feast day of St Joseph (the patron saint of the Métis), which was celebrated in the local parishes on 24 July. While the feast day for St Joseph had been celebrated in the local parishes from the late nineteenth century, the National Métis Festival and "Grand Pique-Nique" were an innovation of the L'Union nationale métisse. It was an occasion to honour the memory of Riel, to remember and celebrate Métis culture and history, and to provide an occasion to invite local politicians and dignitaries to lobby for their causes and raise money. In addition to speeches, there were various sports events, fiddling, folklore displays, and other cultural happenings.[20] These celebrations became, in effect, ritual dramas in which the modern Métis (particularly the young) could participate in the events and culture of the past. As such, they were equated with tradition and came to represent national identity. By the early 1930s L'Union nationale métisse had local chapters in seventeen communities and as many as 300 delegates attended their annual general assemblies. The "Fête nationale" and "Pique-Nique" attracted up to 2,000 at its height in 1934.[21]

For whatever reason, this explosion of activity seems to have abated after the late 1930s. It seems likely that the publication of Trémaudan's *Histoire de la nation métisse dans L'Ouest canadien* in 1935, the Great Depression, and the outbreak of World War II, which diverted the energies of the small group of men who ran the organization, were the main causes. For the Historical Committee, Trémaudan's *Histoire* in 1935 was their crowning glory and with its publication most of their activities ended.[22] The work of the larger union was rekindled in the 1950s, and its work continues to this day.[23]

Histoire de la nation métisse dans l'Ouest canadien

From its inception it had been the intention of the Historical Committee to write a history of the Métis, particularly covering the events of 1869–70 and 1885. The purpose was a recital of the "true facts" to counter the slanderous accounts of the enemies of the Métis, whose only purpose had been to vindicate the governments of the day. In general, they hoped to change the public opinion that held the Métis were greatly inferior to other groups, but more particularly they wanted to write an inspiring account of the deeds of the French-Canadian Métis to imbue the new generation of Métis with the "true knowledge" that their fathers and forefathers, who had been treated as criminals and bandits, were by their heroism, sacrifice, and devotion the founders of the Canadian west. History would be enlisted to inspire in a new generation of Métis a pride in their ancestry and past and allow them to "hold their heads high." According to this view, the Métis had acted as a transition between barbarism and civilization and had carried the French tradition to the Canadian west.[24] For these acts they deserved recognition as a national group. This history, in effect, was to be the capstone of their project to re-establish a national tradition.

The members of the Historical Committee proved adept at collecting historical material (primarily the correspondence of Riel) and of defending Riel and the Métis in the newspapers and journals of the day, but they had neither the time nor the inclination to complete a full-length history. Two of its members who styled themselves as historians (Guillaume Charette and Camille Teillet) were both professionals who were simply too busy to do the writing.[25] By 1924 it was decided to approach Auguste-Henri de Trémaudan, a French-Canadian immigrant to Manitoba who had been educated in France. In Manitoba he had worked as a journalist and lawyer and had published a number of books and articles on Riel and the French in the Canadian west.[26] For a number of years Trémaudan had collected materials on Riel and the Métis in the west,[27] but by 1924 he had moved to California because of his ailing health. After negotiations, which took over two years, Trémaudan agreed to produce a manuscript of 400 pages in French[28] within a year if he were paid $750 and all the books he had sold to the Historical Society when he left Manitoba were shipped to him in Los Angeles. In return Trémaudan agreed to follow a detailed outline prepared by Camille Teillet. This outline divided the proposed manuscript into three parts: (1) Events preceding 1869; (2) Troubles at Red River; (3) The 1885 Rebellion. The committee also reserved the right to provide corrections and give suggestions. By late 1926 Trémaudan had begun work on the history.[29]

The interesting part of this story concerns the major interventions the Historical Committee made in the production of the book that was eventually published in 1935. They presented a very carefully crafted narrative of the Métis national tradition. At points their version simply followed Trémaudan's sympathetic portrayal of Métis history, but at other points it substantially embellished or subverted Trémaudan's work. It was this fashioning of Trémaudan's manuscript that made it effective tradition. The Historical Committee used Trémaudan's account and his documented facts to construct an exclusive myth of origin and continuity and endow the Métis with prestige, common purpose, and group identity.[30]

The radical revision of the Trémaudan manuscript requires a somewhat detailed explanation, as both his preface and the committee's introduction deny any tampering beyond normal editorial procedures. The committee, in a particularly effective but somewhat distorting introduction, noted that, had they written the book, the presentation would have been different, but that the facts related were exact and their importance and relevance were judged from Trémaudan's point of view. Despite their differences, they approved the *History* in its entirety. They also noted that because of his failing health Trémaudan was unable to complete the work, and a last chapter on 1885 was appended by the committee based on interviews with the participants of the 1885 Rebellion.[31] In fact, Trémaudan did complete an entire revised draft of his manuscript prior to his death, but the committee pushed him to substantially revise sections of his book and omit particular events; they not only added an appendix to the work but performed radical surgery on Trémaudan's final manuscript. In the period shortly before his death, these intrusions nearly led him to withdraw from the project.[32]

With this in mind it is necessary to explain Trémaudan's preface, in which he writes that, when it became known that he was working on the *History*, there were rumours that he was writing at the dictates of the Historical Committee – almost "under the rod." To these allegations Trémaudan replied that he had received no instructions other than to write the truth to the best of his knowledge and information, and that he assumed full responsibility for the contents of the book, which he had meticulously checked and verified.[33] This preface was written prior to 25 April 1928, however, when he had not yet completed the first draft of the manuscript, and at a point the committee had reviewed only the first seven of a projected fourteen chapters. The major disputes with the committee were still to come, and Trémaudan wrote his preface at this early date only because Father Adrien Morice had contacted him to let him know that the projected book was causing some uneasiness in certain quarters and that his independence was being questioned.[34] Six months later he would have written an entirely different preface.

No substantial disagreements between Trémaudan and the Historical Committee arose prior to February 1928, when he had nearly finished his manuscript and the committee had finished editing and revising the first seven chapters. At this point Trémaudan was told that his manuscript was too long; they wanted a clearer, more concise and simple account. He was also advised to be less polemic in his anti-English rhetoric, as the goal of the history was to convince the English of the just grievances of the Métis. As Camille Teillet put it, "One does not capture flies with vinegar." His four chapters on the 1885 Rebellion should be cut to two and he was instructed not to deal with Riel's religious views and purported madness, the occupation of the Batoche church by Riel's men, the Frog Lake Massacre, the detention of the nuns, and the issue of Riel's indemnification of $35,000 from the federal government. Rather, the emphasis should be on the collaboration with the English in the early movement of 1884, Riel's diplomacy, the call to arms, the battles of 1885, Riel's capture and trial, and the fact that the Rebellion had achieved all the aims of the Métis and freedom for the west. The "thorny questions" should be omitted and dealt with in another book.[35] Trémaudan's immediate response was that his view on Riel's madness was his own, and the committee could do what they wished. He did make substantial revisions, however, noting that almost every page contained corrections.[36]

Another dispute arose in the fall of 1928 when the committee had completed its reading of the entire manuscript and sent it back with corrections and suggestions for major revisions. The goal of their history, they informed Trémaudan, was the rehabilitation of the Métis, so that the Métis race would be recognized as equal to all others. Therefore, the language should be more moderate and less anti-English. As well, the book was meant to be a popular history that would be read widely by young people and find its way into the curriculum of the school system. To this end it should be much shorter and simpler. The treatment of 1885 should be briefer and deal only with politics. Trémaudan was instructed to leave out entirely the question of Riel's madness and his religious views.[37] The author's first response was to resist any more major revisions. He suggested instead that the committee could write a foreword, noting the points on which they disagreed with the author and presenting their alternative arguments in two appendices. On the matters of length and clarity, Trémaudan also refused to budge. The manuscript, he argued, was written clearly and he had revised and softened his language as much as he could. If the committee could show him where cuts could be made without compromising the narrative, he would consider it, but to his mind it was not possible. As to writing for the youth – this was a joke. The young did not read and, if they read, they did not read history. He had not written it for the schools and had never been told to do so. Concerning his anti-English and anti-Protestant rhetoric, he was of the opinion that in dealing with the "Orangistes" one should never take off one's gloves – they were fanatics.[38]

The committee did not accept Trémaudan's solution, and Samuel Nault noted that it was impossible for them to accept the author's suggestion that the committee could present its dissenting views as appendices. Everyone knew that Trémaudan was their historian and, if they openly displayed their differences of opinion, the committee and their goals would suffer. The public would believe that the committee was wrong. Therefore, it was necessary for both parties to come to some agreement. Nault noted that the committee was still not satisfied with his treatment of 1885 and was adamant that he omit any mention of Riel's religious views and the question of his madness. Any discussion of these topics would not advance their cause.[39]

This dispute drove a major wedge between Trémaudan and the Historical Committee, which Samuel Nault tried to bridge in the next few months. He implored Trémaudan to make some concessions and he would work at his end to have Teillet, the major force for revision on the committee, moderate his demands. The one area where they would not bend, however, was their demand that he leave out the treatment of Riel's religious ideas and his purported madness. In return the committee would endeavour to send him historical evidence to support their views on the issues of the prisoners of Batoche, the offer of $35,000 indemnification to Riel, and the Frog Lake Massacre.[40] The committee, Nault went on, also would send amendments to the texts, which he hoped Trémaudan could accept. They could accept some water in their wine if he could.[41] It is apparent from the succeeding correspondence that Trémaudan did make some of the requested revisions; by March 1929 he had submitted a new manuscript,[42] and the final typescript contains no discussion of Riel's religious views and the only mention of madness is in relation to Riel's trial, when his lawyers introduced the insanity defence. As well, the four chapters on 1885 had been reduced to three.[43]

When the Historical Committee had completed its corrections of this last manuscript version at the end of March 1929, they sent it to Trémaudan, along with the interviews they had conducted at Batoche, for a final revision. Over the summer of 1929 the author apparently made some minor revisions, but baulked at any more major changes. He noted in September 1929, a few months before he died, that he was too ill to continue; if the suggested changes had to be made, he advised the committee to publish the book as authored by the committee, explaining his role. This advice, of course, the committee refused to follow.

The Historical Committee's role in shaping the form and content of Trémaudan's manuscript did not end here. When the committee had finally retrieved the manuscript from the author's family,[44] they were faced with the difficult prospect of publishing it in the midst of the Great Depression. Their initial attempts to have the book produced in Paris (Trémaudan's first choice) came to naught and by 1934 they had settled on publishing it in Quebec. Their publisher, Albert Lévesque, wanted the manuscript cut even more to cut costs, eliminate repetition, and to improve its prose style. It is clear that both the Historical Committee and Lévesque had a role in the final product.[45] Close to 50,000 words were deleted from the manuscript and the committee added an appendix answering exactly those questions that they had forced Trémaudan to excise from his manuscript and on which they had disagreed with him.[46]

The resulting book, while lacking in analytic subtlety, was a highly effective story, declaration of faith, even catechism of the Métis Nation. In this it was a very conscious product of both the sensibilities of Trémaudan and the explicit goals of the Historical Society outlined above. In its form or rhetorical strategy it resembled the hagiographic epic where the truth of the account is more assumed than proved[47] and the narrative owes more to mythic and literary criteria than to historical fact. This connection between the rhetorical strategy of the hagiographic epic and *Histoire de la nation métisse* is intentional and can be seen in the way the book was reshaped at the editing and publication stages (see the comparison in Table 5.1). This was the quality that gave the *Histoire* its emotional weight.

The plot of the hagiographic epic or life of a martyred saint is always structured as a binary opposition between pagan/Christian, good/evil, and vice/virtue, where values are not shaded but absolute. It is told in the first person plural, with the narrator identifying with the martyr's support group; the role of the impartial observer is not a narrative option, since the act involves all of society and polarizes everyone. Hagiographic epics emphasize speech and privilege discourse. Athletic metaphors are common, as the martyred saint is no passive victim, but a willing and energetic participant in the contest, and individual identity is submerged into a corporate one.The conflict is not between individuals but between good and evil. The spirit of martyrdom is always a social one – it celebrates community and the values depicted are those of an entire society. The purpose is not the glorification of an individual but the affirmation of the ideals for which the saint has given his life.

Table 5.1 Comparison of the 1929 manuscript and the published history

Manuscript, 1929	Book, 1935
Chapitre I: Les Aborigènes pp. 9–26 (10,360 words) Chapitre II: Apparition des Blancs 1618–1782	Première Partie: 1618–1782 La Nation Métisse: Sa Formation I. L'Ancêtre Maternelle: L'Indienne II. L'Ancêtre Paternel: Le Blanc III. Le Fruit des Alliances: Les Métis
19,600 words: 13.5%	pp. 31–69 (10,00 words): 10%
Chapitre III: Voyages et Établissements 1750–1820 pp. 44–64 (10,920 words) Chapitre IV: Luttes, Avanies et Développements 1814–1844 pp. 65–86 (12,040 words) Chapitre V: Emancipation et Obstruction pp. 87–107 (12,040 words)	Deuxième Partie: 1750–1869 La Nation Métisse: Sa Vie I. L'Invasion Étrangère II. L'Organisation Primitive
35,000 words: 24%	pp. 73–147 (20,925 words): 22%
Chapitre VI: Les Métis pp. 108–24 (9520 words) Chapitre VII: Organisation et Résistance 1867 pp. 125–42 (9,520 words) Chapitre VIII: Le Gouvernement Provisoire de Rivière-Rouge 1869–70 pp. 143–62 (10,640 words) Chapitre IX: Oeuvres et Chute du Gouvernement Provisoire, jan–août 1870 pp. 163–88 (13,440 words) Chapitre X: Les Canadiens au Manitoba 1870–79 pp. 189–202 (7,280 words) Chapitre XI: Les Métis de la Saskatchewan: L'Insurrection de 1885 (1862–85) pp. 203–221 (9,800 words) Chapitre XII: Suite et Fin de L'Insurrection, mars–juillet 1885 pp. 222–45 (12,880 words) Chapitre XIII: Le Martyre d'un Peuple 1885–86 pp. 246–66 (11,2000 words)	Troisième Partie (1869–86) La Nation Métisse: Son Martyre I. Les Origines et L'Object du Drame II. Les Péripéties du Drame III. Le Dénouement du Drame
84,280 words: 58%	pp. 151–376 (60,750 words): 64%
Chapitre XV: Conclusion pp. 267–79 (6440 words): 4.5%	Conclusion La Situation Nationale de Métis pp. 377–90 (3800 words): 4%
Total Words: 145,320	Total Words: 95,475

Notes: The calculation of the words in each section is only approximate and is included for the sake of comparison. The word count was calculated by taking the average number of words per page in the first three pages of the section and multiplying this average by the total number of pages in that particular section.

And the drama of martyrdom is played out in public, where the martyr bears witness to the social and political context of the times and challenges the entire social fabric of society. The martyr's death is far from being the central narrative interest, but instead is only one element in a complex tale that progresses inevitably to a confrontation between good and evil. The climatic centre of the hagiographic epic is not the moment of death but the interrogative scene in which the tyrant and martyr face each other in public, and the martyr's speech of defiance and confession of faith represent a victory over evil. The resulting death is therefore a vindication rather than tragic defeat. The function of the hagiographic epic is not to convert or win God's mercy, but rather to restate the polarities of the drama, reminding the audience of the ideological basis of the conflict.[48]

While Trémaudan implicitly borrowed these forms, devices, and narrative strategies, the Historical Committee accentuated and made them explicit and corrected Trémaudan where he strayed from the formula. Both would have known that the hagiographic epic or "passio" would be familiar to the Métis reading public schooled in the hagiographic tradition of the Catholic Church. They would have had a common horizon of expectation, a proper respect for the heroic behaviour depicted, and an understanding of the proper function of its themes. The hanging of Riel in 1885 is transformed in the published book into the martyrdom of the entire Métis Nation. The tripartite division of the book breaks the history of the Métis Nation into "Its Formation," "Its Life," and "Its Martyrdom."

Given the centrality of conflict and confrontation in the martyr plot, it is not surprising that some of the largest cuts in the manuscript by the Historical Committee were made in the section dealing with the origins of the Métis Nation. Trémaudan's long and simplistic account of the birth of the Métis Nation as resulting from the mixing of blood is pared to its bare essentials to accentuate the noble character of the Métis derived from both maternal and paternal ancestors. Here, in very stark terms, the Métis are introduced as all that is good and just in the west.[49] The Métis men were tall with dark piercing eyes and almost colossal builds, demonstrating endurance, tenacity, and Herculean strength that spoke of their nobility and pride. Métis women were graceful, shy, and modest. Their settlements epitomized family, hospitality, comradeship, and, as a race and nation between the Indians and Europeans, they fostered friendly relations – the foundation of tolerance and understanding. Blessed with an implacable logic and a finely tuned sense of justice, liberty, and equality, they idealized their rights. They also had a great love and respect for the Catholic religion and its priests, and morality was highly esteemed. Little wonder, Trémaudan muses, that they would offer unyielding resistance to Canadian authorities who had seized their lands.

While it is clear from this early depiction where good and evil reside in the fable, and clear also where the narrative is heading, Trémaudan has a lot of history to cover before the Canadian state enters the story. Prior to this time the Métis encounter some lesser evils and undergo some testing in the course of which they demonstrate their higher heroism and the apotheosis of the people. The first disruption of the peaceable kingdom is by the fur trade companies, which invade the west in a search for wealth, ignoring the rights of the western Natives and victimizing the Métis in the violence of the fur trade competition. The Métis eventually stand up to the imperial Hudson's Bay Company, forcing it to back down in 1849 and acknowledge the rights of the Métis. This sets the stage for the last act of the drama – the battles against the Canadian state – which takes up close to 70 per cent of the book.

The movement of English Canadians westward in the 1860s and the purchase of Rupert's Land by Canada set up the final two battles between good and evil, between justice and injustice. The adventurers from Ontario and the Canadian state are portrayed as cheats, criminals, and thieves bent on invading the Métis homeland, seizing their land, and subjugating the populace. That they do not immediately succeed is due to the heroic and saintly leadership of Louis Riel. Riel's achievements and victories are chronicled in great detail as Trémaudan invents dialogue for Riel to dramatize his leadership and ordeal. All of Riel's actions are beyond reproach as he unites the settlement to achieve rights for all. Yet even when he saves the west for Canada by turning back the Fenians in 1871, he is rewarded with ingratitude and exile.

Despite Riel's victory in 1870 and the passage of the Manitoba Act, Trémaudan continues, a new era of persecution began in the period after 1870, as the Canadian volunteers initiated a "reign of terror" that hounded Riel out of the country, dispossessed the Métis in Manitoba, and repeated this depredation in Saskatchewan. Treated with contempt and criminal neglect, the Métis called Riel back from the United States to fight for their rights. That violence broke out in the North-West in 1885 was, according to Trémaudan, entirely the fault of the federal government. Had Riel wanted, he could have followed Dumont's plan and destroyed Middleton's army by guerrilla warfare, but Riel did not want to act like a savage. Forced into a corner, the Métis fought courageously against overwhelming odds and, despite being defeated, they compelled the government to acknowledge their rights and the rights of western Canada in Confederation. Though Riel could have fled, he chose to give himself up to confront his oppressors one last time in a courtroom. In this last confrontation Riel forced the country to face the truth and adopt measures to remedy the lamentable situation of the Native people in the west and acknowledge the full rights of the Métis Nation. The book's description of the trial is a masterful treatment of the binary oppositions of good and evil: west against east, Quebec against Ontario, Catholic versus Orange, and French against English. Though he was found guilty and sentenced to hang, Riel's death was not in vain. His eloquent defence of Métis entitlements and his martyrdom won rights for the west and for the sacred cause of the Métis Nation.

This pared-down summary of Trémaudan's narrative, while it leaves out a great deal of detail, does suggest the degree to which he followed the emplotment of the hagiographic epic. Our point here is not that he distorted history, but that the story he told was not dependent on historical accuracy and was not falsifiable by reference to real historical events. It is in this light that the Historical Committee's insistence that Trémaudan leave out all mention of Riel's religious ideas that implied heresy makes sense. They, better than the author, who was caught up in the duties of the historian, understood the function his narrative was to play – celebration and edification to promote identification with the Métis Nation. The problem the committee had had with previous French-Canadian and clerical histories of Riel and the Métis, no matter how positive they had been, was that on the subject of the 1885 Rebellion they had all backed away from endorsing Riel's religious views and saw in them at least a hint of apostasy or even madness. For the book to function effectively as a hagiographic epic, these qualifications had to be excised.

Conclusion

After the publication of *Histoire de la nation métisse dans l'Ouest canadien*, Father Adrian Morice, a prolific historian and ethnologist in his own right, wrote a book-length critique of it. While over half of his diatribe was directed at the historical inaccuracies of the committee's appendix, where they had tried to refute every charge that had been levelled at Riel, Morice also took a hard run at the author. The main body of the work, he argued, was honest, but riven with errors of fact and grammar. Trémaudan was a tired and sick man when he wrote the book and a man who was unsure of religious questions. He had been pressured, Morice charged, to write what the committee wanted to hear. To begin with, he noted, the Métis constituted a race, not a nation. They had no common language, religion, habits, culture, territory, and government. He criticized Trémaudan for providing no coherent account of the formation of Métis ethnicity and for having no footnotes to back up his factual assertions. As well, he catalogued a long list of factual errors, omissions, deliberate distortions, and invented conversations. Riel had been whitewashed, the government had been unfairly demonized, and Trémaudan had been turned into a mouthpiece for the St Vital Métis.[50] Morice's criticisms created barely a ripple at the time and are hardly read today. He did not seem to understand, or he understood all too well, that the effectiveness of the hagiographic epic (or heritage in David Lowenthal's formulation) is not dependent on factual accuracy and thrives on omission. As Lowenthal has pointed out, "heritage the world over not only tolerates but thrives on and even requires historical error. Falsified legacies are integral to the exclusive purpose of group identity."[51]

In the midst of the Depression, the Historical Committee managed to raise close to $1,500 dollars by subscription to print 1,500 copies, which were distributed widely in Quebec and western Canada. Although scholars today largely ignore Trémaudan's work, preferring Marcel Giraud's monumental and richly referenced study of the Métis,[52] it is Trémaudan's epic that is more widely read[53] and by far more influential. The book succeeds and is read today not in spite of its factual errors and omissions, but because of them. It succeeds because it presents an epic narrative that has relevance to today's struggles. Its themes of virtuous victims, loss, and the martyrdom of a hero and a people at the hands of the state are a powerful tool in the political struggles for national recognition and achievement of political agendas. The loss of ancestral autonomy, cultural legacies fatally flawed by subjugation, and a legacy of oppression validate present identity far more than victories would do.

These themes were first championed by the members of L'Union nationale métisse Saint-Joseph as they tried to rehabilitate the idea of a Métis Nation and win recognition and respect for the Métis and French of western Canada. The idea was later popularized by the publication of Trémaudan's hagiographic epic, which was carefully shaped and moulded by the Historical Committee of the National Union.

The present-day formulations of the "historic Métis Nation" are a direct descendant of this formulation with its emphasis on the western base of Métis Nationalism, its sense of grievance against the Canadian state, its stress on victimization, and its moral claim to restitution based on the "inexcusable government handling of Métis land rights." It is both a powerful rhetorical strategy and an effective politics of identity.

L'Union nationale métisse Saint-Joseph of the 1930s, however, was only one step in the process that created the present-day formulation of the Métis Nation. While the National Union insisted on purging all mention of Riel's messianic religion, it maintained an emphasis on the French language and tried to rebuild its bridges with the Catholic Church. These two pillars of Métis identity would remain intact until a new generation of Métis leaders in the 1960s and 1970s tried to build a pan-Métis movement shorn of Catholicism and the French language.

PART THREE

Government Policy and the Invention of Métis Status in the Nineteenth Century

The claim of dynamic nominalism is not that there was a kind person who came increasingly to be recognized by bureaucrats or by students of human nature but rather that a kind of person came into being at the same time as the kind itself was being invented. In some cases, that is, our classification and our classes conspire to emerge hand in hand each egging the other on.[1]

The, Manitoba Act, which brought Manitoba into Confederation in 1870, also created a new status category for Natives of mixed ancestry. By this act[2] 1.4 million acres were granted for allocation among the children of half-breed heads of family residing in Manitoba on 15 July 1870. This land grant was justified in the Manitoba Act as being expedient towards the extinguishment of Indian title to the lands of the province. As this land grant was interpreted after 1870, each Métis child was to be given 240 acres of land. Having justified the land grant to extinguish Indian title of Métis children, the government was faced with the problem of how to extinguish Indian title of Métis parents, as they were not included in the land grant.[3] This was accomplished by federal legislation: 37 Victoria, chapter 20, assented to on 26 May 1874. This act provided for a grant to Métis heads of family (both women and men) of 160 acres of land or scrip[4] for $160 receivable in payment for the purchase of Dominion lands. As these programs were extended to the North-West Territories after 1885, scrip was issued to those adults and children who could document that they were of Indian-European ancestry and who had been born in British or Canadian territory. The program was designed to provide the Métis of the North-West Territories with access to land and was granted in extinguishment of Métis claims to Indian title. These massive administrative programs, administering the Métis land grant of the Manitoba Act and the scrip programs of the NWT, constituted the governmental roots of a modern Métis ethnicity or status. These programs, which lasted well into the twentieth century, not only created a massive administrative, statistical, and genealogical archive, but named and defined an ethnicity or identity to which the Métis ascribed in order to receive benefits.

While Métis communities and individuals in the nineteenth century had a wide variety of cultural and economic affiliations with vague ethnic boundaries that did not admit of discrete either/or divisions, the scrip program demanded distinct and absolute boundaries. By the time scrip and treaty commissioners had travelled to northern Saskatchewan and Alberta in the period 1887–1907, they found few differences between the Indian and Métis populations, who were much intermarried. They offered the "mixed-bloods" of the region the choice of extinguishment of their Aboriginal title either by entering treaty or taking scrip. Once they chose, however, they were bound by their decision. In a sense, a type of person came into being at the same time as the "Métis scrip" category was being invented. Scrip and treaty administrative practices that defined and counted collective identities in an all or nothing manner enabled/forced people to see or organize themselves in light of these categories. As Ian Hacking has demonstrated, the power of categories rests in their capacity to impose the realities they ostensibly only describe. Once defined and labelled "Métis" or "Indian" for the purposes of extinguishment, administrative action, and benefits, these categories took on a life of their own. They both closed and opened the possibilities for future action. Classifying people changes them and can even change their past and become part of their essence – a looping effect.[5]

This type of dynamic nominalism, in relation to the process of Métis scrip taking, also had self-ascriptive aspects. At treaty time, individuals and families could choose their relationship to the government (a permanent relationship in treaty as a ward of the state or a one-time grant of land rights and citizenship) and the ethnic label that was attached to their relationship (Indian or Métis). In deciding, they chose not only their future but to some extent their past, as the process of categorization and its acceptance enables humans to redescribe their pasts and create new narratives and personal stories.[6] As such, the process of scrip taking from the 1870s to the 1920s represented not only a recognition of a Métis identity, but in many cases the start of Métis identity formation.

6 The Manitoba Act and the Creation of a Métis Status

During the debate over the passage of the Manitoba Act in Parliament in the spring of 1870, the opposition Liberals were both confused and concerned about section 31 of the bill – the clause that would eventually apportion 1.4 million acres of land to the "children of Half-breed head of families" residing Manitoba on 15 July 1870 and justified as being expedient towards the extinguishment of Indian title to the lands of the province. For the Liberals, and indeed for most observers of Canadian Indian policy, the section represented a clear departure from previous government policy. From at least the 1830s the Canadian government had allowed individuals of mixed European/Native ancestry and who lived with and as Indians to enter treaty and live on reserves. Those who did not were regarded as having exactly the same rights as all other citizens – in other words, no special status. Speaking to section 31 of the act (the Métis Land Clause), Alexander Mackenzie, the Liberal leader, noted: "A certain portion [would] be set aside to settle Indian claims and another portion to settle Indian claims that the half-breeds have. But these half-breeds were either Indian or not (hear). They were not looked upon as Indians, some had been to Ottawa, and given evidence, and did not consider themselves Indians. They were regularly settled upon farms, and what the object could be in making some special provision for them that was not made for other inhabitants was more than he could understand."[7] Edmund Burke Wood, the Liberal MP for South Brant, was even more baffled by the Métis land grant, confusing it with a reservation to extinguish the Indian title of "Indian Tribes."[8] Macdonald had to explain that the land grant "was not for the purpose of buying out the full blooded Indians and extinguishing their titles," but was for their "mixed-blood" descendants, who would be dealt with in the same way as the United Empire Loyalists had been by giving small grants of land for them and their children.[9] By 4 May, when a redrafted version of the bill was finally circulated to the members of Parliament, Macdonald would add that this land grant would "go toward extinguishing the Indian title," but that Métis claims were separate from Indian claims.[10] By these small steps the Conservative government of John A. Macdonald began, inadvertently, to define a new Métis status that encompassed some claim to Aboriginal title and land rights in the west. Despite strenuous Liberal opposition, the Manitoba Act passed final reading in the Commons on 10 May 1870 and received royal assent on 12 May.

Born of the political exigencies of the Riel Resistance of 1869–70 and the difficulties of getting a Métis land grant through Parliament, the 1.4-million-acre grant, in extinguishment of Indian title, created a new category or status that the government almost immediately began to qualify. Adams Archibald, the first lieutenant governor of Manitoba, and the official in charge of implementing the grant, noted in late 1870, "I presume the intention was not so much to create the extinguishment of any hereditary claims (as the language of the Act would seem to imply) as to confer a boon upon the mixed race inhabiting this province."[11] John A. Macdonald, commenting fifteen years later on the rationale of the Manitoba Act, was explicit on this point. Whether the Métis had land rights or not was not so much the question, "as it was a question of policy to make an arrangement with the inhabitants of that Province, in order, in fact, to make a Province at all – in order to introduce law and order there, and assert the sovereignty of the Dominion." The phrase "in extinguishment of Indian title" that was used to justify the 1.4-million-acre land grant was an incorrect one, since they did not consider themselves to be Indians. "If they are Indians," he said, "they go with the tribe; if they are half-breeds they are whites, and they stand in exactly the same relation to the Hudson's Bay Company and Canada as if they were altogether white." Whether they had land claims or not, he noted, "it was necessary that peace should be restored; it was necessary that a Government should be established, it was necessary that the new Province of Manitoba should be organized; and therefore this grant of 1,400,000 acres was made to the half-breeds having possessory rights along the Assiniboine and the Red Rivers."[12] Macdonald, and the federal government, hoped that Manitoba would be the exception and would not set a precedent for Métis rights across the west. In this hope they were sadly mistaken.

The rest of this chapter will explain how the Manitoba Métis grant came about, and how its implementation created a process of categorization and acceptance that would define Métis ethnicity for decades to come. Despite the debates that have arisen over the advisability of a Métis land grant and subsequent Métis scrip programs, and the degree to which they were faithfully implemented,[13] there can be little argument that the Métis themselves embraced the various programs and insisted they be extended throughout the northwest.

The Métis Land Grant in Manitoba

That Métis Aboriginal and land rights became enshrined in the Manitoba Act is somewhat surprising, given they formed no part of Riel's or his Provisional Government's position prior to their negotiations in Ottawa. This omission was in part due to the fact that in defeating the Dease and Hallet factions for control of the Resistance in the summer of 1869 (see chapter 4), Riel was forced to oppose their Aboriginal rights position as well. His opposition to Dease and Hallet and his Métis Nationalism, which owed much to Quebec Nationalism (see chapter 4), thus resulted in a list of demands that included protection of the French language and Catholic schools and provincial status. Those demands related to land that were discussed in the various conventions held by Riel in Red River during the winter of 1869–70 included homestead and pre-emption rights, local control of public lands, respect for and confirmation of local customs, and provincial status.[14] The issue of the extinguishment of the Indian title of the Métis was never discussed in Red River and arose only during the negotiations in Ottawa that resulted in the drafting of the Manitoba Act. The three Red River delegates, Father N.-J. Ritchot, John Black, and Alfred Scott, began serious negotiations in Ottawa on 25 April 1870. When it became clear that the federal government would not surrender control of lands and resources to the newly created province, discussion shifted to compensation for the loss of control over public lands. As Ritchot noted in his journal, control over lands in Manitoba could not be given up without compensation, and in these discussions he first raised the rights of the Métis. In asking for provincial status and rights, he noted, the Métis should not lose their rights "as descendants of Indians."[15]

From this point on, discussion shifted to a land grant for the Métis population to extinguish this alleged title as the compensation demanded. Ritchot would later admit that Métis title, because of their

Indian blood, was not quite certain, but that in order to find a satisfactory solution, it was deemed best to regard it as certain. It was the only way, Macdonald and Cartier told Ritchot, to get a Métis land grant through Parliament.[16] The legitimacy of this concern was more than justified by the Liberal opposition to the Manitoba Act in the House of Commons. Alexander Mackenzie, the leader of the Liberal opposition, noted in relation to what would become section 31 of the Manitoba Act (Métis Land Grant) that he could find no reasonable explanation for this reservation. It was unasked for by the people of Manitoba and no one in the Commons had "vouchsafed an explanation as to who this demand for reservations came from."[17]

Métis Scrip in Manitoba

As this land grant was interpreted after 1870, 240 acres of land was to be given to each Métis child as opposed to all Métis residents. Having justified this land grant in the Manitoba Act as the means to extinguish the Indian title of Métis children, the government was faced with the problem of how to extinguish Indian title of Métis parents, as they were now excluded from the land grant.[18] This was accomplished by chapter 20 (37 Victoria), assented to on 26 May 1874. This act provided for a grant to Métis heads of family (both women and men) of 160 acres of land or scrip for $160 receivable in payment for the purchase of Dominion lands. Under the provisions of this act regulations were made and approved by Order in Council (OIC) of 23rd March 1876: "in view of the great dissatisfaction which has been caused in Manitoba by the locking up of large and valuable tracts of land for distribution among Half-Breeds, thus seriously retarding the settlement of the country, cannot recommend the setting apart of further tracts of land for such purpose, and suggests, therefore, that *scrip* issue to satisfy all claims under the Act above quoted."[19] From this point on Métis heads of family in Manitoba would only have the option of being given scrip for $160 receivable in payment for the purchase of Dominion land in satisfaction of their claims arising out of the extinguishment of the Indian title.

The use of scrip as compensation for Métis claims was probably borrowed from the United States, where a significant Métis presence resulted in various "half-breed" clauses included in the Indian Treaties concluded in the United States between the 1820s and 1870s. These clauses were inserted at the insistence of the tribal leaders who signed the treaties. While not official parties to the treaties, these "half-breeds" were given some recognition in them by cash payments, grants of land, or scrip.[20]

Scrip would also have been known to the Métis of Red River. When the Red River Métis heard that the American government was planning to negotiate a treaty with the Pembina and Red Lake Ojibwa (Chippewa), many decided to relocate to the American side of the boundary to take advantage of the concomitant benefits.[21] During the negotiations the Métis claimed that "it was they who possessed the country really, and who had long defended and maintained it against the encroachments of enemies."[22] The treaty that was signed between the United States and the Pembina Chippewa on 20 September 1851, however, did not include the Métis as signatories, as the government believed it should not treat with people whom it regarded "as our *quasi* citizens." The government negotiator did stipulate that he would not object "to any just or reasonable arrangement or treaty stipulation the Indians might choose to make for their benefit." As a result, the Chippewa inserted a clause into the treaty that $30,000 be given to their Métis relatives.[23] However, the treaty was not ratified by Congress. When a treaty with the Red Lake and Pembina Bands was finally ratified by Congress in 1863, it included a "halfbreed" clause that provided some compensation for "mixed-blood" relatives who were considered not a part the band, but citizens of the United States. In 1864 it was amended to read "that, in lieu of the lands provided for the mixed-bloods by article eight of said treaty ... scrip shall be issued to such of said mixed-bloods as shall so elect, which shall entitle the holder to a like amount of land ... in lieu of all future claims for annuities."[24]

Canadian government officials were certainly familiar with the American precedent in treaty making, and it is possible that they saw the scrip process as a useful expedient in settling "half-breed" claims. It was a process that did not tie up land from settlement, it was easier to administrate, and it was a process with which the Métis were familiar. From the American example, both the Métis and the government would have been aware that the issue of scrip was immediately followed by speculative buying of the same. To discourage speculators, David Laird, the minister of the interior, stipulated that the scrip be delivered only to the person entitled to it who had the proper identification, or to any person producing a properly executed power of attorney[25] from the claimant to receive the scrip.[26]

Administrating the Métis Land Grant and Scrip in Manitoba

One of the reasons why the federal government decided to grant scrip to Manitoba Métis heads of family in extinguishment of their Indian title instead of outright grants of land, as had been the case with the Métis children's grant, was the long delay and administrative nightmare involved in finalizing those Métis children's allotments. They began to be allotted only in 1876 and were approaching completion only in 1880, effectively tying up huge blocks of land in Manitoba for a decade. This process is explained below both to understand why the government preferred scrip as the means to transfer land to the Métis, and to show how it initiated a Métis administrative archive that would shape Métis rights and identity for the next sixty years.

The process of selecting the lands for the Métis land grant was far from straightforward. Lieutenant Governor Archibald, reporting in December 1870, gave the first indication of where the Métis wished to locate their grant. He noted that the English-speaking and Protestant parishes and the French-speaking and Catholic parishes wished to keep this division in the allocation of lands. For this reason he recommended that the French (Catholic) reserves be located south of Fort Garry (forks of the Red and Assiniboine Rivers) and the English (Protestant) reserves north of the fort.[27] Less than a week later Molyneux St John, reporting to Archibald on the appropriation of lands for the Métis grant, noted that there was a difference of opinion on where the Métis wished to locate their lands. "Some persons desire to take their share in the neighbourhood of the lands now occupied by themselves; others would prefer to receive it in parts remote from their present holdings with the view of obtaining Hay and better grazing country."[28] As well, from the initial selections that the Métis made in the summer of 1871 it is obvious that the Outer Two Miles of the river-lot parishes (hay privilege), and even some river-front land, was included in these selections.[29] The first Dominion Lands regulation on this subject was the Order in Council of 25th April 1871, which stipulated that the lieutenant governor would designate townships, out of which individual grants would be made by drawing lots.[30]

The matter was made more complicated and contentious when another Order in Council, passed on 26 May 1871, stipulated that, since the survey could not be effected in time to facilitate immigrants already on their way to Manitoba, it was expedient to allow them to claim land in advance of the survey as long as the entries were made for quarter

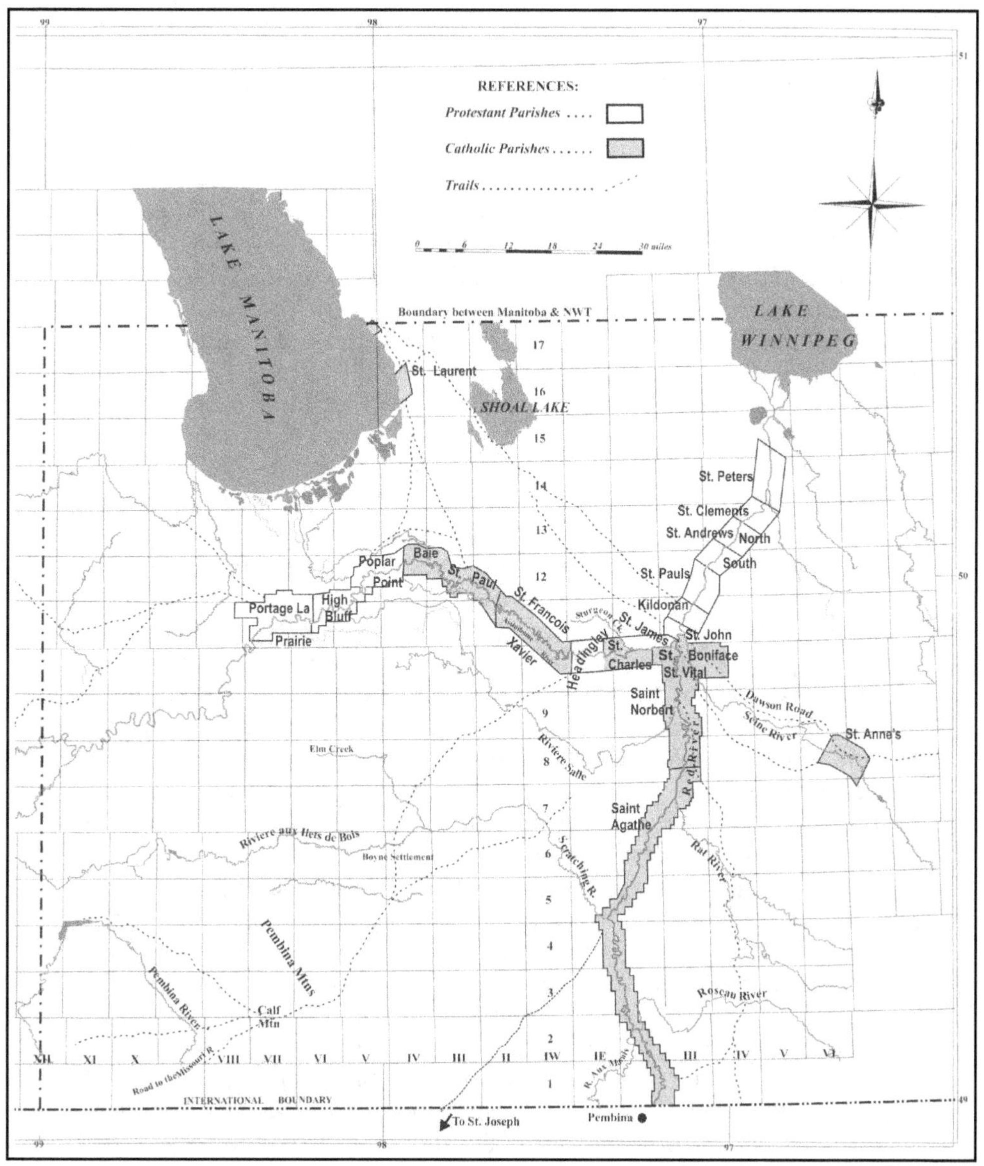

6.1 Red River parishes circa 1870. This map is adapted from J. Johnston, "Map Shewing the Townships Surveyed in the Province of Manitoba and the North-West Territories in the Dominion of Canada, December 31, 1874." LAC.

sections according to the land regulations.[31] When settlers from Ontario began moving onto the lands desired by the Métis, trouble arose. The flashpoint at this early date was an area some thirty miles south of the Assiniboine River along a small river known as Rivière aux Ilets de Bois. This was a location the Métis of St Charles and St François Xavier had been accustomed to using for hay, wood, and sugaring. Archibald eventually convinced over half of the 80–100 squatters in the area to move elsewhere, but enough remained that the Métis began to become suspicious of the government's good faith.[32] Prior to Archibald's selection of Métis reserves in the summer of 1872, when entries on these reserves were prohibited, settlers also located on lands desired by the St James Métis and those of High Bluff and Poplar Point. When possible, the government tried to mitigate the effects and generally tried to accommodate Métis demands as well as they could, given the protection that the OIC of 26th May 1871 had given to these settlers.

In an effort to protect the lands they wanted to have included in their land grant, the Métis of the French parishes began to hold parish meetings to choose the land they desired as reserves and to publish these spontaneous demands in *Le Métis*.[33] In the face of these actions, and in response to a letter addressed to him by the representatives of five Métis parishes asking for assurances in regard to their land grants, Lieutenant Governor Archibald wrote to the members of the Manitoba legislature, stating that in making his choice of Métis reserves he would be guided by the selections made by the Métis themselves. His letter was published in the newspapers of the province.[34] In response to this announcement the Métis in a number of English parishes also held meetings to choose their reserves.[35]

Archibald's proposed course of action, while meeting some censure in Ottawa, was finally adopted, with some qualifications, by the OIC of 15th April 1872, which noted: "it is important that these lands should be selected and set apart at the earliest moment, to prevent a possible conflict of interest that might arise with immigrants that will go into the province in the spring."[36] Under the authority of this OIC, Archibald would select reserves for the Métis based on their published requests, taking care that "only a due proportion of the Wood lands of the Province be included in the 1,400,000 acres of land to be granted to the Half Breeds."[37] As well, the OIC of 26th May 1871, which had permitted squatting prior to survey, would cease to have effect with respect to those lands reserved by Archibald for the Métis grant. However, the rights of those who had already made legitimate entries for land under the OIC of 26th May 1871 would be protected. In mid-July of 1872 Archibald was authorized to begin the selection of the Métis reserves, as the surveys of townships were now sufficiently advanced to permit him to do so.[38] His prompt announcement to this effect and his rapid selection of reserves (July 22) quickly quieted the discontent that had been brewing over the delay.[39] Archibald described his method in the following way.

> In fixing the number of Townships to be withdrawn I ascertain it by allotting a Township to every 150 Half Breeds. The assignment of Two lots in each Township to Schools, and two to the Hudson Bay Co. diminishes the Content of a Township by 2,560 acres, and leaves 20,480 acres to be divided. This will not quite suffice to give to 150 persons 140 acres each, but is sufficeintly [*sic*] near to act upon. On this basis it will require for the Half Breeds of what are called the French Parishes, and who number 5620 about 39 Townships, and for those of the English Parishes, numbering 4219 about 29 Townships: in all 68 Townships.[40]

Archibald would later note that in making these selections he had not committed himself to a final choice of any particular townships, and that the Métis had been made to understand that the only effect of the selection was to have the townships withdrawn from the market, pending the inquiries required to determine a final selection.[41]

Archibald was unable to select reserves for all the parishes in 1872, as some of the English parishes on the Red River north of Fort Garry had not yet made their selections. He noted that he had "intervened only for the Parishes which have made application. I did not think it wise to assume the initiative, and invite deputations from the Parishes; but wherever they have held meetings of their own accord, and named delegates to me, I have received them, and discussed with them the propriety of any selections suggestions."[42] Five parishes in Red River remained to be dealt with, but they were so situated as to create little difficulty in choice. There was an abundance of room and no danger of collision with settlers.[43] These remaining five parishes did not make their decisions until 1873 and therefore were dealt with by Archibald's successor, Alexander Morris.

Although the spontaneous demands of the Métis regarding their reserves are difficult to map, given the local place names used to delineate these lands (metes and bounds) some indication of their location and extent can be determined. Comparing the descriptions to Archibald's reservations, it is clear that Archibald tried to accommodate these demands and was fairly successful, but that there was not a perfect fit, as most parishes requested far more land than their populations warranted or the Manitoba Act provided for. In almost all cases Archibald reserved lands that were within the areas requested by the Métis. Though the Métis of St Charles did not receive the lands they had requested along the Rivière aux Ilets de Bois, they did receive two townships along the Sale River that they had also requested, thus fulfilling the requirements of that parish. Only in the cases of Headingly, High Bluff, and Poplar Point did Archibald substitute some alternative townships close to the parishes in question. It does not appear that these alternative selections resulted in any discontent after 1872, or at least no evidence of continuing discontent has been found.

Following Archibald's preliminary selection of reserves for nineteen of twenty-four parishes in July and August 1872, both the Métis and the government were anxious for the drawing of individual allotments to begin. Alexander Morris, preparing to take over the duties of lieutenant governor from Archibald,[44] noted in late 1872 that the inaction in granting lands to the Métis due to the delays of the survey was still a source of disquiet, and that he was of the opinion that his administration should be given the authority to announce that the allocation of the Métis land grant would proceed in early 1873.[45] However, Morris still had to reserve sufficient land for the five parishes that had not indicated their preferences (Kildonan, St Paul, St Andrew's South, St Andrew's North, and St Peters), and by the time this task was completed other issues had arisen that would further delay the distribution of the 1.4 million acres of land.

By early 1873 Morris had completed the reservations of land for the grant, and on 22 February 1873 he began the drawing of the individual allotments.[46] This drawing would not get very far. Problems and delays arose almost immediately with relation to the hay privilege (the outer two miles behind the parish lots) which had been included in the spontaneous selections of the Métis for their land grant and consequently had been included in Archibald's and Morris's reservations. As the implications of this allotment began to dawn on the Métis, they began to hold meetings to protest any inclusion of the Outer Two Miles (OTM) in the Métis land grant until claims to the hay privilege and rights of common were adjusted. In the view of the Métis the OTM should go to the river-lot owners under section 32 of the Manitoba Act, and they wanted these rights of common adjusted before there was any distribution of the 1.4 million acre grant. They considered that the ownership of the OTM was essential to the river-lot residents; if the OTM were alienated from them, they would be forced to leave their homes.[47] The government, which did not want the conclusion of the Métis land grant delayed any longer, could not understand why the Métis could not take their hay privilege or rights of common in scrip.[48] The government eventually relented, faced with the evidence of the report of the Hay Commission that rights of common existed[49] and the resistance of the Métis to accepting scrip as compensation. This agreement was formalized by the OIC of 6th September 1873, and a public notice was sent to the various parishes to the effect that in those localities where the hay privilege had been recognized by the laws of Assiniboia, lot owners would be compensated in land commencing at the rear of their respective lots and extending outwards no more than two miles and no wider than their front lot.[50] This verdict, in turn, necessitated a re-survey of the OTM and the allocation of extra land for the Métis grant. The new allocation was completed by Lindsay Russell, the assistant surveyor general, who sent the list of additional lands to Morris in August 1873.[51]

In the interim the government had also decided that Métis heads of family should be excluded from the Métis grant, which, by a strict reading of the Manitoba Act, was intended for the benefit of the children of Métis heads of family. This decision was made at the request of the inhabitants of Manitoba and was widely supported by the Métis communities and the Catholic clergy.[52] It further delayed the grant, as all allotments made thus far had to be cancelled and it was now necessary to grant the land to fewer individuals in larger allotments. The redrawing of allotments resumed in the fall of 1873 and Morris expected to complete it before the end of the year. It was not to be, however, as it was subsequently decided that a commission be appointed to determine who was eligible for the children's grant, in effect undertaking another more detailed census. As a consequence, the final drawing of individual 240-acre allotments did not recommence until 1876 and would not be completed until 1880.[53]

The enumeration of Manitoba Métis eligible for either a land grant (children) or scrip (heads of family) began in 1875 and was authorized and governed by the OIC of 26th April 1875. This OIC set up a commission composed of John Machar, a Kingston lawyer, and Matthew Ryan, a Montreal lawyer, and included their secretaries, Amédée E. Forget of Montreal and Henry Goodhue of Danville, Quebec. They visited each parish in the province, after giving notice of the time and place of the

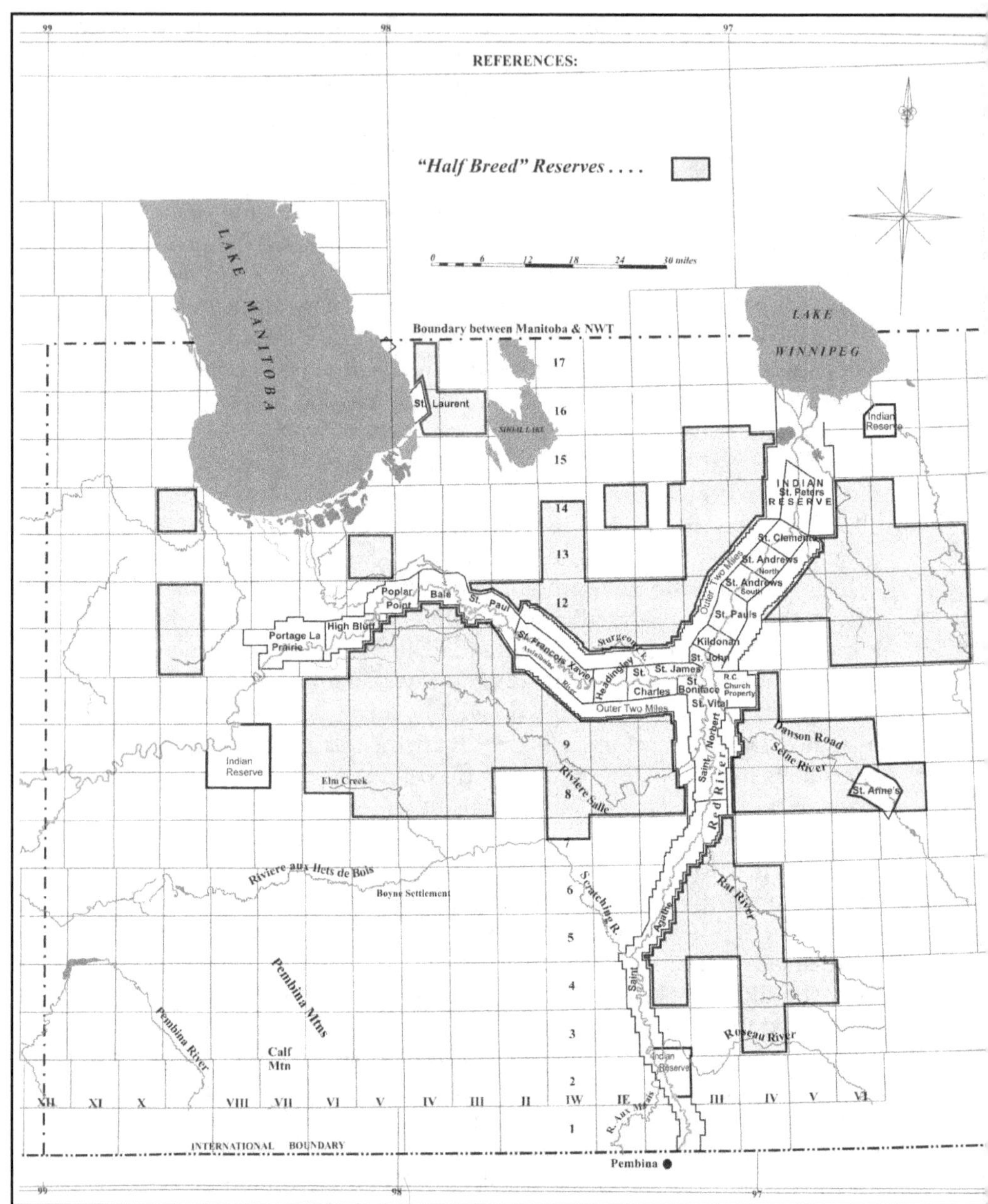

6.2 Métis reserves set aside by Lieutenant Governors Archibald and Morris, circa 1874. This map is adapted from J. Johnston, "Map Shewing the Townships Surveyed in the Province of Manitoba and the North-West Territories in the Dominion of Canada, December 31, 1874," LAC.

sessions, and worked from lists derived from the 1870 Census and earlier applications. Applicants had to apply and each application had to be attested to by two affidavits of householders in the parish. If claimants could not appear before the commission sitting in their parish, they could also apply at other sittings or before a Dominion Lands agent. This work was mostly completed by the end of 1875, but given that many Métis out on the plains had not been able to apply, the commission was extended for two years to allow these claimants to come forward.[54]

This enumeration process marked the beginning of a massive Métis land and scrip archive, which over the next sixty years not only would act to determine Métis eligibility for these programs, but also represented an ascriptive process defining Métis ethnicity. In applying, Métis individuals not only made their genealogical claims to Métis status and identity, but also disclaimed Indian status. These forms have been transcribed below to show this dual nature.

FORM A (a Half Breed Child over 18 Years)

I, Josue Breland of the Parish of St. Frs Xavier in the County of Marquette East in the Province of Manitoba, farmer make oath and say as follows:

1. I claim to be entitled to participate in the allotment and distribution of the 1,400,000 acres of land set apart for Half-breed children, pursuant to the Statutes in that behalf.

2. I was born on or about the month of March A.D. 1855 at the parish of St. Frs. Xavier in said Province; and am now of the full age of ___________

3. Pascal Breland, a half breed, is my father and his wife Maria Grant, a half breed, is my mother;

my said father was the half-breed head of a family resident in the parish of St. Frs. Xavier in the said Province, on the fifteenth day of July, A.D. 1870.

4. I was not the head of any family at the last named date and I have not made any claim other than the above in this or any other Parish, nor have I claimed or received as an Indian any annuity monies from the Government of the said Dominion.

his Josue X Breland mark

Sworn before me at the Parish and County aforesaid on the fifth day of October A.D. 1875, having been first read and explained in the French language to the said deponent who seemed perfectly to understand the same, and affixed his mark in my presence.

Matthew Ryan, Commissioner.

Supporting Affidavit:
We Pascal Breland of the said Parish, in said County and Province, farmer and Casimir Dauphinais, farmer of the same place severally make oath and say as follows:

1. We are respectively house holders in said Parish St. Frs. Xavier
2. We severally know the within named claimant, who has this day made the within affidavit in our presence. We know he is the person, he represents himself to be; and we believe the several statements in said affidavit to be true.

Signed Pascal Breland
Casimir X Dauphinais mark

Sworn before me at the Parish aforesaid, on the fifth day of October 1875
Matthew Ryan, Commissioner[55]

FORM C (a Half-breed Head)

I, Marie Breland of the Parish of St. Frs Xavier in the County of Marquette East in said Province, wife of Pascal Breland, farmer make oath and say as follows:

1. I am a Half-breed head of a family resident in the Parish of St. Frs Xavier in the said Province, on the 15th day of July, A.D. 1870, and consisting of myself, husband and children and I claim to be entitled to such head of family to receive a grant of one hundred and sixty acres of land or to receive Scrip for one hundred and sixty dollars pursuant to the Statute in that behalf.
2. I was born on or about the 15th day of July A.D. 1820 in the N.W. Territory in said Province.
3. Cuthbert Grant, a half breed, was my father; and his wife Marie Desmarais, half breed, is my mother.
4. I have not made or caused to be made any claim of land or Scrip other than the above in this or any other Parish in said Province, nor have I claimed or received, as an Indian, any annuity moneys, from the Government of said Dominion.

her Marie X Breland mark

Sworn before me at the Parish and County aforesaid on the 5th day of October A.D.1875, having been first read over and explained in the French

language to said deponent who seemed perfectly to understand the same and affixed her mark in my presence.
Matthew Ryan, Commissioner
(noted below Claim No. 1120. Scrip issued 20th August 1876)

Supporting Affidavit:
We Robert Morgan of the said Parish in the said County and Province, farmer and Casimir Dauphinais of the same place severally make oath and say as follows:
1. We are respectively house holders in said Parish, St. Frs Xavier
2. We severally know that within named claimant, who has this day made the within affidavit in our presence. We know she is the person, she represents herself to be; and we believe the several statements in said affidavit to be true.
Robert Morgan
Casimir his Mark X Dauphinais

Sworn before me at the Parish aforesaid on this fifth day of October 1875.
Matthew Ryan Commissioner[56]

When this enumeration process was mostly complete by 1876, the process of redrawing the 240-acre children's allotments began again on a parish-by-parish basis. They were drawn in secrecy under the supervision of the lieutenant governor and the results were entered in separate notebooks for each parish, which then were sent to Ottawa. This redrawing proceeded slowly, both because of the required presence of the Dominion land agent, who was not often available, and because of the transition to a new lieutenant governor, but by 1880 most allotments had been drawn.[57]

By contrast, the administration of the Manitoba Métis scrip program proceeded rapidly, if less transparently, after it was decided that Métis adults would not be included in the distribution of 1.4 million acres of land, and that their claim to Aboriginal title would be extinguished by way of scrip. The type of scrip that was eventually issued to the Métis in western Canada fell into two categories: money scrip and land scrip. Both were intended to give the recipient a certain amount of Crown-owned land. These scrip certificates were issued in different monetary values (i.e., $80, $160, or $240), or in amounts of land (i.e., 80 acres, 160 acres, or 240 acres). When the first Métis scrip was issued in Manitoba in the 1870s, Dominion land was valued at $1 an acre, so that a $160 scrip

Table 6.1 Manitoba Métis land allotments and scrip

Manitoba Métis children's allotments				Manitoba Métis heads of family scrip	
Land allotments	Scrip[a] $240	Total land	Total scrip	Scrip $160	Total scrip
6034	993	1,448,160	$238, 300	3186	$509, 760

[a] Scrip was resorted to in relation to the Children's Grant when the 1.4 million acre grant was found not to suffice for the number of children eligible for the 240 acre grant.

Source: N.-O. Coté, "Grants to Half-Breeds in the Province of Manitoba and the North-West Territories, Comprising the Provinces of Saskatchewan and Alberta in Extinguishment of the Indian Title, 1870–1925, and Grant of Scrip to Original White Settlers, 1874–1894," (1929) Department of the Interior, LAC, RG 15, D-II-1, vol. 227, file 0, pt 4.

certificate would get the bearer the same amount of land as a 160-acre scrip certificate. As the value of land increased, however, money scrip was good for a correspondingly smaller amount of land.

The different types of scrip also had different regulations governing their use, which in turn affected their value on the scrip market. Until land prices rose at the turn of the century, money scrip was always more desirable to speculators because there were fewer restrictions on its use. Money scrip could be sold easily and its rights could be transferred, as it was defined as personal property rather than real property or real estate. Land scrip was more restricted by regulations that discouraged easy sale and therefore speculation. It could be used only to locate land in the name of the Métis grantee.

In total, 3,186 scrip certificates were issued to Métis heads of family in Manitoba (see Table 6.1). Most were issued quickly; by one estimate 80 per cent were issued by the end of 1876.[58] A market for Métis scrip soon developed in Manitoba as speculators from inside and outside the province hired agents to buy up the scrip. Winnipeg newspapers carried daily advertisements to buy and sell scrip, and prices were quoted regularly. Scrip became, in effect, a land-backed currency. From information given in the newspapers, it appears that scrip started selling for around $40–65 for a $160 scrip claim in 1876, rose to around $80 in 1877, and stood at $90–120 in 1878.[59] While the impressionistic evidence suggests that most Manitoba Métis heads of family sold their scrip quickly, there is little remaining evidence as to who picked up the scrip, who received powers of attorney to draw scrip, or the ways in which the purchased scrip was used.

Extending Métis Status and Scrip Westwards

Although there has been a good deal of debate over whether the federal government granted the Métis of Manitoba the various benefits of land and scrip to which they were entitled under the Manitoba Act, and whether this land and scrip actually benefited the Métis,[60] there can be little argument that the Métis wanted these programs and that they wanted them extended into the North-West Territories. Because of the rapid sale of and speculation in Métis scrip in Manitoba, the Canadian government was ill-disposed to duplicate this program in the North-West Territories. That they eventually did so in 1885 is testament to the persistent demands of the northwest Métis that they be treated exactly like their brethren in Manitoba. In their memorials and petitions to the government the Métis demonstrated not only that they wanted a scrip program, but also that they understood that this was the compensation due them for extinguishment of their rights to Indian title.

The first documentary evidence that the Métis of the northwest wished lands in compensation of their rights as Métis is an address to the lieutenant governor, Alexander Morris, at a public meeting of the Métis on 5 May 1873 held at Fort Qu'Appelle. This address, praying for protection in preventing strangers from disturbing them on their lands, included a short and vague reference to their land rights. "We ask of you, our Lieutenant-Governor, to give us lands in compensation of our rights to the lands of the country as Métis."[61] The reference is vague in the sense that many of the Métis of Qu'Appelle were Manitoba Métis who had left after 1870 and would have been eligible for Manitoba Act grants. More specific references to scrip and the specific rights of northwest Métis (Métis resident in the North-West Territories on 15 July 1870) began to arrive in Ottawa only after a commission headed by Matthew Ryan to investigate Manitoba Métis claims in the North-West Territories wrapped up in 1877[62] and when the rapid disappearance of the buffalo began to produce real distress on the plains. The timing of the onslaught of petitions after 1876 was also probably related to the fact that the country was not opened for homesteading until after the signing of Treaty 6 in 1876.

Beginning in 1878 the government began receiving petitions from the various communities of the North-West Territories explicitly asking for the same land and scrip rights that the Métis of Manitoba had received. The first of these came from the Métis of St Laurent, who, after holding a public meeting on 1 February 1878, presented a petition to the lieutenant governor of the North-West Territories requesting "that there be granted to each half-breed head of family, and to their children, who have not participated in the distribution of scrip and lands in the Province of Manitoba, a like amount of scrip and like land grants as in Manitoba."[63] In almost identical words the Métis communities of Prince Albert (February 1878), St Albert (1878), Manitoba Village, NWT (1880), Edmonton (1880), and Qu'Appelle Settlement (1881) requested the same land rights and scrip as the Manitoba Métis had received.[64] The one recorded exception to this request for scrip came in the petition of the Métis of Cypress Hills, who asked instead for a reserve of land to establish a permanent home along the forty-ninth parallel measuring 150 miles long and 50 miles wide.[65] As well, increasingly these petitions, memorials, and resolutions connected the granting of Métis land and scrip with the extinguishment of the Indian title of the Métis.[66] The agitation, petitioning, and resolutions continued to 1885.[67]

The point of the foregoing recitation of claims and petitions is to show that by at least 1880 many of Métis of the North-West Territories were demanding scrip and land in compensation for the extinguishment of their Indian title. They understood very clearly the land and scrip rights accorded the Métis of Manitoba and that these rights had been given in extinguishment of Indian title, and they wanted the same compensation.

Given Alexander Mackenzie's belief that "half-breeds were either Indian or not" and that they should have no special rights not given to other settlers,[68] it should not be surprising that his Liberal government (1873–78) made no move to recognize Métis rights possessed by way of Indian title. In response to the petition of the Métis of Lake Qu'Appelle at treaty time in 1874, Alexander Morris, lieutenant governor of the North-West Territories, assured the Métis that the federal government would respect the rights of the Métis to the lands that they had cleared and cultivated, "because it has always been the custom to regard the rights of actual possessors of the lands." With respect to the lands that the Métis might wish to take in the future, he noted, as soon as Indian reserves had been allocated, they would have the same rights as other settlers to take up these lands.[69] In response to the petition of the Métis of St Laurent, NWT, dated 1 February 1878 asking for scrip and land such as the Manitoba Métis had received, David Mills, the minister of the interior, replied that he did not see upon what grounds the "half-breeds" could claim to be treated differently from the "white" settlers of the territories. Where settled, lands would be assigned to them in the same way as they were to "white" settlers, "but beyond this, they must not look to the Government for any special assistance in their farming operation."[70]

The Conservatives, coming back into power after the election of 1878, might have been expected to view this question somewhat differently, given that it had been John A. Macdonald and George-Étienne Cartier who had negotiated the terms of the Manitoba Act, which had provided for the Métis Land grant in extinguishment of Indian title. Macdonald, however, had by 1878 taken a different view in relation to the rights of the Métis of the North-West Territories. In 1885, while defending his government's record between 1879 and 1885, Macdonald backtracked somewhat from the position that the Manitoba Act recognized Métis claims to Indian title.[71] Having let the genie of Indian title out of the bottle in the Manitoba Act, Macdonald and the Conservatives would try valiantly to stuff it back, at least partially, after 1878. Macdonald appears to have believed that the arrangement made in Manitoba was not necessarily applicable to the North-West Territories with regard to a Métis land grant and scrip.[72] However, his ministry was being pushed by its own officials to do something about Métis claims in the territories. In a confidential dispatch dated 20 December 1878, J.S. Dennis, the deputy minister of the interior, recommended that it was expedient "to deal with the claims to consideration preferred by the half-breeds of the North-West Territories," and that "it must be freely admitted they have a claim to be satisfied." The question was how best to satisfy this claim to benefit the "half-breeds" and, at the same time, to benefit the country. Dennis was of the opinion, given the experience in Manitoba, that it was unwise to provide an absolute grant of land to Métis parents and children. After describing the various classes of Métis in the northwest, Dennis recommended one of three courses of action:

> 1. To treat them as wards of the Government in effect, making a treaty with them, as with the Indians, and look forward to their remaining for many years in their present semi-barbarous state.
> 2. To give them an absolute issue of scrip, to a reasonable extent, to each individual, and then let them take their chances of living or starving in the future; or
> 3. To offer them certain endducements to settle on land and learn to farm – especially to raise cattle.[73]

According to Dennis, the first option would be in the interests neither of the government nor of the Métis, and it was very doubtful if the

Métis would consent to it if it were proposed. The second alternative, he opined, would result in a bigger disaster than occurred in Manitoba, as the Métis had no idea whatever of thrift or of the necessity for making provision for the future by locating scrip and securing land for the benefit of his family. Once the buffalo had disappeared, the government would be faced with an impoverished population, with no means of subsistence, and who would prove a standing menace to the peace and prosperity of the territories. The third alternative, he argued, was open to the government and represented the best chance of successfully establishing the Métis upon the land, assuming the Métis were willing to give it a trial. In recommending this solution, Dennis referred to the resolutions of the Council of the North-West Territories of 1878, which had recommended against setting apart a reserve of land for the Métis, or of granting negotiable scrip.[74] In reply to this memorandum, John A. Macdonald instructed Dennis to further investigate the matter by consulting with knowledgeable experts in the North-West Territories, including Archbishop Taché, and Lieutenant Governor Laird. Without exception, all recommended against granting negotiable scrip. The most detailed response came from Archbishop Taché. After admitting that the Métis of the North-West Territories had a claim to favourable consideration, he noted that they should not be compared with Indians, as they had neither the tastes, habits, nor instincts of the Indian, and that they were a "sensitive race" who were easily humiliated with regard to their origin. Having said that, he recommended that the best mode of settling them on the land was to provide reserves for them, and that each Métis should receive two non-negotiable scrips for eighty acres of land each to be located by them in any one of the reserves created. This land, he argued, should be entirely inalienable and not liable to taxation and mortgage.[75] Most of the other replies to Dennis opposed Taché's schemes for inalienable colonies. Hugh Richardson noted that some Métis families would prefer to locate themselves and act independently, while David Laird noted that, where the Métis expressed a desire to settle down together, a block of land should be reserved for a short time only. He believed it would be a mistake to lock up land for a period longer than two or three years.[76]

While there was unanimity among those who advised the government not to issue negotiable scrip, which would quickly fall into the hands of speculators,[77] there was no consensus on how the government should otherwise settle Métis claims. What the government did do was include in the Dominion Lands Act of 1879 subclauses (e) and (f) of section 125, which stated,

> (e) To satisfy any claims existing in connection with the extinguishment of the Indian title, preferred by half-breeds resident in the North-West Territories outside the limits of Manitoba, on the fifteenth day of July, one thousand eight hundred and seventy, by granting land to such persons, to such extent and on such terms as may be deemed expedient.
>
> (f) To investigate and adjust claims preferred to Dominion lands situate outside of the Province of Manitoba, alleged to have been taken up and settled on previous to the fifteenth day of July, eighteen hundred and seventy, and to grant to persons satisfactorily establishing undisturbed occupation of any such lands, prior to, and, being by themselves or their servants, tenants or agents, or those through whom they claim, in actual peaceable possession thereof at the said date, so much land in connection with and in satisfaction of such claims as may be considered fair and reasonable.[78]

For the first time the government officially acknowledged the necessity of satisfying existing Métis claims in connection with the extinguishment of Indian title in the North-West Territories, but nothing was said about how this might be accomplished. While the Métis were clamouring for both scrip and land grants, the government did little between the passage of this act and 1885 other than weigh the options.[79] From John A. Macdonald's defence of his government's policies in 1885 it seems clear that whatever policy would emerge with regard to Métis lands it would not include scrip. The Scrip Commission of 1885 appears to have been forced on the government by the increasing scale of Métis agitation in late 1884 along with the return of Riel to Canada. In 1885 Macdonald admitted that the government had been forced, against its better judgment, to make a scrip offer.[80]

With Métis agitation on the increase and with reports coming in to Ottawa that something should be done, an OIC dated 28th January 1885 (PC 135) was passed establishing a commission to enumerate those Métis "who would have been entitled to land had they resided in Manitoba at the time of the transfer and fyled their claims in due course under the Manitoba Act, and also of those who though residing in Manitoba and equitably entitled to participate in the grant, did not do so." The purpose of this enumeration was to settle equitably the claims of the Métis of Manitoba and the North-West Territories. The nature of this settlement, including the granting of land and scrip, was fleshed out only on 30 March 1885,[81] as the first violence of the Northwest Rebellion erupted.

Thus, by the early spring of 1885 the Canadian government had decided to deal with the Métis of the northwest much as they had with the Manitoba Métis: grant scrip redeemable in Dominion land in extinguishment of Métis claims to Indian title. In extending the scrip program westward the government reaffirmed a separate Métis status and inaugurated a program that would involve the Department of the Interior, Indian Affairs, and the northwest Métis for the next fifty years. This process of defining Métis rights and negotiating what its limits would be, along with the administrative course of applying for and granting this scrip, would define Métis identity in the west until at least the 1960s. For the Métis, entering treaty or taking scrip was a choice that determined not only their status and rights, but those of their descendants as well. These decisions, however, made in the context of economic hardship and limited opportunities, were not always carefully considered. This becomes very evident in the next two chapters, where we examine the permeability of treaty and scrip status for the Métis.

7 Extinguishing Rights and Inventing Categories: Métis Scrip as Policy and Self-Ascription

Although métissage was nearly universal in the fur trade, the biracial descendants of the fur company servants did not automatically assume a Métis identity; indeed, many of these offspring were assimilated among the Home Guard Cree, Ojibwa, Assiniboine, Blackfoot, Chipewyan bands of the northwest. The emergence of distinct Métis communities demanded a sequence of events and decisions that directed these children of fur traders along divergent paths (see chapter 2). One of these decisions was that of taking Métis scrip. It is often assumed that the process of taking Métis scrip was simply the confirmation of a Métis identity or the recognition of a Métis community already in existence. In some localities, such as Red River, Batoche, and St Albert, this was certainly the case, but in other localities the government program to grant scrip in extinguishment of Métis claims to Indian title created Métis communities where none had existed before.

By the end of the nineteenth century both the government and missionaries were cognizant that a great deal of racial mixing had occurred in the northwest and that Indian bands could have a significant number of members of mixed ancestry. For example, in planning for the negotiations of Treaties 8 and 10 and the granting of Métis scrip in these regions the government was confused as to the numbers of Indians and Métis they would be dealing with. In 1902 J.A. McKenna, the eventual commissioner who negotiated Treaty 10 in 1906, noted that many of those families and individuals regarded as "Indian" in northern Saskatchewan by the Indian inspectors and Roman Catholic priests could prove "they had white blood" and would "elect to be treated as Halfbreeds."[1] In 1906, when McKenna negotiated Treaty 10, most of his premonitions proved correct. He noted in his report that "the Indians dealt with are in character, habit, manner of dress and mode of living similar to the Chipewyans and Crees of the Athabasca country. It is difficult to draw a line of demarcation between those who classed themselves as Indians and those who elected to be treated with as Halfbreeds."[2]

For these and other reasons, in those treaties negotiated after 1885, the year that Métis scrip was introduced in the North-West Territories, individuals of mixed ancestry were given the choice of taking treaty and becoming "status Indians" or taking scrip and becoming "Métis." Individuals who had previously considered themselves Indians could now became Métis if they could prove some European ancestry. Even those previously in treaty, now often left treaty to take scrip. As noted in chapter 6, Métis scrip constituted the governmental roots of a modern Métis ethnicity.

Also as noted in chapter 6, the federal government was hesitant to duplicate the scrip program in the North-West Territories because of the rapid sale of and speculation in Métis scrip in Manitoba. Although the government did acknowledge in the Dominion Lands Act of 1879 that the Métis had claims to "Indian title" in the North-West Territories that needed to be satisfied, officials were uncertain of how to do this. Given the experience in Manitoba, almost all government officials and Church leaders advised against granting negotiable scrip that would be quickly bought up by speculators. Thus, between 1879 and the outbreak of the Rebellion of 1885 little was done other than weigh the various options. That the government eventually chose to grant scrip in early 1885 to settle Métis claims resulted from Métis demands to be treated as their brethren in Manitoba had been (see chapter 6).

This chapter is an attempt to clarify how the various Métis scrip programs from 1885 to 1921 were formulated as policy, how this policy formation further defined a "Métis status," and how adherence to that status became a part of Métis identity. The evolution of Métis scrip is a complex and convoluted process and the focus here is on policy formation and its impact on Métis identity. The various scrip commissions that held hearings in the North-West Territories from the 1880s to the 1920s not only created a massive administrative, statistical, and genealogical archive, but they named and defined an ethnic category to which the Métis ascribed in order to receive the benefits of scrip.

This discussion, for the most part, eschews the analysis of the speculation in scrip, which has generated its own archives and debates,[3] because it does not directly impact the questions of Métis identity in this period. Speculation in scrip and the charges of fraud are complex issues, which would require a very lengthy treatment not possible here. The debates and questions related to the speculation in Métis scrip are dealt with here only insofar as they impacted the revision of scrip policy. This is not to say that the issues related to the speculation in Métis scrip are unimportant, but they are beyond the purview of this chapter.

The 1885 Scrip Commission and the Evolution of Scrip Policy

With Métis agitation on the increase and with reports coming in to Ottawa that something should be done, an Order in Council (OIC) dated 28th January 1885 (PC 135) was passed establishing a commission to enumerate those Métis "who would have been entitled to land had they resided in Manitoba at the time of the transfer and fyled their claims in due course under the Manitoba Act, and also of those who though residing in Manitoba and equitably entitled to participate in the grant, did not do so." The purpose of this enumeration was to settle equitably the claims of the Métis of Manitoba and those of the Métis of the North-West Territories.

Three commissioners were appointed to carry out this enumeration in mid-March, and W.P.R. Street, after agreeing to head the commission, was summoned to Ottawa to receive his instructions. He arrived on 25 March shortly before the first reports of the battle at Duck Lake,[4] which marked the beginning of the 1885 Rebellion. With the news of violence at Duck Lake on 27 March, Street apparently noted to his superiors that the powers of his commission were probably not enough to quell the discontent. He requested more powers for the commission and received permission to enumerate, take evidence, and settle the claim on the spot – that is to hand each Métis his scrip certificate before he left the room when it was decided he was entitled to it.[5] These new powers were encompassed in the OIC of 30th March 1885 (PC 688), which set the initial policy for the Métis land grant based on subclause (e) of clause 81 of the Dominion Lands Act of 1883, which provided the Governor in Council the power to satisfy any claims existing in connection with the extinguishment of Indian title of the Métis of the North-West Territories.[6]

This land grant, while greater in scope than anything previously promised to the Northwest Métis, was less than the Métis in Manitoba had received. There the Métis heads of family were given both title to the land they had occupied and scrip for $160 redeemable in Dominion land. Under this Order in Council those Métis heads of family who already occupied 160 acres of land could claim this land but would get no scrip and would, in effect, be treated like ordinary settlers who had no Aboriginal rights to be extinguished. Each Métis child, however, would receive scrip for $240 redeemable in Dominion land.

On the same date that the Order in Council was passed, A.M. Burgess, the deputy minister of the interior, issued detailed instructions to W.P.R. Street on how the commission should proceed. It was to hold sittings in accordance with the itinerary prescribed, adopting a route northward from Qu'Appelle, and to advertise the date and place of the various sittings by means of posters in both French and English, which were to be distributed throughout the territories. The commission was also instructed to take applications of those Métis met en route without reference to prearranged sittings. The commissioners were instructed that they would receive applications from claimants who were in treaty, and arrangements were made to have Indian agents from the various districts attend the commission sittings to advise the commissioners. Anyone in receipt of annuities or on Indian rolls was not eligible for scrip. The commissioners were further instructed to inform treaty Indians that they were not eligible to be enumerated as "half-breeds," and to explain to them that when, under the provisions of the Indian Act, they made an application for enfranchisement, they would be dealt with by the government equitably and liberally.

For a Métis claimant to receive scrip the following evidence had to be furnished by affidavit and substantiated by the sworn affidavits of two reliable witnesses: (a) he was a half-breed head of a family[7] resident in the North-West Territories previous to the 15th day of July 1870, or (b) that he was a child of a half-breed head of a family resident[8] in the North-West Territories previous to the 15th day of July 1870 and born before that date. For those who met these conditions and had attained the full age of eighteen years, the commission would grant them a certificate to that effect and report the same to the minister of the interior. In the case of a claimant who had not yet attained the full age of eighteen years the commission would, upon the production of evidence as to his birth date or age at which he would attain the age of eighteen, issue a certificate.[9]

W.P.R. Street and the other two commissioners, A.E. Forget and Roger Goulet, met in Winnipeg on 5 April and very quickly determined that there was a problem with the terms of the Scrip Commission, which, they argued, could only lead to further Métis discontent and would present a stumbling block to the success of the commission. Street explained to the minister of the interior that, should a Métis head of family already be in possession of 160 acres, he would receive nothing more than if he were an ordinary settler (homesteader) and thus get nothing for his claim as a Métis. Inasmuch as the government was purporting to deal with the Métis as if they had some general rights beyond those of ordinary incoming settlers, great dissatisfaction and disappointment would be created. He suggested he be granted the power to enable the commission to allow the Métis to claim the land occupied by them under the homestead provisions and in addition to give him his scrip for the $160 or $240, as the case might be, for his Indian title.[10] D.L. MacPherson, the minister of the interior, immediately telegraphed back saying there was no objection to the suggestion of giving both scrip and allowing occupants to acquire title through possession.[11] The commission party left Winnipeg by train on 7 April and arrived at Qu'Appelle, where they set up their headquarters at the Indian Industrial School at Qu'Appelle Lake on 9 April. They immediately held a meeting with a delegation of the Métis leaders of that locality at which time a number of problems emerged. Street noted in a telegram that the Métis would refuse money scrip for their children ($240 scrip redeemable in land), demanding that they be issued scrip for 240 acres of land, more in keeping with the land grant Métis children had received in Manitoba. The Métis then tried to make the same argument relating to $160 scrip for Métis heads of family, but the commissioners pointed out that their offer was in accord with treatment received in Manitoba. They agreed and did not further press the point. To placate the Métis the government amended the policy to allow the issue of land scrip, and this change was incorporated in a new Order in Council dated 18 April 1885 (PC 821) amending the Order in Council of 30 March.

With these concerns dealt with, the way was open to begin taking applications. Street noted many years later that even then the Métis were extremely suspicious and were slow to believe that the commission had the power not only to take evidence but also to grant them scrip on the spot. It was not until the first scrip certificate for $160 was given and Charles Alloway, an agent for a banker in Winnipeg, stepped up and offered $80 for it, that this suspicion was removed. The recipient gladly accepted the offer, and the $80 was handed to her. The news quickly spread that the commission was actually offering something that could be turned into real cash and from that time on the commission was besieged with claims.[12] Interestingly, given the

Métis demand that their children be given land scrip, almost all Métis children elected to take the $240 money scrip.[13] This was no doubt related to the fact that land scrip was less attractive to speculators at this time and consequently they paid a lower price for this type of scrip. In 1885 land was still cheap and land scrip, being regarded as real estate as opposed to personal property, was more difficult and time consuming for speculators to acquire and locate, given the location requirements.[14] This situation would change after 1900, when land prices were much higher.

Having been given the authority to grant land scrip, the commissioners were immediately asked in what manner these land scrip certificates granted to children could be converted to Dominion land. As Street noted to the minister of the interior, many of the claimants were children in arms and, if they waited until they were of age, there would be no land left.[15] The department replied that only the legally constituted guardian of the child was entitled to locate land scrip for children, and it was further stipulated that certificates for land scrip (which recorded only the application and initial approval) would not be accepted at land offices to locate Dominion land, but that the recipient had to wait for the actual scrip note to be delivered.[16]

A more vexing problem for the commission and the Department of the Interior had to do with those "half-breeds" who wished to leave treaty to take scrip. Because this issue will be dealt with at some length in the next chapter, it is mentioned here only to indicate that a process whereby "half-breeds" in treaty could withdraw to take scrip was put in place by the time the Scrip Commission had left Calgary.

In their final report for 1885, the Scrip commissioners noted they had taken 1,694 applications encompassing 1,815 separate claims. Of these all but 232 were for money scrip. Money scrip certificates totalled $279,200.94, while land scrip certificates totalled 55,260 acres. Despite their best efforts, however, they noted that in every locality persons remained who were unable because of illness or absence, or other causes, to bring their claims forward. There were also many persons in treaty who expressed a desire to withdraw from treaty to take scrip, but who had been unable, at the time, to obtain their discharge. In addition to these claimants there remained a large settlement of Métis at Lac La Biche who had not been visited by the commission, owing to the disturbed state of that part of the country. The commission recommended that arrangements be made in the following spring to allow these Métis to make their claims.[17]

The 1886–1889 Scrip Commissions

On the recommendation of the final report of the 1885 Scrip Commission, Roger Goulet, one of the commissioners, was appointed on 1 March 1886 as the sole commissioner to investigate and settle the scrip claims of those Métis who were unable to appear before the North-West Half-breed Commission in the previous year.[18] His detailed instructions differed little from those issued to the previous commission but they incorporated the changes made in the field in 1885, which have been detailed above.[19] However, Goulet was told to be especially careful at Lac La Biche to obtain the most direct proof that the claimant was, on the 15th day of July 1870, actually a resident within the territory now ceded by the Indians under treaties. Lac La Biche was on the boundary between Treaty 6 territory and those unceded portions of the North-West Territories, and the department did not want to extend the scrip commissions into areas not yet ceded by treaty.[20]

The bulk of the claims that were received in 1886, and almost all the problems that were encountered, dealt with "half-breeds" leaving treaty to take scrip. As a result, the subsequent discussions over scrip policy involved not only the Department of the Interior but also the Department of Indian Affairs and more closely tied scrip policy to Indian policy – particularly in the areas of civilization and extinguishment of Indian title.

In Goulet's final report to the Scrip Commission of 1886, he noted that he had received and investigated 1,414 applications, of which 1,164 had been allowed. Of these, 602 were from "half-breeds" who had withdrawn from treaty; only 290 were from persons who had never participated in any grants to Indians, and 267 were made by the legal representatives of deceased Métis who had died at a date subsequent to the 15th day of July 1870 and who, had they been living, would have been eligible for scrip.[21] Dealing with "half-breeds in treaty," however, had so delayed the commission that it got no further than St Laurent on the South Saskatchewan River during the summer of 1886. Owing to these delays and the lateness of the season, Goulet was unable to visit Fort à la Corne, The Pas, Cumberland House, Grand Rapids, Norway House, Beren's River, Fort Alexander, Manitoba House, and Fairford. To complete the settlement of these claims he recommended that arrangements should be made early next spring to hold sittings in these locations.[22]

In 1887, Goulet was appointed as chairman of another scrip commission, and N.-O. Coté, secretary to the previous commission, was

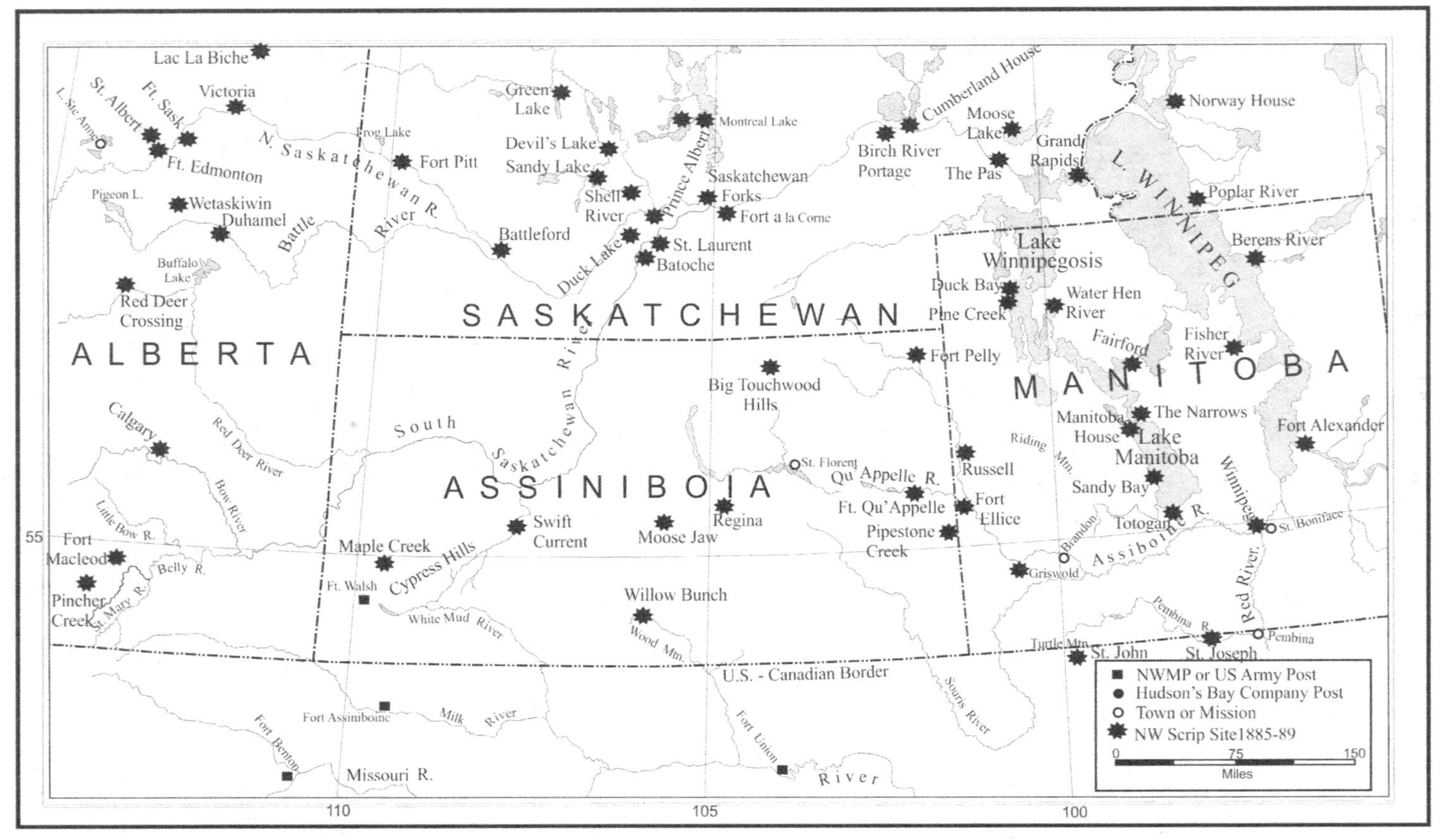

7.1 Locations of Métis Scrip Commission Hearings, 1885–89.

appointed as a member to investigate the remaining Métis claims in the North-West Territories.[23] The Department of the Interior, cognizant that most of the claims would be from "half-breeds" leaving treaty, took special steps to ensure that the Department of Indian Affairs continued the same practice as had been adopted in the previous summer with regard to the granting of discharges from treaty, making sure that an inspector from one of the various Indian agencies accompany Goulet and Coté to every commission hearing.[24] Reporting from Grand Rapids on 13 August 1887, Goulet noted: "all the claims which have so far been dealt with by us, with the exception of ten cases, have been preferred by persons who were previously members of Bands of Indians under Treaty."[25] On returning to Winnipeg, they made another trip to Green Lake and Fort Pelly. They dealt with 565 applications for scrip, of which 31 were disallowed and 321 were granted to persons who had obtained their discharge from treaty (see Table 7.1).

When in November 1888 arrangements were made to conduct negotiations with Green Lake Indians for an adhesion to Treaty 6 (signed 11 February 1889), it was also arranged that one of the two commissioners appointed to negotiate the adhesion be empowered to investigate claims to Métis scrip in the region just surrendered.[26] This scrip commission, though it handled relatively few claims, was significant from a policy perspective. The scrip process at Green Lake signified that Indians and Métis living in an area should be dealt with in one process, and that Indian claims were given a conceptual priority; that is, the

Table 7.1 Statement of claims dealt with by the North-West Half-Breed Commission, 1885–87

Year	Claims	Claims allowed	Money scrip issued	Land scrip issued
1885	1815	1678	$279,200.94	55,260 acres
1886	1414	1164	$261,689.14	2,640 acres
1887	565	405	$81,804.15	3,120 acres
Tot.	3794	3247	$622,694.00	61, 129 acres

Note: This tabulation did not include 256 claims made in January and February of 1887 at settlements on Lakes Manitoba and Winnipegosis, of which 188 were allowed and satisfied by an issue of scrip certificates amounting to $40,620.

Source: N.-O. Coté, "Grants to Half-Breeds in the Province of Manitoba and the North-West Territories, Comprising the Provinces of Saskatchewan and Alberta in Extinguishment of the Indian Title, 1870-1925, and Grant of Scrip to Original White Settlers, 1874–1894," (1929), Department of the Interior. RG 15, D-II-1, vol. 227, file 0, pt 4, pp. 4–7.

commissioners could deal with Métis scrip claims only after receiving the Indians into treaty.[27] Prior to 1889 there had been no direct connection between the extinguishment of Indian title and land grants to the Métis, even though the latter were rationalized in terms of the former.[28] In the numbered treaties of 1871–77 the commissioners were not authorized to deal specifically with Métis claims, though they did accept Métis into treaty. Similarly, the scrip commissions of 1885–87 had little to do with Indians other than grant scrip to those Métis who had withdrawn from treaty. By 1888, however, the Departments of the Interior and Indian Affairs were trying to rationalize the process and clearly connected the extinguishment of Indian title through treaty to the granting of scrip to the Métis. As A.M. Burgess, the deputy minister of the interior, informed the Indian Department in 1888, the Métis of the Athabasca district were not yet eligible for scrip, as the territory had not yet been ceded by treaty.[29]

However, the scrip settlement of 1889, in conjunction with the Green Lake Treaty 6 adhesion, left untouched the different chronological qualifications of the Indian and the Métis. All Indians entering treaty in 1889 were paid annuities, but only those Métis born before 15 July 1870 were eligible to receive scrip. The entry of Manitoba into Confederation in 1870 remained the cut-off date for scrip eligibility rather than the date of treaty signing. This condition would not be amended until 1899, with the negotiations leading to the signing of Treaty 8, and would create additional problems for past scrip commissions.

This would be the last "Half-Breed Scrip Commission" until the Treaty 8 Commission was established in 1899. All told, between 1885 and 1888, scrip had been issued to 854 heads of family, the representatives of 264 deceased heads of family, 1,862 children, and the representatives of 466 children born in the territories before 15 July 1870 but who had died since that date. Of these figures, 1,292 persons were formerly "treaty half-breeds" who had secured discharges.[30]

Trying to Close Off the Scrip Program, 1888–1894

The Department of the Interior was anxious to finally close the scrip process, but by 1888 the department was hearing of more agitation in the North-West Territories to expand the scrip offering. The Métis of Saskatchewan argued that those Métis born between 1870 and the granting of scrip in the North-West Territories in 1885 should also be eligible for scrip. This position was endorsed by the Legislative Council of the North-West Territories. The petition enumerating other demands of the Métis around Batoche noted, "This we will consider as an act of Justice due to our people and that all their rights may be recognized as in Manitoba and that the children born in the intervals of 1870 and 1888 may have right to 240 acres of land each as had been granted to those born before 1870."[31]

To investigate these concerns A.M. Burgess, the deputy minister of the interior, travelled to the various Métis communities in the North-west. He found that there was an almost unanimous opinion "that the Government should come to their relief by granting scrip, as recommended by the Legislative Council of the North-West Territories, to all the Half-breed children born in the country between 1870, the date of the transfer, and 1885, when the Government commenced to enquire into and deal with the claims of the Half-breeds as a special class in the community."[32] He noted, however, that with the exception of Father Fourmond, the Catholic missionary at St Laurent, all missionaries of the various Churches opposed this proposal. The Métis, they argued, had no adequate conception of the real value of money, and that any sum given them would be dissipated in a short time and would lead to increased discontent with their condition, and they would be more unwilling than ever to settle down to hard work. Burgess opined that Métis were indebted to white traders and that this might account for their supporting another scrip commission for those born between 1870 and 1885. Taking into account all these factors, he found it hard to understand how this proposal had obtained the support of the Legislative Council of the North-West Territories and recommended against any new scrip commission,[33] and indeed no scrip was granted to the Métis born between 1870 and 1885 until the exigencies of making Treaty 8 in 1899 forced the government to reverse its policy. Instead, the government tried to close down the scrip process by limiting the time within which applications would be received, and notice was given that application for scrip not filed by 1 May 1894, "shall cease and determine."[34] However, this attempt to close off the scrip process foundered on the Treaty 8 negotiations of 1899.

The Treaty 8 Scrip Commission and the Crystallization of Scrip Policy, 1899–1901

The establishment of the Treaty 8 Scrip Commission of 1899 marked the first time a major scrip commission operated in tandem with the negotiation of an Indian treaty.[35] One result of this joint undertaking was that Indian affairs and treaty concerns would play a larger role in the scrip process than had been the case before. This development in turn forced both the Department of Indian Affairs and the Department of the Interior to more clearly define the boundaries between treaty and scrip and between Indian and Métis. The exigencies of treaty making in 1899 also led the Department of the Interior to change its scrip regulations, which reopened the scrip process in those parts of the North-West Territories that had already been dealt with. These changes and dynamics are dealt with in some detail below because they set the stage for, and regulations of, all future scrip commissions.

In 1899, when it was finally decided to negotiate Treaty 8, the government had a clear set of objectives and a pattern for treaty making. They included the blanket extinguishment of Aboriginal title to secure the peaceful exploitation of resources by the incoming Euro-Canadian community, provision for the allotment of reserves, and the establishment of a relationship between the Indian peoples and the government to facilitate the civilization policy.[36]

The Department of Indian Affairs, by 1899, regarded the Métis as an important element of the treaty process. They were an integral component of the northern Native community, interlinked by marriage, family, and lifestyle. Given that the treaty was intended to extinguish Indian title and maintain peace, the department recognized that the Métis would have to be considered. A.E. Forget[37] clearly linked the extinguishment of Indian title with the extinguishment of Métis title, and he reported in April of 1898 that Bishop Grouard had told him that the government had to be prepared to deal simultaneously with the Métis and the Indians or the Métis might dissuade the Indians from signing.[38]

At first the government believed the best policy would be to encourage the Métis to enter treaty. A.E. Forget recommended that as many Métis as possible be taken into treaty rather than be given scrip.[39] As noted by the Order in Council of 27th June 1898 (P.C. 1703), which authorized the negotiation of Treaty 8, this strategy "would be more conducive to their own welfare, and more in the public interest ... than giving them scrip." Métis would be allowed into treaty if they so desired on the judgment of the commissioners, who would decide which Métis would be dealt with as Indians.[40] This approach was somewhat of a reversal of the past policy of both Indian Affairs and Interior, which had encouraged withdrawal from treaty to take scrip in the period 1885–88.

It was likely the result of the growing belief that scrip had provided no permanent benefit to the Métis, and that the Métis and Indians in the Treaty 8 area lived a similar lifestyle.

In order to convince the Métis to enter treaty it was decided that those Métis choosing not to enter would be dealt with according to the terms of earlier scrip commissions in Manitoba and the Northwest, which meant that the claims of those Métis born after 1870 would not be recognized unless they entered treaty. This early strategy nearly derailed the treaty process in 1899. The reports of the North-West Mounted Police (NWMP) made it clear that the Métis were discouraging other Natives from accepting treaty, would not enter treaty themselves en masse, and would not accept the terms of the scrip offer.[41] Writing to Clifford Sifton in April 1899, J.A.J. McKenna, one of the appointed treaty commissioners, noted that the commissioner charged with effecting a settlement with the Métis would find it very difficult to do so under the scope given him by the Dominion Lands Act, the only statutory provision on the books that dealt with Métis claims. This provision (subsection F of section 90) referred only to those Métis residing in the North-West Territories on 15 July 1870, and hence recognized the claims only of Métis who were twenty-nine years of age or older. The consequent dissatisfaction among the Métis, he wrote, could lead to their using their influence with the Indians in such a way as to make it difficult to negotiate a treaty at all.[42] The minister agreed with this assessment and noted that whatever rights the Métis had, they had "in virtue of their Indian blood." The first interference with these rights occurred when a surrender was made of the territorial rights of the Indians and, while differing in degree from Indian rights, Métis rights in unceded territory "must be co-existent, and should properly be extinguished at the same time."[43] The fears that the Métis themselves would not enter treaty and would disrupt the treaty process pushed the government to offer a new scrip settlement in May of 1899. In effect, they would offer scrip to all Métis living in the proposed treaty area who had not received a settlement elsewhere. The government also decided to create a separate "Half-breed Claims Commission" to accompany the treaty commission.

This was done by OIC of 6th May 1899, which stipulated that all Métis residing in the Treaty 8 district who had not previously received scrip must be eligible for scrip. As well, no distinction would be made between Métis children and Métis heads of family. In the past Métis children were eligible for scrip worth $240 or 240 acres, while Métis heads of family were eligible for scrip worth $160 or 160 acres. The OIC of 1899 stated, that every Métis occupier of land would be confirmed in possession to the extent of 160 acres, and that scrip, redeemable in land, would be granted to each Métis for either $240 or 240 acres. To be eligible he had to be "permanently residing in the said territory at the time of the Indian Treaty and not to have previously received scrip in extinguishment of his claim."[44] The same OIC also appointed James Walker and J.A. Coté to investigate these Métis claims.

These new regulations were also applied to those Métis born in the territories between 15 July 1870 and 1885, and accordingly the Dominion Lands Act was amended by Act 62–63 Victoria, chapter 16, cap. 4, assented to on 11 August 1899. By a further OIC of 2nd March 1900 (P.C. 438) four commissioners were appointed to investigate the claims of the Métis who were born between 15 July 1870 and 1885 in the organized Districts of Assiniboia, Alberta, and Saskatchewan, and that portion of Manitoba lying outside its original boundaries.

When the Treaty 8 Scrip Commission reached Lesser Slave Lake in June of 1899 and began deliberations with the Métis gathered there, they realized some further changes would have to be made to the scrip policy. Given the criticism the federal government had endured because of the rapid sale of children's money scrip to speculators in the Northwest, the government had changed the form of money scrip to require a legal assignment before its sale. On 22 June 1899 the Métis of Lesser Slave Lake held a meeting during which they decided that they were opposed to this type of scrip certificates (Form 'A'), which required an assignment of the certificate before issue of scrip to anyone but the person named on the certificate. This regulation would have made it more difficult to sell the scrip of their children. Father Lacombe, who attended the Métis meeting as an intermediary and adviser, wrote to the commissioners urging them to change the form of the scrip certificate. He noted that he had come to the conclusion that trouble would arise if parents were not able to make use of their children's scrip. He further noted that, while he had previously believed that it would be better to prevent the parents from using their children's scrip and freely disposing of their own, the conditions were now different. Making it harder to sell Métis scrip would only lower the price received for this scrip and the Métis were determined to sell it anyway. Very few would take land scrip, and the money received for selling their scrip would be used to buy cattle for the families. To persist with the current form would only cause more dissatisfaction and make it very difficult to extend the treaty.[45]

On the same day both the treaty commissioners and the Métis scrip commissioners held a meeting at Lesser Slave Lake to consider this question. They noted that, since the Métis were determined to take money scrip for themselves and their children with the object of selling it, the requirement of an assignment would have the effect only of lowering the price, and they decided to make the scrip certificates "payable to bearer." They reasoned that the requirement, which had been intended to benefit the Métis, would in this case be turned to their disadvantage, and that the dissatisfaction caused would impede the work of the treaty commission. The Métis, they concluded, had shown much intelligence and industry and were better able to look after their interests and those of their children than the Métis in the older parts of the Northwest.[46]

The treaty and scrip commissions that departed from Edmonton on 29 May 1899 were a large delegation, and the timing and location of the commission's visits were advertised ahead of time with notices sent out and posted in church halls, land offices, and trading posts. As well, clergy, traders, and government officials were expected to pass on this information to local Métis populations. In all localities visited by the scrip commission, applications were allowed only after Treaty 8 had been signed in that district. The reason for this delay was that the government hoped that many Métis would take treaty rather than scrip (see Table 7.2).[47]

Table 7.2 Declarations and scrip certificates issued in 1899

Place	Total declarations	Money cert.	Land cert.	Land declarations
Lesser Slave Lake	276	562	33	71
Peace River Crossing	62	110	8	26
Fort Dunvegan	22	53	–	9
Wolverine Point	16	35	–	4
Fort Vermillion	56	166	2	49
Fort Chipewyan	68	130	2	1
Smith's Landing	15	17	–	–
Fort McMurray	6	18	–	–
Lake Wabascaw	27	62	2	2
Pelican Portage	12	5	1	–
Grand Rapids	1	1	–	–
Calling River Portage	13	36	–	–
Athabasca Landing	28	–	–	–
TOTALS	602	1195	48	162

Source: "Report of the Half-breed Commissioners, September 30, 1899," LAC, RG 15 D-II-I, vol. 771, file 518158.

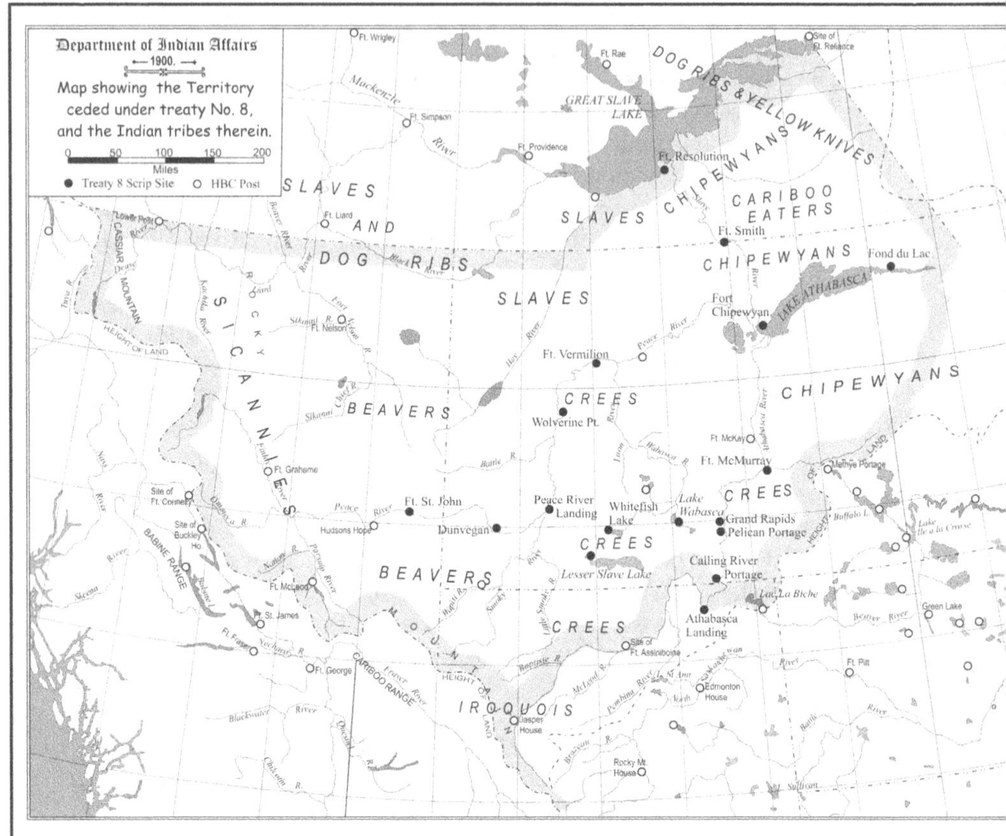

7.2 Locations of Treaty 8 Métis Scrip Commission Hearings, 1899–1901.

Not all Métis could be contacted during the summer of 1899 (the commission was in the field from 29 May until 23 September) and, as a result, subsequent commissions were appointed to contact the remaining Métis in the Treaty 8 area. In 1900 the minister of the interior and the superintendent of Indian affairs decided that adhesions should be taken during the 1900 annuity payments, and they appointed James A. Macrae as treaty commissioner. He was also given the authority of scrip commissioner to investigate any outstanding claims and report back to the minister.[48] Scrip certificates for those who were allowed them were then issued and distributed by Henry A. Conroy, the Indian inspector for the Treaty 8 district, who delivered them during the annual treaty payments of 1901; he would continue to take scrip applications during treaty payments until 1908.[49] In 1909 the Department of the Interior decided not to investigate any further claims to Métis scrip in any area covered by Treaty 8, as it was considered that the Métis of that territory had been given every opportunity and ample time to submit evidence in support of their claims.[50]

After 1899 the policies regarding whether a Métis individual would be allowed to take treaty or scrip began to change. The distinction between Métis scrip recipients and treaty Indians in the region covered by Treaty 8 was almost impossible to make on any genetic or genealogical basis. Persons from the same family were given the option of taking either treaty or scrip, and in some cases one sibling chose treaty while the other took scrip. As well, in some cases where siblings applied for scrip the Department of the Interior might allow one claim and insist that the other take treaty. The issue was further complicated in the sense that both Indian and Métis followed a similar way of life that involved hunting, trapping, freighting, and fishing.

Given this genealogical and occupational convergence, the main basis for differentiating between the two populations was self-ascription, and it was certainly clear to treaty commissioners in 1899 that there were self-identified "Métis" who refused to enter treaty. Thus, while there was an arbitrary element in deciding between treaty and scrip, the Métis knew who they were and, in most instances, the choice of scrip was a de facto declaration of Métis ethnicity.

This somewhat haphazard policy regarding the choice between treaty and scrip, and the ability to move back and forth between treaty and scrip, was tightened in the years after the 1899 Scrip Commission. In particular, it was decisions on the eligibility for scrip made by J.A.J McKenna in 1901 that brought about some changes to this policy. McKenna made these rulings in reviewing the applications taken by James A. Macrae in 1900. In his review of these 381 additional claims McKenna disallowed a large number and thereby set a new policy. He disallowed thirty-two claims on the basis that the claimants should be classed as Indians.[51] A portion of these claims came from the Whitefish Lake Band, whose members had not come in to take treaty in 1899. According to James Macrae, who took the applications, all the claimants were Indians who were disposed to take treaty but were prevented from doing so by the unwillingness of the band to give its adhesion to Treaty 8, and so they had done the next best thing and applied for scrip.

Macrae, although he took the applications, advised that the Whitefish Lake applicants be treated as Indians.[52] McKenna agreed and disallowed their claims, arguing that, no more formal adhesions were necessary. These Indians and any others who had not already been put in the treaty lists would be taken in the ordinary way and paid arrears. Mr Conroy was so instructed. The same rule would apply to all who had been refused scrip because they were regarded as Indian.[53] On this basis McKenna disallowed another thirty scrip claims.

By 1903, however, McKenna was having second thoughts about this policy, as many of the "half-breeds" from Whitefish Lake and God's Lake continued to insist on their right to take scrip. He noted that the government, "having entered so long ago upon the course of treating Halfbreeds as a distinct class with a claim to the soil, I cannot see how we could reverse the policy at this late date."[54]

Reflecting this change in thinking, the minister of the interior overturned an earlier disallowed scrip application. Elise Monitoose and her daughter Isabelle Newahso had initially applied for scrip in 1900 and had been denied on the basis that they should be classified as Indians. They had renewed their application in 1906 to H.A. Conroy, who reported at that time that the claimants were "half-breeds" and that their claims should be allowed. The minister recommended that, as the two claimants "declined to be enumerated as Indians, – that their claims be dealt with on the same basis as were the claims of the Halfbreeds who were residents in 1899 of the territory covered by the said Treaty No. 8; and that he [the Minister] be authorized to issue scrip."[55]

In addition to the disallowed claims mentioned above, McKenna disallowed another fifty-one claims that Macrae had allowed in 1900. Those refused were from claimants who had been discharged from treaty by Macrae and had been approved by the Indian commissioner. Macrae in each case had recommended the issue of scrip, but McKenna disallowed each one. By 1901 McKenna had come to the conclusion, with the assent of the Departments of Indian Affairs and Interior, that it was "not advisable to disturb the conditions existing in that country by discharging a group of persons from Treaty and giving them scrip." If mixed ancestry alone was grounds for giving a discharge from treaty and granting scrip, the issue of scrip would never be closed, as the vast majority of Natives in treaty had some "white blood." McKenna noted that at treaty time Aboriginals were given the choice of having their territorial rights extinguished by treaty (and a perpetual annuity) or taking scrip if "half-breeds." "After electing," he commented, "they should be bound by the election, and if anyone of them who elected to be an Indian should wish to leave treaty, and he be considered fit to leave treaty by the Indian Commissioner, it is only fair to regard his claim as having been extinguished, and if he loses, he loses as a result of his election ... When he is discharged from Treaty he becomes an ordinary citizen of the country having no claim as an aboriginee."[56] In a later report to the minister of the interior dated 31 May 1901 McKenna reiterated this point, which was approved by Order in Council of 6th June 1901.[57]

Thus, prior to 1900 it had been customary, if they were otherwise eligible, to grant scrip to Métis who had withdrawn from treaty. After 1901, however, a Métis who had once joined a band of Indians under treaty and subsequently was discharged from it was debarred from receiving scrip as a Métis, it being contended that all such claims had been extinguished by his accepting the benefits of an Indian treaty up to the date at which he voluntarily surrendered them. However, the Department of the Interior did make some exceptions after 1906. These were treated as special cases and each was dealt with by an Order in Council.

The Alberta/Assiniboia and Saskatchewan/Manitoba Scrip Commissions of 1900–1905

As has already been mentioned, following the work of the 1885–87 scrip commissions, representations had been repeatedly been made to the minister of the interior on behalf of Métis of the North-West Territories that their children, born between 1870 and 1885, should be entitled to the same treatment as those born prior to 15 July 1870. These claims were consistently rejected by the government using 15 July 1870 as the cut-off date, as the Dominion Lands Act then in force (the only statutory provision for dealing with Métis claims) referred only to those Métis residing in the North-West Territories on that date. When in 1899 this cut-off date threatened to derail Treaty 8 talks, it was decided to offer scrip to all Métis living in the proposed treaty area up to 1899. The Order in Council of 6 May 6th, 1899, which made this change in policy, also noted that the Legislative Council of the North-West Territories had passed a resolution in 1897 to the effect that in the opinion of the Assembly all "half-breeds" born before 1885, the date of the settlement of the "half-breed" claims in the territories, were entitled to scrip, and the government had given it due consideration. Having decided that Indian and Métis rights were coexistent and should properly be extinguished concurrently and given that Métis rights in the territories were not so extinguished, it was resolved that Métis rights were "held to exist after the extinguishment of Indian title and up to such time as action is duly taken for their extinguishment."[58] As such, the minister recommended that new scrip commissions be appointed with the power to investigate claims and grant scrip certificates to those Métis born between 15 July 1870 and the end of 1885 in those portions of the North-West Territories already ceded.[59] Like the Treaty 8 Scrip Commission, these new commissions made no distinction between Métis children and Métis heads of family, granting each either $240 in money scrip or 240 acres in land scrip.

The biggest issue that emerged from these scrip commissions, however, had not even been anticipated when they were set up. This concerned the eligibility of those Métis who had been born in the Canadian northwest between 1870 and 1885 and had subsequently moved to the United States. Lack of foresight, the inconsistent application of rules that were eventually established, and makeshift attempts to correct errors led to more than a decade of administrative tie-ups. This issue would also result in charges of fraud and the establishment of a judicial commission to investigate these charges.[60] Interestingly, it was speculators who acted as the greatest advocates for the expansion of Métis scrip rights and speculators who initiated the charges of fraud against other speculators.

The Order in Council of 2nd March 1900 appointed two separate commissions to deal with the new scrip issue: one for the Districts of Alberta and Assiniboia and one for the District of Saskatchewan and that portion of the territories included in the Province of Manitoba as constituted now, but not in 1870. J.A.J. McKenna of the Department of Indian Affairs and James Walker of Calgary were appointed commissioners for the Districts of Alberta and Assiniboia, and J.A. Coté of the Department of the Interior and Samuel McLeod of Prince Albert were appointed commissioners for the District of Saskatchewan and Manitoba.[61] J.A. Coté later fell ill and resigned and on 21 March was replaced by N.-O. Coté of the Department of the Interior.

In order to facilitate the work of the two commissions, further instructions were sent to J.A.J. McKenna ordering that all four commissioners were to meet in Regina on 12 May to discuss their work and come to an understanding as to the procedure to be followed, so that both commissions could proceed upon uniform lines. He was also instructed that, in those cases where the parents of Métis children had received scrip and afterwards were placed on lists as Indian treaty annuitants, their children – if they were born between 1870 and 1885, were not on Indian annuity lists, and were not living as Indians – were eligible for scrip. With regard to powers of attorney and assignments he was told to remember that the issue of scrip was designed to meet the claims of the Métis. It was in their interest that the acceptance of powers of attorney and assignments had been authorized and was not done to suit the convenience of speculators. Therefore, when there was doubt in any case as to whether the scrip certificate should be given to the Métis or to the person presenting a power of attorney or assignment, the Métis was to be given delivery.[62] Hearings commenced in mid-May, but on 5 June McKenna telegraphed from Qu'Appelle that there were three times the expected number of applications.[63]

As well, another more serious problem had arisen. In 1900, when the scrip commissions were established, it was not anticipated that scrip would be granted to the Métis residents of the United States, although they were not specifically barred by the Order in Council of 2nd March 1900 if they had been born in the North-West Territories between 1870 and 1885. The Saskatchewan Commission under N.O. Coté allowed these claims, but they encountered no more than a few dozen. The Assiniboia/Alberta Commission under McKenna, which held many more sittings close to the United States border, was deluged with the claims of American Métis who had crossed the border to apply. McKenna, unlike Coté, disallowed their claims.[64] When this discrepancy came to light, McKenna immediately telegraphed the minister of the interior, explaining that he had taken the position that only children of "Manitoba Half-breeds" who were born in the North-West Territories and who were now living therein had claims. In dealing with the Métis who came over from the United States, he took the position that those of them who had changed their residence previous to the settlement of 1885 were debarred from the benefits of the present settlement on the grounds that their removal to the United States was good evidence that they were not making any use of such territorial rights in the north-west as the Crown was called upon to extinguish. McKenna asked the department for a ruling on the matter, and on the residence question the department decided in favour of the Saskatchewan Commission in allowing the American claims.[65] This decision, however, does not seem to have changed McKenna's mind, as he reserved and disallowed large numbers of claims on account of American residence or because

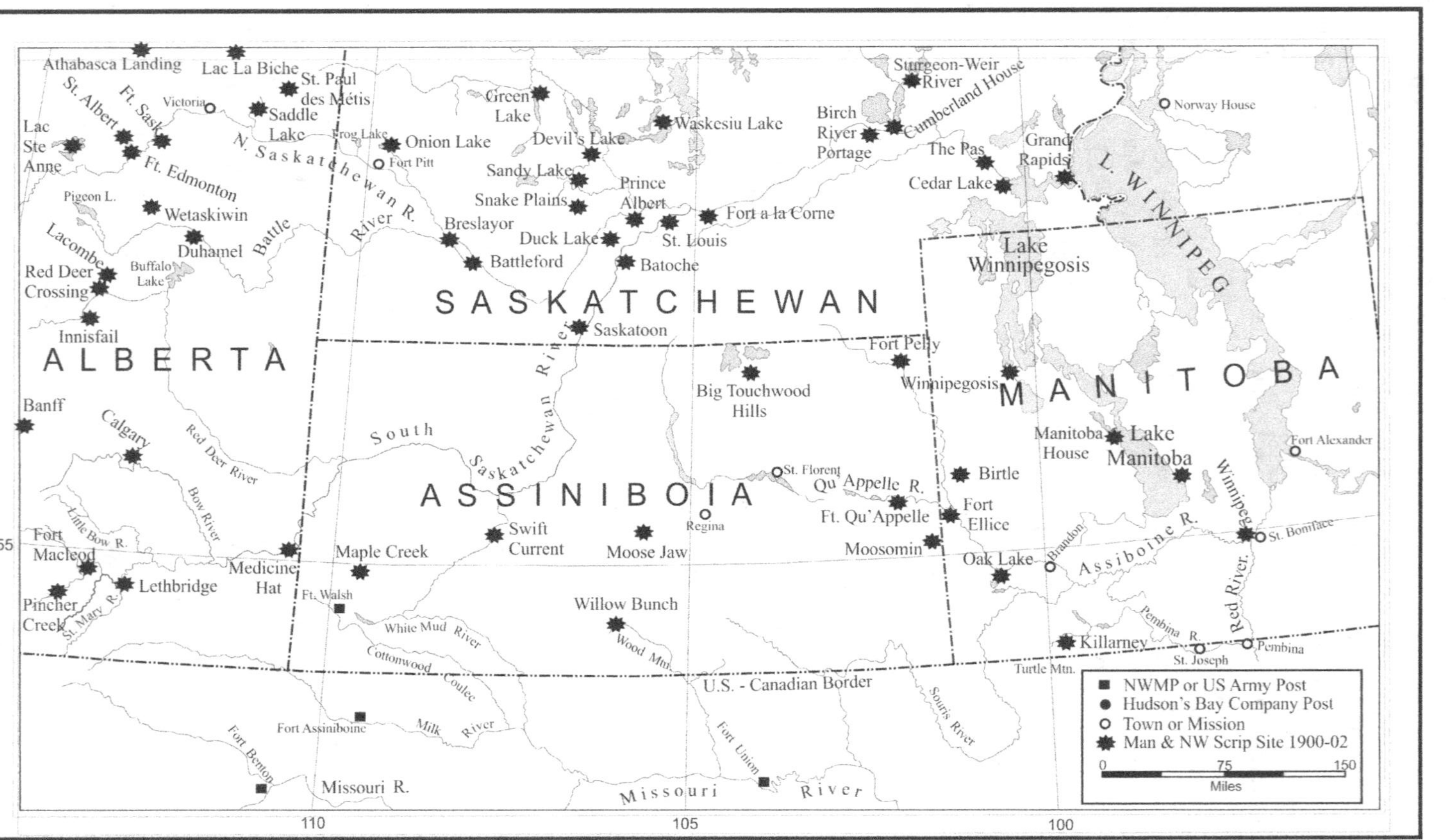

7.3 Locations of Manitoba and North-West Métis Scrip Commission Hearings, 1900–02.

of residence on an American Indian reservation.[66] McKenna's actions and report were approved by Order in Council of 6th June 1901, in effect reversing the decision taken in mid-season to allow the American claims.

In all, the Assiniboia / Alberta Commission dealt with 3,505 distinct written applications representing the claims of 4,397 Métis. Of the 3,306 claims accepted, 1,315 were for money scrip totalling $315,000 and 1,991 were for land scrip totalling 477,840 acres.[67] The Saskatchewan Commission investigated 2,111 claims, allowing 1,990. Of those allowed 1,336 were for money scrip amounting to $344,266.55, and 492 were for land scrip amounting to 117, 680 acres.[68]

As a number of claimants were unable to appear before the two commissions in the summer of 1900, the commissioners recommended special sittings at a few key points during the summer of 1901. By Order in Council of 16 March 1901 (PC 575) J.A.J. McKenna was appointed sole commissioner to deal with claims of those Métis of the territories and Manitoba who had been unable to apply the year before. This Order in Council also ordered all reserved claims be referred to McKenna to be dealt with on their merits. Given his views on American residence and the Privy Council's endorsement of these views a few months later,[69] a large number of the scrip claims of Métis resident in the United States were disallowed.

In all, 2,122 further claims were dealt with, of which 1,326 were allowed and 796 were disallowed.[70] This result might well have closed off the scrip process in the North-West Territories, as the Order in Council of 16 March 1901 (PC 575) had also recommended that public notice be given to the effect that "all claims to land and scrip on account of Aboriginal rights of Half-Breeds in the portion of Manitoba aforesaid and in the North-West Territories that are not presented to Commissioner McKenna with the necessary proof be barred." That this did not occur was due largely to the lobbying efforts of speculators who had invested large amounts of money in buying up the scrip claims of those American Métis that McKenna had disallowed. This campaign, focused on McKenna's alleged mishandling of these claims, would reopen the process in 1904 and would plague the Department of the Interior for another ten years.

Appeals in regard to McKenna's disallowance of Métis claims due to American residence began to come into the department almost as soon as the work of the 1900 season had been completed. The banking firm of Alloway and Champion, who had an interest in almost 200 such claims, submitted a request for a review of some of them, and the cases were sent to Roger Goulet with the instruction to take such evidence as Alloway and Champion could offer in support of these claims. Goulet reported favourably in respect to some but rejected others. When the issue was referred to the department's law office, the chief clerk, T.G. Rothwell, rejected Goulet's recommendation on the accepted claims for scrip.[71] As already noted, this course of action was implemented when the OIC of 6th June 1901 endorsed McKenna's actions and his interpretation of eligibility of Métis residing in the United States.[72]

Pressure to revisit these claims continued from the legal representatives of scrip buyers and by 1903 there appeared some cracks in the department's position. James Smart, the deputy minister of the interior, was in agreement that the claims rejected by McKenna should not be reopened, but he did admit that there was some merit in the case of Canadian Métis who had applied for treaty rights in the United States (Turtle Mountain) and had been rejected as being Canadian and were now rejected for scrip as being American.[73] N.-O. Coté, in his reply to Smart, noted he could offer no more information regarding these cases because there was no written evidence taken by McKenna, as the claims had been rejected with a great many others upon preliminary examination.[74] According to the mode these claims were dealt with by McKenna, unless the claimant was born after 15 July 1870 and was a resident of the North-West Territories in 1885, his claim was not entertained. Coté did note, however, that departmental policy until 6 June 1901 (the date that McKenna's views were endorsed by OIC) had been that once residence was established to have been the Canadian North-West Territories on 15 July 1870, American residence or the fact that the claimant may have been classified, at the time the application for scrip was made, by the United States authorities as a person of "mixed blood" living upon reservations set apart for such persons, did not prejudice in any way their right to receive scrip from this department. Coté wrote that the claims of the Métis were dealt with on this basis by the Saskatchewan Commission.[75]

The decision of the Department of the Interior to review McKenna's disallowance of claims based on American residence occurred in 1904 after it had received a legal opinion from J.S. Ewart.[76] Ewart, writing on behalf of scrip buyers, noted that Métis born between 1870 and 1885 and who resided in the territories until 1885 should have been entitled to scrip and that their removal afterwards to the United States or any other place or their participation in the benefits of any funds or benefits of any sort could not in any way derogate from the validity of their the claims, which had been established by their birth and residence as aforesaid. In his opinion McKenna had acted erroneously in excluding from scrip any person merely because he had taken up his residence on Indian reservations in the United States and participated in the benefits of Indian life thereon. McKenna, he noted, was charged with the duty of reporting for scrip those persons who, according to the terms of the Order in Council then in force were entitled to them, and that it was beyond his power to exclude them for the reason given them. McKenna had "no more right to exclude any one for that reason than because after 1885 he had the misfortune to lose a leg."[77]

This legal opinion was forwarded to the deputy minister of the interior on 11 July 1904 and N.-O. Coté noted that, in reviewing McKenna's actions, he found there were 214 persons whose claims were disallowed after the usual evidence on the basis of residence in the United States, and that a further 156 claims of the same class had been rejected on preliminary examination with no written evidence taken.[78] Shortly thereafter, on 12 August 1904, an Order in Council was passed to re-examine these claims. It stated that McKenna's actions and the OIC that had endorsed them had withheld scrip from persons whose claims had fully matured in the year 1885 and were therefore in the nature of a vested right, given that these claimants had moved out of Canada. For this reason, removal from Canada did not constitute any valid reason for a refusal to recognize property rights fully matured before such removal took place.[79]

This OIC, although it called for the reconsideration of those Métis claims rejected because the applicant who had left Canada to take up residence on Indian reservations in the United States and participated in the benefits of Indian life thereon – did not speak to the claims of those Métis who had taken up residence in other parts of the country or the United States prior to 1885. However, N.-O. Coté, who was appointed to review these disallowed claims, took a much broader view of the question and by October 1904 had begun to review all claims McKenna had disallowed on the basis of removal from the North-West Territories. As he explained to the minister, he understood that the OIC of 13th August 1904 included a review of McKenna's disallowances irrespective of the removal of the claimants to the United States prior to 1885, provided such claimants had been born in the North-West Territories between 1870 and 1885, and that, at the time of their birth, their parents had their permanent residence in the North-West Territories, which had been the practice in the past and was the manner in which he and Macleod, as joint commissioners, had dealt with similar claims in the Saskatchewan District in 1900. Clifford Sifton informed him that the intention of the OIC had been to confine the claims to be reconsidered to those that had been disallowed on the grounds of applicants having taken up their residence on Indian reservations in the United States, or on account of their admission to the United States Indian schools. Under the circumstances, however, Sifton confirmed Coté's action and authorized him to deal likewise with the rest of the claims disallowed by McKenna.[80] The real problem, as Coté saw it, was that as soon as the Order in Council of 13 August 1904 was passed, scrip speculators began to send in new claims of those American Métis claimants who had never appeared before any scrip commissioner. There were 500 new orders for delivery of scrip and more were arriving daily based on evidence collected by the scrip buyers themselves. One example of this type of claim were the claims of brothers and sisters of persons who had appeared before McKenna, but who themselves had not appeared because of McKenna's adverse decisions. Coté noted that, while this contention might be reasonable at first glance, the number of orders that had already reached the department was out of all proportion to the number of claims rejected by McKenna, and that it would be very difficult to deal properly with all of these claims upon documentary evidence. This situation was brought to Sifton's attention, so that the minister could decide whether to confine the investigation of claims only to those on McKenna's list. Sifton's decision, in handwriting across the top of Coté's memorandum, stated, "There is no justification for going outside of the list of persons who filed their claims before Mr McKenna. The attempt being made to bring in other claims should be summarily shut off."[81] By the summer of 1905 Coté had finished his review of the claims rejected by McKenna, of which he allowed 136, disallowed 170, and reserved 69 (see Table 7.3).[82]

Table 7.3 Review of McKenna's disallowed claims on the basis of OIC of 13 August 1904

Disallowed claims on evidence			Disallowed claims on preliminary investigation		
Allowed	Disallowed	Reserved	Allowed	Disallowed	Reserved
122	108	26	14	62	43

Treaty 9 and the Geographic Limits of Métis Scrip

In the nineteenth century the federal government never recognized Métis land rights outside the three prairie provinces and the North-West Territories, but there is little documentation that provides a clear rationale for this decision. Thomas Flanagan has suggested that the explanation probably lies in pragmatism. That is, outside the prairie provinces and the North-West Territories the federal government did not control public lands and therefore could not compensate the Métis with scrip redeemable in Dominion lands. The other factor he cites is that only on the prairies did the Métis constitute a large and cohesive political force that could pressure the government.[83] The records of the scrip commissions and the records related to the negotiation and signing of Treaty 9 in northern Ontario between 1901 and 1906 support this suggestion and make it clear that the government had no intention of extending the Métis scrip program into Ontario.

When in 1901 the federal government began considering treating with the Indians north of the Robinson-Huron Treaties in northern Ontario, the Department of Indian Affairs requested advice from J.A.J. McKenna, then working as a scrip commissioner in the North-West Territories. McKenna, in his letter to Clifford Sifton, noted that in the petitions received from the Indians of the territory they represented themselves as residing in Ontario and Keewatin, while the map he had received showed the territory as located in Ontario and Quebec. McKenna suggested that any treaty that was made should exclude the Keewatin Territory, and the treaty-making should be delayed until the North-West Scrip Commissions were finished their work. His reasons for these suggestions had to do limiting Métis land rights and scrip to the northwest.[84] Sifton approved of these suggestions and wrote in the margins of the letter "I doubt if we can do anything for Halfbreeds in Ontario & Quebec."[85] In McKenna's final report as scrip commissioner for Manitoba and the northwest, he noted that a number of claimants had come before him from Rat Portage and vicinity and had been summarily rejected. As Métis rights in the province of Ontario had never been recognized, he said, great care had been taken to avoid the creation of a precedent that might be used as the basis of a demand for recognition of such rights.[86]

As the planning for what would become Treaty 9 proceeded, the only other mention of Métis rights in the area appeared in a report from the deputy minister of Indian affairs to Clifford Sifton in 1903. He noted that if any claims were made by Métis, as distinguished from Indians, the province of Ontario should grant such claimants "160 acres in fee simple under conditions that will admit of land being located in advance of survey."[87] The federal government, however, had to obtain Ontario concurrence in any treaty-making in that province, and in the Ottawa/Ontario negotiations of the next two years all mention of Métis rights faded from view. In the agreement formulated between the two in 1905 there is no mention of Métis rights or scrip, nor did treaty negotiators receive any instructions related to this issue.[88]

When the commissioners[89] travelled to northern Ontario to negotiate the treaty in the fall of 1905 most of the "half-breeds" that appeared before them were allowed into treaty. At Moose Factory, however, a number of "half-breeds" working for the Hudson's Bay Company were not allowed in treaty on the grounds that they were not living the "Indian mode of life."[90] These Moose Factory "half-breeds" then petitioned the Government of Ontario for help, specifically mentioning Métis scrip:

> We the undersigned, halfbreeds of Moose Factory, beg to petition the Government of Ontario for some consideration as we were told by His Majesty's Treaty Commissioners that no provision is at present made for us. We understand that script [*sic*] has been granted to the half breeds of the North West Territory
>
> We have been born & brought up in the country, and are thus by our birth and training unfit to obtain a livelihood in the civilized world. Should the fur traders at any time not require our services we should be obliged to support ourselves by hunting.
>
> We therefore humbly pray that you will reconsider your present arrangements and afford us some help.
>
> Andrew Morrison
> George McLeod
> William McLeod
> William Moore
> William Archibald[91]

The Government of Ontario sent the petition to Ottawa, which in turn returned it to Ontario with the explanation that "half-breed title" was of the same nature as Indian title, and that these individuals had been refused treaty because they were not living as Indians. The only thing that might be done, they suggested to Ontario, was to admit them into the Indian treaty if they thought it advisable. Ottawa also noted, "but as they are residents of the Province and would come under the same category as the rest of your Indian adherents of Treaty No. 9 and would be paid by your Government, it is a matter which you will have to decide."[92]

In April of 1906, the province of Ontario decided to allow the "non-treaty half-breeds" of Moose Factory 160 acres of land with the stipulation that this land had to be selected in the district where they resided, and the plot could not interfere with Hudson's Bay Company posts or Indian reserves, nor could it be selected from lands required for railways or townsites.[93] No records have been found as to whether this land was ever granted, but it is clear that the federal government had no intention of expanding the Métis scrip program into Ontario. This rejection and the inability of Métis there to self-ascribe to Métis status are certainly two of the reasons why Métis identity in Ontario until the 1960s was much more ambiguous than in the west.

Treaty 10, Treaty 5 Adhesion, and Treaty 11 Scrip Commissions

The scrip commissions connected to Treaty 10, Treaty 5 adhesion, and Treaty 11 did not deviate much from the scrip policies that had been put in place by 1901. Regulations were in some cases spelled out in more detail, but in the main they followed the policies and procedures set out in the Treaty 8 Scrip Commission. The primary innovation that was made was the cessation, after 1906, of allowing the scrip commissioner to make decisions regarding the granting of scrip at the time of application. From 1907 on, scrip commissioners only took applications and collected evidence, leaving to ministerial discretion which claims were accepted. Scrip was then delivered in the following year or years. The other main innovation occurred with regard to Métis compensation in Treaty 11, where, in lieu of scrip, the Métis were granted $240 outright.

As early as 1902 both the Department of the Interior and the Department of Indian Affairs began to receive requests from missionaries, Indian agents, and Métis for a new treaty and scrip offering to be made to extinguish Indian title in those unceded areas east of Treaty 8 and north of Treaties 5 and 6.[94] In 1902, J.A.J. McKenna noted that there had been great distress in the country during the year before, owing to floods, and that relief had been granted through the Hudson's Bay Company. He was of the opinion that in the event of another bad season there would be another demand for help, and that it would be better to bring the Indians of the area into treaty (as would eventually be done) than make a further charitable grant.[95] There were, all told, some 2,000 Indians and 235 Métis in the area under consideration, though McKenna noted that many of those enumerated as Indian would in all probability decide to take scrip.[96] David Laird, the Indian commissioner for the North-West

Territories, was of the opinion that any new treaty or scrip offer should await the resolution of the autonomy question and the formation of the new provinces of Saskatchewan and Alberta so as to better define those territories that needed to be ceded.[97] The question that was not resolved until 1906 was whether to let the Indians of the area take an adhesion to Treaty 8 or negotiate a new treaty. The Department of Indian Affairs eventually opted to make a new treaty with the Indians of northern Saskatchewan to which the Indians of Northern Manitoba could at a later date take adhesion.[98]

By the Order in Council of 20th July 1906 J.A.J. McKenna was appointed commissioner to negotiate a new treaty (Treaty 10) with the Indians of northern Saskatchewan and Alberta, and also to act as commissioner to deal with the Métis claims of the ceded region. The terms of this scrip offer were almost identical to those of the Treaty 8 Scrip Commission,[99] and the commissioners were given the power to take evidence under oath, summon people by subpoena, and compel production of papers to determine the claims of the Métis in the region ceded and to issue scrip to those eligible. In all, McKenna took 541 applications for scrip, of which 498 were allowed, and scrip certificates for these claims were issued on the spot.[100] In his final report, however, McKenna noted that not all Métis had been able to make claims and that provision should be made to give them an opportunity to apply.[101]

With a view to carrying out this recommendation Thomas Alexander Borthwick, who was appointed to take adhesions to Treaty 10 in 1907, was also appointed to investigate additional claims for scrip. He was authorized "to investigate, in accordance with instructions to be given him, such claims for halfbreed scrip as may be preferred before him, and report upon such claims to the minister of the interior and superintendent general of Indian affairs, and, to that end, be authorized to take evidence under oath, to summon persons before him by subpoena and compel the production of papers and writing."[102] Unlike McKenna, however, he was not empowered to issue scrip certificates on the spot. Rather, it was the minister of the interior who was given the authority to decide finally on evidence submitted by Borthwick and to issue scrip that would be delivered at a later date.[103] Borthwick was also instructed that he was not to allow any Indians who had entered treaty in the previous year to leave treaty and take scrip, and he was to inform all who might have a claim to scrip but who elected to be paid as Indians to understand that they had made the choice once and for all, and that in future the department would not be inclined to reconsider their cases.[104]

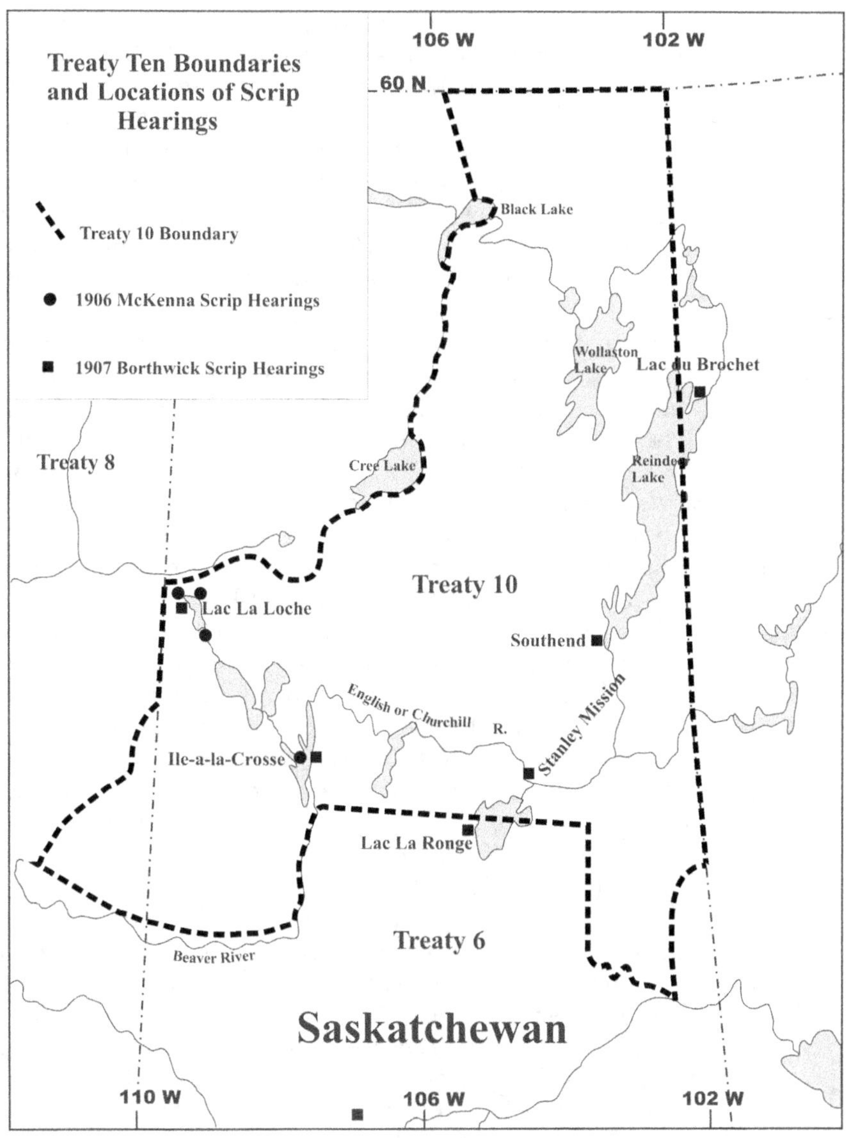

7.4 Locations of Treaty 10 Métis Scrip Commission Hearings.

When it was decided in 1908 to deal with Aboriginal title in northern Saskatchewan and Manitoba, the Department of Indian Affairs informed the Department of the Interior that it intended to take adhesions to Treaty 5 in the coming season and that they might wish to deal with the scrip claims of the Métis of the territory at the same time.[105] As it had been the practice of the Department of the Interior since 1889 to deal with scrip claims at the same time as treaties were negotiated, it was decided to appoint Reverend John Semmens, the treaty commissioner for the Treaty 5 Adhesion Commission, to take applications for scrip.[106]

The specific instructions sent to Semmens did not deviate very much from those of previous scrip commissions, but given that there had been numerous previous treaty and scrip commissions in the region, Semmens was advised that particular care be taken to ensure that the claimant was a Métis, not a member of any band of Indians under treaty. Semmens was also instructed to inform the Métis claimants that the evidence taken would be dealt with later by the Department of the Interior, and that no assurance could be given by him that their claims would be allowed. As well, the Métis were to be informed that land scrip was not transferable and had to be located in person by the grantee thereof at the office of the agent of Dominion lands in whose district the land that might be selected was situated. It was only after the location of the scrip had been made that the locator, provided he was of the full age of twenty-one years, could assign his land. Powers of attorney, agreements of sale, or assignments affecting Métis scrip in any manner, or any claims thereto, were not under any circumstances recognized by the department. As regards the delivery of scrip, he was to advise the Métis claimants that, should their claims be recognized, orders for the delivery of their scrip would not be considered by the department, as it was proposed to have the scrip delivered to them personally by Semmens when he visited the region the next year. However, when applying, the Métis could authorize Semmens to deliver their scrip to them the next year at a fixed place.[107] These extra measures (among others) regarding powers of attorney, the delivery of scrip, and the location of land scrip had been put in place to eliminate any appearance of favouring scrip buyers and to counter the charges that scrip buyers were using both powers of attorney and "impersonation" to get around the requirement that Métis recipients of scrip had to locate land scrip.[108]

In all, Semmens took approximately 200 applications[109] for scrip in the summer of 1908, which were forwarded to the Department of the

Interior for consideration and decision. The department decided that the majority of these claims were applications from "Manitoba Half-breeds," who had no claim because they had received their land rights in Manitoba;[110] consequently, it disallowed most of them: 123 claims were disallowed, 21 claims were reserved for further evidence, and 31 claims were approved. In the event of new applications being made for scrip, Semmens was instructed to obtain all necessary evidence in support of these claims, and he was mildly rebuked for not having provided sufficient information the previous year. Semmens was also informed that the applications he would take in 1909 would not be finally disposed of until the adhesion to Treaty 5 had been completed at Fort Churchill and York Factory, and scrip would be issued the following year to the claimants personally by an officer of the government.[111]

In 1910 and 1911 Semmens took an additional 65 applications for scrip amounting to 111 separate claims.[112] These were adjudicated under the authority of the Order in Council of 24 May 1911,[113] by which 86 claims were allowed.[114] This scrip was to be delivered personally to grantees by C.C. Calvery, Indian agent at Norway House, and by Inspector Starnes of the North-West Mounted Police (NWMP) to grantees at Fort Churchill and York Factory.[115]

When the decision was made to begin treaty negotiations with the Indians of the Mackenzie River District in 1921, it was again decided to extinguish Métis claims at the same time. The Order in Council of 12 April 1921 authorized the Treaty 11 commissioner to also deal with claims arising out of the extinguishment of the Indian title of the "Half-breeds" resident within the territory covered by the proposed treaty. Unlike the mandate of every previous scrip commission, however, all eligible claimants were to receive a one-time cash grant of $240 in lieu of the usual money or land scrip. The OIC stated that the rights of "half-breeds' in the territory to share in this grant were considered to have been extinguished if they had previously entered treaty or been granted scrip. If both their parents had previously been granted scrip, they were also ineligible if they had been born after their parents had become eligible for scrip. If only one of their parents had taken scrip, however, they were still eligible for the $240 grant.[116] In all, there were 172 claims allowed in the Mackenzie River District, totalling $41,280. The compensation in these cases was paid to the claimants by officers of the Department of the Interior on their annual visits to that territory.[117]

Conclusion

With the settlement of these claims in the 1920s, the Department of the Interior believed that the claims of the Métis, arising out of the extinguishment of the Indian title, were drawing to a close. In an effort to shut down the process, legislation was passed in 1921 stating that no prosecution could be taken after three years from the time of the commission of any offence relating to or arising out of the location of land that was paid for in whole or in part by scrip or was granted upon certificates issued to "Half-breeds" in connection with the extinguishment of Indian title.[118]

Between 1925 and 1929, N.O Coté, involved for more than forty years in the Department of the Interior's dealings with Métis scrip, would write a number of long memoranda detailing the departmental memory of the scrip program. According to Coté, 1921 marked the "closing of half-breed claims." By his tabulation 2,609,772 acres of land or land scrip had been granted, as well as $2,885,157.00 in cash or money scrip.[119] From his perspective the rights and claims of the Métis arising out of the extinguishment of the Indian title had been most liberally treated by royal commissions and the department.[120] From a departmental policy perspective there is little to disagree with in this evaluation. Outside of the delay in instituting a scrip program for the North-West Territories between 1874 and 1885, the department was responsive to the Métis demands, changing their scrip policy to meet their demands. As well, the government took purposeful steps to protect Métis land rights acquired through scrip. While it may be argued that scrip was an inappropriate method to extinguish the Métis claims to Indian title, it was the mechanism that the Métis desired. From 1878 to 1906 the Métis consistently requested that they be granted scrip in extinguishment of their rights. Those Métis who wished to enter treaty were generally allowed to do so and until 1900 were also allowed to leave treaty to take scrip. In 1901, however, the Department of the Interior realized that to allow "Treaty Half-breeds" to leave treaty to take scrip would be to make the scrip program a permanent one. To avoid doing so, the government passed an OIC prohibiting those Métis who left treaty to subsequently receive scrip. The Department of the Interior never intended Métis scrip to be an ongoing process, but wanted it to be a "once and for all" extinguishment. As such, Métis scrip, like the treaty process, must be seen within the context of the overall policy of the Canadian government to "civilize" and incorporate Native peoples into Canadian society and extinguish Aboriginal title. Just as important, the scrip program also became an aspect of Métis self-identification. In the period from 1885 to 1920 government treaty and scrip commissions had offered the "mixed-bloods" of the northwest the choice of extinguishment of their Aboriginal title either by entering treaty or taking scrip. In a sense, a type of person came into being at the same time as the "Métis scrip" category was being invented. Scrip and treaty administrative practices that defined and counted collective identities in an all-or-nothing manner enabled/forced people to see or organize themselves in light of these categories. Once defined and labelled "Métis" or "Indian" for the purposes of extinguishment, administrative action, and benefits, these categories took on a life of their own. They both closed and opened the possibilities for future action. As such, the process of scrip taking represented not only a recognition of a Métis identity, but in many cases was a part of Métis identity formation.

8 Indian Treaty versus Métis Scrip: The Permeability of Status Categories and Ethnicities

In the conceptual world of both American and British North American Indian policy persons of mixed European-Native ancestry could be recognized under certain circumstances as Indian or non-Indian, depending on their lifestyle and membership in a particular community. In the process of "civilizing" and "incorporating" Indians there was no room for a separate Métis legal status, though it was hoped that "mixed-bloods" would play an intermediary role in this transition.[1] Colonial governments admitted persons of mixed ancestry into treaties and defined them as "Indian," but they did so only when these "half-breeds" lived with Indians and were considered members of a band. Those Métis that assumed an identity separate from Indian or European and who lived away from an Indian band were not considered Indians. By law, they were ordinary citizens with no special privileges. The difference between the United States and British North America was that, in the latter, hybridity and métissage were viewed in a more positive light as a transitional stage that would further the goals of incorporating Native peoples into the general population. This positive view of métissage, at least before 1885, would play an important role in the political events related to the transfer of Rupert's Land from Great Britain to Canada in 1869–70 when the Métis were able to win some claims to Aboriginal status separate from Indian status.

The story of the invention of Métis Aboriginal status has already been told (see chapter 6) and the focus here is how the alternatives of Indian treaty status or Métis scrip both bedevilled Canadian policy makers until the twentieth century and made Métis identity a much more contingent entity. After 1870 not only did the Canadian government have no clear policy regarding whether people of mixed Indian and European ancestry should be classed as Indian or Métis, but it allowed individuals to change their status after choosing one or the other. Consequently, persons of mixed ancestry could choose either Indian treaty or Métis scrip and, in many cases, they took both. This haphazard policy regarding the choice between treaty and scrip and the ability to move back and forth between the two statuses not only made the policies of extinguishment of Métis claims and the civilization and enfranchisement of Indians problematic, but ushered in a new era of instrumental ethnicity where government policy increasingly shaped how individual Métis identified themselves. These individual choices would in turn affect the identity of future generations of Métis.

The issue of Métis entering treaty in Canada[2] arose overtly in 1850 when William Benjamin Robinson was commissioned to negotiate a treaty with the Ojibwa on the eastern and northern shores of Lakes Huron and Superior. These treaties were seen as expedient in consequence of the discovery of valuable minerals in the region and the desirability of extinguishing Indian title to facilitate mining operations. This became more urgent in late 1849, when a band of Indians and Métis attacked the mining installation of the Quebec Mining Company on the eastern shore of Lake Superior at Mica Bay (see figure 8.1).[3]

Though the agreement on terms did not come easily, the two treaties were signed in September of 1850 and included a gratuity, perpetual annuities, hunting and fishing rights over the ceded territory, and reserves for the various bands.[4] The rights of the Métis of the region were also discussed and Chief Shinguacouse attempted to secure reserve land for "half-breeds" at 100 acres per head. Robinson refused to consider this option, however, as his instructions were to treat with Indians. He did suggest that, while the total amount of reserve acres would be calculated by the number of Indians in a band, if the band so wished, they could give the Métis land in the reserves. He also noted that money would be paid to the chiefs and that once it was in their possession they might give as much or as little to the Métis as they pleased.[5] Asked if they could permit persons of mixed ancestry to join the band and share in annuity money, Robinson suggested that this could be done and the matter was resolved by requiring the Métis to declare themselves as either Indian or non-Indian.[6] This position was in line with what government practice had been since the 1830s. Those persons of mixed ancestry who lived a "tribal life" and were accepted as members of the band with whom they lived, were considered Indian.[7] While this practice would become more contentious after the 1850s, it does not

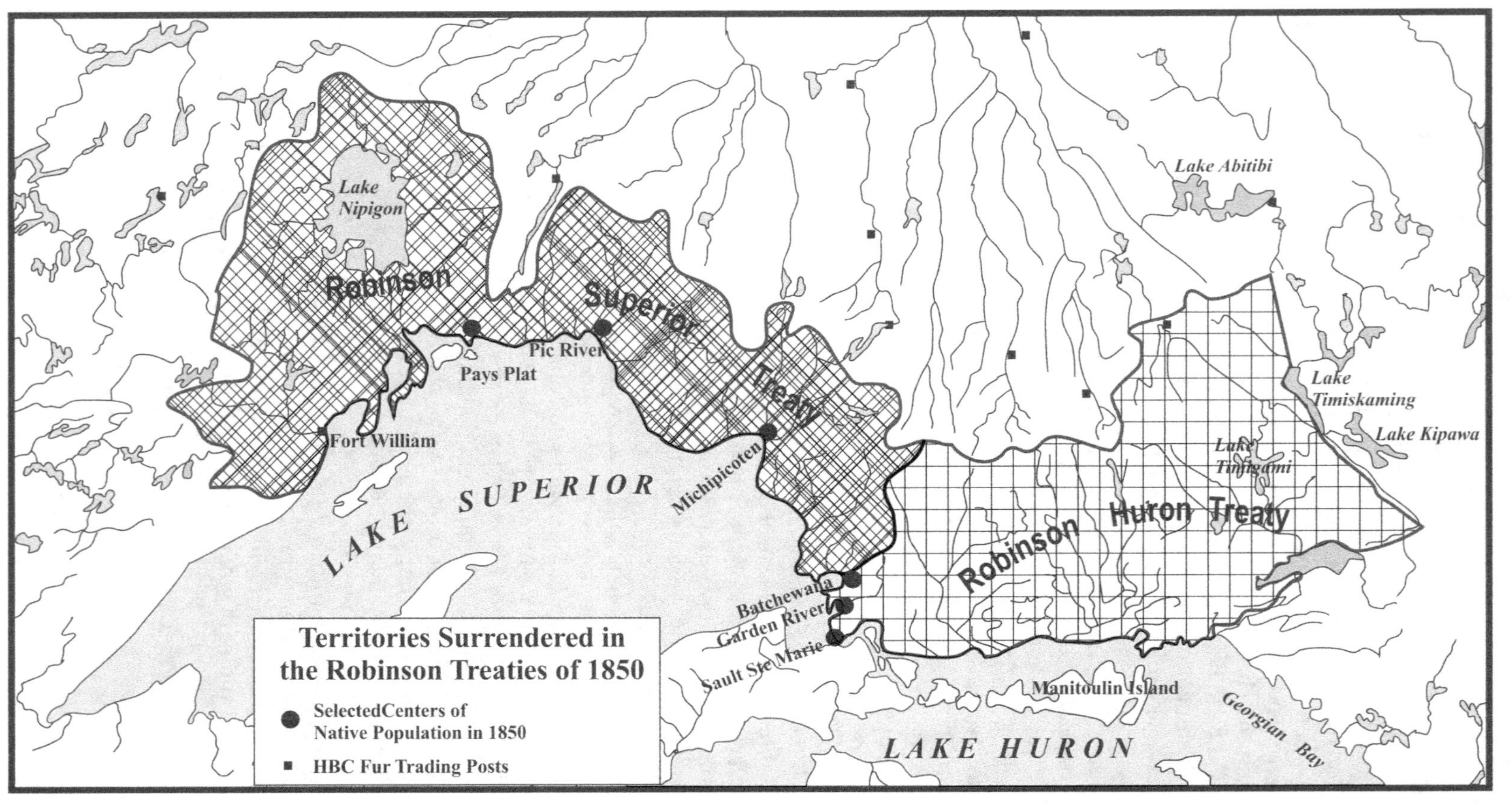

8.1 Territories surrendered in the Robinson Treaties of 1850.

seem to have changed either in the Robinson Treaties or in the numbered treaties in the west.

At the time of the signing of the 1850 Robinson Treaties the number of Métis living with Indian bands was not large. In his report on the Indian population of the region Robinson noted there were 1,240 Indians, including 84 Métis, on Lake Superior, and 1,422 Indians, including 200 Métis, on Lake Huron.[8] Several years prior to the signing of the Robinson Treaties Chief Shinguacouse of the Garden River Band invited the Métis of Sault Ste Marie to join his band and promised that, if they did, he would work for them to get presents and share in their claim. At that time almost all the Métis declined the offer, as the Métis community had its own economy and identity and felt no need to adopt an "Indian" status.[9] In the 1840s most of the Métis along the St Mary's River were old Hudson's Bay Company employees who had settled with their Native families on narrow strips of land on the river where they built small cedar cabins at a location that would become the town of Sault Ste Marie. Here they followed a way of life that relied on hunting, fishing, and voyaging and included small-scale horticulture with some cattle and horses. Over the next few decades, however, as more Euro-Canadian and American settlers moved into the region and as their hunting and fishing economy declined, many of these Métis families began to move to the Garden River Indian Reserve and other reserves along the North Shore of Lakes Huron and Superior. Based on their kinship ties, they were accepted into these bands and began to collect annuities as Indians.[10]

By the 1870s these dynamics had increased the annuitants of numerous bands in the Robinson Treaties, so the value of annuities per member declined (the total amount of money set aside for yearly annuities had been set at a fixed amount in 1850). The Robinson Treaties, however, contained augmentation clauses that provided for both a decrease in annuities if numbers fell below a certain number and an increase if economic conditions changed. As a result, representations were made to the Canadian government to increase annuities, and in 1875 annuities were increased to the maximum of $4 per person.[11] This action significantly increased the costs of treaty payments for the federal government, which in 1892 approached the Ontario government to assume their share of these increased annuities.[12] While the latter admitted their liability for these increased annuities, they objected strongly to the number of Métis that had been added to the yearly paylists since 1850, and in 1892 they sent Edward Borron to investigate the issue with a view to removing the Métis from these treaty rolls.[13]

Borron's and the Ontario government's position, in line with the Pennefather Commission on Indian Affairs of 1858[14] and Canadian legislation of 1869[15] and 1876[16] defining Indians, argued that the majority of Métis on these annuity rolls were descendants of Indian women who had married a "white" man and thus were barred from Indian status. The federal government maintained a more "liberal" policy of inclusion, and the dispute was eventually decided by arbitration in 1894–95.[17] In this arbitration Ontario's liability was limited somewhat, but Chancellor Boyd, writing for the arbitrators, more or less followed the rules of membership that the federal government had followed, namely: "It was not desirable to define with minuteness who are Indians" in advance of any particular case which arose for decision, and that in general he would favour the application of the "rule so as to include among Indians those of other blood, who are not only married to Indians, but were adopted by the tribe as members and as such lived in tribal relations with the other members at their common place of residence."[18] Thus, throughout the period in which the numbered treaties (1–8) were being negotiated in the northwest, the Canadian government showed little interest in playing a gatekeeping role as to who was allowed into treaty.[19] This was left to the bands themselves and little stood in the way of Métis entering treaty. As the rest of this chapter will demonstrate, not only did treaty commissioners and the Indian Department ignore legislation barring Indian women (and their children) who had married "whites" from entering treaty and collecting annuities, but they ignored legislation stipulating that Métis not be allowed into treaty.[20]

Indeed, a large number of the Métis scrip applications that were received in the period 1885–87, and most of the serious problems related to the scrip program, dealt with Métis leaving treaty to take scrip. As a result, discussions over scrip policy involved not only the Department of the Interior but also the Department of Indian Affairs and more closely tied scrip policy to Indian policy – particularly in the area of civilization and enfranchisement. As early as 1871 government negotiators noted the large number of Métis entering treaty, even in areas where they were eligible for Métis land grants through the Manitoba Act. Wemyss Simpson paying Indians at Brokenhead River after the signing of Treaty 1 noted that "a number of those residing among the Indians, and calling themselves Indians, are in reality half-breeds, and entitled to share in the land grant under the provisions of the Manitoba Act." After he explained that, if they took treaty, they and their families would be ineligible to receive a Métis land grant, only a few changed their minds. The reason, according to Simpson, was the fact that "the mass of these persons have lived all their lives on the Indian reserves (so called), and would rather receive such benefits as may accrue to them under the Indian treaty, than wait the realization of any value of their half-breed grant."[21]

This was also an issue in the Treaty 2 region in the Manitoba Interlake, where the Métis lifestyle was largely indistinguishable from that of their Saulteaux (Ojibwa) kin.[22] Both their kinship ties and lifestyles were so close that the majority of individuals of mixed ancestry in the Interlake self-identified as Indians and entered treaty as part of various Ojibwa bands.[23] This was especially the case outside the bounds of the 1870 "postage stamp province" of Manitoba where the Métis were not eligible for a Manitoba Act land grant. As Joseph-Alfred-Norbert Provencher, the Indian commissioner noted, this problem assumed a special feature where the Métis existed in numbers. There "they wish to be acknowledged as special Bands, distinct from Indian Bands which surround them, taking at the same time, their share of the privilege granted the Indians."[24] This issue also showed up in the Treaty 3 region, where an adhesion in 1875 involved a group of Métis from Rainy Lake under the leadership of Nicholas Chatelaine, who opted to become status Indians and signed an adhesion to treaty. They received their own reserve on Rainy Lake and all the benefits and annuities of the treaty.[25]

Alexander Morris, who negotiated Treaties 3, 5, and 6, tried to make some distinction between Métis and Indian statuses, but was largely unsuccessful. During the negotiations leading to the signing of Treaty 6 in 1876 a number of representations were made for the Métis to be allowed into treaty. Alexander Morris noted that there were three classes of Métis in the North-West Territories: "1st those who as at St Laurent, near Prince Albert, the Qu'Appelle Lake and Edmonton, have their farms and homes; 2nd, those who are entirely identified with the Indians, living with them, and speaking their language; 3rd, those who do not farm, but live after the habits of the Indians, by the pursuit of the buffalo and the chase." The first class, he noted, would be recognized as possessors of the soil and confirmed by the government in their holdings, the second class had been recognized as Indians and allowed into treaty, but that the third class would be more difficult to deal with. Though a few were identified with Indians he recommended against their being brought into the treaties.[26] This gesture at discrimination was largely ineffective. As David Laird, the Indian commissioner of the

North-West Territories, pointed out in 1878, it had been difficult to distinguish Métis who had adopted Indian habit from "Full-blood" Indians at treaty time.[27] Indeed, thousands of Métis had joined treaty from the early 1870s on, not only because of their close relationship with some Indian bands, but also because their economic base, the buffalo, was disappearing, and the Canadian government had not yet formulated any policy of scrip for the Northwest Métis.[28]

By 1878 some of these Métis in treaty were attempting to withdraw, but no mechanism existed to do so. David Laird noted that, if they did withdraw, they were excluded from other rights. He argued that it was "desirable that Métis be allowed to leave treaty if they return gratuities and annuities paid them or perhaps should be allowed to do so without penalty." In any case he wished to be advised how he should treat such cases.[29] It was in response to these questions that amendments to the Indian Act (1880 and 1884) were passed, allowing Métis to leave treaty and take scrip with no penalty.[30] Many mixed-bloods in treaty perceived the offering of money scrip, which could be sold and converted into a large sum of money, as preferable to a long-term relationship with the federal government and small treaty payments on a yearly basis. As the *Edmonton Bulletin* noted in October of 1885: "When the Indians in this neighbourhood were first paid treaty money a large number of persons who were actually half-breeds classed themselves as Indian for the purpose of securing the $5 a year payment. Many of these now see the disadvantages accruing from their condition as Indians and desire to abandon it. This desire is to be facilitated by the Indian department as much as possible by securing for those parties scrip as half-breeds."[31] Thus, in 1885 when "North-West Half-breed Scrip" became available, many of the mixed-bloods in treaty chose to change their status to Métis or half-breed and take scrip.

The issue of withdrawal from treaty to take scrip arose first in the summer of 1885, at which time it was still a minor concern. Under their original instructions of 30 March 1885 the commissioners had been instructed to refuse all applicants who were in receipt of annuities or on Indian band rolls. To those that enquired they were to state simply that they were not eligible to be enumerated as "half-breeds," and to explain to them that when, under the provisions of the Indian Act, they might make an application for enfranchisement, they would be dealt with by the government equitably and liberally. By early May 1885 W.P.R. Street was requesting additional guidance. At Qu'Appelle they had received many applications from mixed-bloods who had taken treaty and who wished to be enfranchised. Told that, when they were enfranchised, they would be dealt with by the government equitably and liberally, they asked how they could become enfranchised and what the government would then do for them. Street also wanted to know, before they left Calgary for the north, precisely what the government would do for those who became enfranchised. He suggested that those leaving treaty receive the same as the Northwest Métis minus what they had received in annuities and allowances. He went on to say that, if the government wished to encourage those Métis who had taken treaty to leave the treaty, some definite statement to this effect would be desirable.[32] By 6 May 1885 Street had begun to receive declarations from those mixed-bloods wishing to leave treaty,[33] and a few days later he again implored the government to take more concrete action on this question. They were daily meeting Métis who wished to be allowed to leave treaty and who had requested over and over to be allowed to do so, but had received no answer. When the Indian agent at Fort Qu'Appelle was questioned, he had replied that the problem lay in Ottawa.[34]

By the end of May of 1885, the Indian Department finally clarified the issue when Deputy Superintendent General Lawrence Vankoughnet wrote, in a letter to the minister of the interior, that the Indian Act of 1880 had been amended and that under section 4 (47 Victoria, c. 27) all that was required to effect the withdrawal of the parties named was to have their declarations certified by the two witnesses on oath before some person authorized by law to administer oaths. These declarations, or certified copies of them, should then be sent to the Indian commissioner of the North-West Territories at Regina, so the affected parties could be struck off the pay lists.[35] Thereafter, the commission began to issue scrip certificates to those who had withdrawn from treaty under these regulations. However, this new policy initiated a long debate within both the Department of the Interior and the Department of Indian Affairs, and between departments, as to who would be allowed to leave treaty to take scrip. This debate, given the relatively small numbers involved in 1885, did not much affect the scrip commission in 1885, but it would dominate the proceedings in 1886 and 1887.

On the recommendation of the final report of the 1885 commission, Roger Goulet, one of the 1885 commissioners, was appointed on 1 March 1886 as the sole commissioner to investigate and settle the scrip claims of those Métis who had been unable to appear before the North-West Half-breed Scrip Commission in 1885.[36] A minor change in the instructions given Goulet involved those Métis who had participated in the 1885 Rebellion. In the previous year the commission had been instructed that these Métis should receive no consideration. After some debate,[37] the Department of the Interior informed Goulet that he should deal with the applications from Métis who had participated in the Rebellion of 1885 in the same manner as he would other claims – that is, to accept or reject them on their merits.[38]

This change in scrip policy was also connected to a new attitude within the Indian Department aimed at punishing those Indian bands and individuals who were thought to have participated in the 1885 Rebellion. In order to prevent further revolts and to establish the authority of the government, the department embarked on a policy of rewarding "loyal" bands and punishing "disloyal" ones. This new practice was initiated by Hayter Reed, the deputy Indian commissioner in the North-West. Sent to Indian Commissioner Edgar Dewdney on 13 July 1885, this memo articulated some seventeen or eighteen points on the "future management of Indians."[39] These proposals, which were later amended somewhat by Edgar Dewdney, Lawrence Vankoughnet (deputy superintendent-general of Indian affairs), and John A. Macdonald (superintendent-general of Indian affairs and prime minister), became policy by the end of 1885.[40]

These proposals, after it was noted that all those Indian bands that had not participated in the Rebellion would be treated as before, listed more than a dozen actions that could/should be taken re-establish the authority of the government and punish those bands that had participated in the Rebellion.[41] These actions included abolishing the tribal system of the bands that were considered rebellious, suspending the annuities of "rebel bands," disarming "rebel bands" by confiscating rifles and issuing shotguns instead, prohibiting members of "rebel bands" from leaving their reserves without a pass, dispersing Big Bear's band among other bands, instituting a policy of work for rations, selling the horses of "rebel bands" and using the proceeds to buy cattle for those bands, and striking all "Half-breed members of Rebel Bands" off the annuity pay sheets. Some of these proposals were modified before they became policy. For example, the confiscation of rifles was made voluntary and more emphasis was placed on the distribution of ammunition, and "Half-breed members of Rebel Bands" were not struck from band membership lists, but were to be offered an "inducement" to withdraw from treaty. As it turned out, this "inducement" would be the offer of land scrip to these "Half-breeds" once they had withdrawn from treaty. As "rebel Half-breeds" had been refused the opportunity to apply for scrip in the spring and summer of 1885, the proposed "inducement" necessitated a change in scrip policy to allow all Métis, rebel or not, to apply for scrip in 1886.

Some historians have argued that it was these new punitive measures that "compelled" the Métis exodus from treaty to take scrip. This is the position articulated by Heather Devine,[42] and, given that these measure certainly made life on reserves more difficult for those "Half-breed members of Rebel Bands" (see Bobtail band, below, under "The Bobtail and Papaschase Bands"), they undoubtedly had some role in Métis leaving treaty. It seems unlikely, however, that it was the sole, even the primary, reason for their withdrawal. As already noted, "half-breeds" in treaty had been trying to withdraw from the late 1870s. As well, the amendment to the Indian Act in 1884 eliminating the need to repay annuities for those Métis withdrawing from treaties had been instituted to allow "enterprising" Métis to become "self-supporting citizens," and, in response to an increasing scale of requests by "half-breeds" to leave treaty to take scrip in the spring of 1885, both the Department of the Interior and the Department of Indian Affairs had established a policy permitting withdrawal from treaty to take scrip. This policy was in place by May of 1885, two months prior to Reed's memorandum to Dewdney.

The most pressing issue facing the Scrip Commission of 1886 was the flood of applications they received from "half-breeds" leaving treaty. As early as August 1885, the commissioner of Dominion lands at Winnipeg sounded a warning bell that the policy of allowing "half-breeds" to leave treaty and receive scrip without having to pay back the annuities they had received while in treaty had resulted in numerous petitions from the St Peter's Band near Winnipeg to leave treaty for scrip. He noted that, if it was the intention of the Indian Act to allow all "mixed-bloods" in treaty to leave for scrip without paying back their annuities, there would be a wholesale exodus. Such an outcome, he noted, might be more advantageous to both Métis and the Indian Department if thereafter they would not be called on to support these people. He further noted that this was not very likely, as after expending the proceeds of their scrip grants many would return to the Indian reserves where they had been residing and constitute a burden on both the band and the government.[43] This note of concern prodded the Department of the Interior to seek further clarification from the Indian Department as to the meaning of the Indian Act in relation to leaving treaty and what procedures should be followed to prevent abuses.[44] Indian Affairs replied that the intention of the 1884 revision to the Indian Act had been to allow "half-breeds" to withdraw from treaty without refunding annuities. It was felt that the repayment of annuities had "acted as [a] bar to the withdrawal of many enterprising Half-breeds who might otherwise cease to be Indians and become self-supporting citizens." However, having once withdrawn from treaty and accepted scrip, they became to all intents and purposes ordinary Canadians and as such could not be permitted to reside upon an Indian reserve. Their names would be erased from the treaty pay lists and this action would prevent the likelihood of their ever again receiving annuity money as Indians.[45]

The Department of the Interior tried to convince the Department of Indian Affairs to embody their guidelines and protections into an amendment of the Indian Act, particularly "providing that no treaty-taking half-breeds shall be allowed to retire from the treaty and claim the rights of a non-treaty half-breed unless upon a report from the Indian Agent or the Indian Inspector, that he has for a certain number of years previous to his application been self-supporting."[46] Interior also requested better legislation with regard to "half-breed" minors in treaty and Indian women who were wives of "non-treaty half Breeds."[47] The deputy superintendent of Indian affairs was sympathetic to this course of action, but the lateness of the parliamentary session and John A. Macdonald's view that legislation was unnecessary, given the detailed instructions sent to the Indian commissioner of the North-West Territories and the various Indian inspectors and their agents regarding the procedure to be followed, resulted in no legislative enactments being made prior to the appointment of Roger Goulet as scrip commissioner for 1886.[48]

The first intimation that there were serious difficulties with the commission's work in 1886 was Goulet's report from Calgary on 19 June that there were numerous applications from "half-breeds" in treaty who had not yet received their discharges and were consequently refused. These "stragglers," as he termed them, were causing him considerable problems, as they followed the commission from place to place sowing discontent. This group, he explained, were "half-breeds" who had abandoned the band of Indians with which they had formerly received annuities, and consequently it was almost impossible for them to appear before the Indian agent for the district to which they belonged as Indians to receive their discharge as prescribed by the regulations in place. Given the problems this group was causing, Goulet requested the Indian commissioner of the North-West Territories to instruct agents to grant discharges even if they were not from that district. This the Indian commissioner refused to do.[49] On 23 July Goulet again requested that these "stragglers" be allowed to withdraw from treaty on the authority of T.P.

Wadsworth, an inspector of Indian agencies for Treaty 6 then travelling with Goulet, but again he was refused.[50] Hayter Reed, the assistant to the Indian commissioner of the North-West Territories, explaining the reasoning behind this refusal, noted that "stragglers" could not be discharged in the manner requested by Goulet, because to do so would open the door to fraud. Agents could know nothing about "stragglers" belonging to other districts and, by discharging them, would create a massive headache in trying to locate these stragglers on other pay sheets so as to strike them off the rolls. There was also the danger, he said, of granting discharges to people who eventually would necessarily be thrown back for support at the hands of the government.[51] This explanation satisfied the Department of the Interior, and the deputy minister informed Goulet that he must work within the previous instructions.[52]

More significant problems came to light after Goulet and his commission headed north from Calgary. Not only did scrip applications from "half-breeds" formerly in treaty increase dramatically, but reports began coming in from Indian agents across the west that "half-breeds" were withdrawing from treaty in large numbers.[53] T.P. Wadsworth, an inspector of Indian agencies, telegraphed Edgar Dewdney, the Indian commissioner, on 4 July asking, "are all Indians who represent they are Half-breeds and leading same mode of life as Indians to be allowed discharges? If so, there will be a perfect exodus from Beaver Hills and probably other places. Agents require positive and immediate instructions."[54] In a follow-up letter of 7 July Wadsworth elaborated on the problems he was having. He noted that the number of applications for discharges from treaty were far beyond the expectations of the department,[55] and that Indian Agents felt they had no option but to grant discharges, given that the "alleged half-breeds" had "no difficulty in proving themselves 'half-breeds,' the evidence being only in the form of statements by friends." Wadsworth had informed these agents not to grant any more discharges until he had had a chance to speak to the Indian commissioner, and he noted that this course of action had caused great dissatisfaction among those wishing to withdraw. He also warned the commissioner of problems in the future if clearer guidelines were not forthcoming. Papaschase's Band all wished to withdraw, and Enoch and his band also wished to withdraw. If these departures were allowed, he opined, it would only send "so many paupers out into the country" and lead to an epidemic of withdrawals in other places. He suggested that a representative of the Indian Department be attached to the scrip commission to rule on all applications for withdrawal. Doing so would relieve the agents of the responsibility, for if Indians were forced to stay in treaty by the action of the agent, that agent's influence in the band would be damaged.[56] Dewdney replied immediately that no discharges should be made by any Indian agent until he had consulted John A. Macdonald, the superintendent general, and that he should instruct agents at Edmonton, Peace Hills, and Victoria not to issue any more discharges until further advised. In particular, he wanted to find out how the department could exercise discretion under the Indian Act to justify a refusal to permit withdrawal. As well, Wadsworth was instructed to accompany Goulet and become "jointly responsible as to Half-breeds receiving discharges from Treaty."[57] The scrip commissioner's (Goulet) response to this injunction was to request a quick and clear resolution to the issue. In his opinion treaty "half-breeds" who could clearly show they were "half-breeds" and who did not lead same mode of life as Indians should be given every facility to withdraw from treaty. He strongly recommended that some person be appointed to sign discharges and accompany the commissioner down the Saskatchewan River to Lac La Biche. Immediate action was very important, as the refusal to grant discharges altogether would create great dissatisfaction.[58]

Shortly thereafter the superintendent general travelled to Regina to confer with Dewdney, who then sent a telegram to Goulet stating "Treaty Half-breeds who clearly show that they are Half-breeds and who do not lead the same mode of life as Indians should be allowed to withdraw from treaty. Others should not be allowed." As well, every person accepting discharge should be informed at the time that he forfeited all Indian rights and had to leave the reserve and give up his house and all other improvements without compensation. The consent to these conditions should be written on discharge and signed by the withdrawing Indian. Inspector Wadsworth would travel with Goulet to adjudicate these withdrawals.[59] Goulet agreed with most of these new orders, but noted they had created much dissatisfaction among "a large number of person[s] who although living like Indians are Half-breeds and as such claim to be entitled to participate in the grant of scrip." He also reported that he had consulted a great many prominent persons in the North-West and they all agreed with the intent of the policy but feared that by refusing this class of applicants "what they so earnestly ask for: their discharge and their scrip, might make them very discontented." He also noted that a large number of these "half-breeds" had been allowed their discharge before any distinction had been made between a treaty "half-breed" leading a life identical to that of the Indians (living on the reserve, receiving rations and treaty payments), and a treaty "half-breed" receiving the Indian annuities but who provided for his subsistence by farming, freighting, or hiring out as a labourer. If some of these early discharges proved capable of making their own living, then the restrictions that had been placed on the "granting of discharges to that class of Half-Breeds might, with advantage, be removed."[60]

For T.P. Wadsworth, the Indian inspector in charge of approving Indian withdrawals in the Treaty 6 area, these instructions were not clear enough. He requested a further explanation as to what "mode of life as Indians" entailed. All Indians he noted were engaged more or less in agriculture. Were Chief Papaschase and his brothers to be granted discharges? They farmed and sometimes lived in lodges in summer and houses in winter. A clearer definition, he said, was necessary, and direction on Papaschase would help guide action in other cases.[61] In reply the Indian commissioner telegraphed "I think Pass-pass-chase and brothers might be granted discharges."[62] On the basis of these instructions, Wadsworth proceeded with his duties of adjudicating withdrawals from treaty, but noted in a later report that, since instructions had been received on the 17 July, forty heads of family had received discharges from treaty, and that those who were refused became very angry, behaved badly, and declared they would never again live on any reserve.[63]

Throughout the 1886 scrip season both the Department of the Interior and the Department of Indian Affairs tried to get some control over the situation and make some sensible distinctions that would be in the interests of the Métis, the Indians, the government, and the public, but the door was still fairly open to Métis withdrawing from treaty in large numbers. The Indian Department, given its policy of civilization and enfranchisement, did not want to close any door that would bar the withdrawal of enterprising "treaty half-breeds" who might otherwise cease to be Indians and become self-supporting citizens; the Interior Department did not want to slow down the process of the final extinguishment of "half-breed claims"; and both were being pressured by the treaty "half-breeds" to be allowed to withdraw from treaty. Given this situation, Goulet's scrip commission continued to grant large numbers of scrip certificates to Métis who had withdrawn from treaty.[64] His final report noted that he had received and investigated 1,414 applications of which 1,164 had been allowed. Of these 602 were from "half-breeds" who had withdrawn from treaty; only 290 were from persons who had never participated in any grants to Indians, and 267 were made by the legal representatives of deceased Métis who had died on a date subsequent to the

15th day of July 1870 and who, had they been living, would have been eligible for scrip.[65] Goulet did note that great precautions had been taken to ascertain whether or not the applicant for withdrawal would be capable of supporting himself and family without the assistance of the government.[66] Dealing with "half-breeds" in treaty, however, had so delayed the commission that it got no further than St Laurent on the South Saskatchewan River during the summer of 1886. Owing to these delays and the lateness of the season, he was unable to visit Fort à la Corne, The Pas, Cumberland House, Grand Rapids, Norway House, Beren's River, Fort Alexander, Manitoba House, and Fairford. To complete the settlement of these claims he recommended that arrangements should be made early the next spring to hold sittings in these locations.[67]

In 1887, Goulet was appointed as chairman of another half-breed commission, and N.-O. Coté, formerly secretary of the commission, was appointed as a member of the commission to investigate the remaining half-breed claims in the North-West Territories.[68] The Department of the Interior, cognizant that most of the claimants would be from "half-breeds" leaving treaty, took special steps to ensure that the Department of Indian Affairs continue the same practice as had been adopted the previous summer with regard to the granting of discharges from treaty, making sure that an inspector from the various Indian agencies accompany Goulet and Coté to every commission hearing.[69] Reporting from Grand Rapids on 13 August 1887, Goulet noted that "all the claims which have so far been dealt with by us with the exception of ten cases, have been preferred by persons who were previously members of Bands of Indians under Treaty."[70] They dealt with 565 applications for scrip, of which 31 were disallowed and 321 were granted to persons who had obtained their discharge from treaty. In all, the scrip commissions from 1885 through 1887 had investigated 3,794 applications and allowed 3,247 of them. Of these 1,292 persons were formerly treaty "half-breeds" who had secured discharges.[71]

The discharge of treaty "half-breeds" and granting them scrip had created problems for both the Department of the Interior and the Department of Indian Affairs almost from the first, and these problems continued into the twentieth century. In the expectation of receiving scrip the treaty "half-breeds" of Sandy Bay on Lake Manitoba, representing almost the entire band, withdrew from treaty in 1886. Their story illustrates not only the problems the government had in adjudicating treaty and Métis scrip, but the interchangeability of these two statuses and how government categories increasingly played a role in Métis self-identification and identity after 1885.

The Sandy Bay Band

The Métis/Indians of Sandy Bay had their origins in the fur trade of the early nineteenth century when freemen Canadiens began to penetrate the southern Interlake of Manitoba and marry into the Ojibwa bands of the region. When the fur trade in this region waned in the two decades after the merger of the Hudson's Bay Company and North West Company in 1821, these freemen families either moved to the Red River Settlement or were absorbed into the Ojibwa bands resident in the Lake Manitoba region.[72]

When the fur trade rebounded in the wake of expanding markets and the free trade movement of the 1840s, Métis families moved back into the southern Interlake. One of the wintering foci for these groups was the Whitemud River near its mouth on Lake Manitoba. Associated with the Métis communities at Baie St Paul, St François Xavier, Portage la Prairie, and Ojibwa bands along the western shores of Lake Manitoba, these Métis communities included the Beaulieu, Desjarlais, Desmarais, Flamond, Folster, Houle, Locouette, Lavasseur, McKay, Mousseau, Richard, Roulette, Sinclair, and Spence families. According to their scrip applications in 1887, they followed a way of life that included fur trading, hunting, and fishing in a region bounded by the plains to the south, Riding Mountain to the west, and Lake Manitoba to the east. Important places in this region included the Big Grass Marsh, Big Point, and Sandy Bay on Lake Manitoba, and settlements such as Westbourne, Portage la Prairie, Baie St Paul, and St François Xavier, where they married and baptized their children (see figure 8.2).[73] With the decrease in game in the southern parts of this region and the retreat of the buffalo westward, many of these families moved further northward to locations on the shores of Lake Manitoba where the fisheries provided a more secure subsistence. This move also pulled them into an Ojibwa way of life.[74]

Not surprisingly, most of these Métis families took treaty in the early 1870s. No longer primarily resident in the 1870 "postage stamp province" of Manitoba[75] and therefore ineligible for a Manitoba Act grant, treaty status offered them a reserve, annuities, and aid. Not present at the signing of either Treaty 1 or Treaty 2 in 1871, they were entered onto the annuity rolls of Yellow Quill's band because of their orientation to Whitemud River and Portage. However, these Métis had no desire to settle on Yellow Quill's proposed reserve on the Assiniboine River or to take direction from Yellow Quill, whom they did not consider their

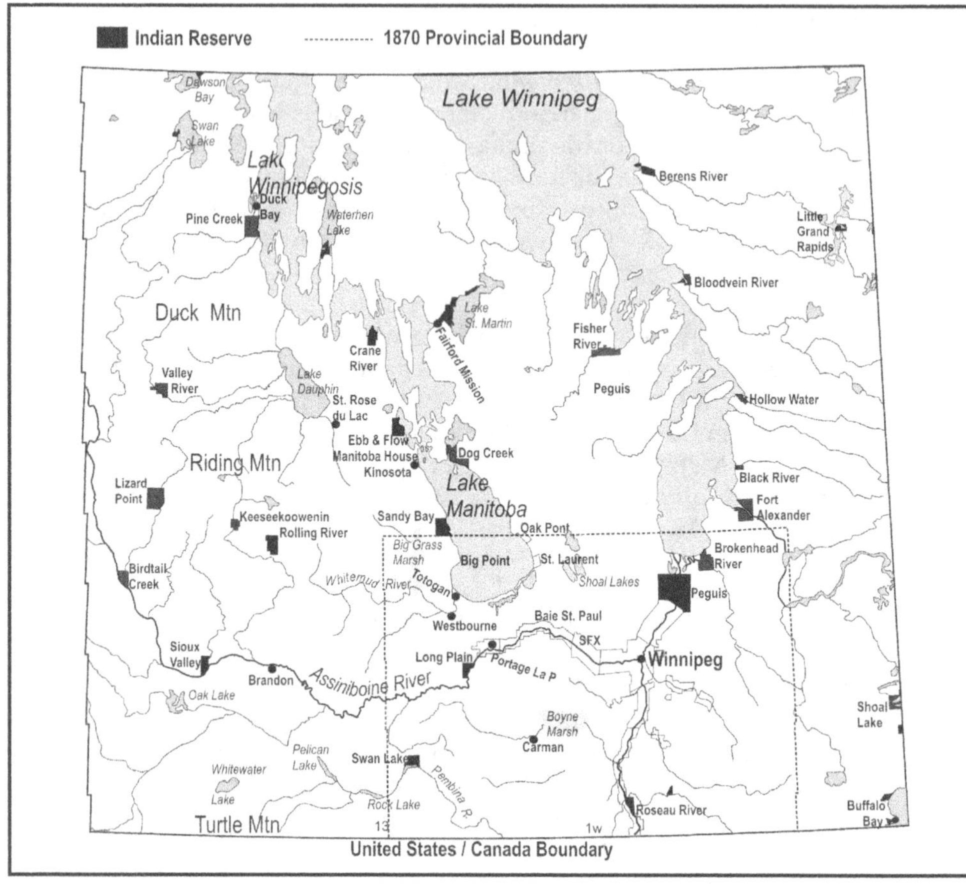

8.2 Manitoba in 1886 showing Indian reserves and the 1870 provincial boundary.

chief, and they argued they should be recognized as a separate band with a reserve on Lake Manitoba near the Whitemud River.[76] Until 1875 this band of Métis/Indians remained at Whitemud River and received their annuities at Totogan. Meeting with Alexander Morris in 1876, they told him they were a Christian band, would never join Yellow Quill, and wanted a reserve at Big Point. Told that Big Point was not available, as there were already settlers there, they accepted a reserve at Sandy Bay, which was surveyed in 1876.[77]

Between 1876 and 1886, when the majority of the band withdrew from treaty, little progress was made in developing the reserve beyond building some houses. Water levels in Lake Manitoba were four to five feet higher than usual and thus flooded most of the arable and hay lands of the reserve, with the result that the majority of band members abandoned the land until 1883, when water levels began to recede.[78] This may account for the willingness of the Métis in treaty to withdraw after Métis scrip became available in 1885. When Roger Goulet arrived in the community in January of 1887 to take applications for scrip, all but three families applied for scrip, but they did request that they be allowed to locate their land on the reserve, as the other families had left. When informed that this was impossible, they finally decided to accept the conditions as endorsed on their discharges and accepted scrip.[79] They continued to hold out hope, however, that their application to the minister of the interior to open their reserve for ordinary settlement would allow them to stay on the lands they had settled on. In this they were encouraged by Goulet, who said he would pass on their request and would urge the Department to consider that their accepting of the conditions of discharges from treaty should not be taken as prima facie evidence of their final abandonment of said reserve. He also recommended that their application be granted if at all feasible.[80] A year later the whole community was in crisis, as they had ceased farming, not knowing whether they would be left in possession of their homes. In desperation they enlisted the aid of Manitoba government officials, who contacted the Department of the Interior.[81] When they finally received an answer from the department it was a flat denial of their request. The minister of the interior noted: "The Half-breeds to whom you refer have withdrawn from treaty and got their scrip, or are entitled to it. They cannot therefore obtain homesteads upon the Reserve, which is no longer theirs. There is really no question to decide because they are exactly in the position of any ordinary white settler in the North West. My own impression is that it was a pity they withdrew from treaty, but that was their own act and having thus chosen to be Half-breeds instead of Indians, they have no right upon an Indian Reserve."[82]

However, the matter did not end there. One year later the Sandy Bay Métis were again petitioning the minister of the interior, noting that when they had withdrawn from treaty they had been assured that all their children would receive scrip, and now they found that only those born before 15 July 1870 were eligible. Families were being separated as they became wanderers, their community was falling victim to alcohol dealers, and they no longer had any schools for their children, as they were out of treaty. They asked that the reserve be thrown open for settlement or that they be readmitted into treaty.[83] Lawrence Vankoughnet, the deputy superintendant general of Indian affairs, wrote to Edgar Dewdney, noting that three courses of action were open, given that the Métis of Sandy Bay were refusing to vacate the reserve. The first was to eject them forcibly; the second was to readmit them to treaty and give them back their reserve but withhold annuities until they had repaid the value of the scrip they had received; and the third was to obtain a surrender of the reserve from the three remaining families in the band and open it to settlement. The best plan, he thought, would be to readmit the Sandy Bay Métis to treaty.[84] Indian Affairs acted quickly and by mid-January 1891 the inspector of Indian affairs for Manitoba was informed that he could readmit the Sandy Bay Métis on the condition that the value of the scrip they had received be deducted from annuities until the full amount had been repaid.[85] Sixty-five individuals then were readmitted to the Sandy Bay Band by the end of 1891. Not all who wanted back in, however, were granted readmission. In 1894 the Indian agent for Sandy Bay noted that François Desmarais, the former chief of the band, had applied for readmission for himself and his family. On enquiring further, however, the Department of Indian Affairs discovered that Desmarais had homesteaded in the Fort Ellice district, had seventy-five acres under cultivation, and had been living on the homestead ever since he had withdrawn from treaty. Indians who had left treaty and were able to provide for themselves were not candidates for readmission and it was decided not to readmit the Desmarais family.[86]

This issue was also a problem for the department in other parts of the west, and Indian Affairs was trying to formulate a policy in regard to those "half-breeds" who had been discharged from treaty and had taken scrip but who did not want to leave the reserve or now wanted readmission to treaty. With regard to those scrip takers who refused to abandon their reserves, the Department of Indian Affairs received a legal opinion from the Department of Justice stating "a half-breed who has been admitted into treaty has the option of withdrawing therefrom, and thereby becoming entitled to any privilege which attach to his status as a half-breed, or of remaining under the treaty and retaining such privileges as he is entitled to thereunder as an Indian, but that he must elect one status or the other, and cannot as a matter of right claim the privileges attached to both."[87] On the question of readmission to treaty the department advised its agents that they could allow a few treaty readmissions, but cases should not be precedents for "wholesale readmissions." Both the scrip commissioners and the Indian agents had warned scrip takers of the consequences of withdrawal from treaty.[88] Any application for readmission to treaty had to be forwarded to the Indian Department, and the agent should provide full particulars regarding each case. Only then was action to be taken. A measure of leniency might be extended to those who were incapable of providing for themselves, but each individual case had to be inquired into.

The Bobtail and Papaschase Bands

Other examples that demonstrated the vagaries of the department's policy and position and the indeterminacy of Métis identity were the cases of the Bobtail and Papaschase bands in Treaty 6. Chief Bobtail, also known as Kiskayu and as Alexis Piché, was the son of a former North West Company "half-breed" servant known as Piché or Peechee, who on "going free" associated more with the Cree bands in the vicinity of Fort Edmonton than with other freemen.[89] He married a Cree woman named Opeh-tah-she-toy-wishk,[90] with whom he had at least five children, all of whom were raised in a Cree context despite being given Christian names at baptism.[91]

By the 1840s Piché and his family could be found in the Cree encampments of Maskepetoon and Walking Bear,[92] and by the late 1860s and early 1870s his two sons, Bobtail (Alexis or Kiskayu) and Ermineskin (Jean-Baptiste or Kasikusiweyaniw), had become Cree leaders in their own right.[93] Bobtail, having married into the Cardinal family of Lac La Biche, also had a following among the Métis of that region.[94] In the early 1870s Bobtail's band was oriented to the area around Victoria Settlement / Saint-Paul-des-Cris in the winter and southward across the plains in the summer.[95] As the buffalo withdrew ever further to the southwest, however, Bobtail and his band left the Saint-Paul-des-Cris region to follow them.[96]

By the time Treaty 6 was being planned in 1875–76 it was understood that Bobtail and his band would have to be brought into treaty.[97] That they were not present at the signing of the treaty at Fort Pitt was explained by the fact that Bobtail had either not received timely notice or considered it too far to bring his band in from the neighbourhood of the Red Deer River.[98] In 1877, however, Bobtail did attend the negotiations for Treaty 7 at Blackfoot Crossing and had an interview with Lieutenant Governor David Laird, who was also a treaty commissioner. Bobtail noted that he and his band had not been included in any treaty, and he expressed a wish to have a reserve near Pigeon Lake. On learning that this location was within the limits of Treaty 6, and that it would be best to keep the Blackfoot and Cree as separate as possible, Laird determined that it would be more expedient for Chief Bobtail and his band to give their adhesion to Treaty 6. An instrument to that effect was accordingly executed and signed on 25 September 1877.[99] Shortly thereafter the bands, under the leadership of Bobtail, Ermineskin, and Samson, asked to have reserves at the place of their usual fall camp on ridge of Bear Hills along Battle River (see figure 8.3). They eventually settled down on these reserves in 1879–80, when the buffalo had entirely disappeared from Canadian territory.

Though settled on a reserve and living within a Cree context, Bobtail and almost his entire band would withdraw from treaty in 1885–86 to take Métis scrip. The reasons for this seeming anomaly were several. By 1885 not only were Bobtail's relations with the Canadian government very rocky, but so too were his relations with the other bands on the Bear Hills reserves. His band had shrunk in numbers since signing treaty in 1877, while the bands of Ermineskin and Samson had increased, with the result that, when their respective reserves were surveyed in 1885, Bobtail's was the smallest and he considered this a blow to his prestige.[100]

The 1885 Rebellion heightened Bobtail's discontent in treaty. It was Bobtail who, in the years leading up to 1885, was the most discontented with the terms and benefits that had accrued to his people through treaty and was the chief most associated with the "troubles" that occurred on the Bear Hills reserves during the Rebellion. Both this heightened sense of discontent and the reprisals that followed the suppression of "rebellion" must be taken into account in order to understand Bobtail's decision to leave in 1886, even though the other chiefs at Bear Hills decided to remain in treaty.[101] As early as May of 1885 he informed Agent Lucas that he would not come for his rations anymore and threatened that, if he was not better treated, he would join his friends at Battleford.[102] This dissatisfaction, combined with his disappointment over the survey of his reserve in August and September of 1885, the arrest of his son Coyote at annuity time in 1885,[103] and the non-payment of annuities to 119 men because of misconduct in 1885 were a hard pill to swallow.[104]

Other factors also influenced Bobtail's decisions. In the summer of 1885, prior to the survey of the Bear Hills reserves, the first North-West Half-Breed Scrip Commission came through the Peace Hills / Edmonton areas. Although Bobtail and his immediate family did not take scrip at

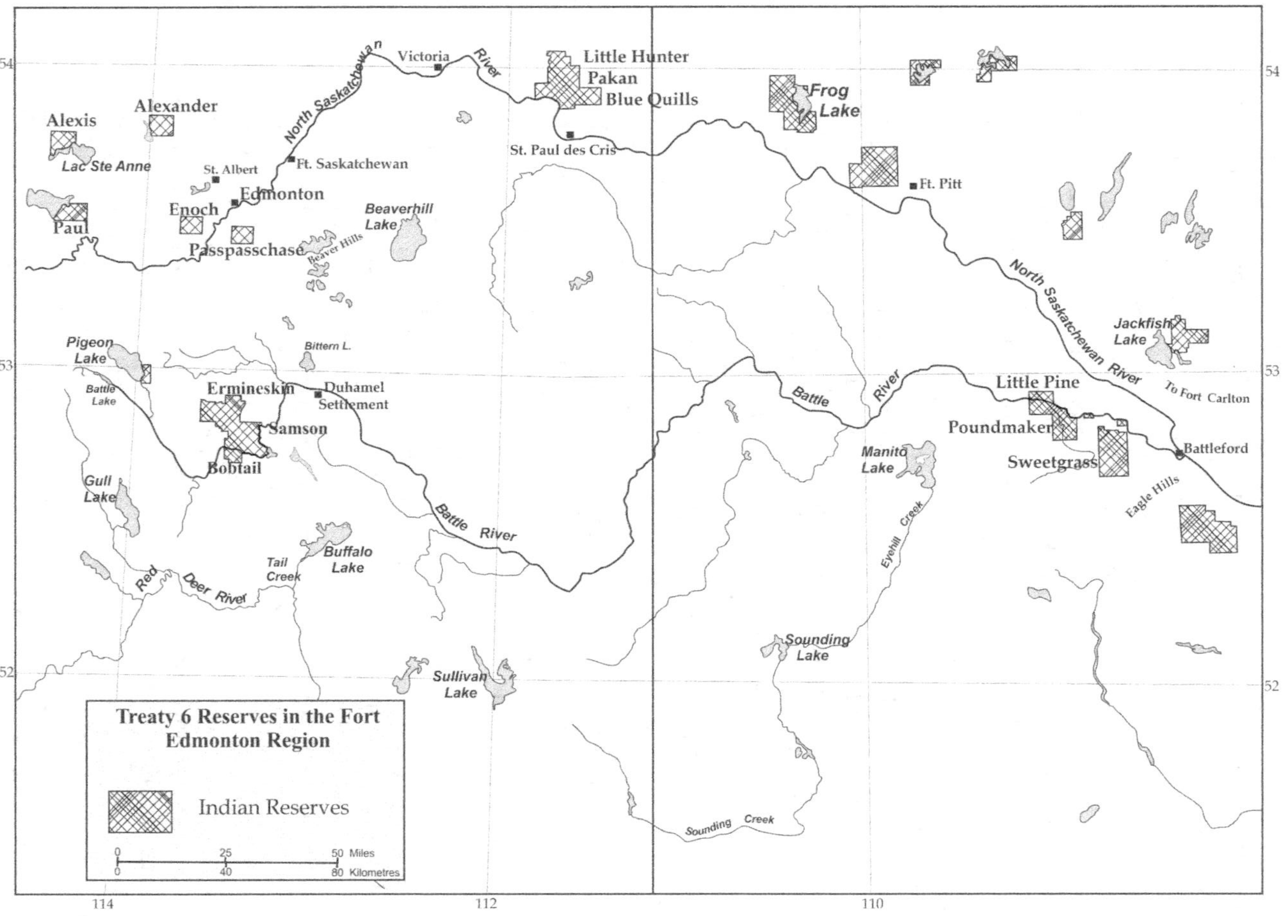

8.3 Treaty 6 reserves in the Fort Edmonton Region.

this time, a number of his band members and their families did so.[105] They included Alexis Josie (married into the Piché family), Isaac Cardinal, Jean-Baptiste Cardinal, Alexis Cardinal, Susan Bremner (née Cardinal), and Baptiste Degrasse.[106] What is interesting about these withdrawals is that they are almost all by Cardinals, related to Bobtail through his wife, and one (Josie) married into the Bobtail family. In 1886, Agent Lucas noted that one of the reasons that Bobtail and his extended family took scrip in 1886 was that several members of these families had taken scrip in 1885, and as the earlier withdrawals were not allowed to live with their family and friends on the reserve, all the families decided to take scrip.[107]

Another reason for taking scrip, given the very hard years of 1880–85, was the monetary benefits that scrip offered. Each family was eligible for a $160 scrip per head of family, and $240 scrip for each child. On this basis, a family of five would be eligible for scrip worth $1,040 to be used in the purchase of Dominion land. If they chose to sell to scrip buyers at discounted prices they would still have received in the neighbourhood of $540 cash in 1885 and $820 in 1886.

By the spring of 1886, it was apparent that Bobtail and his family would be leaving treaty to take scrip. By 25 June Lucas was busy taking evidence and writing applications[108] for discharge from treaty for Bobtail's party, including Jean-Baptiste Cardinal, Beehy Cardinal, Isabel Durand Cardinal, Betsy Cardinal, Monyue Dumais, Pierre Durand Miscenas, François Piché (Coyote), Alexis Piché (Bobtail), Susette Piché, Cécile Piché, Angèle Piché, Alexis Piché, Michael Piché, Marie Piché, and Baptiste Piché.[109]

By the fall of 1886 Bobtail's reserve was nearly empty. The pay sheets for his band lists only thirty-four individuals paid in October of 1886,[110] and Agent Lucas noted that only one to three families still worked the land.[111] By February of 1887, he reported that only two families of Bobtail's band farmed on the reserve; the rest stayed around Calgary and Blackfoot Crossing, coming back to the reserve only to draw their annuity monies.[112] That summer, however, a new dynamic emerged when Bobtail and some of his family and followers asked to be readmitted into treaty and allowed back onto their reserve. Hayter Reed, the assistant Indian commissioner, wrote to the superintendent general of Indian affairs in June of 1887, stating that Bobtail, who had been freighting for the Hudson's Bay Company, was now reputed to be destitute. In view of these circumstances, the condition of Bobtail's followers, and the obvious objections to leaving an indigent group of persons in a state of destitution away from controlling influences, the commissioner was of the opinion that it would be advisable to readmit Bobtail and his followers to the treaty, or at least to allow them to live on their old reserve, upon such terms as the department might deem proper to extend to them. If this were done and if annuity money were again paid to them, an amount should be retained equivalent to the value of the scrip they received.[113] This suggestion was approved by the superintendent general.[114]

In allowing Bobtail and his followers to return to treaty, however, the Indian commissioner exacted harder conditions than those that had been imposed on the Sandy Bay Band. Edgar Dewdney, the Indian commissioner, noted in his dispatch forwarding the agreement that in readmitting some members of the Bobtail band great care was exercised in taking only those whom the department considered would benefit by being treated as Indians.[115] Though readmitted to treaty in 1887, they would not be eligible for annuities until the department saw fit to do so, and they would have no claim to their former reserve lands.[116] While more draconian than most readmission arrangements, they did fall within the parameters set by the department. It instructed its agents that readmissions could be allowed, but none were precedents for "wholesale re-admissions," and it noted that each individual case had to be inquired into.[117]

Why the Bobtail band agreed to these hard conditions is not immediately clear, but T.P Wadsworth, the Indian inspector for Treaty 6, provides something of a clue. He noted that Bobtail's Indians were treated no differently than Treaty Indians, except that they had no regular occupation – they lived on the reserve, they drew rations, they did not work, and they left the reserve at will.[118] Eventually, Agent Lucas was instructed to encourage Bobtail's people to settle with Ermineskin's followers and to obtain the formal consent of that chief and the headmen of that band to this addition.[119] By 1890 the Bobtail band had been entirely absorbed into the Ermineskin and Samson bands.

Another pattern of ethnic positioning along the treaty/scrip continuum was the example of Chief Papaschase and his band in Treaty 6.[120] Although there is no documentary evidence of this band's having existed prior to the treaty period, it did sign an adhesion to Treaty 6 in 1877 and was granted a reserve just south of the Edmonton settlement. From fur trade and Métis scrip records it is possible to determine that a good number of the band members, including Papaschase and his family, were Métis of Cree origin. According to Richard Hardisty, the chief factor of Fort Edmonton, Papaschase and his family had lived at Lesser Slave Lake until 1855, where they worked as tripmen on the boats of the Hudson's Bay Company (HBC) between Edmonton and York Factory. After 1855 they had gradually settled near Edmonton, where they farmed a little, hunted, and worked intermittently for the HBC.[121] In this they pursued a way of life that straddled the more sedentary lifestyle of the Métis of St Albert and the more mobile Plains and Wood Cree. In his scrip application of 1886 Papaschase identified himself as John Quinns Gladu, born at Lesser Slave Lake in 1838 to John Quinns or Kwenis and Lizette, both "half-breeds."[122] Supporting the contention that Papaschase's band was a product of the treaty-making process (formed at treaty time to secure a separate reserve) is that fact that the other members of the band who were not part of Papaschase's extended family came from many different points in Alberta and Saskatchewan.[123] Richard Hardisty noted about the Indians around Fort Edmonton who took treaty in 1877: "the main tie ... which binds the Cree band is residential juxtaposition of the Individual at the time the band was formed. Most of its members might with equal propriety belong to any band other than that with which they are actually connected. They form a heterogeneous assemblage."[124]

The reasons for entering treaty in 1877 would have been similar to those of the thousands of Métis who took treaty between 1871 and 1885. The buffalo were nearly gone from the Canadian territories, other game resources were disappearing, and freighting opportunities were declining as the railway moved westward. Treaty, in the absence of any scrip program in the North-West Territories, offered the best prospect of aid and land to establish a new way of life. Those Métis and Indians unaffiliated with a band would either have to join other bands going into treaty or create their own. It is likely the latter option is what occurred in 1877 when the Papaschase band signed an adhesion, with John Quinn / Papaschase as its chief.[125]

When Métis scrip became available in 1885, offering a means to acquire both land and money without a wardship relationship to the federal government, almost the entire Papaschase band chose to withdraw from treaty and become "Métis." Though we don't know the specific reason why Papaschase chose to leave treaty, we do know that he, his family, and a large majority of his band were adamant that they be allowed to do so. It is also clear that life on the reserve south of Edmonton was not living up to its promise. There was a high rate of turnover in the membership of the band,[126] and in comparison to the other reserves and bands in the Edmonton district the Papaschase band was making little progress in agriculture.[127] While only a few families opted out of treaty in 1885, this turned into a large-scale exodus in 1886, as fully 100 members withdrew and applied for scrip that year.[128] Including Chief Papaschase and his family, this withdrawal constituted well over half of the band and all of the headmen. When the flood of applications to leave treaty became known, the Indian Department tried to slow the exodus,[129] but Papaschase and his band members were adamant that they were "half-breeds" and that they be allowed to leave treaty and take scrip.[130] This concerted pressure convinced the Indian Department to allow Papaschase and his family to leave treaty and take scrip.

These withdrawals left only ten adult men, twenty-five women, and forty-five children in the band; without most of their former leadership, they requested to be transferred to the Enoch band with whom they were paid during the 1887 annuity payments.[131] The Papaschase band thus ceased to exist in any practical sense and the Indian agent for the district was instructed to obtain a surrender of the Papaschase Reserve from the remaining members of the band. This proved to be difficult, as only three voting male members of the band resided on the Enoch Reserve and the rest lived on other reserves or elsewhere.[132] The agent eventually secured a surrender in 1888 signed by the three men living on the Enoch Reserve.[133] In contrast to the Sandy Bay and Bobtail band histories, Papaschase band members did not apply for re-entry into treaty. According to one source, Papaschase was living in the Métis colony at St Paul des Métis in the early twentieth century.[134]

Conclusion

The movement of individuals between treaty and scrip categories was more or less closed off in 1901 when, in the aftermath of the Treaty 8 and North-West Scrip Commissions of 1899 and 1900, the government realized that to permit movement between treaty and scrip would forever leave open the issue of scrip. For this reason, the taking of treaty or scrip became a once-and-for-all decision. Although the Métis were generally given the choice of extinguishment by treaty or scrip, once they chose, they were bound by their choice. If they chose to enter treaty and thereafter received their discharge, they became ordinary citizens of the country with no claims to scrip, as their Aboriginal claims had been extinguished.[135] The Department of the Interior did make some exceptions to this rule, granting scrip to former treaty recipients after

1901, but these cases were treated as special and each was dealt with by a separate Order In Council. Increasingly, after 1900, the economic and social problems of the Métis would be managed by the creation of Métis colonies. The first of these was that of St Paul des Métis (see chapter 10).

The mix-up over treaty and scrip categories that had dogged the government between 1871 and 1899 was significant in several respects. In the process of settling this issue the government began to clearly define what constituted Métis ethnicity and how this ethnicity or status related to treaty Indians. More important for the Métis, government policies related to treaty and scrip forced them to choose who they were (status Indian or Métis), and as a result created a new process of Métis self-definition. In leaving treaty to take scrip, Métis individuals were required to affirm that they were Métis; they named their parents and children (living and dead), and they noted all the places they had lived and where their children had been born. Person by person, family by family, they articulated a collective consciousness and identity that affected their families and communities for generations. That some would change their minds and re-enter treaty is not surprising, but increasingly this option was closed to them after 1900.

9 The United States / Canada Border and the Bifurcation of the Plains Métis, 1870–1900

The Plains Métis had been a borderland people in the British west and American west for more than fifty years prior to the 1870s, and to the extent that they recognized the border as a meaningful entity it was a British/Canadian or American construct to be manipulated. The Métis lived, worked, and hunted on both sides of the line and recognized its existence only when it was to their benefit. After 1870, however, the border began to play an ever increasing role in their consciousness and identity. As the buffalo began retreating both westward and southward, and as the American and Canadian governments began to police and patrol the border with increased vigilance, the Métis became drawn into what Richard Maxwell Brown has called the "Western Civil War of Incorporation."[1] This "Civil War," which created an ordered capitalistic society in the west between 1850 and 1910, had a distinctly international aspect on the northern plains, as this was the time when the international boundary was surveyed, patrolled, and defended. It was thus both a war of incorporation that created two countries out of a single region and a war that involved the Canadian state as well as the United States. It is a process that can be profitably seen as a bifurcation of the Plains Métis.

Prior to the 1870s the American/British border on the northern plains was of little consequence to the Métis who exploited the buffalo herds in this region. The Plains Métis who first came to prominence in the Red River / Pembina region began to spread westward in the 1840s and 1850s as the buffalo began to withdraw from the more easterly parts of the northwestern plains and as the number of the Red River Métis began to increase rapidly.[2] By the 1850s and 1860s their wintering villages could be found anywhere in the ecological zone where the buffalo wintered, irrespective of the international boundary (see figure 9.1).

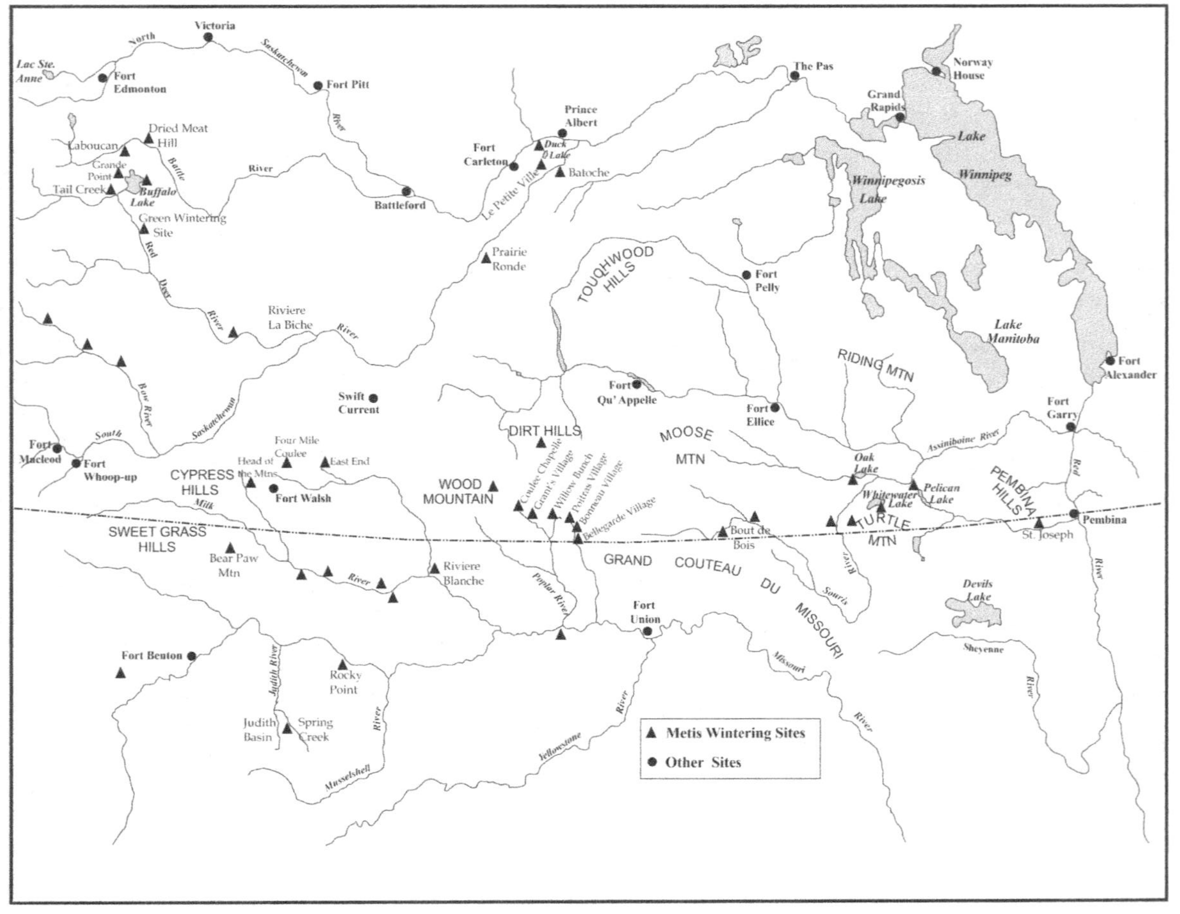

9.1 Métis wintering sites on the Northwestern Plains, 1840s to 1880s.

The Convention of 1818 that had established the 49th parallel as the boundary between the United States and the British possession went largely unrecognized by the Native peoples of the northern plains. For the Métis the main repercussion was that the Hudson's Bay Company (HBC), realizing that their Pembina post along the border was now in American territory, moved it to the Red River Settlement and put pressure on the Roman Catholic Church to relocate its mission at Pembina to Red River, bringing the Métis with them. The HBC feared that if left at Pembina the Métis would take advantage of their new citizenship to flout the company's monopoly and go into the trade themselves. Even though the majority of the Pembina Métis did relocate to Red River in the British territory, they lived and hunted where they wished and where it was safe to do so. Given that the Plains Métis way of life was almost wholly dependent on the buffalo – they acted as provisioners for the fur trade and later became heavily involved in the buffalo-robe trade[3] – they travelled as far as necessary to find the herds they needed. In the 1830s, 1840s, and 1850s they hunted in Sioux territory as far south as Devils Lake and as far west as the Grand Coteau. They had permanent villages in the Red River Settlement, Pembina, and St Joseph, but by the 1840s, 1850s, and 1860s they were hunting as far west as Turtle Mountain, the Souris River Basin, Wood Mountain, Milk River, and the Cypress Hills, and the distance from their former villages necessitated the establishment of temporary wintering villages near the buffalo. From the 1840s onward these wintering villages stretched from the Souris (Mouse) River in the east to the Cypress Hills in the west, and from Devils Lake in the south to the North Saskatchewan River in the north.

These wintering villages provided Métis traders with a secure base of operations to trade with the various bands of Plains Indians in the region, and they provided the Métis buffalo hunters with safety and a community where they could live with their families, who constituted the labour for the production of buffalo robes. The size of these communities could vary in size from a few families to large encampments with hundreds of inhabitants. In September of 1845, Father Belcourt, travelling with the Red River buffalo hunt to the Sheyenne River, noted a considerable group of Métis around the Souris River, where they had established their hivernant camps.[4] Five years later, Belcourt again noted a concentration of Métis around the area of Turtle Mountain and on the Souris plain. They were in the process of gathering their winter provisions and erecting their winter shelters. He noted

9.2 Métis wintering site at Wood Mountain, 1872–74. Archives of Manitoba, Boundary Commission (1872–74) 170 (N14103).

30 houses at the foot of Turtle Mountain, another 15–20 families further up the mountain, and as many as 400 Métis camped on or near the Souris River. They located here in winter because of the abundance of buffalo, which also found winter shelter and pasturage in this locale.[5] These encampments consisted of huts, roughly constructed but adequate to protect them from the weather and to afford them room for goods and furs. They also had to settle in sufficient numbers to protect themselves from hostile bands of Sioux, Assiniboine, and Blackfoot. They built their cabins in late fall and abandoned them in spring when they returned to the Red River Settlement or American trading centres to trade their furs and robes. They would spend a month completing their business and then leave for the plains to take part in the summer buffalo hunt or return to their wintering quarters. Often they returned to the same site year after year when the buffalo remained in the area.

The basic social and material components of these hivernant villages were much the same across the western interior, particularly in the vicinity of the 49th parallel. Most consisted of Métis hunters and their families, a few Métis traders, and by the 1850s a mission priest at the larger sites. The houses that sheltered this population were rude shanties built very quickly using only an axe and a crooked knife. These shanties were virtually identical to each other and consisted of one room. They were built of rough poplar or spruce logs mortised at the corners of the building. The walls were approximately six feet high in front and a little over five feet behind. A large clay fireplace or chimney took up the space of one of the exterior walls. Doors and windows were simply cut out of the solid log walls, and a door could be built from the boards of a cart. Windows consisted of a piece of parchment, and the roof was covered with straight poles, over which was placed a thatch of marsh grass weighed down with loose earth. The lowness of the building was sometimes ameliorated by digging out the ground for two feet.[6] Wealthier traders living in these villages, however, would have multi-room dwellings with gabled roofs. These dwellings were often the site of religious services and dances and accommodated not only the trader's retinue of relatives and followers, but also his trade goods. He usually had a second dwelling to serve as a storehouse for gunpowder, furs, robes, leather, and provisions.[7]

From the time the Métis began expanding southwestward in the 1830s there were almost yearly conflicts with Sioux and some major

9.3 A larger cabin at a Métis wintering site at Wood Mountain, circa 1874. LAC, George M. Dawson fonds, C-81781.

battles.[8] By 1858, however, the Chippewa (Ojibwa), Métis, and Dakota met in a Grand Council north of the Sheyenne River and west of Devils Lake to set tribal boundaries and establish peace among the three groups. The Métis were recognized as a legitimate band in the region and were represented by Jean-Baptiste Wilkie (aka Norbexxa) of St Joseph and were given the right to hunt in Sioux territories.[9] The other factor that diminished Sioux/Métis conflicts was the "Minnesota Massacre" of 1862 ,which put the Sioux at war with the U.S. Army. The Sioux needed allies among the British Métis, who were their main trade source for guns and ammunition, and in 1863 the Sioux travelled to St Joseph to reaffirm the peace treaty. Although these treaties significantly reduced the hostilities between the Sioux and Métis and allowed the Métis access to buffalo hunting grounds north and south of the border, the expansionary nature of both the Métis and Sioux in these years led to sporadic conflicts into the 1870s.[10]

Prior to the 1870s the border was no impediment to the Métis, who manipulated it for their own purposes. For example, when the Red River Métis heard that the American government was planning to negotiate a treaty with the Pembina and Red Lake Chippewa, many decided to relocate to the American side of the boundary to take advantage of the benefits of this treaty.[11] During the negotiations the Métis claimed that "it was they who possessed the country really, and who had long defended and maintained it against the encroachments of enemies."[12] However, the treaty that was signed between the United States and the Pembina Chippewa on 20 September 1851 did not include the Métis as signatories, as the government believed it should not treat with people whom it regarded "as our *quasi* citizens." The government negotiator did stipulate that he would not object "to any just or reasonable arrangement or treaty stipulation the Indians might choose to make for their benefit." As a result, the Chippewa inserted a clause into the treaty that $30,000 be given to their Métis relatives.[13] The treaty was not ratified by Congress, however, and many of those who had claimed U.S. residence returned to the Red River Settlement in British territory.[14] The Métis's cavalier attitude to the border was expressed more explicitly to General Isaac Stevens, who, while exploring a route for a railway from the Dakota Territory to Puget Sound, encountered a number of Métis buffalo-hunting camps on the Dakota plains in the summer of 1853. The first group he met was from Pembina, but the second group, led by a hunt chief named De L'orme (Delorme), had come from the Red River Settlement in British territory. He told Stevens that they had a right to hunt in American territory, being residents of the territory on both sides of the boundary line. Stevens reported:

> they claim the protection of both governments, and the doubt as to the position of the boundary makes them uncertain as to the government upon which they have the most claim. During the hunting season they carry with them their families and their property. Many children are born during these expeditions, and they consider that children born upon our soils during the transit possess the heritage of American citizens. Strongly impressed in favor of American institutions, they desire to be noticed by our government, and feel a desire to meet and confer with a commissioner sent by it to treat with them.[15]

By the 1860s the boundary was becoming of increasing importance. Advancing American settlement, Sioux hostilities in Minnesota, and the Canadian government's interest in acquiring the British northwest made the border a major factor in determining the responsibilities of the various governments in recognizing and protecting the rights of the various Indian groups in the region. As both the Métis and the Indians were increasingly using the border to shield themselves from reprisals by the 1870s, it is not surprising that both governments would want better control of the border region. Within a few years the western boundary between the United States and Canada had been surveyed, and both the U.S. Army and the Canadian North-West Mounted Police (NWMP) were patrolling the border, significantly limiting cross-border traffic. These factors, combined with the southwestward retreat of the buffalo, would increasingly force the Plains Métis to occupy wintering settlements south of the 49th parallel. In 1878 prairie fires swept a wide area of grassland in the boundary region between Montana and what today is Alberta. The buffalo moved south and what was left of the northern herd remained south of the border between the Milk River and the Judith Basin. The large herds never returned to Canada.[16] Not only were the last remnants of the northern herd increasingly concentrated in northern Montana, but escalating military vigilance along the international boundary by both the American Army and the NWMP forced the Métis to choose an American residence. While the American army and NWMP were primarily interested in stopping the arms and whisky trade that was stirring up Indian hostilities, this increased vigilance also ended the Métis practice of taking their buffalo robes across the border to American traders at Fort Benton.[17] Given these factors, it became much more convenient for the Métis to claim American residency.

9.4 Métis hunting camp on the plains, 1874. LAC, George M. Dawson fonds, C-81785.

9.5 Métis plains hunters in the 1870s. Archives of Manitoba, Boundary Commission (1872–1874) 215 (N14134).

9.6 Métis plains traders in the 1870s. LAC, Natural Resources Canada fonds, C-004164.

The Plains Métis had begun wintering in Montana in the 1860s, locating their communities on the Milk River where the Rivière Blanche (Frenchman's Creek or Whitemud Creek) branches off into Canada.[18] By the early 1870s Métis settlements were springing up all over the Milk River country. Father Lestanc, who had built a mission at Wood Mountain for the Plains Métis, was forced to relocate to Montana, as most of his group had left Wood Mountain. In 1871 he reported that there were sixty families wintering at Rivière Blanche and by 1873 his camp alone had ninety families. He noted that no one knew precisely where the border was or if they were living in American or Canadian territory.[19] George M. Dawson, travelling with the British Boundary Commission in 1874, met numerous Métis groups between Wood Mountain and Montana and noted that Wood Mountain had "seen its palmy days. Buffalo & Indians already too far west. Most of the families speak of wintering next at Cypress Hills."[20] On 19 July 1874, he visited a Métis camp on the Milk River that numbered 200 lodges and 2,000 horses. This group of Plains Métis was wintering on Rivière Blanche well within the United States, and he observed that they traded their goods via the Missouri River posts.[21]

The presence of these Canadian Métis in Montana worried the U.S. Army and Indian agents. Convinced that the Métis from Canada were trading whisky and guns to the Sioux and using the border to shield themselves, the U.S. Army resolved to eliminate this traffic.[22]

A.J. Simmons, the Indian agent at the Milk River Agency in Montana reported:

> the halfbreeds are building winter quarters on Frenchmans creek, about forty-five miles from the Agency and about ten miles north of Milk river and about the same distance more or less above the junction of said creek with Milk river. That two white men name Geo Fisher and Kerley were with them: that forty carts from the north had arrived there loaded with goods and liquor: that Geo Fisher was expected daily with upwards of twenty carts from Pembina loaded principally with liquor and that Kerley had gone to some point on the Missouri river below with ten carts for ammunition and liquors and was expected to return about the 20th instant.
>
> This information is reliable and this gang of illicit traders and outlaws must be suppressed at whatever trouble or expense. They are building houses for winter quarters where these supplies will be stored and from thence they will send small trading outfits to all the Indian camps, their

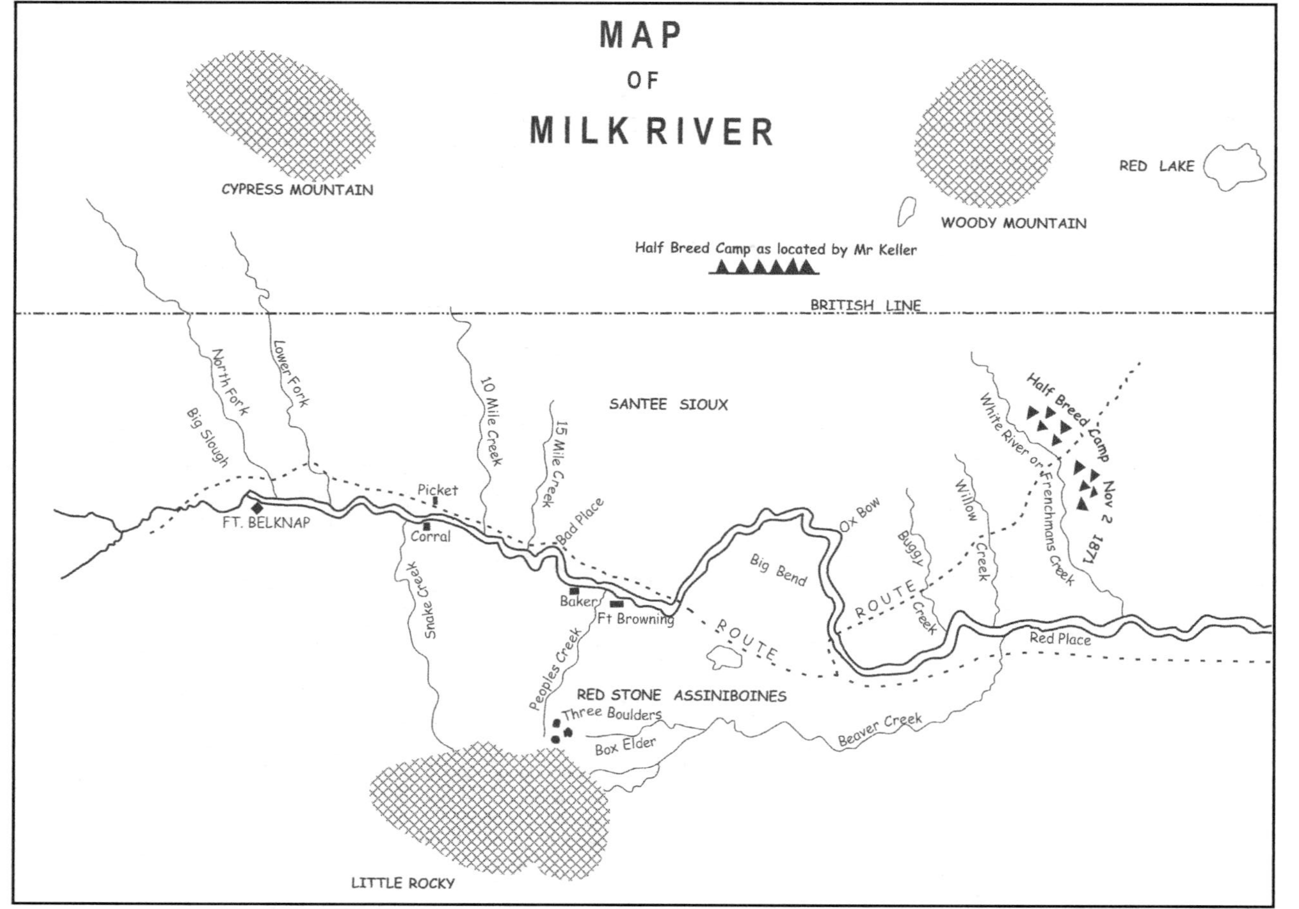

9.7 Sketch of the Milk River Region.

> principal articles of traffic being liquors and ammunition. They will supply the peaceable Indians who can get ammunition from their traders with liquor in exchange for horses and robes and then encourage them to steal other horses from the whites and they will furnish the Teton Sioux and other hostile bands with ammunition with which to make war upon us. Their influence with these Indians is great and they incite them to mischief and depredations upon our citizens, having urged Sitting Bull to resist the construction of the North Pacific Rail Road. So long as Sitting Bull's people remain hostile they have the exclusive trade and barter with them from which they derive large profits and so long as these Indians can procure ammunition from this source, it will be found a serious obstacle in the way of their effecting peace with the Government.[23]

On 19 October 1871, the 7th Infantry, stationed at Fort Shaw, was ordered to proceed to the Milk River, where this large group of "British" Métis had established their wintering villages. The 7th Infantry was ordered to destroy all trade goods, and drive the Métis out of the country. The army arrived at the Rivière Blanche on 1 November, where they found a camp of several hundred Métis. The settlement, consisting of houses and lodges scattered along four or five miles of the river, was burned as well as the whisky and trade goods valued at $10,000, and John Kerley was arrested. The Métis were told that they were in violation of American law by selling liquor and ammunition to Indians and were thereby helping the Indians to make war on the United States. They were ordered to leave the country and not return. The Métis, for their part, argued that the whisky and ammunition were the property of American traders who had only recently joined them, and they had lived on the plains (including the United States) all their lives. Besides, they argued, they could not move north, as the plains were burnt. They begged to be allowed to remain, promising they would allow no traders among them. In consideration of their good conduct on this occasion and realizing that the destruction of the entire camp would have inflicted great hardship and suffering, the army allowed the Métis to remain in their settlement if they obeyed American laws.[24] These problems, however, did not end in 1871[25] and, until the buffalo finally disappeared in 1882, both the American army and the North-West Mounted Police tried to nationalize their respective Native groups. These nationalizing campaigns resulted in an extended crisis for the Plains Métis, which eventually forced them to choose either an American or a Canadian residence and nationality.

By the late 1870s, with both governments trying to keep their Natives on reserves/reservations and having to deal with the hostile Sioux led by Sitting Bull, the Métis were again seen as a problem by the American authorities. By 1878 complaints began coming into army headquarters from U.S. officers and Indian agents that the "Canadian" Métis, camped along the Milk River below the Fort Peck Reservation of the Gros Ventres and Assiniboine, were keeping the buffalo away from the reservation Indians, who were starving and too afraid to hunt below for fear of the Sioux. These reports noted there were up to 500 Métis settled on the Milk River, that they were favourably disposed to the Sioux, and that, given these conditions, they should be expelled from American territory.[26] On the basis of these reports Major Guido Ilges was dispatched in the late fall of 1878 to arrest, confiscate the goods of, and remove the Canadian Métis wintering near Fort Browning and Medicine Lodge. On the basis of these orders Major Ilges captured a camp of Métis coming from the Big Bend on the Milk River, where they had been hunting with the Teton Sioux. Ilges noted that all the party were "foreigners" and consisted of forty-six Métis. He confiscated forty carts, eighty horses, and fourteen rifles. To make an example of them he escorted the party to the border and warned them never to return, and subsequently, he burnt their winter homes on the Milk River. He then turned over the captured property to the U.S. deputy marshal.[27]

The problem was not that easy to settle. Most Métis considered themselves to be Natives of both countries and many had been born on American soil. A further complication was the connection of some Métis to the Assiniboine bands living on the Fort Peck Reservation, whose families requested that their Métis relatives be allowed to stay. Assiniboine chiefs and Agent Lincoln from the Fort Peck Reservation requested that Gabriel Azure and Pierre Berger and their followers (forty families) be allowed to remain below the forks and hunt on the north side of the Milk River.[28] As a result of the Métis determination to continue to hunt the buffalo on American soil and the American Army's inability to continually patrol the border meant that the Métis continued to winter in the Milk River area and either evaded the army patrols or claimed American citizenship. In 1879, when 140 Métis were stopped by the U.S. Army in Montana and asked what nationality they were, all but ten replied they were American. The ten, who declared they were British, were escorted across the border, and the others were advised to go to the Judith Basin.[29]

The final act in this drama was played only after almost all the major buffalo herds had been destroyed in 1881–82. The Métis played a cat and mouse game with the American Army between 1878 and 1881, slipping into Canada when the army pursued and then returning to hunt when the soldiers retreated to their posts;[30] the game became economically and tactically untenable when the most of the buffalo disappeared. By early 1882 there were only a few small herds left, and consequently it was relatively easy for the U.S. Army to locate Métis wintering camps. One of the last substantial herds was located near the Big Bend on the Milk River and both Métis and Cree were camped nearby. As these camps kept the buffalo away from agency Indians, they were seen to be creating great hardships for Indians on U.S. reservations. Shortly thereafter the American secretary of state wrote to the British authorities proposing a policy whereby both Canada and the United States would compel both their Indians and Métis to stay on their own side of the border. The U.S. secretary of state noted that he concurred with the army that force should be used to relocate trespassing Canadian Natives.[31] To this end another army expedition was sent to the locality in the spring of 1882. Finding a number of Métis wintering villages on the creeks and rivers north of Milk River from Price's Crossing to Campbell's Houses (primarily of the Rivière Blanche and Rock Creek), the army burnt the cabins and drove the Métis across the Canadian border towards Wood Mountain. In all, the U.S. Army burnt 296 cabins that spring.[32]

By 1882 the buffalo herds had disappeared, even in Montana. This represented a real crisis for the Plains Métis and they were faced with hard decisions as to what to do next. Those who had close kinship connections to tribal groups in Montana, such as the Blackfoot and Flathead, went into treaty and tribal society.[33] Some Métis who had come to Montana from Manitoba and North Dakota went back and reinvented themselves as the Turtle Mountain Chippewa and took treaty in 1892.[34] Others moved north to Canada and took scrip[35] after 1885, but a large number remained in Montana and refused to leave.[36]

Those Plains Métis who remained in Montana after 1882 did so not only because there were employment opportunities, but also because a significant number had come to see the United States as a homeland – something the Canadian northwest no longer was. By the late 1870s and early 1880s the border had become more than a line on a map; it had become something of a state of mind with its own mythology. This new way of looking at the border and the Canadian northwest had begun shortly after the Riel Resistance in Red River and the transfer of the British northwest to Canada in 1870, and it crystallized with the military suppression of the Riel Rebellion in the northwest in 1885.

With the arrival of troops in Red River in the summer of 1870, the increasing pace of Canadian immigration to Manitoba, and the delays in fulfilling the land grants to the Métis promised in the Manitoba Act, many of the Plains Métis came to believe that they had been treated unjustly by the Canadian government. This feeling only increased, as the government was slow to acknowledge Métis rights in the northwest. By 1873 numerous reports were coming back to Alexander Morris, the lieutenant governor of Manitoba and the North-West Territories, that the Indians and Métis of the Canadian northwest were full of anxiety and uneasiness regarding the intentions of the Canadians towards them. Robert Bell, who wrote a report for Morris on the state of the west, noted that the notion that "the English have ceased to be their friends appears to be fostered and [illegible] if not promoted by the half breeds." The Métis, he wrote, wanted nothing to do with surveys, treaties, railways, or settlement, and they considered the Canadians cowards.[37] When Pascal Breland was appointed by the Canadian government to undertake a mission to investigate the presence of the Sioux at Wood Mountain, he met with numerous Plains Métis who would eventually settle in Montana.[38] He was informed that the state of affairs on the plains was critical and dangerous. In regard to the Métis, Edward McKay told him that the Métis, who lived and hunted on both sides of the border, had little respect for and trust in the Canadian government and were close to taking the law into their own hands. They were spreading rumours that the government wanted to exterminate the Indians and rob them of their country. The Métis, he said, "have so little public spirit that it is utter nonsense to depend on them for assistance." Talk of their being loyal, he said,

> is outrageous as the majority don't know what it means and most of them scorn the idea. If they do not display their disloyalty on all occasions it is only because they are sometimes afraid. Louis Riel is still their idol and should he or any smart fellow come out to lead them there will be a grand row ... They do their utmost to throw difficulties in the way of the peaceful settlement of the country and if they do not break into open rebellion it is only for want of the occasion and through fear. They are becoming bolder every day under the inactive policy of the government and if the call be given a rebellion worse in every respect than the last will spread like a fire on the plains.[39]

Many of the most troublesome Métis, he noted, were those who had left the British territory several years ago and had since been living on the American side. They had recently returned to Wood Mountain to excite the Métis and Indians against the Canadian government and British rule. They promised assistance from the United States if the Métis and Indians refused to permit the Dominion from disposing of their lands.[40]

This discontent was evident as far north as St Albert on the North Saskatchewan River. A large group of St Albert Métis wintering at Buffalo Lake told Bishop Grandin in 1875: "we know too well that we have nothing to hope from the Canadian Government except ill-will and contempt. The facts which have occurred, and are still taking place, at Red River are proof of it. Rather than be ill treated (brow-beaten) like our parents, we have decided to locate ourselves on the territories of the United States. With that object, we have chosen an excellent place, where we shall soon fix ourselves, if you will allow us a priest." Grandin refused this request, but noted that the Métis were still planning to head south and cross the border when the time was right.[41]

These simmering hostilities continued through the 1870s and, when Louis Riel returned to the west in 1878, he quickly saw the potential for a new offensive against the Canadian state. From his base in Carroll, Montana (a settlement in the heart of the badlands or "breaks" of the Upper Missouri near the Judith Basin), Riel planned an invasion of Canada by the Métis allied to various Indian bands. This invasion would be the prelude to the establishment of a confederacy of Métis and Indians in the Canadian northwest.[42] Riel immediately sent for Ambroise Lépine, his former adjutant general from Red River days, who agreed to meet Riel at Fort Assiniboine in late 1879 or early 1880. Archbishop Taché, knowing that Lépine had gone west to meet Riel and aware of the potential trouble the two could create, immediately contacted Lépine and warned him against meeting Riel. Not wanting to offend the Catholic Church and aware of the risk to his own safety if he got involved with him again, Lépine returned to Manitoba without meeting Riel. As he wrote to Taché, it would not take a very large spark to light a fire in the west, as the Métis were very unhappy with how they were being treated by the Canadian government.[43] To Riel he wrote that he was not prepared to sacrifice more for the Métis, as he had already seen the noose at close hand and was not prepared to risk all again.[44]

Riel was just as unsuccessful in convincing the Montana Métis and Indians to support his plan, and after a year or two he moved on to other projects.[45] Riel's plan to attack Canada and establish a Métis and Indian confederacy, farfetched as it may have been, does indicate the degree of Métis discontent with the Canadian government and provides some explanation of why the Métis of Montana had no interest in returning to Canada after the buffalo had disappeared.

These Montana Métis, the remnant of the buffalo-hunting Plains Métis, settled in a variety of railway towns along the line of the Great Northern Railway (Fort Buford, Poplar, Oswego, Wolf Point, Havre, Chinook, Harlem, Malta, Glasgow, Kipp, and Box Elder). Given that the Great Northern ran parallel to the Milk River, some of these towns such as Malta, Havre, and Glasgow were, in fact, very close to old Métis wintering sites. As railway towns they offered the Métis work as construction workers, dirt movers, and wood choppers, and for a time there was money to be had in collecting buffalo bones. Others settled away from railway centres where it was still possible to hunt small game and farm (Dupuyer, Teton River, Sweetgrass, and Choteau). Still others settled at Lewistown, Fort Benton, St Peters, St Ignatius, Augusta, Hill, and Fort McGinnis, homesteading and working as labourers on ranches and farms and in freighting.[46] Some indication of the distribution and concentration of these settlements of Plains Métis in Montana can be observed in figure 9.8.[47]

One of the larger Métis settlements in Montana was located in the Judith Basin at Spring Creek (now known as Lewistown). It was settled by Plains Métis buffalo hunters led by Pierre Berger. These families originated in the Red River / St Joseph region of Manitoba and North Dakota. As the buffalo retreated westward, this Métis band[48] had relocated first to Wood Mountain, and then to Milk River. By 1879 they were wintering on the Milk River between Harlem and Chinook, but as the herds were growing smaller every year Pierre Berger began looking for a better location to winter, one where his people might settle permanently. The larger wintering camps on the Milk were breaking up, so Berger and twenty-five families decided to move to the Judith Basin, where the last big herds were located and where there were other smaller game and plenty of timber.[49] Here they hunted the buffalo and, when they disappeared, took up homesteads. Within a few years they were joined by other Plains Métis hunters from the Milk River, increasing the settlement to more than 150 families. The latter group had been told by the American Army to either leave the country or settle somewhere

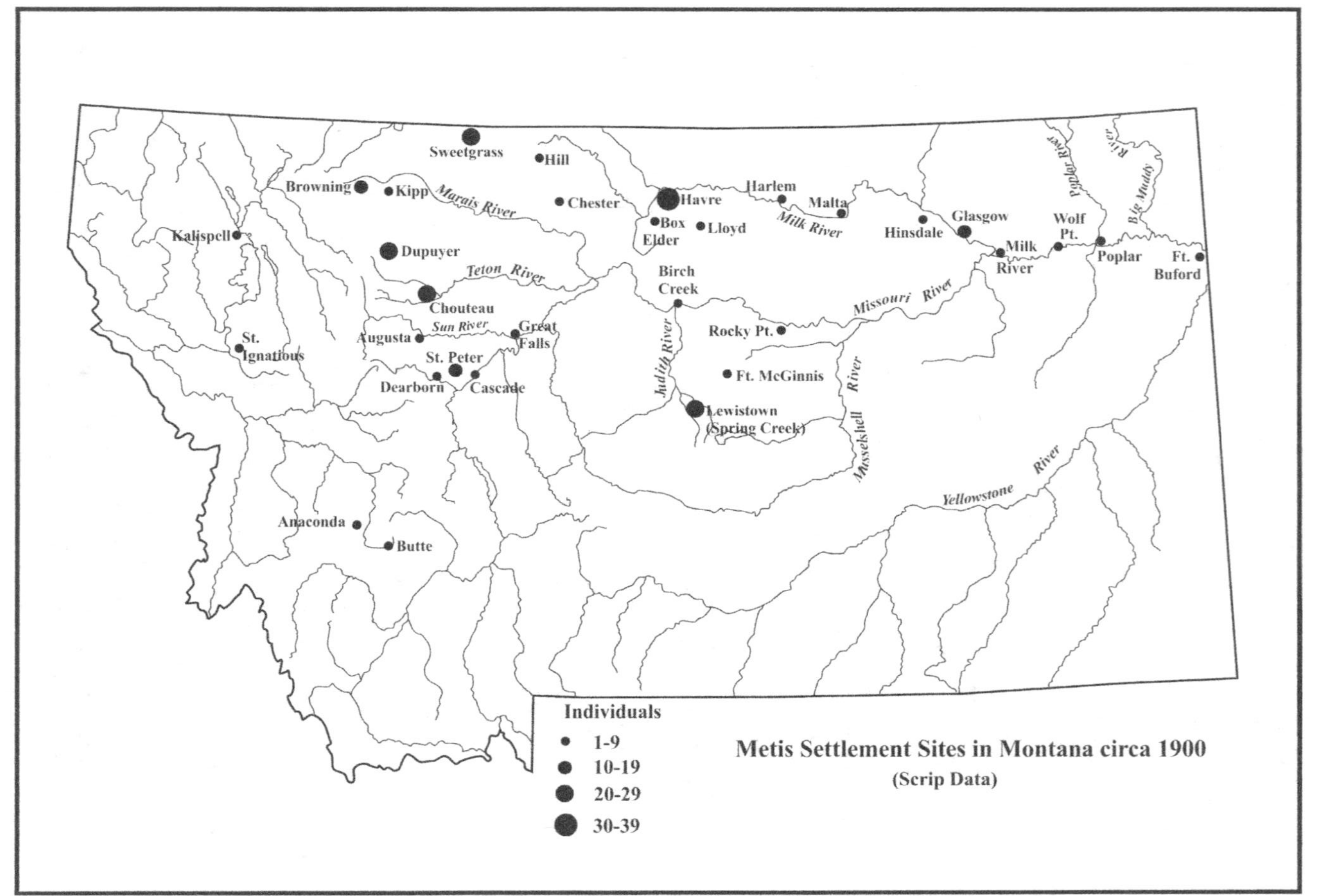

9.8 Locations of Métis settlements in Montana, circa 1900. LAC, NW Métis Scrip Applications.

permanently.[50] These Métis raised stock or worked on area ranches after more settlers moved in.

The crystallizing event that changed a trans-border people into the Montana Métis who regarded the border as protection from the Canadian government was the 1885 Northwest Rebellion. After the Canadian military crushed Riel's forces at Batoche in the spring of 1885, hundreds of Indians and Métis fled south to escape the prosecution they were sure would follow. These Métis, settling among the Métis who had been in Montana for at least a decade and a half, reinforced the mythology of the evils of the Canadian government. Approximately sixty Métis refugee families settled on Dupuyer Creek south of the Blackfoot Reservation,[51] and another group chose the south fork of the Teton River near Choteau. Hiding in the canyons for fear of being sent back to Canada, these Métis lived off the land, hunting small game, "woodhawking," selling buffalo bones, and working on area ranches and farms.[52] Their anti-Canadianism and fear of deportation stayed with the Montana Métis for good reason. In 1896 the American government decided to solve the social problems created by these "indigent" Canadian-born Cree and Métis by forcibly shipping them back to Canada. In all, 537 persons were shipped by rail to Canada, but almost all returned, slipping back across the border over the next few weeks.[53]

Those Plains Métis who settled permanently in Montana had been transformed, over the course of a decade and a half, from a borderland people into American Métis. They willingly and deliberately chose an American residence and citizenship at least in part because of their belief that they had suffered an injustice at the hands of the Canadian government, and that their rights and livelihood were better protected in the United States. This, despite the fact that the American government did not recognize the Métis as a separate group and accorded them no special political or economic rights. By 1885 the border had assumed almost mythical status as protection from prosecution by the Canadian state.

The action of choosing U.S. residence and citizenship had repercussions on how these Métis conceptualized their sense of identity. By the end of the first third of the twentieth century the American Métis identity had diverged or bifurcated in significant ways from those Métis living in Canada. Because the Manitoba Act and the various Métis scrip commissions had recognized that the Métis in Canada had some claim to Aboriginal title, Métis identity by the second half of the twentieth century increasingly came to be defined in political or constitutional terms.

While some of the American Métis were able to apply for scrip in Canada (as former residents), it gave them no Aboriginal status in the United States.[54]

In the immediate aftermath of the disappearance of the buffalo and the 1885 Riel Rebellion, life for Métis on either side of the U.S./Canadian border followed similar patterns. Families and communities adjusted to life after the buffalo and adapted to agriculture, ranching, labour on the railway, woodcutting, and other occupations, which included hunting and trapping where they were still viable. As Martha Harroun Foster,[55] Heather Devine,[56] and Brenda Macdougall[57] have shown, whether they lived in Montana, Alberta, or Saskatchewan, Métis identity continued to be located in the webs of kinship and family networks that provided them with economic and social stability and a sense of who they were.

With the increase of American and Canadian settlement in the transborder west, however, and the dominance of binary racial categories that emphasized "white" or "Indian" identities, terms such as "Métis" or "Michif" became problematic by the early twentieth century. As Martha Harroun Foster has noted: "For the Spring Creek Métis, like all Montana Métis, there was simply no opportunity or advantage to declare a Métis identity while fighting for rights as Native Americans or for U.S. citizenship. Even the words 'Métis,' 'Michif,' and 'Mitsif' went out of use and were seldom heard in Montana after the 1930s ... Denied a way to express their unique identity, negotiating an Indian identity came close to meeting their needs and self perceptions ... A private Métis identity survived, centered on strong kinship ties and a sense of community."[58]

Similar dynamics were also at work north of the U.S./Canada border, but in Canada the political and constitutional recognition that the Métis had a separate claim to Aboriginal land rights provided the space for political action and the political reformulation of Métis rights and identity. This is a space or arena that is investigated at some length in the later chapters of this book. It is also a dynamic that increasingly set the Canadian Métis apart from their counterparts in the United States.

PART FOUR

Economic Marginalization and the Métis Political Response, 1896 to the 1960s

Whatever the economic benefits of the various Métis scrip programs, and they did direct a significant amount of money to Métis families at a time when the plains economy was floundering, these programs did not achieve their primary economic purpose[1] – to provide a land base for the Métis in aid of their transition to a settled economy. Instead, almost all Métis sold their scrip (money and land) and relied on the homestead system to gain access to farmland if they desired it. Homesteading, however, required that improvements be made to the land in order to acquire a patent, and in the aftermath of the collapse of the Plains Métis economy (hunting, fishing, trading, freighting) due to the disappearance of the buffalo, rapid settlement, and the building of the railway, many Métis families were not able to prove up and became landless. This was not a case of a people unwilling to adjust to a new economy, but the result of an economic transformation that occurred with such overwhelming rapidity that many individuals and families simply could not adjust. Not only did the buffalo disappear after 1879, but the freighting economy was wiped out when the railway arrived in the 1880s. In the face of these calamities and new state regulations[2] that further impinged on the ability of the Métis to support themselves during this transition, many simply abandoned their homesteads for labour jobs or to move to the north where hunting and trapping were still viable.

It was in response to this crisis that Father Lacombe and the Catholic Church petitioned the federal government in 1895 to create a Métis reserve to "redeem" the landless Métis. The creation of this reserve, known as St Paul des Métis, would not become a matter of policy, as Indian reserves were, but was considered an act of charity. The reserve was not held in trust for the Métis by the Crown but was leased to the Catholic Church and left to its control. More important for the purpose of this study, the reserve had a debilitating effect on the way the Métis were perceived by outsiders and, in some cases, even by their own leaders. Designed to aid and rehabilitate the Métis and facilitate their transition to an agricultural economy, the administrators of St Paul des Métis established criteria that defined the Métis as "poor" and "landless" – that is, the Métis were seen less as an ethnic category or group and more in terms of a "social problem." This phenomenon of Métis as pathology and problem would remain a prominent feature of governmental interaction with the Métis throughout the first half of the twentieth century.

Although St Paul des Métis was dissolved in 1909, its precepts were resurrected with the formation of Métis settlements in Alberta in the 1930s and in Saskatchewan in the 1940s. In both instances the pretext was another financial and social crisis, and in both cases the Métis were defined in pathological terms. For the Plains Métis the economic crisis of the Great Depression was exacerbated by the Natural Resources Transfer Agreement (NRTA) of 1930, which transferred responsibility for natural resources from the federal government to the prairie provinces. For those Métis squatting on Crown land in northern Manitoba, Saskatchewan, and Alberta this move proved disastrous, as the provinces, anxious to expand agricultural productivity, opened vast expanses of Crown land to homesteading. While the Métis themselves could have taken advantage of these homesteading opportunities, it required capital they simply did not have, given the crash of commodity prices, particularly fur. They were doubly disadvantaged in that most were ineligible for direct relief, as residence provisions of the relief acts worked against trappers who lived outside organized districts or in areas too far remote to access relief even if they resided within organized districts.[3] These dynamics produced the misery and abject economic and medical conditions that pushed the governments of Alberta and Saskatchewan to reconsider the concept of Métis reserves.

The latter efforts, however, were different from St Paul des Métis in that the Métis had a greater role to play in the organization and control of such colonies, at least in Alberta. Largely powerless in the 1890s, when St Paul des Métis came into being, by the 1930s the Métis had political organizations that were in the forefront of advocating government intervention to help the poor and the landless Métis. The economic crisis of the late 1920s and the 1930s acted as a catalyst among Métis leaders and the culmination of this political activity was the formation of Métis colonies in Alberta and Saskatchewan. These political organizations would have a long-term influence on the resurgence of Métis political consciousness in Canada, but in the short term they demonstrated that Métis identity as pathology had been internalized by some Métis leaders.

This perception of Métis in terms of pathology continued into the 1950s, 1960s, and 1970s, when the provincial governments of Alberta, Saskatchewan, and Manitoba launched a series of studies investigating the conditions of native people in the northern parts of the provinces. This led to an invasion of academically trained investigators, mainly sociologists, economists, and anthropologists, who produced a series of government-commissioned reports designed to influence government policy in the north. Their findings and reports both were informed by and continued to reify the perception of the Native population, particularly the Métis, in pathological terms: "maladapted," "poverty-stricken," and so on. While these studies and reports did not always result in any perceptible government action, they had an impact on the perception of Métis by outsiders and by the Métis themselves.

10 St Paul des Métis Colony, 1896–1909: Identity as Pathology

The idea of a Métis reserve or colony did not originate with Father Lacombe in 1895. It had been a part of the Catholic Church's agenda since the negotiations leading to the Manitoba Act in 1870. This agenda was based on the belief that the Métis were by nature improvident and too attracted to the hunt to settle down and farm – a view shared by the Government of Canada. Viewed as children, it was believed they needed to be taught to accept agriculture. In 1869–70 both Bishop Taché and Father Ritchot believed that the lands the Métis received in Manitoba should be inalienable for a significant time. These ideas, inimical to the Métis, did not make their way into the Manitoba Act, but resurfaced when the federal government began considering extending Métis land rights into the North-West Territories in 1878.

The question, as noted earlier in chapter 6, was how best to satisfy these rights. While there was unanimity among those who advised the government not to issue negotiable scrip, which would quickly fall into the hands of speculators, there was no consensus on how the government should otherwise settle Métis claims.[4] As a result, the government did little more at this point than amend the Dominion Lands Act in 1879 to include an acknowledgment that the Métis of the North-West Territories had land rights by way of their claims to Indian title, and that the government would take steps to investigate these claims.[5] The decision to grant negotiable scrip in 1885 was brought about by the demands of the Métis to be treated like their brethren in Manitoba and the increasing scale of Métis agitation in late 1884, forcing the government to take some action.

The rebirth of the Métis colony idea arose in the aftermath of the 1885 Rebellion, when the disappearance of the buffalo combined with the building of the Canadian Pacific Railway (CPR) eliminated the traditional Plains Métis economy of hunting and freighting, and scrip, granted in the immediate aftermath of the Rebellion, had been mostly sold off. Father Lacombe, the indefatigable supporter of the Métis, made overtures to both his ecclesiastical superiors and government officials to do something to "rehabilitate" the Métis, who Lacombe now claimed were mostly "destitute." By 1895 Lacombe found supporters in both the Roman Catholic Church and the government. Government officials were becoming worried that a landless and destitute Métis population in the west spelt trouble. A.M. Burgess, the deputy minister of the interior, noted in 1895 that the advent of colonization and railway building west of Red River and contact with "a population 'superior' to themselves" had been "ruinous" to the Métis. He noted further that government policy had exacerbated the problem when Métis in treaty had been allowed to withdraw from treaty to take scrip. These Métis had proven unable to maintain themselves by their own independent exertions and remained "unfitted on the one hand by natural instincts to settle down to the pursuits and avocations of the white man, they are precluded on the other by their temperament from permanently joining the Indian tribes on their reserves without distinct disadvantage to both parties concerned." As a result, Burgess was compelled to concur with Father Lacombe that their condition was worse in every respect from that of the Indians, and that without amelioration he had "very grave apprehensions for the future." In consequence, he heartily endorsed Father Lacombe's proposal for a Métis colony as "an act of true charity and of humanity to make a final effort for the reclamation of these people."[6]

These views are perhaps not surprising, coming from a government official, but they were echoed, more or less, by Father Lacombe, the supposed defender of the Métis. In his proposal for a Métis colony, entitled "A Philanthropic Plan to Redeem the Half-Breeds of Manitoba and the North-West Territories," he noted that "the contact of that little nation with the white population has been fatal to the former" and that the future looked very dark, creating trouble and unease for the whole country. He acknowledged that the Métis were "well and justly treated" by the government "but unfortunately owing to their natural improvidence, they have wasted what they received." It is in this light that he humbly begged the government to endorse his plan "for the redemption of the half-breeds" – namely, a Métis colony.[7] While it might be expected that Lacombe would play up the fairness of the government and the improvidence of the Métis to gain governmental approval of his plan, these views are echoed in his other writings. In 1901, on a fund-raising mission in Quebec, he addressed his audience on the state and future of the Métis. Quick to defend the Métis from their detractors he praised their intelligence and ability to learn. They were, he said, generous to a fault and their hospitality was proverbial. His love for his people, however, did not blind him to their defects, the most prominent of which was the "facility with which they allow themselves to be drawn into pleasures of all kind." From this characteristic arose a considerable loss of time, a neglect of duties, and an inconstancy of character and lack of control, which rendered them fickle and improvident and deprived them of "a part of the numerous advantages that otherwise they could reap from the present conditions of the country." He did not attribute this to any innate flaw, but rather, that "the life of adventure, in which they had been brought up, had not prepared them to face the new order of things brought by foreign immigration and the disparition of the buffalo." The future, Lacombe noted, did not bode well for this race/nation. They seemed disinclined to farm and its labours filled them with disgust. As immigration increased in the prairies, the Métis gave way, and without help they would soon be without homesteads in their native land and would disappear. The remedy, Lacombe noted, would come from the Catholic clergy, who had gathered the Métis together in a colony, where they were given land but could neither sell nor mortgage it. It was a colony administered by the Catholic hierarchy, where the Métis would be taught domestic economy, trades, and especially farming.[8]

Here, in a nutshell, were both the problems and the legacy of the St Paul des Métis Colony. Grounded in a view of the Métis as a people unwilling to adjust to the new economy of the west, the administrators of the colony gave them no say in its organization or running, they assumed they knew better than the Métis about what was good for them, they gave them no ownership in the land (until the colony was closed), and when the colony "failed"[9] the fault was assumed to lie with the Métis themselves. This experiment in social engineering had defined the Métis as a crisis-ridden people in need of reclamation, and the failure of the experiment, in turn, left a legacy of seeing Métis ethnicity as pathology. There is a counter narrative, but it is one inimical both to the political concerns of the Métis today and to government and Church understanding of the experiment that was St Paul des Métis. This view holds that the Métis conceived the colony in very different terms than did the Catholic hierarchy. Based on Lacombe's promises they conceptualized it as an economic support mechanism that would allow them to follow their traditional pursuits – that is, their hunting, trapping, trading, freighting, and fishing. When the Church, more particularly the colony manager, failed to provide the support they expected, they blamed the failure of the experiment on the Church.

In telling this story we have paid a good deal of attention to the details of land management and occupation. These were important issues in the minds of the Church administrators of the colony, the whole purpose of which was to inculcate the ideals of a settled life and an agricultural economy. When the Métis who came to St Paul des Métis pursued a different agenda, the Catholic hierarchy gave up on the colony and decided to use the land to promote French-Canadian settlement. Established to wean the Métis from their "improvident" ways, the colony instead served to reinforce the Catholic Church's view of the Métis as nomadic, resistant to change, and beyond rehabilitation.

On the basis of Lacombe's and Burgess's views the federal government in 1896 enacted an Order in Council reserving four townships in the district of Alberta for the reclamation of the Métis of Manitoba and the North-West Territories.[10] This act, in effect, created the colony of St Paul des Métis along the lines requested by Father Lacombe. The one difference was that Lacombe had initially requested land in the Buffalo Lake District, but A.M. Burgess, the deputy minister of the interior, felt that this land was in too close "proximity to existing settlements, and the ever increasing demands for lands in that district by white settlers" would be counterproductive to rehabilitating the Métis. This land, Burgess believed, would be unsuitable for the purposes desired, and the Métis would be better served by "a tract of land outside of the territory to which the current immigration is now ... directed."[11] Indeed, he convinced Lacombe that a better site could be found east of Edmonton and north of the North Saskatchewan River. After some inspection Lacombe chose four townships (townships 57 and 58, Ranges 9 and 10 west of the fourth meridian – see figure 10.1) in the Egg Lake District. Lacombe considered this a good location because it was away from "white" settlement; it was good farmland; it had plenty of timber, hay, and water; and it was close to the Saddle Lake Indian Reserve, where the Catholic Church had a mission.[12] Under the terms of the Order in Council this land was leased for twenty-one years to the Roman Catholic Episcopal Corporations of St Boniface, St Albert, and Prince Albert; Father Lacombe; and two lay people named by the Catholic Church. The land could then be subleased to destitute Métis families in blocks of forty acres (later changed to eighty acres) under regulations established by the original lessees. Out of this land four sections were to be set aside for the Catholic Church to establish a residential school for the Métis.[13] The intent was to make the Métis self-supporting by agricultural training and education, but the land was retained by the Church so as to prevent the Métis from selling or bartering it.[14] Finally, the government allocated $2,000 to provide seed grain and implements for the most needy of those Métis who moved to the colony.[15]

Although Lacombe claimed to have letters from 200 Métis in the Dakotas and Montana who wanted to move to the colony,[16] only eight families were on the land by the fall of 1896.[17] Ten more families arrived in the spring of 1897 and by 1898 there were thirty-two families[18] in the colony. This number increased to eighty families in 1904, after which time the numbers went down before the colony was opened to general settlement in 1909.[19] These numbers suggest a less than enthusiastic reception by the Métis to the Oblate Plan, even at the peak of the colony's population. An examination of who settled St Paul, what their motivations were, to the extent that they can be determined, and the Métis complaints about how the colony was run help explain this anomaly.

According to Métis scrip applications taken from Métis at St Paul des Métis in 1900,[20] most came from the Edmonton / St Albert district (36 per cent), Battle River / Duhamel area (17 per cent), and Fort Pitt / Battleford region (14 per cent). A few Métis had been in treaty but had withdrawn after 1885, and a significant number were former plains buffalo hunters or the children of buffalo hunters.[21] While some were undoubtedly poor, there is evidence that many of the Métis who settled at St Paul were neither poor nor landless and a number had taken out homesteads prior to moving to St Paul. The question of why they came to St Paul des Métis then arises. An examination of those who came from Battle River / Duhamel provides something of an answer.

Duhamel (also known as the Laboucane Settlement) had its origins as a small Métis settlement in the mid- to late 1870s after the buffalo had disappeared from the Canadian prairies. A number of the buffalo-hunting Métis families from the Fort Edmonton region who used to winter at Buffalo Lake and Tail Creek established a settlement on the banks of the Battle River where it bisected the trail from Winnipeg to Fort Edmonton. These included the families of François Gabriel Dumont and Abraham Salois. Here it was possible to engage in small-scale horticulture, hunt and fish, trade in furs, and participate in the carting business on the trail

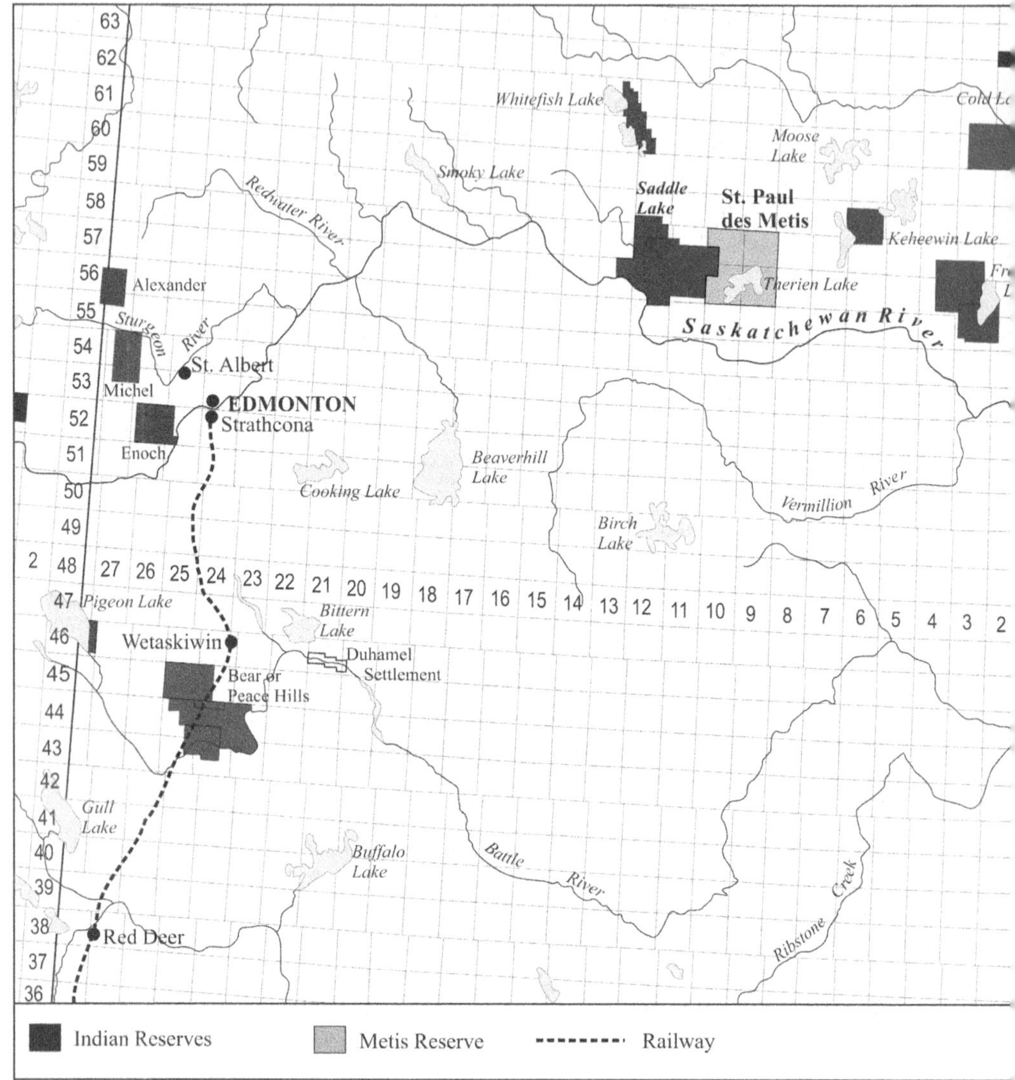

10.1 Location of St Paul des Métis relative to Edmonton and Indian reserves, circa 1896.

from Winnipeg to Edmonton. This settlement also became home to a number of prosperous Métis traders and merchants such as the Laboucane brothers.[22] According to Father Adéodat Thérien, the manager of the St Paul Colony for its entire history, Métis from Duhamel, including almost all of the prosperous Laboucane family, began moving to St Paul beginning in 1898. Their motivation, according to Thérien was that too many "white" settlers had moved into the Duhamel region, presumably ending all prospects of hunting and trapping, while the Calgary to Strathcona railway completed in 1891 had ended the freighting business in the area. After selling their land at Duhamel, they came to St Paul with cattle, horses, and presumably other assets.[23]

The question then turns to why the Métis were attracted to St Paul des Métis under the sponsorship of the Catholic Church when they were not permitted to own land in the colony. A number of answers are suggested by the activities that the Métis did participate in. At St Paul, a relatively unsettled area until 1904, it was still possible to hunt, and there was easy access to fishing lakes and trapping areas to the north. As well, there were labour opportunities with surveying parties that were busy in the region until 1907. Finally, until the Canadian Northern Railway was completed to Edmonton in 1905, there was freighting work between Vegreville and Edmonton. These factors suggest that for many of the Métis who moved to St Paul, farming was not a high priority and hence owning land was even less of a priority. The presence of the Catholic Church as the patron of the colony also was seen as providing services and material goods in times of need. This view is supported by the inspection report made in January of 1899 by A.A. Ruttan, a Dominion land surveyor. While Ruttan reported that the future prospects of the colony looked good, notwithstanding the scarcity of implements, his agricultural statistics do not add up to any kind of success. He reported that at the end of 1898 only 363 acres had been cultivated, including the mission farm; since there were forty families there in 1898, this averages out at only nine cultivated acres per family. Given these figures, it is not surprising that Ruttan noted that a significant portion of the food for the Métis families came from hunting and fishing.[24] It was other aspects of Ruttan's report, however, that provide an explanation for how the Métis saw the Church's role in their economic lives. In a meeting with the settlers, Ruttan noted that they did not like the day school in the colony, which did not serve their purposes. They needed a boarding school, they said. They could not clothe their children and send them to school daily, but needed a boarding school, which would provide food and clothing to their children and free the parents to hunt and fish. Were a boarding school to be established, they noted, many more Métis would move to the colony.[25]

This perspective also explains most of the complaints that the Métis had against the Catholic Church in general and Father Adéodat Thérien, the manager of the colony, in particular. In his letters to his superiors Thérien repeatedly notes that the Métis were upset that he was not dispensing credit or providing economic support in clothing and food to the extent they thought proper. In particular, they believed that the Church had fabulous wealth at its disposal and could not believe Thérien did not have the money, tools, and cattle to make their lives easier. As Thérien noted, the Métis had hoped to be fed and clothed by the Church and believed that this is what Lacombe had promised them when they had been recruited.[26] From Thérien's perspective these attitudes were a sign of indolence, which if encouraged would produce a nation of beggars. He deliberately set out to be very parsimonious with charity, not to give credit, never to pay with cash, and in this way to make the Métis rely on their own labour to farm. He considered it an economic education,[27] but probably, more than anything else, it contributed to the hard feelings between the Métis and the Catholic Church.[28]

Here in a nutshell was the basic problem of the colony. On the one hand the Catholic Church and the Canadian government saw the colony as a rehabilitation program to turn the Métis into a settled agricultural population, bringing them into the mainstream of Canadian society, while the Métis saw the colony as a way in which to maintain their distinctive hunting, trapping, freighting, and small-scale horticultural economy. Thérien and the Métis were closest to being on the same page when, as a stopgap measure, Thérien used his political connections with Frank Oliver to get contracts with surveyors, who agreed to use Métis labour.[29] By 1904–05, however, Thérien had lost hope of turning the Métis into sedentary farmers or of transforming St Paul into a Métis farming colony.[30]

Yet there were other reasons, besides Métis intransigence in becoming sedentary farmers, for the colony to close its doors and open the reserve to outside settlement. The colony was a significant financial drain on Catholic Church funds, by 1904–05 settlement was encroaching on the colony from all sides, and by the same date the Catholic Church was trying to find ways of colonizing the west with French-speaking and Catholic settlers. All of these factors influenced the Church to give up its experiment in Métis rehabilitation and colonization.

Recognizing that the Métis of St Paul wanted a boarding school for their children and believing that the best way of transforming the Métis into an agricultural sedentary people was through education, the Oblates prematurely opened a boarding school in the colony in 1899, which quickly enrolled forty-eight students, increasing to sixty-four later that fall. Unable to house this number without a new building and unable to fund the expense of feeding and clothing this many pupils, the school had to close in the spring of 1900. Thérien and four other settlers petitioned the federal government for a grant of $60 per student to run a boarding school,[31] but the government refused[32] and Thérien and Lacombe were forced to travel east to raise funds. A new school would eventually be opened to students in 1902 and officially opened in the fall of 1904. The school, impressive as it was, was a major drain on the colony's finances and, when it was destroyed in 1905 in a fire set by Métis students, there was no serious thought of rebuilding the uninsured school. Psychologically crushed by the fire,[33] Thérien later noted that the fire marked the beginning of the end of Lacombe's dream to rehabilitate the destitute Métis of the west.[34]

By this time the isolation of the colony was also ending. The Canadian Northern Railway now ran some thirty miles south of the colony and settlers were taking up most of the open land east and west of it.[35] The first sign of trouble from this quarter occurred in 1904, when seven settlers, misdirected by a Dominion Lands agent in Edmonton, took up lands in the Métis reserve, in effect, illegally squatting on land not open for homestead or even occupation by non-Métis. Eventually, the squatters applied to the Department of the Interior for entry onto these lands; the department directed their applications to the board of trustees of the colony with the advice that they had the authority to evict the squatters. At this point, Thérien was somewhat open to the option of letting the squatters stay if the colony was compensated with other lands, as most of the squatters were French Canadian. Lacombe, on the other hand, was adamant that they be expelled, as he foresaw that, if they were allowed stay, it would be the end of the reserve. This began a long debate between the Episcopal Corporation that governed the Métis colony and the federal government, and between Thérien and Lacombe about what to do about the squatters, who had made improvements on the land. The federal government was consistent in referring the matter to the Catholic Church, which had authority over the reserve through the Order in Council of 1895. Thérien, for his part, slowly convinced Lacombe that squatters on the reserve were not a bad thing if they were

10.2 St Paul des Métis – convent and school, 1901–05. Provincial Archives of Alberta, Oblate Collection (OB2096).

French and Catholic and if they provided a good example to the Métis trying to farm on the reserve. By late 1906 he had made at least a dent in Lacombe's blanket opposition when a Mr Fouquet was given permission to stay and the Department of the Interior was requested by Thérien to grant him a homestead.[36] For Thérien, the writing was on the wall. He had come to believe by 1907 "that to keep the colony alive and keep the area Catholic and French-speaking, non-Métis should be allowed into the colony."[37] From that point on Thérien began working with a colonization agent in Quebec and redoubled his efforts to convince Lacombe of the merits of opening the colony to settlement.

Thérien's reasoning had three parts. First, the Oblates and Catholic Church could not afford to continue subsidizing Métis colonization, and rebuilding the boarding school was out of the question. Given the meagre financial resources of the colony, Thérien had decided shortly after the fire that only well-established Métis should be allowed to settle there.[38] This policy already represented a major step back from Lacombe's vision of rehabilitating the destitute Métis of the west. The financial problems of the colony were, in Thérien's mind, compounded by the ambivalent attitude and reluctance of the Métis to farm full time. Finally, as the pace of settlement heated up, it became more important for Thérien to put French and Catholic settlers on the ground than to hold out for larger-scale Métis settlement in the future. According to Thérien, these arguments finally persuaded Lacombe in 1908 that the Métis colony would have to be sacrificed to preserve a French and Catholic settlement,[39] and in June of 1908 Thérien wrote to Frank Oliver, then the minister of the interior, that the Oblates wished to open the colony to homesteading.[40]

On the basis of communications with Bishop Legal of St Albert, Frank Oliver had an Order in Council signed into law to the effect that all unoccupied lands in the reserve be thrown open for settlement as soon as the claims of the Church and the Métis had been settled.[41] In particular, the Department of the Interior agreed with Legal's request that, given the Church's considerable expenditures in the colony for buildings and salaries,[42] it would be granted outright four sections of land on which their church and other buildings stood.[43] The Order in Council also stipulated that an investigation be made to determine the various claims of the Métis in the reserved tract who had been granted lots by the Oblates and to determine any other rights of bona fide occupants (squatters) who had complied with the ordinary homestead conditions.

Pursuant to the Order in Council of August 1908, Samuel Maber was sent to the colony to investigate all the various claims. His report dated

22 January 1909 noted that sixty-three Métis families had legitimate claims in the colony. Twenty were heads of family settled on eighty-acre allotments but who had received patent for homesteads elsewhere. These claimants he recommended should be allowed grants of eighty acres. Fifteen heads of family resided on eighty-acre allotments but held entries for homesteads outside the colony and should likewise be granted only eighty acres in the colony. Twenty-eight other heads of family had eighty-acre allotments, but had not exhausted their homestead rights and therefore should be eligible for a 160-acre grant in the colony. Finally, nineteen Métis claimants were non-resident and therefore had no right to consideration. He noted that most claimants had substantial homes on their claims and recommended that they be given title without a fee but subject to settlement duties.[44] In this investigation Maber also reported on each squatter, allowing those who met with the residency and building requirements of homestead entries (See figure 10.3). At this point, the Oblates gave up their lease for the colony on 2 March 1909 and on 10 April the reserve was opened to settlement.[45]

In order to ensure that the open land in the reserve went to French Catholics, Thérien continued to work with an immigration agent in Quebec and was assisted by Frank Oliver, the minister of the interior, in keeping the opening of the colony quiet until it was announced in the newspapers on 1 April 1909. When the land office opened for applications on 10 April, there were 400 applicants lined up, most of them French Catholics brought in by Thérien.[46] In a space of less than twenty-four hours St Paul des Métis had ceased to be a Métis reserve and had become a French-Canadian Catholic parish.

Whether one views St Paul des Métis as a failure or a success, and regardless of where one places the blame for the closure of the colony, the dominant discourse regarding St Paul des Métis in the decades after 1909 was that authored by Thérien and the Catholic Church. This discourse faulted the Métis, who, with some exceptions, were unwilling or unable to adjust to sedentary agriculture. Defined at the outset of the experiment as a "crisis ridden" people in need of "reclamation," the experience at St Paul des Métis did nothing to alter the Church's diagnosis/prognosis. While the Catholic Church had proven it was not up to the task of reclamation, or at least couldn't afford it, in the 1930s both the Alberta and the Saskatchewan governments would continue to see the Métis in pathological terms and make similar attempts to reclaim them for society. These efforts, and the Métis response to them, form the basis of the next two chapters.

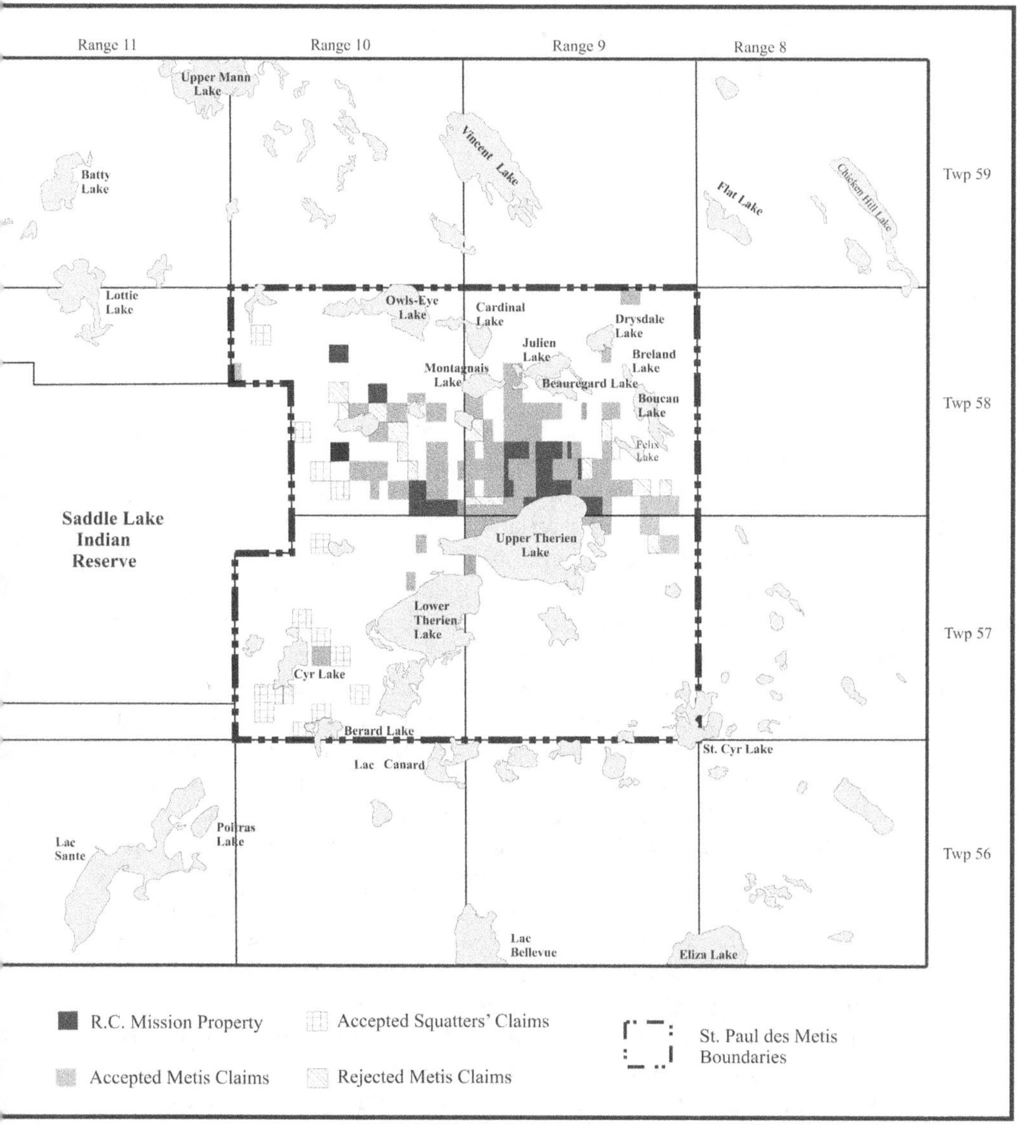

10.3 St Paul des Métis Colony showing the final disposition of land prior to the dissolution of the colony in 1909. LAC, RG 15, D-II-1, vol. 708, file 360530.

11 Political Mobilization in Alberta and the Métis Population Betterment Act of 1938

The 1930s saw the beginning of a renewed political and ethnic reformulation among the Métis of the prairie provinces – particularly in Alberta and Saskatchewan, where Métis organizations began to form in response to new political and economic pressures. By this time, Native political organizations were becoming commonplace in Canada; there had been various Native associations and brotherhoods representing treaty and/or non-treaty Indians as well as Métis in existence since the 1920s and even earlier. But the 1930s would prove to be a particularly appropriate time for the Métis to begin organizing. They were facing many problems. Some, of course, like those associated with the beginning of the Great Depression, were not unique to them. But the Depression and the concomitant rise of working-class militancy would prove to have significant effects on the Métis, as several of their early leaders, particularly in Alberta, were influenced by the growth of various workers movements, unions, the Communist party and Marxism. But there were other pressures on the Métis that *were* unique to them – pressures faced by neither their Indian nor their non-Native relatives and neighbours. First and foremost was the Natural Resources Transfer Agreements (NRTA), passed by the Parliament of Canada in 1930, which gave Manitoba, Saskatchewan, and Alberta jurisdiction over Crown lands and natural resources. These agreements supplanted the various Dominion Lands Acts under which the federal government had been managing Crown lands to this point. This was of major concern to the Métis, because it meant that the Métis scrip programs, which had been constituted under the Dominion Lands Acts, were to all effects becoming null and void. The NRTA transferred federal responsibility for the Métis scrip program to the provinces, which meant the end of the scrip program, an abandonment of Métis claims by the federal government, and refusal of the provincial governments to take up these same claims. This was one of the prime causes of Métis political mobilization on the prairies. Until the passage of the NRTA, the scrip programs had undergone several extensions and reformulations, which may have given the Métis the idea that scrip was part of their permanent patrimony, available to each forthcoming generation.

Linked to this assumption was the perception the general populace had of the Métis, as illustrated by the thinking behind St Paul des Métis. Rather than being regarded as a well-established indigenous population with useful roles in the economy, claims to Aboriginal rights, and some political power, they were seen as a group unwilling or unable to adjust to the demands of the new economy and sedentary agriculture. This view of the Métis as a social problem and a drain on the economy would be adopted by both the Alberta and the Saskatchewan governments.

In Alberta, the impulse to form a political organization also may have been a residual effect of St Paul des Métis. While the colony experience may not have been a beneficial one for the Métis, the memory of it and the role it may have played in perpetuating a sense of Métis identity may well have provided the spark that led to the formation of the Métis Association of Alberta approximately twenty-three years later, and the establishment of Métis Settlements in central and northern Alberta a few years after that.

As we shall see, the growth of the Métis Association of Alberta also owed much to the existence of a strong leadership consisting of several individuals with complementary organizing skills – although, ironically, several of these leaders would prove to have motivations and ideas not that different from those manifested at St Paul des Métis by Frs Lacombe and Thérien. Far from promoting Métis identity, nationhood, and culture, these early leaders saw the objectives of the Métis Association of Alberta as centred on providing relief and assistance to an indigent Métis population that needed some means of assistance if they were ever to hope to adjust to the needs and new economy of the dominant society. Indeed, the first concrete result of the Métis Association's activities was the formation of a set of Métis colonies, much like those originally envisaged for St Paul des Métis. It would be a great many years – the mid-1960s to be exact – before any move would be made by the Métis Association that went beyond providing social assistance and began introducing ideas of defining and/or refining a Métis identity, or the idea of the Métis as a nation. However, the beginnings of the Métis Association of Alberta illustrate the first steps taken by the Métis of western Canada towards delineating and developing the political entity and concept of Métis familiar to us today.

Early Leadership: The "Big Four"

As the Métis began to feel the full effects of the Natural Resources Transfer Act, the changing economy and nature of Alberta society, several Métis communities set up local councils in an attempt to deal with problems of land title, relief, medical services, and hunting and trapping regulations. One such group was from the Cold Lake area of eastern Alberta. Fishing Lake, a Métis community situated on a forest reserve, was to be opened up to settlement.[1] Based on their previous experiences at St Paul, the Métis became convinced that, if this happened, they would lose the land to non-Native settlers.[2]

Convinced that they needed a more educated person to be their intermediary, the group invited Joseph Dion of Gurneyville to one of the meetings in Cold Lake in 1930. Dion, a nephew of Big Bear, was an enfranchised treaty Indian born on the Kehewin Reserve near St Paul. Dion was a schoolteacher, and it was because of his Native background and education that the Métis approached him to be their spokesman. Although he was not completely comfortable with the role of political leader, his sense of duty to Native people led him to initiate a series of meetings in the area, eventually generating a group of local representatives from various Métis settlements across northern Alberta.[3] These activities began to attract the interest of various provincial and federal politicians.

Dion and Deschene began to petition the provincial government on behalf of the Métis, requesting free land, education, medical care, and hunting and fishing permits.[4] Eventually, their efforts bore fruit – at least to the extent that personnel in the Department of Lands and Mines decided to conduct a questionnaire to quantify the economic status of the Métis in the province, determining the size of the families, whether or not they had received scrip or had homesteaded, and so on.[5] The nascent Métis organization was chosen as the vehicle to deliver the questionnaire, even though it had no formal organization or constitution and was still unchartered.[6]

But the success of the movement began to attract more and more interest from concerned Métis. In 1932, a new person became involved in the Métis cause: Jim Brady. Brady contacted Dion by letter in May of

1932, stressing the need for formal organization and strong community locals. His ideas on organizing and strategy were very useful to Dion, who at the time was travelling to several Métis communities in northern Alberta in attempting to organize a more formal Métis association. These meetings culminated in a provincial convention, set for 28 December, which would see the birth of a formal, provincially based, Métis political organization. L'Association des Métis d'Alberta et des Territoires du Nord-Ouest, the original name of the Métis Association of Alberta (now the Métis Nation of Alberta), was formally established at that meeting. At least thirty-three members from thirty-three districts were present at that meeting.[7] The stated aims were to convince the government to fulfil their requests as outlined in Dion's submissions.[8]

Joseph Dion was elected as the first president; Malcolm Norris, Felix Callihoo, and Henry Cunningham were the three vice-presidents; and J.P. Brady was the secretary-treasurer. The election of Peter Tomkins Jr as vice-president two years later completed the make-up of the "Big Four" as Dion, Brady, Norris, and Tompkins, came to be known – the men who, more than any others, developed the Métis organization and the direction it was to take for most of its formative years.[9] The four men are interesting in their own right, but their involvement in the Métis movement also reveals much of the nature of Métis/Indian society in the 1930s and 1940s, including how the Métis were perceived by others and how they perceived themselves. Their characters, influences, and motivations have been described in detail by many authors,[10] so a brief sketch will suffice for our purposes.

Joseph Dion was born in 1888 on the Onion Lake Reserve. He attended a Catholic-run Indian residential school, which proved to be one of the great influences in his life. He remained a devout Catholic till he died. As a young man he enfranchised – that is, he voluntarily gave up his Indian status; he became a schoolteacher and taught at the Keheewin Indian reserve from 1915 to 1939.[11] Malcolm Norris, the first vice-president of the organization, was born in 1900. He was the son of an Edmonton trader who had moved there in 1852. Norris's mother was a Métis woman. Malcolm Norris had planned on attending university, but his father's early death made that financially impossible. Norris, like many of his fellow activists in the Métis Association, held a variety of jobs throughout his career. None of the leaders was able to pursue a full-time career in Native politics – such a position was unheard of in Canada in the 1930s. Norris served briefly with the North-West Mounted Police (NWMP) in 1918 and then worked for many years as a

11.1 The provincial executive of the Métis Association of Alberta, 1935. Front row, left to right: Malcolm Norris, Joseph Dion, James Brady. Back row, left to right: Peter Tomkins, Felix Calihoo. Glenbow Archives, PA-2218–109.

trapper and trader in northern Alberta and the Northwest Territories. During World War II he served in the Royal Canadian Air Force.

Jim Brady was born near St Paul in 1908. He came from a well-educated and politically active family. Like Norris, he was the child of a Euro-Canadian father and a Métis mother. His father was born in Dublin, and married Philomena Garneau in 1905. Jim Brady Sr was a prominent member of local society, serving as postmaster and Dominion lands claims officer. He ran unsuccessfully in 1917 in the provincial election as an Independent Liberal. Brady's mother was the first Métis registered nurse in Alberta, graduating from Misericordia Hospital in Winnipeg. Her father had taken an active part alongside Riel in 1873 and later had homesteaded and lived at St Paul des Métis. In 1913 he unsuccessfully stood for election as a Liberal. Thus, Jim Brady came from a family with an above-average education, and a tradition of political involvement. Despite this background, he worked as a labourer for most of his life, with occasional stints as a civil servant. Like Norris and the others, he had to subsidize his political activity through regular employment. Brady joined the army in 1943. He lived in Saskatchewan for the remainder of his life, where he continued to play a major role in Métis politics until his death in 1967.[12]

Peter Tomkins was born in the Peace River area of northwestern Alberta in 1890. Like Norris and Brady, his father was non-Native, and his mother Native. His father had been captured by Riel's men in 1885 while he was repairing telegraph lines. While in detention he met with Riel and was influenced by him enough to become an ardent supporter of the Métis cause. He later married Chief Poundmaker's daughter, whom he had met when he was a prisoner of the Métis.[13]

Of the "Big Four" three had non-Native fathers and Native mothers. Two of these women were Métis, one Indian. The fourth member, Dion, was Cree, and an enfranchised or non-status Indian. Thus, none of the Big Four had two Métis parents and could not be classified as coming from a strictly Métis background – at least not the way Métis background is calculated today. Also, all were influenced by mainstream society to a much greater degree than the average grass-roots Métis. Even Dion, who was a full-blooded Cree, was influenced by the dominant society. His early residential school upbringing and Catholic influences distanced him enough from his Native background that he enfranchised and became a schoolteacher. It is difficult to know if these people would be accepted as Métis politicians today – especially Dion – since there was a purge of non-status Indian politicians from the Métis organizations in the 1980s. But it is evident that the Métis movement of the 1930s was not a purely nationalist one; non-status Indians were seen as much a part of the movement as were the Métis.

The coming together of the Big Four at the beginning of the Métis Association was a happy circumstance of complementary personalities, characteristics, and good timing. Several authors have commented on how each of the four leaders reinforced the other; the qualities of one seeming to complement those of the others.[14] All were influenced by European or western traditions, but there were fundamental differences in which traditions they adopted and how they were applied. Joe Dion's most prominent characteristic was his deep commitment to Catholicism. Perhaps because of the influences he received as a child at residential school he believed that the future of Native people lay in their assimilation – at least economically – into the dominant society. His own choices – becoming enfranchised as a young man, becoming a schoolteacher in denominational schools, retaining close connections with the clergy – reflect these same values, but he never supported total cultural assimilation. He supported Métis and Indian cultural events: in the 1930s, he organized a group of Métis dancers to perform in eastern Canada, and he continued to help organize the annual pilgrimage of Métis and Indians to Lac Ste Anne.[15] He became involved with the Métis because, as a Native schoolteacher, he was exactly the sort of educated and literate person the Métis would feel comfortable in turning to. His kindness and compassion would not let him refuse their requests. His obviously sincere religious conviction probably was also comforting to a great many of the Métis who were themselves deeply religious. At a time when the clergy were actively discouraging political activity of the Métis and their association, Dion's participation helped to legitimize the political struggle for many of them. He may not have been the most effective or astute politician (correspondence of Brady and Norris shows they were often critical of his political leanings and savvy) but he was able to win the affection and trust of the Métis in a way that the other leaders were not.

Both Norris and Brady, on the other hand, were influenced by socialism and interpreted the history of the Métis and their contemporary situation accordingly. However, the Métis were only part of their concern: they wanted social justice for all working people. Despite the similarity of their political interests, the two men were quite different in nature. Norris – whose nickname was "Dynamite" – probably was the most outgoing and charismatic of the four. He was famed for his oratory and quick wit in public meetings and was equally at home in English or in Cree. He was the most urbanized of the four, having lived in Edmonton consistently during this period. Despite his obvious success in adjusting to mainstream society and his interest in provincial politics and socialism, he was fiercely proud of his own Native heritage and of the Métis's place in history. Brady, on the other hand, was much more of a recluse, never marrying, often living by himself and avoiding contact with friends and family alike. His contributions to the Métis cause lay not in public meetings or face to face confrontation, but in his historical writings, application of strategies, and role as a theoretician. His focus was different from Norris's as well. While Norris was interested in applying socialist principles to mainstream politics, especially at the provincial level, Brady was much more interested in practical applications at the local level, spending much of his time advocating, forming, and managing various cooperatives in the Métis settlements and in Saskatchewan.[16]

Pete Tompkins, like Dion, was more interested in achieving immediate and practical relief for the Métis than in grand theoretical political issues, but he was sympathetic to Brady's and Norris's ideas. He was the one most responsible for the Métis Association's channelling relief to the Métis and pressuring charitable organizations for their assistance. He has been characterized by many as "the great peacemaker" among the Big Four – able to reconcile differences and aggrievement – and was of great help in preventing the association from splitting apart under the different philosophies and leadership styles of the administration.[17] Tompkins's background was that of a non-status or non-treaty Indian, rather than a Métis. This was not a problem when the Métis Association was first being developed, because the whole issue of Métis nationalism had yet to be raised. But under contemporary conditions that determine who is or who is not a Métis, such as those put forth by the Métis National Council, it is possible that Tompkins, or even Brady and Norris, would not be recognized as traditional Métis leaders.

Métis Identity and l'Association des Métis d'Alberta et des Territoires du Nord-Ouest

Given the background of the four most prominent leaders, what does the formation of the Métis Association tell us about Métis identity in the 1930s? Murray Dobbin seems to feel that the new organization represented a rejuvenation of Métis nationalism, and that to be "Métis" at that time in Alberta meant to be French and Catholic: "A large majority of the leadership of the new organization were French Métis. This factor and the French name of the organization recalled the history of the Métis national struggles, which had always drawn their militant leadership from among the French Métis. While the organization quickly became known by its English derivative (the Métis Association of Alberta) due to the general dominance of the English language, the convention testified to the fact that, in Alberta, Métis nationalism was French and Catholic."[18]

Yet while it is true that a perusal of the list of initial councillors indicates a preponderance of French names,[19] the fact that the Big Four were primarily English speakers and the fact that the association quickly became known as the Métis Association of Alberta belies this. In fact, even before the 1932 convention, Jim Brady and the St Paul Métis had produced a provisional constitution for the proposed Métis organization, which stated that membership was open to all British subjects with Indian ancestry, whether treaty Indian, non-treaty, or Métis.[20] Although the Métis Association did not formally register under the provincial Societies Act until 1961[21] several versions of a constitution had been prepared, all following the Society Act's guidelines.[22] Each version of the constitution indicated that the association was not seen as a strictly Métis organization, at least not as Métis is defined today by the Métis National Council. Membership was inevitably defined as open to "Métis, Non-Treaty Indians, or any person of mixed White and Indian blood." In fact, this fundamental definition was the operating definition of the Métis Association until 1984.[23] Early correspondence from Dion usually pleaded the case equally for both Métis and non-treaty Indians.

Evidence of how the Métis were perceived at this time comes from two main sources: (a) the personal correspondence of Brady, Norris, Tompkins, and Dion, and (b) the proceedings of the Ewing Commission, which was inaugurated in 1934 to assess the socio-economic circumstances of the Métis population of Alberta. It is probably safe to say that the Big Four and the other leaders of the Métis Association were concerned more with social welfare than with Métis nationalism. The fact that membership was open to non-treaty Indians as well as anyone with Métis or mixed ancestry testifies to this fact. Dion, himself an enfranchised Indian, had no direct interest in reviving a sense of Métis nationalism, although he had done some things to encourage it, such as sponsoring a Métis dance troupe to travel around the province. The same motivations of social justice seem to have been the main activating forces for Brady, Norris, and Tompkins. While proud of their Native heritage, they seemed mostly concerned with providing land for the indigent Métis. Their correspondence often shows a certain amount of distance between themselves and the Métis, little interest in proclaiming themselves to be Métis or building pride in being Métis, and almost no interest in distinguishing the Métis from other Native peoples.

Their writings reveal that the Big Four were very much part of the dominant, non-Native society. They were reasonably successful in that society – much more so than most of the Métis whom they were attempting to represent – and had absorbed some of the conventional wisdom about Native peoples common to the dominant society, in particular the ideas that the Métis and other Natives were "primitive and child-like" members of a "dying race" whose only hope was to adapt and adopt the customs and values of the dominant society. Dion, in a letter to A.G. Reid of the Department of Lands and Mines, Alberta, circa 1933, stated that "a man cannot hitch a wild horse alongside a well-broken and grain fed horse and expect the former to do as good work as the latter."[24] Continuing the equine analogy, Dion at another time said "Knowing our people as I do, I think that I can safely compare them to a short winded race horse, who will raise Hell and go like blazes for a little while."[25] He also regarded them as children, to whom he owed a filial duty: "I may have to work for the welfare of the little children for many years to come."[26] The attitudes that convinced Dion to enfranchise and spurn the government benefits due a treaty Indian also compelled him to warn the government "against the consequence should the half-breed get into the habit of expecting relief always, *he is an Indian* and if given an inch will demand a mile."[27] To Dion, the enfranchised Indian, the Métis was simply a Native; there *was* no Métis nationalism as far as Dion was concerned.

Norris and Brady also demonstrate a certain distance from the Métis, as well as an almost patronizing attitude towards them. At one point, Norris echoes Dion in seeing the Métis as helpless wards or children: "When one considers the number of unfortunate souls involved it is extremely difficult to throw up the sponge in despair, without feeling a little guilty, like forsaking helpless children."[28] Norris often talks about the Métis as if he is not one of them, criticizing their political naiveté, stating that the association would become a "joke" if he and Brady left it in their hands: "Knowing the Metis as I do, all talk and no give, you can expect them or rather many to swell their throats with anticipation of appointments and material benefits. Poor misguided fools. The best brains we have among us is none too great to battle with the trained politicians & clergy. Still in their ignorance, they think it is a simple task. However, it is our duty to uphold the Assn that we can place this matter in their hands with fair warning after which it will become the joke and plaything of every political party in the country."[29] Again, continuing the analogy of the parent to child, or at least a form of noblesse oblige, he felt it was his and Brady's duty to continue their efforts on the Métis's behalf "not for our sakes but for the hundreds of poor beggars involved. Endeavour in the meantime to stay the ship."[30]

Norris has no qualms describing the Métis as having limited abilities, a childlike psychology, and unable to look out for themselves. In discussing the possibility of the Ewing Commission's mounting an inquiry into Métis conditions, he counsels against it, because of the "limitation" of the Métis and their "Halfbreed psychology" and the fact that the leaders would not be there to run interference:

> Listen, Jimmy, you know what an inquiry of individuals would result in. A collection of data irrational, inconsistent. Worthless to our cause and in all probability detrimental to our movement. I base this opinion on my knowledge of Metis people, their limitations and Halfbreed psychology. White people are always represented by a Barrister for the simplest of procedures. Therefore, I am absolutely opposed to this sort of inquiry. They the commission are no doubt aware that we have not the means to tag their party around to be on hand to council [*sic*] and advise the individuals testifying before the Commission.[31]

Norris reiterated his characterization of the Métis when testifying at the Ewing Commission. He even seems to have accepted the common wisdom that the Métis, in rejecting or squandering their chances for scrip, were the authors of their own misfortune. "Unfortunately there exists the discrimination of Metis who through lack of foresight relinquished their right of possession with the fool [*sic*] blooded Indian for script [*sic*] which speedily passed into the hands of people of superior training and foresight. Others again have refuted their Treaty to accept enfranchisement, who are thus classified Metis and fool [*sic*] blooded Indians as fully enfranchised citizens of the country, and are not considered as wards of any kind."[32]

The willingness to recognize both non-status or non-treaty Indians and Métis as equally legitimate clients of the association underlines the fact that the leadership were not overly concerned with creating or recognizing Métis nationalism. As already mentioned, Dion himself was a non-treaty, enfranchised Indian. The interchangeability between Métis and Indian status continued after the association was formed. The association leadership would often contemplate claiming any non-treaty group in the province as a potential membership source, in order to further legitimate the status of the organization and its claims. When he heard that the Department of Indian Affairs was contemplating adding some Indians living at Trout Mountain, along the Wabasca River, Long Lake, and Chipewyan Lake to treaty, Brady wrote to Pete Tompkins:

> It is the intention of the Dept. to make an effort to bring these people under Treaty when the next Treaty payments are made in that area ... We should make an effort, by hook or crook, to reach these people before the Treaty payments take place and induce them to join our fold, thereby enhancing

our problem in the eyes of the Dominion as well as the Provincial Government. You can readily realize what a reaction this would be to the Government and a tremendous influence it would make to our claim. If it is possible to make diplomatic advances in that direction, before the Department of Indian Affairs arrive with their gospel of Treaty it would be in our opinion a politic move ... It would be necessary, of course, that any gravitation of these people to our movement appear to be of their accord and impulse.[33]

The attitude of the Big Four and the rest of the leadership is consistent with their role in the association and their relation to the Métis population as a whole. While the association may have been initiated by the homeless and near destitute, its leadership quickly became dominated by working- and middle-class Métis, of whom Dion, Brady, Norris, and Tompkins were but the best-known examples. These were the same classes of Métis that had played a prominent role in the earlier struggles of 1869 and 1885.[34]

Elites often play an important role in defining ethnicity, and it is their values that often come to the fore in characterization of the group. One of the ways this can be seen is in the struggle of the leadership to have the name "half-breed" expunged from general use, to be replaced with "Métis." The minutes of the first meeting do not suggest a definition of the Métis, but it does reject the "odious" name of "Half-Breed": "(Chairman, Felice Calihoo): I would suggest that we give this Association the appellation of 'L'Association des Métis d'Alberta et des Territoires du Nord-Ouest.' The term 'Metis' applies particularly to our people. The word 'Half-Breed' is suggestive of a person of any mixed descent, and to many of us is of an odious nature."[35]

This attitude was made explicit in the Métis Association's written report on the history of the Métis, submitted to the Ewing Commission as *A History of the Half-Breed Claims and Petitions as Prepared by the Members of the Metis Association*,[36] although the official title of the various scrip acts forced them to use "Half-Breed" in the title. Within the report the authors objected to an article in the *Edmonton Bulletin* of 13 January 1934, which used the term "Metis Breeds," claiming: "The term Breed displays gross ignorance of the traditions and history of the West."[37] It is not clear from this example whether they objected simply to the term "Breed" or "half-breed" as well, but throughout the early history of the association, various leaders would periodically attempt to discourage popular use of the term "half-breed." Norris commented approvingly on the use of "our term Metis" rather than Halfbreed in the Métis Betterment Act of 1938. "I presume you are aware that *An Act Respecting the Metis*

Population of the Province (Note official recognition of our term Metis in preference to Halfbreed) was passed at a special session last fall."[38]

W.J. Calihoo was still fighting the use of the term in the press in 1945: "a Metis, Thos Letendre, was run over by a truck & killed. Of course, the papers had to mention he was a half-breed. I couldn't stand the insult any longer. I wrote both the Journal & Bulletin, asking the editors why was it that the Press without fail stresses the Metis nationality, calling him a half-breed a name belonging to animals ... I got a response shortly from both editors, expressing regrets of the papers & that no more nationalities be exposed from now on, over 4 months has passed since this episode & believe me no more half-breed is ever mentioned in the papers."[39]

However, as we shall see in later chapters, the use of the term "half-breed" continued well into the 1950s and 1960s.

Métis Identity and the Ewing Commission[40]

At least in part because of political pressures initiated by the Métis Association, Dion, Norris, and Brady, the provincial legislature agreed to look into the socio-economic status of the Métis of Alberta. In 1932, the Department of Lands and Mines issued a questionnaire investigating the economic status of the Métis. A resolution to investigate the conditions of the Métis had been passed by the Alberta Legislative Assembly in 1933, and several reports to the minister of lands and mines had already suggested that land might be set aside for the use of the Métis. The final result of this was the creation, by an Order in Council of 12th December 1934, of a three-man commission to make inquiries "into and concerning the problems of health, education and general welfare of the Half-breed population of the Province."[41] The commission was headed by the Honourable A.R. Ewing, a justice of the Supreme Court of Alberta. The other two members were E.A. Braithwaite, a medical doctor who had worked as a civil servant for the public health services in Alberta, and J.M. Douglas, an Edmonton politician. The Royal Half-Breed Commission, or the Ewing Commission, as it quickly came to be called, was not only to make use of the material already collected, but to hold meetings in some of the smaller towns in northern and central Alberta[42] and to conduct a main set of hearings in Edmonton, where testimony was invited from clergy, medical practitioners, politicians, representatives of the Métis Association, and other interested parties.

The hearings of the Ewing Commission provide an insight into prevailing conceptions about the Métis that were current in the 1930s.

11.2 Members of the Métis Association of Alberta with MLAs and Catholic Church leaders, photographed during the Ewing Commission. Back row, left to right: Joseph M. Dechene (MLA), Felix Calihoo, Lenoida Giroux (MLA), Pete Tomkins Jr. Front row, left to right: Jim Brady, Rev. Father Falher, Joe Dion, Bishop Guy, Malcolm Norris, Pete Tomkins Sr. Glenbow Archives, NA-1899–8.

We have the testimony of clergymen, doctors, politicians, the Métis leadership, and occasionally some of the Métis themselves. Generally, the results tell us more about the preconceptions the non-Native population held about the Métis than about how the Métis defined or thought of themselves. Even the Métis leadership was sufficiently separated from the rank and file that their definitions were from the outside.

One of the first questions to be addressed at the hearings was the definition of the term "half-breed" (the term "Métis" was rarely used in the hearings). This discussion clearly documents the general view of the Métis held by members of the commission, as well as of some of the leaders of the Métis Association. Three criteria were quickly established as being of importance in identifying the "half-breed": the percentage of Indian blood, whether the individual was living the life of an Indian, and whether the individual was capable of supporting himself/herself.

The general view of who was or who was not a Métis or half-breed and the place of non-treaty Indians in relation to the half-breed population can be seen clearly in the initial discussion of the commission:

BISHOP D. GUY: The term of half-breed is well understood I take it. There are two kinds of half-breeds, you have the non treaty Indian and the half-breed –

THE CHAIRMAN: Right there My Lord, there would appear to some difference of opinion, should the non treaty Indian be treated as a half-breed, as far as this Commission is concerned I mean of course.

BISHOP D. GUY: Well, what is one to do, the treaty Indian of course is different, –

THE CHAIRMAN: The Half-Breed Association, what does that include?

BISHOP D. GUY: Members of the Association? Half-breeds and Non Treaty Indians. In some families, in the same family you might have treaty Indians and non-treaty Indians, that is the difficulty in the schools. I have been identified with this Indian problem since 1913, and I can assure you that it is a problem.

THE CHAIRMAN: I can well understand that, you have always treated non-treaty Indians as half-breeds?

BISHOP D. GUY: Yes, that is so. In the beginning of course, well perhaps it is not much use going back to the beginning, the days of the issuing of scrip –

THE CHAIRMAN: We had some discussion about that yesterday. I said then, I do not see much use in raking that up and trying to apportion blame. That will not help us much to-day. I was wondering whether the terms of our Commission were wide enough to include the non-treaty Indian with the Half-breeds? Do you think it wide enough?

BISHOP D. GUY: Yes, it should be, there seems to be no difference.

THE CHAIRMAN: You think we are safe?

BISHOP D. GUY: Oh yes.

MR PENNOCK: In the original petition to the Honourable Reid, reference is there made to the conditions amongst the Half-breeds and Non-treaty Indians.

THE CHAIRMAN: Oh does it, I didn't see that. I don't see that in the recommendation of the Commission. However, His Lordship thinks we are safe. Might I ask this, in defining a half-breed, might I suggest that it does not mean what it says, literally, one of half blood. How far would you go My Lord, in defining a half-breed? As one of partly Indian blood?

BISHOP D. GUY: Any one who has Indian blood? Yes I think so, anyone with Indian blood, without being a treaty Indian, yes I think they would come in that category. It is very difficult to give such an exact definition that everyone will be satisfied. Some people with Indian blood might resent being called half-breeds, what is one to do?

MR JAMES BRADY SR: You are asking about the definition of half-breed. I remember in our district in the old days, people coming to Montana, and I have known people share in the land grants in Montana who were only 1/16 extraction. That of course was in the States, and that raised the Indian totals in the States, but that need not be a definition in this country of course.

MR PENNOCK: That was anyone with Indian blood in their veins?

MR BRADY: Yes sir.

MR NORRIS: Anyone living the life of an Indian providing of course he had Indian blood?

MR BRADY: Yes.

THE CHAIRMAN: Let us get back to the half-breed. Would you say the definition anyone having Indian blood in their veins and living the normal life of a half-breed comes within the definition of "half-breed?"

MR NORRIS: Yes, I think that is right.

THE CHAIRMAN: You see, you must include "living the life of a half-breed" otherwise, there are a large number of men in Edmonton, some occupying responsible positions, who are not intended to be included in this investigation.

MR PENNOCK: And their conditions are not deplorable.

BISHOP D. GUY: I think Sir, that there are a lot of Metis who are living lives that would not come within that definition, "living the normal life of a half-breed."

MR NORRIS: For the purposes of this investigation it is rather difficult to give a definition –

THE CHAIRMAN: When I said "living the normal life of a half-breed" I meant of course, living the life that one usually associates with a half-breed. I do not think that we can tie ourselves down to exact definitions, we must draw the line somewhere of course, but we may find that we cannot adhere to the definition that we do make, in making a proper investigation into conditions.

THE CHAIRMAN: All right then, we have got to a definition, perhaps Bishop Guy will now be good enough to tell us something about conditions, starting with education first.[43]

Several things are revealed in these exchanges. First, the term most commonly used at the time was "half-breed," not Métis. The use of the term was not limited to the members of the commission; most of the witnesses, including the representatives of the Métis Association themselves used the term, sometimes interchangeably with "Métis" even though their association had long been opposed to the "odious" term.[44]

It was also decided by all parties that non-treaty Indians should be considered as part of the commission's mandate. Bishop Guy's earliest words to the commission stated that there were "two kinds of half-breeds, you have the non-treaty Indian and the half-breed." Joe Dion told the commission: "The most destitute amongst the Metis today are the direct descendants of Indians who left treaty in favour of scrip." Mr Pennock, a lawyer acting for the Métis Association pointed out that the original Métis petitions included the non-treaty Indians in their submissions. While it may have been an exaggeration to suggest, as Bishop Guy does, that "there seems to be no difference" between non-treaty Indians and Métis, it should be remembered that there was a long association between the two groups, one that would continue for many years, until constitutional recognition of the Métis in 1982 with no provision for non-status Indians made the political union impractical.[45]

All sides also agreed that an essential aspect in defining Métis or half-breed was the presence of Indian blood – although it was also quickly established that blood was not the only criterion. "Lifestyle" was equally important. There was some discussion over proportion of blood – how much Indian blood was needed to qualify a person as a "half-breed." After a short discussion, it was decided not to specify an arithmetical quantity – any amount of Indian blood, no matter how small, was sufficient. After all, it was not the presence of Indian ancestry that was important; "lifestyle" or, more precisely, degree of assimilation was the determining criterion. Even Norris agreed; "if he has one drop of Indian blood in his veins and has not been assimilated into the social fabric of our civilization he is a Metis."[46]

It became clear that the commission was not interested in those Métis who were already self-sufficient. No consideration of Aboriginal or

Indian title was made in the proceedings – the only consideration was of need; the terms of reference were strictly those of social welfare, not entitlement by virtue of Native ancestry. (However, they did refer to Aboriginal rights in the final report and recommendations.)

Apparently, being economically self-sufficient was not "normal" behaviour for the Métis; the commission had decided that the most important criteria for inclusion was "living the normal life of a half-breed." The implications were that if there was no demonstrable need – that is, if the person was not indigent – he or she was not a "Metis," but was merely a citizen with some Indian ancestry, no matter what he thought of himself in cultural or social terms.

On several occasions individual witnesses, including Brady and Tompkins, suggested that most of those Métis who were descendants of the Red River Métis did not need the help of the province or the association.[47] As Brady stated in his testimony, most of the people needing help were the non-treaty Indians: "Well, there is one thing you have to remember, the original Half-breed, the Red River Metis, the majority of these people are still carrying on, they are still more or less able to hold their own. The majority of the destitute people today among the Metis were formerly treaty Indians, they are Indian through and through, except for the names, they are still Indians."[48] It soon became clear that a two-tier model of Métis society was emerging – those who needed governmental assistance and those who did not – although the commissioners' and the Métis leaders' models were based on very different criteria.

The leaders of the Métis Association – Brady, Tomkins Sr, Dion, and Norris – took the general position that there were two types of Métis: the "Red River" or "agricultural" Métis and the "nomadic" Métis. This position was reiterated by J.M. Dechene, the MLA for Beaver River. Dobbin credits Brady as the sole author of this dual-class analysis of Métis society and suggests that he coached the other executive members before their testimony.[49] Whether or not Brady was the originator of this idea, he certainly discussed it many times, in the commission hearings and in his writings.[50]

This analysis takes the view that the Red River Métis were relatively well established – the elite of Métis society – while the "nomadic" Métis were the destitute, landless, and unintegrated Métis. The Red River Métis (both the French and the English/Scottish subgroups) consisted of the people who had settled in the North Saskatchewan River valley after the 1885 Rebellion and included most of those who had settled on the St Paul des Métis Reserve after 1896. Most of these people had made a transition from being dependent on the fur trade to either commercial endeavours or agriculture, and many of them were well educated. Of course, some were more successful than others, and there were those who, deprived of their lands or unable to make a transition, were in need of assistance. But generally, they were economically self-sufficient and were not considered to be the concern of the half-breed commission. The Red River Métis were distinguished from a newer group of people, some of mixed European and Native ancestry and some non-treaty Indians who had either been missed in treaty negotiations, had refused to sign treaty, or had been struck from the treaty lists. This was the group designated as "nomadic," because their means of subsistence was primarily based on hunting, trapping, and fishing, rather than agriculture. The nomadic Métis were particularly vulnerable in the southern area of the province, the North Saskatchewan River and below, where they were primarily squatting, living on road allowances, or living on Indian reserves. This group suffered from malnutrition, disease, and lack of medical treatment and was particularly dependent on outside help.[51] As far as Ewing and the other commissioners were concerned, it was the nomadic Métis who properly constituted the concern of the half-breed commission.

As Dobbin points out in his analysis of Brady's scheme, the basic distinction between the two groups lay in how well they were adapted to the dominant economic structure:

> Brady's description of two broad classes of Metis did not fit the orthodox Marxist view of class. It was an analysis which recognized implicitly the colonial reality of many Metis and a continuing national liberation movement. An individual's class position was based on how they related to the mainstream society. Thus Brady does not talk about a Metis working class as such – the working class Metis were included in the category of "progressive" just as farmers and small businessmen were. All these economic classes were part of the Canadian mainstream and were therefore "progressive." The nomadic Metis – a large proportion of whom were actually ex-treaty Indians – were outside the mainstream. As described earlier some Metis were on the borderline – entering one or the other of these two classes depending on economic conditions.[52]

Brady's analysis assumed that the more "progressive" Métis could/should have a leadership role in helping the more destitute of the Métis make an effective adjustment to contemporary society, and that the ideal mechanism for this would be the Métis Association.[53] To some extent, up to that time this was exactly how the Métis Association had been working. According to Dobbin, most of the local leadership came from the land-owning "Red River" class and it was their support that made the work of the "Big Four" possible. The Métis Association was potentially of great importance; its existence and success could demonstrate to the commission that the Métis were capable of governing themselves and becoming productive citizens. Brady and Norris's greatest fear was that the commission would recommend a simple relief plan for indigent Métis, creating government-run reserves for them without any provisions for self-government and without a role for the Métis Association in the administration of the reserves. As it turned out, their fears were justified.

Another two-tier scheme, one suggested by several non-Métis and based on different criteria than those suggested by Brady and the Métis Association, was presented to the commission. Here, the Métis were divided into "northern" and "southern" Métis. The group that supported this definition included Bishop Breynat, Father Coudert, F. Falkener (MLA for Stoney Plain) and Inspector Christianson, who worked for Indian Affairs.[54] This scheme was assimilationist in nature and based on the idea of the "vanishing Indian" common at the time; stressing a contrast between the traditional Native way of life and the modern European way. Falkener expressed the distinction clearly. The "northern" Métis people still successfully lived a traditional lifestyle, trapping, hunting, and fishing, and were by and large still self-sufficient. They were contrasted with the "southern" Métis – those who were living in areas already settled by whites – who no longer could support themselves through hunting, trapping, and fishing, but had not successfully adapted to white society, in areas of either agriculture or other economic pursuits.[55] It was the living conditions of the southern Métis that elicited the most concern, but those who took this point of view felt that the way of life would eventually decline in the north as well as in the south.

So the Ewing Commission was treated to at least two distinct views of the Métis: the historic-economic-based model espoused by the leaders of the Métis Association, and the assimilation-based model espoused by Falkener, Bishop Guy, and the chairman of the commission itself. At first glance, it might seem that the two views were similar; both were two-tier models, dividing the Métis into two somewhat observable groupings; both were descriptive of how the Métis related to mainstream society;

and both posited an economically independent group that did not need the commission's attention. But the association's model was conceived in terms of historical, social, and economic forces and was to some extent the construct of insiders (albeit with the qualification that Brady, Norris, and Tompkins could best be characterized as partial insiders). It also suggested a relationship between the "progressive" Métis, who were fully participating in the mainstream economy, and the "nomadic" Métis, who were yet full participants in the economic system.

The assimilation model, on the other hand, was the product of a totally non-Native perspective. It was the perspective of the dominant society and was informed by the prevailing view of the time: the "vanishing Indian," based on a simplistic contrast between "primitive" society and "civilization." This view was not that the Indian would *physically* disappear, but that the Indian *way of life* would disappear and, inevitably, that the Native would become an almost invisible part of mainstream society. This vision did not see a role for the "progressive" Métis leading the rest of the Métis; in fact, once a Métis made it into the "progressive" group, he or she ceased to be a Métis at all; at least in the sense that the commission defined Métis.

The assimilation-based interpretation of the Métis placed the blame for their present situation squarely on the shoulders of the Métis themselves and their failure to adapt to the demands of the new, dominant society. From the start it was this view – the one expressed primarily by the non-Native witnesses – that held the most sway with the commissioners. They refused to consider seriously Brady's model or any analysis that perceived the Métis's present situation as accruing from colonialism, problems with scrip fraud, or discriminatory practices of the dominant society. Ewing dismissed any evidence regarding scrip fraud and the subsequent alienation of land from the Métis people, stating that he did not "know that any good can accrue by attempting to place the blame for any particular state of affairs that exists today."[56] Rather, it was the shortcomings of the Métis themselves – their character and well as their economic inflexibility – that was the cause:

MR PENNOCK: You were speaking of the Half-breeds owning land. I suppose the great trouble with the Half-breed is, he is irresponsible.

BISHOP GUY: Yes, like his white brother, he loves money but he cannot keep it.

DR BRAITHWAITE: He just lives from day to day?

BISHOP GUY: Yes.[57]

It should be pointed out that Mr Pennock was the barrister representing the Métis Association, and even he characterized them as "irresponsible" and therefore to blame for their own problems.

The view of the Métis as childlike and irresponsible was endemic in testimony offered the commission by a variety of witnesses. In a written submission to the inquiry, Dr Quesnel, a physician residing in Lac La Biche, offered some evidence on the high level of disease among the Métis. These statistics had been downplayed by the provincial Department of Health, so his testimony about the high rates of venereal disease and tuberculosis was seen by Brady and Norris as potentially valuable and supportive of the Métis's case. But even here, the disease rate was made to sound as if it were the Métis's fault. Dr Quesnel's characterization of the Métis makes them seem almost subhuman, and he doubted they had the ability to become farmers: "Their appalling ignorance makes them unfit to understand the first item of our laws of hygiene and sanitation. This same ignorance which has persisted amongst them for centuries, has made them indolent and given them a sub-normal mentality; all these deficiencies are conducive to laziness; laziness predisposes to poverty; and poverty in an ignorant, indolent race, means filth and filth brings disease ... poverty is responsible for a restricted diet and as they have no disposition for farming, they are even too indolent and lazy to spade up a garden."[58] It was also felt that they were incapable of improvement. The commissioners seemed to take the view that education would be wasted on them:

MR DOUGLAS: What is your opinion regarding the value to the half-breed of giving him an education?

BISHOP BREYNAT: I don't think he should be given too much education. Too much is bad for some of them. He needs just a little help – I think just until they are 13 or 14 years old probably.

MR EWING: I agree with you there, too much would be a bad thing.[59]

Implicit in this view is that the Métis, if not disposable, were certainly not a particularly valuable part of society; nor were they worthy of too much public expenditure. Little concern was expressed over the health of the Métis, even less than over their educational needs. Although there was much testimony about the high rates of venereal disease, scurvy, and tuberculosis among the Métis from Bishop Guy, Drs McIntyre and Quesnel, and the Métis Association executive, the commission tended to downplay or ignore the evidence in favour of that of Dr Orr, a physician with the provincial Department of Health. In one of the more cynical statements about the value of the Métis to society, Dr Orr suggested that "the cost of a travelling doctor would be prohibitive unless the Venereal Disease Vote was very greatly increased."[60]

This condescending attitude, if not the contempt towards the Métis displayed by the commission, was reflected in the way in which Norris and the other representatives of the Métis Association were treated and in the weight given their evidence. Whereas most of the non-Métis witnesses were treated courteously, the Métis executive was treated in a peremptory and less respectful manner. While other witnesses were allowed to express various views uninterrupted, the executive were often interrupted or cut off. Judge Ewing seemed hostile to the executive, particularly Norris.[61] Despite the fact that they were better educated and better off than the average Métis, there was little reason to doubt their bona fides. They were Métis themselves (or in the case of Dion, an enfranchised Indian), lived in or were familiar with the areas of Alberta that were being discussed and had travelled extensively throughout the region in their capacity as representatives of the Métis Association. Yet their qualifications were challenged several times. They were asked about the percentage of all the Métis in the province their membership represented and whether there was any opposition by the Métis to this new organization. The question itself was certainly a reasonable one, but the intent behind the question seemed to be designed to undermine or discredit the association rather than to validate its representativeness.[62]

Other witnesses, such as the clergy who testified about education, clearly had a vested interest in gaining or regaining control of Métis education, yet their motives or qualifications were not questioned in the same way that the Métis's leaders were. Contempt and hostility towards the leadership was also expressed by some of the witnesses as well as the commissioners:

> MR DOUGLAS: Regarding this education problem. We have heard different representatives, Malcolm Norris and some other chaps. They do not seem to be very favourable to church schools being formed –
>
> BISHOP BREYNAT: You cannot go by his advice anyway. That is the type of man that does not know – he is a very poor man. He would not know anything about it.[63]

Of course, the paternalism and condescension exhibited towards the Métis was not confined to the proponents of the assimilationist model alone. To some extent this characterization of the Métis was shared by the leaders of the Métis themselves. Brady and Norris, despite their belief that the Métis were in a state of poverty and vulnerability through forces beyond their control, seemed to share the prevailing view that the Métis were primitive and childlike. Malcolm Norris told the Ewing Commission: "The half-breed is after all but a child, in many cases his mentality is only that of a child, insofar as business and finance is concerned, and you can readily see the dangers he becomes liable to just as soon as he endeavours to deal with the white man on terms of equality in matters of business."[64] It may be that Norris felt compelled to take that position because the atmosphere at the hearings was so heavily weighted in favour of the assimilationist model that the association members may have felt that arguing against it was a lost cause.

But some of the leaders, particularly Dion, seemed convinced that the ultimate objective of the Métis Association was indeed assimilation:

> EWING: The Metis population should be willing to contribute their labour ... and when they get in position to be able to do so, they should be willing to contribute by way of taxes and any other way they can.
> DION: We have often discussed that amongst ourselves, that seems to be the general feeling, we want finally to be able to be assimilated.
> EWING: To put the half-breed back to where he belongs and to finally assimilate him into the citizenship of this country?
> DION: Yes.
> EWING: So that he may be a self-sustaining citizen of this country?
> DION: Yes. That is what we hope for finally.[65]

Dion probably did not want the Métis to be totally assimilated. It is more likely he wanted them to become self-sufficient and independent – in other words, integrated but not necessarily assimilated. But Ewing's none-too-gentle prompting seems to have backed Dion into a corner where he felt compelled to advocate total assimilation.

Despite the differences of opinion and theoretical outlooks expressed by the witnesses at the commission, it appears that all sides, including the executive of the Métis Association and the commissioners themselves, were agreed on one thing: the Métis were unable to look after themselves. Not only was their traditional means of subsistence failing them, but they were incapable of changing on their own. They were unable to compete economically or socially and needed protection from the rest of society, at least for a period of time. There were differences among the witnesses and the commissioners as to the *reasons* for the destitution of the Métis, as well as *how* the land issues would or could be settled. Norris and the Métis Association executive believed the Métis were not to blame for their present situation. However, since Ewing had disallowed any discussion of historical circumstances such as problems in the scrip program, it was difficult for them to defend their own people. They wanted land set aside and a system of local self-government bolstered with a role for the Métis Association as a province-wide umbrella organization and administration for the Métis. The rest of the witnesses seemed to focus the blame for the present situation on the Métis's own shortcomings. They were also in favour of setting aside land, either to be administered by the Church or to be administered as part of public welfare. The Church-run scheme was simply to protect and isolate the Métis from the rest of society, while the public welfare scheme was seen as a way of "rehabilitating" the Métis, eventually bringing them into mainstream society.[66]

Final Report of the Ewing Commission

The Ewing Commission issued its final report on 15 February 1936.[67] It was surprisingly short, just fifteen pages. Despite Ewing's disinclination to entertain testimony regarding scrip or other historical grievances, the report opens with a brief description of the history of the Métis and owns that, although the Métis's Aboriginal rights had been extinguished through the issue of scrip, the vagaries of the federal program had led to the present impecunious state of the Métis. The report adds that the scrip program had shown that the Métis did not have the "land hunger" that would cause them to seek and keep ownership of land, and that lack of experience in modern business techniques would likely result in further loss of any new land they were given title to. It is also clear that the particular group of Métis the report was concerned with were the "nomadic" Métis – those who lived "the life of the ordinary Indian" and included non-treaty Indians. The commissioners were not concerned with the "respectable" Métis who had made a successful transition to farming or business.

The report then tackled the social conditions of the Métis as the commissioners saw it. Considerable space was devoted to a discussion of health problems. The report cited Bishop Guy's testimony, but dismissed the statistics on the incidence of venereal disease presented by the secretary of the Métis Association as an overstatement. The commission concluded, "while the health situation is serious, it is not, except as to the particular diseases mentioned (tuberculosis, venereal disease), more serious than among the white settlers."[68] The report also discussed education, detailing some of the suggested remedies such as boarding schools and Church-run schools, and cited that 80 per cent of Métis children received no schooling whatsoever.

The commission was now ready to offer its solutions. The commissioners reiterated the ambivalence many witnesses felt about the ability of the Métis to become productive farmers. However, they pointed out that a considerable number of Métis *had* become successful farmers, and they concluded that in order to survive, the rest of the Métis had no other option but to become farmers as well. But adapting to a farming life would require education and assistance; hence, "some form of farm colonies is the most effective and ultimately, the cheapest method of dealing with the problem."[69] However, the commission realized that this was not a total solution; it recommended that individuals who were making a reasonable living from hunting and trapping and who had no desire to become farmers, as an alternative to joining a colony, could ask the government for the use of a parcel of land not more than 320 acres in size.

Although the commission took pains to stress that this was a welfare scheme, not an acknowledgment of any claim based on Aboriginal rights, the report reveals an interesting ambivalence on the part of the commissioners towards the issue of Aboriginal rights. In the commissioners' opinion, Aboriginal rights had been extinguished through the issue of scrip. They were of the opinion that this should not change; that they "should not submit a scheme which would give the half-breed the status of Indian and thereby make him a ward of the government."[70] (It is difficult to see how the provincial government would have had the authority to give Indian status to the Métis in any case.) Yet the commission did recognize a limited Aboriginal right as far as hunting and fishing were concerned: "The Commission is of the opinion that as the Metis were the original inhabitants of these great unsettled areas and are dependent on wild life and fish for their livelihood, they should be given the preference over non-residents in respect of fur, game and fish."[71] Despite this seeming recognition, the allotment of a parcel of land in a colony was a "privilege," and "no half breed would have an inherent right"[72] to join any Métis colony.

The commission was consistently unclear about the status of the Métis or of the rights flowing from that status. While the report makes it clear that the Métis were to be considered ordinary citizens, they were not treated as such. For example, they were denied the regular access to welfare: "no half-breed would be compelled to join the colony but if he did not join he could have no claim to public assistance."[73] Despite the recommendation that the Métis not be made wards of the government, the report consistently treated them as dependants. The report denied that the Métis had any Aboriginal rights, yet it made some concessions on hunting and fishing in recognition of them. This ambivalence about the place of the Métis in Alberta society was to persist for many years, and placing a proportion of them in colonies would do little to alter that ambivalence. The status of "Métis" was not clarified by the Ewing Commission, but it inadvertently revealed many of the contradictory concepts about them, which it perpetuated in its recommendations for government policy.

The Métis Population Betterment Act, 1938

The Alberta provincial legislature passed the Métis Population Betterment Act on 22 November 1938. The preamble to the act states that it was based on recommendations of the Ewing Commission for the betterment of the general welfare of the Métis population, and through negotiations with representatives of the Métis population of the province. Métis folklore has it that the act was, in fact, written by Dion and Tompkins, "in the Cecil Hotel in Edmonton" using the federal Indian Act as inspiration. It was continually rewritten and revised by them as various sections were approved or rejected by government officials.[74]

The act contains an official definition of Métis, and for many years, the various versions of the Métis Population Betterment Act and its successor, the Métis Settlements Act (1990) were the only government acts that attempted to define Métis.[75] Under the original act: "'Métis' means a person of mixed white and Indian blood but does not include either an Indian or a non-treaty Indian as defined in *The Indian Act*, being chapter 98 of the Revised Statutes of Canada, 1927."

There had been some discussion about including non-treaty Indians with Métis in the commission hearings, but the act specifically rejects non-treaty Indians, at least those who fall under the Indian Act (note: at that time, the concept of "registered" Indian did not exist, as the Indian Registry was not introduced until the 1951 revision of the Indian Act). In keeping with the sentiments expressed from the beginning of the commission, the new act did not apply to all Métis, but only to those

Métis "who are unable to secure out of their own resources a reasonable standard of living." In 1940, the act redefined the term "Métis" as a person with not less than one-quarter Indian blood, but who was neither an Indian nor a non-treaty Indian according to the Indian Act.[76]

The Métis Population Betterment Act, as it was written, nominally encouraged local self-government, although it simultaneously seemed to reject, or at least ignore, the existing Métis Association as a vehicle for that self-government. Section 4 (1) of the act empowered the minister "to promote the formation of one association or more composed of members of the metis population of the Province who are unable to secure out of their own resources a reasonable standard of living." No mention was made of the pre-existing Métis Association, even though it had been in operation for several years. The constitution and by-laws of the government-sponsored association(s) were to determine the qualifications and conditions for membership in the association and, subsequently, the colony. A board consisting of not more than five persons was to provide control of the business and affairs of the association. The constitution also was expected to make provision for election of the members of the board and to determine the length of their respective terms of office. The aims and objects of the association were "to cooperate with the Minister in preparing and formulating schemes for the betterment of the members of such association, and for their settlement on lands set aside for that purpose by the Province." Note that, as they were actually constituted, the associations were set up as strictly local organizations, one per colony. No provision was made for any sort of unifying province-wide organization, although the act did not specifically rule such an organization out. That role was a natural one for the Métis Association of Alberta to fulfil, but this was not to be, at least not for several years.

Subsequent versions of the Métis Population Betterment Act simultaneously increased the powers of the minister and decreased the powers of the Métis boards. The 1940 revision, in addition to changing the definition of Métis, increased the administrative powers of the minister, although it also deleted the phrase that indicated only destitute Métis could benefit from the plan. In 1941 a third amendment allowed the government to create game preserves in the settlements. In 1942 a fourth amendment empowered the government to designate the lands of a colony as an "Improvement District." This allowed the imposition of a minimum tax on each member, although they were supposedly immune to normal provincial assessment and taxation. In 1952, the act was amended to drastically change the structure of the colony boards. Instead of being made up of four individuals elected from the members of the Settlement Association, the board now was to consist of a chairman, who would be the local supervisor of the area as appointed by the Métis Rehabilitation Branch of the Department of Public Welfare, and four Settlement Association members, two of whom would be appointed by the minister and two of whom would be elected by the members of the Settlement Association. This arrangement gave the minister a great deal of control over the board and reduced the number of members to be elected by the members themselves to two.[77]

The local control hinted at in the first version of the act proved to be illusionary, and the structure of the boards made the Métis Association more and more irrelevant. This is not to say that the association had no part to play in the early development of the colonies, or that they did not attempt to create a role for the association. The association was involved in the early negotiations. Shortly after proclamation of the Métis Population Betterment Act, the minister of public health was designated as its administrator. He formed a joint Métis-Government Committee to select appropriate areas to be reserved as colonies. According to some authorities, the members of this committee comprised representatives of both the Métis Association (Dion, Brady, Norris, and Tomkins) and the government (Buck, Rees, and MacKenzie), but Dobbin doubts the participation of Brady and Norris.[78] This committee recommended twelve possible sites as settlement areas. In the following years, eleven of these sites were set aside by Order in Council for the use of the Settlement Association, but three of the sites were eventually rescinded. At present there are eight Métis settlements.[79]

Conclusions

The concept of who was a Métis, what it meant to be a Métis, and when and why one might adopt the identity of Métis began to be modified as the beginning of the twentieth century saw an increasing change in the social structure of the western prairie provinces and the Northwest Territories. From an early time, state definitions of ethnicity and Nativeness began to impinge on Métis identity, as lifestyle and other factors began to distinguish between Métis who took treaty, Métis who took scrip, and Métis who passed back and forth between the two categories, taking treaty at one point, forsaking it at another, and reapplying for treaty once again. In addition, the development of a non-Native settler society began to isolate the Métis from mainstream society, which, as a result of fishing and hunting regulations, created an increasing separation from the natural resources the Métis were traditionally dependent upon. The situation was exacerbated by the passage of the Natural Resources Transfer Agreement, provincial regulations as to the eligibility for relief, and arbitrary expulsions of Métis and Indians from treaty. These conditions created a growing population of Native people separated from Indians, separated from non-Natives, and separated from means of making a living, who were ripe for political and/or ethnic mobilization.

But political mobilization was to prove only partially successful as far as triggering a regrowth of Métis national identity in the beginning of the twentieth century. While the formation of L'Association des Métis d'Alberta et des Territoires du Nord-Ouest, the original name of the Métis Association of Alberta (now the Métis Nation of Alberta), seemed a promising start for Métis Nationalism, the values of its own leadership, particularly that of Brady, Norris, Dion, and Tompkins, who were heavily influenced by non-Native political and social ideals and the prevailing attitudes towards the "vanishing Native" and its concomitant disparagement of the value of Native identity, ensured that Métis nationalism would make only a faltering start in the 1930s.

The Ewing Commission also proved to be a handicap to the formation of a Métis identity or Métis nationalism. Refusal to allow testimony on past injustices and economic problems, a determination to define Métis through poverty rather than any cultural or ethnic standard, plus a conflation of Métis and non-treaty Indian (values which were, to be sure, somewhat reflected in the testimony of the Métis leadership as well) also discouraged the formation of a positive Métis identity.

The Ewing Commission gave rise to the Métis Population Betterment Act of 1938. This provided a state-regulated definition of Nativeness, defining Métis first as a person of mixed white and Indian blood who was neither an Indian nor a non-treaty Indian as defined in the Indian Act, and later (1940) as a person with not less than one-quarter Indian blood, but who was neither an Indian nor a non-treaty Indian according to the Indian Act. Despite this definition, the wording and application of the act limited the meaning of the term "Métis" to the indigent; there was no inherent right to be recognized as Métis, nor was there any recognition of rights flowing from the status of Métis.

The Métis Population Betterment Act and the creation of the Métis colonies did little to further Métis self-determination; in fact, it set it back several years. It sounded the death knell, or at least, the near death,

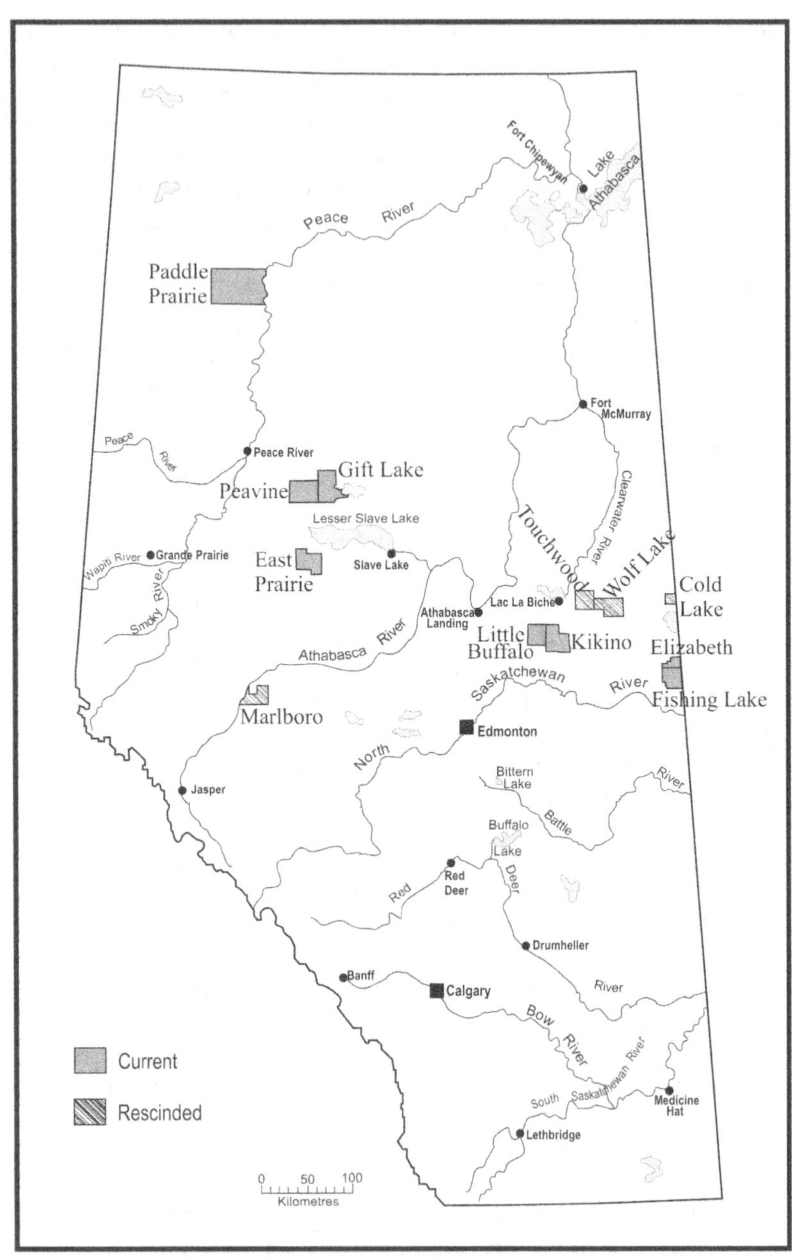

11.3 Métis settlements in the province of Alberta.

of the Métis Association. One might think that its success in bringing the plight of the Métis to the attention of the government and initiating the move towards the creation of the settlements might have given the association a great boost and cemented its position as the vehicle of a new Métis political movement. But the opposite was true. The association was almost moribund by the time the Ewing Commission published its findings. Because the association was wholly self-supporting, with no funding from the government, all of the members had to donate their own time and money. Once the association had interested the government in the plight of the Métis, there was little for it to do. It had been almost dormant in the few months prior to the setting up of the Half-breed Commission, and in the few months prior to the release of its report, both Brady and Norris were in the north, working, and had little time to devote to association business.

It is not unusual for a voluntary organization to disband or become inactive once it has achieved its objective. Once land began to be made available, the ostensible reason for the association's existence ended – at least in the eyes of some of the executive. Not so, however, for Norris and Brady; the important thing for them was for the Métis to become self-governing. The report of the Ewing Commission and the subsequent Métis Population Betterment Act effectively scotched that idea. Dion and Tompkins were less interested in the issue of self-government, and the association began to falter because there was no new goal that united all of the leaders. This is not to imply that the association disappeared or that the executive totally abandoned it. The association, or individual members of the executive, was involved in the early stages of implementing the colonies. But eventually, the association was shunted out of any direct involvement. Although it continued to exist, if in name only, for many years, it was not until the mid-1960s that it again became an important vehicle for Métis political action. This stifled any real growth in Métis nationalism until that time. To some extent, the association itself may have been the instrument of its own demise. First, it had succeeded in achieving the major goal of land grants, obviating one of the main reasons for its existence. Second, it had colluded in the creation of the image of the Métis as a helpless dependant. How could it now insist that these "children" would be capable of governing themselves? And third, none of the leaders had expressed any real desire to create a sense of Métis identity; in fact, as we have already seen, they felt apart from the Métis themselves. At any rate, the climate was not yet ripe for a Métis ethnic or political revival, nor was there much opportunity in the upcoming decade of the 1950s.

12 The Liberals, the CCF, and the Métis of Saskatchewan, 1935–1964

The situation of the Métis in Saskatchewan at the end of the nineteenth and the beginning of the twentieth century parallels that of the Métis in Alberta and the other prairie provinces in many ways, particularly in their increasing marginalization from the dominant society. The Métis were in some danger of completely disappearing – if not as an actual ongoing separate population, then as a publicly recognized ethnic group or subgroup of Aboriginal peoples. Increasingly, the boundaries between Métis and Indian were being erased in the public's perception. The newly arrived Euro-Canadian immigrants did not tend to view the Métis as the older non-Native population had – as a separate category from both Canadian and Indian. They tended to conflate Métis and Indian into a single category of "Indian," despite the fact that the Métis were beginning to face particular problems not faced by treaty Indians. This melding of both groups into a general category of "Native" was accompanied by the loss of economic importance brought about by the Great Depression and – for the Métis in particular – the passage of the Natural Resource Transfer Agreement (NRTA), which transferred natural resources to the prairie provinces and, with the transfer, responsibility for Métis scrip programs. The NRTA also had a psychological effect on the Métis of the prairies. In one fell swoop the federal government renounced its responsibility for the Métis, transferring their scrip claims to the provinces, while the provinces had little intention of assuming any responsibility for the Métis outside of the most limited social welfare issues. In effect, the NRTA created a constitutional/political crack through which the Métis would fall. In one sense the Métis political resurgence of the 1930s was a response to this new indifference.

The diminished economic importance of the Métis was accompanied by an almost total political marginalization. While Indians by definition were outside the political sphere, as they had no vote (being viewed as wards of the state), the Métis, although having the right to vote, were almost as invisible. They rarely voted and seldom ran for public office. Their marginalization took different forms in different parts of the province. While Indians and Métis were still involved in the fur trade, lumber industry, and fishing in the north, Métis in the south were facing some hard economic choices. The new agricultural economy was directed towards opening the west to immigration. The new immigrants would open up new farmlands and provide the labour for new businesses and industry. Farming, though advocated for both the Métis and the reserve Indians, did not become a viable option for either group. For the western Indians, whose traditional mode of production had been hunting and trapping, the difficulties of adapting to a farming economy in the southern parts of the province were obvious, even to the government and the Euro-Canadian populace at large. But contrary to popular perceptions of the time, farming was not a viable option for the majority of Métis. Relatively few Métis made a living as full-time farmers in this period, as they mostly worked as freighters and labourers when not hunting or trading.

The so-called settler mentality was also a factor in the declining status and fortune of Native peoples in the western provinces. By "settler mentality" I mean something similar to the values Elizabeth Furniss isolates in her characterization of the frontier narrative, a binary structure of opposing forces that contrasts the "heroic" acts of the first European settlers v. "hostile" Natives, a narrative coloured by the concepts of man vs. nature, civilization vs. savagery, and rugged individualism in the face of an outside (urban) government.[1] While frontier narratives as defined by Furniss will typically romanticize indigenous peoples, linking them with the "natural" world and lamenting their destruction by the forces of European expansion, this does not guarantee convivial relations between settler populations and indigenous peoples. The immigrants flooding the area held much more negative feelings towards Natives than had the original fur traders who had been the major contacts with Native people prior to the incoming immigration population. The newcomers held that European culture was naturally superior to the Native culture, and that Native people were naturally inferior. Ironically, many of the new immigrants coming into the west – particularly those from eastern Europe – themselves were victims of this racist assumption of "white" superiority. In the shifting parameters of racial boundaries, many of these people, such as Ukrainians and Poles, were designated as not being "white" themselves. But that did not stop them from harbouring and perpetuating negative stereotypes about Native people.

The result was that by the 1930s, the Métis were marginalized in even the depressed economy of the times. Although the Métis had long been adapted to working for wage labour (unlike much of the Indian population in the west), they began to find themselves systematically excluded from employment opportunities, bank loans, and credit from stores. Of course, some Métis were able to make the adjustment to the new economic reality. These were generally full-time farmers, businessmen, and some labourers, mostly English speaking. But one of the ways that enabled these individuals to make the transition was to jettison their Métis identity – to "pass for white." There were at the time sound reasons to deny or hide one's Métis identity, especially a French Métis identity following 1885, as there was widespread anger directed at those who had taken part in the 1885 resistance.

The Saskatchewan Métis Society

In the face of this growing marginalization in the 1930s, the Métis of Saskatchewan, like the Métis in Alberta and Manitoba, began to organize and form Métis associations. Murray Dobbin[2] suggests that as early as 1931 a group of Métis from Regina, led by Joe McKenzie, began meeting to address the problems they were facing as Métis. Like the early associations in Alberta, the major issues they raised concerned land and scrip. At this time, the last scrip issue was still within living memory – only about twenty-five years before. In the 1930s, many Métis believed that much of their Aboriginal title to the land was still intact, and/or that they had not been properly compensated for Aboriginal title they had surrendered. Another common perception in Saskatchewan at the time was that distribution of scrip was to continue for each generation.[3] This was not true according to any existing scrip legislation or Order in Council, but the belief may have been fostered to some extent by the fact that the cut-off dates for eligibility for scrip in the Northwest Territories had been extended so often. The Métis's various concerns over scrip lasted for years and eventually precipitated a Canada-wide investigation into the scrip issue conducted in the late 1970s by the Department of Indian Affairs, the Native Council of Canada, and several of the provincial Métis organizations from the Maritimes, Ontario, Manitoba, Saskatchewan, and Alberta.

One might wonder why, if so few Métis were farmers, or were interested in becoming farmers, the subject of scrip was so important to them. After all, the market price of scrip was fairly low. Perhaps they saw it as recognition of their Aboriginal rights. Or simply that, in the dire financial straits they were in, even a small sum would seem significant. At any rate, the early meetings of the nascent Métis association were concerned mainly with the scrip issue. However, it was several years before these meetings resulted in anything substantial; no claims against government were initiated until the 1940s.

According to Dobbin, a small group of Métis in Regina met in 1935 or 1936 to form the Saskatchewan Métis Society (SMS). Joe Ross, a labourer from Regina was elected chairman, and Henry McKenzie Sr was elected secretary-treasurer. There were seventeen people at this inaugural meeting. Also in attendance were other members of the McKenzie family, Mr and Mrs Ed Klyne, Mrs Ray Dixon, Martin Knudson, and Flora Diotte. The beginning of the Saskatchewan Métis Society was similar to that of the Alberta Métis Association, in that several local Métis organizations began forming independently in various communities. These groups then amalgamated to form a provincial organization. By 1937, there were several locals organized in the Regina area. Lebret was probably the first to organize, but there were others as well. According to Ross, the Métis did not seek public attention at first; they wanted to organize among themselves before approaching government or making any public claims: "We wanted to see first where we stood and how we could present ourselves. We held off until we knew we were going to be a chartered organization." [4]

Unlike Alberta's association, which drafted several versions of a constitution without consulting a lawyer but never formally registered under the provincial Associations Act until the 1950s, the Saskatchewan leaders went to some pains both to write a constitution and to register early on. In the fall of 1937 they consulted a lawyer, T.H. Newlove, who helped them draw up a constitution. The aims of the association were fairly typical of the early Métis organizations in Alberta and Manitoba: to organize to improve social and economic conditions; to preserve Métis culture; to help create and perpetuate a history of the Métis in Saskatchewan in keeping with the Métis's own perception of themselves, and to encourage the formation of SMS locals, or affiliation with already existing local Métis associations that "held similar aims and objectives."[5] Joseph Z. Laroque, a Métis from Lebret, was chosen as the first president.

Joe Ross was designated as the organization's fieldworker. His task was to organize a province-wide Métis association. As was the case in all of the early Native organizations – Métis, non-status, or status – there were no funds available. Organizing was done with little money; mostly out of the leaders' own pockets or dependent on small donations or association fees. However, in this the SMS had one advantage over similar organizations, as its fieldworker had access to free travel. Being legally blind, Joe Ross was entitled to a free railway pass, which enabled him to travel around the province and organize various locals. His efforts proved fruitful; by the end of 1938, there were at least thirteen functioning locals in Regina, Lebret, Estevan, Crooked River, Meota, Willowfield, Crooked Lake, Touchwood, Shell Lake, Ituna, Glen Mary, Battleford, and Saskatoon.[6]

While the Métis in the three prairie provinces generally were similar in their cultural makeup and faced similar political and economic concerns, there were regional variations, which were reflected in the early development of their political organizations, and the Saskatchewan Métis Society differed from its Alberta and Manitoba sister organizations on several significant issues. One of the most important was membership. Whereas the Métis Association of Alberta (MAA) was open to all Métis as well as non-treaty Indians, the SMS, from the beginning, limited its membership to those who identified as Métis or half-breed only, although the non-Indian portion of their background could include English, Scottish, or French. At this time, the only Manitoba association was L'Union nationale métisse Saint-Joseph, which limited membership to francophone Métis.

Although all three provinces demonstrated a split between Métis in the northern and those in the southern parts of the provinces, this divide seemed to be much more significant for the early organizations in Saskatchewan than it was for those in Alberta or Manitoba. The Métis in the north and south had somewhat different needs and conditions in Saskatchewan. Those in the southern part of Saskatchewan were more acculturated to the dominant society. Most could speak English, rather than French, Cree, or Mechif, and they regularly interacted with the larger society in business and wage labour. The northern Métis were more oriented to bush life, still making their livelihood through hunting and trapping.

The Saskatchewan Society also differed from its sister organizations in that it appeared to have closer ties to established political parties.

The early pioneers of the MAA – Norris, Brady, and Dion – were not officially tied to any of the established political parties in the province. Brady and Norris in particular were associated more with smaller left-wing movements and associations. But in Saskatchewan, several of the influential leaders, particularly Joseph Z. LaRocque, had close ties to the Liberal Party. This did not always work to the organization's advantage; some Métis avoided the organization because of its perceived ties with an established political party, because either they were not Liberals or they distrusted all political parties.

This close tie to the Liberal Party also led to another difference between Alberta and Saskatchewan: although the SMS limited its membership to Métis only, it was far more influenced by non-Métis advisors than was the MAA. After the SMS identified land and scrip as two of its major concerns, it began to solicit advice from outside its ranks. One such person was Zacharias Hamilton of Regina, secretary of the Saskatchewan Historical Society. Although not a Métis himself, Hamilton was married to a Métis woman. He also had close ties to the Liberal Party. Hamilton offered the fledgling Métis Society advice on both research into land claims and advice on how best to pressure the government. He was assisted in both issues by several other interested non-Métis, including A.T. Hunter, J.A. Gregory and B.J. McDaniel of Regina. All of these men were members of the Historical Society as well as the Liberal Party, and Gregory and McDaniel were in fact elected Liberal members of the legislative assembly.

The early organizers, like those in Manitoba and Alberta, found it difficult to attract members either from groups that had become financially successful or from those that were more or less indigent. Many Métis denied their heritage – especially those who had achieved some success in business or the workforce. This problem was not unique to Saskatchewan. The task of building ethnic pride was one of the objectives of Métis organizations everywhere, and one that took many years to achieve. Denial of one's Métis or Indian heritage was quite common in Canada at least up to the 1970s. In an interview with Dobbin, Joe Ross stated that that was one of the major problems in the early years of organizing: "There were all kinds of people who wouldn't admit they were Métis – couldn't talk to them at all – they wouldn't have anything to do with you. A lot of these people felt 'Well, I'm doing fine, why should I be bothered with anything like that?'"[7] Those who were not successful were even more alienated from the political and economic mainstream, and it was difficult to persuade many of them that any action would be successful.

The SMS and the Patterson Liberals

The SMS was quite successful during the period 1938–39. There was much discussion in public and the legislature over the state of the Métis, and it is probable that a good deal of this was instigated by the activities of the SMS. The 1939 SMS Annual Assembly heard personal addresses from Premier William Patterson, the mayor of Regina, and representatives of the Anglican and Roman Catholic Churches. A new executive was elected, including Mike Vandale of Saskatoon as president and Joe Ross of Regina as vice-president and organizer. Among the many resolutions passed was one petitioning the Dominion government for recognition of the Métis's land claims. The resolution stated in part:

> And whereas through the encroachment of settlement the Metis have been deprived of their original means of subsistence and are reduced, they and their children, to the most abject poverty;
>
> Therefore, be it resolved that the Saskatchewan Metis Society ... hereby humbly petitions the Government of the Dominion of Canada to grant to the Metis of Saskatchewan for extinguishment of their title to this country, adequate assistance to establish themselves in agriculture, industry, and other means of making a livelihood for themselves and their children .
>
> And be it further resolved that any settlement made by the government to the Metis people, shall not infringe on the franchise the Metis people now enjoy."[8]

The SMS Assembly also authorized the executive to meet with the provincial government to seek assistance for its land claim.

This resolution provided another example of differences in strategies and outlook between the Métis in Saskatchewan and Alberta. While the Saskatchewan Métis were aware of the plans for the Alberta Métis colonies, and while there was some support for a similar plan in Saskatchewan from the Liberal, Co-operative Commonwealth Federation (CCF), and Social Credit Parties (the idea had been discussed in the legislature in early 1939, with support from all parties), the SMS itself seemed to reject the idea. They may have had some good reasons. The society executive regarded any provincial land grant as a relief measure, and they preferred to deal with the federal government, where their claims would be based on Aboriginal title rather than on need.

However, the SMS may have been receiving some mixed messages from their advisors on the validity of their Aboriginal claim. While the resolution quoted above, written by one of the Historical Society's members, refers to "extinguishment of their title," Dobbin suggests that Zachariah Hamilton and the other members of the Saskatchewan Historical Society were generally of the opinion that Aboriginal title had already been extinguished by the various scrip programs, and that all that remained was a "moral claim."[9] However, the Métis Society chose to proceed as if they still had an unextinguished Aboriginal title. This allowed the provincial government to treat any Métis claim as a federal responsibility and slough off any provincial responsibility. This was underscored when Liberal MLA J.A. Gregory, who was also the president of the Historical Society, stated in the legislature that he felt the Métis were a federal responsibility, although he was contradicting himself somewhat, as the Historical Society's report, which he was partly responsible for, suggested that the Métis had no federal claim. Dobbin is quite critical of the leadership of the SMS at the time, suggesting that they were far too much influenced by their non-Métis advisors. Nevertheless, one could argue that it takes time to develop the political acumen that is now possessed by contemporary Native political leaders, and that some of the shortcomings of these pioneer Métis activists could be due to lack of experience or to the diffidence that some of the leaders may have felt towards their better-educated and supposedly better-informed advisors. It probably wasn't education that was needed as much as self-confidence: many of the most powerful Métis leaders who came forth in the 1960s and 1970s, such as Stan Daniels and Jim Sinclair, had little formal education, but that did not stop them from taking on the most powerful politicians on both the provincial and the national scenes, and holding their own. However, this self-confidence apparently had not yet been developed by the early leaders.

To address the ongoing concerns of the Saskatchewan Métis a meeting was held in June 1939 between the SMS and the Liberal premier of Saskatchewan, William Patterson.[10] The province was represented by the premier and two cabinet ministers, and the SMS was represented by its executive, and its two advisors, Z. Hamilton and A.T. Hunter. The meeting did not go well for the Métis. They began by requesting that the provincial government set up a commission to study the conditions of the Métis. The premier replied that he did not see the necessity for such a commission, and the Métis and their advisors dropped the topic without much of a fight. They further weakened their own case by putting aside issues that clearly were the responsibility of the province – relief and education – to concentrate on explaining the Métis's land claim against the federal government. They asked the premier for financial help in pursuing this claim. This may have been a tactical error on the part of the SMS executive. There is some evidence that the Saskatchewan government was already considering setting aside land for several Métis colonies as had been done in Alberta, but the SMS's insistence on pursuing a federal claim mitigated against the Society's having much input into how the proposed colonies would be set up or administered. Nor did their insistence that their claim was a federal, not a provincial, one give Patterson any pressing reason to fund their land claims project. Although the Liberal government did eventually institute a Métis colony, probably little of this decision was due to efforts of the SMS. Although the SMS executive and their non-Métis advisors were not successful in obtaining any money from the province to help them pursue their federal case at that meeting, the province did eventually provide the SMS with a grant of $10,000 to help take their case to Ottawa. This was in 1940 – almost a year after Patterson's first meeting with the SMS. The society eventually hired the Regina law firm of Noonan and Hodges to look into the claim, but WWII intervened and, on the advice of Z. Hamilton, the claim was put on hold for the duration of the war.

Why was the SMS so set upon the strategy of obtaining land from the federal government rather than from the province? Dobbin suggests it was "pride and historical justice." He also suggests that the SMS may have been aware of the shortcomings of the idea of the Métis colonies. They probably realized that they would be situated on secondary lands in the north rather than in the prime farmlands in the south. The Métis in the south wanted to stay where they were, and the Métis in the north likely did not want farmlands at all. Laurie Barron, for example, doubts that many Métis in either part of the province wanted farmlands. He thinks they were already more concerned with moving to urban areas and joining the labour force.[11] Nevertheless, Dobbin thinks that "if they had been given good political advice they may have accepted the Province's rehabilitation scheme."[12] That was unlikely, as the early leaders seemed to make an important distinction between being granted land by the federal government in recognition of their Aboriginal title and being granted land in recognition of "need" by the provincial government.

While the SMS seemed to be making progress in the early 1940s – a grant from the provincial government to begin land claims research and an increased membership (a list of SMS locals from 1940 indicate that the SMS had twenty-eight locals and a reported membership of over 2,500[13]) – several seeds were already in place that would weaken the organization and subvert its political power for years to come. First, WWII had a drastic effect. Not only was public attention diverted from internal issues such as relief, education, and welfare of Natives, but many active or potential Métis leaders and spokespersons were drawn away into the war. This distraction compounded the leadership problem already prevalent in the SMS: no really powerful or effective leader had emerged to rally the Métis of the province. The decision to postpone their land claims until after the war also weakened the SMS.

However, the biggest cause for the disintegration of the SMS was a split between the northern and southern Métis in the province. The division became more pronounced as the war effort halted the activities of the SMS. There were also definite leadership problems. At the Annual Assembly, held in Saskatoon in June 1940, Thomas Major, a Métis from Lebret, was elected president. He had been reluctant to run, but was persuaded to let his name stand because of perceived interference from several non-Métis at the Assembly, including Zacharias Hamilton from Regina and Wilma Moore of Saskatoon. Shortly after he had been elected, he joined the army and was posted outside the province. He had little time to devote to the society during his service and, even when he returned from the war, he showed little interest in taking up the reins as president. Major felt he was a liability to the SMS because of his ties to the Union of the Unemployed and other more radical political movements.[14]

Many members were becoming impatient with the society's lack of progress on land claims issues and its dependence on non-Métis advisors, whose motives they distrusted. Toby McGillis, of the Willow Bunch local, wrote to former president Joe LaRocque complaining of the association's dependence on "English" advisors: "why do you have Englishmen run your business for you, you are supposed to be educated enough to run your (own) business affairs. When as you know, they are mostly working for themselves ... We don't know half of what's going on having them going ahead to do as they like. In Alberta I heard they would have never gotten their land, if they hadn't gone ahead and speak for themselves ... now they have what they wanted already but we don 't seem to make any headway."[15]

This concern was to prove well founded, especially for the northern faction of the Métis Society, where the role of at least one non-Native in the organization expanded from being a mere advisor to becoming an actual member of the executive. Sometime in 1941 or 1942 a group of northern Métis held a meeting in Saskatoon and attempted to take over the SMS. Although only a minority of the SMS, and acting without the sanction of the SMS executive, they declared the meeting to be the Annual Assembly. One of the people involved was Wilma Moore, a non-Métis who had been active in both the Liberal and the Conservative Parties. Many of her family were Presbyterian ministers, who had been active in Métis and Indian communities for years. The group elected a new executive: R.O. St Denis was elected president, and Wilma Moore elected secretary (despite the fact that the SMS constitution specifically forbade any non-Métis from holding office in the organization).[16] Dobbin casts Moore as the instigator of this palace coup, but it does not seem likely. His interview with her[17] reveals her to be – to say the least – imperceptive and confused, with little understanding of government structure or Native issues. Nor can this coup be blamed – as Dobbin also does – for instigating the long and bitter dispute between the north and south that characterized Métis politics of the time. That division was in place for a long time and for more fundamental reasons than the holding of this meeting, which was more likely a reflection of the division rather than the cause of it. Nevertheless, shortly after the Saskatoon meeting, Moore wrote to the standing secretary of the SMS, Spence Isbister, informing him that she was now secretary and demanding the papers of the SMS. Isbister replied:

> It is difficult for me to understand how I can do what you suggest because ... I am still secretary of the SMS ... At an executive meeting held some time ago ... it was decided that for the present time, owing to war conditions there should be no annual meeting held. In the meantime the regularly elected officers were to continue to hold their offices ... the annual meeting can only be called by the president or the vice president ... at the request of a certain number of members ... May I also point out that our Constitution provides that no one can hold office unless they are of Metis origin.[18]

Nevertheless, for a time at least, the centre of operations of the SMS shifted to Saskatoon.

The reorganized SMS held another convention in 1943, at which time the new executive made explicit the reasons for the reorganization, namely, that in its view the original SMS had ceased activities. They sent a letter to Noone and Hodges demanding the completed brief.

The lawyers, annoyed at being rushed, complained to Z. Hamilton, although Hamilton no longer held much if any influence with the SMS, since power had shifted to Saskatoon. Nevertheless, according to Dobbin, the brief as completed by Noonan and Hodges closely followed the original views of Hamilton, that the Métis had no enforceable claim other than a moral one. The brief advised the Métis that they should "stress ... present conditions ...and needs rather than ... compensation for past rights and alleged injustices."[19]

The executive of the Saskatoon Métis took possession of the brief in July of 1943, but it quickly became obvious that its members lacked the judgment or experience either to understand its implications or to design any feasible alternative strategy. Even though the brief suggested that the Métis had no enforceable claim, the executive approached the Patterson government asking for funds to allow them to take the brief, as it was written, to Ottawa. Perhaps fortunately, they were refused. However, shortly after the CCF came into power (July 1944) they again approached the provincial government and this time were awarded a small grant of $500 to cover expenses for the trip to Ottawa. The inexperience of the executive was such that they were not even sure of what branch of the federal government they should submit the brief to. Moore reveals that while she was in Ottawa as part of the delegation, she was uncertain about who took the brief or who read it.[20] At any rate, nothing came of their expedition. The federal government reiterated that it considered all Métis land claims had been satisfied with the issuance of scrip, and that any further responsibility for the Métis lay with the provinces, not the federal government. The Ottawa trip marked, to all intents and purposes, the end of the SMS. After the executive returned from Ottawa, Wilma Moore lost interest in the organization and dropped out. She soon moved to British Columbia. The rest of the executive also became inactive, there was no longer any real grass-roots membership to speak of, and the SMS became, for the most part, an organization in name only.

The CCF and the Métis

By 1944, the SMS was at its lowest point since its incorporation in 1937. Despite its close ties to the Liberal Party and its reliance on advisors with close ties to the Liberal Party, there was little to show for this political affiliation after its first seven years of operation. The SMS had received only token assistance from the Patterson government in its land claims case against the federal government (a grant of $10,000) and had had little or no input into the establishment of the two Métis colonies at Green Lake and Lebret that had been initiated by the province. When T.C. Douglas led the CCF to a resounding victory over the Liberals in the 1944 provincial election, the SMS's prospects were about as low as those of the Liberal Party to which they had once pinned their hopes.

Much has been written about the CCF's influence on Native issues[21] but the party showed little interest in them while it was building up support in the years leading up to its victory in 1944. Only one person – Tom Johnson, CCF MLA for Touchwood – had discussed the topic of the Métis and their place in Saskatchewan society. There had been several opportunities for the CCF to make inroads into the Métis community, but they had ignored them. Joe Ross, one of the founders of the SMS, had CCF connections and was continually trying to get the party to address Métis issues. In May of 1944 – well into the election campaign – the SMS executive agreed to advise their constituency to vote for the party that offered the Métis "the best opportunity to improve their conditions."[22] Joe Ross wrote to CCF secretary A.O. Smith to inform him of this policy, suggesting that the Métis could swing the vote in at least five constituencies. He also advised that, despite the resolution passed by the executive, the current president of the SMS, R.O. St Denis, and the secretary, Wilma Moore, were advising the Métis to vote for the Conservatives.

In response, Smith wrote to T.C. Douglas, passing on Ross's suggestion that the CCF consult with the Métis to develop a Métis platform. Douglas did not feel that such consultation was necessary, and nothing was done. This was a presentiment of things to come, as the relationship between the Métis and the CCF was destined to become a rocky one. The CCF Party president wrote to Ross: "It has been suggested to me that you draft a letter addressed to the Métis people urging their support for the CCF."[23] However, no real effort to gain the Métis vote was made, and no reason was suggested to Ross as to why the Métis should support the CCF.

Basically, the grass-roots constituencies of the CCF were farmers and workers. The CCF did not need – or did not think it needed – to reach out to the Métis or to learn the specific needs or desires of the Métis. Of course, after they were in power and attempted to initiate programs in northern Saskatchewan such as the Fur Marketing Service, they discovered too late that they did not understand the needs or desires of the Métis and as a result were alienating a significant portion of their northern constituency. There has been some suggestion that this lack of knowledge was due to an ingrained racism within the CCF hierarchy, but that is an unsatisfactory explanation.[24] It was more likely simple political expediency: the CCF was attempting to identify and build up a political base and constituency and did not see the Métis as fertile ground for adding to its membership. As it turns out, they were correct. The Métis became almost universally opposed to the CCF. Whether that hostility was because of the party's early neglect is not clear, although it could not have helped. It was more likely due to several unpopular policies the CCF had initiated in the north.

Although by now the SMS was an organization in name only, it occasionally could show some signs of life and initiate some political response. In answer to several requests from Fred Delaronde, the sitting president of the SMS, T.C. Douglas called for a meeting between Métis leaders and the provincial government to be held in Regina on 30 July 1946. Representatives from every part of the province were invited to attend – although no money for travel or accommodations would be provided by the government. Each district was free to send as many representatives as they wished – an offer easy to make, since no travel funds were being provided. The local committee in Lebret was drafted to help delegates find accommodation. The meeting was held during Exhibition Week in Regina, purportedly because many Métis would be already in town during that time.[25] However, this was hardly a propitious time to call a convention; any accommodation to be had would be at a premium and attending a conference instead of the exhibition was hardly an enticing idea. As a result, only about thirty representatives of some seventeen Métis communities were able to attend.

The meeting was chaired by Morris Shumiatcher, law officer of the attorney general and personal assistant to T.C. Douglas. Shumiatcher had already been instrumental in the formation of the Union of Saskatchewan Indians and had a good understanding of treaties and Aboriginal rights.[26] His opening remarks indicated that he also had a good understanding of the present condition of the SMS: "the Government is anxious to deal with the representatives of the Metis who are elected in a free and democratic fashion. Now the Saskatchewan Metis Society has been in existence for several years. As I understand, today it represents primarily the Metis of the northern part of the Province. The Metis round Lebret and round Regina have not participated actively in this organization during the last year or two."[27]

He also made clear what he expected from any organization of the Métis – representation from all parts of the province. "The Government (is) anxious to ascertain what people best represent the Metis population of the Province as a whole. That is, it may be that the (SMS) does, it may be that it doesn't, but the Government does not wish to treat with any society or organization unless it is reasonably certain that it does represent the Metis population of the Province as a whole and not merely one segment of a group."[28] He stated that until the Métis were able to forge a strong, representative political organization, the government would not consult with them. However, he was anxious to reassure the Métis that the government had no interest in using whatever organization developed out of this meeting for its own political gain, as in the past this had been a barrier in building a unified Métis society.[29]

Despite its initiative in calling this meeting, the CCF government did not seem as committed to fostering a province-wide organization for the Métis as they were for the status Indians. Perhaps it was because it became obvious at this meeting that (a) the northern and southern Métis were deeply divided, and (b) there was no leader (at least, no leader who appeared at that meeting) who seemed capable of bridging the gap and putting together and heading up an effective organization.

The meeting almost immediately broke down into a bitter conflict between Métis of the north and those of the south. Joe Ross claimed the northern group was breaking the SMS constitution by electing people who were not present at the meeting. The discussion then turned to the question of whether the SMS should continue to serve or if a new organization should be set up. Several other grievances were aired, including both the fact that the original SMS had been on hold during WWII and whether or not the northern group was justified in wresting control of the SMS for that reason. A motion was quickly put forth by Martin Knudson of Regina, seconded by Joe Ross, declaring non-confidence in the existing SMS. After a sometimes acrimonious discussion, the motion was defeated and the SMS was recognized as the official representation of the Métis people of Saskatchewan. But it quickly became evident that the SMS was in a very sad state. The past president, R.O. St Denis of Saskatoon, was not even able to say with certainty how many locals were presently active (there had been fifty-three before the war). Wilma Moore, the erstwhile secretary, had dropped out of the SMS by that time and was not present at the meeting.

It was also becoming quite evident that the breach between the north and south was unlikely to be healed. In an effort to get past the internal squabbling of the Métis at the meeting, Shumiatcher suggested the formation of a committee to be chosen from those present to act as a representative for the Métis of Saskatchewan until such time as the SMS could become reorganized. But neither side wanted to reconcile. Knudson suggested that the committee should consist of people close to Regina. Joe Ross agreed, complaining: "These people from the north, presently ruling this Society, have endeavored in every way possible to block the people from the south to have any say in the Society's business ever since they got hold of it." His solution was to limit the committee to three members, all from Regina, on the rationale that Regina was the seat of power and the society couldn't afford to bring people in from the north to attend every meeting.[30]

Shumiatcher, obviously exasperated, stated, "Mr Ross, I don't see how you are going to attempt to have all your members (of the committee) in Regina. If you do that the people in Prince Albert will have the same objection you have ... Your complaint is that the Metis Society is run by people from the North. Now you are going to set up a committee of people from the South, and the people in the North will have the same complaint."[31] It was becoming obvious that there was little enthusiasm – from either the north or the south – to work together to provide a province-wide organization.

It was finally decided that the committee would consist of six members, including the president of the SMS, who sat as chair and an ex officio member of the committee. The committee as it was chosen seemed a reasonable one – it had members from both the north and the south. Schumiatcher expressed satisfaction with the way the committee was structured: "it seems to be fairly representative; [the committee members] come from all parts of the Province, and the South is certainly represented."[32] They then agreed that the committee should meet in October of that year (1946). As far as is known, the committee never met. The meeting probably convinced the CCF that an effective Métis society was not likely to be developed any time soon. There did not appear to be much interest from the Métis population at large and no effective leader capable of healing the breach between the north and south was forthcoming. It probably had been a mistake to vote to continue with the old organization. Beginning afresh with a new organization may have been one way to heal the old resentments between the north and the south.

In November 1946, two members of the committee, M.W. Knudson of Regina and R.O. St Denis of Saskatoon, requested $1,000 to reorganize the SMS, but the government refused.[33] The reason for this response may have been that the government was concerned that the request came from only two members and did not represent the committee or the Métis of the province as a whole. With this exchange, the SMS became, to all intents and purposes, defunct in1946. It would be many years later – 1964, in fact – before an effective Métis organization would begin to develop in Saskatchewan. Few policy initiatives for the Métis were undertaken between these dates, except for the foray into Métis colonies. Schumiatcher suggested that the government establish a royal commission to look into Métis conditions (this proposal had also been made at the 1946 Métis conference by Knudson and St Denis), but it was never came to pass. The CCF had established a committee of the legislature in 1945 to look into the problems of the Métis and had promised some action, but it rejected the idea of a commission.

The refusal of the CCF to support the SMS – or the failure of the SMS to convince the CCF that they were worthy of support – did not totally end efforts of the Métis to organize in the 1940s and 1950s. Malcolm Norris, who had come to Saskatchewan to work for the CCF government in northern Saskatchewan, eventually settling in Prince Albert, attempted to resurrect the SMS. Norris was also instrumental in bringing Jim Brady to Saskatchewan. Norris encouraged Métis in several communities in the north to set up SMS locals. He called for a general meeting of the various SMS locals in Saskatoon to take place in June of 1947, almost a year after the CCF-sponsored provincial meeting. Twelve people attended, representing eleven communities. But the meeting only reiterated the weakness of the SMS: the executive was totally inactive. Reinventing what had been done just a year before, the group formed a provisional council to try to build up the organization. But it came to nothing. In 1949, Joe Ross once again tried to resurrect the SMS, calling for a province-wide meeting. This attempt, too, failed.

The late 1940s and 1950s were generally a low point in Métis political activity throughout the prairies. The time was not ripe for political activity of minorities (at least not of Native minorities). Some conditions had improved since 1930s, when many of the organizations were founded, but not to the extent that there was a role for a strong Métis political association. There were, of course, committed individuals throughout the prairies who kept up the fight – Adrian Hope, using the remnants of the Métis Association of Alberta to represent the Métis colonies in Alberta, Norris and Brady sporadically advancing Métis organization in Saskatchewan – but for some reason, political apathy among the majority of Métis subverted any real progress.

There were, to be sure, some specific problems facing Métis political organization in Saskatchewan. The division and resentment of north vs. south and the lack of an effective leadership are but two examples. One could argue, perhaps, that the upgraded government services under the CCF improved conditions for many Métis, making political activism unnecessary. However, it can easily be shown that this was a time of deep political discontent among the Métis, particularly among northern Métis. Their discontent was aimed directly at the CCF government. Yet this dissatisfaction did not manifest in any concerted political action. It was not until 1964, when Malcolm Norris and Donald Nielson founded a new group, the Métis Association of Saskatchewan, that Métis political organization again was manifested. A year later, another organization, the Métis Society of Saskatchewan (not the old SMS) was generated in Regina. When the two organizations amalgamated in 1967 under the name Métis Society of Saskatchewan (MSS), the political activity of the Métis in Saskatchewan was back on track. That organization is still extant today, although it has undergone many permutations and name changes.

The CCF and Métis Identity

Part of the reason for the lack of enthusiasm either for promoting Métis organizations or for consultation with Métis can perhaps be found in the outlook of Douglas and other members of the CCF. At the 1947 Métis conference, the premier posited an egalitarian philosophy and seemed to suggest that any sort of enhanced ethnic identity for any sector of the population would be counterproductive. "The Government of Saskatchewan has pretty well worked on the belief that we have a responsibility for all the people who live in the Province ... we cannot divide people up, and what affects one affects all."[34] O.W. Valleau, minister of social welfare, followed up in his opening address at the conference: "I think that you will agree with me that all any person or any group of persons should have is an even break, an even chance with the other fellow. I do not think that anyone wants an advantage, or that the government should be requested to give anyone an advantage." Valleau alluded to the futility of the Métis claiming special status because of their mixed heritage, since in his view, almost anyone could claim "mixed" heritage, himself included: "You have the handicap of what you think, possibly more than we consider, the handicap of being a mixed people. I do not see why it should have to be. It is quite likely there is nobody here whose blood is more mixed than mine. I think the bulk of mine is white, but when you get French and German and Dutch and I believe some Irish ..."[35] He then went so far as to deny that the Métis even qualified as a separate ethnic or Aboriginal group: "I am not at all sure myself that the idea of a group settlement (with regard to land) is the wisest thing. *You see, you people are not a definite race apart.*"[36] Moreover, in his opinion, the Métis were destined to disappear, and this was desirable: "The ultimate solution will be absorption into the general population. I don't think there is any doubt about that. There will come a time when there is no distinction between Metis and white men. You will be absorbed through inter-marriage."[37]

The CCF's emphasis on education was a recognition that the Métis needed to be brought up to speed with the rest of the population, but they were not interested in creating an enhanced ethnicity.[38] Nevertheless, the CCF, perhaps inadvertently, helped reify a Métis sense of identity and otherness. First, by commissioning extensive social science research into the north and hiring V.F. Valentine, an anthropologist, to study the Métis, a general picture of the Métis began to be constructed from the outside (see chapter 13). Second, many of the policies introduced by the CCF, in particular the Fur Marketing Service, totally alienated the Métis, uniting them in at least one thing: a total opposition to the CCF. Of course, that was not the party's intent; the CCF was concerned about the Métis, and developed several programs for them, but none was aimed at enhancing their separate ethnicity. Such a policy would go against the egalitarian principles of the CCF.

The Saskatchewan Métis Colonies

The CCF's reluctance to work through the Métis Society did not mean that they had no interest in working with the Métis or designing special programs for them. But their interest in assimilating the Métis naturally made them reluctant to work with a Métis organization that would want to enhance the ethnicity of the Métis. Most of the work with the Métis was through the Department of Social Welfare and Rehabilitation (DSWR) a creation of the new CCF. One of the major initiatives of the DSWR was the setting up of several Métis colonies.

The CCF did not initiate the idea of Métis colonies. They had existed in Alberta for several years, and two were already in place in

Saskatchewan. The previous Liberal government under W.J. Patterson had set up a colony at Green Lake, located in the Île-à-la-Crosse district in north central Saskatchewan in 1940, and there was a similar operation in Lebret, a Métis settlement in the Qu'Appelle Valley operated by the Oblates.[39] The rationale of these earlier Saskatchewan colonies was more or less adopted by the CCF government in 1944 and consequently requires some explanation.[40] The Liberal government in Saskatchewan during the Depression was faced with a "Métis problem" that stemmed from the destitution of Métis families squatting on road allowances in makeshift huts. The catalyst that made this impoverishment a political issue was that the municipal councils were under severe financial distress and viewed Métis squatters in their districts as a further financial burden. Unable to pay taxes, these families constituted a drain on the social assistance programs administered by the municipalities, and these municipalities in turn requested help from the provincial government. Picked up by the press, the economic, social, and health concerns of the Métis became a political issue that the Liberals tried to allay by establishing a Métis colony at Green Lake in 1940–41. It was a solution based on the premise not unlike that of the earlier experiments in Alberta – that through a process of resettlement and agricultural training the Métis could be "rehabilitated" and transformed into productive members of society.

The Green Lake Colony initially involved some 125 Métis families in the immediate area around Green Lake who had formerly made their living by hunting, trapping, and gardening. With the inroads of Euro-Canadian settlement, however, this mode of life was no longer viable. The "rehabilitation" plan called for the expulsion of settlers from the area by giving them land in other districts and the moving of Métis families onto these farms, with each family given forty acres on a ninety-nine-year lease from the provincial government. For those Métis interested in wage labour there was an option to receive a town lot in the hamlet of Green Lake, but the main goal of the plan was to encourage the Métis to farm. This plan also involved a large central farm operated by Métis heads of family under government supervision. This "model" farm was intended to instruct the Métis in farming techniques and to provide other assistance in the form of livestock and animal feed. The Catholic Church was also involved, as it was seen as an important agent of social change in a population that was largely Catholic. Though this colony initially served the Métis of the Green Lake region, the government believed that the colony might also be a solution for the Métis problem in southern Saskatchewan either as the prototype for other colonies or as the destination for the resettlement of southern Métis.

Unlike the colonies in Alberta, however, the Green Lake Colony, and subsequent Métis colonies in Saskatchewan, was not intended to be permanent and certainly not a Métis homeland. Administered as a local improvement district by the Department of Municipal Affairs, the colony was seen as a transitional institution whose goal it was to rehabilitate the Métis into the mainstream agricultural economy of the province. Once that result was achieved, the "Métis problem" (and presumably identity) would disappear and the local improvement district would evolve to municipal status.

Thus, when the CCF took office in 1944, precedent and policy had been set on both the "Métis problem" and its solution. Very early on the Douglas government endorsed the Green Lake Colony and began planning colonies in southern Saskatchewan. The government purchased the Lebret Métis Farm from the Oblates in 1945,[41] assumed control over its operations and expanded its holdings to two sections. The intent was to make it a model farm to instruct Métis families in the district. Approximately nine families worked for wages at the farms, supporting about sixty-five people as well as providing advice and machinery to other Métis colonies. By the late 1940s there were colonies at Crooked Lakes, Lestock, Crescent Lake, Baljennie, Willow Bunch, Duck Lake, and Glen Mary. While Green Lake remained under the control of Municipal Affairs, the other colonies came under the control of the newly created Department of Social Welfare and Rehabilitation.[42]

Interestingly, little consultation with the Métis themselves seems to have taken place regarding these colonies. In 1946 at the Métis conference called by the CCF, Tommy Douglas referred offhandedly to Lebret: "Mr Valleau will probably be telling you something about the experiment which has been made of the farm at Lebret. If that experiment seems to please all parties concerned, that may be the solution to be tried in other places."[43] He seemed to be inviting consultation from the Métis present, but none seems to have taken place.

As Laurie Barron has argued, the CCF's philosophy in running the Saskatchewan Métis colonies (like that of their Liberal predecessors) was different from the approach of the Alberta government. They were to be temporary, educational, and aimed at integrating the Métis into the general population, not permanent ethnic enclaves like those in Alberta.[44] The colonies were designed as model farms, perhaps inspired by the model farms that had been set up on many Indian reserves in the prairies and with the same object – to teach mixed farming techniques. In the case of the Métis, this would allow them to integrate into the farm communities, presumably as hired hands, before getting farms of their own. The minister of social welfare waxed eloquent on his own experiences as a hired hand, as well as pointing out that many other members of the CCF cabinet had also been farm hands: "don't think for a moment that going out as a hired man is something any one need be ashamed of. Since sitting down here at the back I was going over in my mind the number of those who sit around the Cabinet table who were hired men at some time or another and I think that the majority have at one time or another worked as hired men."[45] However, since the conference had indicated that the CCF was reluctant to provide farmlands to the Métis, because they thought veterans had a stronger or more pressing claim to land than the Métis did, it is difficult to see how this supposed integration into farm ownership was to be accomplished: "if I had the power to give every Métis family in the province a quarter section, I don't know that I would be prepared to do that."[46]

As already noted, by the late 1940s there were seven colonies in operation besides the ones at Green Lake and Lebret, all being run by the DSWR. Culturally specific education programs were provided for the Métis children: basic literacy augmented by vocational training deemed appropriate to the rural economy. No attempt was made to accommodate any Métis who was contemplating moving to an urban environment or aspiring to any sort of profession beyond labourer.[47] The CCF seems to have had a preconceived idea that the Métis were naturally a rural people. Valleau expressed some puzzlement over this: "I have been rather wondering during the last two years why so few of your people seem to adjust themselves to living in towns and cities, you seem to cling to the rural areas."[48] He wondered if it was because "you do not like the towns, or whether it is because of the handicap of lack of education which makes it difficult for you to earn a living in town."[49] It is interesting that he should pose such a question, yet preside over a system that did not provide the sort of education that would facilitate a move to urban areas.

By the 1950s, the colonies were mostly abandoned. Cost was the factor most commonly cited for this, but Barron suggests some other reasons. First, he feels that the CCF had misinterpreted Métis desires. In the 1940s, most Métis were turning away from farming towards wage labour. Those who wanted to remain farmers were more interested in privately owned

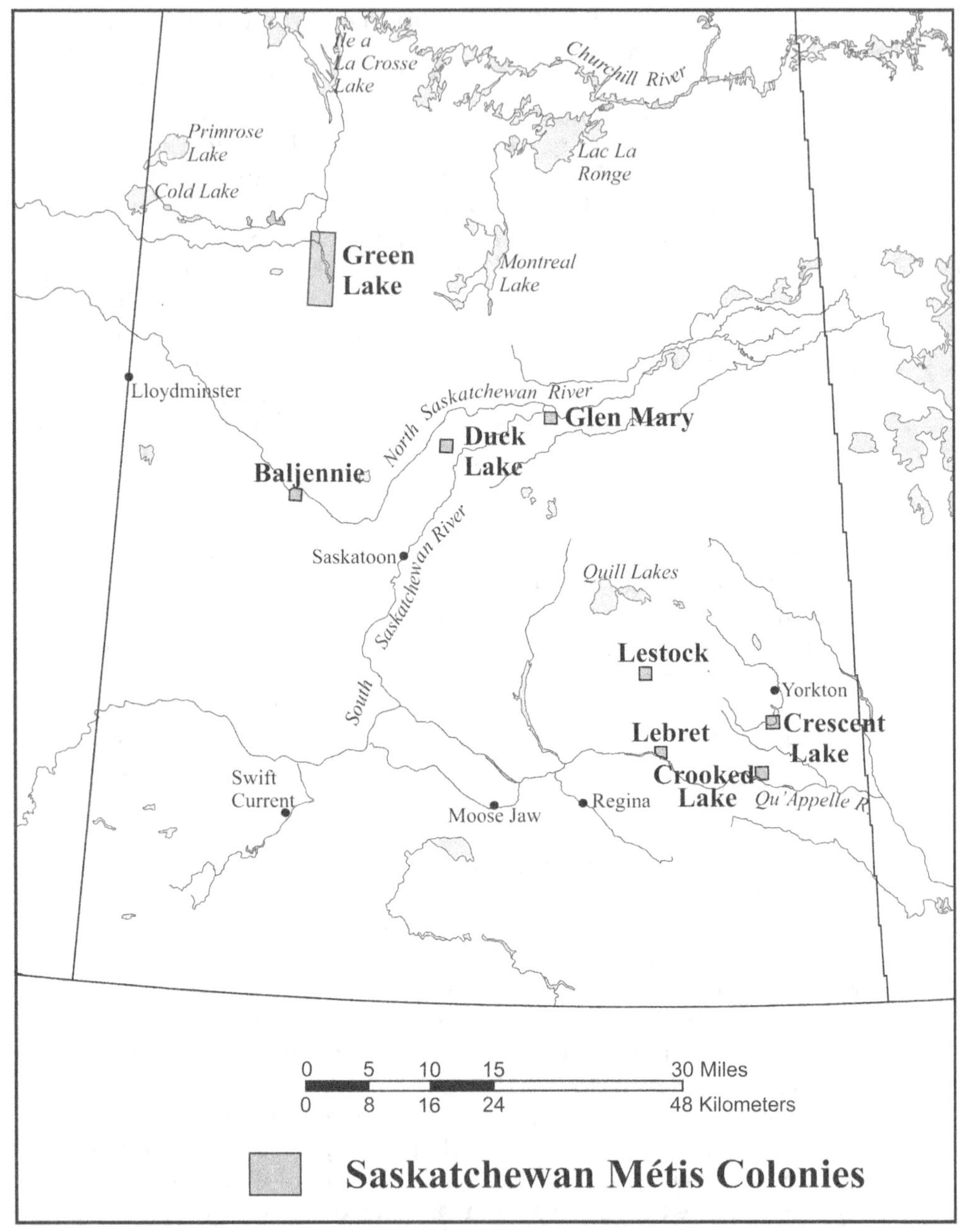

12.1 Location of Green Lake Métis Colony and other Métis colonies in Saskatchewan.

farms rather than the cooperative model the CCF was advocating. Second, Barron blames the CCF, or at least most government employees "especially at the local level," for discouraging individualism and initiative – the very reason the farms were instituted. He argued that it was because government employees had doubts about the competence of the Métis, which led to a systematic discouragement of local councils and individual business activities. Euro-Canadians were encouraged to move into Green Lake, for example, and take over many of the entrepreneurial roles such as storekeepers. Local officials did not always implement government policy. Newcomers to the colony were mistrusted by the local government supervisor. Barron also suggests that welfare payments were restricted in Green Lake to encourage the Métis to keep working in the colony, because the government was the biggest employer in the area. The idea was to keep them working and reduce wage expectations.[50]

Also, the colonies had a weak economic base. Most were located on marginal lands. The Métis were drawn away to better employment opportunities in urban areas. They would leave in the summer when there were employment opportunities elsewhere and return to the colonies in the winter, where some social assistance was available. Green Lake was an exception – there the Métis would go north rather than to urban areas, but otherwise, the pattern was the same; they would leave when there was an economic opportunity elsewhere and return in the off season for the social benefits available there. By the beginning of the 1960s, there was a general understanding that the colonies weren't working, that not all Métis wanted to be farmers, and that the colonies were encouraging a form of segregation. This situation "was the first step toward redefining the Métis problem as an urban phenomenon."[51]

CCF: Colonizer of the North?

Much has been written on the CCF's northern policies and their effects on Native people (Dobbin, Barron, Quiring). Part of the reason for this relatively prolific amount of research is undoubtedly a curiosity over the sorts of policies a nominally "socialist" government might develop with regard to a Native population. There is no doubt that the twenty years of CCF administration (1944–64) had a profound effect on the social organization of the Métis and Indian populations in Saskatchewan. Whether these changes were more or less harmful than those that inevitably would have occurred under another administration is a matter for speculation. It is useful to remember that this was a period of increased penetration into the north across Canada, and that similarly drastic changes could be observed elsewhere.

Under the CCF, northern Saskatchewan was administered mainly by the Northern Affairs Branch of the Department of Natural Resources (DNR). Other government offices included Education, Cooperatives, and Social Services. The minister in charge of DNR during its formative years was Joe Phelps, who was committed to the "complete socialization of all natural resources."[52] He attracted several like-minded individuals to work in administrative positions in the north and enticed Jim Brady and Malcolm Norris to leave Alberta to work for the DNR. The state of northern Saskatchewan when the CCF came to power was certainly a cause for concern. The major sources of income were the fur, fishing, and lumber industries, none of which was capable of providing a reasonable yearly income. School attendance was abysmal – less than 50 per cent of children regularly attended school. Many communities lacked year-round road access and many airfields were in a state of disrepair.

The CCF embarked on a plan to rejuvenate the existing fur, fishing, and lumbering operations, as well as attempt to open up the north to mining and other industry. In 1944, the Natural Resources Act was amended to give the provincial government the power to guide economic development and to actively regulate and determine enterprises such as the fur industry. Most commentary agrees that these policies, although well motivated and designed to alleviate pre-existing conditions that were truly deplorable, were nevertheless wrong-headed and ultimately harmful. They also were not particularly effective; the CCFs own review of the trapping and fishing industries, carried out in 1961, revealed little progress in increasing income.[53]

These policies were based on a misunderstanding of Native and Métis culture, social structure, and economy and on the preconceived ideas the dominant society commonly held of Native society at the time. Barron describes Douglas's notion of the last frontier as "laced with ethnocentrism and paternalism."[54] Quiring agrees that "ethnocentrism appeared even more strongly in the CCF than in some other sectors of society," and that Douglas and others in his party "thought the Aboriginal's hunter-gatherer, nomadic life style represented a low form of economic, political and social organization."[55]

Another common characterization of the CCF is as colonizer – Dobbin, Barron, and Quiring all use the term, although not in the same way. If by colonization one simply means domination of one region by another, one can hardly argue with the characterization, but domination can be political, social, economic, or cultural, and it is useful to distinguish the sort of domination one is writing about. If one uses the term in the sense of deliberately setting up an extractive economy – transferring wealth from the periphery to the core – the characterization hardly holds water for the early years of CCF rule. As Dobbin points out, the region was not set up fully as an extractive economy; it was not completely "underdeveloped" in the way that A.G. Frank would use the term, but it was closer to being "undeveloped" because capital had not yet penetrated the area to any great extent.[56] Despite that caveat, Dobbin characterizes the CCF's role in the north as the entrenchment of a colonial regime in which the Department of Natural Resources replaced the Hudson's Bay Company (HBC) as colonizer.[57] The difference was that the old colonial relationship was simple: the HBC provided credit to the trapper in return for his/her labour. The CCF replaced that with a more complex relationship, forcing the Native to sell furs to the government's Fur Marketing Service and demanding centralization, taxes, royalties, compliance with conservation laws, acceptance of resource allocations, and attendance of children in school, in exchange for transfer payments.[58]

Barron also uses the term more or less in its economic sense, referring to the "vested interests that had benefited from Native marginalization," and he states: "Indeed, the CCF was itself a colonizing force in its treatment of Native people!"[59] He also was referring to the Fur Marketing Service and similar CCF policies, and the paternalism the CCF was demonstrating in its assumption that the Native nomadic lifestyle should be changed. This observation seems to have been shocking enough that Barron felt it was necessary to add an exclamation point to the end of that sentence, although why it should come as a surprise that a government of the 1940s would not display the sensitivity and perceptions of the 1990s and twenty-first-century analyses of colonialism is difficult to understand. Quiring also continues the characterization of the CCF as colonizer and in fact incorporates the term into the title of his book. He does not define it explicitly, but he seems to use it as a synonym for external political and economic control.[60]

When the CCF turned its attention to the north, the most important part of the Métis economy was the fur industry, and that was to remain the case for most of the time the CCF held power. According to the study of the fur industry by economist Helen Buckley, the trapping industry was still most important among the Native population in 1961. Over 95 per cent of those involved in the fur industry as trappers were Native, and the majority of those were Métis.[61] Her report was completed several years after the CCF had turned its attention to the fur industry, but the problems it outlined (low prices, a market whose centre was located outside Saskatchewan) were there from the beginning.

The DNR quickly set about ameliorating the most egregious of the social problems of the north by developing a series of systematic programs dealing with the distribution of land, the conservation of wildlife, education, health, agriculture, and collective marketing.[62] The DNR attempted to restructure natural resource exploitation, especially fur trapping, fishing, and the forest industry to improve the income of the predominantly Indian and Métis population. Anthropologist Victor Valentine suggests that these programs were designed not only to raise the living standards of the Métis, but to "wean them from their nomadic hunting and gathering existence."[63]

Of the traditional industries being practised in the north when the DNR began operating there, trapping was by far the most significant. According to Valentine, the reasons were structural and cultural: "these people came into being because of the quest for furs and their economy, as well as social organization, is traditionally based on trapping."[64] In addition to explaining these patterns through "tradition," Valentine also suggests that it would be in the interests of the fur trader to discourage the Métis from expanding into other economic ventures. So there were historical and structural reasons for the patterns seen here, based on the Hudson's Bay Company's fur trade practices. Fishing was of considerably less economic importance to the Métis. Lake fish made up a considerable part of their traditional diet, but few Métis actually took part in commercial fishing. Their involvement in the lumber industry was very limited as well.

The outlook for trapping in northern Saskatchewan in 1944 was grim, particularly for Indian and Métis trappers. The major problem was the depletion of fur; over-trapping had led to the almost complete extinction of beaver in some parts of the province, and there were no effective measures in place to enforce conservation. This situation was partially due to an increase in the number of trappers: many non-Native trappers had entered northern Saskatchewan, pushing the Indian and Métis from their traditional territory. Native trappers setting out on their traditional trap lines often discovered that it had already been trapped out by newcomers. The introduction of a lease system, through which a trapper received the right to trap a particular area for ten years, did little to protect the Native people, as most leases went to non-Natives.[65]

The DNR took several steps to alleviate these problems. First, in 1944, with the help of the federal government, it set up the Saskatchewan Fur Marketing Service (SFMS) in an effort to rationalize the industry and help break up the HBC influence in the communities. The SFMS was an attempt to create an orderly marketing system that would stabilize and increase the income of Métis and Indian trappers. It was also there to enforce defined quotas on beaver and muskrat. By requiring that all beaver and muskrat be marketed through the SFMS, the DNR could check the harvest in any area against the quota set. The means for setting these quotas was introduced in 1946 when, in a joint effort between the provincial and federal governments, the Northern Fur Conservation Program was established. Under this agreement, the whole of northern Saskatchewan (north of 53°lat.) was turned into a conservation block. The federal government was involved because of its responsibility for treaty Indians, and it paid for 60 per cent of the costs of the program. Under this scheme, northern Saskatchewan was divided into several conservation areas that would carry a fixed and limited number of trappers. Trapping was restricted to members of the fur block, who had to be resident in the area (living there at least one year). Each block was to be administered by a five-person council, which determined membership in the block and served as liaison between the trappers and the DNR. The council was also responsible for assisting in determining the quota of furs to be harvested on a yearly basis by providing data on animal population and habitat conditions, but the actual quotas were set by the DNR Research Division in Regina.[66]

Although the SFMS had been designated as a way to increase the income of Métis and Indian trappers, its arbitrary nature and unintended side-effects quickly alienated the trap line population. It had the unintended result of uniting the Métis into an almost universal opposition to the CCF, to the point that "to be called a 'C.C.F.'er' is an anathema."[67] However, Valentine and Young report that, at least where conservation practices were concerned, the program was a success. The number of beaver marketed in 1952–53 was over 10,000, compared with 1,000 in 1944.[68] Nevertheless, the Métis were implacably opposed to the block conservation program and the SFMS. This opposition could have had the effect of mobilizing them to organize politically, but there is no evidence of that happening. Instead, it seemed to infuse the population with a feeling of ennui or disenchantment with all political activity.

The major impact of the SFMS was that the trapper could no longer trade with the HBC or with private traders. He/she had to sell the fur to the local government field officer. Valentine claims that the program worked in the technical sense – the trapper ultimately got more money for his fur. However, this result was offset by the fact that he did not get all his money immediately. There were two payments, the first being 50 per cent of the market price at the time the furs were sold to the field officer. The second instalment came after the furs were sold by the SFMS. Since they were sold at market value, this protected the Service from paying the trapper more than the eventual market value of the fur. However, a drastic drop in the market between the time the trapper sold his furs to the Service and the time the Service sold them to a dealer could lead to some confusion and disappointment. Also, and more important, the trapper had to wait much longer to get full payment than had been the case under the old arrangements with the HBC or private traders. And the extra money – if indeed there was extra money – was of little help.

The compulsory marketing system, by preventing trappers from receiving credit at the HBC, had some far-reaching effects on the social organization of the Métis. Credit was the major underpinning of the fur trade economy for Métis and Indian trappers. Prior to the creation of the SFMS, the HBC would give a trapper credit for an entire trapping season. This allowed him to provision himself and his family and remain on the trap line for the whole season. At the end of the season, when the trapper returned with his yearly catch, the value of the goods received would be subtracted from whatever price the trapper received for the value of his fur. After the few necessities needed to pursue trapping were made, whatever surplus cash the trapper received was regarded, for the most part, as disposable income, to be used for entertainment and displays of conspicuous consumption.[69] When this money was spent, it was time to return to the trap line – financed by a new line of credit with the trading post. This system had worked for almost as long as there had been a fur trade in Canada, but it was now disrupted because the HBC could no longer purchase beaver or muskrat directly from the trader. This restriction in turn made the trader unwilling to extend credit to the trapper, since there was no way he could compel repayment.

Here are some comments in the Métis's own words, as conveyed to Valentine in the summer and fall of 1952. An elderly man living in a family camp near Portage La Loche had this to say: "The Fur Marketing Service is no good, mister. I heard a man got 16 rats and he get a cheque for sixty-two cents! Some got nothing ... It's no good for the people, mister. Before we go to the Hudson's Bay Company and have lotsa credit and grub to last, now the widows got no money even to buy glass for the house. Mister, it's no good. Can't get no credit, no nothing."[70] An elderly man living with his family near Île-à-la-Crosse told Valentine through an interpreter: "The big trouble with the Fur Marketing Service is that it ruins a man's credit. At one time a man could go to the store and buy enough grub for the whole summer with his rats. But now all he can get for twenty-five rats is enough grub to go back and catch thirty more. When the cheques do come, the stores gets them all anyway. To get credit we have to sign the cheque over to them."[71]

Valentine and Young describe in some detail how the trade patterns with the HBC had integrated and underwritten the traditional social organization and economy of the Métis, particularly the way the "excess" cash supported the roles of men and their prestige system:

> One of the curious aspects about the attitude of these people to money is the way in which prestige is acquired from it. The adult male Metis established his status in the eyes of his fellows, not by acquiring money, but in disposing of it. This also applies to material goods such as clothing, hunting and fishing equipment. In this trait one is reminded of the "Potlatch" of the Indians of the Pacific northwest.
>
> One of the ways used in disposing of his money, and thereby establishing his social position, is through the purchase of liquor. There are no exact figures to be had illustrating the total picture in this respect, but a survey completed by the provincial anthropologist in one community showed that something like one-third of the family income was spent in buying beer during the year 1953. The significant fact here is not the amount of liquor consumed (for alcoholism is rare among these people) but rather the amount that is purchased and given away. The same type of reckless attitude shows through in their gambling.[72]

Although Valentine and Young seem unable to control their middle-class disapproval of such "reckless" behaviour, they are able to show how the changes introduced by the SFMS drastically altered Métis social organization. There was more to it than simply the disruption of the prestige system of the Métis male; Valentine and Young also point out that the Métis had extended kinship bonds, and that an important aspect of the surplus cash was also to enable an individual to give assistance to family members, or to receive assistance when it was needed. This entire kinship support structure was threatened by the introduction of the SFMS.

Under the new system, the Métis could get only enough credit from the HBC or a private trader to go out on the trap line for a week or so. This necessitated many trips back to the community, to sell the few furs caught, get a small amount of credit from the HBC, and go out for another few weeks. Furthermore, since the second part of the payment from the SFMS came in the form of a government cheque sent through the mail, those whose residence was not close to a post office also had to make a special trip to a settlement centre to collect their money. Since the exact date when the cheques would arrive was not certain, it often meant camping out in the vicinity of the post office for several weeks at a time. The result was extra expenses, which ate up or negated most if not all of the extra money they might have received under the new marketing system. Valentine also points out that the system actually increased the amount of money paid out in relief, because many trappers overspent while hanging around the central area waiting for the government cheque to arrive.

One of the stated objectives of the block conservation scheme – besides the conservation of fur-bearing animals – was to put an end to the Indian and Métis nomadic lifestyle and to confine them to permanent settlement areas. It seems to have succeeded on that count; in 1962 Buckley was able to report that "with few exceptions, Indian and Métis peoples are no longer migratory."[73] But why centralization of the Native population was so important to the CCF remains in question. Several writers have put it down to simple ethnocentrism, claiming that Douglas and others in the CCF simply believed "in the superiority of Euro-Canadian ways"[74] Dobbin, Barron, and Quiring all have attempted to locate much of the rationale for the CCF's northern policy in the character of the CCF itself – in its obligation to "agrarian social democracy, its Fabian roots, its populist character, its social gospel dimension, and its particular egalitarian focus"[75] to quote Dobbin. This might be so, but Native populations were facing forced centralization in all parts of Canada, not just from CCF governments. Given the tenor of the times, it is likely that the Métis and Indians would have faced the same pressure to centralize under any other government. It is much more probable that the CCF followed this conscious policy of centralization simply because it seemed a more efficient way to deliver services.

Nevertheless, the block conservation program caused considerable problems for the Métis. First, it confined them to one particular area in which they could trap and hunt, areas not always consistent with their traditional hunting/trapping grounds. To get the right to trap in one of the fur blocks, a trapper had to be sixteen years of age or older and a British subject. A woman had to demonstrate that she supported a family on her own to be allowed to trap. Although there was some attempt to accommodate those who trapped the area traditionally, Native people were not necessarily given preference over non-Natives, although to prevent "itinerant" trappers from invading the area licences were granted only to those who had been residents of the area for at least twelve months. Second, the forced move to settlements, formerly just centres for trade and church, with few permanent dwellings, brought about some new problems for the north: overcrowding, disputes over land, and increased health and sanitation problems. As part of the centralization process, the CCF also attempted to encourage farming, but this was not successful, partly because the land was not suitable and partly because the Métis did not desire it.

The administration also tried to invigorate the commercial fishing industry by buying out some of the private operators, building freezer and filleting plants, and establishing a fish marketing service. This enterprise was not much more successful than the SFMS. Fewer Métis were involved, as almost none had ever been full-time fishers. The fishing industry in Saskatchewan was very insecure, and the policies of the CCF could do little to improve it. The main market was located in the eastern United States, and Saskatchewan had to compete with fisheries in other provinces and on the Great Lakes for freshwater fish, to say nothing of the competition from ocean fisheries. There were problems with transporting the fish, and a large proportion were infested with a parasite (*triaenopherous crassus*) that made the flesh unpalatable.[76]

All of these initiatives of the CCF, though undoubtedly well intentioned, were for the most part ineffectual and wildly unpopular. The SFMS was roundly despised, and Barron states that the Saskatchewan Fish Marketing Board (SFMB) also "became one of the most hated features of government policy in the north."[77] In an attempt to bring Native people on board, Joe Phelps, minister of the DNR, hired Malcolm Norris and Jim Brady to act as mediators between the CCF and the Native population. This may have been a good idea, but there is little evidence that it was particularly successful. Brady was nominally hired as a conservation officer. However, he was encouraged to help establish fishing and lumber producer co-ops in Cumberland House. Brady was a supporter of co-ops and had already helped start some in Alberta.[78] Malcolm Norris helped establish a trappers association, and he and others conducted meetings in various communities to discuss government programs.[79] Both Brady and Norris were of the mind that the policy of ending the nomadic lifestyle of the Native population and moving them to settlements was in the best interests of the Métis. Nevertheless, neither was able to sway the Natives' opinion of the CCF and its policies and, in any case, they themselves were often quite critical of the CCF. In 1960, after the provincial election, Brady wrote to Norris declaring with a certain amount of satisfaction: "After twenty years of monumental blundering, the CCF in the north [is] no longer a political force. The Indians and Métis detest them."[80] While both Norris and Brady are remembered with respect and affection by the Métis, there is little recollection of their links to the CCF.

The CCF was able to do little towards improving the infrastructure of the north; after the party had been in office for many years many communities were still isolated or served by poorly maintained roads. This is hardly surprising, as Saskatchewan was rather impoverished at the time and funds were limited. Despite the considerable efforts of the CCF, few inroads were made in terms of capital investment. However, the concerted attempt at centralizing Native people was having some effect. The CCF's efforts in the north dropped significantly after the 1948 election. The unpopularity of the government's policies could not be made clearer: they lost both northern seats, and Joe Phelps, the head of DNR, was defeated in his southern riding. The situation did not improve for the CCF for years in the north; the results of the 1952 elections reveal that the Métis were voting almost unanimously for the Liberals.[81]

The CCF continued to sponsor social science research in the area in an attempt either to design new Native policy or to evaluate what had already been done. However, perhaps because of the lack of progress many of these reports revealed, a certain amount of ennui ensued, and little new policy was developed after 1950. Valentine's description of the effects of the SFMS was devastating. Buckley's 1962 report on the state of trapping and fishing in the economy of northern Saskatchewan, based on fieldwork begun in 1960, revealed that sixteen years of CCF administration had resulted in little more than creating or perpetuating third-world conditions.[82]

Buckley paints a picture of economic gloom for the Métis and Indians of Saskatchewan in the early 1960s, holding out little hope for them from either the new mining enterprises or the tourist industry. Trapping, the mainstay of the Native economy, also offered few prospects, despite the work of the SFMS, and the conservation program and centralization of the population only increased the problems. By the 1960s transfer payments had become the largest portion of income for most Native families. Buckley itemizes these problems:

> 1. By making it possible for more people to survive, we have brought about a large increase in the Native population. As the current generation of children reaches maturity, population is likely to increase even more rapidly.
>
> 2. Chiefly through schools, we have tied the people to the settlements, so that the traditional means of support – trapping – has become much more difficult to pursue.
>
> 3. Our main contribution towards redressing the balance between increasing numbers of people and decreasing returns at trapping has been government allowances. Although practising the most rigid economy, the cost of social aid mounts year by year. The sum total of federal and provincial welfare payments comes to twice the value of the fur harvest in an average year. A whole new generation is learning to live on welfare payments of one type or another.
>
> 4. Through increased contact, we have permitted a glimpse at the standard of living which obtains in the south. Any young man can see that the trapper's life, however industriously pursued, will never provide a car, or a modern house, or a better future for his children. The typical youth may well go into trapping, for lack of other jobs, but he cannot be expected to pursue his vocation with the same satisfaction that his parents and grandparents had.[83]

The reality was that two economies developed in the period covering the 1940s to the 1960s –Native and non-Native. Of course, this disparity was not simply the fault of the CCF. Buckley points out that many of the problems were not within the power of any provincial government to solve, in particular control of the world market. Prices for fur had fallen disastrously between 1949 and 1960. But another reason, the "silent revolution," which accompanied the adoption of village life and the large increase in population, did come about as a result of provincial policy.

Conclusions

Many changes occurred in Saskatchewan during the period from 1935 to 1964. The economic decline of the traditional Métis economy (fur trapping, hunting, fishing) brought with it poverty and marginalization. In response, the Métis organized and made several attempts at forming associations to re-instil pride in being Métis and to change their economic fortunes. For the most part these efforts came to naught and, combined with government programs that did little to improve the lives of most Métis and, indeed, worked against any renewed Métis identity or nationalism, Métis political organization more or less died out in the 1950s, probably because of a combination of a lack of funds, few tangible results, and the split between the north and the south. This state of affairs would last until new developments in the 1960s re-energized Métis politics.

For most of the period under examination the CCF was in power. The net result of the party's policy of centralization and economic development had little positive impact on Métis families and communities. It largely replaced the old trading economy with that of transfer payments. An extreme form of dependency had been created in northern Saskatchewan. This did not necessarily mean that the Métis population was simply "living on welfare." Buckley's figures show that transfer payments such as the Family Allowance (which were made to all Canadians) simply constituted a larger proportion of the northerner's total income, because their income from other sources such as trapping was so low.

Nevertheless, rather than empowering the Métis population economically, the CCF seemed to have increased its dependency. As well, the overt attempts at centralizing the Native population, through transfer payments and the requirement that children attend school, disrupted the existing social structure. The fur-marketing system disrupted the old settlement patterns even further. The two-tiered payment scheme limited the amount of credit available to the trapper, forcing him/her to make many short trips back and forth to the trap line, thus limiting the size of the trapping area. The forced wait at other settlements where there was a post office also disrupted traditional settlement patterns. The new government presence in the north meant new expenses for the Métis – income tax, licence fees, royalty fees, and other charges, mostly collected by the DNR. Alcoholism increased. All of these factors have led several commentators to the conclusion that the lifestyle of the Métis suffered under the CCF's tenure. Dobbin states it explicitly: "In examining the policies of the CCF as they affected the daily lives of northern native people, there is no question that, overall, life became more difficult. While health care and education improved, living standards did not."[84]

This assertion may be true, but the decline in lifestyle, if there was one, is difficult to measure and difficult to blame on CCF policy alone. The living conditions of the northern Natives in Saskatchewan, while indeed reflecting an unacceptable poverty level, were comparable to northern populations across Canada, and attempts at ending the Native population's near total dependence on a fur industry that was incapable of providing a living wage can hardly be condemned out of hand. The increased life expectancy, reflected in the growing population, indicated that, in at least some aspects, life had been improving. However, evidence shows that most Métis people themselves were convinced that their conditions were deteriorating. Some of the interviews recorded by Valentine in July 1952 are indicative of this Métis point of view. There was much longing for the "good old days," which in their terms meant pre-CCF days. For example, an elderly Métis at Île-à-la-Crosse had this to say:

> In the old days, we used to work then. As far as livin' was concerned we could get fish meat and berries. It was okay then. We never lived off the store but off the land. The old mans used to tell us what to do how to make a living and all that. They have councilors now. It's not like the old days, then it was free and you could go any place to make a living and now you can't. We were the boss of what we took out of the bush. It belonged to us but now with this compulsory stuff, it doesn't belong to us. This government has just taken everything away from us and never gives us work. There is no wages here. All we got to live on is the rats we catch in the winter for all summer.[85]

Most Métis people had little doubt about who was to blame for this decline in their way of life: it was assuredly the CCF. A man in his early sixties, living with his family at Canoe River described the situation (through an interpreter):

> The trouble with the government is they don't give any work to the people. They come up north here and take away our living. One time, when the Liberals were here, there used to be at least work for a man in the summer. But now they send a bulldozer in to do this work. The last work we had was to build a dam up here about three years ago. No, the people don't like the C.C.F. because there is no work and the compulsory rat business. Yes, the C.C.F. government has taken away our living. We have to buy a license to catch fish to eat and it has stopped the people killing ducks to eat.

> Some say they are going to let the people in the north starve because they vote Liberal.[86]

Nevertheless, at least some younger Métis saw benefits from the CCF's presence in the north and their consolidation into larger more permanent settlements. One young man living with his family at Sandy Point talked of the many changes he'd seen in his own community since the CCF came to power – everything from schools, stores, and movies:

> The people around here just remember the work the Liberal government gave them at .60¢ a day. Today we get .60¢ an hour. Yes, the other government done very little for the north. I remember when I was a kid, the people used to walk from Snake Lake to Beauval for ten or twelve pounds of flour and sugar ... Now there is everything in Snake Lake, schools, stores, moving picture show – everything. I can remember [when I had] to take a plane to Snake Lake, with my family it cost over $50.00 and they made me leave 24 pounds of flour on the ice. Now I betcha I can go there and back for about $20. The people here don't know what's good for them ... the C.C.F. government did lots for the people in the north but they can only see the old ways.[87]

The early 1960s found the Saskatchewan Métis in dire straits – undereducated, underemployed, and without a political voice of their own. Yet there were some encouraging signs – a new leadership was slowly emerging and, in fact, the Métis were on the cusp of a political reawakening. The Saskatchewan Métis were soon to launch one of the most successful provincial organizations in Canada, which would become a prime vehicle for the new-found and powerful Métis nationalism that would develop in the 1970s.

13 Social Science and the Métis, 1950–1970

Section 1: "Discovering" the Métis

Attitudes towards the Métis – and attitudes among the Métis about themselves – began to undergo a fundamental change across Canada in the latter half of the twentieth century. An important influence on this change came about in the late 1950s and early 1960s, when the Métis were being discovered, for a second time by social activists, service organizations, and government officials, but for the first time by social scientists. The emerging field of applied anthropology and other applied social sciences, plus the introduction of government-sponsored research reports and policy reviews led to an invasion of newly trained sociologists, economists, and anthropologists into the northern parts of the prairie provinces (see Table 13.1).

These activities were part of a general increase in applied social science in North America. Program evaluation – the systematic application of social science research tools to analyse the impact of public sector programs – began to be implemented in Canada in the mid-1960s to the late 1970s.[1] Social scientists working for Canada's federal and provincial governments began to evaluate selected government programs at around the same time as similar practices were being initiated in the United States. Government program and/or policy evaluation offered many new employment opportunities for graduate students or newly minted PhDs willing to work for government agencies. Not all social scientists were comfortable with working for government agencies, as there was no guarantee of having any meaningful input into final policy, nor could they control the way the information they collected would be used. Despite such concerns, applied social research grew

Table 13.1 Social science research among the Métis, 1950–70

Author(s)	Date	Area
Valentine	1953, 1954, 1955	NW Saskatchewan
Valentine/Young	1954	Northern Saskatchewan
CASW	1949/1954	Manitoba
Howard	1958	Turtle Mountain, N. Dakota
Hlady/Poston	1959	Rural Manitoba
Boek/Boek	1959	Winnipeg
Hlady	1960	Northern Manitoba (Cedar Lake)
Kew	1960	Northern Saskatchewan (Cumberland House)
Worsley/Buckley/Davis	1961	Northern Saskatchewan
Buckley	1962	Northern Saskatchewan
Card/Hirabayashi/French	1963	Northern Alberta (I.D. 124)
Slobodin	1963	Northwest Territories
Spaulding	1965, 1970	Northern Saskatchewan (Île-à-la-Crosse)
Davis et al.	1965, 1967	Northern Saskatchewan
Knill and Davis	1962	Northern Saskatchewan
Hatt	1966, 1969	Northern Alberta (Lac La Biche)

quickly in the mid-1960s, and social scientists of all political stripes were beginning to work in the field of policy analysis in Canada.

There is a fairly long tradition of applied research and policy analysis on Canada's Native peoples at the federal level, particularly in the case of First Nations. Much of this is well known and has been discussed in various histories of applied anthropology in Canada.[2] However, what is less known is the impact of policy analysis research done at the provincial level, especially on the Métis in the prairie provinces in the 1960s. Native peoples – specifically the Métis – became the object of a set of studies in Alberta, Saskatchewan, and Manitoba.[3] This chapter is concerned with the way social scientists began portraying the Métis from 1950 to 1970 and how these studies both elucidated and contributed to a new reformulation of Métis identity.

The suggestion that social scientists can create, modify, or reify an ethnic group or other social unit simply by studying it is not far-fetched. To some degree, the act of representation – of making a particular group the object of study described in a text – *destroys* or at least *supplants* the original, making the textual representation more "real" than the group itself. Representation, in this case analysis by social scientists, puts parameters around the object, thereby simultaneously simplifying and ordering reality, in the same way that an India ink drawing of an archaeological artefact may look more "real" or at least reveal more essential details (essential, that is, to the archaeologist) than a photograph of the artefact, or even the artefact itself.

One of the functions of theory and scientific analysis is to iron out and make comprehensible the innumerable vicissitudes and variations of the natural world. For example, a description of the Métis as an "ethnic group"[4] attempts to create a logical and intelligible order out of an extremely complex set of social relationships bordering on seeming chaos. But this description or analysis then runs the risk of becoming a substitute for reality. It begins to operate like Jean Baudrillard's description of the operation of signs: "It is no longer a question of imitation, nor of reduplication, nor even of parody. It is rather a question of substituting signs of the real for the real itself, that is, an operation to deter every real process by its operational double, a metastable, programmatic, perfect descriptive machine which provides all the signs of the real and short-circuits all its vicissitudes. Never again will the real have to be produced."[5] And in some cases the real *cannot* be produced. After all, now all we have left of the Métis population of the 1950s are the written descriptions of them hidden away in government reports and scientific papers.

So, the social scientist, to some degree *manufactures* a social reality when he or she describes a particular group.[6] The very production of a "scientific" or an "applied" study of a subset of society such as the Métis makes it "real" and influential, even if it is composed of "inventions rather than observed facts."[7] The effect is felt as much by the objects of the study as it is by the readers of the government reports or academic papers. The very act of entering and interacting with a community of people – through interviews, and especially participant observation, but also by writing about the community – will change not only the investigator's view of the subjects, but the subjects' views of themselves. The actions of the varied sociologists, anthropologists, economists, and political scientists who were set loose on the Métis in the 1950s and 1960s began to change the boundaries and outlines of the group. The fact that most of these early efforts were funded by government – the research was specifically commissioned to inform public policy, rather than simply to add to the general body of knowledge – probably contributed to the effect. The reports were at least read, if not immediately acted upon, by government bureaucrats who interacted with the Métis and non-status Indians on a daily basis. The attitudes, opinions, and prejudices expressed in these reports were sure to affect both government policy and public perception.

One of the most obvious and easily demonstrated changes effected by these social scientists was the replacement in government and academic circles of the term "half-breed" with "Métis"–with or without the acute accent on "e." This process of reclassification was soon adopted by the Métis themselves, but the first changes were initiated by government officials and social scientists, even though at the time that these studies began, "half-breed" was by far the most common terminology. The change was undoubtedly due to a certain squeamishness and a preponderance of middle-class values on the part of the social scientists, social workers, and others who were first interested in the Métis. The Manitoba Branch of the Canadian Association of Social Workers, in their 1954 study (first undertaken in 1947) openly admitted that the major reason they adopted the term "Métis" was because they considered the more common term "half-breed" to be degrading: "The term 'Metis' which is used throughout the study ... is used in preference to the more commonly used term 'half breed' because of the disparaging connotations of the latter term, which we feel expresses an attitude central to much of the difficulty experienced."[8]

The Manitoba social workers were not alone in their reluctance to use the common parlance. A similar sentiment was expressed in an early economic and social survey of northern Saskatchewan: "For people of Indian-White ancestry, who are not legal 'treaty' Indians, 'Half-breed' is the term most widely used in the North, though no term is in universal use. However, this name has derogatory implications for some people. *We therefore prefer the less widely used term 'Metis,'* since it has proud connotations."[9] And in 1963, a study on the incidence of tuberculosis among the Métis of northern Alberta stated: "In our experience with persons of Indian ancestry, the term 'Breed' or 'Half Breed' is as appropriate as the word 'Metis' and is usually not considered offensive or in poor taste in communities with large mixed populations. In this study *the term 'Metis' is used because it is the more common in Canadian writing* referring to persons of white and Indian ancestry."[10]

The anthropologist Philip Spaulding explained his use of the term Métis in Île-à-la-Crosse, Saskatchewan, as a "euphemism for half-breed": "Although the name 'Métis' is not used by the people of the settlement to describe themselves, I have adopted it here in conformity with its general use by administrators, missionaries, and social scientists as a euphemism for 'half-breed' and as a means of distinguishing treaty 'Indians' from non-treaty 'Indians.'"[11]

So social science and administrators began a process of "Métisfication," aggressively expunging the term "half-breed" from government reports, if not general use. As we shall see, they were soon joined in this renaming by the Métis themselves. But not all Métis objected to the older terminology, nor did they welcome the new identity wholeheartedly. Emma Larocque, a Métis from Alberta and professor of Native studies at the University of Manitoba, does not care for the term, and attributes the tendency of the Métis to take on the new terminology to the prejudices inherent in colonialism: "I prefer 'Halfbreed' to 'Métis' because I feel that 'Métis' is so aristocratic and I, happily, do not come from an aristocratic Halfbreed background. We never used the word 'Métis' until I came to Manitoba, and some very colonized Métis were highly offended by the term 'Halfbreed.'"[12] In the same spirit, Maria Campbell named her 1973 autobiography *Halfbreed*. While the title may have been chosen for its provocative stance, the fact remains she does not use "Métis" anywhere in her autobiography, except when referring to the political organizations she worked for, such as the Métis Association of Alberta. She routinely refers to her people as "Halfbreeds" or "Breeds," once as "Road Allowance People,"[13] and once as "*Awp-pee-tow-koosons*" ("halfpeople," a derisive term used by the Cree).[14]

In Manitoba, the term "half-breed" remained very much in common use. A social and economic study of the people of Indian ancestry in Manitoba undertaken in 1958, for example, demonstrated that 118 out of 123 people in rural Manitoba who identified as either half-breed or Métis preferred the term "half-breed" or "breed" to describe themselves.[15] A small number of these, or 7 of the 118, qualified their answer by identifying as "part Indian," "French and Saulteaux," "Cree Scotch," "Scotch and Indian," or "Half Scotch." According to Hlady and Poston, this was to avoid the "less desirable connotations ... connected with 'Breed' or 'Half-Breed.'"[16] Often there was a European designation in addition to "half-breed" or "breed." In the 123 half-breed and Métis responses, French was mentioned 39 times, Scotch 17 times and English twice. Hlady and Poston took this response to mean that there was an attempt on the part of some half-breeds or Métis to associate themselves with their European nationality while retaining "half-breed" as an indication of the Indian portion of their background. Only four persons stressed their Indian heritage without noting the European. The investigators" interpretation was that this may have been a sign the respondents felt "a need to stress the European portion of one's heritage ... in talking with Whites." Or, it may simply have indicated that they were comfortable with their identity and nomenclature as half-breeds.

But the most significant point of this survey in terms of nomenclature was that only three persons (1 per cent) in the study group identified themselves as Métis. To the investigators, it was obvious that "the singular absence of the word, 'Metis' as a nationality indicates that this is not the way the study group thinks of itself."[17] However, they admit to the possibility that, since the interviews were in English, the English equivalent "half-breed" may have been used. As an aside, I recall that in the 1960s in Winnipeg, I was once admonished by an Aboriginal person: "Don't you call me a Métis! I'm a half-breed!"

Despite the widespread use of "half-breed" there are indications that at least some Métis – whether "colonized" in Larocque's terms or not – objected to the term. This reaction may have varied on a regional basis. Richard Slobodin reported for the Northwest Territories: "The Northern Metis is in a more difficult position in self-identification; 'Metis' is not common parlance north of Fort-Simpson, and 'halfbreed' is a term that Northern Metis avoid."[18] But in the same paragraph he adds: "It is interesting that Red River Metis not uncommonly refer to themselves as "breed" and "halfbreed" without apparent strain or pain." We also discovered in our own interviews in the NWT that many people were comfortable with the term "half-breed." A Métis activist in Hay River, NWT, reported that, until her husband began working for the Métis Nation, NWT, in the 1970s: "I didn't know what a Métis was. I was always a half-breed. And suddenly I was being told that they can't call us half-breed anymore."[19]

But Fred Hatt found that some colony Métis in the Lac La Biche area of northern Alberta objected to "half-breed": "The Metis dislikes the word 'half-breed,' even though his origin may be derived from a mixture of relationship between the Whites and Indians. He sees the term 'half-breed' as referring more to animals than men. As one man said, 'after all, we're not half-men, we're full men.'"[20] This objection may always have been present; as we saw in chapter 11, the Métis Association of Alberta rejected the term in its inaugural meeting, and periodically some of its members would write to newspapers objecting to it. But it was not universally condemned until the 1970s at the earliest – after the Métis had been exposed to the work of social scientists and government officials imported from the south.

Why did the term "Métis" begin to gain popularity in the 1960s? Why did it begin to overtake "half-breed?" Without too much imagination, we can understand why a social scientist working in the 1950s and 1960s might feel uncomfortable with a terminology ("half-breed") he/she was encountering daily. "Half-breed" is equated with "mongrel." "Purebred" has superior connotations. If the researchers used "breed" in their writing, their superiors, or colleagues, may have considered them to be racist. Anyone writing a report for the government would want it to be accepted as a good piece of research, untainted by any touch of racism. A researcher thought to be racist (or even insensitive) would not get another contract. Therefore, even if a researcher's informant regularly called himself/herself a "breed" the researcher would be extremely reluctant to use the current terminology. What was desperately needed was a value-free term, and "Métis" became the designation of choice. When it began to be used in the 1950s and 1960s, the very rarity of the term (and the fact that it was a non-English term) made it value free.

In fact, the conditions that made the term so adaptable and malleable in the 1950s, 1960s, and 1970s continued until very recently. Aboriginal/European populations as far flung and unconnected to the Métis as the eastern United States and Labrador and the Maritimes in Canada have adopted the term.[21] Since "Metis" had not been used historically in those areas, it seemed value free to the local population, a term that had no objectionable or racist connotations and one that could easily be assumed without consequence. However, the Métis have begun to object to outsiders appropriating their name, and some groups, such as the Labrador "Métis" are now dropping the use of the term.[22]

Etic (Outside) Definitions of the Métis

Now that we have established that the early researchers of the Métis in the 1960s almost universally eschewed the words "breed" or "half-breed" in favour of "Métis," the question that remains is: what did they *mean* by "Métis"? Many researchers found it rather nebulous and ambiguous and in fact often expanded it to include other concepts. Various people with Native ancestry who had no demonstrable links with Red River Métis, such as non-status Indians and non-treaty Indians, began to be conflated with the Métis – still coupled with middle-class reluctance to use a term associated with racism. Note that Philip Spaulding, whose quote above explains his use of the term Métis as a "euphemism for half-breed," also combined the concept of Métis with non-treaty Indian. This conflation of "Métis" with non-status Indian or non-treaty Indian was the beginning of a pattern that was to continue until the 1980s and had profound implications for Métis political organization for many years.

Spaulding was not the first to combine the categories of Métis and non-status or non-treaty Indian. Many government and social agencies made the same assumption. For example, note the definition of Métis that the Canadian Association of Social Workers (CASW) developed in the 1950s: "It was recognized from the start that the Metis group is not clearly defined ... The operations of the legal and social factors rather than the racial ones are seen clearly in the fact that *the child of the marriage of a Treaty Indian woman and a white man is considered a Metis child, while the child of a Treaty Indian man and his white wife is Treaty Indian*."[23] In fact, "the child of a marriage of a Treaty Indian woman and a white man" would more likely be a non-status Indian rather than a Métis, but the CASW deliberately chose the term "Métis." To some extent this was a natural reaction; the agencies were concerned more with their legal responsibility (provincial vs. federal) and the socio-economic status of their clients than with any niceties of social or ethnic identification. Both Métis and non-status Indians had similar needs as far as these agencies were concerned.

Some investigators solved the problem of distinguishing between Métis and Indian simply by ignoring it, preferring to speak of the Métis-Indian population as a whole. Many of the sources on the Métis we have from this period are provincial government reports detailing social and economic conditions in the northern or southern portions of Saskatchewan.[24] Most of these reports primarily dealt with unemployment and job creation. For these concerns the distinction between Métis and Indian was unimportant, since the two groups occupied, or were assumed to occupy, the same or similar socio-economic positions. Michael Kew, for example, who wrote a detailed ethnographic and economic report on Cumberland House in 1960 for the Saskatchewan Department of Natural Resources, employed a class analysis that merged the Métis and Indians residents of the area in opposition to outside power structures: "economic and political power has from the beginning emanated from the 'outside' – and the people exercising that power have been overwhelmingly White."[25]

But many of the researchers investigating the Aboriginal population of the prairie provinces in the 1950s and 1960s, north or south, recognized the Métis as distinct from the Indian population. V.F. Valentine's study of the Métis, undertaken at the behest of the Saskatchewan Department of Natural Resources, was one of the earliest anthropological investigations into the Métis. As far as defining the Métis, Valentine was unable to go much beyond stating that they were a group of people "who in thought and mode of life are neither Indians nor white men,"[26] although he also noted that "the Metis is more akin to the Indian than he is to the white man in his mode of life."[27] Valentine at least acknowledged that there was a significant difference between the two groups. Still, his definition of Métis was primarily a racial, not a cultural, one. Any mixed marriages resulted in "Métis" by his reckoning. On the other hand, there was a social aspect to his construct of Métis, because any person who was treaty was excluded from the category of Metis: "While most of the Indians have 'mixed blood,' they are not considered to be Metis. At Fond du Lac, for example, there are many who can trace their ancestry to earlier fur traders, but were included in the treaty arrangements along with the local Chipewyan Indian bands."[28]

Later studies were able to address the differences between Indian and Métis in more detail. The social and economic study of the people of Indian ancestry in Winnipeg used self-ascription as well as ascription by others to distinguish between the two populations. The investigators used a questionnaire that asked: "Is your background straight Indian or partly Indian?" "Those having no Indian in their background at all were not interviewed further. All those answering that they were partly Indian were classified as Metis, unless they were treaty or their names had been on a band list. *A few people clearly identified by informants as being part Indian were also included, even though they did not admit their background or had forgotten it.*"[29]

It is interesting to note that in the Manitoba study "Indian" was treated as an undifferentiated group – that is, tribal differences (Cree, Saulteaux, Chipewyan, or Sioux) were not considered significant in this survey. Nor was a distinction made between people who identified as Métis and those who did not; all who identified as partly Indian were classified as Métis, whether they used that term to describe themselves or not. In fact, as the above quote notes, some people who did not admit to an Indian background were included, despite their own self-identification, if they were identified as having a mixed ancestry by others. This is an early example of how the term Métis was being imposed from the outside, leading to its florescence in the 1960s and 1970s. Note also that no attempt was made to contrast Métis with non-status Indian. Besides self-ascription and ascription by others, the study used location as a means of identification, applying an "area probability sample" based on knowledge of where most Native people lived in Winnipeg.[30]

The study of people of Indian ancestry in rural Manitoba that ran concurrently with the urban study in Winnipeg also used ascription by others as well as self-ascription as the working definition of Métis. However, this study put more emphasis on self-ascription than the city-based one did; no people were included if they did not identify as Métis or half-breed: "Although Metis is defined as 'anyone of mixed blood,' all persons of mixed White and Indian background do not identify themselves, or are identified by others as such. For research purposes, it was necessary to develop a working definition ... It was decided that the study would include 'Those people who identify themselves or are identified by their neighbours or work associates as Metis or Half-Breed.'"[31]

Card, Hirabayashi, and French, in their study of the Métis in Northern Alberta,[32] did not use self-identification as a criterion for isolating the Métis. Instead, they attempted to discover the *external markers* that identified a person as Métis. Like many others who have tried to delineate ethnic groups though external markers, they found it to be a difficult if not impossible task.[33] It was fairly straightforward to divide the residents of I.D. 124 into ethnic groups, as long as they linked the Indians and Métis together. They had no difficulty in distinguishing among the Chinese, European, and French Canadians of the district, but admitted that it was very difficult for outsiders like themselves to differentiate between Métis and Indian: "Determining who is a Metis or Breed and who is an Indian in I.D. 124, is, however, a complex task which a number of local residents, particularly those of Indian ancestry, appear to undertake effortlessly and unerringly. Assigning or assuming Metis or Indian status is not a simple matter, but involves specific knowledge acquired frequently by observation or hearsay. As interpreted by the writer, this knowledge is derived by the use of five [*sic*] criteria or indicators of what constitutes a Metis and what an Indian."[34] Actually, Card et al. listed six criteria, not five: (1) physical characteristics, (2) culture or style of life, (3) place of residence, (4) legal status, (5) language, and (6) reputational history.

Under "physical characteristics" Card et al. recorded stereotypical physical markers such as skin colour, eyes, hair, and facial features. However, they quickly discovered, as have many before them, that such markers are almost useless in isolating any population, because the supposedly defining features actually shift imperceptibly from one group to another. To demonstrate, Card et al. presented several photos, all of Métis, whose physical characteristics shifted from "Indian" to "white," making any racial identification impossible.

They did no better when investigating "culture or style of life" as a possible distinguishing feature. While there were a few markers, such as Tea Dances, which were more the purview of Indian than Métis, very little set them apart. Card et al. did note the generally disparaging attitudes the local non-Native population had towards both the Métis and the Indian lifestyles, and the fact that the local non-Natives did not or could not distinguish between the two groups.

"Place of residence" was another potentially useful distinguishing feature, since those who were living on the reserve were by definition status Indians. However, off reserve was another story. Indians and Métis lived in the same communities, so residence there meant only that the person was likely to be Native. There are communities in northern Saskatchewan that have separate residential areas for Métis and Indians,[35] but this distinction apparently did not hold true for I.D. 124 in Alberta. Language also was of little help; most Natives in the area, Métis or Indian, spoke Cree.

"Reputational history" may be a useful criterion in small communities where people know each other quite well. But as Card et al. pointed out, it is unlikely that the local non-Natives, who had difficulty in distinguishing Métis from Indian, would have access to this information, which was complicated by migration in and out of the communities, and by changing legal status of Indians who either moved off reserve or changed status though marriage; 12.1 (b) of the Indian Act, which rescinded Indian status from a status Indian woman marrying a non-status Indian or non-Indian, was still in force at the time (it was dropped on 28 June 1985).

From the criteria listed, it is clear that Card et al., like several other investigators we have already seen, combined Métis with non-status or non-treaty Indian. However, they did notice that "Metis who have migrated from St Albert or who trace ancestry to Saskatchewan Metis have some distinctiveness in reputational history over Metis who are local products, and who frequently have close relatives among Treaty Indians, or have been themselves at one time under Treaty."[36] This observation indicates that there may have been a core group of Métis living in the area – people who would indeed identify with links to Red River and Louis Riel – and who felt themselves to be separate from the non-status and/or non-treaty Indians of the area. But Card and his colleagues' list of outward markers was not sensitive enough to draw them out, other than this brief hint. Undoubtedly, criteria based on self-identification would have been more capable of differentiating between them.

At any rate, Card et al. rejected physical characteristics, lifestyle, and language as being too similar for the two groups to provide an accurate point of departure. In their opinion, only residence, legal status, and reputational history were capable of accurately distinguishing the Métis from the treaty Indian, but they added that the reputation criterion was useful only for local persons who already have an extensive knowledge about individuals of Indian ancestry.

Card et al. were not the only ones to make such an observation. Peter Worsley, working in Saskatchewan, also pointed out that outsiders had difficulty in distinguishing between Indian and Métis. "Physically, many of the people termed 'Metis' or 'half-breed' are as white as many of the 'Whites.' It is the *socially-known* element of Indian ancestry, as well as its physical visibility, that makes a person 'Indian' or 'Metis.' Were his ancestral history not known, it would sometimes be difficult to distinguish him from a White."[37]

Card et al. admitted that the investigating team could see little overt or significant difference between the two groups, except for their legal differences: "Without Treaty, reservations and the Indian services of government, there would be little basis for distinguishing between Indians and Metis who are Native to the Lesser Slave Lake area." However, that does not mean that the distinctions were not there, or that they were not important to the members of the groups. Card et al. also pointed out that the distinction was not of great importance to the non-Native residents of the area: "stereotyping takes place among the whites which has a tendency to equate Metis and Indian, despite differences that do persist."[38]

To some degree, it is surprising that Card, Hirabayashi, and French even bothered to look for a distinction between Métis and non-treaty Indian, since the major reason for the study was to examine the rate of TB among non-treaty Native people. Under those criteria, the difference between a Métis and non-treaty Indian was not of much practical interest to the investigators, since there would not have been any significant difference in access to health services. Nevertheless, from this report we can gather some important clues about perception of the Métis and about their self-identity in the 1960s. One can also see why, at around this time, ethnic studies led by Fredrik Barth and others abandoned cultural markers as a means of delineating ethnicity, turning to boundary maintenance instead.[39]

The distinction Card et al. mentioned in passing – between Métis from St Albert vs. local non-status Indians – is reflected in Slobodin's work on the Métis of the Mackenzie District in the Northwest Territories.[40] Slobodin also noticed a difference between Métis who were of local origin and those who had links to the historic Métis population from the prairies. He developed a useful terminology to distinguish between them; "Red River" Métis and "Northern" Métis (reminiscent of Jim Brady's distinction between "Red River" Métis and "nomadic" Métis).[41] "Red River" Métis refers to "those families which derive genealogically, and usually in tradition, from the historic population which had its centre in *la nation métisse* of the western plains."[42] Slobodin includes within the term those not of Red River derivation, but who lived among and had assimilated to the older Métis population. The Northern Métis refers to "those families deriving from miscegenation within the northern part of the Mackenzie District"[43] and includes both Indian/European and Eskimo/European individuals. Slobodin notes that "among Metis of the southern Mackenzie District, old traditions of Metis nationality and of the insurrections retain a vitality surprising to this observer."[44] These distinctions persist to this day in areas like northern Manitoba, but they are being diffused by the activities of political organizations, which seek to include northern Métis in their ranks both because the people of the area need political representation, and because their presence swells the ranks of the organizations.

Slobodin was able to portray a clearer distinction between the two mixed-blood populations than Card et al. were (other than what could be explained by the differences in location between northern Alberta and the NWT) because of differences in the methodology and motivations for the study. Slobodin was engaged in a typical participant-observation field study, which was of much longer duration and involved more intensive technique and covered interviews, conversations, and observations taken from the period between 1938 and 1962.[45] These features alone were enough to give Slobodin the advantage that Card admitted his research team lacked – the "reputational history," which was available mainly to local persons or those who had acquired an extensive knowledge about individuals of Indian ancestry.

Slobodin also compiled a list of more or less observable distinctions between the Red River and Northern Métis, including remote miscegenation vs. relatively recent miscegenation; variations in European ancestry, Native ancestry, religion, recognition of European or Indian kin, surname groups, mobility in terms of residence and employment; valuing independence vs. valuing authority and hierarchy; and, finally, validation through identification with Métis tradition vs. validation through either (a) identification with white father and Euro-Canadian power institutions, or (b) prestige and leadership among Aboriginal relatives.[46] These distinctions also support Card et al.'s observation about the necessity for detailed local knowledge: many of the differences Slobodin delineates are not necessarily obvious to the casual observer.

Some researchers simply ignored the issue of definition. Philip Spaulding[47] provided a detailed description and analysis of the northern Saskatchewan community of Île-à-la-Crosse, based on a series of visits between 1961 and 1965. He did not define Métis per se (and, as mentioned above, the term "Métis" was not customarily used in this community at the time). Rather, he described the Native population as a whole (which happened to be predominantly non-treaty or Métis) in opposition to the non-Native community.

Although Arthur Davis provided much interesting information on the Métis of Northern Saskatchewan in the mid-1960s, he was not specifically interested in the Métis. In selecting the respondents for their study of northern urban Natives, Davis and his colleagues made no significant distinction between Métis and Indian – although they tried to keep track of them.[48] Davis saw the Métis and Indians as differing biologically, but not culturally. He did suggest that self-identification was the key to defining and identifying Métis. Persons having some Indian ancestry, yet passing in the community as "white," were of no interest: "sociologically, such people are not Metis or Indian – regardless of their biological ancestry – because they do not see themselves as such, nor are they so defined by others in the community."[49] However, some ascription was used in the study, based on the experience of one of the fieldworkers. In his study of urban Métis in Prince Albert, Davis was assisted by Jim Brady, the long-time Métis politician and co-founder of the MAA:

> Brady estimated the total Metis and Indian population in Prince Albert to be about 1,700. However, he classified about one-fifth of these as "assimilated" – that is, as persons having some Indian ancestry, yet passing in the community as White ... Our interviewer made his estimates, using his own knowledge of Metis family names, the local city directory,

> and the advice of two or three long-time Metis residents. As Mr Brady put it – after moving into town – "I could soon tell you which Ridleys (a fictitious name) in town were Metis and which ones were really White."[50]

Davis follows Spaulding and many others when he delineates the "two solitudes" of non-Native and Native in the communities, and that there was something of a caste system at work: "most of the Metis and Indians we interviewed in these three Saskatchewan urban centres still held ethnic pictures of themselves which indicated uncertainty, confusion, self-rejection and resignation ... This fact reflects ... the generally recognized (by both Whites and Non-Whites) inferior status of Metis and Indians in Saskatchewan communities."[51] In his study of Cumberland House this view is reflected by Kew, who, as Hatt stated,[52] converged ethnicity and class. Some of the researchers considered so far concentrated on those who identified as Métis, and some simply used the term arbitrarily. Some saw the Métis in terms of social problems. But all these definitions are primarily ascriptive.

Emic (Inside) Definitions of the Métis

Some researchers extended the attempt to define the Métis to a consideration of how the Metis defined themselves. A good example was Hatt, who studied the residents of the Alberta Métis colonies in the early 1960s and 1970s.[53] At one level, he had little difficulty in isolating the Métis; since he was studying colony residents, he could simply rely on the provincial definition of Métis as provided under the 1952 Métis Betterment Act, and which determined whether or not an individual was eligible to live in one of the colonies: "'Metis' means a person of mixed white and Indian blood having not less than one-quarter Indian blood, but does not include an Indian or a non-treaty Indian as defined in the Indian Act (Canada)."[54] Freed of the responsibility of deciding who was a Métis and who was not, he was able to concentrate on what made a Métis a Métis. He devoted considerable time to analysing the meaning and implications of the term, particularly in his government-sponsored report on the Métis of Lac La Biche.[55] Hatt looked at the term from two perspectives: from the perspective of the outside society (etic) and from the opinions of the Métis themselves (emic). From both points of view, "Métis" was generally conceded to refer to people whose parents were some mixture of Indian and European, but Hatt felt this definition was of little practical value. As he pointed out, "there are countless

Albertans who are of mixed 'Indian blood' who neither appear to be or see themselves as Metis. And they are not Metis."[56] He recalled that the half-breed commission of 1935 added the rider: "living the normal life of a half breed" as the operational definition of "half-breed."

Hatt also outlined the difficulty of the official definition used by the Métis Population Betterment Act of the time, particularly the reference to the provision of having not less than one-quarter Indian blood, in terms of accurately measuring an individual's racial mixture: "This, naturally, depends on reputation and memory. The particular operation in this calculation involves the 'amount' of 'Indian blood' in each of the parents, and then dividing that 'amount' by two in order to ascertain the 'amount' of 'Indian blood' in a particular offspring."[57] Stan Daniels, the former president of the Métis Association of Alberta, once told me that, when applying for residence in one of the Métis colonies, it was common for the "darkest-looking" person in the family to make the application.[58] The major difficulty according to Hatt was that the issue of blood quantum was entirely irrelevant, because it "ignores the salient features involved in the problem of definition of the Metis."[59]

Hatt attempted to clarify matters by delineating between the legal and the social definitions of Métis. According to him, the social definition of "Métis" or "half-breed" was simply an individual who occupied a position somewhere in the middle of the Indian-white dichotomy, combining those characteristics – skin colour, facial structure, clothing style, name, occupation, and place of residence – that supposedly differentiated one group from the other. The fact that this is a fiction, that it is in reality almost impossible to consistently and accurately recognize either "Indian," "Métis," or "white" characteristics does not mean that the idea was not prevalent in the Lac La Biche area at the time.

When Hatt attempted to explain what the term "Métis" meant to the Métis themselves, he was not able to find a much clearer definition. The Métis did claim they could delineate three types of people: white, Indian, and Métis. For example, in the discussion of "whom one should marry," three categories of response emerged: "one's own kind," "a treaty," or a "white." In answer to the question "what makes a Metis a 'Metis,'" there was "general agreement" that the Métis was a person whose parents or other ancestors were Indian and white. However, Hatt noted that often respondents said they "didn't know" – as if it were hard to state in definite terms of what a Métis consisted. Hatt did not mention this point specifically, but it is worth noting that "don't know" is often a response to a "pushy" question or an indication that the respondent finds the question or the answer unwelcome or simply too much trouble to bother answering in detail, rather than displaying a genuine lack of knowledge. Another problem is that Hatt did not offer a numerical breakdown of how many Métis he polled on the question or if he asked them all precisely the same questions.

Many Métis apparently offered Hatt physiological distinctions. Physical characteristics that supposedly distinguished the Métis were high cheekbones and colour of the skin. But at the same time, skin colour was offered as the basis for the distinction between Indian and Métis. "some thought the Metis was light – like the White; others thought he was dark – like the Indian."[60] But the Métis were consistently seen as a product of mixed blood. As noted by the three-way distinction the Métis made (Indian, Métis, white) the Métis did distinguish between Indian and "white" populations. Hatt (like Card and Worsley, above) suspected the Métis could make a finer distinction between themselves and the Indian population than the non-Natives of the area could make, likely based on specific knowledge of family background.

Thus, Hatt suggested that the Métis in the Lac La Biche area in the 1960s were unable or unwilling to say what makes a person a Métis. Some saw themselves as more like "whites" in contrast to Indians; some saw themselves as more Indian, while others saw themselves as different from both. Yet he could tie this only to the idea of mixture of blood or differences in facial or skin characteristics; no cultural differences (Michif, dress, music) were used. Hatt was forced to say that the major source of the definition of Métis was a negative one: a Métis was neither Indian nor white. Hatt essentially fell back on the same compromise that Valentine used. "That's essentially who the Metis is. He is distinguishable as not White, by certain features designated 'Indian.' Yet he is distinguishable as not Indian by certain features which are defined as 'White.'"[61] For the remainder of his report, Hatt used the term "Metis" to refer to "a group of people who are offspring of both White and Indian parents … who are probably recognizable (in the broadest sense) as both 'Indian' and 'White'; and would tend to identify themselves as Metis rather than Indian or White."[62]

Hatt's suspicion that the Métis could make a finer distinction between themselves and the Indian population than he or the non-Natives of the area could make is probably well founded. If we turn to writing by the

Métis themselves – for example, Maria Campbell – we find they have no difficulty in distinguishing Métis from Indian:

> There was never much love lost between Indians and Halfbreeds. They were completely different from us – quiet when we were noisy, dignified even at dances and get-togethers. Indians were very passive – they would get angry at things done to them but would never fight back, whereas Halfbreeds were quick-tempered – quick to fight, but quick to forgive and forget.
>
> ... We all went to the Indians' Sundances and special gatherings, but somehow we never fitted in. We were always the poor relatives, the awp-pee-tow-koosons (half people). They laughed and scorned us. They had land and security, we had nothing.[63]

Section 2: Characterizing the Métis

The previous section detailed the beginnings of social science research into the Métis in the early 1950s. Much of this early research was concerned with attempts at isolating and identifying the social boundaries of the Métis. Although these early studies betrayed some general confusion over who was and who was not Métis, the distinctions between Métis and non-status Indian, and how (or if) they differed culturally from status Indians, the studies themselves were partly responsible for legitimizing the idea that the Métis were a separate and recognizable segment of the Native population in Canada and helped sketch the first drafts of the ethnic boundaries that were beginning to coalesce around them.

In this section, we consider *how* the Métis and their communities were portrayed in these early studies. What was the nature of Métis society and culture as perceived by these investigators? In general, we will find that it was hardly a prepossessing one. The Métis that emerged from this research were maladjusted, powerless, poverty-stricken, uneducated, and at the mercy of a non-Native overclass. In effect, the portrayals did not go much beyond the "social pathology" models that were so characteristic of the Ewing Commission two decades earlier. Here is a typical portrayal:

> There can be few sights more depressing than one's first view of a north-Saskatchewan native community. Ramshackle cabins and shacks alternate with patches of brush and weeds. Chickens and dogs and kids pursue their

> separate goals oblivious to the buzz of flies around the outside privies or the curses of impatient adults. People wander aimlessly about searching for something to engage their interest or simply sit and wait for something to happen. There is a general impression of disorder, disorganization, and apathy – and over all, the taste of squalor and poverty.
>
> And down the road, insulated by both social and physical distance, stand the neatly painted and well-fenced houses of the government administrators, commercial operators, and mission personnel, whose task it is to share with the native population the fruits of modern society.[64]

While there may be some validity to this portrayal, it should be remembered that the picture that emerges from Métis writers such as Maria Campbell and from some academic research is much more optimistic and life affirming, while not ignoring social problems and poverty.

But why such a negative portrayal? To gain some insight and understanding of these characterizations, we must first examine why the studies were undertaken and their nature. The Métis were of special interest to the provincial governments, since it was held at the time that they, along with non-status and non-treaty Native people, were a provincial responsibility. Thus, most of the research done on the Métis between 1950 and 1970 was of an applied nature – usually undertaken at the behest of provincial governments or social welfare agencies, with the manifest goal of informing and designing public policy for Native people. In the main, the research investigated preconceived "social problems" defined as such either by the government agencies themselves or by the researchers. Perhaps, then, it is not surprising that the picture is so negative: researchers tend to find what they are looking for. For example, the Manitoba study of the living conditions of the Métis and off-reserve Indians in that province was undertaken "with a view to discovering whether their social integration and economic advancement could be facilitated."[65] In other words, it was already assumed that they were not well integrated into society, and that their "social integration and economic advancement" was required.

Perhaps the best example of the interrelationship of government policy and applied research in the 1950s and 1960s is found in Saskatchewan in the works of Valentine, Buckley, Kew, and Worsley, referred to above. While this research was couched in terms of social problems, specifically the economic situation of the Native population, there was an additional and specific political component to the studies not present in the other provinces. Most of these studies were undertaken by the Cooperative

Commonwealth Federation (CCF) government, which was in power from 1944 to 1964. During the first part of their tenure – from 1944 to 1960 – several policies were introduced that impacted dramatically on the Métis, particularly the Saskatchewan Fur Marketing Service, a compulsory marketing system for beaver and muskrat furs, and the Block Conservation System, a system of allocating land for trapping aimed at conservation. Much of the research was therefore aimed at understanding the reason that these and other "beneficial" programs were not achieving the measure of success expected of them and, not incidentally, at identifying ways to increase the popularity of the CCF in the northern regions of the province.[66]

Within a few years after the CCF took office, opposition to CCF policies by the Métis had become widespread and implacable. The results of the 1948 and 1952 provincial elections made this particularly obvious; the CCF lost both northern seats in 1948, and the 1952 CCF votes were particularly low in the predominantly Métis communities studied by Valentine.[67] In what may have been an attempt to garner Métis support, the well-known Métis activists Malcolm Norris and Jim Brady were hired to work for the Department of Natural Resources. Brady was taken on as a conservation officer and to establish cooperatives in the village of Cumberland House.[68] In conjunction with these economic efforts, Brady also held regular adult education classes, initiated an informal village council, published a community newsletter, and set up a local credit union. Norris was hired to conduct social and economic surveys of all northern settlements, identifying individuals who would be able to give help to local governments in the future.[69] This may have been why they were hired, but they were fighting an uphill battle as far as gaining points for the CCF with the Métis. Maria Campbell, who remembers Brady from the time and portrays him as a champion of the Métis, doesn't mention anything about his work for the government or his programs, other than the fact that he held out the promise of land from the government. She also recalls that her father followed him for a while, then became completely discouraged. She also mentions that her father had been an object of ridicule by other Métis while he had supported Brady.[70]

Research on the Métis of northern Saskatchewan was begun by anthropologist V.F. Valentine in 1952, when the Department of Natural Resources initiated a research project into "Métis personality, society and administration": "The practical aim of the project was to study the Métis both as an individual personality and as a member of a particular network of social relations, in order to discover on the basis of scientific research, how the effectiveness of northern policies and programs might be increased from the standpoint of improving Métis welfare."[71] Valentine clearly documented the impact of the CCF's policies. The major flaw of the Fur Marketing Service was its disruption of the traditional Métis economic structure, which was based on a system of credit from the Hudson's Bay Company or private traders. Although Valentine claimed that the Métis actually got a higher cash value for their furs under the new system, the timing of the payments and the lack of availability of credit disrupted the seasonal round, which effectively prevented the Métis from spending as much time on the trap line as previously.[72] The Block Conservation System was a supposedly democratic system by which the trappers were to decide for themselves the number of muskrats and beavers that could be taken from each conservation block to sustain the yearly yield. But the system was too restrictive for the Métis; residence requirements limited Métis trappers to one particular block, which often prevented them from trapping in traditional areas, and the blocks also required the purchase of a trapping licence. Valentine demonstrated how the block system disrupted the settlement patterns of the Métis.[73] The policies of the CCF, although introduced with the aim of improving the economic situation of the Métis, resulted only in widespread resentment and anger, to the extent that "to be called a 'CCF'er' is an anathema."[74] Maria Campbell's account of growing up in northern Saskatchewan at the time includes many examples of the hatred and contempt the Métis held for the CCF and its policies.[75]

In addition to his analysis of government policies, Valentine's other contribution was his ethnographic portrait of the Métis, probably the earliest done by an anthropologist in the prairie regions (Slobodin's work, which started earlier, was in the NWT). As might be expected from what is very much a preliminary study, it is sketchy and at times contradictory, but it remains a rare and informative picture of the Métis in the 1950s. Beginning in 1952, Valentine studied the Métis in four regions of northern Saskatchewan: Buffalo Region, Lac la Ronge Region, Cumberland Region, and Athabasca Region. While he found recognizable differences between the Métis of these regions in terms of ethnic background and geographic and economic conditions, his portrait of Métis communities and their relations with both non-Natives and Indians showed a fair amount of consistency from community to community. Setting the tone for many subsequent portrayals of northern communities, Valentine depicted the relations between Native and "white" (Valentine's term) in the communities of northern Saskatchewan in the 1950s in terms of a caste system. In Valentine's version, the Indian was relegated to the position of inferior caste, the non-Natives to the ruling caste, and the Métis relegated by both groups to the position of "outcast."[76] Valentine attributed the Métis's distinctiveness to this status:

> They are neither fully-accepted members of either group and, as a consequence, have developed group characteristics which can be described only as being Metis. The majority, however, while they refer to themselves as being "Half-breeds," prefer to identify themselves with the white men rather than with the Indians whom they consider as inferior beings. Like the majority of white men, the Indians regard the Metis with considerable suspicion and contempt, and do not feel comfortable in their presence. This again, however, varies in intensity from region to region.[77]

While strained at times, Valentine's metaphor of caste is not totally inapt. (But it is confusing: sometimes the Métis are referred to as "outcasts," sometimes as a "superior" caste to the Indian). It does capture the unequal power structures and social positions that existed in Métis communities at the time, demonstrated in other works such as those of Spaulding[78] and Hlady.[79] Even the disagreement of members over which group is "superior" to the other – since the Métis considered themselves superior to the Indians and the Indians considered themselves superior to the Métis – is reminiscent of the caste system. Valentine's work is particularly useful because he devoted a great deal of time to the relations and the distinctions between Indian and Métis. His portrait shows that whatever the cultural content of Métis vs. Indian, there was a socially significant distinction between them, with a definite boundary being maintained between the two Native groups in northern Saskatchewan communities. As we shall see, not all social scientists who worked in the northern regions of the prairies were able to make the distinction. Valentine does, however, conflate Métis with non-status or non-treaty Indians, which somewhat muddies the portrayal.

At the time of Valentine's research, the legal position of treaty or status Indians gave the Métis certain advantages in the "caste" system. Because it was illegal for treaty Indians, but not for Métis, to purchase liquor, the latter were able to obtain alcohol for their Indian relatives. They often acted as bootleggers, usually at double the cost price. A public reaffirmation of this social distinction was symbolized by the presence of beer parlours; the Métis were allowed on the premises, but the Indians were not.

Another aspect of the different legal status was section 12 1(b) of the Indian Act – the regulation that stripped a treaty woman of her status if she married a "white," a non-status Indian or a Métis (this section remained in effect until 1985). Valentine identifies this as a reason for the increase of the Métis population; both non-Native man/Indian woman and Métis man/Indian woman marriages contributed to the Métis population. Strictly speaking, this would be an increase in the non-status Indian population rather than the Métis population (at least it would be so the way Métis is reckoned today), but apparently at the time of Valentine's research (or in Valentine's interpretation) both recent non-Native/Indian marriages as well as historical Métis populations were subsumed as Métis.

The attitudes non-Natives displayed towards the Métis and Indian also were revealing, and could be demonstrated in many communities other than the ones Valentine worked in. Many non-Native respondents informed Valentine that Métis were different from whites because of their inheritance of "Indian characteristics," which when listed implied laziness, apathy, untrustworthiness, and generally a lower intelligence quotient, as well as cultural backwardness.[80]

A common feature of the northern settlements that many other investigators, such as Hlady and Card et al., have commented on was job status. Again, it was reminiscent of a caste system: non-Natives held positions such as administrator, priest, storekeeper, pilot, technician, school teacher, police officer, doctor, and nurse. Those held by Métis – such as trapper, fisherman, waitress, and a host of casual labouring jobs – had less power and prestige. The overclass usually rationalized the differentiation by claiming that the average Métis either was not suitably trained or was unreliable.

According to Valentine, "whites" also discouraged their children from associating with Métis children. They were particularly reluctant to send their children to the same school because they feared that the Métis children were infected with contagious diseases such as TB, and they felt the school standards were lowered to fit the Métis child, who often entered school speaking an Indian language rather than English. Very often they sent their children to boarding schools in one of the large population centres to the south.[81] ChristineVan der Mark portrayed a similar situation in a northern Alberta community in the 1940s, albeit in a novel.[82]

Valentine also portrayed a class-within-caste system. The non-Natives that the Métis did mingle with were in the lower classes, "such as he meets in the pool room, beer parlour, cheap restaurant and boarding-house."[83] He also pointed out that many Métis who tried to emulate a "white" lifestyle, chose that of the lower class. He reported that in the Uranium City area, pool shooting was believed to be a desirable "white-man" habit, capable of enhancing the prestige of the individual, since it was a "white" man's innovation. However, the Métis and Indians who spent time in the pool hall did not understand that most Euro-Canadians "regarded time spent in the pool room during working hours as being time misspent, practised by hoodlums, bums and other undesirable types of people."[84]

The separation of Métis from the "whites" within the community, Valentine felt, contributed to the lack of success typically experienced by those who left the Métis settlement to attempt to work in a southern population centre. Unused to "white" society and "white" norms, they typically failed to adjust, and returned to the north bitter and disillusioned. They then faced the condemnation of the "whites" in their own community, who criticized them for coming back and becoming "more Indian than the Indians." This pattern was also illustrated by Van der Mark in her novel.

Valentine portrays something that Maria Campbell would later raise: the force of public opinion and public ridicule within the Métis community, which limited any attempt at changing one's social status: "the common opinions expressed on how one should behave have the force of law. Should any individual treat them with contempt, he would be immediately ridiculed and shunned by his friends."[85] This was particularly true of any Métis recognized by government officials as leaders. The Métis would mock and taunt them with derogatory accusations such as "CCF spy" or trying "to act like a big-shot white man." Because these people would not only be ostracized from Métis social life but denied access to the dominant society because of caste barriers, they often found themselves completely isolated from both groups.[86] One of the strongest uniting forces of the Métis of the area was their opposition to the CCF, which, as we have seen, stemmed particularly from the introduction of the Fur Marketing Service and the Block Conservation System. Anyone expressing support for the CCF was sure to become the object of ridicule. Campbell illustrates this point with her depiction of the Metis local member of the provincial legislature who, after he won the election, "joined the Baptist church, painted his old car blue and started wearing suits."[87]

Valentine illustrated one of the major points of distinction between Métis and Indian or "white": definite in-group and out-group feelings that delineated the Métis from other groups. To be a Métis, one had to accept the common values and attitudes of the group or else suffer ostracism. In the main, Valentine illustrated the feeling as it separated the Métis from the non-Natives, but Campbell also illustrated it for Indians as outsiders. Thus, the concept of Métis as a readily identifiable group in the prairies of the 1950s is obviously not an "invented" or artificial dichotomy. However, we can see that the designation of "Métis" (as opposed to "half-breed") and the creation of a mythology to help delineate the group, which happened in the 1970s, may well be a recent "invention," or at least ethnic boundary development. Valentine tantalizingly mentions a few traditions and cultural markers such as gambling, which the Métis regarded as their own, but he does not give many details, although he attributes these to Euro-Canadian society: "In the more remote places games introduced by early traders, and now forgotten in the South, are still played. Like the music and square-dance steps introduced by the early traders, the Métis believe these outmoded games to be their own cultural creations."[88]

Contributing to this feeling of separateness was the fact that the majority of Métis regarded themselves as being continually cheated and duped by the administration in particular, and by the "white" folk in general. The in-group feelings were such that in cases of minor infractions of the law, a Métis would seldom report the offence to the RCMP even if the offence was against himself. Should he do so, he would be considered a traitor and be accused, sarcastically, of being an imitator of the Euro-Canadians. Individuals feared ridicule. Hence, public opinion, expressed by their own kind, was the strongest governing force in their social life.[89] Valentine leaves us a picture of the Métis, dissatisfied but unable because of formalized inequality to improve their situation.

It is here that Valentine's orientation as government employee becomes apparent. While on the one hand he understands why the Métis are resistant to the changes being introduced and is able to explain this attitude in terms of the interdependence of their various economic endeavours, he also takes the position that change is inevitable, and "the people must change."[90] He even suggests that the reason for their resistance might be lack of intelligence or education or of being "too set in their ways."[91] So he exhorts the administration not to falter – or else "the people would become more and more a welfare problem."[92]

If the first phase of the CCF's administration in the north was marked by a well-meaning but intrusive and ultimately harmful disruption of Métis life, the second phase, from 1950 to the defeat of the CCF government in 1964, was characterized by a almost complete policy vacuum.[93] Ironically, this was the period when a great many research projects on the social conditions of the Native population of northern Saskatchewan were initiated by the government. Many of these studies were undertaken by the Centre for Community Studies (CCS) a research organization established by the CCF government in 1958, in conjunction with the University of Saskatchewan. A three-year economic and social survey of northern Saskatchewan, begun in 1960 and financed by the Saskatchewan Department of Natural Resources and the CCS, yielded several reports detailing the conditions facing the Native population of the north .[94] Despite the fact that Jim Brady was hired as one of the field workers, supposedly because of his expertise in Métis issues,[95] almost none of this work was aimed directly at the Métis. Most of it examined the Native population as an undifferentiated whole, treating the Métis and Indians as a single socio-economic entity.

While the political orientation of the researchers varied, many of their reports were couched in terms of colonialism or metropolis-hinterland structures and were often critical of past and present CCF policy. Although they made many recommendations for change, few if any of them were acted upon, and by mid-1963 political interference from the CCF began to be felt within the Centre for Community Studies. The CCF and the Centre even sought to prevent many of the reports from being published, although some were later published by Western Washington State University in 1967.[96]

Not all of the research into the Métis in Saskatchewan in this time period was government sponsored, but much of it echoed the social pathology models already produced by government studies. Spaulding's ethnographic study of the Métis of Île-à-la-Crosse in the 1960s,[97] while not subsidized by the government, provided a picture of Métis village life similar to that of Valentine, who had been there a decade earlier. We see again the familiar picture of social inequality: non-Natives assuming or allocating to themselves a higher social position and the Métis recognizing and attempting to come to terms with their own vulnerability and powerlessness in the face of government regulations and economic dependence.[98] Spaulding also reiterates Valentine's characterization of the community as exhibiting the kind of opposition and exclusivism characteristic of caste communities.[99]

Spaulding paints an unprepossessing picture of Métis village life – rife with "drinking and drunkenness, expressions of hostility, pre-marital and extramarital sex activities and like practices."[100] He calls attention to a general perspective shared by a number of social scientists concerning the state of social order in northern Canadian Indian, Inuit, and Métis communities – a condition more than one had referred to as "northern slums" and "lower-class life styles": "The deviant acts – drinking, fornicating, fighting – large families, borrowing of personal property, reliance on social aid, etc., are used to bolster a belief that the Metis are comparable to the impoverished classes of Canadian and American urban slums. Indeed, the expression 'sub-arctic slum,' is frequently used by administrators to characterize Île-à-la-Crosse and other northern Saskatchewan villages."[101] According to this perspective, high rates of alcoholism, minor crime, illegitimacy, marital maladjustments, aggression, and other putative signs of disorder prevail in a large number of northern communities. While not doubting the accuracy of these descriptions, Spaulding disagreed with analyses like Honigmann's,[102] which interpreted lifestyles that violated the moral norms held by Euro-Canadian society as "social disintegration." Rather, Spaulding saw them as patterns of *adaptation* in northern communities undergoing changes in their relationship with the larger society.

Basically, Spaulding used an acculturation model to explain the Métis lifestyles he observed in the 1960s. He suggested that the evident social disruption was a result of a clash between Métis traditional values and norms and those that were consistent with the requirements of village life. The resultant behaviour pattern represented an outgrowth of the difficulties the Métis had faced and were facing in adjusting to the demands of village life; he seems to see it as a transitional point on the way to a more complete adaptation. Spaulding's point is that these behaviours are *adaptations*; they are not indicators of social disintegration but rather activities that have adaptive significance during a period in which traditional norms and values are being reformulated into behavioural guidelines of greater utility and significance in the context of village life. Specifically, the so-called deviant activities represent the efforts of the Métis to establish a more meaningful social order, which, at the same time, is consistent with major traditions.

Spaulding portrayed a prestige system among the Métis that was different from that of the larger society. Prior to village life, trapping, hunting of large game animals, and knowledge of efficient survival techniques were the main sources of prestige. Success was indicated through the ability to maintain large families or residential units. A man of relatively great ability in exploiting the physical environment, and of great strength and stamina, could attract a large following, particularly if he was generous and shared the products of the hunt. Such a man – one who demonstrated skill, judgment, strength, generosity – was in Métis terms a "big man," or *ogimow*.[103] This was the same prestige system that operated among the Indians, but Spaulding was not concerned with distinguishing between or comparing the two.

He felt that these values became transformed with adaptation to village life. Although the old sources of prestige (skill in hunting, etc) may have lost their relevance, the institution of the *ogimow* and some of the concomitant practices and values survived. Métis men holding minor administrative posts and other kinds of permanent employment asserted their claim to the title of *ogimow*. This was a logical progression, since by contrast with others Métis they were men of wealth and, consequently, they were expected to share their good fortune. Great value continued to be placed upon the rearing and maintenance of large families and the solidarity of the male sibling grouping. Above all, the sexual capacity of men was valued and, like generosity, it had to be demonstrated with a fair degree of constancy.[104] These concepts led to a value system many non-Natives found to be deviant and maladaptive.

"White" attitudes towards Métis were similar to those described by Valentine and others. The non-Natives often expressed anger and exasperation because, in their view, the Métis did not exert greater efforts to help themselves. There was a genuine feeling of resentment that the Métis did not appreciate the "help" that the larger society was trying to provide, coupled with a suspicion that any efforts to create an economically viable community in Île-à-la-Crosse would fail in any case. However, it was felt that this failure would most likely be due to a lack of natural resources in the area; not because of any intrinsic shortcomings of the Métis.[105]

Spaulding was able to demonstrate two categories of Métis attitudes towards "whites": those held by people who were old enough to have spent part of their adult lives in the bush and those held by Métis who had been reared entirely in the villages or who had spent only their immature years in the bush. The older people still harboured a strong resentment – bordering on a chronic state of anger – against the "white" government for introducing changes that made untenable their old lifestyle in the bush. This loss was still personified as being the fault of the CCF: "The CCF government took away our living." Although the strength of their resentment had died down somewhat by the time of Spaulding's study, the fact that it continued as a dominant theme in Métis attitudes after more than twenty years suggests the magnitude of changes Métis were forced to make in resettling in the village. The younger generation was torn between ties with the older generation and a sense of identification with the larger society. They inherited from their parents a large measure of ambivalence and distrust of non-Natives, but they also internalized many Euro-Canadian values in schools and the desire to "make something of themselves" and to leave the village for success in the outside world. Many times, they returned home having failed.[106] As already indicated, similar observations have been made by Valentine and Van der Mark.

Spaulding's portrayal of the Métis of Île-à-la-Crosse ignored one important issue: the difference between Indian and Métis. How did the Métis differentiate themselves from Indians? According to the picture provided by Spaulding, they did not. Spaulding did mention that the Métis attributed any differences between themselves and non-Natives (which included poverty and activities defined by Euro-Canadians as "deviant,") to their Indian heritage. Despite modifications they may have been forced to make to survive in the "white man's" world, the Métis viewed their behaviour as intrinsically "Indian."[107] It would be reasonable to assume that they then emphasized their differences from Indians through non-Native characteristics, but Spaulding does not report any such actions. In fact, in his writings, he seems to have amalgamated Métis and Indian within the concept of "Native" – although he always refers to them as Métis.

Some of the work in Alberta was government sponsored. Hatt's 1967 report was prepared for Human Resources Research and Development, Executive Council, Government of Alberta. It was targeted specifically at the Métis in the Lac La Biche area. While the concept that the Métis represented a special problem in terms of human resources and the programs designed to serve them seemed to come from the government's side, Hatt justified his research with the hope that presenting Métis perceptions of the situation to government agencies would lead to an increased basis for understanding differences and developing effective programs.[108] The research of Card, Hirabayashi, and French[109] was sponsored by the Alberta Tuberculosis Association in association with the University of Alberta Committee for Social

Research. According to Card, the research was informed by three major values. The first was "the value of good health, particularly freedom from the ravages of tuberculosis, and a concern about the persistently high incidence of the disease among Alberta Metis." The second value was "sound and reliable knowledge," and the third was the "absolute worth of individuals."[110]

Card et al. also characterized the Métis lifestyle as maladapted; they seemed to suggest that any deviance from the larger society was evidence of some sort of shortcoming. While the three writers had some different perspectives, they all shared a general agreement that the Métis did not "measure up." French begins by asking, in essence, "Why can't they be more like us?" "This section of the report will attempt to deal with reasons why the Metis seem unable to approach a way of life considered standard and normal by the larger Euro-Canadian society, and why efforts made in the past by the various agencies of the larger society seem to have had little noticeable effect in gaining a more desirable life for these people."[111] The answer, French goes on to say (in direct opposition to Spaulding) is not the retention of Indian traits because, in his view, very little Cree culture was retained by the Métis of I.D. 124. Echoing Valentine, Worsley, and others, Card, Hirabayashi, and French centred the "problem" of the Métis around the adoption of "lower-class" values:

> The main hypothesis of this section is that the Metis have adopted the values of the lower classes of the larger society so that they do not function in a manner markedly different to lower-class persons throughout North America regardless of the racial or ethnic groups to which these persons belong. The passive acceptance of disease ... and other unpleasant life situations seem to indicate an internalization of lower-class norms and values which include poor self-conceptions, feelings of unworthiness, apathy toward the external environment and a very circumscribed point of view. [112]

Card, Hirabayashi, and French grounded their research in the social stratification and class analyses popular in American sociology of the 1950s and 1960s. Hirabayashi, for example, posited a built-in conflict as the Métis assimilated "middle-class values," which created frustration, owing to their lower-class position in the hierarchy.[113] He suggested that, when the Métis were exposed to the dominant urban middle-class values of the larger society, their reactions were a result of three vectors: the "Indian cultural traditions" of the Métis (which French, on the other hand, felt were negligible), their historical colonized roles, and their present lower-class status.[114] The result was "apathy"– a lack of aspiration and withdrawal based on a realistic assessment of one's life-chances. Hatt[115] draws a parallel between this interpretation and Merton's version of *anomie*,[116] which also deals with situations wherein people's goals are beyond their means. Like Spaulding, Hirabayashi suggests this is an "adaptive" model by people on the fringes of the larger society: "the Metis ... are responding *positively* to their motives and aspirations and are very much involved in the environment *as perceived by them*, an environment related to the larger society only in a fringe way."[117]

The most striking conclusion that these researchers have reached is not only that there is something lacking in the Métis way of life but, echoing other commentators such as Valentine, that it *cannot be allowed to remain unchanged*.

> As concluded in this report, the focal problem of tuberculosis control among Metis is changing Metis status. This is a short-hand way of saying *that all aspects of Metis life, those which contribute directly to health and those which contribute indirectly, the economic, social and cultural, need to be modified.* Status most simply means standing or ranking. It is a social evaluation of the importance of the Metis, an evaluation based on their low positions in Alberta occupations and communities, and on the way they perform the roles they are assigned or which they assume. Their low health status and known high incidence of tuberculosis is also reflected in their low general status of "Metis."[118]

This suggestion of the need for change goes beyond the need for change necessary to lower the rates of TB among the Métis.

Most studies undertaken in this time period (1950s–1970s) from all of the prairie provinces emphasized the marginality of the Métis. The entire focus of the social and economic study of the Indians and Métis of Manitoba[119] was based on the preconceived conclusion that the Native population was not contributing to the economy in the fullest sense. Hence, whether the Métis were studied in Winnipeg (Boek and Boek) or rural Manitoba (Hlady and Poston) the work was basically a compendium of social shortcomings. In his summary report, Jean Lagasse isolated poverty as one of the main elements in identifying Métis: "To be classified as a Metis a person must have some Indian ancestry.

The presence of Indian physical characteristics is not important although it helps to identify as Metis some persons who might otherwise not be detected. *A second condition to being classified as a Metis is living under poor circumstances.*"[120] He stated that the great majority of the people included in the study lived in poverty. The only Métis included in his study who achieved a high standard of living were the members of the upper class in predominantly Métis communities and a few families in predominantly non-Native communities.

It is evident from this overview that all the studies of the Métis in the prairies shared a common point of view: the Métis were maladjusted, they were neither benefiting from nor contributing to society in any meaningful way, and something had to be done. But beyond that, there was not necessarily agreement on either the cause or the cure.

Theoretical Issues

While most investigators and analysts of the Métis in the period 1950–70 agreed on the general picture of the northern communities – a caste-like division between non-Native and Native, with non-Native administrators holding the majority of power, not all couched their analyses in the same theoretical terms. Many – such as Valentine, Spaulding, and Card, Hirabayashi, and French – explained the Métis position in terms of unsuccessful or partial acculturation and a clash between "Indian" values and "white" values, suggesting that the present situation was but a way station on the road to a better integration with modern society and feeling it was their place to initiate changes to "improve" this integration. But other researchers, such as Worsley and Davis, were not content to explain the position of the Métis simply in terms of a clash between indigenous patterns of behaviour and Euro-Canadian behaviour or a lack of economic development. These researchers preferred to explicate the situation of Canada's indigenous population (both Indian and Métis) in terms of the processes of colonialism: "Northern Saskatchewan, in fact, presents several classic features of a colonial area. Perhaps the nearest analogy is to northern Australia. The more one examines its problems, the more strikingly one finds the closest social resemblances in areas as physically unlike Northern Canada as Melanesia or tropical Africa."[121]

Worsley et al. seem to agree with researchers who portrayed the Métis as "having adopted the values of the lower classes in the larger society"[122] but their explanation and identification of the processes involving patterns of colonialism differs markedly, nor do they see it as a process of acculturation: "Another striking resemblance is to the underprivileged people in the rural and urban 'lower depths' of the advanced societies. Much of the psychology and social behaviour of the Indian or Metis of the North reproduces the characteristic patterns of the slum-dweller and the unemployed of Glasgow, Toronto or New York. *We would be rash to assume that the distinctive behaviour-patterns of the Indians can be entirely explained in terms of the indigenous Cree and Chipewyan cultural inheritance, significant as this may be.*"[123] Most of the reports of the Centre for Community Studies by Buckley, Worsley, Kew, Davis, and their colleagues agreed that economic development in the north (mining, tourism, etc.) had passed the Native population by, that government services such as education and family allowances had encouraged abandoning nomadic lifestyles for permanent settlement in communities and had helped destroy traditional hunting and trapping patterns, but had not provided commensurate employment opportunities. Their picture of the north was as disheartening as any of the others, but their analyses were different.

A.K. Davis, in particular, elaborated on the colonial model with several articles utilizing metropolis-hinterland models.[124] Using the concept of underdevelopment (as opposed to undeveloped) that owed much to older works such as the staples theory of Innis as well as the works of Andre Gunder Frank, Davis's approach eschewed "cultural pluralism" as explanation and local self-development as cure.[125] The theoretical stance was an interesting one, but it was insensitive to certain nuances such as cultural/social differences between the Indian and Métis. In fact, most of Davis's work as well as that of most of his colleagues did not even attempt to distinguish between the Métis and Indians, usually treating them as a single economic class:

> The Metis-Indians are but one of a number of seriously disabled groups in Canada. Those groups – the unemployed, the undereducated, young people, small farmers, certain ethnic groups, many of the aged – together constitute a culture of loosely knit but often reinforcing deprivations – the "Other Canada," which ... may well include 20–25 percent of Canada's population ...
>
> The "Metis-Indian problem" is at the very least a "White-Indian" problem. Indeed, it may be defined more accurately as a problem of modern Canadian society, because the latter has moulded and dominated the Indian communities ever since the beginning of the fur trade. In general, it is the First

> Canada – the economic and institutional order of urban-industrial Canadian society – which defines and produces the Other Canada.
>
> ... Our focus, we repeat, should not be upon the Metis-Indians, but on the structure and functioning of the Canadian social system as a whole.[126]

Conclusions

In summation, while social scientists "discovered" the Métis in the 1950s, 1960s, and 1970s, their initial insights were limited. Most of the work was of an applied nature, underwritten by provincial governments or social agencies in Manitoba, Saskatchewan, and Alberta. There were also, however, a handful of purely ethnographic studies such as Slobodin's work in the NWT. These works taken together may or may not have been responsible for the demise of the word "half-breed" in the 1950s and 1960s, but they certainly contributed to it, or at the very least they reflected changes of opinion in society that were occurring at the same time.

Regardless of why the research was undertaken or of differences in the theoretical orientation of the investigators, the picture of Métis communities that emerged was fairly consistent: caste-like power structures with non-Natives in positions of power, where the Native population (both Indian and Métis) shared the bottom position, exhibiting both powerlessness and poverty. In some interpretations, the Métis occupied an intermediary position between "whites" and Indians; in others, the investigators saw the Native population as an undifferentiated whole. Some of the research was from an acculturation perspective, some was from a class analysis or used a model of colonialism, but the picture of the Métis communities that emerged from these different perspectives showed a remarkable similarity. The one or two examples of Métis writing from the period – Maria Campbell in particular – adds a perspective that much of the other analysis lacks. Of particular importance is the sense of community held by the Métis and the distinction between Indian and Métis they recognized between themselves, which the metropolis-hinterland and colonial analyses in particular seem to have overlooked.

The social conditions portrayed and the unhappiness with and passive resistance to the Saskatchewan provincial government's policies in the north evinced by the Métis in the 1950s are possibly a foreshadowing of their eventual coalescence into a political entity – one of the many motivating factors that eventually led to Métis political activity and ethnic assertiveness in the 1960s. While it is true that there was almost no Métis political activity in the 1950s – perhaps a result of the repressed and powerless position they held in the society, as shown by the various ethnographies we have just considered – that inactivity could not, and would not, last forever. Looking back at this portrayal of the Métis today, it is possible to suggest that the forced isolation, differentiation, and lack of power they experienced must have contributed to a deep sense of dissatisfaction, which eventually boiled over and formed the basis of the resurgence of Métis ethnicity in the 1960s and 1970s. There had been evidence of their ability to coalesce politically in the 1930s and 1940s, and although there was very little activity in the 1950s, it was only a matter of time until their potential for organization was reawakened. This shift was evinced by the formation of the northern Métis Association of Saskatchewan in 1964, the southern association in 1965, and the amalgamation of the two in 1967, as well as the founding of the Manitoba Métis Association in 1967 and the resurgence of the Métis Association of Alberta in the same general time period.

PART FIVE

Politics, the Courts, and the Constitution: Reformulating Métis Identities since the 1960s

The reformulation of Métis identities accelerated tremendously in the mid-1960s and continues to this day. These changes can be closely tied to the regeneration and growth of Métis political organizations, which also began in the 1960s. At that time, the organizations often represented an amalgamation of Métis and non-status Indians and, in fact, many of the most prominent leaders in the associations identified themselves not as Métis, but as Indian. For example, the Manitoba Métis Federation was begun by an enfranchised Indian, and many of its early leaders regarded it as a non-status Indian association, despite the fact that nominally it was a Métis association. Similar processes can be seen in Alberta, Saskatchewan, and elsewhere, as can be seen in the names of organizations such as the Association of Métis and Non-Status Indians of Saskatchewan and the Ontario Métis and Non-Status Indian Association. During this time period groups in other parts of Canada, such as Labrador and the Maritimes – which had no tradition of a separate Métis population or, at least, had no separate population that historically identified itself as Métis – began to use the term "Métis" to refer to themselves, although this trend has recently begun to recede.

Thus, the ethnic boundaries of the Métis have shifted considerably in the last fifty years. When the Manitoba Métis Federation began its operations, almost anyone of a mixed Aboriginal and non-Aboriginal background, however recent (even first generation), could, if they chose, identify themselves as Métis, and join the association – as could non-status Indians or non-Aboriginal spouses of Métis. The same or similar criteria for membership and definitions of who was or was not a Métis could be found in most of the other provincial Métis organizations of the time. The definition of Métis today – at least for those

Métis whose associations are part of the Métis National Council (MNC) – is much more stringent. According to the MNC, to be recognized as a Métis one must be able to demonstrate a link to a historic Métis population or to an ancestor who had received Métis scrip and/or acceptance by a recognized Métis community. Many factors have contributed to this change in ethnic boundaries: the inclusion of Métis as one of the recognized Aboriginal peoples in the Canadian Constitution; several court cases in Ontario, Manitoba, and elsewhere determining Métis Aboriginal rights and land claims; and the growth of Aboriginal organizations in areas of Canada whose membership had not traditionally used the term "Métis" but were beginning to do so in the 1970s.

This politicization has resulted in the Métis managing their own identity in new ways, with new parameters. To illustrate some of these changes, we have chosen to look at two examples outside the prairie provinces: the Métis of the Northwest Territories and the Métis of Ontario. The various organizations in these areas are interesting in that some of their members can trace their heritage to the Red River Métis population, but they have also tried to accommodate a large mixed-blood group, as well a non-status Indian population, that does not identify with the Red River Métis tradition. These diverse groups formed political alliances with the Métis in pursuit of land claims and economic development. In some cases they have also claimed ethnic identification as Métis.

We end this section, and this book, with a consideration of how the Métis distinguish themselves from other Aboriginal populations, through the selection and manipulation of particular symbols or historic figures: a specific flag, the identification of important historic figures such as Louis Riel and Gabriel Dumont, and cultural artefacts such as the Métis sash, the Métis cart, and traditional music and dance.

14 A Renewed Political Awareness, 1965–2000

The mid-1960s represent the beginnings of a remarkable shift in the political fortunes of the Métis. After years of surviving outside the consciousness of mainstream Canadian society and totally without political influence – a group that was often described as the "forgotten people" by its own spokespersons, politicians, and historians[1] – they began a process of reinventing themselves and of thrusting themselves back into the consciousness of Canadian society. They were not trying to become assimilated into that society, but were attempting to become recognized as a distinctive strand woven into the Canadian fabric – a "nation" with an idiosyncratic past and distinctive rights. In one of the most startling turnarounds in Canadian history, they either rejuvenated the old Métis political organizations or created new ones and began the slow process of forcing recognition of their special place in Canadian society.

This was not an easy task. It is difficult today, now that the Métis have achieved constitutional recognition as Aboriginal people, to appreciate the obstacles Métis politicians faced in the 1960s: either outright ridicule or denial that they existed as a group. Even when they were acknowledged as a separate entity, they were repeatedly told that they were merely a cultural or ethnic group, with no special rights or status – certainly no Aboriginal rights. At first they could find no level of government willing to listen to their claims. The provincial governments (with the exception of Alberta, which had been maintaining the Métis colonies) refused to acknowledge that the Métis were different from any other rural ethnic community. Even if they accepted the Métis as an Aboriginal group, the provincial governments would promptly declare them to be the responsibility of the federal government. The federal government, in turn, took the position either that the Métis were not an Aboriginal group or that, if they were, any Aboriginal rights they possessed had been terminated years ago by the Manitoba Act or the scrip provisions of the various Dominion Lands Acts. This made them a "political football" in the words of Angus Spence, one of the early Métis politicians and the first elected president of the Manitoba Métis Federation (MMF).[2] But this initial denial of their existence did not stop the new political mobilization the Métis were launching in the mid-1960s.

However, their political awakening was not an isolated event. They were joined with, and sometimes driven by a parallel political awakening of status and non-status Indians and Inuit as all Canada's Aboriginal peoples became politically mobilized. Many of the early political organizations became rejuvenated, and many more completely new ones sprang up, to promote the interests of Native peoples in a way unprecedented in Canadian society. This rejuvenation was part of a universal awakening, as all around the world ethnic and Aboriginal groups began to demand the right to self-determination and self-identification. This was the time of "Black Power," Chicano mobilization, and the American Indian Movement (AIM) in the United States, for example. But these indigenous and ethnically based movements were not limited to North America; they were part of a world-wide phenomenon, representing the interests of disparate groups such as Lapps (Sami), Chicanos, Australian Aborigines, and the Chamorro of Guam. The most striking feature of these movements was the newly found assertion of the ideal of self-determination. Once regarded as the proper purview of the nation-state, in the 1970s the idea grew that self-determination could and should be the goal of any group that felt justified in demanding it or who wished to free themselves of the shackles of the nation-state. Renewed interest in Scottish and Welsh independence in the United Kingdom and Basque nationalism in Spain encouraged this attitude. Canadian nationalism was no longer capable of stifling the desire of self-determination within Quebec, or even in the western provinces. This widespread assertion of minority rights began to influence Canada's Aboriginal population, which had long been interested in claiming rights to self-government, usually as part of a package of recognition of Aboriginal rights.[3]

The rallying cry behind this seemingly universal demand for self-determination was often justified by the inferior economic, political, or social position of the group vis-à-vis the larger society; but the major impetus as often as not seemed to come from the growing idea that people inherently have the right of self-determination or of recognition of their uniqueness regardless of their economic or social position. I do not mean to suggest that the worldwide spread of the idea of minority independence was the only reason Native political movements rose to such prominence in Canada in the 1960s. The political organizations that were to become the mechanisms of the political movement were already in place and had been there since the 1930s. I am suggesting that this new political climate did provide a sense of encouragement and legitimacy to the movement and brought more people into the fold. There were other stimuli to the Native political movement, of course, such as a growing educated and professional middle class among Native people in Canada. However, while some of the early urban-based Native political movements were the product of university-trained Aboriginals, the most powerful and influential leaders in the 1960s were usually not university educated.[4]

While the growing ideal of self-determination led to a renewed interest in the Native organizations, two great boosts to their revitalization came from the federal government, led by the Liberals and Pierre Elliott Trudeau (1968–72). First, the 1969 White Paper galvanized the status Indian organizations into restructuring and reorganizing in order to lobby against the propositions of the bill, which sought to repeal the Indian Act. Their growing strength inspired and encouraged similar organizations from the Métis, non-status, and Inuit. Second, and perhaps even more important, the same Liberal government began to legitimize the organizations through the infusion of federal and provincial monies to back their infrastructure and basic operations. This process began in earnest with the Trudeau government's emphasis on multiculturalism, participatory democracy, and citizen participation. Many ethnic groups and interest groups besides Aboriginals were supported through the various new federal programs, but the funds provided to Aboriginal groups were extremely important in mobilizing these organizations and generating a Native middle-class leadership. This support took many forms (even including volunteer work by members of the Company of Young Canadians) but the major impetus came from "core funding," later known as the Aboriginal Representative Organizations Program, or AROP, under the secretary of state. The program was created in 1971 to cover the basic operating costs of the emerging Native political organizations. It originally provided funds for one national status Indian and one national Métis and non-status Indian organization (MNSI) and for one status and one MNSI organization in each province. The money was intended to provide the basic costs of running the organizations (hence "core"): office rental, equipment, and supplies; salaries of the executive and staff; and basic travel and meeting costs.

This massive public funding of Native political organizations remains unique to Canada, and its effects can hardly be overemphasized. It was partially a result of the nature of the Canadian political structure and the particular place of Native people in Canadian society. While there was a growing recognition of the need for Canada to deal with what was seen as legitimate concerns of Native people, there were few mechanisms in place that would allow the federal government to deal with a recognizable and representative Native leadership. The few Native people who became members of Parliament could not fill the gap created by a lack of Native leadership. The regionalism that defines the role of a member of Parliament within the Canadian political system made them incapable of speaking for the wide variety of Native peoples found throughout the country. The government needed a credible (and tractable) leadership with a demonstrable and convincingly legitimate power base from which it could negotiate. This need was particularly important when the Trudeau government was anxious to discuss the repatriation of the Canadian Constitution and other constitutional matters in the 1970s. The vacuum was partially filled by the various status, non-status, and Métis organizations that were being reorganized or developed at the time.

Of course, an alternative suggestion as to why these organizations were funded is that they provided a potential means of controlling or constraining Indian and Métis political activity. It is true that government funds have the potential to manipulate the organizations through the administration of funds, by specifying the terms and conditions under which money can be spent, what it can and what it can't be requested for or used for, and how it is accounted for. These features provide a ready means of control.[5] However, while it is possible to demonstrate that the government can attempt to manipulate and control these interest groups through funding, it should come as no surprise that, once they have been established, such organizations quickly take on a life of their own, going in directions that the government may not have foreseen or even desired.[6] One such result, probably unforeseen by the federal government, was the Métis organizations lobbying for, and achieving, recognition as one of Canada's Aboriginal peoples in the new Canadian Constitution (not all early Métis leaders saw themselves as Aboriginal peoples) and second, as organizations that actively pursued recognition of Aboriginal rights (such as hunting) in the courts. Indeed, the Métis forming a national organization – the Métis National Council, separate from the Native Council of Canada – was not only unforeseen but was initially (and unsuccessfully) opposed by the federal government.

The Prairie Métis Associations

As a direct result of government funding, there was a revitalization of existing political organizations and the appearance of new organizations at both the provincial and the federal levels. A wide variety of Métis and non-status Indian associations became politically active and politically influential in the prairie provinces in the 1960s and 1970s, among others, the Métis Association of Alberta (now the Métis Nation of Alberta); the Federation of Métis Settlements; the Saskatchewan Métis Society (from 1975 to 1988 known as the Association of Métis and Non-Status Indians of Saskatchewan, then the Saskatchewan Métis Society once again until 2000, when it became known as Métis Nation – Saskatchewan); the Manitoba Métis Federation. The operations of these organizations have been extremely significant for the development and negotiation of ethno-Aboriginal identities and the meaning of Métis in Canada today. Before we proceed, a brief history of some of the more influential organizations is in order.

As we saw earlier (see chapter 11), the Métis Association of Alberta (MAA), which was formed in 1932, had its beginnings as a federation of many local Métis community organizations. It enjoyed some early success, despite an indifferent and sometimes hostile provincial government. The MAA was at least partially responsible for the formation of the Ewing Commission, which recommended the setting up of the Métis colonies, now called the Métis Settlements. However, the MAA was quickly sidelined after the province set up its own system of settlement councils. The Alberta government refused to deal with the MAA or allow it to act as a representative of the colonies, although it cherry-picked a few of the more amenable of the MAA's leaders (particularly Pete Tompkins and Joe Dion) to run the colonies. Malcolm Norris and Jim Brady were probably considered too intractable or radical, although Brady was hired briefly as a superintendent at Wolf Lake.

Hampered by a lack of funding and sporadic leadership, the MAA managed to hang on in one form or another until the 1960s, although it was not much of a force. It would be many years before it would be able to regain the influence it had prior to the setting up of the Ewing Commission. Adrian Hope attempted to resurrect the association in the 1960s, making it the voice of the Métis colonies.[7] He remained president of the association until 1967. Around that time, government money was starting to become available to various Native political organizations in Canada, and, by his own admission, Hope felt that a new type of leader would be necessary in the new circumstances of government funding.

One of the first conditions placed on the MAA as a result of core funding was the requirement that it broaden its base. It could no longer remain as the sole voice of the Métis colonies, as Adrian Hope had wanted. The new leadership had to agree to represent all Métis within the province of Alberta. This meant a radical shift in the MAA's focus. From its earliest beginnings it had been centred in northern Alberta; now it was required to extend its activities to the southern part of the province as well. This shift in itself is an indication of how government funding created or reformulated organizations according to its needs, as opposed to the needs, desires, and perceptions of the Métis themselves.

The restructuring of the MAA did not sit well with the residents of the Métis settlements. They had never been particularly concerned with issues outside the settlements or with general Alberta Métis issues. This situation lasted well into the 1990s.[8] They felt the new MAA was neglecting their particular interests, especially as the colonies were involved in a claim for gas and oil royalties from the Alberta government of the time. Their feelings of isolation or special interest led the residents to create the Federation of Métis Settlements in 1975, leaving the MAA to serve the interests of the Métis outside the colonies. Since the 1990s, the MAA has been known as Métis Nation of Alberta – a name change of some significance, as attitudes to the nature of Métis identity have changed, and the concept of nationhood for the prairie Métis has taken hold.

The history of Métis and non-status Indian organizations in Saskatchewan is probably the most volatile of the three prairie provinces in terms of organizational change and criteria for membership. The Saskatchewan Métis Society (SMS) began meeting sporadically in the early 1930s and was formally organized in1937, with Joe Z. Larocque as its first president.[9] While it was not able to match the early success of its sister organization in Alberta in terms of land claims or the creation of

Métis colonies, it did manage to get some attention from the provincial government. It differed from the MAA in one major way: its clientele. From its beginning, the SMS was strictly a Métis organization, devoted to instilling national pride in being Métis, and did not accept non-status or non-treaty Indians as members.[10] This policy was in marked contrast to that of the MAA, which did accept non-treaty Indians into its ranks. It also flew in the face of the ideas of many non-Métis officials and political leaders of the time, for example, Church officials and members of the Ewing Commission in Alberta, who saw "no difference" between Métis and non-treaty or non-status Indians.

The organization enjoyed some early success: its first high point was in 1940, when it was able to claim 28 locals and a membership of 2,500. However, this achievement did not last long; the organization quickly disintegrated, owing to disruptions of World War II, dissension between northern and southern leadership, and some suspect political advice from some non-Métis advisors. The Saskatchewan government experimented briefly with Métis colonies, inspired by the pattern established in Alberta, but the role of the SMS in the process was peripheral at best, since some of the consultants it was relying on and some of its own leadership publicly questioned and subverted the idea of Métis Aboriginal rights and the need for land. This attitude eventually contributed to the almost total disappearance of the organization.[11] It was revived somewhat when Malcolm Norris moved to Saskatchewan in 1947 to take a job with the provincial government. Norris began organizing locals in northern Saskatchewan, where the SMS previously had been inactive. But it was not until 1964 that the organization finally started to take on a form that enabled it to be politically effective. In that year, Malcolm Norris founded a separate organization serving the north, the Métis Association of Northern Saskatchewan, and acted as its first president. Jim Brady, who had also moved to Saskatchewan, filled a smaller, but nevertheless supporting, role in this organization by organizing the La Ronge local of the association. One year later, in 1965, the Saskatchewan Métis Society was reconstituted in Regina, with Joe Amyotte as president. The two organizations amalgamated in 1967, laying the groundwork for what eventually was to become the present day Métis Nation of Saskatchewan.

The organization underwent many permutations before becoming the MNS. In 1975, the Saskatchewan Métis Society changed its name to the Association of Métis and Non-Status Indians of Saskatchewan (AMNSIS) as a public recognition of the fact that not only did non-status Indians face many of the same political and social problems as the Métis (this was prior to the constitutional recognition of Métis as one of Canada's Aboriginal peoples) but that many non-status or non-treaty Indians were already members, including the president, Jim Sinclair. For quite a few years, Métis and non-status Indians worked side by side, making it one of the most progressive and successful of the provincial Métis organizations. But many never forgot that the organization was, in its original format, a Métis-only organization. In 1988, a group of Métis managed to seize control of AMNSIS. After a province-wide referendum, 53 per cent of those who cast ballots voted to split the AMNSIS into two separate groups, one representing Métis and one representing non-status Indians. The name of the new Métis organization was the Métis Society of Saskatchewan. As of 2000, the organization's name has been changed to the Métis Nation-Saskatchewan, and it claims to represent the interests of approximately 80,000 Métis people in Saskatchewan.

After the dissolution of AMNSIS, several different organizations attempted to fill the gap for non-status Indians in Saskatchewan. One organization that existed briefly was the Assembly of Aboriginal Peoples of Saskatchewan (AAPS), which was incorporated in September of 1988. Its function was to represent the "excluded Indians" (i.e., non-status or non-treaty) of Saskatchewan. This was not the only organization dedicated to serving non-status Indians; the Native Council of Canada (NCC) had earlier tried to establish a provincial branch. That organization also fell by the wayside, but was eventually replaced when the NCC was reformulated as the Congress of Aboriginal Peoples (CAP). The Saskatchewan affiliate of that organization is now known as the Aboriginal Council of Saskatchewan.

The name changes of the Métis organizations in Saskatchewan offer a brief history of the evolution of the name Métis in the twentieth century and the political circumstances that have affected it. It began as an exclusively Métis society, then changed to one with both Métis and non-status Indians, then went back to a Métis-only society, and finally became a Métis "nation." The changes involve more than simple nomenclature; they are a reflection of changing political conditions and of how individuals either make ethnic choices for themselves or have choices made for them by others. The tie between Métis and non-status Indian is particularly illustrative of the changing concepts of the term Métis. For a time, at least, the tie had the potential of representing more than a simple political alliance between the two groups. There was an actual *identification* as Métis on the part of many non-status Indians; the boundaries between the two were for a time quite blurred, and the decision to cross over (or to be forced across) was a traumatic and distressing decision for many individuals. This issue will be discussed in more detail below.

The history of Métis organization in Manitoba is quite different from that in Saskatchewan or Alberta. Although the Manitoba Métis Federation was not formed until 1967, making it the youngest of the three prairie province Métis associations, Manitoba is home to the earliest Métis organization in Canada: L'Union nationale métisse Saint-Joseph du Manitoba. Many of the activities of the National Union have been discussed in chapter 5. It was founded in 1877, and its goal was to develop a concept of the Métis Nation that would ensure Métis culture would remain strong and francophone. It organized a national holiday (24 July) and a day to commemorate Louis Riel's death (16 November). In the 1920s, it commissioned A.-H. de Trémaudan's *Histoire de la nation métisse dans l'Ouest canadien*, which was eventually published in 1935. But by the 1960s, the organization was almost moribund[12] (although it rebounded later), and in any case, the objects and constituency of L'Union nationale métisse Saint-Joseph du Manitoba were far different and much too narrow to confront the issues facing the Métis and non-status Indians who founded the Manitoba Métis Federation.

The Manitoba Métis Federation, like the Métis Association of Alberta before it, had its beginnings in various local social organizations found in the small Métis communities in the province. However, in Manitoba, most of the communities were based in the southern and central parts of the province, rather than in the northern parts of the province as in Alberta. The MMF began as and remains a federation of small, community-based organizations, or "locals." Prior to the formation of the MMF, the leaders of the Métis locals had little opportunity to meet on a province-wide basis. The only mechanism that allowed for such meetings with any regularity was the annual Indian and Métis Conference that was sponsored by the Community Welfare Planning Council of Winnipeg. While this venue was an important first step in politicizing Manitoba's Aboriginal population, it was not totally satisfactory to the Métis, who felt their special problems and issues were being ignored in favour of those of status Indians, whose representatives outnumbered them at these conferences. Typically, the conferences would concentrate on treaty rights, band councils, and self-government issues on reserves.

Nevertheless, these conferences were instrumental in initiating discourse between the many Métis locals throughout the province and in giving a political bent to local organizations that primarily had a social rather than an activist function. The major issue that galvanized the Métis into exerting a united political pressure in the late 1950s and early 1960s was housing. In the late 1950s, the annual Indian and Métis Conferences began to put pressure on the provincial and federal governments to address the issue of inadequate housing for Native people in remote areas of Manitoba.[13] Housing programs had recently been introduced on reserves by the federal Department of Indian Affairs. Whatever the shortcomings these programs may have had, they provided a level of housing that was in stark contrast to what was typical in the remote, primarily Métis communities not covered by housing program. The Métis in these areas – Duck Bay, Camperville, Thompson, The Pas, Berens River – began to form housing associations, which worked through the Indian and Métis Conferences to apply pressure on the Manitoba provincial government to set up a special housing program for remote areas. Similar activities in other provinces reinforced their case; in 1966, the Saskatchewan government introduced its own Remote Housing Program, and the Métis housing associations seized on the Saskatchewan example to bring further pressure to bear on the Manitoba government.

By this time, the housing associations had amalgamated to form the Manitoba Métis Housing Association and they initiated housing surveys in sixteen Métis communities. The March 1967 Indian and Métis Conference tabled a list of eleven resolutions and proposals, which included a brief encouraging the province of Manitoba to address the issue of housing in remote areas.[14] This Indian and Métis conference proved to be the last one in which the two groups met together. The housing issue made it painfully clear that, while having many problems in common, they needed very different solutions in terms of government services available to them. However, the break did not happen at that conference. It happened several months later, in October 1967, at a communications workshop, which had as its supposed goal developing "better communications between Indian communities, Indians and Métis, and Indian, Métis and whites."[15] Prior publicity for the workshop mentioned issues such as setting up a Native newspaper. Nothing indicated in advance what was to happen at this workshop – the formation of two new political organizations that changed the political status of Native people in Manitoba for years to come. There were about ninety delegates, and status Indians, mostly chiefs and band counsellors, made up two-thirds of the delegates and the Métis making up the remainder. Once again, the Métis were outnumbered.

The events that took place at that workshop have now entered into the folklore of the Métis of Manitoba. Because the large majority of delegates were status Indians, the discussions inevitably gravitated towards issues of concern primarily to status Indians, in particular, a resolution to resurrect the moribund Manitoba Native Brotherhood. This organization had been around in one form or another since 1935, but had not been active since 1962, the last time it had elected any officers. The question arose as to whether the organization should invite the Métis to participate, or whether it should devote itself strictly to issues of status Indians. The tenor of the discussion was making it clear to the Métis that the time had come to form their own political organization. Stan Fulham recalls how Angus Spence, a rancher from the Eddystone Bacon Ridge area stood up and vented his dissatisfaction with the state of affairs: "Angus said 'you know, there's nothing here for me. For the Métis people. We're talking about matters of importance to the Indian people, but there's nothing here for us. I'm walking out of here. I'm going across the hallway, to this other room. I would like other people who have my concerns to come and join me; Métis people who feel there's nothing here for us.' He walked out and 27 other people went and joined him. I can't think of all the names of the people who did, but Adam Cuthand would have been one of them."[16] Variations on this story can be heard from many Manitoba Métis who are knowledgeable about the history of their organization. Some of the people who were present at that inaugural meeting, in addition to Adam Cuthand (who was not a Métis, but an Indian from Saskatchewan who had lost his status when he became an ordained minister), were Ferdinand Guiboche from Camperville, Joe Keeper, George Monroe (head of the newly formed Indian-Métis Friendship Centre, which had been officially opened at this workshop) Tom Eagle, coordinator of the workshop, and many others.[17]

But the activities of the status Indians were just as far-reaching. The treaty delegates unanimously supported a motion calling for a reorganization of the Manitoba Native Brotherhood. The new organization was dubbed the Manitoba Indian Brotherhood. Chief Dave Courchene of the Fort Alexander reserve was named the president of the newly formed organization, along with four regional vice-presidents. One of the vice-presidents was twenty-two-year old Phil Fontaine, band manager of the Fort Alexander Reserve and former member of the Company of Young Canadians. Fontaine was later to become the national chief of the Assembly of First Nations.

Early Activities of Organizations

One of the most profound influences on the growth of Métis nationalism and ethnicity in the twentieth century comes from the development of the Métis political organizations at the national, provincial, and local levels. Unfortunately, while we have some understanding of the evolution of the provincial and national organizations, we have little information on the nature of the early community-based groups that were the precursors of the wider political organizations. While there seemed to be an important political component to them, it is likely that they were primarily oriented towards social and cultural functions. This certainly was the case in Manitoba.

Stan Fulham, the first executive director of the Manitoba Métis Federation (1970–74) and manager of the Kinew Housing Corporation from 1974 to 1981, remembers the early locals in Manitoba very well. Long before the formation of the MMF, he recalls that there were local Métis organizations in The Pas, Berens River, and Camperville, the John Bosco local in Winnipeg and in many other parts of Manitoba.[18] A typical example was the Fort Ellis local in St Lazare. Like the other locals existing at the time, it was not an overtly political organization. Its main purpose was to organize various sports activities and an annual picnic held at the old Fort Ellis grounds. These functions remained an important part of the local activities even after the formation of the MMF. Stan Fulham remembers that one of his first tasks as executive director of the newly formed MMF was to help the Fort Ellis local get buffalo meat for their big picnic.

These locals were usually quite small. John Fiddler, the first vice-president of The Pas local, said that there were only a handful of people that regularly attended meetings;[19] he too indicated that they used to meet primarily for social reasons. This impression fits with my own early observations of the locals. In 1971 I worked for the Manitoba Métis Federation as a researcher on a remote housing evaluation program and in the course of that research visited several Métis communities in northern and southern Manitoba. Earlier, in 1970, I had conducted anthropological fieldwork in several other Métis communities in northern and southern Manitoba.[20] I noticed in all these situations that most people who were aware of the MMF identified it primarily (or only) as the organizer of one of the weekly bingo games or of a picnic or dances. It should be pointed out that the recreational function remains one of the most important aspects of the MMF locals to this day – and the same is true for many of the locals in the other provinces. This should not be surprising; not all people are interested in politics or are able to formulate or are interested in articulating ideas of identity, and there are many other important functions a community-level organization must serve, political organizing being only one.

Fulham attributes the strong social and cultural content of local activities to the peculiar social position of the Métis at the time. As he put it, their members had one thing in common: they were socially isolated. They were Native people living in a primarily Native community, but their main commonality was that *they were not Indians*. According to Fulham, they were not stating their "Métisness" with any particular fervour; they were emphasizing their "Nativeness" and separateness from status Indians. Fulham says that the political functions of the organizations did not come to the forefront until the formation of the umbrella provincial organization.[21]

Be that as it may, the existence of these locals helps to explain how and why the Métis communities managed to survive the first half of the twentieth century, maintaining a strong cultural identity while remaining under the radar of the rest of Canada. These early manifestations of Métis collectivity, which eventually evolved into the provincial political organizations (and eventually into the Métis National Council) were a reflection of this ongoing community spirit and identity as Métis and at the same time helped to perpetuate it and foster the identification in the next generation.

But the organizations did not do much about *changing* the concepts of Métis identity or the parameters of Métisness until they began to amalgamate and operate on a provincial level as overtly political structures. The potential effect on the reformulation of ethnicity was noticed at the beginnings of the MMF and was not greeted with universal enthusiasm. According to Fulham, Jean René Allard, MLA for Rupert's Land and a long-time member of L'Union nationale métisse Saint-Joseph du Manitoba who had served as its leader, objected to the MMF when it was first organized. Specifically, he disliked the use of the name "Métis" because he felt it should be restricted to people of French and Indian origin who were Roman Catholic. Noting that the leadership of the early MMF comprised people such as Angus Spence, Adam

Cuthand, and Stan Fulham, he felt that these people were not entitled to the use of the name "Métis."[22] Nevertheless, the die was cast, and the change in meaning of the term was unstoppable once the process of political union had begun. The MMF, being a provincial federation of many regions, communities, and ethnic ties (French, English, Scottish, as well as other European mixtures later in the twentieth century), had a marked and reformulative effect on Métis conceptions of identity. The organizations in Saskatchewan and Alberta had a similar effect, as non-status Indians, people who were part Indian but whose non-Native ancestry was neither French, nor English, nor Scottish, and people who had simply married into the Métis community became active in the new provincial associations.

National Organizations: The Métis National Council and the Congress of Aboriginal Peoples

There are two organizations that claim to represent Métis in the national scene: the Métis National Council (MNC) and the Congress of Aboriginal Peoples (CAP). Both associations had their origins in the Native Council of Canada (NCC). The Native Council of Canada was formed in 1970 to represent the national interests of the Métis and non-status Indians of British Columbia, Alberta, Saskatchewan, and Manitoba. It had a great deal of difficulty in remaining a cohesive force. In addition to the usual problems inherent in any national Canadian Aboriginal organization of balancing the interests of different regions and provinces, it had the added challenge of attempting to represent two very different groups: Métis and non-status Indians. While there were times when the NCC could claim to represent almost all of the Métis and non-status Indian organizations across Canada, there were other times when there were more provincial organizations outside its purview than in.

The situation came to a head in 1983, shortly after the 1982 repatriation of the Canadian Constitution. Not only was the legal and cultural divide between the Métis and non-status Indians magnified by the inclusion of the Métis in the constitutional recognition of Canada's Aboriginal peoples, alongside the simultaneous exclusion of non-status Indians, but the leadership of the NCC had passed completely out of Métis hands. In 1983, neither the president nor the vice-president of the NCC was Métis; in fact, the vice-president was not even non-status, but a status Indian from British Columbia. This meant that the Métis were completely shut out of the upcoming first ministers conferences that had been scheduled to identify and define the Aboriginal rights so recently granted constitutional protection. The Métis were supposedly represented by the NCC, but the two seats reserved for the NCC were to be filled by the president and vice-president, neither of whom was Métis. So, the three prairie Métis organizations, joined by the Federation of Métis Settlements, quickly formed a new national Métis organization, the Métis National Council (MNC) and demanded their own seats at the table.

The federal government, in the person of the justice minister, Mark MacGuigan, at first refused to recognize the newly emergent organization, apparently preferring to keep the Métis and non-status in the same organization. But after a threatened boycott and legal action, the government relented and the MNC became the official representative of the Métis, not only at the first ministers conferences, but subsequently on all other matters regarding Métis on the national scene. The Native Council of Canada continued its operations until 1994, when it changed its name to the Congress of Aboriginal Peoples. It now claims to represent the interests of urban and off-reserve Indians, some dissident prairie Métis organizations, Métis peoples outside the prairies, non-status Indians, and Bill C-31s.

Conclusions

The 1960s mark a second florescence of Métis political organization in the twentieth century in the prairie provinces – at least for Alberta and Saskatchewan. In Manitoba, the situation was somewhat different, as the Manitoba Métis Federation (MMF) was not incorporated until 1967. But the MMF was not the first Métis organization in that province; it was preceded by L'Union nationale métisse Saint-Joseph du Manitoba, which formed in 1888, almost eighty years before the MMF began operations. So, the MMF, too, in a sense represents a second coming of a Métis association in Manitoba and parallels the movements in the other provinces as the Métis began to reinvent themselves in the 1960s. The growth of these provincial Métis organizations was accompanied by something new – an expansion beyond provincial lines as several of the provincial organizations attempted to amalgamate into a national, Canada-wide organization, first manifested by the Native Council of Canada (NCC). The NCC eventually split into two organizations, the Métis National Council (MNC) and the Congress of Aboriginal Peoples (CAP).

These organizations, along with the many First Nations organizations whose development accompanied those of the Métis, have become an essential part of the Canadian political process on the national and provincial levels. Canada is unique in the number, breadth, and power of Native political organizations within its borders, but they have developed to meet specific needs and political realities. Canada's classification and registration of its Native population resulted in a confusing conglomeration of status Indians, non-status Indians, and Métis, each with different histories, cultures, and claims to Aboriginal rights. Each of these groups needed a mechanism with which to approach and negotiate with the Canadian government in order to pursue their rights and improve their conditions. Participation in the regular political field was impractical or, at best, a partial solution. Native people as a whole made up a small minority within Canada and were scattered across the country in small and often isolated communities. Electing truly representative MLAs or MPs who could effectively speak to the special interests of Métis and status and non-status Indians was a difficult if not impossible task. Native political organizations on the provincial and national levels remained the only effective way Native peoples could lobby the governments in their own interests.

The development and influence of these organizations since the 1960s has been remarkable. They have achieved heights of influence and effectiveness probably undreamt of by those who began the first tentative steps of organizing in the 1930s. What made this growth possible was the massive influx of funding from the federal and provincial governments, particularly federal core funding under the Aboriginal Representative Organizations Program (AROP). A second source of income and political influence arose as the organizations began to administer various government housing and education programs. There are many reasons why the federal and provincial governments were willing to provide these funds. The organizations filled many functions in the Canadian political scene. First, they allowed the governments to deal with the Native population as corporate groups. Besides providing a useful mechanism for negotiating land claims and other Aboriginal rights, they could act as delivery agents for various government services such as housing and education. They also helped put a public face on Native leadership, providing that leadership with a means of legitimizing itself in the public eye through internal elections. As a result, many of the leaders became recognizable as important players on the Canadian political scene. Also, from the government's point of view, the organizations could be seen as a means of potentially controlling the Native population, through providing or withholding the funding necessary for their operations.

When the Métis groups began to reform in the 1960s, their main problem was defining their constituency. They often began as an alliance between Métis and non-status Indians. At first, this partnership seemed to work well, as the two groups faced a similar problem, namely, that the federal government refused to recognize the Aboriginal heritage or rights of any group other than Indians registered under the Indian Act. Both the Métis and the non-status Indians felt that they too had Aboriginal rights and they banded together to pursue them. However, their alliance was an uneasy one at best, and it quickly broke down after the Métis became recognized as one of Canada's Aboriginal peoples in the Canadian Constitution (along with Indians and Inuit), leaving non-status Indians as the sole group of Aboriginal people in Canada without government recognition. The split had actually started during constitutional negotiations, when the Métis organizations broke off from the NCC to form the Métis National Council. After constitutional recognition, the Métis in provincial organizations such as the Association of Métis and Non-Status Indians of Saskatchewan (AMNSIS) quickly followed the lead of their national organization in redefining their membership, purging non-status Indians from the associations, and refashioning them as Métis-only.

The Métis associations filled many different roles as they began to develop. As we can see from the MMF, much of the early activity, especially on the local level, was of a social and cultural nature – organizing picnics, Métis Day celebrations, weekly bingo games, and the like. As the organizations grew in influence and political strength, they took on many more substantive roles such as reformulating ideas on Aboriginal rights and land claims and pursuing various forms of economic development. But for our purposes, their most significant feature has been the reification and redefinition of ethnic boundaries – restating what it meant and means to be a Métis in the twentieth and twenty-first centuries.

15 Reformulated Identities, 1965–2013

"Métis," as the term has come to be understood in Canada today, has its roots not solely in the nineteenth century, but also in the renewed and revitalized Native political activism that began in the 1960s and 1970s. Although many factors have combined to shape twentieth- and twenty-first-century Métis identity, undoubtedly the major influence is the existence of Métis political organizations and pressure groups and the corporate and political elite who evolved alongside them, who pursued Métis Nationalism and Aboriginal rights with an increasing fervour throughout the 1960s, 1970s and 1980s. Their actions resulted in the recognition of the Métis as one of Canada's Aboriginal peoples in the repatriation of the Canadian Constitution in 1982, but there were many definitions of what or who constituted a Métis identity that were experimented with on the way to constitutional recognition, and there have been many changes since recognition was achieved, changes that in fact are still ongoing. Today, the term encompasses groups that were not part of the original nineteenth century definition (such as English and Scottish "half-breeds"), while excluding others that only a few years earlier had been included, such as non-status Indians. So, although today's Métis share the same name as the "New Nation" of the nineteenth century, have appropriated some of its history, and are at least partially rooted in past conceptions of "Métisness," the modern group has a very different make-up and political awareness than the ancestral group it supposedly descended from. "Métis" is very much a modern concept.

Why did an increase in political activity result in such a radical shift in ethnic boundaries and values? Undoubtedly, the major impetus was that the Métis, perhaps for the first time since the 1890s, were starting to take control of their own definition of self. We have already seen that in the first half of the twentieth century, the Métis were perpetually being defined by others – by the Ewing Commission in the 1930s and by social scientists, historians, and other academics in the 1950s and 1960s. Not surprisingly, when the Métis began to assert their own definitions, they proved to be different from those of outsiders. While some of the imposed definitions became accepted by Métis leaders and the early organizations (much as the concept of "status" became accepted by Indians), many outside concepts began to be rejected with growing political sophistication and self-confidence. But it was not a sudden change; it evolved, and went through many permutations in the twentieth century. As we have already noted, this was part of a world-wide assertion of Aboriginal self-determination and self-identity.

Of course, political organizations and political mobilization are not the only variables that affected Métis identity in the twentieth and twenty-first centuries. Government policy and definitions (the Manitoba Act, the various Dominion Lands Acts, the Indian Act and its amendments, and constitutional recognition) are equally important variables. Modern land claims and court cases on the nature of Métis Aboriginal rights are an important factor, as is the existence of other mixed-blood populations in Canada that have begun to adopt the term "Métis" to describe themselves. Individual choices – to be or not to be Métis – are another variable, as are disputes over these personal and collective claims. Individual choices over whether to claim to be Métis or not have become more complicated, as the term "Métis" not only has grown to be socially acceptable and desirable, but has come to offer some economic advantages as well. All of these factors, and probably others, have combined to change the meaning of the term "Métis." This chapter is an attempt to explore the most influential of these factors in the period after 1965.

The flexibility of Métis identity should come as no surprise to students of ethnic change and ethnic group dynamics. The central ideas running through most analyses of ethnicity since the 1960s are that ethnicity is neither stable nor permanent, it is sensitive to the political environment, and a collective ethnic identity emerges out of political struggle. The concept of ethnic adaptability began with Barth's notion of ethnic group boundary maintenance, which suggested that ethnicity was to some extent permeable, allowing people to "cross" boundaries; assuming or discarding ethnic identities according to need.[1] This in turn implied that ethnic boundaries needed some conscious effort to maintain, which morphed into the idea that the boundaries could and would change according to political and economic expediency. From there it was only a short step to the idea of the "invention" of tradition and ethnic groupings. But it should be remembered that outside of academic circles, the idea of ethnicity is very different: it is usually seen as something immutable through generations, based on bloodlines and an extension of kinship. The Métis are no exception. Like most ethnic groups, they cling to the notion that ethnicity is a matter of blood or descent, and they have little patience with suggestions that their ethnicity smacks of political expediency.

The Métis of western Canada test and illustrate the boundaries of all current theories on ethnicity and nation-building. The structure and function of their collectivity is dependent on a complex mixture of state definitions, pressure group politics, court-imposed definitions, ethnic boundary maintenance, and reactions to colonialism. In the pages that follow, we shall consider some of the major forces that have impacted Métis ethnicity in the twentieth century, including activities of the Métis political organizations, government policy, court definitions, ethnic symbolism, disputed ethnicity, and group vs. individual choices in ethnicity.

Organizational Activity and the Definition of Métis

One of the most obvious mechanisms of change in the concepts of Métis identity is the Métis political organizations and their activities at the regional, provincial, and national levels. The process is most clearly seen in the various definitions of Métis engendered over the years. These definitions, which at first merely determined who could or who could not become a member of the organization, eventually morphed into definitions of who was or who was not a Métis. From the beginnings of twentieth-century Métis political mobilization, there were many conflicting views of Métis identity and who should or who should not be represented by the emerging organizations. This conflict is reflected in the various criteria for membership as articulated by the organizations. One of the earliest examples is provided by the Métis Association of Alberta (MAA). Its 1932 constitution accepted all British subjects with Indian ancestry as members, whether they were treaty Indians, non-status Indians, or Métis.[2] The 1940 constitution[3] does not distinguish between Métis and non-treaty Indians – all were members of the "Red Race" and all were welcome to join. There was a strong element of "Indian" values in the document, with references to the Great Spirit, and brotherhood among all Native peoples of the North American continent.[4] This emphasis was perhaps due to the influence of Malcolm Norris, the most likely author of the document, whose own values and identities did not necessarily include a total identification with the Métis. An "active member" of the Métis Association of Alberta was defined as a "Métis, Non Treaty Indian, or any person of mixed White and Indian blood." The constitution also enjoined that "every member hold to the ancient Indian code; love and help thy brother," and that any person who complied with these conditions was entitled to "become an active member on the recommendation of two (2) members in good standing and whose application is ratified at a regularly called meeting." However, the Alberta definitions should not be taken as proof of a universal acceptance of the equivalence of Métis and non-status in all the prairie provinces. In the same time period, the 1930s and 1940s, the Saskatchewan Métis Society (SMS) billed itself as a Métis-only organization, and non-treaty or non-status Indians were not eligible to join that organization.

The inclusive definition articulated by these early MAA constitutions was the one that held sway for some time and continued well into the next wave of Métis political activity, which began in the 1960s. There was much controversy over what or who constituted a Métis, even among the Métis themselves. When I first started attending meetings of Manitoba Métis Federation (MMF) locals in 1970 and 1971,[5] I was struck by the regularity with which discussions centred on who was or who was not eligible to join the federation, who the federation was supposed to represent, and indeed who was or who was not a Métis. It was also a concern at the provincial level of the federation – a 1969 workshop for the MMF executive devoted a major part of its discussion to the confusion between unregistered Indians (for whom there was no other representative organization in the province at the time) and those considered "true Métis."[6] This uncertainty was exacerbated by the fact that Adam Cuthand, one of the founding members, was not a Métis, and that other leaders were descended from Scottish or English half-breeds rather than French Métis. Similar concerns were being discussed in the Saskatchewan and Alberta organizations at the time.

Probably because of this confusion over identities (but also because early government funding encouraged a wide membership of both

Métis and non-status) the earliest definitions were as broad as the 1940 MAA definition. They generally stated or accepted that anyone of mixed white/Indian ancestry was eligible to join the provincial Métis association. Little attention was paid to time-depth or generation; a first-generation Métis or a non-status Indian, or even in some cases a non-Native spouse was as welcome to join as was someone who could trace his or her ancestry back to the early days of the Red River Settlement. For example, the Manitoba Métis Federation's 1969 constitution stated that any unregistered person of Indian descent who was eighteen years of age and over was eligible to become a voting member of the federation. Membership was also open to any non-Indian over eighteen who was married to a person of Indian descent (status of the Indian person was not specified).[7]

While some of the early definitions specified a white/Indian ancestry, this requirement was soon broadened to include any non-Native ancestry. For example, in Alberta one area of the province has a long-standing mixed black/Indian population. At an assembly of the Métis Association of Alberta in the early 1970s, a person of mixed black/Indian ancestry stood up and asked, "What about me? I'm part Indian. Aren't I a Métis too?" After a lengthy debate, it was decided that he was indeed a Métis, and the MAA constitution was changed to read "any person of mixed Indian and *non-Indian* blood, or any non-status Indian or their spouse ... sixteen years of age or older, residing in the province of Alberta, is eligible for membership in the Association."[8]

It is true that the definitions cited above are statements of eligibility for membership in the Métis associations, rather than definitions of Métis per se, but the emphasis on non-Indian/Indian ancestry rather than on a connection to a historic Métis (French or otherwise) population became the accepted definition of ethnicity as well, at least for a time, as long as such a person wanted to claim to be Métis. As late as 1982, the Alberta Federation of Métis Settlements defined Métis as "any person of mixed Indian and non-Indian ancestry who identifies as a Métis."[9] Save for the qualification of self-identity, the definition is the same as the one developed by the MAA almost ten years previously, nor is it far removed from the 1940 definition. This concept of Métis was deemed acceptable by the majority of MAA members for many years, and there was little conflict between Métis and non-status members at the time. In the three years I spent working for the MAA (1978–80) I did not witness a single expression of antagonism between a Métis and non-status Indian – or even an acknowledgment that there were problems or differences between the two.

However, soon after the repatriation of the Canadian Constitution, and the inception of the Métis National Council (MNC), a new definition of Métis began to be developed by the prairie organizations. At the 1984 annual Assembly of the MAA, the following bylaws regarding the definition of Métis was passed: "A Métis is an Aboriginal person who declares himself/herself to be a Métis person, and can produce satisfactory historical or acceptable legal proof that he/she is a Métis, or has traditionally held himself/herself to be a Métis, and is accepted by the Métis people as a Métis."[10] All mention of non-status Indians was dropped, as well as references to mixed ancestry. Both the inclusion of "Aboriginal" and the dropping of non-status was at least partially a consequence of section 35(2) of the Constitution Act of 1982, which included Métis but did not include non-status Indians as Canada's Aboriginal peoples. The term "Métis" was also expanded to include those who traced their descent from English and Scottish half-breed populations of the Red River of the nineteenth century, as well as the French Métis.

When the revised definition was adopted, the vice-president of the Métis Association of Alberta publicly stated that this did *not* mean that all non-status Indians would have to leave the association. Perhaps acknowledging the strong commitment to the Métis cause that many non-status Indians had made within the organizations for the fifteen to twenty years prior to the 1984 change in membership regulations, as well as the spirit of the traditional definition of the MAA, she stated that "if they identify themselves as Métis and are accepted by the Métis community, then they have absolutely no problem."[11] Thus, it seemed that there was still an opportunity for some non-status Indians to take on the identity of Métis if they so desired. But at least one category of non-status was unlikely to be able to maintain their position within the associations: professional politicians who happened to be non-status. Their public position made them extremely vulnerable to attack from Métis political opponents who could (and did) accuse them of being "Indian" rather than Métis, and therefore unqualified to speak for the Métis.

The Métis National Council's definition, developed at around the same time, was undoubtedly an influence here. The existence of the MNC and its definition eventually resulted in a relatively uniform definition of Métis currently being used by Métis prairie organizations, but the process took some time. The original MNC definition of Métis stated:

> 1. The Métis are:
>   - an Aboriginal people distinct from Indian and Inuit;
>   - descendants of the historic Métis who evolved in what is now Western Canada as a people with a common political will;
>   - descendants of those Aboriginals who have been absorbed by the historic Métis.
> 2. The Métis community comprises members of the above who share a common cultural identity and political will.[12]

While this early definition did not use the term "nation" (the final step in the evolution of Métis identity in the twentieth century), note the distinction between Métis, Indian, and Inuit, another reference to s. 35(2) of the Constitution Act, 1982. It is significant to note that all of the definitions of Métis that have been developed by the prairie and national organizations since the MAA changed its definition in 1984 have dropped any reference to "mixed-bloodedness" (see further discussion below).

The provincial organizations then began to refine the MNC definition to reflect the regional and special legal concerns of their own constituency. The 1992 constitution of the MMF defined Métis as

> 1(b) "*Metis*" means an Aboriginal person who self-identifies as Metis, who is distinct from Indian and Inuit and:
>
> i. is a descendant of those Metis who received or were entitled to receive land grants and/or scrip under the provision of the Manitoba Act, 1870, or the Dominion Lands Acts, as enacted from time to time;
>
> or
>
> ii. is a person of Aboriginal descent who is accepted by the Metis Nation.

Perhaps the most significant aspect of this new definition and of other definitions that were emerging at around this time other than the dropping of reference to mixed-bloodedness was the addition of the word "Nation," as in *the* "Métis Nation." The reference to the western Métis as a distinct nation was an important addition to the concept of Métis. One of the earliest manifestations occurred in the early 1990s, when the Métis Association of Alberta changed its name to the Métis Nation of Alberta. The term then began appearing in the definitions of Métis being developed since the 1990s and, as mentioned previously, the Métis Society of Saskatchewan became the Métis Nation-Saskatchewan in 2000. While the Manitoba Métis Federation retains its original name, its 1992 definition makes it one of the first organizations to refer to itself as a "Nation." Although the Métis have used "Nation" to describe themselves before, it is possible that the recent resurgence of the term among the prairie Métis organizations was also influenced by the growth of the term "First Nations" as adopted by status and treaty Indians. The use of "Nation" also serves to distinguish themselves from other groups of Aboriginal populations who are either laying claim to the term "Métis," or are using it as a general catch-all for mixed Aboriginal/non-Aboriginal populations, a usage that later became reified by the *Report of the Royal Commission on Aboriginal Peoples* (see below).

The other important characteristic of the Manitoba definition was that the terminology was becoming more and more legalistic. The references to the Manitoba Act and the Dominion Lands Act are undoubtedly there because the Manitoba Métis Federation has been pursuing a land claims case through the courts since the 1980s. The current definition is quite a change from the beginnings of the original MMF, the membership of which was open to "any unregistered person of Indian descent." As the Saskatchewan Métis share a great deal of common history with those in Manitoba and are also interested in pursuing land claims on their own, the current definition of the Métis Nation-Saskatchewan (as amended in1997) is almost identical to its Manitoba counterpart.[13]

In keeping with the legalistic requirements of the new Métis identity, the definition of the Métis Nation of Alberta, as of 2004, required a prospective member to produce an ancestor who had received scrip during the late 1800s under the Manitoba Act or the Dominion Lands Act or an ancestor from up to five generations back who was recorded as a Métis by the government or a Church. It would also accept a statutory declaration from another Métis. As in the previous definition, the member must "hold himself/herself to be a Metis, and be accepted by the Metis people as a Metis."[14] A new feature was an appointed fourteen-member Métis senate that had, among other duties, the responsibility of deciding on a person's eligibility to claim Métis status and join the organization.

The "National Definition of Metis" as adopted at the 18th Annual General Assembly of the Métis National Council in 2002 also embraced the idea of a Métis Nation and in fact narrowed the concept down to a specific "historic Metis Nation." "Metis" now meant a person who self-identifies as Métis, is distinct from other Aboriginal peoples, is of historic Métis Nation ancestry, and is accepted by the Métis Nation. While the definition itself is fairly succinct, there are several caveats and sub-definitions associated with it, which complicate it considerably. The "historic Metis Nation" is defined geographically as "the Aboriginal people then known as Metis or Half-breeds who resided in the historic Métis Nation Homeland." The historic Métis Nation Homeland itself refers to "the area of land in west central North America used and occupied as the traditional territory of the Metis or Half-breeds as they were then known." "Metis Nation" means "the Aboriginal people descended from the historic Metis Nation which is now comprised of all Metis Nation citizens and is one of the 'aboriginal peoples of Canada' within the meaning of s.35 of the Constitution Act 1982." And finally, the definition explains that "distinct from other Aboriginal peoples" means distinct for "cultural and nationhood purposes."

An earlier draft version of the MNC definition was even more explicit in its definition of the historic Métis Nation, tying it to a specific date of "on or before December 8th 1869, the date of the proclamation of the Provisional Government of the Metis in the North West Territories."[15] An alternate date that was also proposed in the same document was the proclamation of the Métis Nation at the Battle of Seven Oaks in 1816. The document is quite forthright about why a specific date is important:

> Specifying a date can be useful for several reasons. One reason is that by reiterating our historic moments in our formative documents (we hope that eventually this national definition will be included in our Metis Nation Constitution) we reinforce our own history and our own important Metis historical moments. It is helpful to emphasize when the Metis Nation came into being and by stating this date, the Metis are saying we are not just descendants of Indians, we are descendants of a pre-existing Metis Nation which was self-proclaiming and self-determining. This date is recognizable by Metis people and by the Canadian state. Further the inclusion of a date is the practice used in modern land claim and self-government agreements.[16]

The region includes the Red River Settlement (Manitoba), Saskatchewan, Alberta, Montana, and North Dakota. This regional definition may prove to be too narrow for some of the members of the Métis National Council, particularly those from Ontario and British Columbia, and it may preclude potential members from the Northwest Territories as well.

Since at least 1993, the Métis National Council has been proposing the establishment of a national Métis registry, to be used to identify those eligible to participate in the electoral process governing Métis political institutions and to receive benefit from the programs and services delivered by Métis organizations. The registrar would have the legal responsibility to add or delete individuals from the registry.[17] The MNC felt that "there (is) strong support ... for a centralized registry of Metis citizens, not just an enumeration. An enumeration only provides for a one-time count of Metis people, whereas a national registry will allow for the Metis Nation to maintain control of its citizenship, as well as provide credibility and consistency for the Metis definition adopted by the MNC and its governing member organizations."[18] This invites parallels to the federal government's registry system for status Indians, and could lead to a *new* category in Canada: "Registered Métis" and, inevitably, "non-Registered Métis" or non-status Métis, to mirror the category of non-status Indian. This is just one of the many indications that the definition of Métis is becoming narrower and narrower. There is a danger that the organizations will create a new set of disaffected Métis who, for one reason or another, are not seen as bona fide members of the Métis Nation, regardless of where they reside in Canada.

In fact, there is already good evidence that such a disaffected Métis population exists. Not all Aboriginal pressure groups have rejected the notion prevalent in the 1970s that any "nontribal indigenous group" (to borrow a phrase from Chris Andersen[19]) has the right to be regarded as Métis. There are several groups and categories of Aboriginal people in Canada that are either non-status or at any rate not "Indian." Many of these groups have a mixed Aboriginal and non-Aboriginal ancestry, but that is not necessarily the key to their separateness. Nevertheless, many of them began to lay claim to the term "Métis." The Congress of Aboriginal Peoples (CAP), formerly the Native Council of Canada (NCC), cast a much wider net than the Métis organizations, by attempting to represent *all* Aboriginal peoples who are excluded from various definitions – from governmental definitions such as those in the Indian Act to organizational definitions such as those in the MNC.

The CAP claims it is the national representative of over 800,000 off-reserve Indian, Inuit, Métis, non-status Indians, and those Indians who have regained status under Bill C-31. What the CAP's constituents have in common is that, despite their Aboriginal background, they are often excluded from government policies and programs for Aboriginal peoples. Among the groups the CAP claims to represent are "Metis people [who] are located in all of the provinces and territories of Canada. These persons, who may or may not be entitled to status under the Indian Act, are Metis culturally, historically, and for purposes of constitutional recognition. Some of this group are a distinctive mixed blood population, others are closely identified with the history and culture of the French/Cree Metis in southern Manitoba and central Saskatchewan in the 1860s. [Others include] ... Bush Cree/ Metis; 'Bay-Metis' in Northern Ontario, and Gwitchin Metis in the northern McKenzie."[20]

The attitude of those who are excluded from the "Métis Nation" of the prairies can be seen in "The Other Metis," a website dedicated to "Providing Information on Metis Peoples Everywhere in North America." This site is the creation of Martin Dunn, a former researcher for the Native Council of Canada, the Ontario Métis and Non-Status Indian Association, and the Royal Commission on Aboriginal Peoples. Although Dunn himself is a descendant of Red River Métis, he disagrees with the exclusionary definition developed by the MNC. He feels that the Acadians were the first Métis, and he likes to point out that half-breeds existed long before the Red River Settlement was founded. He estimates that at least 17 per cent of Canadians qualify as Métis under the old Native Council of Canada guidelines.[21] On the first page of the site, the name "The Other Metis" is explained:

> There are virtually millions of people *of mixed Aboriginal and non-Aboriginal ancestry* [emphasis added] in Canada and the United States. Some of these people identify themselves as Metis and some do not. This site is dedicated to those individuals, communities, and Nations who want to assert their Metis identity and heritage as a living and valuable contribution to modern life.
>
> As the title of this site implies, the emphasis of the information presented here will be related to those Metis who are not represented by the better known Canadian prairie Metis organizations and their national organization, the Metis National Council. It is these "other" Metis who most need the opportunity to present their case.

As has already been mentioned several times in this volume, the emphasis on "mixed-bloodedness" is problematic in terms of its being an ethnic marker, as *all* populations are "mixed." Nevertheless, it remains a significant ethnic distinction to many, as Dunn's definition indicates.

This split between the "Métis Nation" from the prairie provinces and other groups claiming a Métis identity in the rest of Canada has also been addressed by the *Report of the Royal Commission on Aboriginal Peoples* (RCAP). The RCAP acknowledges that the appropriateness of applying the term "Métis" to everyone is problematic, and that many members of the historic Métis Nation believe that, because the term has been associated most often with them and their ancestors, they have a right to its exclusive use. These Métis believe that other non-tribal indigenous people, or Canadians of mixed Aboriginal/non-Aboriginal ancestry and culture should be described in some other way. But the other mixed-blood and/or non-tribal populations in Canada point out that in terms of dictionary definitions, "Métis" simply means "mixed." They contend that when the term was inserted in the constitution in 1982, it was intended to apply to all Métis people.[22] The RCAP definition of Métis attempts to accommodate both groups by recommending that "Every person who (a) identifies himself or herself as Métis and (b) is accepted as such by the nation of Métis people with which that person wishes to be associated, on the basis of criteria and procedures determined by that nation, be recognized as a member of that nation for purposes of nation-to-nation negotiations and as Métis for that purpose."[23]

This definition obviously takes much of its inspiration from earlier organizational definitions, particularly in terms of self-identity and acceptance from the community. However, it ignores the issues of scrip or tracing ancestry back to the Red River population. Where it breaks new ground is in its inference that there may be more than one Métis community, indicated by the phrase "by the nation of Métis people with which that person wishes to be associated." The RCAP report explicitly acknowledges that there are many distinctive Métis communities across Canada, with more than one culture:

> in deference to the legitimate concerns of Métis Nation members who trace their roots to the western fur trade, we have tried to differentiate these two Métis worlds as much as possible by referring to one as the Métis Nation and to the other by terms such as other Métis, Labrador Métis, and so on ... There are many distinctive Métis communities across

> Canada, and more than one Métis culture as well. Geographically, the homeland of the Métis Nation embraces the three prairie provinces as well as parts of Ontario, the Northwest Territories, British Columbia, and the north central United States. Another Métis people, at least as old as the Métis Nation, is located in Labrador and has maritime traditions. Although the origins of that population are venerable, the application of the term Métis to it is relatively recent. Other Métis communities are found in Quebec, Ontario, Nova Scotia, New Brunswick, British Columbia, and the North. Some have significant links to the western Métis Nation while others do not.[24]

The RCAP report accepts the idea that the Métis people of Labrador are probably in a position to exercise the rights and powers of nationhood. It claims that the Labrador Métis community exhibits the "historical rootedness, social cohesiveness and cultural self-consciousness that are essential to nationhood, and they are developing a political organization that will allow them to engage in effective nation-to-nation negotiation and to exercise self-government."[25] The RCAP admits that the way of life of the Labrador Métis is very similar to that of the Labrador Inuit and Innu, but posits that the Métis culture is sufficiently distinct to mark them as a unique people, and that they are likely to be eligible for nation status under the recognition policy proposed by the RCAP.

The Labrador Métis afford an excellent example of how organizations and pressure groups can affect, or even manufacture, identity change. The name "Métis" was only recently introduced to Labrador; previously, this population was referred to as the Settlers or Liveyers of Newfoundland-Labrador. Their origins are similar to those of the Métis in that they are an Aboriginal and European mix and developed a lifestyle and identity separate from both their Aboriginal and their European ancestors. However, the Native "blood" of Settlers is more likely to be Inuit rather than Indian.[26] This population of mixed bloods in Labrador has a long history, but the first application of the name "Métis" came about in 1975, when the Native Association of Newfoundland and Labrador changed its name to the Indian and Métis Association of Newfoundland and Labrador (IMANL). In part, the name change can be directly attributed to the activities of the Native Council of Canada. Yvon Dumont, formerly the lieutenant governor of Manitoba and one-time president of both the Manitoba Métis Federation and the Métis National Council, was probably the first to apply the term

"Métis" to this group. It happened when he was a young fieldworker for the Native Council of Canada, sent to assist in setting up the structure of the Labrador non-status Indian organization.

As a fieldworker, Dumont was responsible for helping with their organization; assisting them in becoming incorporated, suggesting structures for the board of directors, and recommending a format for their constitution. As Dumont recounts the story, when the question came up of what to call the new association, it was at his suggestion that the name the Labrador Métis Association was chosen. This probably was the first time that the leaders of that Aboriginal community referred to themselves as Métis. Looking back on the choice many years later, Dumont admitted that it was probably a mistake, and he stated that only those people comprising the Métis Nation should be entitled to use the term "Métis."[27] The association did not remain long under that name; it split into two organizations, and "Métis" was dropped from both. However, another organization, the Labrador Métis Association, was formed in 1985, to represent mixed-blood Settlers for southeast and central Labrador.[28] In keeping with the claim to nationhood asserted by the prairie Métis and the MNC, the Labrador Métis Association changed its name to the Labrador Métis Nation in 1998. John Kennedy attributes this in part to the opinion expressed in the RCAP that the Labrador Métis also exhibited characteristics essential to nationhood.[29]

The authors of the RCAP report itself were aware of how political activity on the part of the organizations can affect identity, as discussed in their survey on self-identification. This point was demonstrated in the Newfoundland census figures, which showed that more persons reported Métis identity than had Métis ancestral origins. The RCAP explanation for this discrepancy was that, when asked to specify their origins, some Labrador Métis chose to answer the origin question on the census form in terms of their early Inuit or Innu ancestry, while they identified themselves as Métis in the Aboriginal peoples survey. RCAP concluded that many Labradorians reported Métis identity in this survey because of the high-profile organizational and advocacy activities of the Labrador Métis leadership at the time the survey was being conducted.

One of the most interesting aspects of Kennedy's work is his recounting of the changing attitudes the Settlers evinced towards their Aboriginal background between 1979 and 1983, brought about in part by the activities of the Labrador Métis Nation. When he first began his research, the settlers either avoided the issue or even indicated that they were ashamed of their Aboriginal ancestry. By 1983, they were eagerly asserting their Aboriginality, a process that Kennedy attributes both to the ethnic liberation occurring around the world, and to the benefits of obtaining a "Métis card," which would recognize the Aboriginal rights of Labrador Métis to harvest certain species of wildlife.[30] As in the early days of prairie Métis political organization, membership criteria were sweeping. A Métis was defined as "a person with Indian (Naskapi, Montagnais) and white ancestry, and a person of Inuit and white ancestry and their descendants who are recognized by the Association as Metis or to a person called an 'Original Labradorian,' that is, who settled in Labrador North of the Pinware River prior to 1940, who has remained there since, and their descendants."[31] As Kennedy points out, by this definition any Métis falling within the category of "original Labradorians" need not have *any* "Native blood."

The search for an appropriate form of self-identification is not over for this group. Although many individuals in Labrador continue to identify themselves as "Métis" in the census and elsewhere, the organizations that represent them are beginning to question the use of the term. In 2010 the Labrador Métis Nation changed its name to the NunatuKavut Community Council "to reflect its members' Inuit heritage." NunatuKavut translates as "Our Ancient Land" in Inuktitut."[32] The people represented by the NunatuKavut council are now identified as the Southern Inuit.[33]

These examples illustrate that political organizations can affect and indeed have affected Métis identity, not only in the prairies, the home of the historic Métis Nation, but in other parts of Canada as well. But it is clear those political organizations in and of themselves can be only part of the story. They are as much a *reaction* to political and social change as they are an agent of change. Many other catalysts are likely to be just as important, such as government policy, personal choices of individuals, economic and emotional considerations, and disputes over who may or who may not claim a particular ethnicity.

"Racialization" and Contemporary Definitions of Métis

How important is the concept of mixed ancestry to historic and contemporary definitions of Métis? Andersen has examined the "racialized" logic governing the identification and definition of Métis in Canada over the years.[34] By referring to the "role of racialization in the last five centuries of colonial rule," Andersen is questioning the idea that mixed ancestry is the major (or perhaps only) defining factor of being Métis. He prefers to concentrate on the forming of a political unit whose members identified as Métis: "Métis identity is first and foremost about historical and contemporary political self-consciousness and struggle as Métis and the ability to produce 'intersocietal norms.'" The over-emphasis on mixed race as the primary defining characteristic of the Métis explains much, from the current trend of imposing the identity of Métis on historic upper Great Lakes non-tribal indigenous fur trade settlements, whether or not they may have regarded themselves as such, to considering why contemporary groups who are clearly not Métis have taken on the identity.

The above anecdote concerning Yvon Dumont's adapting the term "Métis" to cover the Labrador situation is particularly relevant in this regard. Why did it seem so natural to import "Métis" and apply it to the Labrador group? The obvious parallels between the Métis and the group in Labrador are their mixed ancestry and feeling of separateness from the other Aboriginal populations in the area. Still, why is it that the Labradorians (and Yvon Dumont himself) placed such a high priority on their mixed ancestry, ignoring other aspects such as culture, tradition, and sense of community? The separateness that they felt from other Aboriginal groups and mainstream society was a direct result of racism and colonialism. Treated as separate from the non-Native population, they were also regarded as separate from the indigenous one. In the vernacular of state-imposed criteria, they were neither fish nor fowl under the prevailing colonial definition of "Inuit" or "white" in that particular geographical area. Searching for some sort of alternative identity, it seemed only natural for them to adopt the available term of "Métis." It "felt right" to them because of the obvious similarities: the mixed ancestry and separate identity they possessed.

In providing this example, I am not suggesting that mixed ancestry in itself is a defining characteristic of being Métis – quite the contrary. The prairie Métis organizations and the MNC many years ago abandoned mixed ancestry as a criterion in their official definition of Métis. Yet it is pointless to deny that many people identifying themselves as Métis – whether from the prairie provinces or elsewhere – recognize mixed ancestry as an important distinguishing feature of their identity. The question remains; *why* is this regarded as such an important feature? Andersen suggests that the emphasis on mixed ancestry originally came from the state, not from the people themselves. He feels that historical colonial authorities tried to subdue the region by imposing a "biological-cum-cultural differentiation" between "half-breeds" and "Indians" and that historians, by accepting that these settlements were recognized as something separate, accept (and thus conceal) these activities. In doing so, he claims, ethnohistorians "take over as tools of analysis the reified products of the ethnoracial struggles of the past." Andersen believes that "in presenting mere separateness as a basis for Métis identity, ethnohistory marginalizes an otherwise obvious hallmark of Métis 'groupness': political self-consciousness as Métis and attachment to a self-ascribing Métis people."

This may well be so, but his argument is not completely compelling. This point of view presupposes that the distinction of separation due to mixed ancestry came *only* from the colonial authorities' racialized ideas; it ignores the fact that the distinction may well have been self-ascribed by the Métis themselves, and that the distinction was simply reflected in colonial definitions. His concern applies to the contemporary situation as well. We have seen several examples of contemporary groups such as the Labradorians and people in the Maritimes appropriating the name Métis specifically *because* of their mixed ancestry. This may well have come from the legacy of the last five centuries of colonialism and racism and the internalization of same by the colonized. But regardless of where it came from, the idea of mixed race is still the elephant in the room in discussions of contemporary ideas about Métis identity, and it will not disappear despite Andersen's concerns. As we shall see below, it has also been regarded as an essential criteria of Métis identification in several important court cases, including *Powley* and *Daniels v. Canada*. Identifying it as a legacy of colonialism does not relegate it to irrelevance, nor does it simplify the issue of contemporary Métis identity for the analyst.

Further to the issue of identity, Andersen is particularly critical of scholars who suggest that "mixed-race" people other than those in/at/from/attached to Red River ought to be able to self-identify as Métis because Métisness is ultimately about racial intermixing and subsequent separateness from tribal communities. Since these dynamics occurred outside Red River as well as inside it, descendants who choose to self-identify as such, wherever their historical settlements exist, should possess equal access to its symbolic prestige. This viewpoint raises several issues, particularly the idea that a scholarly analysis should presume to insert itself into the contemporary fray of whether or not a group has a right to call themselves Métis.[35]

While in the past the link between the historic Great Lakes groups and Red River may have been tenuous at best, that does not preclude the possibility that they are today *becoming* linked, through the same process of developing a political self-consciousness as Métis and attachment to a self-ascribing Métis people that Andersen feels distinguished the historic Red River Métis from other "nontribal indigenous fur trade settlements" in the past. But Andersen's point is not that this historic group was not legitimately "Métis," but that it was not Métis for the reasons that Hele and other scholars have cited: their "mixedness."

Federal Government Policy

In Canada, state definitions of Aboriginality have influenced Native identities since at least 1850, as legal, semi-legal, formal, and semi-formal definitions have affected Aboriginal group identity and group membership. Official designations of ethnicity and/or race – the identification of specific populations for census taking and for designing exclusive policies such as affirmative-action policy or immigration policy – is a common feature of governments around the world,[36] and Canada is no exception. But Canada's policy of defining Native peoples is unique. It differs from that of the United States, for example, in that tribal differences of Indian groups are ignored in favour of an all-inclusive "status Indian" designation. Even the later appellation of "First Nations" emphasizes the collectivity rather than individual tribal or cultural differences. Further, not all Native people are recognized as "status," or as First Nations, leaving a residual group of "non-status Indians," half-breeds, and Métis, who for years were defined primarily by not being under the administration of the Indian Act. This wasn't necessarily a denial of a person's Aboriginality by the federal government; the half-breed scrip program claimed to extinguish Métis claims to "Aboriginal title" and hence recognized some Aboriginal rights of part of this population. But as years passed and recollection of the scrip program faded from public and government memory, recognition of Métis Aboriginality faded or was denied. And, because the original Indian Act of 1876 and the definition of "Indian" have been continually revised by the federal government, the official perception of who was a Métis, half-breed, or non-status Indian has varied over time.

The most influential pieces of government legislation that have affected Métis identity are (a) governmental definitions of Indian, including those in the Indian Act of 1876 and its various amendments (particularly Bill C-31 in 1985); (b) The Manitoba Act of 1870 and the various Dominion Lands Acts of 1872 and onward;[37] and (c) the constitutional recognition of Métis as one of Canada's Aboriginal peoples in 1982. While some of the above legislation mentioned the Métis (or "half-breeds") specifically, most of it, particularly legislation defining "Indian," did not, leaving the Métis as an undefined residual category, supposedly outside the responsibility of the federal government.[38]

The first attempt to define "Indian" took place in 1850, when the legislatures of Upper and Lower Canada passed parallel acts "for the protection of Indians from imposition and the property occupied or enjoyed by them from trespass or injury." The definition was revised in 1851 to include any person deemed to be Aboriginal by birth, blood, or adoption; any person reputed to belong to a particular band or body of Indians; and any woman who married an Indian. This definition was subsumed under the first Indian Act, passed in 1876.

After 1850, the government began keeping lists of the names of Indians who were members of bands recognized under government legislation as Indians. Usually, any Métis who was accepted by an Indian band could be included in these lists, but was considered an Indian, not a Métis. Many Métis also had the option of taking treaty under the same conditions, again becoming Indian in the eyes of the federal government, while others took the option of scrip. Some were able to make the choice more than once, perhaps originally taking treaty as Indians, then leaving to take scrip, perhaps even going back to treaty at a later date. But it was not long before the government closed that loophole, further reifying the legal difference between Métis and status Indian. In the 1940s, the government began a purge of treaty and band lists, arbitrarily removing many Métis and Indians who may have been legitimately entitled to treaty and/or band membership. This elimination added to the ever growing population of Métis, and non-status Indians who were landless, without special recognition from the government, and with few resources with which to face the future. Herein lies one of the defining factors of Métis ethnicity – or at least the seeds of a potential Métis social/political movement – a closing off of "Indian" as an alternative status

The present notion of status, or registered, Indian dates back to the 1951 revision of the Indian Act, which authorized the establishment of a centralized record of all persons entitled to be registered as Indians. The register was to consist of two lists; a Band List, containing the names of all individuals who were members of an Indian band and entitled to be registered as Indians, and a General List, comprising everyone who was not a member of a band, but who was still entitled to be registered as an Indian. Basically, the list contains the names of all people the government is willing to recognize as someone it has responsibility for under the Constitution Act, 1867. The exclusion of Métis and non-status Indians from this registry is what led to their similar political position vis-à-vis the federal government and their political union, which lasted for many years until the Constitution Act, 1982 recognized Métis but not non-status Indians as part of Canada's Aboriginal peoples and rendered their political union irrelevant.

An observer unfamiliar with Canadian practice might view the Indian Act merely as peculiar legislation that excludes certain Native people (Métis and non-status) from some government services. Such a view, however, would fail to take into account the extent to which the term "Indian" as defined under the Indian Act has been internalized, reified, and even sanctified by Canadian Indians. Today, many status Indians (and even many non-status) regard status as a *confirmation of their identity as Native people* – often the only, or official, confirmation. While this may be interpreted as yet another example of a colonized people accepting the labels imposed upon them by the colonial superstructure, the sincerity and depth of feeling engendered by the notion of status cannot be denied, and it continues as a potent force in today's political scene.

The second category of government policy to affect Métis identity was the various acts that recognized that the Métis had a claim to "Indian title," namely, the Manitoba Act,1870 and various Dominion Lands Acts. But they were not necessarily regarded as a confirmation of the Métis as a separate Aboriginal group. According to Sir John A. Macdonald: "That phrase [the extinguishment of the Indian title] was an incorrect one, because the half-breeds did not allow themselves to be Indians. If they are Indians, they go with the tribe; if they are half-breeds they are whites, and they stand in exactly the same relation to the Hudson['s] Bay Company and Canada as if they were altogether white."[39] Nevertheless, the recognition of Aboriginal or Indian title in these documents continues to be an important source of Métis identification, particularly in Manitoba and the other prairie provinces (see below). But undoubtedly, the greatest piece of legislation affecting Métis identity has been their recognition as one of Canada's Aboriginal peoples under section 35(2) of the Constitution Act, 1982.

Section 35(2) states: "In this Act, 'Aboriginal peoples of Canada' includes the Indian, Inuit and Métis peoples of Canada." The most significant aspect of this definition from the standpoint of Métis identification is the absence of any mention of the non-status Indians of Canada.[40] This omission by itself does not mean that non-status Indians are excluded from the Constitution. Neither Indian, nor Inuit, nor Métis is defined in the act, and it could be argued that the term "Métis" was intended to include the category of non-status Indian.[41] Alternatively, "non-status" conceivably could be subsumed under the category of Indian.[42] At the time the Constitution was being repatriated, legislation was already being considered to change some aspects of the Indian Act with regard to who was eligible for status, particularly along sexual lines; the eventual result was Bill C-31, the Act to Amend the Indian Act, 1985. This act indeed allowed many non-status Indians to regain status, particularly women who had originally been status Indians but who had lost their status through marriage. However, not all non-status Indians were eligible to regain status, and new non-status Indians could still come into being. There is some evidence that the architects of the Constitution Act may have thought that any non-status Indian not eligible to regain status under the Indian Act would or could be subsumed under the definition of Métis, but this has not proved to be the case, and the ranks of non-status Indians in Canada continue to swell.

Constitutional recognition of Métis but not non-status Indian proved to be the catalyst that ended the tenuous political alliance of the two groups.[43] The alliance had never been particularly strong to begin with; the Native Council of Canada, the ostensible voice of the Métis and non-status on the national scene at the time always had a great deal of difficulty bridging the vast regional and cultural differences between Métis and non-status Indians across Canada. However, while the constitutional definition had a profound effect on the political alliance of the two groups, and therefore on the eventual definitions of Métis, which excluded the non-status, it should be remembered that the constitutional definition was *not* simply imposed on Native people (at least, not the Métis and non-status) but was the result of lengthy negotiations between the Métis and non-status organizations and the Canadian government.

As part of the preparation for the repatriation of the Constitution, the Government of Canada authorized the Native Council of Canada to initiate a series of public meetings aimed at formulating policy in the areas of constitutional reform regarding Canada's Métis and non-status

Indian populations. This was known as the Métis and Non-Status Indian Constitutional Review Commission and was established in July 1980. The purpose of the commission was to provide an opportunity for Métis and non-status Indian Peoples in all parts of Canada and regardless of organizational affiliation to participate in the formulation of policy regarding constitutional reform. These proceedings and the recommendations of the commission are a likely source for the recognition of Métis, but not non-status Indians, as one of Canada's Aboriginal peoples.[44]

In the summary of the recommendations of the commission, entitled *Native Collectivities: Who Is a Native?* the commission recommended that "the constitution should recognize the existence of Indian, Inuit and Metis collectivities and their right to develop in accord with their own aspirations."[45] (Note the lack of direct mention of non-status Indians in this recommendation.) The commission also recommended "broad, realistic and equitable definitions" of Indian, Inuit, and Métis for the purposes of the Constitution and subsequent legislation "in order to avoid the fragmentation of Native collectivities which has hitherto occurred." These definitions were to include notions of: "descent from common ancestors; a common and continuous history; a form of social organization "rooted in distinctive modes of economic enterprise"; distinctive cultural attributes, values, and a willingness to identify as part of the Indian, Inuit, or Métis collectivity.[46]

It is apparent from the report of the commission that the assumption was that these definitions would eventually eliminate non-status Indians, most of them being subsumed under the category of Indian and a smaller group having the right to identify as Métis. The commission called for a survey of non-status Indians to determine how many would wish to regain registered status and of these how many would wish to live on reserves. The commission then called on the federal government to reinstate those non-status Indians so desiring on band lists or on the general list, to permit those non-status Indians preferring to move onto reserves to do so, and to enter into negotiations with band councils and provincial governments to adjust the size of reserves and their budgets to meet the subsequent increase in reserve population. It also recommended that those non-status Indians preferring to remain off-reserve be entitled to the same rights and privileges as status Indians living off-reserve. The commission also recommended that non-status Indians should be fully involved in discussions leading to revision of the Indian Act. Clearly, the commission felt that, for the purposes of constitutional reform, non-status Indians should be considered the same as status Indians.

Many non-status Indian witnesses themselves demanded the adoption of a broad definition of Indian in the constitution to encompass *all* people of Indian ancestry who identified as Indians, not only those registered under the Indian Act. Gary Gould, president of the New Brunswick Association of Métis and Non-status Indians expressed their aspirations: "The non-status Indians see the future lies in creating for themselves a distinctive identity as Indians, not as non-persons negatively defined on the basis of their exclusion from government created and imposed definitions of who 'is' and who is not an Indian."[47]

Most significant for our purposes is recommendation number 7: "those non-status Indians who reject registration under the Indian Act have the right to be considered Metis for the purposes of the constitution and subsequent legislation." This and the other recommendations concerning non-status Indians likely provided much of the impetus for the subsequent inclusion of Métis and the concomitant exclusion of non-status Indians in the constitutional definition of Canada's Aboriginal peoples.

Many of the recommendations anticipate the formulation of Bill C-31. The commission lamented the fact that negotiations on revisions to the Indian Act involved only the status Indian organizations and the federal government, and that non-status Indians and Indian women's organizations were being denied participation in these discussions. The commission recommended that the patrilineal bias in the Indian Act should be terminated, including the repeal of section 12(1)(b), the illegitimacy rule, the "double mother rule," and all other clauses that discriminated against Indians on the basis of gender and male descent. It proposed that the Indian Act should be revised so that Indian men and women acquire or lose status in the same way. If either an Indian woman or a man married a non-Indian, she or he should retain status, whereas the non-Indian spouse should not gain status. The commission probably assumed that these recommendations, if followed to their logical conclusion, would eliminate the category of non-status Indian. However, that was not to be.

There was a fundamental difference of opinion between First Nations on the one hand and the Métis and non-status Indians on the other regarding the proposed Charter of Rights and Freedoms and the repatriation of the Canadian Constitution. The Métis and non-status saw the charter and repatriation as an opportunity to redefine their relationship with the Canadian government and to have themselves recognized as Aboriginal peoples and have their Aboriginal rights, including the right to self-government, recognized. They were joined by several Aboriginal women's groups, who also desired change, particularly in the discriminatory sections of the Indian Act regarding marriage, and who were concerned by the lack of women's voices in the constitutional debate. But many First Nations and individual status Indians preferred the status quo. They feared that the charter would violate or impinge upon the special relationship they felt they had with the Queen and the British government as well as the Canadian government. They also feared that their rights to self-government, legal systems, languages, and cultures would not be recognized under a repatriated Constitution.[48] In 1979, a delegation of 347 chiefs and elders from across Canada travelled to England to ask the Queen and the British government to reject patriation of the British North America Act to Canada until their concerns were addressed. They also wanted the First Nations to be recognized – along with the French and English – as a founding race and an equal partner in constitutional questions. Although the delegation failed to meet with the Queen, they were successful in garnering much positive publicity for their cause on both sides of the Atlantic.[49]

It is ironic, however, that despite all the efforts made to distinguish between Métis and non-status Indians, including the elimination of the category of non-status from the Constitution, the federal government continues to associate Métis with non-status Indians. This can be seen by the existence of the office of Federal Interlocutor for Métis and Non-Status Indians, a division of the Privy Council Office. The role of Federal Interlocutor was created in 1985 to "provide a point of contact between the Government of Canada and national Aboriginal organizations that represent Métis and non-status Indians."[50] The official description of the Federal Interlocutor's role carefully equates Métis, non-status Indians, and urban Aboriginal people. The role includes "bilateral relations with national Métis and non-status Indian organizations; tripartite processes with off-reserve Aboriginal groups and the provinces; and, finding practical ways to improve the life chances of Métis, non-status Indians and urban Aboriginal peoples." The Federal Interlocutor also provides funding to support Métis, non-status Indian, and off-reserve Aboriginal organizations. While there are undoubtedly many practical reasons for the federal government to combine the services of Métis, non-status Indians and urban Aboriginal peoples under one division, it also indicates that the Métis have not yet managed to completely extricate themselves from association with non-status Indians and may never be able to do so in relation to government jurisdiction.

Policies of Provincial Governments

Policies of provincial governments have influenced Métis ethnic boundaries as well. This was well illustrated in Alberta in 1934, when the Ewing Commission was set up to investigate the causes of Métis poverty and to suggest certain remedies. Although the commission came about at least in part as a result of lobbying by the Métis themselves, the final determination of who was or who was not a Métis lay squarely in the hands of the commissioners, not their Métis witnesses. In the 1930s the political climate was open to recognize only one type of Métis existence, one that clove to preconceived characterizations of "Métisness" and "Nativeness," including being "helpless," "poverty-stricken," and "childlike." The Ewing Commission refused to acknowledge persons as Métis if they were economically self-sufficient. If they were financially independent, they were merely individuals with some Indian background, not Métis. During the preliminary discussions, it was decided by the commissioners and some of their witnesses that the term "Métis" should also include non-status Indians – that to all intents and purposes, "there was no difference between them." The Métis and their leaders were forced to go along with these characterizations or forgo any chance of establishing a land base in Alberta.

The Ewing Commission set the stage for the only example in Canada of a government actually attempting to define Métis through legislation. In 1938 the province of Alberta passed the Métis Population Betterment Act,[51] which established several Métis "colonies" or settlements and contained a definition of Métis that stated, "a Metis means a person of mixed white and Indian blood but does not include either an Indian or a non-treaty Indian as defined in *The Indian Act*." A 1940 revision of the act defined Métis as a person with "a minimum of one quarter Indian blood, but who was neither an Indian nor a Non-Treaty Indian according to the Indian Act."[52] This revised definition is unusual for Canada; unlike the situation in the United States, blood quantum has not often been used to determine Aboriginality in this country. This definition was used for administrative purposes only, to determine if an individual was eligible to live on one of the provincially established Métis settlements. It was of no practical use in identifying whether a person was or was not Métis, since most Métis did not regard the definition as a legitimate criterion and rejected the idea of quantifying Native ancestry as a condition for Métis identity. As Elmer Ghostkeeper, a former president of the Settlement Association, pointed out, "a literal interpretation of the Act's definition would exclude even Louis Riel from membership in a Metis Settlement Association."[53] Despite the opposition to this definition, it remained on the books for a surprisingly long time, until the Métis Settlements Act, 1990,[54] defined Métis as "a person of aboriginal ancestry who identifies with Metis history and culture." According to Garry Parenteau, one-time Métis Settlements General Council vice-president, the provision denoting one-quarter Indian blood was eliminated "because Native blood cannot be measured."[55] This current definition – primarily on the basis of self-identification and acceptance from the Métis population – is more in keeping with the way political organizations are now defining Métis.

Canadian Courts and the Definition of Métis

In recent years, there have been several court cases involving either Aboriginal title or Aboriginal rights of the Métis, and these also have affected Métis identity. In discussing these cases, I should point out that I am making no attempt to analyse their legal merits. Nor am I am concerned with how these cases have defined Métis Aboriginal rights. I simply wish to explore how the courts have defined Métis. It would appear that the courts have usually accepted self-definition as sufficient proof. In a case concerning the land rights of the Métis under the Manitoba Act, 1870, one of the judges in the Manitoba court of appeal made the following statement: "Twaddle J.A.: ... let me make it clear that, for the purpose of this appeal, I assume the truth of all allegations of fact contained in the statement of claim. Those allegations include the allegation that all half-breeds of 1870 were 'Métis'; that the Métis of 1870 were a distinct people; and that all their descendants are included within the undefined group of persons constitutionally recognized today as 'the Métis people.'"[56] In a dissenting opinion in the same case, the following statement was made: "O'Sullivan J.A.: ... the existence of the Métis people is asserted in the Constitution as of the present, not simply as of the past. Each individual plaintiff can, I think, prove indisputably his membership in the Métis nation. Their genealogical records are unparalleled in modern societies.[57] This judge also felt that the Métis organizations were in a good position to represent the interests of the

Métis: "it is impossible in our jurisprudence to have rights without a remedy and the rights of the Métis people must be capable of being asserted by somebody. If not by the present plaintiff [Manitoba Métis Federation], then by whom?"[58]

However, there was some indication that a more systematic method of determining who is or is not a Métis would be welcomed. In a 1994 case involving the hunting rights of two Métis charged with violating the Wildlife Act near Wanless, Manitoba,[59] the Provincial Court judge stated that the two defendants ("acknowledged Métis") had unextinguished hunting rights and directed the Crown to enact new legislation, "which would provide for the registration of those Métis who rely on subsistence hunting as a way of life." Such legislation might make life easier for those charged with upholding game laws, but the Manitoba Court of Queen's Bench found that the direction to create a registry for Métis persons under the Wildlife Act was unconstitutional in light of the provisions of s. 91(24) of the Constitution Act, 1867, which assigns exclusive legislative authority to the federal Parliament over "Indians and Lands reserved for the Indians." That judgment bears on the issue of whether or not Métis should be considered "Indians" under s. 91(24) of the Constitution Act, 1867, which was unclear at the time, but was decided in the affirmative in 2013 in *Daniels v. Canada*. This case is discussed in more detail below.

In *R. v. Blais*[60] the accused Métis was convicted of hunting in southern Manitoba, in violation of the provincial Wildlife Act. The principal in the case was Ernie Blais, former president of the Manitoba Métis Federation and leader of a breakaway organization, the Métis Nation of Manitoba. Mr Blais deliberately precipitated this case, informing wildlife officials and the media that he intended to violate the act, and giving specific information about where and when he was going to do so. He was attempting to force the courts to widen the finding of *R. v. McPherson* to include southern Manitoba and to have the term "Indian," as used in the 1930 Natural Resources Transfer Agreement (NRTA), apply to Métis hunting rights at the same level as treaty Indian hunting rights. Paragraph 13 of the NRTA stipulates that the provincial laws respecting game apply to Indians, subject to the continuing right of the Indians to hunt, trap, and fish for food on unoccupied Crown lands.

Once again, the claim to being Métis by the individuals in question was accepted by the court at face value. However, the judge commented that an appropriate definition of Métis might be taken from the wording of the Métis Nation Accord, which was accepted by federal, provincial, and Aboriginal leaders in 1992 as part of the Charlottetown Accord. The Charlottetown Accord was rejected in a national referendum, of course, and is not legally binding. But the judge felt that the definition contained in the Métis Nation Accord was a useful political answer to a political question.[61] The definition is as follows: "Métis means an aboriginal person who self-identifies as Métis, who is distinct from Indian and Inuit and is a descendant of those Métis who received or were entitled to receive land grants and/or Scrip under the provisions of the *Manitoba Act, 1870* or the *Dominion Lands Act* as enacted from time to time."[62] Note that this definition is very similar to that of the Manitoba Métis Federation and the Métis National Council. In other words, it is very much a definition of the "historic Métis Nation," excluding the Labrador Métis and the "other" Métis.

Mr Blais lost his bid to have the term "Indian" include Métis under the NRTA, and both subsequent appeals in provincial courts were unsuccessful. Finally, on 19 September 2003, the Supreme Court also held that his appeal should be dismissed.

One of the most significant cases for defining both Métis Aboriginal rights and the term "Métis" is *R. v. Powley*.[63] The case involves two men who shot a bull moose north of Sault Ste Marie, Ontario. One of the men was in possession of an Ontario Métis and Aboriginal Association (OMAA) card. This card indicated that he claimed Aboriginal rights to hunt under the Robinson-Huron Treaty, as well as "the right to harvest natural resources that my family has done since time immemorial." One of the questions the court had to decide was: are the Powleys Métis for the purposes of s. 35(2) of the Constitution Act, 1982? In order to determine the answer, the judge reviewed earlier cases, particularly *R. v. Blais*. After reviewing this material, the court decided on its own definition of Métis: "Without a universally accepted definition of Métis to be found, I shall attempt to distil a basic, workable definition of who is a Métis. Accordingly, I find that a Métis is a person of Aboriginal ancestry; who self-identifies as a Métis; and who is accepted by the Métis community as a Métis."[64] The Métis Nation Accord definition was considered by the court, but the section limiting Métis to those who had or were eligible to receive scrip was dropped. This is hardly surprising, since that definition would automatically have eliminated Mr Powley and all other Métis from northern Ontario. The court found in favour of the Métis. The Crown appealed the case to the Ontario Superior Court of Justice, which also found in favour of the Métis. The Court of Appeal for Ontario also found in favour of the Métis.

The case finally came to a conclusion on 19 September 2003, when the Supreme Court of Canada handed down its ruling, once again in favour of the Métis. This ruling has had a profound effect on the place of Métis in Canadian society, going to the heart of Métis identity. By now, the Métis were being defined as: "distinctive peoples who, *in addition to their mixed ancestry*, developed their own customs, way of life, and recognizable group identity separate from their Indian or Inuit and European forebears ... develop[ing] separate and distinct identities, not reducible to the mere fact of their mixed ancestry."[65] It is significant, especially in consideration of the discussion regarding the "racialization" of the definition of Metis that the court found it necessary to add the proviso "mixed community." Most prairie Metis organizations had eliminated this aspect from their list of defining criteria of who was or was not a Metis. The court also defined Métis communities as "a group of Métis with a distinctive collective identity, living together in the same geographical area and sharing a common way of life." The court went on to state that in addition to demographic evidence, proof of shared customs, traditions, and a collective identity is required to demonstrate the existence of a Métis community that can support a claim to site-specific Aboriginal rights. It also held: "the development of a more systematic method of identifying Métis rights-holders for the purpose of enforcing hunting regulations is an urgent priority. That said, the difficulty of identifying members of the Métis community must not be exaggerated as a basis for defeating their rights under the Constitution of Canada."[66]

One of the implications of this ruling is that it left the door open for *any* group of mixed bloods in Canada that can demonstrate a collective identity, shared geographical area, and common way of life to lay claim to being a Métis community. Indeed, just a few days after the Supreme Court's decision was announced, several newspaper articles reported that various groups in the Maritimes, such as Acadians and others, were considering making claims to Aboriginal rights based on the criteria specified in the Supreme Court's decision.[67]

Andersen has demonstrated how the Powley decision developed this "legal" definition of Métis and the repercussions this definition has had on ethnohistorical analysis in particular, and the perception of Métis generally: "Importantly, as in all powerful fields, part of the juridical field's legitimacy lies in its nearly unparalleled ability to name and to have such naming recognized in the perceptions and practices of actors other than its own. To do so, it rarely produces meaning out of whole cloth (as it were). Rather it refracts symbols, meanings, and identities already in circulation elsewhere."[68] More to the point being discussed here, once the Supreme Court had defined Métis, the term assumed some very specific meanings over and above any that may have been contemplated by Métis political organizations or Métis people themselves. For example, Andersen points out that the Powley definition did not require that any contemporary Aboriginal group attempting to lay claim to being Métis demonstrate a historical self-identification as Métis. The group needed only "to prove their ancestral community's separateness from adjacent tribal communities." Despite the fact that the Supreme Court specifically stated that Métis identity was not simply reducible to the mere fact of their mixed ancestry, Andersen has no qualms about attributing the logic of this definition to the court's preconceptions "about the essential 'mixedness' of Métis identity."[69]

Daniels v. Canada, 2013 FC6

On January 2013, in a case that may prove to have even more significance for Métis identification than *Powley*, a federal court ruled that Métis and non-status Indians were indeed "Indians" under subsection 91(24) of the Constitution Act, 1867.[70] It had long been a contention of many Métis and non-status Indian activists, historians, and even some government officials, that both Métis and non-status Indians properly fell under the designation of "Indian" as the term was understood under the 1867act. While the federal government was free to define who was or was not an Indian under the various permutations of the Indian Act, this did not necessarily mean that those excluded from the Indian Act were also excluded from the category of "Indian" under the Constitution Act. This issue was a vital one for both Métis and non-status Indians because it would determine whether they were a federal or a provincial responsibility. In 1969, the Congress of Aboriginal Peoples (CAP) along with three individuals filed a suit against the minister of Indian affairs and northern development and the attorney general of Canada to settle the issue. The case was finally decided in 2013.

Although the ruling was hailed as a victory by CAP, it was not received with complete enthusiasm by the prairie Métis or their organizations. Although most Métis welcomed the idea that the federal government had the same responsibility for Métis and non-status Indians as it had for status Indians, they were dismayed by the way "Métis" was defined by the court. For the purposes of the declaration, the judge relied on a 1980 government definition, which conflated Métis and non-status and in effect defined Métis as "as a group of native people who maintained a strong affinity for their Indian heritage without possessing Indian status."[71] The concept of Métis was thus reduced to one of mixed ancestry, ignoring the historical aspects that delineated the Métis culturally and politically from other mixed-ancestry populations. Lawyer Jean Teillet, in an early reaction to the judgment called it "brutal and wrong in every way ... [The judge] virtually erased the Métis nation ... He's just said 'You don't mean anything. All you are is people who care about your Indian heritage.'"[72]

The Federal Court also relied on the definition of Métis as developed in *Powley*, but that did not help the prairie Métis to any great extent, as *Powley* concerned an individual from Sault Ste Marie and therefore, by definition, could not reinforce for the Métis an exclusive prairie or western origin. While self-identification as a Métis and acceptance of a Métis community are recognized as critical in *Powley*, the most central aspect of the prairie Métis criteria for identification – an ancestral connection to the historic Métis community of Red River – remains absent. The court probably added to the Métis's discontent when it identified, again quoting *Powley*, mixed ancestry as the "sine qua non" of Métis identity.[73] Furthermore, in *Daniels*, the court attached great importance to the fact that the one plaintiff in the case who could unequivocally be identified as a Métis not only stressed his ties to the Métis community but also to his First Nations heritage.[74] All in all, the prairie Métis are probably correct when they state that the message that ultimately comes from the *Daniels* decision is that Métis are merely a variety of non-status Indians, distinguished from non-status by their mixed ancestry, who stress their Indian heritage. However, this conclusion does not imply (as some have suggested)[75] that *Daniels* means that any individual with some Indian background can lay claim to the identity of Métis. There remains the criterion that some collectivity calling itself Métis must accept that person as a member.

Daniels has reopened a question for the public that many thought had long been settled: "who are the Métis?" If Métis and non-status Indians were now "Indians," what does this mean for Métis identification? While it may not be a problem to those who identify as Métis, it certainly is of concern to the general public and the federal and provincial governments. We are brought back full circle to the 1960s, when the early Métis organizations were struggling over self-identification, trying to convince the public and government that they were a legitimate Aboriginal entity separate from both First Nations and non-status Indians.

The confusion is compounded by the nature of the *Daniels* case, which of necessity involved the cooperation of both Métis and non-status individuals, and by the nature of the organization that acted as plaintiff, the Congress of Aboriginal Peoples. CAP, from its beginning as the Native Council of Canada, has been an organization that cast a wide net in its definition of Métis. After all, it attempted to represent both Métis and non-status Indians, in fact, any Native individual or collectivity that fell outside of the Indian Act. As a result, CAP extends recognition of "Métis" groups to those whose background differs from that of the prairie Métis associations. Because of the way CAP structured its evidence, the court accepted that "the term Métis was and is used well outside of Western Canada."[76]

As of this writing, it is too early to fully appreciate the implications this ruling may have on the Métis, as the case is destined be heard by the Supreme Court of Canada. However, from the standpoint of the Métis, most of the objections to the way they were characterized in *Daniels* have now been addressed. When the case went to the Federal Court of Appeal (FCA) in 2014,[77] the Métis National Council and other Métis organizations seized the opportunity to claim intervener status and influence the court in its definition of Métis. There were several agendas pursued by the different Métis organizations, but there was a general desire to preserve the integrity of the Métis Nation definition of "Métis" while still being recognized as "Indian" for the purposes of the Constitution Act, 1867. For example, the Métis Nation of Ontario asked that their status under s. 91(24) be upheld, but that "the Court decline to define the Métis other than to say that the individuals included as Métis within section 91(24) are the members of the Métis peoples of Canada," and the Manitoba Métis Federation asked that the judge's declaration be restated to separate reference to non-status Indians from the declaration.[78]

The Federal Court of Appeal rendered its decision on 17 April 2014, upholding the finding that Métis were included in the meaning of the term "Indian" within the scope of s. 91(24) of the Constitution Act, 1867. However, the FCA overturned the declaration as it applied to non-status Indians, concluding that such a declaration "lacked practical utility,"[79] in part because the reasons for excluding people from status are many and complex, and determining the reason each class of individual was excluded from the Indian Act would have to be done on a case-by-case basis.[80]

While the federal government and non-status organizations were obviously displeased with the finding, the Métis organizations were satisfied for the most part, because not only had they retained their inclusion in s. 91(24), but they had also succeeded in overturning the race-based definition of "Métis" used in the original decision.[81] The FCA acknowledged that an interpretation of section 91(24) "requires the term Métis to mean more than individuals' racial connection to their Indian ancestors ... The Métis have their own language, culture, kinship connections and territory. It is these factors that make the Métis one of the Aboriginal peoples of Canada."[82] The judge also cited *Powley*'s criteria of Métis identity as a means of identifying Métis, characterizing those as "inconsistent with a race-based identification of the Métis."[83] The Métis organizations probably would have been content to let the FCA's findings stand, but the federal government and non-status organizations were not. They applied to the Supreme Court of Canada for leave to appeal the decision, which was granted on 20 November 2014.[84] Once again, the Métis organizations will be forced to intervene, to make sure their interests and identity are protected.

Ethnicity as a Rational Choice: Mandatory Ethnicity vs. Assumed Ethnicity

We began this chapter with a consideration of the forces affecting the reformulation of Métis identity in the latter half of the twentieth century. To this point, we have considered only outside, or imposed, criteria – federal and provincial designations as well as various court cases. But we have not yet considered *internal* or individual choices. Why does someone choose to be recognized as a Métis, sometimes in the face of intensive social pressure *not* to identify as such? What compelled a Howard Adams or Maria Campbell to proclaim themselves Métis and to work towards recognition of the Métis as separate and identifiable group within Canada, when at the time they chose to do so, a high social cost was involved? Not surprisingly, not all Métis followed Adams's or Campbell's lead. In a 1958 Manitoba government survey of people of Aboriginal background in the province, fieldworkers attempting to locate Métis informants were repeatedly told of individuals who "were no longer half-breeds," individuals who had shed the social and economic stigma of being Métis.[85] It is hardly surprising that some Métis decided to discard their Native background at that time. Many reports from the 1950s and 1960s portray the Métis of northern Saskatchewan and Manitoba as poverty stricken, powerless, and at the mercy of a non-Native overclass. What is more surprising, perhaps, is that so many Métis decided to maintain their identity in the face of this position in the social hierarchy. But it is not always easy to discard one's identity. Decisions to cross an ethnic boundary or remain within it are complicated by many forces, from both inside and outside the ethnic conclave.

Mandatory ethnicity is often embedded in the social structure. This certainly was the case for prairie and northern Métis in the early 1950s. V.F. Valentine depicted the relations between Natives and non-Natives in the communities of northern Saskatchewan in the 1950s in terms of a caste system, where the Indians were relegated to the position of inferior caste, the Euro-Canadians positioned as the ruling caste, and the Métis consigned by both groups to the position of "outcast."[86] The most important aspect of a caste system, and the one that led Valentine to use caste as a metaphor for describing Métis society, is the difficulty in changing or breaking the boundaries imposed by the system. Despite the attempt that many Métis made to escape poverty by moving out of the northern communities to make a new life for themselves in the south, their identity as Métis made it difficult for them to adapt or be accepted by the majority population. Inevitably, the lack of support from other Métis and overt hostility from the non-Native majority drove these people back to their original communities. Dropping one's identity as a Métis was one solution, but it was extremely difficult to do successfully at that time. Valentine gives several examples of this in his work. Another portrayal of this pattern, also by a non-Métis, but from outside the academic community, can be found in Christine Van der Mark's novel *In Due Season*.[87] This insightful portrait of Métis/non-Native relations in northern Alberta deals in part with an individual's unsuccessful attempt to leave a small Métis community to try to make a new life in the south.

Mandatory ethnicity can come from internal as well as external sources. Maria Campbell, whose autobiography, *Halfbreed*, portrays the same period and community described by Valentine, illustrates not only the bigotry and prejudice the Métis experienced from non-Natives and Indians alike and the genuine feelings of separateness and uniqueness the Métis felt, but also the elaborate system of ridicule and public condemnation Métis would face from their own people if they tried to shake off their Métis ancestry and "act white." These pressures – from within and without – explain why the identity of Métis was maintained even when the social cost of being Métis was very high.

Quite a different set of circumstances can take hold when an ethnic identity starts to offer advantages rather than disadvantages, as the concept of Métis did in the 1960s. At that time, more and more people began to identify as Métis. There were two phases to this change. When the benefits were mainly symbolic, only a small number of people were attracted to the prospect of identifying as Métis, but the range of people who were attracted was quite wide. In the 1960s and 1970s, many officers in the Manitoba Métis Federation, for example, were non-Métis; either they were non-status Indians or, in some cases, totally non-Native (non-Native spouses of Métis were often chairs of Métis locals). The most popular Métis newspaper of the time (*New Nation*) was owned and operated by a non-status Indian. In the second phase of this change, there were economic as well as symbolic advantages to being recognized as Métis, as the newly formed political organizations began to provide housing, employment (including employment as paid political leaders), and legal and social services, including scholarships and bursaries for post-secondary education. At this point, the number of people claiming a Métis identity increased dramatically.

As can be imagined, when Métis identity passed from merely having some cachet and being personally satisfying to having some economic advantage, there was much more competition for the privilege of calling oneself Métis. Being Métis suddenly became much more heavily regulated, both socially and politically, by the Métis themselves. The political organizations, which once defined Métis as anyone having some Aboriginal and non-Aboriginal ancestry, began imposing restrictions in terms of pointing to origin and group values to exclude certain formerly accepted members. Several people who had once been welcomed as Métis, or at least not questioned closely about their background, now found themselves cast out or in a socially unrecognized position.

This scenario was played out many times and at many different levels in the 1980s. A good example is provided by the Association of Métis and Non-Status Indians of Saskatchewan (AMNSIS) when it was remodelled as a Métis-only organization. The history of AMNSIS is a capsule of the changing boundaries of Métisness from the 1960s to the 1980s. Starting out as a Métis organization – the Métis Society of Saskatchewan – it changed its name to AMNSIS to reflect the growing number of non-status Indians who were both in the organization and taking on the identity of Métis. After the recognition of Métis as one of Canada's Aboriginal Peoples in the Canadian Constitution, and the exclusion of non-status Indians, the organization purged itself of non-Métis, reverting to its former name of the Métis Society of Saskatchewan.

The story of Jim Sinclair, who was president of AMNSIS, is a good example of the conflict of roles or disjuncture of identity that could occur at the personal level. He had been president of the Saskatchewan organization for an extremely long time (much longer than normal for a president of a Native political organization) and was almost unassailable by his political enemies. His one weakness was his identity. He identified as an Indian, not a Métis. As Métis identity became more focused and exclusionary (in part because it became more "valuable" as an officially recognized ethnic entity) it became easy for his opponents to ask: "What's an Indian doing leading the Métis?" It is important to note that when that question was asked, he was portrayed as an *Indian*, not a non-status Indian, to further distance him from the Métis fold. Ironically, Mr Sinclair had been one of the staunchest supporters of having the Métis recognized as one of Canada's Aboriginal peoples, but this recognition was what led to both his political downfall and his exclusion from the Métis organization. His story illustrates a typical case of a disjuncture between individual ethnic identity and available social choices. To be fair, he never claimed to be Métis; he chose to be a politician in a Métis organization and attempted to change the parameters of the organization to reflect the presence of non-status Indians and to bring more non-status into it. The fact that he was successful for such a long time is testimony to the flexibility and fluidity of ethnic borders.[88]

The issue of self-identification continues into the twenty-first century. Today it has been complicated by the development of several groups claiming to be "Métis" in Canada and the thorny issue of whether membership in one such nation allows for membership in another. This problem has been exacerbated by the increasing movement of individuals who, in the course of travelling from one region of Canada to another in search of employment or education, find themselves in a different Métis territory. I observed one such incident in the spring of 2011, when an individual from Nova Scotia, who identified as a Métis in that province and who had membership in either the Eastern Woodland Métis Nation Nova Scotia, or the Sou'West Nova Métis Council, attempted to join the Manitoba Métis Federation. He was shunted back and forth between the Winnipeg local office and the provincial head office, without success. He had documentation showing his Mi'kmaw ancestry and was attempting to use this as proof that he was Métis. He could not understand the difficulties he was having in getting an MMF membership. A prominent Métis politician from the southwest region of Manitoba who had been in the provincial office that day and was observing this incident told me: "I finally put my hands on his shoulders, looked him in the eye, and told him: Sir, I'm sorry, *but you are not a Métis.*" The man's membership was ultimately denied. He may still think of himself as a Métis, of course, but he is not accepted as such in the prairie provinces. Ethnic boundaries may shift over time, but they are not universally permeable.

The Limits on Ethnic Forces

Despite the circumstances that favoured the maintenance of Métis as a viable ethnic group in the twentieth century and have made them a much more visible group in Canada in the last thirty years, many Métis are surprisingly pessimistic about the chances for the Métis to continue as an ethnic group. For all the forces that are operating to distinguish and maintain a separate ethnicity, there are levelling forces that are also at work, forces that tend towards homogenizing Canadian society, forces that may yet reduce the Métis to a memory.

Stan Fulham, the former executive director of the MMF, has stated that the community locals, whether functioning as social clubs, as they did in the early 1960s, or as combination social/political organizations as members of the MMF from the 1960s to the present, no longer were acting as cultural safeguards or preservers of Métis culture and identity by the 1990s. Fulham points to his own community of St Lazare, which has had a local in operation since at least the 1950s. He says that the Métis community there is disappearing through intermarriage, and the activities of the MMF have not affected the process at all. "There has been so much intermarriage between the Métis and the non-Métis that left on its own, in another generation there really won't be too many Métis left. St. Lazare is a classic example. Within the last 25 years, there is not been a single Métis girl or boy who's married another Métis person. They've all inter-married with white people."[89] Fulham sees the same process ongoing in urban centres as well: "The same is true in Winnipeg. When I managed Kinew housing, we had 450 homes in the city [of] Winnipeg. I helped to develop that over the years. And that's all for native families and at one time the majority were Métis people.

I could see what was happening to my tenants. I could see the same thing [intermarriage] happening there. Wherever the Métis are living in a mixed community, they are gradually being absorbed into the dominant community."[90] Fulham's point is well taken, but out-marriage is not in itself a mechanism for ending Métis identity. The Métis politician referred to above who denied Métis identity to the Nova Scotia Native and who is very serious about maintaining Métis identity is married to a non-Métis. However, he feels very strongly that his children are Métis, and they are being raised as such. Fulham sees more danger in the fact that – in his estimation – the *idea* of being Métis is disappearing in the communities. He feels that most young people are not interested in talking about Métis affairs and Métis politics. The most active are from the previous generation and those that remain within the isolated Métis communities, such as Duck Bay or Camperville. While to some extent this outlook may simply be the typical intergenerational pessimism with which the older generation regards the younger, there may be some truth to his observation.

Furthermore, and this may be the more telling point, Fulham feels that the major reason the Métis communities remain Métis is not so much because of a cultural distinction, but because of an economic one. Their isolation is based on welfare. Because they lack any viable economic base, the MMF has functioned to keep them intact over the last twenty-five years of its operations through the various training programs and economic development schemes it has sponsored, aimed at keeping people in these communities rather than moving to economic centres such as Winnipeg and Thompson. Whether that is a desirable or worthwhile goal is a matter of interpretation. While programs like the Remote Housing Program (RHP) may have functioned to keep the communities together, Fulham suggests that it may have been better to simply let the Métis go to where there were jobs. However, the MMF is still officially committed to preserving Métis communities through such programs.

It is difficult to say how long that policy can continue. But even if these communities begin to falter and die out, this is not necessarily the end of Métis identity, although it does suggest yet another stage in the ever changing parameters of Métis ethnicity. The Métis of tomorrow may no longer be based in the small Métis communities of the prairies; they may be fully urbanized and yet still be with us. Alternatively, as more and more of Canada's Aboriginal population begins to lead a primarily urban existence, many of the current differences in status and identity may begin to fall away, in favour of a more generalized Aboriginality. However, as of 2004, most political organizations seemed intent on maintaining the distinctions between Métis, First Nations, and Inuit, eschewing any plans of the government to introduce pan-Aboriginal programs.[91]

At any rate, there is more to identity than economic advantage. Increasingly, the membership of the MMF is made up of people who are successful in their own right without needing the MMF to help them educationally or financially. For those individuals, the emotional bonds of belonging – of being able to identify as Métis – are probably their main motivation in remaining active in the association. This may well the factor that will maintain the identity of Métis in the future.

16 The Métis of Ontario

I always considered myself a Métis Indian. I still consider myself that. Like opposed to being an Ojibwa or Cree or whatever. I consider myself a Métis Indian.[1]

There is only one historic Métis nation and we are the descendants of that historic Métis nation with a distinct geographic homeland.[2]

Perhaps no province better illustrates the contradictions, complexities, and stress inherent in the contemporary definition of Métis than does Ontario, home to a non-tribal or mixed-blood Aboriginal population that for the most part has no direct links with the Red River Métis, but that has explored many avenues in its search for an identity. At times its leadership has pushed for identification as "Métis," either as descendants of Red River Métis or as a separate group of Métis indigenous to Ontario, and at other times it has lobbied for a "special status." The population has a distinct historical presence, with several geographic centres, the major one being around Sault Ste Marie.[3] It usually exhibits a clear sense of separateness from status Indians and at times from non-status Indians, but it has had trouble fitting its peculiar identity into the political demands of the new millennium. And, like the prairie Native population, in the political organizations there has often been a strain between those identifying as Métis and those identifying as non-status Indians.

From 1994 to 2007, there have been two major but separate organizations with two diametrically opposed strategies for Métis self-identification in Ontario. One approach, represented by the Ontario Métis Aboriginal Association (OMAA), attempted to create and represent a population with a unique Ontario mixed-blood ancestry: the "Métis Indians" or the "Woodland Métis Tribe." The OMAA was forced to close its doors in 2007. In its heyday, it and its preceding organization, the Ontario Métis and Non-Status Indian Association (OMNSIA), represented the population that, at least before the before the 1960s, did not necessarily identify itself as Métis, but was identified by itself and others as "half-breed." It also included many non-status Indians and off-reserve Indians. Its national affiliation was with the Congress of Aboriginal Peoples (CAP). CAP is now represented in Ontario by the Ontario Coalition of Aboriginal Peoples (OCAP). Although OMAA has officially disbanded, it still maintains a website that declares that "the Woodland Métis Tribe is alive and well and our dedicated members feel that it is our solemn duty to rebuild our organization."[4] It promises to rebuild the organization without recourse to federal or provincial funding, and a video created by its former president optimistically exhorts interested parties to keep checking the website for further developments.

The other approach to Métis identification is represented by the Métis Nation of Ontario (MNO). Despite some severe financial problems at around the same time as OMAA shut down, it has managed to stay afloat and was still operating as of 2014. It explicitly opts for an alliance or amalgamation with the "Red River" or western Métis of the historic Métis Nation. This approach stresses ties to Red River, or at least appropriates the cultural symbols of the prairie group. MNO, as would be expected, is an affiliate of the Métis National Council.[5]

The demise of OMAA does not negate the fact that there remains a fundamental split in the identity of the mixed-blood population in Ontario. Both of the province-wide organizations claimed to represent the "Métis of Ontario," but both had a very different idea of who their membership was, and what constituted a Métis. Not surprisingly, this divergence has caused problems for the provincial government and the courts, both of which have been grappling with the issue of Aboriginal rights for the Métis. The collapse of OMAA may have resulted in relegating a large proportion of the province's Aboriginal population to non-recognition and non-representation, although with luck, the slack will be taken up by OCAP.

This schism between OMMA and MNO was intensified by the successful demands of the Sault Ste Marie Métis for recognition to hunt and fish, in the court case *R. v. Powley*.[6] Although the case was consistently decided in favour of the Métis through all levels of the court system, culminating in a Supreme Court of Canada decision in September of 2003, the courts were unable to develop a succinct definition of Métis.[7] This decision proved to be a watershed in the struggles of the two organizations. While both MNO and OMAA were involved in the early phases of the *Powley* case and both claimed victory after the Supreme Court decision, MNO was the one to successfully take control of the situation. It has become identified, by both the public and the provincial government, as the major player in *Powley* and as such has been the group the Ontario government seems to be willing to negotiate with on Aboriginal rights' harvesting issues. What this means for that portion of the Aboriginal population not identifying as either members of the historic Métis Nation or Indian remains to be seen.

The History of Métis Political Organization in Ontario

The Métis and non-status Indian movement in Ontario had its beginnings in the early 1960s, in the small community of MacDiarmid, situated on the shores of Lake Nipigon in Ontario, north of Thunder Bay. There, in 1962, a group of Native people – some non-status Indians, some identifying as "half-breed" – formed the MacDiarmid Housing Corporation, under the leadership of Paddy McGuire. The object of this association was to purchase houses from an abandoned airforce base at MacDiarmid and move them into the community, for the benefit of Native families who were living in substandard housing. The project seemed to be successful at first. But according to Mike McGuire, son of Paddy McGuire and one of the original members of the housing association, an ironic twist made the very people who had worked to make the houses available ineligible to receive any themselves. After they had arranged to have the houses moved into MacDiarmid, it transpired that only status Indians would be eligible for them, owing to the vagaries of government funding and status definitions.[8] This was not the first time that members of the McGuire family or others in their community had experienced discrimination because of their anomalous position in society, caught between the non-Native and Indian communities. As children, some of the McGuire family had had trouble in attempting to go to school, being rejected at both the Indian school and the non-Native school.[9] This was a common complaint from half-breed and non-status

Indians in Ontario when they recalled the 1950s, 1960s, and 1970s. They did not belong anywhere: "the white people used to call us the Indians and the Indians used to call us the white people. We couldn't fit in with either one of them."[10]

The experience of the MacDiarmid Housing Corporation was just another example of this two-way rejection, a rejection that extended to their political organizations. The Métis, non-status, and half-breeds who did not fit easily into any recognized social category did not fit into any existing Native political structures either. For a time, non-status Indians were provided seats on the board of directors of the Union of Ontario Indians. But when that group was reorganized in 1969, they were informed by the president of the union that Métis, half-breeds, and enfranchised Indians would no longer be eligible for membership.[11] Paddy McGuire recalled that "he kicked us out in a nice way," suggesting that they form their own Ontario Métis movement, and offering the union's help in obtaining start-up money – but the decision that they had to leave was final. The Métis and non-status Indians could not work in the same organization as status Indians. They were facing the same rejection within the Native political arena as they had elsewhere.

Paddy McGuire and others had already formed the Lake Nipigon Métis Association in 1965. Among the founding members were Paddy McGuire, his son Mike McGuire, and his brother Nate McGuire, Leonard King, and Dennis Leschuk. This small local association was the catalyst that set in motion Métis political activity in Ontario, eventually resulting in the Ontario Métis and Non-Status Indian Association. The Lake Nipigon association was intended for people who were Aboriginal but who did not have Indian status. For lack of a better term, they called themselves "Métis." This name was not chosen for cultural or historic reasons; rather, it was seen as the widest, most general and all-encompassing term that could be used: "It was after we decided we should form an association that we called ourselves Metis. One of the main reasons we called ourselves Metis was to include everybody, because a lot of Metis people were half-Irish half-Indian; some were half-French half-Indian, and the rest were all different races of people. If they were Oriental and Indian they all could be included in this. So the word Metis in Ontario was to include everybody."[12] It is interesting to note the source of the first appearance of the term "Métis." It was almost unknown in Ontario at the time, "half-breed" or "breed" being much more common. The term became known to the members of the Lake Nipigon Métis Association through political activity in the prairies:

> The Lake Nipigon meetings were held in 1965, with my son Mike, my brother Nate, myself, Joe and Dennis. And that all started because we had read in the paper about out west where Jim Sinclair and Dr Howard Adams were doing something about the Metis movement out there. Also, at that time, we didn't know what a Metis was. We thought you had to be half French to be a Metis. We knew we were Half-breed but some people called us Non-Status Indians. *According to them two fellows, we were all Metis*, so that's how we founded the Lake Nipigon Metis Association, because we heard those guys talking about it.[13]

It is significant that McGuire mentions Jim Sinclair, an important force in the mobilization of the Association of Métis and Non-Status Indians of Saskatchewan (AMNSIS), but who himself was a non-status Indian rather than a Métis.

By 1969 there were several local Métis associations in Ontario, but there was no province-wide organization. The impetus for that came shortly after the founding meeting of the Native Council of Canada (NCC) in December 1970 in Edmonton. Mike McGuire had gone to Edmonton as a representative of the Ontario Métis and non-status Indians, but he was not allowed to vote as a representative of a provincial organization, because the existing Ontario organizations were regarded as locals. However, encouraged by the Edmonton meeting, McGuire and others began lobbying for money for a provincial organization. On 27 March 1971, the Ontario Métis and non-status Indian Association (OMNSIA) was formed, consolidating the sixteen locals that had been established throughout Ontario by that time.[14]

Considerable thought was dedicated at the inaugural meeting over what to call the new organization. As he had done with the earlier Lake Nipigon local, Paddy McGuire wanted to make sure that the widest possible net be cast:

> When I founded the Ontario Provincial Association, I instructed the delegates to make sure that both the French name for the people with mixed blood, and the English name for people with mixed blood, be included in the name of our association. So all Half-breeds of French and English would be protected. At the founding of OMNSIA, people thought you had to be part French to be a Metis. Some people still do.

> This is the reason why we named our association the Ontario Metis and Non-Status Indian Association, in order to cover all natives with mixed blood as long as they didn't have legal status.[15]

Mike McGuire remembers it this way:

> There were different names that they wanted to call it. The Ontario Métis Association, they wanted to call it the Ontario Aboriginal Association and I put a name on the floor; the Ontario Métis and Non-Status Indian Association. The reason I put that motion on the floor that day was because some people were enfranchised, some people considered themselves non-status and some people considered themselves Métis and some others considered themselves half-breeds and we had to try to unite these people into one organization. So that name was a good name for a lot of years. It wasn't until '85 when they brought Bill C-31 in that we changed our provincial name to the Ontario Métis Aboriginal Association.[16]

OMNSIA was incorporated in Thunder Bay in June 1971, and the first assembly was held in Sault Ste Marie in October. At this time, most of the Métis organizations, in the prairies as well as in Ontario, were joint Métis and non-status organizations. It would be a few years before the trend to form explicitly Métis organizations would take hold, but the question "who is a Métis?" was becoming more and more of an issue. This was an especially important question in Ontario, where there was little in the way of a distinct Métis history. The population was open to several identity strategies. One of the more interesting ones was suggested in 1980, when Duke Redbird became president of OMNSIA. He attempted to develop a "special status" for Métis and non-status Indians in Ontario, one that would have the Ontario government recognize them as a separate Aboriginal group, with Aboriginal rights to hunt, fish, and trap.[17] Little came of that proposal, however, and soon other political issues changed the direction of OMNSIA, although not before it had launched an important survey into the nature of its constituency and the self-identity of its members (see below).

Despite the fact that most of the Métis of Ontario had no definite links to Red River or the historic Métis Nation, it soon became obvious that OMNSIA shared at least one characteristic with the prairie Métis political organizations: a growing strain between the Métis and non-status Indians. Paddy McGuire began voicing this concern as early as 1980:

> I think a lot of that problem began when we added the words, "Non-Status Indian" at the end of our Association. But the reason for that was that we wanted to cover all the Half-breed people ... Well, a lot of guys took advantage of the word, "Non-Status Indian." Status Indians living off reserve called themselves Non-Status Indians because they have no voice in selecting Council or voting in their Chief ... Then there is a lot of people who will tell you, "I'd like to sell my Indian rights and become a Metis," and a lot of us will accept that because we don't know who a Metis is. And then again, you'll find where there are some Indians that forgot to register and they want to become Metis or a Non-Status Indian, but again, *that's an Indian problem, that's not a Metis problem.*[18]

Although Paddy McGuire was not completely clear as to what constituted a non-status Indian (he seemed to assume that an enfranchised Indian had no right to use the term "non-status"), he was reasonably clear as to the difference between Métis and non-status Indian. For him, Métis was clearly a racial term,[19] while "non-status" or "non-registered" were legal ones. Because of that, he felt that the two groups did not belong in the same organization: "What they should do is educate our members the difference between a Metis problem and an Indian problem and we haven't done that... There is a lot of people living up north who are not registered, they are Non-Registered Indians. They think they are Metis people because they are not registered. They think that anybody who has sold out on their Treaty Rights or anyone who is not registered has actually got Metis rights, but this is all wrong."[20]

These strains were brought to a head in 1985, with the passage of federal Bill C-31. The Indian Act was amended to permit many non-status Indians to regain their status and become registered Indians. As a result, approximately 20 per cent of OMNSIA's members became registered under the Indian Act. In order to reflect this change in their constituency, "and to symbolize the rejection of the Indian Act as a means of categorizing and dividing their people,"[21] OMNSIA dropped the term "non-status Indian" from its name in 1987 and changed it to the Ontario Métis and Aboriginal Association and subsequently to the Ontario Métis Aboriginal Association. As of 2001, OMAA claimed to represent 200,000 Indian and Métis peoples living off-reserve in Ontario.

This commitment to off-reserve Indians was in keeping with the aims and target membership of CAP, with which the OMAA was affiliated.[22] As already mentioned, the organization closed its doors in 2007, although CAP still has a presence in Ontario through OCAP.

For the many years that OMNSIA was the main representative of the Ontario Métis, it never suggested an actual link with Red River Métis for its constituency, nor did its successor, OMAA, other than borrowing the name "Métis." That void was filled in 1994 with the formation of the Métis Nation of Ontario. MNO was founded at a delegates' meeting that brought together people who wished to be identified as Métis (mostly OMAA members) from communities around Ontario. In contrast to OMAA, and OMNSIA before it, MNO offered an aggressive identification not only as the Métis of Ontario, but as a group having a similar background and identity to the historic Métis Nation or Red River Métis. It became affiliated with the Métis National Council as "the only representative body of the Métis in Ontario."[23] In 2001, it claimed that over 380 communities were included in the MNO Registry, and that its registry was the only registry of Métis in Ontario recognized by the historic Métis Nation, represented by the Métis National Council, and that MNO offered "the most legitimate way in Ontario for Métis people to be recognized."[24] Thus, from 1994 to 2007 there have been two provincial organizations purporting to speak for the Métis of Ontario. Both had very different ideas of who their members were. To get a better understanding of how this situation came about, it is necessary to consider the specifics of Métis and non-status Indian identification as they were taking shape in Ontario in the 1980s.

Métis, Half-breed, or "Special Status"?

Hi, my name is Jean Brown. As you can see I am of native blood and sometimes I wonder, I stand back and say, well the white man don't want me, the Indians don't want me, where the heck do I belong, you know?

Jean Brown, Sault Ste Marie [25]

From its inception in 1965, the Métis and non-status Indian political movement in Ontario struggled with the idea of identity and the strategy that could best be used to build a new identity. The above quote, one of many expressed by OMNSIA members in the 1970s and 1980s, should remind us of the importance a lack of identity can have on a personal level.

Many people of Aboriginal ancestry lacking status under the Indian Act have long faced this question of an ambivalent identity in Ontario, and the issue came to a head in the 1980s. The options for Native people outside the Indian Act were limited. They could press for reinstatement as status Indians, they could reject the notion of status altogether, they could lobby for a special recognition of non-status Indians, or they could embrace the notion of "Métisness." All of these options were considered in Ontario at one time or another. As we saw, "Métis" was adopted at the earliest stages of political organization at the Lake Nipigon Métis Association in 1965, but that strategy brought its own problems. What actually did it mean to be called "Métis" during this period of early political mobilization? Was it a race-based, a legal, or a cultural definition? What, if anything, was the difference between a Métis and a non-status Indian? Was there a Métis culture indigenous to Ontario, or was it associated with the west?

These questions are troubling today, but they were even more so in the late 1970s and early 1980s, the formative years for political mobilization of Métis and non-status Indians in Ontario. We have at least three sources that reveal the thoughts and conflicts surrounding the idea of Métis identification at that time. One was a series of meetings that discussed the merits of a "special status" for Métis and non-status Indians in Ontario – a policy briefly pursued by OMNSIA under Duke Redbird's leadership (1980–82). The second is a series of debates that OMNSIA held to discuss issues surrounding the repatriation of the Canadian Constitution, including the definitions of Métis, Aboriginal, and Aboriginal rights. And finally, OMNSIA conducted several surveys, polling its members on both policy issues and issues of self-identification. All three of these sources offer insights into the development of an Ontario Métis identity.

In 1978, OMNSIA launched a preliminary inquiry into determining what special or Aboriginal rights, if any, accrued to its constituency. It quickly became obvious that the first order of business was to classify and identify its constituents. In 1979, after a meeting between OMNSIA and Premier William Davis and his cabinet, the Committee to Investigate the Legal Status of Métis and Non-Status Indians in Ontario was formed. This committee toured five communities (Moose Factory, Sault Ste Marie, Thunder Bay, Fort Frances, and Whitney) to gather information from Métis and non-status Indians about perceptions of their identity and Aboriginal rights. The objectives of the committee included the need to define OMNSIA's constituency for the

Ontario government, to identify the needs and aspirations not being met by existing government policies, and the identification of special provincial responsibilities. The committee was also expected to explain to the government what OMNSIA was, who and how many people it represented, as well as what its constituency wanted and to justify why the Government of Ontario should be involved.

The information gathered at the meetings was combined with documentation from the research project to produce an *Interim Report of the Special Status Committee,* which was presented to Premier Davis and his cabinet during a meeting with OMNSIA in June 1980. In this report, OMNSIA proposed a "special status" for Métis and non-status Indians in Ontario that recognized them as a Native and indigenous people. There was little content to this "special status" as far as defining OMNSIA's membership in any cultural sense of being Métis. It merely recommended an "official" recognition of Métis and non-status Indians as Native people with, in many cases, an Aboriginal relationship to their land: "All persons of Native ancestry in the province of Ontario who are not presently recognized as status Indians, have the right to self-determination as native, indigenous, and aboriginal people. Since they have, historically, and as a result of federal and provincial laws and policies, been deprived of that right, these persons have a claim to legislated recognition of that right to correct past and continuing injustices and inequities in relation to their perceptions of themselves as Native people."[26]

The committee broke this group down into those who needed recognition of Aboriginal rights in relation to hunting, fishing, trapping, or other use of the land and those who did not. It recommended that it be possible for people who had Native ancestry, but who were not recognized as such, either (a) to formally register as a Native person *without* claiming Aboriginal rights, or (b) to register as a Native person *with* Aboriginal rights. The committee also recommended recognition of the Aboriginal relationship to the land that many rural and northern people still maintained and some form of compensation for those who could demonstrate they were historically deprived of that relationship by the unilateral actions of governments. Little came of the idea of "special status" (probably because both the content of special status as presented and the criteria for identification of those eligible for "special status" were rather vague and the legal implications far-reaching). However, the interviews and testimony of those OMNSIA members who spoke at the committee meetings offer a valuable insight into the perception of Métis and Aboriginality in northern Ontario at the beginning of the 1980s.

What is most striking about the testimony is that most of the people who testified at the Special Status Committee hearings mainly spoke to *non-status issues*, rarely identifying themselves as Métis. Many spoke to the question of losing Indian status under 12(1)b of the Indian Act. Although some were concerned about the exclusion of Métis from treaty and status, few actually posited a separate culture or identity for the Métis. Most of the witnesses identified as Indian, not Métis, and the "culture" they stated that they most regretted losing was a knowledge of woodcraft. Reading the testimony from many of the witnesses at the OMNSIA special committee, it is obvious that at this time OMNSIA mainly was acting as an amalgamation of Métis and non-status Indians, the majority being non-status, stressing their Indian background, as opposed to Métis. Many of the respondents matter-of-factly referred to themselves as "Indian," often expressed through an idealized version of the past.

One of the few people who used the term "Métis" at these hearings was Mike McGuire. But even he spoke more about what it was like to be excluded from both Indian and non-Native society rather than having an endemic Métis society to draw support from. He related how, as a child, he and his relatives (a "pile of Indians") were not accepted as Indians, either by status Indians or by the Department of Indian Affairs. One gets the impression that, had he been accepted as Indian, he and his father would never have tried to appropriate or construct a Métis identity or launch a political movement: "The first attempts at Metis organization here in Ontario was some years ago. The main objective we had at that time was special status or to be recognized by the government – not just for what we were historically but for what we are today. At that time we were nothing but a pile of Indians who were not recognized by the Indians or by the Whites ... But since then we've come to recognize what we were and the old man and a whole bunch of us got together and formed a Metis association."[27]

It is worth noting that the phrase usually used throughout the hearing was "Indian, non-status Indian or breed" rather than Métis. To be fair, Métis identity was not the main issue of concern at these meetings; it was, rather, the assertion of hunting and fishing rights. However, some individuals *did* refer to themselves as Métis, like this individual, who contrasted his identity with that of an Indian, making a veiled comment about not being dependent on government handouts through the

Department of Indian Affairs and Northern Development (DIAND). But note also that, although he referred to himself as "Métis" once, he called himself "Breed" or "Half-breed" three times:

> I personally am not in favor of our people joining together with the Treaty Indians in forming one organization. I am also not prepared to risk losing the pride and independency that is mine because I am a Breed. We have always owned our own homes, and always made a respectable attempt to survive as a Breed. We have always done things our own way without any handouts. In other words, we and our ancestors have always paddled our own canoes. Our ancestors were a proud and independent breed, capable of living in harmony with the land, the Indian and the Whites. We stand our ground for special rights and the recognition of ourselves as Half-breeds. Joining the Treaty Indians would be a total loss of our own identity ... We should endeavor to obtain official recognition by all levels of governments throughout this land, and not only as another ethnic group or as another native organization. We should be recognized for what we are, and WE ARE METIS.[28]

Some people who supported a cultural identity separate from that of Indian identified themselves not as Métis, but simply as *Native people different from Indian*. Others totally dismissed that distinction and called for cultural awareness simply as Indian. Métis did not seem to be a large part of the common lexicon of 1979 (despite the fact that Duke Redbird, president of OMNSIA, wrote a Master's thesis published in 1980 under the title *We Are Metis*). Several people, like the woman quoted below, credited OMNSIA with making them aware of and proud of their Indian heritage. In her case, it did not lead her to identify with the Métis (although her brother later became part of the Métis Elders Steering Committee for MNO when it was formed in 1994): "I think there should be more cultural awareness, myself, I never heard nothing about OMNSIA till my brother Olaf got from his local in Batchewana. I never joined till just this year, but I've realized a lot of things about the Indian heritage that I never knew before. I think it should be brought out in the open that you are proud that there is Indian in you. I think that it should just be made more aware to the public that we are proud to be half white, half Indian or whatever."[29]

Many of the Native people who identified as Métis did so because that seemed to be the only identity available: "We are here this evening before you as a proud group of people. A people who are thought to have the best of two cultures, White and Indian. We are asking you, the members of this special committee, to represent us to the Premier of Ontario and members of the government for recognition as Metis people. Not as Indians, because we are not Indians ... We, as Metis people, know who we are. We are Indian descendants. We are also white descendants. Therefore we do not wish to be classed as status Indians but we need a special status."[30]

Some people, however, made claims as *both* non-status Indians and Métis. A person from Fort Frances showed little concern over Métis identification in the first part of his testimony. Rather, he outlined the typical concern of a non-status Indian over the loss of status and the benefits he may have enjoyed as a status Indian: "my dad enfranchised voluntarily because of the static he was getting on the reserve, so he said, 'What the heck, I've had enough of you guys' and left there. But maybe I would've enjoyed some kind of benefits that I might've been able to capitalize on."[31] But in a later part of his testimony, he identified as a Métis. His testimony is particularly interesting in that it shows he consciously took on the definition of Métis. Note his adoption of the Métis version of Canadian history and their contribution to western Canada:

> I am a Metis. As I grew up, the word Metis was seldom heard of ... The white folks called us Indians. Indians didn't call us anything. But I am proud to be a Metis especially since I now know what a Metis is. The average Canadian does not know what a Metis is ... There was a time in my life, not too long ago, when all I could identify with was Indian. But this left me frustrated because I know that I am not an Indian. I am not white but I am not Indian anyway. What am I? Well, first in spite of what Canadians have handed us in the past I still say that I am a Canadian. I'm also a French Metis. I sincerely hope that Canada soon recognizes what our people deserve relative to the sweat they gave to fabricate this Dominion of Canada.[32]

Many people regretted that they did not have recourse to the definition of Métis in their youth, expressing the common feeling of rejection from both non-Native and Indian. But others who recounted their experiences of rejection by both groups did not specifically take on the identity of Métis.

In keeping with the internalization of colonial status discussed in a previous chapter, some witnesses called for a "special ministry" within the provincial government to monitor Métis and non-status Indian affairs.

It is hard to believe that some Métis and non-status were calling for another version of DIAND, albeit at the provincial level. Some not only wanted recognition of "special status" as indigenous people (note that this testimony was given prior to constitutional recognition of the Métis in the Canadian Constitution) but also wanted special parliamentary representatives, as the Maori have in New Zealand. Some wanted Métis identification cards, issued by the government, in other words, a Métis registry. Still, it is not clear whether those recommending a registry wanted recognition *as Métis* or as an Aboriginal person with Aboriginal rights. Later, in the 1990s, both OMAA and MNO would issue such cards on their own, and MNC would propose a national Métis registry of those belonging to the historic Métis Nation.

Perhaps it is fitting to end this section on the special status hearings with a word from Paddy McGuire, the founder of OMNSIA. In his testimony, he expressed a desire to be recognized for "what we are – Half-breeds or Metis." He was advocating a separate identity; but not necessarily one linked to the traditions of Red River: "We're not after special status in a sense that we all want to become treaty Indians. All we want is a little bit of recognition. We want to be recognized as what we are, Half-breeds or Metis. We're getting sick and tired being called Indians anyways."[33]

Although little came of OMNSIA's lobbying for special status, the hearings and the negotiations leading up to it are a valuable source for illustrating the ideas of Métis and non-status identity current at the time. They indicate that only a minority of those who spoke chose to identify as Métis, and that the question of Aboriginal rights was at the forefront in many members' minds. These issues remain important today. Although the Ontario and Supreme Courts have consistently found that the Métis do possess Aboriginal rights, the issue of who is or who is not a Métis has not yet been satisfactorily answered by the courts. But the nature of the controversy seems to indicate that even now, the question of identity ("who is a Métis?") takes second place to a recognition of Aboriginal rights in the minds of most Métis and non-status Indians in Ontario, despite the rhetoric of Métis identity upheld by MNO.

In July 1981, OMNSIA held a "Commission of Inquiry" to debate proposed changes to the Canadian Charter of Rights and Freedoms and the Constitution[34] and to develop an official position for OMNSIA regarding the definition of Aboriginal peoples and Aboriginal rights in the Constitution and the Charter. Much of the proceedings were taped, transcribed, and are available for study.[35] While a great many issues were discussed, Aboriginal rights and definitions of Aboriginal peoples were the main topics of the day. Based on the definitions of Métis and non-status Indians found in the testimony of the delegates, it is probably safe to say that there was considerable disagreement and confusion in the minds of OMNSIA members at the time. Many different ideas were expressed, but the definitions proposed were almost always based on race or legal criteria. Conspicuous by its absence was any suggestion of western Métis culture or values as a basis for Métis identity. In fact, one delegate found the use of the term "Métis" "objectionable."[36]

One common issue was the difference between Métis and non-status Indian. Paddy McGuire, who was one of the commissioners, added to the mix when he suggested that enfranchised Indians had no right to call themselves non-status, and that they had no right to belong to an organization of Métis and non-status. His sentiments indicate the confusion and conflicting ideas of what constituted Métis identity at the time. One person aptly referred to the Métis and non-status Indian population as "People of Nowhere."[37]

This muddle over identity and legal definitions was reiterated in this submission from Lake Nipigon, the founding local of OMNSIA. The speaker outlined the difficulty in distinguishing between Métis, half-breed, non-status Indian, and enfranchised Indian, and the submission reiterated Paddy McGuire's contention that enfranchised Indians had no place in OMNSIA:

> Who is a Metis? … has every half-breed got the right to be a Metis or is it only French half-breeds who have this right? Are other half-breeds Non-Status Indians? What does the law have to say about this? ... Unregistered Indians are Status Indians who are not registered. This is not a Metis problem. They will never get registered by a Metis association. Can an enfranchised person be called a Non-Status Indian and still be within the law of Canada? The Indian Act clearly states that an enfranchised person is no longer an Indian under this Act or any other law of the country. These people will never get back their Indian status by hiding in a Metis association as Non-Status Indians.[38]

It is likely that these feelings of confusion over identity still resonate within Ontario today, which explains why, until recently, there have been at least two organizations claiming to represent the population, as well as a few independent or unaffiliated organizations such as the Red Sky Métis Independent Nation.

On at least two occasions, OMNSIA conducted surveys that gathered information on policy matters, self-identity, and other issues of concern to its membership and leadership as well as the national and provincial levels of government. In 1981 OMNSIA distributed a lengthy questionnaire to the delegates to the Commission of Inquiry that was held at its Annual Assembly.[39] In 1985, OMNSIA decided to carry out a more extensive survey that would include all of its members in Ontario. To that end, it distributed a revised and expanded version of the 1981 survey, which dealt with various matters that concerned the Métis and non-status Indians population in Ontario, particularly self-identity, loss of Indian status, and Aboriginal self-government.[40]

There were several reasons why OMNSIA conducted these surveys. The 1981 survey was carried out as part of OMNSIA's efforts to develop positions on constitutional issues to be discussed at the constitutional conferences that were being held with the government. As for the second survey, 1985 was the year that Bill C-31, the amendment to the Indian Act that revised the regulations on enfranchisement, was passed. Because this legislation would allow many non-status Indians to regain status, it had a potentially profound effect on OMNSIA's membership. In addition, definitions of who constituted the Métis were potentially of central concern, as the government of Canada was debating issues of self-government with the various national and provincial Native political organizations as the four first ministers' conferences on Aboriginal constitutional matters were nearing completion. The Métis National Council and the Native Council of Canada were locked in a dispute over the definition of Métis: MNC favoured a narrow definition based on descent from the historic populations in the west and eligibility for land grants or scrip, while NCC (Now CAP) favoured a wider interpretation, which would include various mixed Aboriginal populations from other parts of Canada, including Ontario.[41] Therefore, the Native Council of Canada had a vested interest in documenting the existence and voice of a Métis population outside the traditional Red River region. Ontario, with its extensive Métis and non-status Indian population, was one of the most important provinces in that regard.

The questionnaires were distributed in various ways. The 1981 questionnaire was published in the OMNSIA house organ, *Special Editions* (9[3]: 25), with an invitation to "anyone who wanted" to fill it out within the month and return it to OMNSIA. However, that issue was primarily designed as the workbook for delegates to the OMNSIA Commission of Inquiry into Aboriginal Rights and the Constitution of Canada, and the questionnaire seemed to be directed mainly at the delegates. Delegates were asked not to answer the questionnaire until after they had attended the study sessions held at the Commission of Inquiry and then to hand in the completed questionnaire to a staff member of OMNSIA on site during the hearings. It is not clear how many people responded to the 1981 survey. The preliminary report stated that 64 per cent of the delegates had submitted their completed questionnaires to the commission, and 114 delegates were named in the same issue, so it is likely that approximately seventy-three questionnaires were filled out. The 1985 questionnaire had a much wider distribution, through the OMNSIA local offices, at general information meetings, and in some cases through direct mail to members. There were 2,004 responses to this second survey.

Both surveys have administrative and methodological design problems. Obviously, the small number of returns on the 1981 survey (73 vs. 2,004) and the less than random method of distribution affect its reliability (the survey was completed mainly by delegates to the OMNSIA constitutional inquiry.) As OMNSIA's own analysis suggests, these delegates were not "average" OMNSIA members; they had high profiles in their communities as active, and often executive, members of their locals.[42] In addition, the questionnaires were completed after the respondents had attended several workshops and informational meetings at the inquiry, which undoubtedly influenced the answers. But the 1985 survey had administrative problems as well, particularly in the way it was distributed by individual locals with little attempt at maintaining a consistent control and in the design of some of its questions. Although the design of these surveys and their distribution are less than ideal, nevertheless they give some interesting insights into the nature of the OMNSIA's membership in the mid-1980s.

For our purposes, the questions of primary importance are those of self-identification. Both questionnaires were almost identical in this regard. They began with two questions. The first question on both was "I consider myself a person of aboriginal ancestry (YES/NO)." In the 1981 survey, the second question was "I am A Status Indian; A non-status Indian; A Metis; Canadian born; Naturalized Citizen; Immigrant," with spaces to allow the respondents to check off their answers. The 1985 survey added the choice of "Inuit" and "Other" for question 2. There was no admonition in either survey to choose only one of the options, and in the 1981 survey, at least, several respondents checked off more

Table 16.1 Respondent self-identification[a]

Self-identification (percentage)	1981	1985
Métis	57.5	36.0
Non-status Indian	34.2	40.9
Status Indian	1.3	13.3
Inuit	n/a	0
Other	n/a	1.0
Canadian born	28.7	6.2
Naturalized citizen	1.3	0.5
Immigrant	0	0.1
No response	6.8	1.7
Total	129.8	100.0

[a] The figures from 1981 are from *Dimensions. Special Editions* 9(4); the 1984 figures are from Peters, Rosenberg, and Halseth, *The Ontario Métis.*

than one. The only way to distinguish a Métis from a non-status Indian in either survey was through self-identification.

In the 1981 survey, just over 90 per cent of the respondents considered themselves to have Aboriginal ancestry, as opposed to 97.7 per cent in the 1985 survey, and almost 58 per cent identified themselves as Métis, as opposed to 34 per cent identifying as Non-status Indian in 1981. This is a reversal of the 1985 survey, which showed more respondents identifying as non-status Indian (40.9 per cent) than Métis (36 per cent) (see Table 16.1). The 1981 survey shows that there was a certain amount of confusion among the respondents about their identity. The fact that a significant percentage did not answer the first two questions (4 and almost 7 per cent, respectively) indicates some Native people were struggling to understand the terminology involved and how it applied to them as individuals. Also, the total (129.8) of the percentages for the second question (choosing a category) indicates a flaw in the structure of the question, since many respondents found it necessary to check more than one category. In 1985 a substantial number checked both options "Status Indian" and "Canadian born." A large number of those who checked "Status Indian" may have been non-status Indians in the process of being reinstated, and many of the "Canadian born" may have been Aboriginal people. It is possible that some of the respondents who checked "other" may also have been Métis and non-status Indians.

A consideration of question two reveals the difficulty of an analysis of self-identification using the data from these surveys. Both surveys lack the ability to distinguish between "Red River" Métis and "Ontario" Métis.

It would have been interesting to see the results if "breed" or "half-breed" had been included in the survey, but political and social considerations made that question unlikely. "Other" had no provision for a write-in answer, which might have yielded "breed" or other self-identifications. Peters et al. are of the opinion that the Ontario Métis "represent a group distinct from the Métis who trace their heritage and identity to their experiences at Red River,"[43] but other than referring to some historical authorities, they can offer no internal evidence to support or refute this claim, because nothing in the survey was designed to elicit such information.

However, the surveys do give us some interesting insights. All of the respondents who answered the questions on registration in 1981 would have registered as Native persons if they had had that opportunity, almost 70 per cent of those people choosing to register as Métis and only 18 per cent choosing Indian. Although no one said they would not register, the 8 per cent who did not indicate what sort of Native they would register as suggests some suspicion of what registration might mean or some indecision over identity.[44] In 1985, more than 97 per cent of Métis respondents stated that they considered themselves to be of Aboriginal ancestry and would legally register as an Aboriginal person given the opportunity. But the second survey allows for some finer analysis because it had questions on language use and cultural and spiritual values. There were no corresponding questions regarding language use or cultural and spiritual values in the 1981 survey. The 1985 survey showed that only a small percentage of Métis respondents used an Aboriginal language at home (Ojibwa, 54.7 per cent; Cree, 27.7 per cent; Algonquin, 1.7 per cent and "Other," 11.7 per cent.) Perhaps significantly, no cases of "Michif" were reported. There was no selection of languages provided; respondents were asked to write in their language. There may have been some cases of Michif subsumed under the "Other" category, but no breakdown of that category was possible. Aboriginal and spiritual values were reported to be important in everyday life for almost three quarters of Métis respondents.[45]

Both surveys also indicated that those who identified as Métis saw themselves as a separate Aboriginal entity from non-status Indians (although neither survey considered the question of *how* Métis saw themselves as separate from non-status). Peters et al. report that, while 60 per cent of the Métis respondents said they wish to be reinstated under the Indian Act or to the band of their ancestry, more than three-quarters indicated that they preferred a legal status different from status Indians. When asked whether they would register themselves as Indian, Inuit, or

Métis, 71.9 per cent of Métis respondents indicated that they would register as Métis. Similar figures were collected in 1981 (70 per cent of those people choosing to register as Aboriginal would register as Métis and 18 per cent would register as Indians). According to Peters et al.: "This suggests that there is a fairly strong sense of Métisness, independent of Indian heritage among Métis respondents."[46] They may be right, but there are many possible reasons why this group might wish to distance itself from status Indians besides an innate sense of "Métisness." Familiarity with overcrowded reserves and the generally poor level of social services available, or an unwillingness to submit to band council politics on reserves may be other reasons. And while there definitely is a feeling of separateness among those who identify as "Métis Indians," there is no indication that this "Métisism" had anything in common with the "New Nation" or "Red River" Métis identity of the prairies. That connection did not occur until the creation of MNO in 1994 .

From the point of view of Métis identity, the most interesting findings of the OMNSIA survey involve the differences displayed between those who identified themselves as Métis and those who identified as non-status Indians. The study revealed that there were only minor differences in gender, number of children, number of single mothers, and any of the other socio-economic and geographic variables measured. Both groups (97 per cent and 98 per cent, respectively) strongly identified as Aboriginal persons, or as persons of Aboriginal ancestry and agreed that they would register themselves as an Aboriginal person if they were given the opportunity. But there were some significant differences between the two groups in terms of origins, use of an Aboriginal language in the home, and desire for reinstatement under the Indian Act.

Family origins seemed to be particularly important in determining whether the person identified as Métis or non-status Indian. Those who identified as non-status Indian were most likely to have come from families of status Indians, having become non-status Indians either by losing status themselves or through a relative. The loss of Indian status was experienced at a personal level; either the person himself/herself had experienced the loss, or it had happened to their parents or grandparents. Non-status Indians were much more likely than Métis to wish to be reinstated under the Indian Act or to the band of their ancestry. Only about 28 per cent of Métis respondents stated they would register as an Indian compared with over 90 per cent of non-status Indians. While it seems likely that this response reflects the relative possibilities for non-status Indians to regain Indian status compared with those of

Métis, it also may reflect a Métis sense of identity separate from Indian heritage.[47] The Métis felt much more strongly than non-status Indians that they should have a legal status apart from status Indians under the Indian Act. In addition, the percentage of respondents stating "Not Sure" is lower for the Métis than for the non-status Indians.[48] "In other words, the Non-Status Indians clearly identify with an Indian status from which they have been legally excluded. *In contrast, the Métis appear to distinguish themselves from the Indians and identify with a separate culture, only one element of which is Indian ancestry.*"[49]

In summary, Peters et al. conclude that "Métis" and "Non-Status" were *not inter-changeable* in the minds of respondents. While both groups had a strong Aboriginal identity, and both supported separate political representation, a Métis land base, and separate institutions, they differed in the desire to achieve Indian legal status, many Métis aspiring to a separate legal status as Métis. Similarly, while non-status Indians supported the idea of a Métis land base, they were much less likely than the Métis to consider moving there.[50] This is an interesting conclusion, but unfortunately, neither of the surveys gives us an idea of what it meant to be an Ontario Métis in the 1980s. According to OMNSIA, the results of the 1981 survey indicate that "the self-identification of respondents as Métis, and the desire to have that identification legally recognized [are] clearly in the majority. These statistics clearly contradict the common assumption that Métis identity is predominant only in the western provinces."[51] What that conclusion ignores, however, is the observation that although the *term* may have been the same, the *content* of being Métis was not necessarily the same in Ontario as it was in the western provinces at the time the survey was taken. As in the later survey, the term "breed" or "half-breed" was not offered as a choice, although a cursory examination of much of the testimony offered at the constitutional inquiry, as well as the earlier testimony on special status, shows that both terms were still in use, and that half-breed was often the first choice rather than Métis.

Cultural Symbolism in Ontario Métis Political Organizations

While the data from the 1981 and 1985 OMNSIA surveys are revealing in that they effectively demonstrated the existence of an Aboriginal group with an identity separate from Indians in Ontario, the surveys did not effectively reveal the cultural markers, historical traditions, or political conditions that sustained this group – if indeed such markers existed. Nevertheless, the data give some clear indications that significant socio-economic differences existed between those identifying as Métis and those identifying as non-status Indian. While the surveys were not able to explain how or why some individuals identified themselves as Métis and others did not, or if there was an appreciable difference between an Ontario Métis identity and a prairie Métis identity, they did reveal that the seeds that led to the eventual split between MNO and OMAA had already been planted, and that the split was predictable and perhaps even inevitable.

For example, the 1985 survey revealed that those identifying as non-status Indians more closely identified with an Indian heritage, particularly with regard to language and spirituality, than did those identifying as Métis. The subsequent rift between the two organizations may reflect a continuance of this cultural differentiation, OMAA more closely supporting non-status Indian and Native values and MNO more closely supporting Red River or historic Métis Nation values.

An examination of the symbolism used by each organization would seem to bear out this conclusion. While the introduction of any divisive political symbolism would have been muted in the 1980s, when both populations were represented by the same organization, it is likely that separatist symbols would become much more pronounced when the different groups began to be mobilized and needed to distinguish themselves from each other. This is evident in an examination of the symbolism used by OMNSIA, OMAA, and MNO.

OMNSIA

The original OMNSIA logo (1971–87) was a fairly elaborate figure, combining an equal number of Indian and Euro-Canadian symbols. It was made up of an inner and an outer circle that contained sixteen stars and the letters OMNSIA. The inner circle contained pictures of a lynx, a book, a bow and arrow, a set of scales, a feather, a maple leaf, and a three-pointed flower – the trillium. These symbols are indicative of who OMNSIA considered to be its constituency at the time. The official explanation of the symbolism, as offered by OMNSIA, clearly represents a mixture of two cultures:

> The Outer Circle is the symbol of infinity. Native people have been here since time immemorial. The Stars symbolize the heavens and the Great Spirit – there were 16 locals in the first OMNSIA group, therefore 16 stars in the emblem. The Maple Leaf is the Canadian National emblem.

> The Trillium is the Ontario flower emblem. The Scales symbolize justice, which the organization seeks for the Metis people. The Lynx is a native Ontario fur bearing animal noted for strength, cunning and survival ability. The Feather represents the Indian heritage of our people. The Bow and Arrow represent the early hunting life of the North American people. The Book – Education – represents the future. The Inner Circle represents the earth.[52]

It is also significant that there are a more or less equal number of non-Native and Native symbols in this logo. Non-Native symbols include the trillium (Government of Ontario), the maple leaf (Government of Canada), the scales of justice ("white man's justice"), and a book (Euro-Canadian "book learning"). Native symbols include a lynx, a feather, and a bow and arrow. Note also that there are no explicitly western or Red River Métis symbols: no Métis flag, no sash, and no mention of Louis Riel. Since OMNSIA was not proposing an explicit link between the Red River Métis and the Ontario Métis at that time, no symbols from the Red River Métis were used.

OMAA

The logo of OMAA offers a significant contrast to the old OMNSIA logo. It consists of the letters OMAA in black, reflected underneath in a mirror image in red, as if the letters were standing next to a lake. Part of the "M" and the two "As" are slanted, so that when they are combined with the mirror image they resemble arrows. The "O" reflected in the lake appears as an infinity symbol. The upper letters are silhouetted against a white sun and a yellow sky with a bird flying above. It is evident that the OMAA represents a different constituency than OMNSIA, or at least sees them in a different light than OMNSIA did. The Indian side of the equation is much more explicitly emphasized, and the membership is referred to as either the "Woodland Métis Tribe," or "Métis Indians." The symbolism of the new logo has a predominantly Native content:

> OMAA's new logo stands for continuing advancement of the OMAA woodland Métis tribe. The logo is made up of the four sacred colors, representing the four races of mankind, the four seasons, directions and the four stages of life. The arrows represent our peoples' determination to move forward and advance their issues and concerns. The upper half of the arrows consists of an "M" and two stylized "A's" formed from the

> traditional tipi sign. The "O" represents continuity in cycles of life and when combined with the mirror image of the OMAA acronym, creates the Métis symbol of infinity. The sun is central to our existence, playing a vital role in the continuity of life. Finally, the flying eagle represents independence and freedom at the heart of their mission.[53]

The symbolism differs drastically from the OMNSIA logo. There are six North American Indian symbols used: tribe, the sacred number four (four races, four seasons, four stages of life), arrows, tipis, sun ("father sun"), and eagle. There is one Métis symbol used: the "infinity" symbol from the Red River Métis flag. The only "white" symbol that remains is the colour white itself (the "white race" is part of the four colours) and (perhaps) the anthropological term "Woodland."

While not part of its official logo, another revealing illustration could be seen at the OMAA site: a braid of sweet grass intertwined with a Métis sash. Although, strictly speaking, both the sash and the sweet grass are prairie symbols, the illustration is a graphic representation of the importance of Native values to the Ontario Métis population. While the sash is likely a nod towards the influence of the prairie Métis (although the sash has Quebec rather than prairie origins), the greater emphasis is on Ontario Native values.

A great many Cree and Ojibwa values inform the stories about both the beginning of OMNSIA and the beginnings of OMAA. Mike McGuire tells a story about how all the founding members of OMNSIA heard a baby crying on the mountain during the founding of the Lake Nipigon Métis Association in 1965. He interprets that as a realization of a legend he had heard from his grandfather that a cry ringing from the hills in the MacDiarmid region would signal the emergence of a "New People."[54] Traditional Indian ceremonies remained an important part of ongoing OMAA activities, including a "Sunrise Ceremony" derived from a tradition of keeping a sample of ashes from all the fires made when a hunter was out trapping.[55] The members of OMAA still go to the Native community for spiritual leadership as well as ceremonies such as the shaking tent.[56]

According to OMAA, its constituency was mainly off-reserve Aboriginal people (status or non-status). About 20 per cent of OMAA's constituents were registered Indians living off-reserve. In this way, they were seeking the same constituency as the Congress of Aboriginal Peoples (CAP), the national organization with which they were affiliated. OMAA stated as its mission: "To represent the political, social and economic aspirations of the Métis and other off-reserve aboriginal people in Ontario."

It should be pointed out that MNO, like OMAA, could demonstrate ceremonial links to First Nations. At a ceremony held in August 2004 at the Turtle Mountain Reservation at Belcourt, North Dakota, Tony Belcourt, president of the Métis Nation of Ontario, was given a Thirsty Dance or Sundance song, commemorating an 1820s alliance of the Assiniboine, Cree, Chippewa, and Michif peoples at Buffalo Lodge Lake in what is now northwest North Dakota. The song subsequently became part of a ceremony commemorating a Nation to Nation relationship between the Métis Nation of Ontario and the Anishinabek Nation in Ontario.[57]

The MNO

MNO has no official logo, but its website features discussions and illustrations on various aspects of historic Métis Nation culture, including the fiddle and sash and the Métis flag. While MNO's aggressive identification with the western Métis represents a break from the original OMNSIA and OMAA strategy, the idea of consciously looking to the west for cultural inspiration is not new. As early as 1978, Duke Redbird, who had been active in OMNSIA politics for many years and was president of OMNSIA in the early 1980s, wrote a Master's thesis (published in 1980) in which he suggested that the half-breeds and non-status Indians of Ontario might wish to look to the western Métis to find an identity:

> In Canada, however, half-breed and many non-status Indians have moved toward the only recognized non-status group … the Metis. This has provided an identity solution for many natives who had lived for years in a limbo world outside the special status reserved for registered Indians. This represents an expanded concept of the Metis people – with an historical continuity borrowed from the original Metis in the West, but based on the reality of native consciousness in North America. "[58]
>
> There is an extant strong identity base that the Metis can build upon – the legacy of Louis Riel. However, the western Metis image and cultural characteristics that now serve as a bridge to connect the Half-breed on a national scale, must not rely solely on the historic context. It must now develop an awareness of values in a modern context, and of the Metis' contribution — not only in Canadian history – but also in present day Canadian life.[59]

MNO seems to have borrowed a page from Redbird's book and turned to Red River as the source of their Métis identity. This is a recent innovation, and even their own website alludes to the fact that the term "Métis" (in the context of Red River Métis) was not always known in Ontario. However, MNO makes the case that the Métis were always here, just not recognized as such. "The Métis Nation of Ontario (MNO) evolved from the rich and dynamic history of an Aboriginal people *long thought to be non-existent in Ontario*. MNO was founded in 1994 at a delegates meeting that brought together Métis from nearly 100 Ontario communities. This dynamic approach has allowed MNO to realize great success in a relatively short period of time. It has drawn Métis people together in ever-increasing numbers, encouraged them to claim their inheritance, and to *establish their identity within the Province of Ontario*."[60]

MNO makes a claim for eastward migration of some Red River Métis, while at the same time pointing out that other mixed communities evolved in Ontario before the western Métis. There definitely is a historical population that they can draw on,[61] but it is not at all clear that these groups were linked to Red River, or that they ever referred to themselves as Métis. That is more likely a modern interpretation fuelled by MNO and the influence of the *Powley* decision:

> The Métis of Ontario have faced the same exclusion and denial of their inherent Aboriginal rights [as the Red River Métis]. Many Métis communities were established from migration after the government's deplorable annexation of the Métis. Other Ontario Métis communities evolved long before the annexation and still survive today, in areas throughout Ontario. Ontario Métis communities have thrived and flourished from the Ottawa Valley to Sault Ste Marie to Kenora. The Métis have a rich and established history in the Province of Ontario. The Métis of Rainy River signed an adhesion to Treaty Three in 1873 conferring the same rights First Nations enjoyed upon the Métis. Presently, none of the promises of lands, rights, or annuities have been fulfilled. As well, other Métis communities across the province still have not had their constitutionally entrenched Aboriginal rights fully recognized.[62]

Another symbol of prairie Métis culture being introduced into Ontario can be seen in the aforementioned acquisition of a Thirsty Dance or Sundance song by Tony Belcourt. This event was "the culmination of a two year search by Mr Belcourt for a traditional Michif song that he could bring to a ceremony to commemorate a Nation to Nation relationship which has recently been forged between the Métis Nation and the Anishinabek Nation in Ontario." As noted above, the song originally commemorated the coming together of the Cree, Assiniboine, Chippewa, and Michif at Buffalo Lodge Lake, in northwest North Dakota, but it has now become part of the Ontario Métis cultural package as represented by MNO.[63] It could also be seen as a deliberate attempt to usurp OMAA's constituency by showing that MNO also has close ties to tribal cultures.

One can easily overemphasize the "cultural invention" of the Ontario Métis. For example, it would not be totally true to suggest that the Ontario Métis have no cultural memory of Louis Riel. Even Mike McGuire, president of OMAA, and one who questions the importation of western Métis values into Ontario, has some family memories that include Riel. He qualifies his story by pointing out that his family is Irish, not French, and that he expresses a certain bemusement over the realization that people can consciously adopt symbols to develop their culture:

> I guess there was communications (with the west) on Lake Nipigon because it was one of the trade routes of the Hudson's Bay Company, to the people of the west. I know my uncle Nate used to talk about how he had three beads off of Louis Riel's string of beads; prayer beads. He had three of them, but I don't know what happened to them. But the funny thing about being a Métis or a half-breed in MacDiarmid is that we're Irish. Like we celebrated St Patrick's Day, one of the biggest days of the whole year. *It's funny how you can develop your own culture, like start up the whole thing.* The rest of the year we lived like genuine half-breed people.[64]

Most of the cultural markers used by MNO are derived from the prairie Métis: the flag, sash, and Louis Riel. But there is at least one aspect exclusive to Ontario: the adhesion of half-breeds to Treaty 3, an important issue for MNO, although the organization has substituted "Métis" for the term "half-breeds," which was the term used in the original historical document: "Treaty No. 3 is a rare example of a treaty that includes the Métis. On September 12, 1875, the Métis were included in a treaty 'adhesion' or add-on to the original agreement. The Métis people were included, according to the written text of the treaty, 'by virtue of their Indian blood' and because of their 'claim [to] a certain interest in the lands or territories in the vicinity of Rainy Lake and the Rainy River.'"[65] But a quote from one of MNO's representatives (Gary Lipinski of Fort Frances) shows that the mixed population was not necessarily separate from the Indians: "'At that point they [the Métis and the Indians] would have been related – family ... You would have looked after your brothers and sisters, and in some cases children and grandchildren. There would have been inter-marriages, friendships, and relationships formed. ... First Nation members include the descendants of local Métis who were absorbed into the little Eagle band and are now part of Couchiching First Nation."[66] Also, as the existence of the Red Sky Métis Independent Nation indicates, there is some tendency for "Status Métis" to distinguish themselves from both Métis and non-status Indians.

The need to postulate a Red River Métis connection represented not only a desire to separate itself from the OMAA while representing a group that clearly separated itself from the Indian population, but it also derives from the fact that the MNO had its national affiliation with the Métis National Council, which held as part of its policy that the only true Métis populations are those of the Historic Métis Nation of the west. Since at least 1999, the MNC was proposing a definition of Métis that stated explicitly that a person must be "a descendant of a Métis person who resided in or used and occupied the Historic Métis Nation Homeland on or before December 8th 1869."[67] Depending on how the "Homeland" would be defined, there was concern that many of those registered in Ontario would not be entitled to identify as Métis under MNC guidelines. As a result, MNO might "be reduced drastically in numbers with severe financial consequences as they lose needed funding from governments."[68] The stressing of Red River ties, therefore, was probably as much a way for MNO to fend off their exclusion from MNC as it was to construct an identity for its membership.

Métis Identity and Aboriginal Rights

A common goal of both organizations was to secure Aboriginal rights (hunting and fishing for subsistence) for their constituents. This was a long-standing issue and a major preoccupation for OMNSIA, the predecessor of both organizations, as demonstrated by its attempts at securing a "special status" for its membership in the early 1980s. It would not be an exaggeration to suggest that this topic may have trumped even the issue of identity for both MNO and OMAA, although many consider identity and Aboriginal rights to be inextricably mixed.

In an attempt to assert their Aboriginal rights, as well as to define who is or is not a Métis in Ontario, both organizations launched respective versions of a Métis registry and a Métis status card. These cards identified the bearer as a Métis and asserted his/her Aboriginal rights to hunt and fish for subsistence. The desire to create a registry of Métis people was likely influenced by the Canadian government's long-standing practice of maintaining a registry of "status" Indians. While proponents of a Métis registry point out that there is a major difference between their version of a registry and the government's, in that the Métis people themselves (or, at least, their political organizations) control the criteria for membership, the potential for creating yet another category of Nativeness in Canada – "status" Métis vs. "non-status" Métis – seems to be counterproductive. Nevertheless, both of the major political organizations of Métis and non-status Indians in Ontario seem to have embraced this course of action.

OMAA began by issuing its version of an Aboriginal status card, which it called a Certificate of Aboriginal Status. Primarily, it was a membership card signifying that the person named on it was a member of the Ontario Métis Aboriginal Association. But it also acted as an identification card – signifying that the holder was a person of Aboriginal ancestry and recognized under the federal Constitution Act, 1982, with "all the rights, opportunities and privileges accorded to aboriginal people."[69] OMAA clearly saw the card as being similar to the "status" card with an identification number issued to status Indians registered with the Government of Canada through the Department of Indian Affairs and Northern Development.

MNO's response to OMAA's status card was the creation of a "Métis Registry" for Ontario. MNO feels that the establishment of a registry will put an end to the question "who are the Métis?" In keeping with its affiliation with the Métis National Council, its definition of Métis is bound by the same restrictions on the definition of Métis imposed by the national organization, including descent from the historic Métis Nation (see below). In a veiled reference to the OMAA, MNO claimed that "unlike organizations which issue cards to anyone who claims to be Métis, MNO applicants must supply proper genealogical documentation and proof of aboriginal ancestry."[70] However, OMAA also claimed that the same sort of proof was needed for its card. MNO stated that its registry would provide "a new wealth of Métis history, and a genealogical database that will serve future generations."[71]

The issues of who is a Métis in Ontario and who represents the Métis of Ontario have been affected by the *Powley* case, and the 2003 Supreme Court of Canada's recognition of the Aboriginal rights of the Sault Ste Marie area Métis. In the wake of that decision, the Ontario government offered an interim agreement in July 2004, allowing Métis to hunt and fish for food without being charged by the Ministry of Natural Resources.[72] The agreement covered a two-year period and was negotiated exclusively with the Métis Nation of Ontario, which agreed to use its Métis registry to issue a maximum of 1,250 harvesting cards to its membership. Since then, the agreement has been expanded and ratified several times. Although the agreement provided for a third party to independently evaluate MNO harvesting registry system, limiting the agreement to MNO membership still has the potential to leave many people of Aboriginal descent in limbo.

Not surprisingly, the agreement was greeted with dismay by OMAA. Henry Wetelainen, the first vice-president of OMAA, suggested that the agreement was reached because both levels of government were concerned over the size of OMAA's constituency and preferred the narrower definition of Métis represented by MNO: "They're scared of the East; they're scared of OMAA and the size of our province."[73] But to some degree, it was inevitable that Ontario chose to negotiate with MNO rather than OMAA. Since its inception in 1994, the Métis Nation of Ontario was able to usurp much of the political influence OMAA previously had enjoyed as the representative of the original Métis and non-status Indian organization in Ontario. This was most obvious in the *Powley* case. Although OMAA was the initiator in that case (the "Métis card" originally used by Steve Powley to assert his Aboriginal right to hunt was in fact issued by OMAA) MNO was able to quickly wrest the *Powley* issue from OMAA in the eyes of both the government and the general public.

But the choice of MNO as the vehicle for registering Métis hunters in Ontario begs some serious questions. Because MNO is affiliated with the Métis National Council, it is bound by the national organization's definition of Métis and its linkages to the historic Métis Nation Homeland. MNO admits as much in its description of its registry of Métis people in Ontario: "The purpose of the MNO Registry is to list Métis people in the Province of Ontario who meet the standards for registration in accordance with criteria established by the Métis National Council that represents the historic Métis Nation in Canada."[74] It will be recalled that the MNC definition (as adopted at the MNC's 18th Annual General Assembly in Edmonton, on 27–28 September 2002) represents the historic Métis Nation, exclusively, who "resided in the Historic Métis Nation Homeland," defined as "the area of land in west central North America used and occupied as the traditional territory of the Métis or half-breeds as they were then known."

It is extremely problematic to consider Ontario as part of that historic Métis Nation Homeland,[75] or that all the MNO's members are "descended from the Historic Métis Nation which is now comprised of all Métis Nation citizens and is one of the 'aboriginal peoples of Canada' within the meaning of s. 35 of the *Constitution Act, 1982.*" Nevertheless, this definition is quoted in full in the MNO's description of its Métis Registry, which in turn forms the basis for the MNO's issuing of harvesting cards. Despite the fact that this definition obviously excludes a significant portion of Ontario's mixed-blood population, the Honourable David Ramsey, minister of natural resources, stated that he felt that the MNO Registry was "a good system" that was "consistent with Métis status checks recommended in the Powley case."[76]

But there is no need to postulate a link to the Red River Métis or a historic Métis Nation Homeland as defined by MNC to meet the criteria for Métis as outlined in the *Powley* case. It will be recalled that while the Supreme Court's decision avoided a clear ruling on who was or was not a Métis, it did define Métis communities as "a group of Métis with a distinctive collective identity, living together in the same geographical area and sharing a common way of life." The court went on to state that in addition to demographic evidence, proof of shared customs, traditions, and a collective identity is required to demonstrate the existence of a Métis community that can support a claim to site-specific Aboriginal rights. There is nothing in that definition that requires a connection to the historic Métis Nation Homeland as defined by the Métis National Council, and, in fact, it supports the conclusion that there may be many Métis communities in Canada, each with its own set of customs and identities. This finding is consistent with those of the 1996 Royal Commission on Aboriginal Peoples, which pointed to separate Métis populations in Ontario, Quebec, Labrador, and the Maritimes.

However, Clem Chartier, when he was the president of the Métis National Council, made it clear that, as far as he was concerned, the *Powley* decision clearly referred to the Métis as defined by MNC. He dismissed OMAA's criticism of MNO and MNC, because OMAA "does not represent the 'Historic Métis Nation,'" although he acknowledged that a few Métis may be members.[77]

At the very least, the *Powley* decision has made it obvious that a clear definition of "Métis" is required under section 35 of the Constitution Act, 1982. But as the Ontario situation demonstrates, this is not necessarily simple or straightforward to achieve, or at least it was not when there were two competing organizations, each representing a constituency with a competing claim for an identity as "Métis" and the benefits that accrue to it. Although it seems that MNO has won the battle for official recognition in Ontario, it may be positing a Métis identity that is at odds with the views of a large proportion of the province's non-tribal Aboriginal population, one that has its own history, distinct from the Red River Métis.

Powley has had an interesting effect on the perception of Métis in Ontario. In chapter 15 it was mentioned that, post *Powley*, many academics, particularly historians, have taken to referring to the Upper Great Lakes fur trade settlements as "Métis" whether or not they regarded or referred to themselves as such. *Powley* has had a similar effect on our perception of more recent Métis and/or non-status Indian populations in Ontario. We now tend to forget, or to gloss over, the fact that the term was almost unknown in Ontario in the 1960s, when the first organizations attempting to represent Aboriginal groups not covered by the Indian Act were forming, and that the contemporary recognition of populations as Métis is only a few decades old.

Who Are the Métis in Ontario?

It is an undeniable fact that there is a distinct Aboriginal people in Ontario, separate from status or "tribal" Indians. The OMNSIA surveys plus much testimony from individuals throughout Ontario all point to the existence of such a group. But what is not clear are the cultural and historical boundaries of that population. Are they part of the Métis Nation or of some other group? Which portion of this group can legitimately lay claim to the term "Métis" and which cannot? It is clear that no single political group can speak for the total population, which is why there have been so many organizations attempting to do so. Neither MNO, nor OMAA, nor its successor OCAP can hope to definitively answer the question "where does the 'non-tribal indigenous population' of Ontario fit in the spectrum of Aboriginal identities available in Canada?" However, it is possible they could settle the question of which portion of this population could be identified as Métis.

MNO is attempting to do so by importing western Métis values and culture to this eastern Aboriginal group. Not surprisingly, some Ontario Aboriginal people who identify as Métis object to this action. Mike McGuire, one of the founding fathers of OMNSIA and president of OMAA, had this to say about MNO's attempt to create an Ontario "Métis" culture:

> Well, I guess Tony Belcourt ... wanted to go more with the Red River things, eh? Maybe MNO, they wanted to say to be Métis, you have to come from the Red River in order to have that identity. But in Ontario we don't identify with that. The Métis people of Ontario; they are the *Ontario* Métis people. They're not from the west. Like, Tony comes from Alberta. He comes into Ontario and says well, here are the values of the Métis people. Well, maybe in the west they do have a different set of values. But in Ontario we certainly don't want to do that. We're a different being here ... So that's how the split [between OMAA and MNO] began. I think it was more of the Western Métis concept, I think that they wanted to put the Western Métis values here.[78]

One should keep in mind this is a statement from the head of a rival political organization, one that had been courting much the same constituency as MNO, although it recognized a somewhat wider base for them. Mr McGuire does have a point, but it can be argued that it was the early political activities of him and his father that first introduced the term "Métis" into Ontario. The name was almost unknown in the province before the early founders of the Lake Nipigon Métis Association became aware of the activities of the western Métis and non-status Indians organizations, particularly AMNSIS, and adopted the term. Several of the founders (Paddy McGuire, George McGuire, Leonard King) have stated that "Métis" was deliberately chosen, because at least in the 1960s and 1970s it was seen as having the broadest base – a term that could include "half-breeds," Métis, "Métis Indians," and non-status Indians alike. This was a strategy that had been attempted before, in the prairies. But, like the situation there, as early as 1980 it was evident that the Métis and non-status Indians of Ontario could not fit entirely comfortably within one organization.

This schism between Ontario Métis and non-status Indians is what led to the eventual formation of MNO. But while it is clear that there were differences between those identifying as Métis and those identifying as non-status Indian, it is still not clear that Métis identity in Ontario is related to that in the prairies. Nevertheless, with the formation of a separate Métis organization, there was the need for a recognizable identity, and that of the western Métis was the obvious one to draw from.

MNO has made a lot of progress in this regard. At least for some, in Ontario the term "Métis" is becoming accepted as part of the larger western definition of the historic Métis Nation. This reformulation of identity is spurred by MNO's affiliation with the Métis National Council, which insists that the term refers only to the descendants of the historic Métis Nation of the west.[79] Another important validation of MNO's efforts has come from the Ontario government, which in 2004 agreed to use their registry as the basis for recognizing those who would be entitled to Métis Aboriginal rights.

We have seen evidence that most of the Métis of Ontario represent a group of Aboriginal people different from those from Red River, or at least a group with few actual links to the historic Métis Nation. We have seen testimony from OMNSIA members in the late 1970s and early 1980s that showed that the term "half-breed" was still being used in preference to "Métis." We have seen that many of the older generation of Métis leaders such as Mike McGuire and Leonard King refer to themselves as "Métis Indians" as well as half-breeds. But to some degree, that distinction may be becoming irrelevant. Ethnic identity is never stable; it continually changes, and it is not (as is obvious from the Ontario scenario) necessarily bound to the past. The adoption of western Métis values cannot and should not be interpreted as "wrong" or "misguided"; it is simply the way Métis ethnicity is being developed in Ontario. A new Métis identity is being forged in Ontario through the political activities of MNO and social change.

The adoption of a western Métis version of identity is in itself entirely understandable. The idea of Métis in the Red River sense is a seductive and attractive one (the portrayal of the "New Nation," the Métis as one of the creators of western Canada, Louis Riel as culture hero). It gives the Métis people of Ontario a sense of pride in an actual ethno-Aboriginal identity as opposed to an "anti-identity" based on rejection from other groups.

Despite the fact that the "Métis of Ontario" as presented by MNO is an identity at least partially based on outside influences and national politics, it also seems to be becoming the reality. The one thing that can be predicted about ethnic or Aboriginal boundaries is that they change with the times. The situation today may demand a Métis identity in Ontario far different from the one originally envisioned by Paddy McGuire and his fellow activists when they started the Lake Nipigon Métis Association in 1965.

17 Organizational Politics, Land Claims, and the Métis of the Northwest Territories

I am a Metis who is a declared Dene and I am also a chief ... I am a good example of unity, working and living in harmony on an equal basis. I am accepted by all the chiefs. There isn't a thought in my mind that I am a Metis when I am with the Dene. We are a people with all or part of the same blood running through our veins.[1]

I was still called a Breed when I went to school. I was a goddamn Breed and that's exactly what they called me. And a Breed I will stay, and I'm not no Dene![2]

I do not derive any comfort from those provisions that the collective Métis identity of the members of the North Slave Métis Alliance will be preserved. My understanding, and the understanding of my advisers, is that if we were to enroll in the Tlicho land claims agreement, we become Tlicho citizens and therefore lose our Métis identity. The Métis are adamant that we are not about to lose our identity at the altar of this land claim.[3]

These quotes nicely capture the fractured nature and depth of emotion that accompanies the question of Métis identity in the Northwest Territories (NWT), where two consistent, albeit conflicting, patterns of identity have persisted for years. On the one hand, there are those Métis who identify with, and can trace their ancestry to, the original Métis of Red River. On the other hand, there are those who express a closer identification with their First Nations (Dene) relatives.[4] As elsewhere in Canada, these patterns of identity have been modulated by political expediency (a need for unity) and a personal sense of self – a need for an ethnic identity.

How the terms "Dene" and "Dene Nation" are currently used in the Northwest Territories is somewhat ambiguous. "Dene" (there are several linguistic variations) is a common term for "person" or "people" in various languages within the Athapaskan linguistic group. But as it has come to be defined by the Dene Nation, the organization representing the First Nations people of the NWT, it has gone beyond its Athapaskan linguistic and cultural origins. According to the constitution of the Dene Nation, "The term Dene means a Chipewyan, Slavey, Louchoux, Dogrib, Hare, Cree or Beaver Indian person whose aboriginal lands or part of these lands were, before January 1, 1921, within the boundaries of the Northwest Territories as those boundaries were on August 29, 1982."[5] Linguistically, the term is anomalous, as it includes Cree, which is an Algonquian language, not an Athapaskan one. But politically, in bringing together all Native people residing in the NWT except for Inuvialuit (Inuit of the western Arctic), it makes perfect sense. In 1982, the term was redefined to include "descendants of the Dene"[6] – subsuming, or potentially subsuming, all Métis residing in the Northwest Territories within the time frame mentioned. Although many favoured a political and ethnic union of all Native peoples within the NWT, the politico/ethnic reality was such that a Métis population continued to flourish. Not all Dene accepted Métis as full-fledged members of the Dene Nation, and not all Métis felt totally comfortable identifying themselves as Dene.

The majority of the Métis located north of 60° lat. live in the Mackenzie Valley, which includes most of the present day Northwest Territories.[7] The majority of the largest urban communities, including Yellowknife, Hay River, Fort Smith and Fort Simpson, are located in this area. In 1999, the Northwest Territories was divided into two new territories. The eastern region became known as Nunavut, and the western section retained the name Northwest Territories, although there had been talk of naming the territory Denendeh (variously translated as "Our Land" or "the Creator's Spirit flows through this Land").[8] Nunavut is primarily home to the Canadian Inuit, who make up the majority of the population there; the western Northwest Territories is home to most of the Dene nation as well as most of the Métis who inhabited the NWT at the time of its division.

The number of Métis in the Northwest Territories is relatively small – 3,585 persons, or 8.7 per cent of the population, according to the 2006 Canadian census. The total population of the Northwest Territories itself is not large (41,055), but the Aboriginal population makes up one of the highest proportions of Aboriginal people in Canada; 50.3 per cent of the total population. The Métis make up a relatively small part of that number, but they constitute the largest enclave of Métis in the three Canadian territories. For example, in the Yukon, only 805 persons, or 2.7 per cent of the population identify as Métis.[9] In Nunavut the number who self-identify as Métis is even smaller: 130 persons or 0.4 per cent of the population.[10]

Despite their small numbers, many of the Métis of the Mackenzie Valley retain a strong and vibrant sense of their own identity and history, which they have exhibited for some time. It was strong enough to make them the first group of Métis to attract in-depth anthropological research in Richard Slobodin's pioneering work,[11] several years before similarly intensive research was undertaken in the prairies. But this sense of identity is not absolute. Many Métis feel themselves torn between identifying as Métis and identifying as Dene. This chapter is an attempt to document the struggle the Métis have made to maintain an identity separate from the Dene in the NWT, a struggle that, in some regions at least, remains active to this day.

Native Organizations

One way to examine the development of an NWT Métis identity in the twentieth century is to trace the development of the NWT Native organizations. While it is by no means a given that separate Native organizations – those representing status and non-status Indians, Métis, and so on – reflect the realities of ethnic or Aboriginal identities already in place, an examination of these organizations exposes very interesting divisions. Much of the history of Native organizations in the NWT concerns a tension between those who favoured a single organization of Métis and Dene (and in some cases the Inuvialiut) and those who supported two or three separate organizations. The three most important organizations that potentially had a Métis membership were the Committee for Original Peoples Entitlement (COPE); the Dene Nation (originally organized as the Indian Brotherhood of the NWT) and the Métis Nation, NWT (originally called the Métis and Non-Status Native Association of the NWT, then the Métis Association of the NWT).

The Committee for Original Peoples Entitlement, which began operation in 1969 and was legally incorporated in March 1970, was one of the first Native political organizations in the western Arctic.[12] Today, COPE is best known and remembered as the organization representing the Inuvialuit and for negotiating the Inuvialuit Land Rights Settlement with the federal government (the negotiations began in 1974, an agreement in principle was signed in 1978, and the final agreement was signed in 1984). Few remember that it began as an organization representing *all* concerned Natives of the area: Métis, non-status and status Indians, as well as the Inuvialiut. In some ways this was a natural way for Native people to organize in the territories. Because there were no reserves, Native peoples of all categories tended to live together in one community, and there was a fair amount of interaction between them and the non-Native population as well. This mingling was reflected in the background of many of the early Native leaders. The co-founders of COPE, Agnes Semmler and Nellie Cournoyea, had Indian, Inuvialuit, and non-Aboriginal forebears. Agnes Semmler, the first president of COPE, was a Gwich'in Métis from Peel River, and Nellie Cournoyea was the daughter of a Norwegian father and an Inuvialiut mother.[13] This mixed ancestral heritage, which was not at all unusual in the territory, is one reason why a single organization representing people with Dene, Métis, and Inuvialiut ancestry made sense. However, government pressure during the land claims negotiations resulted in COPE's changing its mandate to represent Inuvialiut only, and Sam Raddi, an Inuvialiut trapper, took over the presidency. But its early membership included representatives from all native peoples of the area. Wally Firth, Rick Hardy, and Charles Overvold, all later prominent in the Dene and/or Métis political movement, were original members of COPE. COPE was also instrumental in founding other Native organizations. Agnes Semmler and other COPE leaders helped organize the Indian Brotherhood and attended the early meetings. COPE was also instrumental in helping the nascent Métis and non-status Indian organization become established a few years later.[14]

In October of 1969, sixteen Dene chiefs formed the Indian Brotherhood of the Northwest Territories (IBNWT).[15] Its mandate was to represent the Dene, or northern Athapaskan-speaking peoples and their descendants, in their traditional territory, mainly situated in the Mackenzie River Valley. The Dene came to organizational politics relatively late (status Indian organizations such as the Indian Association of Alberta had started as early as 1939), but once they came to the table, they quickly established themselves as one of the most influential Native political organizations in Canada, revising ideas on Aboriginal rights, Aboriginal self-government, Aboriginal identity, and the idea of Aboriginal nationhood. With James Wah Shee, a Dogrib from Fort Rae as president, the organization began by responding to Department of Indian Affairs and Northern Development (DIAND) policies and proposals and attempting to develop new policies, particularly in education. However, the IBNWT was not particularly effective until it turned its attention to dealing with issues regarding Treaty 8 (signed in 1899–1900) and Treaty 11 (signed in 1921–22).

Some of the people involved in the beginnings of the Indian Brotherhood were non-status Indians or Métis (such as Agnes Semmler of COPE, Wally Firth, Charles Overvold, and others). They were pressing the Brotherhood to include all people of Dene descent, including Métis and non-treaty and non-status Indians. However, when the Brotherhood turned its attention to dealing with treaty issues, Métis and non-status were by definition excluded. This proved to be one of the reasons the Métis Association came into being: "Some of us attended the first assembly of the Indian Brotherhood, and we argued for an open membership. They said no. They didn't want to open up their membership. They wanted to organize as treaty Indians. We couldn't sell the idea of an open organization."[16] However, the membership criteria of the Brotherhood were to change in later years.

The Brotherhood took the position that Aboriginal rights in the NWT were still intact, despite the treaties, and one of its first actions was to file a caveat (or legal warning to third parties) respecting continued First Nations interests in lands described in these treaties. This stipulation led to a long and involved series of land claims negotiations, sometimes in concert with the Métis organizations. The Indian Brotherhood took a particularly radical view of Aboriginal rights as far as the Canadian government was concerned. It held that Aboriginal rights negotiations were not simply to do with land, but about the establishment of a political relationship between the Dene and the Canadian state.[17] This opinion was made explicit in 1975, when the famous "Dene Declaration" was passed unanimously at a joint General Assembly of the NWT Indian Brotherhood and the Métis and Non-Status Indian Association of the NWT in July at Fort Simpson, wherein the Dene insisted on the right to be regarded by themselves and the world as a Nation.

The Dene Declaration would prove to have many implications for all the Natives of the Mackenzie Valley, including the Métis. The next year, the Indian Brotherhood at its General Assembly in Fort Simpson, passed a resolution to admit non-status Dene into membership. In 1978, under the leadership of its new president, Georges Erasmus, the Indian Brotherhood formally changed its name to the Dene Nation and its constitution was amended to open full membership "to all those who have formally declared themselves under the Dene registry."[18]

Despite this call for one organization for all people of Dene ancestry, regardless of treaty or Indian status, there were enough people who identified as Métis for a Métis and non-status Indian organization to exist as well. The first territory-wide Métis organization for the NWT came into being in 1972, following the southern pattern of an amalgamation of locals. The organization was first called the Métis and Non-Status Native Association of the NWT, but within a few years its title was simplified to the Métis Association of the NWT (MANWT), although it continued, at least for a time, to welcome non-status Indians as members. In 1991, again following patterns to the south, where the word "Nation" began to be included in most Métis organizations (or, more likely in the case of Métis in the NWT, following the example of the Dene Nation) the association's name was changed to the Métis Nation, NWT (MNNWT).[19] Like its sister organizations in the south, the Métis Association was first set up to address specific concerns of the Métis and non-status Indians. And, like its sister organizations, it soon found itself in difficulties in pursuing the agendas of these two somewhat disparate groups. But as will be seen, the competition between the Métis Association and the Dene Nation over membership exacerbated its problems of membership far beyond those faced by its sister Métis associations to the south.

For most of its existence, the Métis Association was overshadowed by the Indian Brotherhood / Dene Nation. This imbalance was not only due to the fact that the Brotherhood / Dene Nation often claimed that the Métis Association's constituency was a subset of its own, but also due to the fact that many of the Métis Association's members themselves would have preferred to be in the Dene Nation. For much of its existence, the Dene Nation was led by Georges Erasmus, one of the most charismatic and dynamic Native leaders in Canada, who by himself had the ability to overshadow almost any other leader or organization. Second, while the two organizations often worked closely together, this often resulted in the Métis Association being eclipsed by the Dene Nation. The two organizations cooperated mainly in the area of land claims, but occasionally collaborated on other projects, such as a discussion paper regarding the division of the NWT called *Public Government for the People of the North*. In it they suggested that three territories be created instead of only two and that one of the territories be called Denendeh.[20] The Métis Association pursued several land claims negotiations together with the Dene Nation and, while that arrangement was often convenient, it also meant that media attention was concentrated on the more visible Dene Nation rather than on the Métis Association. Over the years, the two organizations were thus involved in a love-hate relationship, particularly over land claims – at times pursuing a joint settlement, at time pursuing separate ones. These strategies were complicated by conflicting responses from the federal government, which at times encouraged joint negotiations and at other times did not. This process came to a seemingly successful conclusion in 1990, when a final comprehensive agreement was agreed upon by all negotiators. The agreement included ownership of 180,000 square kilometres of land plus subsurface mineral rights to 10,000 square kilometres; hunting, fishing, and trapping rights; and a share of resource royalties. The Dene/Métis leadership were satisfied with the agreement (indeed, several negotiators still defend it to this day) and they recommended to their respective constituents that they vote to ratify the agreement. However, this was not to be. The delegates refused to ratify the agreement at the joint Métis and Dene assembly in 1990, which broke into factions. A major bone of contention was the status of Treaties 8 and 11. The Akaitcho Dene First Nations (Fort Resolution, Lutsel K'e, Ndilo, and Dettah) refused to abandon their treaty rights and announced their intention to seek their own regional land claim. This decision put an end to the joint Dene/Métis negotiations, at least on the territorial level.

At that point the federal government, bowing to the reality of the ethnic and tribal divisions in the territory, decided to abandon the goal of a comprehensive land claim, and instead agreed to pursue several smaller land claims on a region-by-region basis. This was a blow to both organizations, but it hit the Métis Association particularly hard. While many of the five regional claims involved the Métis as well as the Dene, MNNWT, as the territorial organization, had only a small role to play in any of these claims. In most cases, regional Métis organizations such as the South Slave Métis Tribal Council[21] sprang up to deal with the particular claims, making MNNWT redundant there as well.

MNNWT began to slip into irrelevance and finally closed its doors in 2001. Its major weakness – tension between Métis, non-status Indians, and people who identified as Métis but were members of a treaty – led to the demise of the organization. Two separate incidents precipitated this end. First, a proposed change to the constitution regarding membership eligibility was narrowly voted in, denying membership to individuals who had taken Indian status under Bill C-31. MNNWT had long accepted "C-31s," as they are known and, in fact, this had been a bone of contention between it and the Métis National Council for years; so this change in membership eligibility was a profound one. Second, a motion was put forward to deny treaty members the right to sit on the board of directors. The confrontation was mainly between members from the South Slave region, who supported the amendments, and those from the other eleven communities in the Métis Nation. The latter representatives eventually forced the resignation of George Morin as president in December 2000.[22] His replacement resigned for health reasons shortly afterward. Finally, on Wednesday, 7 March 2001, after twenty-seven years of service, the Métis Nation of the Northwest Territories ceased operations when the board of directors was unable to fill the group's executive positions. All its assets were handed over to the commissioner of the Northwest Territories.[23]

Gerald Morin, president of the Métis National Council (not to be confused with George Morin, president of the MNNWT) suggested that the collapse of the organization was due to its lack of a fully defined constituency: "Its membership was comprised of Métis people, and non-status and status Indians, so I wasn't surprised. Any organization that's made up of Métis and First Nations is not likely going to work out anyway."[24] Morin went on to state that he hoped there would be a new organization strictly representing Métis that the MNC could deal with more easily. Instead, several regionally based organizations – with somewhat competing ideas of Métis identity, not always consistent with MNC definitions – stepped up to take MNNWT's place.

Although MNNWT no longer functions as an umbrella organization, many of its locals are still active and still identify under their old local identification. For example, the Fort Simpson Métis Council, part of Dehcho First Nations, still identifies itself through its old MNNWT local number, 52. Some locals have become part of regional associations, or at least share membership. For example, the president of the North Slave Métis Alliance (NSMA) has also served concurrently as president of the Yellowknife Métis Nation Local 66 (which also has retained its old MNNWT local number).

The several regionally based organizations that now represent Métis in the NWT came about in various ways, but most had their beginnings in the regional land claims negotiations that the federal government initiated after the collapse of the joint Dene/Métis Comprehensive claim in 1990. Two of these claims have been settled with Métis participation. In 1992, the Gwich'in Dene/Métis settled their land claims, and although the Métis are not identified as such in the claim, they are recognized as beneficiaries. In contrast, distinct Métis political organizations were part of the Dehcho process. In July 1993, the Sahtu Dene and Métis voted to approve the Sahtu Dene and Métis Comprehensive Land Claim Agreement; 85 per cent of the Dene who voted approved, as did 99 per cent of the Métis.[25]

As of 2009, the Dehcho First Nations (sometimes spelled Deh Cho), which represents ten band councils and three Métis locals, was still negotiating a land, resource, and self-government agreement with the Government of the Northwest Territories (GNWT) and the federal government.[26] According to their own literature, the Dehcho Métis see themselves as part of the Dehcho First Nations. They are represented by three Métis locals: Fort Providence, Fort Simpson, and Fort Liard. The Dehcho Métis councils are limited purpose organizations, created to represent the interests of the Métis in the land, resource, and self-government agreement process. For example, the Fort Providence Métis Council, which represents the interests of the indigenous Métis/Dene descendants of the Fort Providence area, works in concert with the Deh Gah Gotie Dene Council. The organization has an elected executive and board of directors. In addition to representing the interests of the Fort Providence Métis in the land claims process, the council also undertakes to preserve and promote the history and culture of the Métis people of the area.

However, not all of the regional land claims negotiations in the NWT have included the Métis. The Tlicho land claim is an example. Métis from several communities in the area formed the North Slave Métis Alliance in 1996 in hopes of taking part in the negotiations for a land and resources agreement in the North Slave Region and the Treaty 11 Area.[27] However, the NSMA was excluded from the process. It had been offered a seat at the Tlicho land claims and self-government negotiating table in 1997, but this offer was withdrawn when the NSMA initiated a lawsuit to halt the Dogrib Treaty 11 land claim process.[28] The lawsuit was subsequently dropped when a new administration took over the NSMA, but by that time the Tlicho claim had been completed without Métis participation. It is the position of the NSMA that despite the settlement of the Tlicho claim, the North Slave Métis claim remains outstanding. The Tlicho settlement contains a clause that states that no Aboriginal or treaty rights of any people other than the Tlicho are affected.[29] But the NSMA claim covers more than the Tlicho territory. The disputed area covers the entire Tlicho Settlement Area, part of the

Sahtu and Nunavut Settlement areas, as well as part of the Akaitcho and Dehcho claim areas.[30]

The South Slave region is another matter. There, the Treaty 8 Dene, the Akaitcho Dene First Nations, decided to pursue a Treaty Land Entitlement process rather than a comprehensive claim. Since this process excluded Métis or non-status Dene who were not covered by Treaty 8, they were left without a negotiation process to address their issues. The South Slave Métis Tribal Council was set up to negotiate a separate claim. In August 1996, the Government of Canada, the South Slave Métis Tribal Council and the Government of the Northwest Territories signed a framework agreement to begin negotiations on land claims and self-government. In July of 2002, seventeen months after the Métis Nation, NWT, shut its doors, the South Slave Métis Tribal Council changed its name to the Northwest Territory Métis Nation (NWTMN). Perhaps a justification for this all-embracing name can be found in the fact that, as one of its founders George Kurszewski points out, the Métis of South Slave comprise the majority of the Métis in the Mackenzie Valley, and the NWTMN is the only Métis organization in Canada that is engaged in land and self-government negotiations.[31] Like the other regional organizations, the NWTMN is interested in more than negotiating claims. It wants to promote and retain a Métis heritage as well.

Southern Influences on Native Organizations in the Northwest Territories

With the possible exception of COPE (Committee for Original Peoples Entitlement) it cannot be said that any of the Native political organizations in the NWT simply arose on its own, in response to local or territorial needs. If it had, it most likely would have followed the example of COPE, and kept a much more inclusive membership base. The existence of separate Métis, non-status, and status organizations, and the relations between them, indicate that these organizations originated at least partially in response to outside pressures as well as local ones. Some of the outside pressures included non-governmental organizations (NGOs), government organizations, and Native organizations that imposed their own ideas about the nature of Native identity. Some examples are the Company of Young Canadians (CYC); the Canadian Association in Support of Native Peoples (CASNP), earlier known as the Indian-Eskimo Association of Canada (IEA); and national and provincial

Native political organizations, particularly the Native Council of Canada and the National Indian Brotherhood. While all of these organizations helped kick-start Native political activity in the form of separate organizations, the Canadian federal government was particularly influential, through its Core Funding Program from the secretary of state and other monies from Indian Affairs. It favoured separate Métis and First Nations organizations, although not always in a consistent manner.

The IEA was originally a non-Native organization established in 1957 under the name National Commission on the Canadian Indian, but it soon was reformulated to include both Aboriginal and non-Aboriginal peoples. It was incorporated in 1960 as the Indian-Eskimo Association. The IEA had several functions, which included fund-raising, organizing workshops to discuss Native housing, community and economic development, providing advice and support in legal matters, and, perhaps most important for this analysis, encouraging Native leaders to form organizations. The IEA was divided into several provincial and regional divisions, including the NWT.[32] In 1972, the name was changed to the Canadian Association in Support of Native Peoples (CASNP). One of the IEA's most enduring contributions was the first comprehensive study of legal issues regarding Aboriginal rights in Canada, the groundbreaking *Native Rights in Canada* by Peter Cumming and Neil Mickenberg, published in 1972.[33]

To achieve its goal of encouraging the growth of Native political organizations in the western NWT the IEA hired Wally Firth and Harry Leishman as executive secretaries. Their specific duties were to help Native people organize. The IEA provided an airplane with floats, and Wally Firth was hired as the pilot. Firth, Leishman, and others visited various communities in the Mackenzie Valley to encourage organization of locals. One of the first was the Thebacha Indian Association (Fort Smith), formed in 1969. According to Rick Hardy, past president of MNNWT, it was Wally Firth, and Agnes Semmler (first president of COPE) who were instrumental in organizing the Indian Brotherhood of the NWT.[34] They and several others, such as Bob Overvold, envisioned the Brotherhood as representing all the Dene descendants of the area. However, at the founding meeting of the Brotherhood, held in 1970, it was decided that only treaty Dene would be represented, so people like Overvold, Firth, and Semmler were denied membership in the organization they helped to create. This lack of a mechanism to address Métis concerns eventually led to the formation of the Métis organization in 1972.

Another early influence from the south came in the form of the Company of Young Canadians. The CYC was created by Lester Pearson's federal government in 1966 as an independent Crown corporation to provide a structure for unemployed or underemployed Canadian youth to do volunteer work. Volunteers were given minimal training in social animation and community development techniques. They received a monthly living allowance plus an additional honorarium of $50 per month which was to be paid at the end of two years' satisfactory service. In 1968, CYC had 225 volunteers engaged in various projects throughout Canada. By 1970, the project was, to all intents and purposes, a dead issue, plagued by bad press and generally perceived as a boondoggle with ill-defined goals and poorly trained volunteers. But CYC provided an important impetus for Native political organizations in many parts of Canada, including Ontario and Alberta.[35] It had a particularly influential role to play in the NWT. Many influential Native leaders in the NWT got their start with CYC, including James Wah Shee and Georges Erasmus. It also included many non-Native people such as Peter Puxley, who later became a research advisor to the IBNWT.

While NGOs like CYC and CASNP were instrumental in encouraging early political activism, the influence of the federal government itself should not be underestimated. The most obvious and significant manifestation was the funds that were coming from the government – from the Core Funding Program of the secretary of state, and from separate funds from DIAND. However, not only did these funding programs foster the beginning of political activism in the NWT, but they also fostered the formation of separate Métis and Dene organizations. Charles Overvold, former president of MANWT, is one of many early organizers to voice his frustration at how the funding requirements were structured to encourage the formation of separate Métis and Dene organizations:

> We wanted to stick together and tried to get organized as one group for the whole Northwest Territories – the Dene, Métis and Inuit. We wanted to try and stick together. We weren't too interested in doing what they were doing down south, where they were splitting up, and the Métis were organizing separately – the Dene or the treaty Indians. We didn't have any Indian reserves up here so we thought, well, we all grew up here in the same communities, why shouldn't we just all go together? We thought we'd be stronger politically if we stuck together, but we couldn't do it

> because of the federal funding. The funding criteria were such that we had to get funding to organize as Métis only and the treaty had to get funding just to organize as treaty Indians.[36]

However, the federal government was by no means consistent in its insistence on separate organizations. Over the years it sent conflicting and frustrating messages to the organizations. At times it forced them to develop as separate entities, and at other times demanded that the Dene and Métis organizations work together. For example, in 1973, the Indian Brotherhood and the Métis Association agreed to seek a single Aboriginal rights settlement on behalf of all descendants of the Dene. This joint action was scuttled when Ottawa demanded that each group negotiate separately.[37] Later, in 1977, when the Indian Brotherhood and the Métis Association presented separate claims, the federal government did an about-face, demanding that the two associations settle their differences and present a single claim. In order to bend the organizations to the government's will, DIAND Minister Hugh Faulkner cut off funding to both – a cut that was to last until April 1980.[38]

The Berger Inquiry also had a profound effect on organizations. The Canadian Parliament established the Berger Inquiry on 21 March 1974 to review plans to build an oil and gas pipeline down the Mackenzie Valley. This inquiry affected the organizations in two ways. First, it mobilized individual Aboriginal people to make presentations, which raised the political consciousness of many people in the NWT. Second, it provided funding to all the organizations to help them make their presentations. At a time when most funding was limited to Core Funding from the secretary of state and some monies being advanced from Indian Affairs for land claims negotiations, the funds of the Berger Inquiry were a substantial supplement.

Both the Métis organization and the Indian Brotherhood employed a similar strategy of helping Native elders to testify before the Inquiry by preparing them to tell their stories, to explain their understanding of the history of the treaties, and to describe the philosophy behind traditional land use. Both organizations used inquiry funds to act as advance parties , preparing the communities for the visit and identifying people who should stand up and speak and give evidence.

But the inquiry also helped drive a wedge between the two organizations. The leadership of the Dene and Métis disagreed on the Mackenzie Valley Pipeline. The leadership of the Métis Association was in favour of it, while the Brotherhood was completely opposed. Richard Hardy, who was president of MANWT at the time, states:

> We were in an ongoing battle with the Indian Brotherhood, at the time the Berger Inquiry was in full swing. The Indian Brotherhood was just adamantly opposed; there was no way in the world that they would ever agree to the construction of a gas pipeline. It wasn't something that you could sit down and discuss terms and conditions with them. It was just "no." Our position was that the pipeline *should* be built. Our vision of the future was in terms of a modern cash economy, that's the way the world was going. We were saying, in order to do that, we have to have projects like the pipeline. But before they could build it the claims had to be settled.[39]

The opposition was quite heated; Hardy states that on at least one occasion, he was physically assaulted during discussions over the issue. It drove other activists, such as George Kurszewski, who had been working with the Métis Association, to join the Indian Brotherhood.[40] The issue was also clouded by attitudes in the south. There, sentiment was so opposed to the pipeline that any pro-pipeline sentiment, especially that coming from a Native organization, was almost completely buried.[41]

Pressure to form separate Native associations in the NWT was also building from the newly minted or newly rejuvenated national and provincial Native political organizations, particularly Métis ones. Charles Overvold recalls that in the early years of formation, in addition to the help from the IEA and CASNP, Métis leaders received considerable help from the Native Council of Canada (NCC) which was already in existence. Overvold recalls Harry Daniels, president of the NCC, travelling to the NWT to encourage a territorial Métis organization. Other leaders such as Gary Bohnet recall visits from Yvon Dumont and from Tony Belcourt, both of whom were with NCC at the time.[42] George Kurszewski mentions Jim Sinclair, who would have been with the Association of Métis and Non-Status Indians (AMNSIS) at the time, as an early influence.[43]

In 1971 Harry Daniels invited fifteen Métis leaders from the Mackenzie Valley to attend the National Assembly of the NCC, even though there was no formal Métis organization in the NWT as yet. The NCC was actively encouraging the establishment of Métis and non-status organizations in all parts of Canada and was helping local organizations to apply for Core Funding from the secretary of state. But there was no money available to bring the early leaders together. Charles Overvold recalls that with the help of Nellie Cournoyea they borrowed $5,000 from COPE, and he and several other Métis leaders went to the NCC's National Assembly in Ottawa as a first step in getting organized: "All we had was this $5,000, so we couldn't even bring people together in Yellowknife and organize ourselves first and then go down. What we did was go straight down to Ottawa. We got together in a small hotel room there, and formed our first organization for the North West Territories Métis. There were 15 of us from around the North; I remember there was Freddie Beaulieu, there was myself, Dave McNabb, and several others."[44] When they returned from the assembly, they organized as the Métis and Non-Status Native Association of the NWT and the organization was incorporated in 1972. They opened a small office in Hay River. Dave McNabb was the first president and Charles Overvold was vice-president. The structure of the organization followed that of similar groups in the south: a federation of locals. Rick Hardy thinks they used the Métis Association of Alberta's structure as a model, which he felt was inherited from union structure.[45] They began to establish more locals throughout the area; Fort Smith was the first local formed, Fort Resolution the next.

It is interesting that the organization first started up because of pressures from outside the NWT. In Hardy's words, "there were no real burning issues that precipitated the formation of the Métis and Non-Status Native Association."[46] It may well have been formed simply as a reaction to the fact that Métis and non-status organizations were springing up in the rest of Canada, and from active encouragement from the IEA, CASNP, and CYC. The formation of the Indian Brotherhood was similarly influenced from the outside, through lobbying by COPE, CASNP, and CYC.

One of the reasons that Hardy felt there wasn't any real need to organize in the period when the Indian Brotherhood and the Métis and non-status organizations came into being was that the Métis and non-status and treaty Indians all enjoyed basically the same Aboriginal rights, because of the system of general hunting licences. The NWT had introduced a general hunting licence in the 1950s, which stated that anyone who was trapping for a living in 1953 and their descendants were entitled to a general hunting licence. All the Dene and Métis people in the territories were included in that group, so there was no real need for them to press for Aboriginal rights at the time. It also explains why there was not much need for separate Métis and Dene organizations.

There was little grass-roots involvement in Métis, Inuvialiut, or Dene organizations until the issue of land claims and Aboriginal rights began to develop in the mid-1970s. In the beginning, the organizations, including the Métis Association, were driven by welfare programs, housing, alcohol education, and so on. It was not until land claims and self-government became an issue that the prominent leaders of the various Native groups became active.

Métis Identity

As in other parts of Canada, the concepts of who would identify as Métis as well as when and why they would choose to do so underwent radical change in the Northwest Territories in the 1970s. The change was mostly orchestrated by activity in the political arena, as various Native organizations began staking out territory, defining constituencies, and redefining what it meant to be Native. But this process took its own direction in the NWT, as the organizations, particularly the Indian Brotherhood / Dene Nation, began to question basic government definitions and conceptions of Nativeness, such as status and treaty, that often went unchallenged in other parts of Canada. This in turn meant that the rationale for separate Métis and non-status Indian organizations was often hotly debated, as the Indian Brotherhood / Dene Nation was far more accommodating towards non-status Indians and Métis than were First Nations organizations to the south and, in fact, often aggressively pursued their membership. The Indian Brotherhood / Dene Nation put considerable pressure put on individuals to cast aside their identification as Métis, non-status Indians, or non-treaty Indians and to accept the all-encompassing designation as Dene. But being pressured to accept an identity as either Dene or Métis did not necessarily simplify matters for everyone or make the choice an easy one. Closer examination reveals that there was as much anxiety and concern over identity in the territories as there was elsewhere in Canada. Who was a Métis? Who was a half-breed? Who was a Dene? What was a non-status Indian and where did he or she belong? Were you born a Métis or could you become a Métis through marriage? These questions plagued the beginnings of Native political organization and the development of a Métis identity in the NWT.

The claims of Native activists within the Indian Brotherhood that there was only one nation of Native people in the Mackenzie Valley – the Dene Nation – was something of an oversimplification, made for political and ideological reasons rather than for any ethnographically defensible ones. Many Métis continued to stress that they had both a Native and a non-Native background, or that they had a single identity as Métis, and that they formed a separate community, regardless of what political gains could be made by declaring themselves Dene. This separate community had been evident long before political organizations began to form in the Mackenzie Valley. In the early 1960s, Slobodin identified a separate "Red River" Métis (his terminology) community in the southern Mackenzie District and noted that "old traditions of Metis nationality and of the insurrections retain a vitality surprising to this observer."[47] He described their cultural and linguistic roots in some detail: "The original Indian-European unions in the genealogies of southern Mackenzie District Metis are as a rule quite remote, dating in many cases from a century ago or more. The Metis here are of French and of Roman Catholic traditions, although some of the old families bear Scottish names, and some families are no longer Catholic. 'Country French' as well as various trade jargons and Indian languages, have until very recently been the preferred modes of speech."[48]

He identifies Fort Simpson as the approximate northern limit of territory occupied by Métis proper and contrasts this "Red River" population with what he terms the "northern Métis":

> The people of "mixed" ancestry in the northern or lower Mackenzie drainage do not share these traditions or characteristics. The very term "Metis" is little known and is seldom applied. The original Indian- or Eskimo-European unions in very few cases date back as far as a century. Non-aboriginal ancestry is much more varied than it is for the southern Metis, including a noticeable minority of non-European (Polynesian, Micronesian, American and African Negro). However, the non-aboriginal nationality most heavily represented in northern Mackenzie genealogies is Scottish.[49]

These "northern Metis" were most likely the ones who would later choose to identify as Dene rather than Métis when the choice was offered to them.

Slobodin also notes: "It is interesting that Red River Metis not uncommonly refer to themselves as 'breed' and 'half-breed' without apparent strain or pain."[50] This observation, based on interviews and fieldwork carried out in 1963, still held sway in the NWT at least into the 1970s. Rick Hardy, past president of MANWT and one of the staunchest supporters of a separate Métis identity in the NWT, stressed both the pride in his heritage and his comfort with the term "half-breed": "We knew we were a distinct people, but the word 'Métis' wasn't used that much. Our primary term was 'half-breed.' It was used in a different context from what ... was used in the prairies. In the prairies, you know, you call somebody a half-breed, it's kind of pejorative. Up here, it's something that was used with a lot of pride. I'm a half-breed."[51] Of course, changing opinions and attitudes towards the term meant that it would eventually drop out and be replaced by "Métis" (see chapter 13). But the mere existence of a group of readily identifiable Métis did not make the ability to defend this identity or the success of a Métis-specific political organization a foregone conclusion, as became evident after the formation of the Métis and Non-Status Native Association in 1972.

The Métis Association and the Question of Métis Identity

The two strands of mixed-blood populations noted by Slobodin – those Métis who could claim cultural and ancestral links to Red River and whose native ancestry was mostly Cree vs. the local or indigenous Métis whose links were mainly with the Dene – caused some difficulties in terms of creating a Métis organization. The "Red River" Métis made up too small a minority to form an effective organization on their own. Only by combining with the "northern" Métis could an effective organization be formed. But this left a lot of their members open to being wooed by the Indian Brotherhood / Dene Nation, once it opened its doors to all people of Dene descent regardless of status or treaty membership. This attempt at amalgamating two very different groups may well have sowed the seed for the Métis Association's eventual dissolution in 2001. At that time, the Métis organizations in the south faced a similar problem of having a mismatched membership base, usually an amalgamation of Métis and non-status Indians. But they were able to reformulate their membership and purge non-status Indians because the Métis population in the south was large enough to continue effective organizations on their own. The same may not have been true for the NWT.

There was considerable anxiety demonstrated over identity in the early days of MANWT's operations. As was common among Métis and non-status Indian organizations in the 1970s in other parts of Canada, the members of MANWT struggled with the ideas of who was a Métis and who was eligible to join the organization. Was there a difference between Métis and non-status Indians? Were spouses and/or treaty members eligible? These issues formed one of the major topics for discussion during the MANWT 3rd Annual General Assembly, held at Fort Simpson in August of 1975. The Métis Association's constitution had been amended the year previously, to the effect that non-Native spouses of Métis were eligible to become only associate (i.e., non-voting) members. But several members at the 3rd General Assembly objected, pointing out that "a White woman married to an Indian becomes an Indian automatically" (this was before Bill C-31), so logically, a Euro-Canadian woman marrying a Métis should also become a Métis.[52] It was also pointed out that by marrying a Métis, a non-Native woman often faced rejection from her own people. If she was then rejected by the Métis, she would become "a person without a country."[53] Rick Hardy, who was president of MANWT at the time, agreed, and he used his own family situation to illustrate. He felt that his father, who was non-Native, should be entitled to be called a Métis as well, because "his mind is as Metis."[54] Other people felt that behaviour and commitment to the Métis community was as relevant to being Métis as was bloodline.[55]

As a result of this discussion, the delegates voted that "the by-laws of the constitution of the Metis Association of the NWT be amended to read 'all persons of Indian descent who are not registered Indians *and their spouses* shall be eligible for membership in the association.'"[56] The motion passed, although it was rescinded before the next General Assembly.[57] Nevertheless, this decision illustrates that as late as 1975 and 1976, there still was much confusion over who should be considered Métis. Questions such as "Should a White woman marrying a Métis automatically become a Métis?" were common and continued at the next year's assembly. An important point is that the issue was considered to be separate from land claims; an individual might be considered a Métis through marriage, for example, but this status in itself would not qualify him or her for any benefits accruing to a land claims settlement.

The issue of whether being a member of a treaty or having Indian status should prevent someone from joining the Métis Association, or being considered a Métis, was another question that plagued the association in its early days. At the 4th Annual General Assembly, held in 1976, several people took issue with the fact that treaty members were allowed to be members of the Métis Association.[58] One reason for this opposition that was often expressed (and remains a comment often heard by Métis people in other parts of Canada as well as the NWT) was that treaty people "had their way paid for them" by the government, and that Métis, by contrast, "have always paid their own way."[59] "We are two different and separate entities socially, politically and culturally. The Metis pay their own way, all the way."[60] But allowing treaty people to be part of the association was defended by others on the basis that "there are some Treaty people who are Half-breeds and who identify as Half-breeds but they're Treaty and they're not allowed to participate in our organization the way it's drawn up right now."[61] In other words, some felt being Métis was a cultural or racial trait, unaffected by whether or not one was a member of a Treaty.

The confusion over who was or was not a Métis is illustrated by the fact that many delegates suggested that non-status Indians should be recognized as Métis. Others suggested that all racial and cultural backgrounds were irrelevant, as long as that person was living the life of a Métis and was part of the Métis community: "Let's decide that. To unite the Metis and Non-Status Indians; the Non-Status people ... I believe that it should be included [in the constitution] that any Indian person or White person, for that matter a Negro person or Japanese person who is living under the culture and brought up with the Metis people is a Metis. If I marry a White woman or an Indian woman and she sleeps in my bed, she sleeps in a Metis bed. She's not sleeping in an Indian bed – that's my house and that's where it's at."[62] This delegate did not think what Native background a Métis held was important: "These kids don't know whether they are Cree, Slavey or what they are. And they don't care ... We're Metis people. We are the same. Forget all the other stuff. You're a Metis or you're not ... There's no difference between a Metis whether he's a Cree, Slavey, Dogrib or what he is. He's either a Metis or he's nothing. Period, it's just simple as that."[63]

There was still much confusion over whether one could become a Métis through marriage or loss of Treaty or Indian status. Again, this uncertainty was expressed mostly through discussions on who could become a voting member of the association, but it still indicates some confusion at the time over what made a person a Métis. Was it lifestyle? Ancestry? Poverty? Culture? All of these definitions were suggested. Many people took the view that if a non-Native married a Métis they became Métis, but there was little talk of a Métis identity per se; the questions seemed to be concerned more with legal definitions of status, treaty, and non-status. However, as we saw above, there was some notion of a cultural or ethnic identity as Métis, since it was suggested on more than one occasion that someone might happen to have treaty, but still be a true Métis – or a "Breed" (the term was still being used in 1976).[64] Some suggested that even full-blooded Indians who weren't treaty be allowed to participate in the organization."[65] The final compromise (at least for that year) was to define active membership as "all persons who are 16 years of age or older, who are resident in the N.W.T., and who are of Indian descent, but are not registered Indians under the Indian Act."[66] Note that in this definition no mention is made of any non-Aboriginal heritage.

Another indication of MANWT's concern with a need to define a Métis identity was the publication of *Our Metis Heritage*, a pictorial treatment of the Métis of the NWT, published by MANWT in 1976.[67] The project was originally conceived to create a history of the Métis of the NWT and to determine who would be eligible for benefits under any forthcoming land claims settlement.[68] The resulting volume was quite different from that originally planned, and is as interesting for what it does not say about Métis identity as what it does say. There is minimal analysis or discussion of what makes someone a Métis. Nor is there any discussion of the history of the Métis population in the NWT. The book is mainly a collection of historic and contemporary photos and short biographies of elders and local people. What little analysis there is comes from one-paragraph lead-ins to the various sections of the book: Metis and the Trapline, Metis and Trading Companies, and so on. This lack of analysis may have been the result of its being Volume 1 of a projected two-volume set. Volume 2 was never completed, partly because of the resignation of its editor, Joanne Overvold, over her disagreement with some of MANWT's pro-development policies.[69] But it may also have been a result of her own personal view of what it meant to be Métis and of the relationship between Métis and Dene. In an interview in 1996 she stated: "When I first heard people talking about organizing as Métis people, and not as native people, I remember feeling a little bit confused about that, based on my experience in Fort Providence, where people really didn't distinguish between Dene and Métis and there [were] very close ties."[70] By the time she resigned from MANWT, she saw Métis identity as mostly divisive: "It was the first time I had experienced or seen Métis nationalism presented in a negative way. My experience had been before that, that the differences were minimal, the ability to relate to Dene ancestry was very strong, and our understanding of our common history and common future was clear. It was the first sort of real time that there was any attempt, conscious, deliberate attempt, to break ties and deny that commonality, and to emphasize the differences and to focus on those differences as a basis of, or justifying, positions or providing a certain direction."[71] Nevertheless, *Our Metis Heritage* is the earliest, and remains one of the few, publications by native people themselves that takes as its topic Métis identity in the NWT.

Dene Nation vs. Métis Nation: Organizational Struggles and Identity

The issue of Métis identity is brought into particular focus by the rivalry between Indian Brotherhood / Dene Nation and MANWT over membership. Once the Brotherhood had abandoned its strategy to represent treaty Indians only and recognized non-status and non-treaty individuals who had Dene ancestry, there was a considerable overlap in potential members of the two organizations. There was also considerable pressure for the two organizations to amalgamate – usually under the banner of the Brotherhood or the Dene Nation. The Dene Nation's argument for this strategy – that uniting all NWT people of Indian heritage would make for a stronger political force – was hard to refute. The only real argument for MANWT's continued existence was the position that the Métis formed a distinct cultural, social, and political unit, and that many of its members did not identify as Dene. But even this position was hard to defend at times as the two organizations began to work closely together.

For a time, there was an almost total permeability of borders between the Métis Association and the Brotherhood / Dene Nation, although it was shortly to be sundered over different attitudes regarding development and the Mackenzie Valley Pipeline. As Joanne Overvold, the editor of *Our Metis Heritage*, recalls:

> At that stage, Rick Hardy was president, and there was a very close working relationship between the Indian Brotherhood and the Métis Association. They sort of divided the work, so that anyone working in one organization was working on behalf of all of us, and vice versa. I happened to be working under the Métis Association on a history project, and it was there at the end of that project, when the big split occurred around the question of support for the Mackenzie Valley pipeline. I remember that it came as a real shock to me, personally, and I took steps to finish the project so that I could leave the Association. By the time I finished the project it was really intense.[72]

She was not the only researcher or politician who worked for both organizations or switched sides over the pipeline issue. James Wah Shee, one-time president of the Indian Brotherhood, worked for MANWT as land claims researcher after his presidency. Bob Overvold, who was at one time the executive director of MANWT, was later named chief negotiator for both organizations during the negotiation of the Dene-Métis Comprehensive Claim.

Some leaders, like George Kurszewski, three-time president of the Fort Smith Métis local and the founding father of the South Slave Métis Tribal Council (now operating as the NWT Métis Nation) felt very strongly that the Dene and Métis should form one organization; that the family ties between so-called Métis and Dene (which, in the political definition being developed by the Dene Nation, included Cree) precluded the need for a separate organization. Around 1975, just after the Mackenzie Valley Pipeline Inquiry, several young activists led by Kurszewski started a movement called the United Native Families, when Kurszewski was president of the Fort Smith Métis Local and a member of the MANWT Land Claims Committee. The United Native Families was created to overcome the pressures that were dividing the Native community and unite the two major organizations by focusing on the family ties between the Native populations in the Mackenzie Valley.

> I was a young president here in the Métis capital (Fort Smith), and I proposed a movement of young people in the Mackenzie Valley. We didn't really have any problems about being friends and seeing ourselves as brothers, so to speak, even though we were treaty Indian, non-status, and Métis. It was a youthful movement that proposed to unite the two organizations. I felt that we should work together. The history of my own family gave me some resolve on this. I had a grandmother who was treaty Indian; she lost her status by marrying a Métis man. My uncles were treaty Indians, so there was a mixture of treaty Indians, non-status, and Métis in my own family. So I saw that really, we don't have all that much difference. We have more in common, so we should work together and we would be stronger with a united front. It was a very good concept, I believe, that was well intentioned by young people trying to keep their families united.[73]

Kurszewski and others who pushed for a joint organization were not denying the existence of the Métis or a legitimate Métis identity, but stressed that this joint organization would be strictly political and would not be based on culture or identity. They claimed that they all still "knew who they were."

That organization, centred in Fort Smith, lasted about a year, but, according to Kurszewski, it posed a threat to the leadership of the Métis Association, and he was removed as president of the Fort Smith local by Rick Hardy, president of MANWT. At that time, Kurszewski and several others who agreed with his position moved over to the Indian Brotherhood, which had changed its constitution to accept Métis and non-status members.

However, most of the pressure to form one organization came from the Dene. This was particularly evident when Georges Erasmus was president of the Dene Nation / Indian Brotherhood. Erasmus, later to become Grand Chief of the Assembly of First Nations and who later headed the Royal Commission on Aboriginal Peoples, had long lobbied for both groups to form one organization. As Rick Hardy put it: "Georges was of the view *that there was no such thing as Métis people, that we were all Indians,* and that we should fold up the Métis Association and all join the Dene Nation."[74] This point of view is particularly interesting, considering that Erasmus could have identified as Métis as easily as Dene.[75]

Yet this attitude was consistent with the Dene Nation's willingness to defy government classifications of status and non-status. For several years, the organization tinkered with its criteria for membership, first allowing non-status Dene into its fold and later allowing Métis as well. The process began in 1976, when the Indian Brotherhood passed an "extraordinary resolution" at its General Assembly in Fort Simpson to admit non-status Indian Dene into membership. Two years later, when the name of the organization was changed from the National Indian Brotherhood of the NWT to "Dene Nation" (1978), the constitution was amended to extend membership "to all those who have formally declared themselves under the Dene Registry." This amendment potentially included anyone of Native descent, status or non-status, Métis, and so on, and it was made even clearer in 1982, when "Dene" was redefined in such a way as to "make all people of Dene descent feel part of the Dene Nation."[76] The term "Descendant of the Dene" included any person who was "a lineal (blood) descendant of a person described (as Dene) whether Treaty, non-Treaty, or Metis." The Dene Nation constitution included Métis "if they were descended from the Dene, or if they (or their parents or grandparents) lived north of the 60th parallel and received scrip."[77]

The 1976 resolution proved to be a particularly significant incident in the history of the two organizations. After the Brotherhood passed its resolution, the MANWT board of directors met in Inuvik to discuss whether or not the Métis Association should dissolve and have all its members join with the Indian Brotherhood, forming one large Dene organization.[78] Many people in both the Indian Brotherhood and the Métis Association were in favour of the merger, but many were not. In addition to the membership issue was the question of whether or not the two organizations should work on a joint land claims document with the federal government. A Special Assembly of MANWT was held in July 1976 for the purpose of determining whether the Métis Association should be dissolved and a new Dene organization in which all persons of Indian descent could join should be incorporated.[79]

Several members of MANWT were in favour of the resolution, including George Kurszewski, whose name had already become publicly associated with the move towards a single organization. Those in favour saw it as a sign of unity among all Native people in the region. They also tended to portray those wishing to preserve a Métis organization as mere political opportunists, more concerned with maintaining their own power base than in pursuing common goals in the interests of all Native people. In an attempt to control public perception, the board of directors of MANWT issued a press release on 26 June 1976, which stated that the extraordinary resolution was not about unity or non-unity, but rather "how best to achieve the legitimate aspirations of the Metis and Non-Status people of the N.W.T." It was felt that this goal was to be achieved by "continuing the Metis Association in its present form and with its present policy of seeking recognition of the Aboriginal rights of the Metis and Non-Status people, in cooperation with the Indian Brotherhood of the N.W.T."[80] The resolution to dissolve MANWT was defeated unanimously at the Special Assembly. A separate motion was passed, also unanimously, that the association remain as the Métis Association of the NWT.[81] At this time George Kurszewski was removed from his position as president of the Fort Smith Métis local.[82]

The issue of whether or not the two organizations could work together on a joint land claims was also coloured by the question of identity. In August 1976, both were discussing approaches to be taken on land claims. The executives agreed to meet at Camp Antler, forty miles north of Yellowknife, to decide how the Indian people and the

Métis people could work together on a joint land claims proposal. Rick Hardy, as president of MANWT, took the position that Métis must be recognized as a distinct group of people, not Indians, not Euro-Canadian. If the Métis Association was to work with the Indian Brotherhood, this basic fact had to be acknowledged and accepted. As far as the Métis Association's taking part in the forthcoming land claims proposal, his position was that if the Métis were to take part, they must have 50 per cent input and the proposal must be a Dene/Métis submission.[83]

At Camp Antler, the Indian chiefs and the Métis board of directors agreed that they would sign a memorandum of agreement setting out the terms that had been agreed on to this point in the meeting. According to Hardy, the board of directors of MANWT wrote up and signed what they understood to be the memorandum of agreement the two sides had approved. The document was presented to Georges Erasmus in person at the MANWT offices. Erasmus took it back to the Brotherhood, but returned later with a substantially different document. The major change involved replacing the phrase "Dene/Metis" with "Dene" alone. There were other changes as well, revealing some substantial differences between the two organizations in terms of what constituted a Native person. It also represented another step in the campaign by Georges Erasmus and the Brotherhood to subsume the Métis Association and all its members into the Indian Brotherhood. Erasmus's position on Métis identity was succinctly stated in the letter that accompanied the Brotherhood's version of the Camp Antler agreement:

> The basis for proposed Dene/Metis government contained in the Metis Association draft would give support to that interpretation of history which suggests there are two native nations in the Mackenzie Valley – one Dene and the other Metis. We do not accept this interpretation. We believe there is only one nation of people – the Dene Nation – which includes all those descendants of the original people of this region, no matter whether they have been referred to as Status, Non-status or Metis by the Europeans. We believe we are all Dene and that to admit otherwise will weaken our collective interest and strengthen the interests of those who wish to ignore our rights.[84]

This caused a near sundering of relations between the two organizations. In reaction, a motion was made to sever all ties with the IBNWT at the 4th Annual Assembly of MANWT, held a few weeks after the

Camp Antler meeting.[85] Many who spoke in favour of this motion did so in terms of identity – that is, being Métis, not Dene:

> I come from the largest family in the Northwest Territories. I speak for them. We are not Dene. We'll never die Dene. Our children will always be Metis ... I'll continue to fight for that fact that I am a Metis. My family is Metis. We come from the largest family in the Northwest Territories, next to the Beaulieus, the Laffertys, the Mandevilles. We are all Metis. This Association was built on the foundation of the Metis people in the Northwest Territories – not on the species of the Indian Brotherhood ... This Association is the Metis Association of the N.W.T. not the Dene Association. Let's vote on my motion that we separate and let's direct this Executive to work for our own cause.[86]

Although the motion eventually passed, the two organizations continued to work together for many years, particularly in the area of a joint land claims. Like a stormy marriage, there were periods of togetherness and periods of strife. Five years later, the dance between them was still going on. In his speech to the 9th Annual Métis Association General Assembly (21–23 August 1981) at Yellowknife, Dene Nation president Georges Erasmus enthused about their current relationship: "The working relationship between the two organizations is so close *that it is really in some ways misleading to state that there are still two organizations* ... We have been working on issues not as if we are two organizations, not as if there are differences amongst our people but we have been looking at issues as if we are one people and that we have a common future in the North and I think this is the only way to approach it."[87] However, the joint Dene-Métis Comprehensive Claim was doomed to failure. When, in 1990, the two organizations failed to ratify the agreement at their respective annual assemblies, further cooperation between them ceased, and eventually led to the end of MANWT/MNNWT.

The Dene Declaration vs. the Métis Declaration

One of the fundamental sticking points between the two organizations was the Dene Declaration, the statement on the right to Dene self-determination, which, among other things, demanded the right of the Dene to be regarded as a nation. It held that Dene Aboriginal rights included the right to self-government, denied that the government of either Canada or the Northwest Territories was the government of the Dene, and proposed the establishment of a special political relationship between the Dene and the Canadian state. The Dene Declaration was passed unanimously by 300 delegates to the Second Annual Joint Assembly of the Indian Brotherhood of the NWT and the Métis Association in July 1975, at Fort Simpson, NWT. The passing of the Dene Declaration was an extremely important event in the history of Native political development in Canada, as it was one of the first statements by an Aboriginal group within Canada demanding to be recognized as a nation: "We the Dene of the N.W.T. insist on the right to be regarded by ourselves and the world as a Nation. Our struggle is for the recognition of the Dene Nation by the Government and the people of Canada and the peoples and governments of the world."[88] While the Dene Declaration makes no mention of the word "Métis," the declaration was passed unanimously by the Métis Association delegates as well as the Indian Brotherhood delegates. But this seeming accord between the Métis and Dene was deceptive. Among other things, the Dene Declaration was the opening salvo of the aggressive campaign by the Brotherhood to subsume the Métis Association and form one large organization representing all people of Indian descent in the NWT. This position flowed logically from the awareness of the processes of colonialism, which is evident in the Dene Declaration: "Colonialism and imperialism are now dead or dying. Recent years have witnessed the birth of new nations or rebirth of old nations out of the ashes of colonialism. As Europe is the place where you will find European governments for European peoples, now also will you find in Africa and Asia the existence of African and Asian countries with African and Asian governments for the African and Asian peoples."[89] The language and tone of the declaration clearly owed much to the rhetoric of post-colonialism current in academia at the time and were at least partially due to the influence of the non-Native advisors to the Brotherhood, including Mel Watkins, an economist at the University of Toronto and former spokesman for the Waffle movement in the NDP, and Peter Puxley, former CYC worker and former student of Watkins. This quality led many critics of the Brotherhood (including many members of the Métis Association) to suggest that the Brotherhood had become the mouthpiece for left-wing academics.[90] But Erasmus and other Dene leaders were perfectly capable of expressing such ideas on their own and, in fact, Erasmus purged the Brotherhood of these advisors shortly after he became president.

Erasmus regarded the various classifications of Native peoples that had become accepted in Canada (status, treaty, non-status, Métis) as the result of colonial rule and government imposition, which did not represent Native ideas of who was or who was not a Native person (although as we have seen, these colonial divisions have become accepted by many other Native groups in Canada). The Dene Nation to this day remains one of the few organizations that have questioned the government-imposed divisions of Native peoples in Canada.

The other major point of the Dene Declaration was a demand for some form of self-government and a rejection of the form of government that had been imposed upon them by the colonial process to that point. Hence: "The Dene find themselves as part of a country. That country is Canada. But the Government of Canada is not the Government of the Dene. The Government of the N.W.T. is not the government of the Dene. These governments were not the choice of the Dene, they were imposed on the Dene."[91] This radical stance against the existing Government of Canada, coupled with the dawning realization that the concept of the Dene Nation was aimed at assimilating Métis and non-status Indians into its fold, proved to be quite troubling to many members of the Métis Association, despite the fact that the declaration had been passed unanimously at the joint assembly (and despite the fact that the Métis Association had subsequently posted several press releases indicating its support of the Dene Declaration). At the Camp Antler meeting, Hardy told the Brotherhood executive that the Métis people were uncomfortable with certain parts of the Dene Declaration, in particular, the statement that the federal government was not the government of the Dene people. He also pointed out that many Métis people did not like to be called Dene. He further stated that in MANWT's opinion, the Dene Declaration was only "adopted in principle" at Fort Simpson, and that subsequently it was never really discussed in detail with people in the communities. He told the chiefs that many Métis were under the impression that Dene wanted to set up their own country and that the Métis people did not agree with that idea.[92]

The 1975 3rd General Assembly of the Métis Association, held just one month after the joint assembly that had passed the Dene Declaration, already revealed some concern and controversy among Métis delegates regarding the concept of the Dene Nation, and many openly disagreed with MANWT's support of the Dene Declaration. Not all the concerns were totally negative; several members supported the idea of dissolving the Métis Association and joining the Dene (although the Dene organization was still officially called the IBNWT, delegates at the 3rd Assembly were already referring to the organization as the Dene Nation). Other people were against this suggestion, and one reaction was a proposal for the Métis Association to develop its own "Declaration of Métis Rights."

At this point, many of the delegates seemed to regard the Dene Declaration as a work in progress, and they discussed the possibilities of modifying it, or at least modifying the approach the Brotherhood was developing towards land claims and self-government, in a working paper.[93] A motion was also passed to initiate a Métis Declaration of Rights Committee "which would be used for input into the Dene Declaration of Rights working paper."[94] Nevertheless, the Métis Association issued a press release dated 1 September 1975, which once again endorsed the Dene Declaration of Rights, although it went on to say that the press "had confused the Dene Declaration with an unofficial working paper being circulated to communities for discussion" and claimed that the Fort Simpson General Assembly and the Fort Norman Métis Assembly "did not take any official position on the working paper."[95]

As we have seen, by the next year (1976), relations between the two organizations were becoming strained, and several people began lobbying for MANWT to sever all ties with IBNWT, partly because of refusal to identify as Dene and partly because of disagreement with the Dene Declaration: "[in] my own Local in Inuvik, we have people ... called Half-Breed, Metis or whatever you want to call them. Now these people do not believe from the country I come from that they are Dene and it's Dene I am against ... because the Dene Declaration ... is not accepted in my country, not one bit."[96] It was becoming increasingly clear that one of the biggest problems the Métis Association was having with the Brotherhood was the Dene Declaration and, in particular, the statement that neither the Government of Canada nor the Government of the NWT was the government of the Dene. At the assembly, Rick Hardy pointed out that Article 2, item c of the Métis Association constitution stated that one of the objectives of the association was "to promote the participation of Metis and non-status Indians in all areas of settlement, municipal and territorial organizations," which he interpreted to mean settlement councils, municipal councils, and the Territorial Council. He felt that this section of the Métis Association's constitution "puts us in direct conflict with the Indian Brotherhood of the NWT because part of our fight is over the Dene Declaration where they do not want to recognize municipal governments, the Territorial

Government, or the Federal Government."[97] This position – that the basic disagreement between the Indian Brotherhood and the Métis Association was over the phrase "the Government of Canada is not the government of the Dene" – was reiterated several times over the course of the 4th Annual General Assembly. These discussions resulted in a motion "that the Métis Association of the N.W.T. totally reject the Dene Declaration and also the Dene statement of principles that are to be presented to the government of Canada on or about the first of November 1976."[98] The motion also resolved "that if any party presently involved in land claims in the Mackenzie valley continues to use the Dene Declaration as the basis of the claim, that the Metis Association will begin immediately to develop a claim that is more in line with the thinking of the people of the Mackenzie Valley."[99]

Four years later, in July 1980, at the Métis Association of the Northwest Territories General Assembly in Hay River, the association finally passed its own Declaration of Rights (it was also passed at the 1980 Dene National Assembly at Fort Good Hope): "We the Métis people of the Northwest Territories do declare that we exist as a national entity. While it is true that our nationalism does not take form of a nation state it is sufficient to define us as a distinctive people. While it is also true that we are descendants of the Dene of the Northwest Territories we are also descendants of the other nationalities. As such we have evolved as a people that are distinct from both groups." The Métis Declaration clearly can be seen as a reaction to, and in some ways a criticism of, the Dene Declaration and certainly a refutation of the idea that there is only one group of Native people in the NWT. The declaration goes on to claim that the Métis have both democratic rights as citizens of the Canadian nation state (in contrast to the Dene Declaration's rejection of the Canadian and territorial governments), which they have "inherited from the newcomers to Canada," and Aboriginal rights, which they have inherited from their Dene ancestors. By issuing the Métis Declaration, the members of the Métis Association of the NWT indicated their desire to enter into negotiations with the Government of Canada to have their Aboriginal rights recognized and made substantive and to gain recognition from the Canadian government as Métis people.

Métis Identity and the Regional Métis Organizations

Thus, despite the attempts to posit a single Native identity in the Mackenzie Valley (per the Dene), the idea of being Métis refused to die out.

Even today, long after the collapse of MANWT, there are organizations and individuals who carry on with the idea of Métis as a separate identity from other Native people in the Mackenzie Valley. It is instructive to note how an NWT Métis identity was maintained after the demise of the territorial MNNWT, given that the association fell because its membership could not agree on a definition of Métis that was acceptable to all in the NWT. It is not surprising that "Métis" is now being defined on a regional basis, and various groups of Métis are being represented by organizations such as the North Slave Métis Alliance and the NWT Métis Nation.

The degree to which the concept of Métis is recognized varies. Under the Gwich'in Comprehensive Land Claim Agreement, Métis are subsumed as Gwich'in beneficiaries, but are not specifically recognized as Métis. Under Sahtu, the Métis are recognized as Métis and have their own land claim based organizations.[100] But other agreements have not involved the Métis at all. The Tlicho claim was negotiated without the participation of the North Slave Métis Alliance, and the South Slave Métis Tribal Council (now the NWT Métis Nation) is negotiating a separate claim from that of the Akaitcho Dene First Nations.

The North Slave Métis Alliance makes a strong case for the existence of an established Métis identity in its area. It has published a well-researched history of the Métis in the North Slave area (in the vicinity of modern-day Rae-Edzo), which includes a detailed section on current Métis identity.[101] The writers describe how the early Métis inhabitants of the area formed a culturally distinct grouping of indigenous people. They trace the emergence of this distinct identity to several factors, including marriage patterns (second- and third-generation French Métis in the North Slave region during the late nineteenth century tended to marry among themselves); economic factors (Métis had distinct roles in the transportation and communication networks); family size (French Métis families were usually two to three times larger than local Dene families); religion (French Métis were Roman Catholic and shared a common cultural heritage and background with the Oblate priests); language (most early French Métis spoke Michif, as well as Cree, Dogrib, and Chipewyan); and differences in the organization of production (French Métis families were particularly successful at combining wage labour pursuits with subsistence hunting and fishing for their families, reflecting the two traditions of skills learned from their Euro-Canadian and Cree/Dene progenitors).

The NSMA defines this unique North Slave culture as an amalgam of indigenous Dene culture mixed with French and Cree: "While the Métis arrivals quickly became immersed in the Great Slave's Chipewyan, Slavey, and Dogrib cultures, they maintained many elements of their French-Cree heritage. As trappers, boatsmen, fort provisioners, and fur-trading middlemen, they spoke as many as seven languages, including French, Cree, and several Dene dialects. A unique North Slave Métis language known as 'Michif,' a mixture of the French, Cree and Dene languages, is still spoken today by many North Slave Métis. In the past, some Métis from the area referred to themselves as 'Mitif.'"[102]

The regional aspect of Métis identity in the NWT is also well illustrated by the Métis members of the Dehcho First Nations, where Métis is perceived differently in different communities. In some communities, the Dehcho Métis exhibit aspects of Dene identity, and in others they lay claim to a connection with the Red River Métis. For example, the Métis Council in Fort Simpson still sports its old MNNWT logo (Local #52) on its website and discusses what Métis identity means in the community. It contrasts the true Red River Métis with mixed-ancestry Dene and suggests that the latter exhibit a mainly Dene culture: "There are two distinct Métis populations in the Dehcho region. In the southern parts of Mackenzie Valley the cultural heritage of the mixed-blood people has been drawn from the French-Indian fur trade culture of the southern Prairies. It can, therefore, properly be called 'Métis.' In the northern part of the valley, however, *a distinctive Métis society did not take root even though there were many people of mixed blood in the region.*"[103] They suggest that the Treaty 11 and scrip processes split the community into Métis and Dene: "One important effect of Treaty 11 on the mixed-blood people was to create and emphasize divisions between them and the Indian population, a division which until then had been blurred. According to the treaty, Dehcho Dene were to become treaty Indians, and the Métis were to have their rights extinguished in return for a scrip payment of $240."[104]

But a somewhat different attitude towards being Métis can be found at Fort Providence, also part of the Dehcho First Nations. There, the council has undertaken to preserve and promote the history and culture of the Métis people of the area. One of its major accomplishments in that regard is the publication of an impressive local history delineating the development of Métis consciousness in the NWT and in the Dehcho area in particular.[105] The volume has a detailed section discussing Métis and the effect of Treaty 11 and scrip on delineating who is or who is not Métis. The Fort Providence Métis attempt to maintain cultural ties with Métis "who live in Northwest Métis Communities along the Mackenzie River as well as the communities around the Great Slave Lake region of the Northwest Territories."[106] The council specifically endorses the original Métis Declaration of 1980 and includes it on its website.

The NWT Métis Nation is another case in point. The NWTMN, which claims to represent the largest Métis community in the NWT, stresses a strong Red River Métis element in their identity, even though they are negotiating for "indigenous" Métis in their land claim. In section 1.2 of the South Slave Métis Framework Agreement of 29 August 1996, "Indigenous Métis" are defined as Métis people who can trace their ancestry to 1921 (the signing of Treaty 11) in the Northwest Territories.[107] In 2000, the organization passed a new Métis Declaration, which reads in part: "We, the citizens of the Northwest Territory Métis Nation, affirm that we are a distinct Métis Nation within Canada, with Aboriginal rights to land, resources and governance throughout our traditional territory."[108] Note that this is a much stronger statement of Métisness than that of the original Métis Declaration, which merely stated that the Métis people of the NWT "exist as a national entity." They are now a Nation, with Aboriginal rights. The declaration goes on to say that they hold these rights because they are direct descendants of the Dene and Cree First Nations and Métis peoples of the Mackenzie and Athabasca river basins, who lived on these lands, and who governed themselves according to their own laws and customs, "from time before memory."[109]

They also proclaim that they are distinct from First Nations peoples by nature of being direct descendants of the first people of European heritage to reach this region, well before Canada became a nation in 1867. And, while they point out their indigenous roots in the NWT, the authors of the declaration also emphasize their connections to Red River and Great Lakes Métis. They state that the Northwest Territories Métis Nation arose independently of, and at the same time as, the Métis fur trade communities that grew up in the American Midwest / Great Lakes region and the historic Métis Nation of the Canadian prairies, and that, eventually, all these communities became linked through trade and marriage ties: "Many of us are related to Métis people from the Great Lakes or Red River who came north in the 1700s and 1800s … We are proud Métis, known historically as 'the free people,' or '*gens libres*' in Michif French."[110] In recognition of their prairie Métis heritage, the

NWTMN commissioned the design of a new Métis sash in 2009. The unique design details different parts of the NWT Métis environment: fireweed, northern lights, the sun, waterways, the boreal forest, and the Métis people themselves.[111]

They acknowledge that one of the reasons for their distinctiveness is state imposed: their being defined as non-treaty and non-status. They identify themselves as direct descendants of those who signed Treaty 8 at Fort Chipewyan, Smith's Landing, and Fort Resolution, but point out that they have never been accorded the benefits of Treaty 8 or recognized as a First Nations people. They define as their own territory the communities of Fort Smith, Hay River, Fort Resolution, and Yellowknife in the Northwest Territories, and proclaim their Aboriginal title and right to self-government: "We did not cede, surrender or release Aboriginal title to the land and resources throughout our traditional territory. We shall always have Aboriginal rights to our land and resources. We also have the inherent right to govern ourselves in matters that are internal to our communities and traditional territory, integral to our distinctive culture and practices, customs and traditions, and with respect to our unique relationship to our land, water and resources, and essential to our operations as governments."[112]

The declaration is much longer than the original Métis Declaration and much longer than the excerpts reproduced here. But it clearly shows that, despite the close ties they enjoy with the Dene, some Métis in the Mackenzie Valley regard themselves as a distinct people, separate from other Native people of the NWT.

Conclusions

The persistence of a Métis identity and Métis claims in the NWT is a remarkable example of resistance and the endurance of ethnicity in the face of opposition. Perhaps in no other part of Canada has the concept of being Métis been under such a consistent and unrelenting attack, yet Métis identity remains a viable strategy in the NWT to this day. This pressure to deny a Métis background was based not on pressures to deny a Native background – something Métis in the latter parts of the nineteenth and earlier parts of the twentieth centuries had to face – but rather, on the pressure to embrace a single Native identity: Dene. It was a pressure based not on exclusion, but on welcoming people into a community. It was also a pressure that made sense politically – there was certainly strength in numbers to be gained if all people of Native ancestry joined together. Yet the desire to be known as Métis remains strong in the Mackenzie Valley, represented by several regionally based Métis organizations and an ongoing sense of cultural belonging and strength.

This survival in the face of the Dene willingness to embrace all people of Dene ancestry and include them in negotiations for a comprehensive land claim is remarkable – and instructive. There is no doubt that the Dene concept had a profound effect on Métis political development and, by extension, Métis identity. The many debates the Métis held over the years regarding the advisability of shutting down the Métis Association of the NWT and joining the Dene Nation testify to that. The implications of the Dene Nation's approach are far reaching and could have been groundbreaking. By allowing all those with Dene ancestry to declare themselves as such under the Dene registry, the Dene were among the first in Canada to repudiate government-imposed standards of Nativeness such as status, non-status, treaty, and non-treaty. This remains one of the most radical challenges to the right of government to determine Nativeness in Canadian history. Had this approach spread to other parts of Canada, the picture of Canada-Native relations would be profoundly different today, in terms of political development and identity politics. At the very least, one could assume that the self-identified Métis population would likely be much smaller than it is now. But probably it would still have survived – just as it has in the NWT today. This bodes well for the idea that a strong Métis identity will persist well into the future.

It is easy to understand the persistence of Métis identity in the cases where the Dene were not so welcoming. It is possible, for example, that the South Slave Lake Métis Tribal Council, which later changed its name to the NWT Métis Nation, exists today in the form it does mainly because the Akaitcho Dene chose to pursue a treaty settlement that excluded non-treaty Dene and Métis from negotiations. But even if that had not been the case, there is no guarantee the Métis would have disappeared. The fact remains that there is a strong Métis presence in the Mackenzie Valley, based on demonstrable historic and genealogical ties. This presence can be seen in the detailed local histories produced by the North Slave Métis Alliance, the Fort Simpson Métis Council, the Dehcho Métis, and the NWT Métis Nation. Contemporary examples of a continuing development of Métis culture includes the rewriting of the Métis Declaration of Rights, the commissioning of a special NWT Métis sash, as well as the ongoing negotiations for land claims. Such initiatives speak to something beyond an attempt to secure Aboriginal rights: a simple pride in a unique Aboriginal background, one that happens to be neither wholly Dene nor wholly Euro-Canadian.

What is equally of interest is the unique approach the Métis of the NWT have used to define themselves. While we can see that, as happened in the rest of Canada, a sense of being Métis rose in tandem with the growth of organizations related to land claims or Aboriginal rights, and that the influence of southern Métis organizations had some effect, the Métis organizations in the NWT went very much their own way. They defied the limited definitions of Métis developed by the Métis National Council and developed their own far more inclusive ethnic boundary, which refused to exclude Métis who had taken treaty or who had taken C-31. In doing so, they chose to forge links with the Native Council of Canada rather than the Métis National Council, which also recognized Métis from Labrador and other parts of eastern Canada. And they developed this unique ethnic enclave while constantly being exhorted to identify as Dene.

The point of this chapter has not been to make any judgment on what constitutes a true sense of being Métis in the NWT or elsewhere, or why people might choose one identity over another. It has simply been to demonstrate that, for the Métis of the NWT, being Métis is a decision based on many competing and conflicting impulses. In that respect, the Métis of the NWT are no different from the Métis in the rest of Canada, and regardless of their origin the sense of a Métis identity is a potent force in the NWT today.

18 Ethnic Symbolism: Reinterpreting and Recreating the Past

Ethnicity, and an individual's sense of belonging to a group, are routinely maintained and rationalized through the use of the particular symbols of belonging: flags, dress, ritual, and written and oral history. The contemporary Métis are no exception. The Métis of western Canada and Ontario have gathered together several important symbols of "Métisness": the historic figure of Louis Riel, the concept of a Métis homeland, the arrowhead sash, the Michif language, traditional fiddle music and song, and a special concept of "Nativeness" with which to distinguish themselves from mainstream society. But the Métis's interpretation of their past and their use of the past to explain their present do not always correspond with historians' or other academics' interpretations, leading to the question of what is or what is not an "authentic" representation of the past.

For many years, academics in a variety of disciplines have been intrigued by the process by which modern accoutrements of ethnicity, particularly changing representations of the past, have come to be adopted as definitions of "authentic" contemporary identity. This resulted in a large body of literature spearheaded by a collection of essays published under the provocative title *The Invention of Tradition*.[1] While that collection of essays was concerned primarily with European and British colonial invented traditions, other authors working in the "tradition-as-invention" model began exploring examples of Aboriginal peoples who were adapting their models of custom, culture, or traditions to create powerful contemporary political symbols.[2] However, the term "invention of tradition" (in some cases the invention of culture), while intriguing, was also unfortunate, in that it implied that many traditions and symbols of ethnicity were somehow spurious or inauthentic, especially when applied to the customs or claims of contemporary Native or Aboriginal peoples.

This implication has led to predictable complaints from Native activists and academics who see the "invention-of-tradition" as politically revisionist and anti-Native, and the model indeed has the potential to be used by those opposed to recognition of Aboriginal rights. This "dilemma of authenticity"[3] has led to heated discussions, not only within the academy, but from the press, concerned Native activists, and the general public.[4] But it is important to note that not all writers contributing to the tradition-as-invention model take the same theoretical approach. Some, like E.J. Hobsbawm and Roger Keesing, seem to suggest that there is a significant distinction to be made between "genuine" and "invented" traditions. Although Keesing admits that "their symbolic power and political force are undeniable," he states unequivocally that the ancestral ways of life being called forth by activists across the Pacific likely "bear little relation to those documented historically, recorded ethnographically, and reconstructed archaeologically."[5] But others, such as Jocelyn Linnekin and Richard Handler, take the position that the "genuine vs. invented" distinction is a false one, and that it is particularly hypocritical to single out Aboriginal examples of invented tradition, because *all* groups interpret the past to suit present needs.[6]

The question of origin and relevance of ethnic symbols is of special concern to the Métis in contemporary Canadian society and is full of irony. Like many modern ethnic or Aboriginal groups, they are striving to demonstrate that they are "human communities so 'natural' as to require no definition other than self-assertion."[7] But they are particularly vulnerable in this regard, since, by their most common definition, they are biologically diverse and the product of at least two "cultures" or traditions (European and Aboriginal) or many ("French," "Scottish," "English," and "Saulteaux," "Cree," etc.), depending on the criteria used.[8] The historic accoutrements and symbols available to the Métis for appropriation are not rooted in some mythic past, but can be traced to specific, and relatively recent, historic occurrences. Still, this has not prevented the contemporary Métis from developing a system of cultural and political symbols that can distinguish them from other Natives and mainstream society.

Some of these markers, like the Métis themselves, demonstrate a mixed heritage: the Red River cart, the arrowhead or L'Assomption sash, Métis fiddle music, and the Mechif language. Some, like the Métis

National Council's discussion over which date best represents the birth of the Métis Nation (either 8 December 1869, the date of the proclamation of the Provisional Government of the Métis in the Northwest Territories, or the proclamation of the Métis Nation at the Battle of Seven Oaks in 1816)[9] are used to distinguish the Métis from non-Native society; others are used to distinguish the Métis from other Natives, in particular, from other mixed-ancestry groups who have recently begun laying claim to the name "Métis."

The "Métis Way": The Indigenous as Comment on the Exogenous

There are two types of invented tradition.[10] One occurs when a dominant group invents a tradition for a subordinate group and then uses that "tradition" to treat them in a particular way (usually occurring in colonial situations, such as the nineteenth-century British invention of African "kingdoms"). The second occurs when people develop (or "invent") their own traditions, usually for the purposes of political mobilization and resisting colonialism. But it is not always easy to distinguish between the two. A good example of this dynamic occurred in 1816–19 when the North West Company (NWC) encouraged the Métis to call themselves an "independent tribe of Natives" and provided them with a flag so as to deflect blame from the company for the Seven Oaks battle. This "National Tradition," invented by the NWC, over the next thirty years would be adopted and elaborated on by the Métis themselves (see chapter 3). Ironically, the ideas colonized people use in creating an idealized past with which to distinguish themselves from the dominant society have often come from the dominant society itself.

Take, for example, the concept of "Native." It is fairly common for the Métis to display their separateness by contrasting themselves with non-Native society, usually through the expression of "Native" values vs. "white" values. Angus Spence, when he was president of the Manitoba Métis Federation in the early 1970s, showed this dichotomy:

> Where I come from, I'm a rancher, you are judged by the number of cows you own. Just on the number of goddamn cows! We live in a society in which the value system is based on material possessions, on your rank, if you want to call it that, or on the amount of money you got – your bank account, your education, so on and so forth. But *our* value system is based on human beings. Human beings are more important than cows, or high academic standing, or the degrees that go with it, or bank accounts, or you name it.

> If you want me to be a little more specific when I say the value system, I would say that the native people live in a more or less communal society, where they believe that they should share, and they do share. For the most part, you go to a Métis home, they will never tell you, "We would like to put you up for the night but there is no room." They'd sleep on the floor, and say, "Oh yeah, we can put you up, you can sleep right here." I'm not saying about all white men, but many white people will come up and say, "Well, we don't have a spare bedroom, so sorry, but we can't put you up." We live very different.[11]

Note that, while Spence's statement is couched as an indictment of stereotypical "white" values, it is not so much an affirmation of *Métis* values as it is of *Native* values. This is not an isolated example. Previously, we noted Stan Fulham's characterization of the early Métis community organizations as stressing their *Nativeness* rather than their Métisness as what set them apart. In the mid-1980s, Dolores Poelzer and Irene Poelzer conducted ninety-six interviews with eighty-three Métis women in northern Saskatchewan communities.[12] Very little was said by any of these women on the subject of Métis identity, but according to the senior author, many of these women, when they did speak of their culture, spoke of it as "the Indian way" (note: *not* the "Métis way"). The "Indian way" apparently consisted of a genetic Indian ancestry, speaking a Native language, and maintaining certain customs and traditions. Thirty-nine of the forty-three women who discussed their ancestry "saw no difference" between being Indian and being Métis.[13] These attitudes seem to indicate that there is a gap between the way the Métis organizations are defining identity and the way many Métis actually feel about their identity. It is true that a few of these women indicated that they preferred to identify as Métis rather than as "white" or treaty Indian, but the number who expressed this sentiment were definitely in the minority. It is frustrating for us that the authors did not appear particularly interested in the topic of identity and did not pursue the matter in any of their interviews.

However, the quote by Angus Spence, the reminiscences of Stan Fulham, and the affirmation of the "Indian way" by the Métis women surveyed by Poelzer and Poelzer indicate that many Métis think of themselves as "Native" before they think of themselves as "Métis." Some of the mixed populations in Ontario (particularly those represented by the Ontario Métis Aboriginal Association [OMAA]) have expressed similar sentiments. But ironically, many of the values associated with the construct of "Native" are as likely to be a "white" invention as an indigenous one. The "Native way" expressed by the people quoted above may have been coloured by one of the dominant society's favourite myths about Native society, the "noble savage," whereby certain supposed aspects of indigenous culture – harmony with nature, simplicity, wisdom, communal values, and a willingness to share – are selected and glorified as commentaries on the intrusive and dominant colonial culture. Albert Memmi[14] and others have commented on the process of dominated peoples reproducing the "conceptual and institutional structures of their domination."[15] Antonio Gramsci's concept of counter-hegemonic discourse[16] incorporating the structures, categories, and premises of hegemonic discourse is also relevant here. First, the colonized are likely to absorb and internalize the premises and categories of the dominant society; second, because the dominant society controls and dictates the institutions and methods to which all sectors of the society must conform in order to lay claim to power, the very process of resistance will be defined and predetermined by the dominant sector.[17]

A classic example of colonized peoples incorporating the premises of the dominant society into their own value system can be seen in the widespread acceptance of the category of "status" Indian by the majority of Canada's Native population. Today the colonial aspects of the term are somewhat hidden by the substitution of "First Nations" for status Indian, but the fact remains that the distinction is one wholly created by the federal government and the Indian Act. This wholesale acceptance of a government distinction means that the Métis's claim to be "Native" is often challenged by other Native groups. It is common, particularly in the prairies, for status Indians or First Nations peoples to denigrate the Métis and to deny that they are Native. A common charge is that they "sold their status for scrip" and now have no right to call themselves Native. While these statements are often expressed in private, by both the grass roots and the leaders, they rarely surface in public.[18] But occasionally, the silence is broken. In 2004, a vice-chief of the Federation of Saskatchewan Indians, who was criticizing an Aboriginal justice commission report, condemned it mainly because it lumped together First Nations peoples with Métis and other "shouldabeens, couldabeens and wannabees."[19] The president of the Métis Nation of Saskatchewan demanded, and got, an immediate apology from the chief of the federation, but the opinions expressed by the vice-chief are hardly new or unique. Still, "Nativeness" remains one of the primary elements of Métis identity, in some cases taking precedence over the concept of Métis itself.

Collective Memories: Riel, Scrip, and Injustice

A defining characteristic of any ethnic group is a collective sense of history – those defining moments of how, when, and where the group came into being. Often, a group's origins are assumed to be clouded by mystery, lost in the mists of some distant and mythological past. This can hardly be the case for the Métis, however, since their origins are fairly recent and well documented. Nevertheless (or perhaps because of it), the Métis have a particularly strong sense of their own history. No one who has worked among the Métis communities of the prairie provinces in the late 1970s and early 1980s, as I and my colleagues in the Land Claims Research Project of the Métis Association of Alberta have done, could be insensitive to this feeling. Issues such as Louis Riel's execution and the scrip program of land distribution did not occur in some distant and mythological past, but were matters of a current and palpably urgent concern, part of everyday life. The basic sentiment of this living history was partly a pride in being Métis, but even more strongly was informed by a pervasive sense of aggrievement, of a sense of injustice and of being victims of Canadian imperialism. This sentiment was often expressed in the perceived martyrdom of their beloved leader, Louis Riel, but was particularly intense in their recounting of the injustices of the scrip program, which was to have provided the Métis with a land base in recognition of their Aboriginal rights, but which in their estimation was denied to them through trickery and dishonesty on the part of the government of the day.

Without a doubt, Louis Riel is the most important historical figure for the Métis. Only Gabriel Dumont comes close to matching his historic and emotional impact. But there is an irony in the Métis veneration of Riel. Riel's religious conception of the Métis Nation, in which the idea of a Métis homeland is seen as a "gift from God" and an extension of French-Canadian nationalism (see chapter 4), is considerably at odds with the way Riel is perceived today. It is a reminder that nation building can be as much a process of selective forgetting as invention.

Not all Canadians share the Métis's view of Riel. Few figures in Canadian history can stir up such divided and emotional reactions. Riel led two resistance movements in 1870 and 1885. He committed his most controversial act during the 1870 resistance, when he presided over the execution of Thomas Scott, one of the road workers sent to the Red River Settlement from Canada in 1869 and who had been captured by Riel's forces. However, it was the second uprising in 1885 that led to his being tried and hanged for treason. Riel's actions and execution and the refusal of John A. Macdonald's cabinet to commute his sentence sharply divided French and English Canada and fuels heated controversy to this day. His execution served to encourage Quebec nationalism and led many Quebeckers to forswear the Conservative Party in favour of the Liberals led by Sir Wilfrid Laurier, a pattern of voting that lasted well into the twentieth century.

Today, Riel remains a hero to the Métis, many French Canadians, and a surprisingly wide cross-section of the rest of Canada.[20] But the process by which Riel came to be perceived in this manner is complex and many-layered. Albert Braz documented how the view of Riel has changed over time to fit the specific social reality and needs of those who have written about him. In particular, Braz noted that the discourse is predominantly carried out by Euro-Canadians, and that Riel "is usually situated not in a Métis context but a Canadian one," wherein he is seen as a revolutionary champion of Native rights and the founder of the province of Manitoba.[21] Many see his defiance of federal authority as a mirror of their own linguistic and nationalist struggles (even the founder of the western-based Reform Party, Preston Manning, is an admirer, who regards the Riel Rebellion as part of a continuing western resistance to central Canadian power). But many others see Riel as a criminal and traitor. He divides Protestants and Catholics, east and west, French and English. He is still able to inspire an almost irrational hatred; newspaper columnists fulminate against him; "I despise the man ... I loathe Louis Riel ... that moustachioed Jesus."[22] Those who attempt to re-examine his role or exonerate him are routinely accused of "rewriting history."[23]

But to the Métis, he is the very symbol of their presence in Canada. Tony Belcourt, president of the Métis Nation of Ontario (MNO), described him this way: "I often think of Riel as being the soul of the Métis nation and I see us as being Riel's people. He embodies our values and what we aspire to be as people, as human beings. He was intelligent. He was compassionate. He was a leader ... a walking spirit of the values of the Métis people."[24] Mr Belcourt's championing of Riel is particularly interesting because, as president of the MNO, he represents a constituency that at first glance has only a passing relationship with Riel. Save for a small contingent of Métis who migrated east to the Rainy River district of Ontario after the first Riel Rebellion, most Ontario "Métis" are from a completely separate historical group (see chapter 16). Yet a visit to the MNO's website shows a long and detailed history of Riel and a discussion of his importance to the Métis, along with similar sections on other symbols usually associated with the prairie Métis, such as the Métis flag and the Métis sash. But this treatment should not come as a surprise. It is in the nature of political symbols to mutate with the times, and Riel has become a symbol to more than just the prairie and French-Catholic Métis. In a very fundamental way, it does not matter if Riel has a logical or demonstrable historic tie to Ontario. Political symbols are empty of content; they need not be "real" in the sense that they accurately represent past actions of actual people, times, or places. They merely need to work as a unifying force.[25] Another factor is that today the Métis, like many other sectors of Canadian society, are mobile and routinely leave the prairies to take up residence elsewhere in Canada. Many Ontario Métis (like Tony Belcourt himself) are transplanted prairie Métis who are carrying their traditions with them, making them a part of Ontario. Tradition, like any other aspect of culture, continues to mutate and adapt.

Louis Riel is undoubtedly the most important historical figure the Métis have. Yet, like many of their symbols, they must fight to keep him as their own. This is not an easy task, as he appeals to a broad spectrum of Canadians besides the Métis. "Everyone wants a piece of Riel ... People in Quebec have their own reasons for identifying with Riel; people within western Canada do ... I think that Riel has taken on a kind of hero-like status ... I don't necessarily identify with the historical elements of his life anymore. To me he's just a symbol of what we're going for ... to allow his people to continue to exist within the federation."[26]

As a symbol of the Métis, Riel has no parallel. But the Métis are not the only ones who claim him. He seems particularly attractive to members of Parliament, who seem to want him for political and emotional reasons. For years, there have been numerous private member's bills introduced in Parliament (at least fifteen between the years 1983 and 2004) seeking to exonerate Riel and/or to declare him a Father of Confederation.[27] It is interesting to speculate why so many MPs, especially backbenchers, have taken up the cause of Riel's exoneration, particularly when one considers, as Braz has pointed out, that Riel's writings indicate a distinct lack of identification with Confederation. (Of course, many other MPs have been just as passionately opposed to the exoneration.) Perhaps the romance that surrounds Riel's own attempts at serving as an MP – twice being elected to the district of Provencher, but never being able to serve, although at one point, despite a warrant for his arrest, signing the register in the House of Commons in disguise – appeals to them.

However, it is understandable that there should be some resentment among the Métis over the "ownership" of Riel and a suspicion as to the motivations behind those non-Métis who claim him: "as the Métis people, Riel belongs to us ... [We] have little else … We have no recognition of our rights and almost no meaningful political advances in over a hundred years – and still they would take away this one thing we have – Louis Riel … cleaned up and set out in a new set of clothes to their liking."[28] Despite the fact that many of the MPs and senators who sponsored or supported the various bills aimed at exonerating Riel were Métis themselves, the bills were often opposed by the mainstream Métis political organizations. Many Métis spokesmen from the Métis National Council and from provincial organizations have voiced either concern or outright opposition to the proposals. The attitude of the organizations and Métis spokespersons sometimes has caught the proponent of the exoneration bills by surprise. For example, MP Reg Alcock and MP Denis Coderre attended a conference on Métis rights sponsored by the Métis National Council in Winnipeg in 1998[29] in order to present their proposed legislation on Riel's exoneration. If they expected a warm reception for their proposed legislation or support from the MNC, they were sorely disappointed. Tony Belcourt, president of the MNO, was particularly antagonistic to the two members of Parliament, publicly berating them and accusing them of attempting to use the issue of Riel to their own political advantage.

There is more to this squabble between MPs and Métis politicians than simply a perceived notion of "ownership" of Riel or a right to use him as a symbol of Métisness. There are practical concerns as well. Gerald Morin, when he was president of the MNC in 1998, said that many Métis leaders were opposed to detaching the issue of Riel's exoneration from broader and presumably more pressing negotiations with the federal government, including land claims, Aboriginal rights, and self-government.[30] Several other leaders and spokespersons have expressed similar sentiments, reasoning that allowing Canada to exonerate Riel would somehow let Canadians "off the hook" for the harm Canada supposedly has done the Métis, without offering more practical compensation for what the Métis see as major grievances over land claims and Aboriginal rights. "Let the stain remain for now until we get what we want, and then exonerate Riel."[31] These people feel that it is better *not* to forgive and forget: "Riel's execution is a stain on the honour of Canada, and those who are the descendants of the people responsible for his death should have to live with it."[32] Gerry St Germain, who not only was Canada's first Métis senator, but when he was an MP was also the first Métis to serve in the Cabinet, had similar reservations about exoneration for Riel. Issuing a pardon, he felt, may make it possible for "those who ignored the importance of Riel's work [to] now find a degree of exoneration in their mistreatment of this great Canadian hero."[33]

However, the reason most often cited for opposition to a pardon for Riel is that "he was never guilty in the first place."[34] "A pardon implies guilt. Pardons are political tools used by governments to advance their own agendas, but people who are granted pardons are not presumed to be innocent and the pardon does not wash away the moral stain."[35] Most Métis politicians want an exoneration rather than a pardon, but they recognize that the two concepts are confused in the public mind. They feel many of the private member's bills, even though they may not use the word *pardon*, are essentially asking for one, or are making the common error of confusing a pardon with exoneration. Not all Métis agree with the stance of the organizations. Métis Senator Thelma Chalifoux feels that Métis leaders who oppose the bills aimed at exonerating Riel are "out of touch with their people."[36] There may be something to that charge. When Denis Coderre was trying to get support for his private member's bill, he was able to claim the support of about 100 members of Riel's family,[37] even though some spokespersons for the organizations, including Jean Teillet, the great-grandniece of Riel, opposed the bills. Paul Chartrand, a Métis law professor, writer, and private consultant, stated the sentiment behind this opposition succinctly when he described Coderre's bill as a "forgive and forget formula that is being offered by strangers."[38]

Despite the practical reasons the organizations may cite to rationalize their opposition to Riel's exoneration – either that they see it as a negotiating strategy or that they do not accept that Riel was guilty of treason – it is likely that the major reasons for the opposition are a sense of ownership and resentment of others presuming to speak for the Métis. As the Anishnabe writer and painter Sherry Farrell Racette asks: "who owns Riel?"[39] Is it Canada or the Métis? This question was forcefully brought home in 2002, when the Canadian Broadcasting Corporation (CBC) and the Dominion Institute, a non-profit organization "devoted to preserving and disseminating information about Canadian history,"[40] staged a "retrial" of Louis Riel. The show, according to CBC publicity, was "based on Canadian law of the present day." Although the charge was still treason, it was not meant to be a simple recreation of the original trial, but a reinterpretation. Practising lawyers played most of the leading roles; Alan Lenczner, QC, acted for the prosecution and Edward Greenspan, QC, for the defence; Guy Bertrand played Louis Riel and Thomas Berger, former justice of the Supreme Court of British Columbia, was the presiding judge. The final verdict was to be delivered by the Canadian public, who were able to use the Internet to vote on Riel's innocence or guilt in the twenty-four-hour period after the trial was broadcast. The program was to run in three parts on three consecutive nights: Part One was a short biography of Riel, Part Two was the actual retrial of Louis Riel, and Part Three was a live discussion by various representatives of the Métis community, reviewing the program and the results of the online voting.

Reaction from the Métis community erupted long before the program was aired. Although the retrial wasn't broadcast until 22 October 2002, it had been taped on 22 August of the same year. The Métis Nation of Ontario released a press statement on the same day the show was taped, condemning the entire proceedings and urging all Métis to refuse to take part in the program as observers or discussants. Foremost of the complaints was that no Métis scholars, lawyers, or politicians had been consulted. Tony Belcourt was quoted as saying:

> It is a mark of the contempt that the organizers of this program have for Riel's people today that they have consciously ignored all Métis people before planning such an outrageous charade ... I am appalled that none of our people, not even any of our Métis lawyers who have distinguished and landmark careers in the legal profession in Canada and internationally were consulted or even considered. It is beyond comprehension and absolutely stunning that the producers of this program would even contemplate holding a disgusting vote on whether or not to again hang Riel.[41]

The point was reiterated by Jean Teillet, Métis lawyer and great-grandniece of Louis Riel: "It is most unfortunate that the CBC has chosen to co-produce and broadcast this ill-conceived show. It recreates the same racism that existed in 1885 when Riel was hung. In 1885 the Prime Minister of Canada, Macdonald, ensured that the Métis Nation could not participate in the trial of their leader and that Riel would not be tried by his peers. 117 years later the CBC will do it again."[42]

Eventually the Métis organizations moderated their position, at least to the extent that some leaders, including Tony Belcourt and Jean Teillet, agreed to appear on the final show as discussants, but not without making the point that they had not been invited before they had made their objections known to the general public. The results of the online poll revealed a generally favourable view of Riel across Canada; almost 87 per cent of voters found Riel "not guilty." But the overwhelmingly high Internet vote in support of Riel did little to mollify the Métis. In fact, the results may not have pleased Métis activists; Riel would be a more valuable, or at least a more exclusive, symbol for the Métis if he were not being embraced by such a large proportion of the Canadian public. As the quote from Jason Madden, above, states: "Everybody wants a piece of Riel." Evidently, whether the Métis want to or not, they are going to have to share him with a large proportion of the rest of Canada.

Scrip, Land, and Homeland

As already mentioned, one of the defining elements essential to being Métis is a sense of historical aggrievement. This sense of aggrievement has two main foci; the execution of Louis Riel and, perhaps even more important, the perception of loss of entitlement to a land base through the scrip program. The idea of a land base is coupled with the concept of a Métis homeland. The emotional significance of this interpretation of their historic past was brought home to me when I was director of land claims for the Métis Association of Alberta from 1978 to 1981.[43] As I and my fellow researchers interviewed Métis families throughout northern Alberta, we were struck by the extraordinary impact that historic occurrences still had on the contemporary Métis. Almost all of the Métis families we interviewed in northern Alberta had stories of how their great grandparents, grandparents, or in some cases their parents had been given scrip; how this scrip was given in recognition of their Native heritage to provide a land base for the Métis and their descendants; and how, in most cases, the scrip was subsequently lost, stolen, or swindled from them. These views, while based on some verifiable events of the past, are as much invented as real. While scrip was intended to provide a land base, the Métis were given a choice of land or money scrip, and between 1885 and 1900 the vast majority of those Métis who were granted scrip chose to take money scrip because it was easier to sell. Between 1900 and 1910, when a larger percentage of Métis chose land scrip (land having risen in value), almost all chose to sell immediately. Thus, few Métis saw scrip as a way of gaining a land base; rather, most saw it as a way of raising money in hard economic times (see chapters 7 and 8). These "facts," however, have not prevented a sense of grievance from developing in subsequent generations.

This obsession with the past has echoes in the various land claims cases the Métis have brought to the courts.[44] The emotional impact of the issue is well illustrated by the Honourable Yvon Dumont, interviewed when he was lieutenant governor of Manitoba, as he described the tears of joy that filled the eyes of the Métis leaders when the Supreme Court upheld their right to pursue their land claims case:

> One of the most satisfying things that happened to me as president of the Manitoba Métis Federation was when we went to the Supreme Court of Canada, on March 2, 1990. Tom Berger was representing the Métis. His arguments were based on documentation provided to him by various land claims researchers, but basically they were the same claims that were made by our ancestors. The seven judges of the Supreme Court of Canada went into the back room, and they came out after 7 or 8 minutes, and unanimously agreed with us. I looked back amongst the Board of Directors, and there were grown men, sitting there with tears in their eyes. This is what they were feeling as Métis people you know? They couldn't believe that all of a sudden, here was the Supreme Court of the land that persecuted the Métis people over the years and after listening to our lawyers making the claims that our ancestors had been making for a hundred years agreed with us, and not with the government lawyer. That to me was very very significant.[45]

The sense of loss of a land base is closely associated with another idea, that of a historic Métis homeland. This concept is so essential to the idea of being Métis, that the Métis National Council has incorporated the definition of a "historic Métis Nation Homeland" as part of its national definition of Métis.[46]

Some scholars, like Keesing, point to the irony of an Aboriginal population taking on the western concept of territory, suggesting that the actual territory, or the perception of territory as essential to the cultural heritage being proclaimed, may have acquired reality only through the colonial process itself.[47] He sees the deep identification with and reverence for land that many Aboriginal groups demonstrate as having been "radically transformed in the course of political struggle and histories of conquest and land alienation."[48] While Keesing is speaking of the Pacific Islands, it is an idea that is at least partially applicable to the Métis and other Aboriginal groups in North America. In the case of the Métis, the idea of a Métis homeland began to be articulated in the decades after 1816 (see chapters 3 to 5). Today this idea of a Métis homeland is firmly part of the Métis idea of self.

Symbols of Mixed Heritage

Certain symbols used by the Métis, like the Métis themselves, demonstrate a mixed heritage. This often leads to accusations of their somehow being "inauthentic." The Red River cart is one such example. No symbol or artefact from the Métis's past is more closely related to the Métis than the wooden, two-wheeled Red River cart they used for their buffalo hunts and general transportation, although it was also used by some plains Indian groups and by many non-Métis as well. The carts are still being built today by Métis craftspersons, to be utilized in special Métis ceremonies or as museum pieces. In 2004, the Red River Métis Heritage Group completed a pilgrimage from St Norbert, Manitoba, to Batoche, Saskatchewan, in five carts especially crafted for the purpose, to celebrate Batoche days.[49] Carts are also being manufactured by Métis in Montana.[50] Many logos of the provincial Métis organizations have featured the cart as an emblem of the Métis. In the 1960s and 1970s, the logo of the Métis Association of Alberta featured a Red River cart in silhouette, along with a dedication to "Louis Riel, a great Métis leader." The Manitoba Métis Federation's logo, developed in the same time period and still in use today, features a Red River cart wheel with a buffalo head and two rifles superimposed over it.

Nevertheless, many writers who wish to challenge Métis claims to a separate identity stress the European origins of the cart, pointing to similar designs in other parts of the world, and intimate the carts were simply introduced to the region by Euro-Canadian traders rather than being developed locally.[51] But today, the identification of the cart with the Métis is accepted almost universally as an emblem of the Métis by Métis and non-Métis alike. Non-Métis are, if anything, even more adamant about the significance of the cart. Anyone who has had a book published on the Métis has likely found it inevitable that the publishers would insist on a Red River cart on the cover, whether that is an appropriate image or not.[52]

But there is more controversy over the use of the other common emblem of Métisness: the L'Assomption, or arrow, sash, today most commonly referred to as the Métis sash. It has become one of the most important symbols of Métis identity. The MNC, MNO, MMF, and many other Métis organizations all feature the sash in their promotional literature and websites, usually giving a brief description and history of the sash, discussing its evolution from a simple and practical article of clothing to a contemporary piece of regalia to be worn at formal Métis cultural and political events.[53] As such, it is a perfect example of an "invented" tradition; the Métis organizations are completely forthright about the adaptation of the sash as symbol and its use in the development of contemporary tradition: "The sash has *acquired new significance in the 20th century*, now symbolizing pride and identification for Métis people. Manitoba and Saskatchewan have both created 'The Order of the Sash' which is bestowed upon members of the Métis community who have made cultural, political or social contributions to their people."[54]

There is general agreement among the various organizations as to the history and origin of the sash. Although it is most commonly associated with the Métis of western Canada, they acknowledge that the sash as such is not unique to the Métis; it had its origins in Eastern Canada and, in addition to the French Canadians, the Iroquois and other Eastern Woodland Indians produced it and used it. The variety usually worn by the Métis was known as the L'Assomption sash, and featured a "ceinture fléchée" or "arrow belt" pattern. It originated in Lower Canada around 1780 in the village of L'Assomption, located northeast of Montreal, where it was handcrafted by French-Canadian artisans for the fur trade.[55] The sashes were finger woven, without the use of a loom, using brightly coloured wool. A typical design had a red band or "coeur" in the centre, paralleled by a series of zigzags forming arrow designs along the length (hence the name "arrow" belt). The most popular colours were red, pale blue, dark blue, yellow, and green. In addition to the sashes available commercially, there were many home-made versions, which could usually be distinguished by a looser weave, coarser wool, and a wider variety of patterns than those available for trade. Many Métis families often developed their own patterns, which then served as a means of familial identification in the manner of Scottish tartans.[56] The sashes were of various lengths; the average was about three metres, but some were as long as six metres. They were traditionally used as a belt, tied around the waist over a coat, but they were also used as scarves, tow ropes, dog harnesses, and tumplines.[57]

Generally, the Métis organizations' literature and websites make no attempt to hide the contemporary nature of the symbolism associated with the sash and, in fact, make it quite clear how the sash evolved into its present form. For example, the Manitoba Métis Federation adopted a new design as its official sash, replacing the traditional yellow yarn with black, which symbolizes "the dark period in which the Métis people had endured dispossession and repression after 1870."[58] The NWT Métis Nation held a competition in 2009 for a distinct sash to identify Métis in the NWT. While the original colours of the sash had no particular meaning, today each colour is treated as having a special symbolism. For Manitoba, red is the "traditional color of the Métis sash"; blue and white symbolize the colour of the flag of the Métis Nation; and green symbolizes fertility, growth, and prosperity for the new Métis Nation.[59] According to the MNC website, yellow, which has been removed from the Manitoba sash, may appear in exceptional situations: "Representing gold, it can be woven onto both sides of a sash presented by the Métis community to an individual it wishes to honor." The NWT Métis Nation sash has chevrons in several unique colours, representing northern symbols such as fireweed, northern lights, the sun, waterways, and the boreal forest.[60] The practice of using the sash as a badge of honour began in 1992 when the Manitoba Métis Federation established the "Order of the Sash" to recognize and honour outstanding individuals and their contributions to the Métis Nation. The Métis Nation of Saskatchewan quickly followed suit with its own version of the Order of the Sash, and the MNC has established a National Order.

Although any group can designate a particular object as a symbol of their uniqueness, there is no guarantee that the object so selected will remain their exclusive property. Such is the case of the Métis sash, which even the Métis admit can be claimed legitimately by the Eastern Woodland Indians and Maritime Natives. The prairie and Ontario Métis adapted the sash as one of the identifying symbols that would separate them from Native and non-Native people, particularly other mixed heritage or non-tribal Aboriginal groups with no historical links to the Métis nation. But this did not prevent the sash from being adapted by the very groups the Métis wished to distinguish themselves from, those that have only recently begun to apply the designation "Métis" to themselves. A good example is found in Nova Scotia. A website produced by the craft coordinator for the province, whose duty it is "to educate and teach ... Métis crafts such as clothing and head dress as well as beaded work," listed the Métis sash as one of the crafts that is being taught in Nova Scotia Native communities.[61] The name "Métis" is of relatively recent origin in this area, part of the aforementioned tendency of mixed non-Aboriginal/Aboriginal groups to search for a value-free word to replace "half-breed." But these groups often appropriate more than the *name* "Métis"; they often appropriate the *symbols*, and even the interpretation of the past that originally belonged exclusively to the prairie Métis. The Nova Scotia website not only listed the Métis sash as one of the emblems of the eastern "Métis," it also reproduced *in toto* the symbolism of the colours developed by the prairie Métis, including the contemporary black thread pattern developed in Manitoba (although the "dark period" the black thread refers to has little relevance for the Maritimes). However, there are no references to the twentieth- and twenty-first-century origins of the colour symbolism in the Nova Scotia site, giving the impression that the colours are "traditional," applicable to the east, and have always had the meanings they have today. We are seeing the "invention of tradition" here twofold; once as it is deliberately developed for a particular situation (Manitoba and the rest of the prairies) and once again as it is adapted almost uncritically to a different area with different historical traditions, but with concepts such as the "dark period of Métis relations" being adapted as part of a total package.

Another symbol that has been retrieved from the past (and used in both Ontario and the prairies) is the Métis flag. This flag is a very deliberately chosen symbol for the modern Métis Nation. In the process of selecting this flag, the Métis leadership of the later twentieth century eschewed the flags Riel had used in 1869–70 (featuring a fleur-de-lis and a shamrock) and at Batoche in 1885 (featuring the Holy Virgin). Instead they chose the flag given to the Métis by the NWC in 1815. This flag, consisting of a white infinity sign on a blue background, is more useful for the needs of today's Métis political organizations, as it is not burdened with the pre-existing national or religious symbols of Riel's earlier flags. It has been interpreted as having two meanings; the "joining of two cultures, and the existence of a people forever."[62]

Métis music and dance, especially fiddling and jigging, and other aspects of Métis culture are also being used as cultural markers and are finding their way into school curricula as well as organizational literature and websites.[63] The Métis and the organizations are adopting and manipulating many more symbols than can be discussed here; the MNC website, for example, has discussions on all of the following aspects of Métisness: the Mechif language, contributions by Métis people, the Métis flag, Louis Riel, Louis Riel Day, the sash, the voyageurs, Métis voyageur games, beading, jigging, the fiddle, the York boat, the Red River cart, the buffalo hunt, and National Aboriginal Day.[64] What all these items have in common is that they address the present, not the past. They define the Métis of today, and their attempts to deal with contemporary society on their own terms, in a way that allows them to remain a distinct sector of Canadian society; very much like a "strand in the sash."

This analysis of Métis political representations of the past has not been to suggest that they are distortions of a "real" past, but to emphasize that the Métis, like all ethnic groups and nations, are always reinterpreting (or "inventing") the past in the interests of the present, and that there is no primordial nation or identity. As Keesing has pointed out, "a reverence for what survives of the cultural past (however altered its forms), and for a lost heritage, is a necessary counterpoint to deep anger over the generations of destruction."[65] Each generation recreates what it means to be Métis.

Conclusion

The unifying theme of this book is the historical emergence of the Métis as a distinct people in North America and their attempts to create and recreate enduring identities from the eighteenth to the twenty-first centuries. These identities, we argue, shifted over time as the Métis sought to adapt to changing social, economic, and political conditions. We argue that Métis ethnicity and identity were not simply products of biology, kinship, and culture, but the product of a dialogical process between how the Métis viewed themselves and how others, including governments, perceived and structured their relations with the Métis. Thus, government policies such as treaties, land claims, status categories, and scrip programs affected both how the Métis positioned themselves ethnically, and their political struggles against the state.

We are not arguing that Métis ethnogenesis is unique in this sense. Ethnogenesis is a common phenomenon. All over the world, ethnic groups have been coming into existence, or disappearing, or expanding, or contracting, as local conditions, government structures in the form of encompassing states, and economic conditions exert their influence. This process started with the development of the nation state and the culture of capitalism. The patterns are recognizable and have been noted in Africa, Asia, and North and South America. The outstanding features of this process involve, but are not limited to, ideas of belonging (including an increasing stress on blood and biological relatedness), ideas of a sovereign existence (which, once recognized by the encompassing state are used *against* that state), and ideas of the importance of territory (often beginning with land claims, which quickly become intertwined with ideas of sovereignty).[1]

Our book therefore begins with a consideration and delineation of the ethnological categories and space in which the Métis were conceptualized and were allowed to occupy in the early development of the Canadian and American nation-states. In general, Euro-American observers saw hybridity in either degenerationist or amalgamationist terms. The "Métis" or "half-breeds" conceptualized as racial categories were seen as a temporary phenomenon that would either revert back to their "Indian" roots or merge with the European race. While "métissage" could be seen as having a salutatory effect on Canadian or American populations, a separate Métis "race" or "nation" was at best a transitional phenomenon. This type of thinking would shape government policy in both the United States and British North America. "Métis" individuals were allowed in Indian treaties if they lived as Indians or were considered Canadian or American subjects and citizens if not. No separate Métis status or category emerged in either country prior to 1870. While Métis ethnogenesis occurred in various parts of North America where economies (generally fur trade related) favoured intermarriage between Aboriginal and European individuals and the development of intermediate broker populations, political recognition of Métis was circumscribed by the British, Canadian, and American refusal to recognize these communities as permanent and possessing specific rights. Only with the Riel Resistance of 1869–70 and the passage of the Manitoba Act of 1870 were the Métis accorded constitutional status as Aboriginal, but not Indian. With this constitutional enactment, policy related to the Métis diverged in Canada from that in the United States, affording the Métis in Canada a political pathway to develop their national aspirations. It is in this sense that Métis scrip became not only a colonial tool of Aboriginal extinguishment, but a marker of Métis Aboriginality. The administration of the various Métis scrip commissions, which operated from the 1870s until the 1920s, thus named and defined an ethnicity or identity to which the Métis ascribed to in order to receive benefits. Within this context, Métis struggles for recognition from the early decades of the nineteenth century through the early twentieth century slowly transformed Métis as a racial category into the "Métis Nation." Earlier racial thinking and categories would continue to permeate the thinking of government officials, and even some Métis leaders, but the Nation idea would increasingly become the predominant one among historians and the Métis.

This transition from seeing Métis in racial terms to seeing them as a Nation was by no means a straightforward or progressive process. It was a transition that was contested (by both the Canadian state and some Métis organizations) and complex. During the economic devastation of the 1930s Métis political organizations began to articulate a kind of Métis nationalism, but in their efforts to gain government assistance for devastated Métis communities they cooperated with government agencies and commissions and in the process were co-opted into again defining Métis in racial terms and the language of social pathology. In securing both government aid and Métis colonies, these organizations lost their national pretensions for a time, and their most aggressive leaders, Malcolm Norris and James Brady, withdrew from Métis politics.

Even in the period from the 1950s to 1970, when the modern Métis political organizations were in their formative stages, Canadian social scientists continued to frame Métis identity in racial and pathological terms. Anthropologists, sociologists, and economists hired to study various northern Métis communities described these communities as "half-Indian," disorderly, and broken, and the Métis inhabiting them as maladapted, poverty-stricken, and powerless. This type of racialization and definition on the basis of social pathology might seem an anathema to the development of a Métis national consciousness, but in some ways it worked in the opposite direction. The volume of social science studies that appeared in this period convinced the various governments that not only were these "broken" communities in need of social services and aid, but they were not about to disappear. Funding came both from provincial governments for housing, health care, and economic development and from the federal government, which, through the secretary of state began funding Métis political organizations that would eventually lead the fight to win recognition of the Métis as a Nation. Finally, these social science studies helped in formulating a new Métis identity by replacing the various "half-breed" terminologies with the somewhat more race-neutral "Métis" terminology.

The growth and development of the Métis political organizations in the prairies, while in some ways unique to Canada, nevertheless functioned to allow the Métis to develop their ethno-Aboriginality in ways similar to those of groups in other parts of the world. While initially concentrating on improving their social conditions (housing, education, economic development), they also embarked on a mission to clarify and assert their place in Canada as a distinct Aboriginal group – distinct from First Nations, Inuit, and particularly non-status Indians, with whom they were politically involved in earlier stages of the 1960s and the 1970s. Their first major objective was achieved when they successfully had their identity as Aboriginal peoples recognized in the Canadian Constitution of 1982. They were then able to use this recognition as a springboard for launching several Aboriginal rights cases (particularly hunting rights, such as were central in *R. v. Powley*) and land claims cases, culminating to date in the Manitoba Métis Federation's Supreme Court victory in 2013, which ruled that the federal government had failed to properly distribute land grants that were promised to the Manitoba Métis as part of the Red River Settlement of 1870.[2] While remarkable achievements in their own right, these court victories represent a familiar pattern easily recognizable to students of ethnogenesis on the world stage. As the Comaroffs have observed, once ethnically defined populations have their sovereignty officially recognized, they tend to assert it against the state, which usually involves or begins with a land claim of one kind or another.[3]

With the incorporation and governmental recognition of an ethnic Aboriginal group comes an inevitable conflict between those who are included and those who are excluded, either by the government or by the group itself. In the case of the Métis, the situation is complicated by the fact that no definition of who was or was not a Métis accompanied the constitutional recognition of the Métis as one of Canada's Aboriginal peoples in 1982. This omission has led to several other Aboriginal groups (usually citing a mixed Aboriginal non-Aboriginal ancestry) to lay claim to the term "Métis." Not surprisingly, the prairie Métis have fiercely defended their hard-won right to call themselves Métis and decried the use of the term by other groups of Aboriginal people in Canada. While perhaps motivated solely by the ethnic ideals of culture and biological relatedness, the recent success in land claims cases by the Métis suggest that financial and territorial interests are likely a part of this hardening of ethnic boundaries. This too is a worldwide phenomenon wherever ethnicity has engendered a territorial or financial benefit.[4]

Whether predicated on notions of "race," "Nation," ethnicity, or financial protectionism, conflict remains over the proper use of the term "Métis." For example, the disagreement over definitions of Métisness that continue to rely on racial distinctions and those that posit identity in national terms was clearly visible in the Native politics of Ontario and pitted one group of Métis against another. Here two opposed strategies of Métis self-identification emerged in the 1980s. The Ontario Métis Aboriginal Association (OMAA) argued that the Métis were a distinct "mixed" Aboriginal people – "Métis Indians" or the "Woodland Métis Tribe" – and often used the term "half-breed" in preference to Métis. The Métis Nation of Ontario (MNO), on the other hand, preferred national imaginaries and allied itself with the western "historic Métis Nation."

The picture of Métis identity was even more complicated or fractured in the Northwest Territories, where the Métis were divided on two conflicting ideas of Nation. One group traced their ancestry to the Red River and asserted a Métis Nationality and the other chose identification with the Dene Nation. This division between two conflicting "Nation" ideas, however, also encompassed different thinking about race. The Métis Nation advocates stressed they had both Native and non-Native ancestry, emphasized older traditions of Métis nationality to the south, and until the 1970s often referred to themselves as "breeds" and "half-breeds" as well as Métis. Those who advocated identification as members of the Dene Nation argued that racial background and "mixture" were irrelevant; as long as a person lived the life of a Native, he or she was a Dene and part of the Dene Nation. Some Dene leaders went so far as to deny that the Métis existed as a separate identifiable group. Again, the major causes of this division centred around land claims and territoriality as well as ideas of identity.

Constitutional developments and court decisions that since the 1980s have opened new avenues for Métis political organizations to articulate definitions of Métis Nationhood have also created discord over the use of the term "Métis." Part of the reason is that the definitions still rely on racial distinctions and terminology. For example in *R. v. Powley*, a Métis hunting rights case, the Supreme Court of Canada defined "Métis" according to both their "mixed ancestry" and their ancestral community's separateness from adjacent tribal communities.[5] While some have cited *Powley* as preserving the idea of Métis by specifying both self-ascription and acceptance from a Métis community, in actuality it allows for *any* group that so desires to call itself Métis. That has not prevented the prairie Métis from declaring themselves to be the "true Métis," but there are other challenges, in particular, the *Daniels* case. The legal verbiage of the case – the original ruling that Métis and non-status Indians are "Indians" under subsection 91(24) of the Constitution Act, 1867 – is confusing enough, probably even leading some Métis to question the difference between Métis and Indian, even though this distinction refers only to their being a legal responsibility of the federal government.

Perhaps more challenging is the definition of Métis the federal court used in this case. The court cited a federal government document from 1980 that defined "the core group of MNSI [Métis and non-status Indians] as a group of native people who maintained a strong affinity for their Indian heritage without possessing status. Their 'Indianness' was based on self-identification and group recognition."[6] The court then stated: "it is those persons ... who are the Métis for the purposes of the declaration which the Plaintiffs seek."[7] As pointed out in chapter 15, this announcement was greeted with trepidation by some Métis spokespersons, who felt that with one stroke of the pen the judge had reduced the concept of being Métis to nothing more than a group of people with some Indian heritage. But it should be noted that this definition was simply for the purposes of affirming that the MNSI were recognized as coming under the Constitution Act, 1867. It does not claim to supplant the definition of Métis as cited in *Powley*. In fact, it is possible that this decision ultimately strengthened the idea of Métis in the courts. The prairie Métis organizations successfully gained intervener status in the case, and were able to convince the Federal Court of Appeal to overturn the lower court's race-based definition of Métis in favor of one more in keeping with the Métis's own idea of their cultural or national identity. However, this case is not yet settled. As of this writing, it is destined to be heard by the Supreme Court.

Despite the court system's tremendous symbolic power in Canadian society,[8] decisions such as *Powley* and *Daniels* ultimately may have little influence on what is obviously a very strong idea – that of being part of a group identity known as the Métis. However one wishes to analyse Métis identity, it is safe to assume that people will keep on identifying as Métis as long as there is a reason to do so. Our analysis of these dynamics – from new peoples to new nations, from racial classifications to national consciousness – has been framed in the context of instrumental ethnicity (situational and strategic). We feel this kind of analysis best illustrates the variety of historical roles played by various Métis peoples at different times and places and serves to emphasize how various Métis leaders, such as Louis Riel, reordered Métis consciousness and politics to adapt to the actions of the Canadian nation state in the period after 1870. As well, this approach allows us the scope to interrogate the dialogical and contested space between Métis as race and Métis as nation up to and including the contemporary period.

It might be assumed that after the constitutional recognition of the Métis as an Aboriginal people in 1982 and the various court decisions that have naturalized and defined the rights of the Métis, the reformulation of Métis identities and ethnicities would coalesce into a more stable essence. Our analysis above suggests the opposite: an *ongoing* Métis ethnogenesis, fuelled by national and global economic and political forces. But the direction this continued ethnic development will take is not clear. If John and Jean Comaroff are correct that ethnicity in general "is becoming more corporate, more commodified, more implicated in the economics of daily life,"[9] then Métis ethnicity should continue to evolve in instrumental ways, fuelled by economic considerations unique to ethnic groups. In commenting on the Maori of New Zealand, the Li of China, the Cajun of Louisiana, and the Native Americans in the southern United States, the Comaroffs have noted the commodification of their often reinvented customs, which they feel is "vital to their survival and sustainability"[10] and is "universal."[11] This observation can be applied to the Métis, even though they have not yet managed to fully commodify their ethnicity and culture, and these forces will continue to shape and reshape Métis identity.

Notes

Introduction

1 *Daniels v. Canada*, FC6 (2013) [para 619].
2 Interview with Métis lawyer and activist Jean Teillet, on *The Early Edition with Rick Cluff*, CBC radio broadcast, Monday, 14 January 2013, downloaded from http://www.cbc.ca/earlyedition/, Tuesday, 15 January 2013.
3 *Daniels v. Canada* [para 130].
4 John Hutchinson and Anthony D. Smith (eds), "Introduction," *Ethnicity* (Oxford: Oxford University Press, 1996), 6.
5 Anthony D. Smith, *The Nation in History: Historiographical Debates about Ethnicity and Nationalism* (Cambridge: Polity Press, 2000), 3.
6 Ibid., 5.
7 Ibid., 22–5. Our understanding of instrumental ethnicity has been shaped by the work of Abner Cohen, particularly his *Custom and Politics in Urban Africa* (Berkeley: University of California Press, 1969), and Paul Brass, *Ethnicity and Nationalism* (London: Sage, 1991). It should also be stated that our instrumentalist perspective is not simply an adopted "theoretical position," but one arrived at through thirty years of work in the field of Métis history. It includes, as concerns Joe Sawchuk, work with Métis political organizations in Manitoba and Alberta since the 1970s and, as concerns Gerhard Ens, work on Métis land claims since the 1980s.
8 Smith, *The Nation in History*, 53. Our understanding of this approach has been influenced by Eric Hobsbawm and Terence Ranger (eds), *The Invention of Tradition* (Cambridge: Cambridge University Press, 1983); Ernest Gellner, *Nations and Nationalism* (Oxford: Blackwell, 1983); Homi Bhabha (ed.) *Nation and Narration* (London: Routledge, 1990); and Benedict Anderson, *Imagined Communities: Reflections on the Origins and Spread of Nationalism* (London: Verso, 1991).

9 These affective aspects of ethnicity are crucial to what has come to be known as an ethno-symbolic approach. This approach asserts that it is necessary to analyse the rise of nations in terms of antecedent ethnic ties and popular formations over the "la longue durée." See Smith, *The Nation in History*, 62–72.

10 The most recent work in this vein is Brenda Macdougall, *One of the Family: Metis Culture in Nineteenth-Century Saskatchewan* (Vancouver: UBC Press, 2010). See also her "Whakootowin: Family and Cultural Identity in Northwestern Saskatchewan Metis Communities," *Canadian Historical Review* 87 (Sept 2006): 429–62. In these works, Macdougall argues that Métis ethnogenesis in northwestern Saskatchewan emerged out of female-centred kin networks that incorporated successive waves of outsider males into a distinct regional and cultural world view rooted in family obligations and responsibility and expressed through reciprocal relations between families.

11 Anderson, *Imagined Communities*, 6.

12 Our analysis of the power of colonial categories to shape ethnic formulations is much influenced by the work of Dipesh Chakrabarty and Ian Hacking. See Chakrabarty, "Governmental Roots of Modern Ethnicity," in Chakrabarty, *Habitations of Modernity: Essays in the Wake of Subaltern Studies* (Chicago: University of Chicago Press, 2002); Hacking, " Making Up People," in *Reconstructing Individualism: Autonomy, Individuality, and the Self in Western Thought*, ed. Thomas C. Heller, Morton Sosna, and David E. Wellbery (Stanford: Stanford University Press, 1986); Hacking, "The Looping Effects of Human Kinds," in *Causal Cognition: A Multidisciplinary Debate*, ed. Dan Sperber, David Premack, and Ann James (Oxford: Clarendon Press, 1995).

13 These works were attempts at historic retrieval, almost salvage ethnography. A.H. de Trémaudan's *L'Histoire de la nation métisse dans l'Ouest canadien* (Montreal: Éditions Albert Lévesque, 1935) was a deliberate attempt to recover a usable Métis past to instil pride in a younger generation of Métis who had all but forgotten their "glorious" history. George Stanley's *The Birth of Western Canada: A History of the Riel Rebellions* (London: Longmans, Green, 1936) portrayed the Métis as a people unable to adjust and doomed with the advance of the settlement frontier. Marcel Giraud's *Le Métis canadien: Son rôle dans l'histoire des provinces de l'Ouest* (Paris: Institut d'ethnologie, 1945) was the most comprehensive inquiry into the origins, rise to prominence, and decline of the Métis, written at a time when he believed they were doomed.

14 George F.G. Stanley, *Louis Riel* (Toronto: Ryerson Press, 1963); George Woodcock, *Gabriel Dumont: The Metis Chief and His Lost World* (Edmonton: Hurtig, 1975); Thomas Flanagan, *Louis "David" Riel: "Prophet of the New World"* (Toronto: University of Toronto Press, 1979; rev. ed. 1996).

15 Joe Sawchuk, *The Metis of Manitoba: Reformulation of an Ethnic Identity* (Toronto: Peter Martin, 1978); Murray Dobbin, *The One-and-A-Half Men: The Story of Jim Brady and Malcolm Norris – Metis Patriots of the Twentieth Century* (Vancouver: New Star Books, 1981); Joe Sawchuk, *The Dynamics of Native Politics: The Alberta Metis Experience* (Saskatoon: Purich, 1998).

16 Joe Sawchuk, Patricia Sawchuk, and Theresa Ferguson, *Metis Land Rights in Alberta: A Political History* (Edmonton: Métis Association of Alberta, 1981); Thomas Flanagan, *Riel and the Rebellion: 1885 Reconsidered* (Saskatoon: Western Producer Books, 1983); D.N. Sprague, *Canada and the Metis, 1869–1885* (Waterloo, ON: Wilfrid Laurier University Press, 1988).

17 Jacqueline Peterson and Jennifer S.H. Brown (eds), *The New Peoples: Being and Becoming Metis in North America* (Winnipeg: University of Manitoba Press, 1985); Gerhard J. Ens, *Homeland to Hinterland: The Changing Worlds of the Red River Metis in the Nineteenth Century* (Toronto: University of Toronto Press, 1996); Tanis C. Thorne, *The Many Hands of My Relations: French and Indians on the Lower Missouri* (Columbia and London: University of Missouri Press, 1996); Nicole St-Onge, *Saint-Laurent, Manitoba: Evolving Métis Identities, 1850–1914* (Regina: Canadian Plains Research Center, 2004); Martha Harroun Foster, *We Know Who We Are: Métis Identity in a Montana Community* (Norman: University of Oklahoma Press, 2006); Heather Devine, *The People Who Own Themselves: Aboriginal Ethnogenesis in a Canadian Family, 1660–1900* (Calgary: University of Calgary Press, 2004); Macdougall, *One of the Family*.

18 Giraud, *Le Métis canadien*.

19 Joseph Kinsey Howard, *Strange Empire: A Narrative of the Northwest* (New York: William Morrow, 1952).

20 See John. E. Foster, "The Métis: The People and the Term," *Prairie Forum* 3(1) (Spring 1978). See also Chris Andersen on the racialized logics governing the use of the term "Métis": "*Moya 'Tipimsook* ('The People Who Aren't Their Own Bosses'): Racialization and the Misrecognition of 'Métis' in Upper Great Lakes Ethnohistory," *Ethnohistory* 58(1) (Winter 2011): 37–63.

21 See John E. Foster and Gerhard J. Ens, "The Metis," *Encyclopaedia of World Cultures*, Vol. 1: *North America*, ed. Timothy J. O'Leary and David Levinson (Boston: G.K. Hall, 1991); Jennifer S.H. Brown, "The Métis: Genesis and Rebirth," in *Native People, Native Lands: Canadian Indians, Inuit and Metis* (Ottawa: Carleton University Press, 1991), 136–47.

1 Race and Nation

1 As Chris Andersen has pointed out, both judicial and administrative discourses have had a tendency, into the twenty-first century, to naturalize a racialized construction of Métis at the expense of an indigenous national construction. For an examination of this dynamic in recent court decisions see his "*Moya 'Tipimsook* ('The People Who Aren't Their Own Bosses'): Racialization and the Misrecognition of 'Métis' in Upper Great Lakes Ethnohistory," *Ethnohistory* 58(1) (Winter 2011): 37–63. For an example of how census categories had a similar effect see Chris Andersen, "From Nation to Population: The Racialization of 'Métis' in the Canadian Census." *Nations and Nationalism* 14(2) (2008): 347–68.

2 Hudson's Bay Company Archives (HBCA), E.2/12; repr. in Andrew Graham, *Observations on Hudson's Bay 1767–1791* (London: Hudson's Bay Record Society, 1969), 145. HBCA, E.2/4.

3 "Petition of Servants of the HBC, York Factory, September 10, 1816," HBCA, E.8/5, fol. 126.

4 For the Great Lakes regions see Jacqueline Peterson, "Many Roads to Red River: Métis Genesis in the Great Lakes Region, 1680–1815," in *The New Peoples: Being and Becoming Métis in North America* (Winnipeg: University of Manitoba Press, 1985), 37–71. See also her "Prelude to Red River: A Social Portrait of the Great Lakes Métis," *Ethnohistory* 25(1) (Winter 1978), 41–67. For the Missouri see Tanis C. Thorne, *The Many Hands of My Relations: French and Indians on the Lower Missouri* (Columbia and London: University of Missouri Press, 1996), 64–97.

5 Shaw and Grant were sons of partners of the North West Company and were serving their apprenticeships, and Pangman and Montour, also sons of partners, were serving as interpreters. See Peter Fidler's journal of 1815. Library and Archives of Canada (LAC), MG 19-E1, Selkirk Papers.

6 Peter Fidler was the Hudson's Bay Company Officer in charge of Fort Douglas at that time.

7 The records of this commission headed by W.B. Coltman can be found in "Papers Relating to the Red River Settlement: viz. Return to an Address from the Honourable House of Commons to His Royal Highness The Prince Regent, dated 24th June 1819 … ," *British Parliamentary Papers. Colonies. Canada* 5 (Shannon: Irish University Press).

8 See John Pritchard, "A true copy of the Original Confession in Police Office, Montreal, 22 February 1817," and W.B. Coltman, "Report relative to the Disturbances in the Indian Territories of British North America, June 30, 1818,"

in "Papers Relating to the Red River Settlement," *British Parliamentary Papers*, ibid., 266, 339, 351.

9 "Observations respecting the employment of illegal Force by the North-West company, the causes which have rendered an Appeal to the Law for redress impracticable on the part of the Hudson's Bay Company," in "Papers Relating to the Red River Settlement," 314. There is evidence that the "half–breeds" in the Hudson's Bay Company system were also beginning to emerge as a separate collectivity, though with a decidedly anti-Métis bias. James Bird, the chief factor of Edmonton House in this period, and the Hudson's Bay Company officer who took over control of the company's operations in the northwest when Semple was killed in 1816, noted from Jack River that "All the Half Breeds (sons of servants of the Company) that are here have expressed a wish to embody themselves under affairs of their own choosing and to come forward to arrest the alarming influences which the Canadian Half Breeds may now acquire by their achievements [*sic*] in Red River; they are perhaps rather inferior in point of numbers to their Enemies yet if collected from all parts of the Country and regularly organized they cannot faile [*sic*]to be a powerful check … I have thanked our young men for their offer & and given them every encouragement in my power to take every measure that may enable them to come forward hereafter with Effect," HBCA, B.60/a/15, fol. 49d-50. Edmonton House journal, 1815–16, 2 August 1816.

10 Since 1816, McGillivray had been at great pains to defend both himself and the North West Company from charges that they had been responsible for encouraging the Métis to attack the Red River Settlement. By asserting that the Métis were an independent tribe of Indians, McGillivray hoped to absolve himself and the company of any blame for the killings.

11 Dispatch from Lieut. General Sir John C. Sherbrooke to the Earl of Bathurst, dated Quebec 11th November 1816, in "Papers Relating to the Red River Settlement," 247. W.B. Coltman noted in his report: "Cuthbert Grant, in his deposition (No. 216,) states also, that after the first expulsion of the colony in 1815, an address had been prepared to the governor of Lower Canada, on behalf of the half-breeds, to inquire of government whether Captain Miles McDonnell, who had called himself governor, had any authority over them or the Indians, of whom signed the address, or any right to possess himself of the lands, and deprive them of their accustomed rights, in order that if it was so, the half-breeds might withdraw themselves to the Missouri, and trade with the Americans there." See "Papers Relating to the Red River Settlement," 385.

12 Winnipeg Post journal, 7 April 1827, HBCA, B.235/a/8, fols 22–22d.

13 Letter from James Sinclair et al. to Alex Christie, Governor of Red River Settlement, 29 August 1845, HBCA, D5/15, fol. 139a. This letter was signed by twenty-three Métis. The HBC view is summarized by Alexander Christie, the governor of the Red River Colony; Letter of Alex. Christie, Governor of Assiniboia, to Messrs James Sinclair, Bapti Larocque, Thomas Logan and others, 5 September 1845, HBCA, D5/15, fols 139a–139b.

14 Alexander Kennedy Isbister was born at Cumberland House and was the son of an Orcadian clerk of the HBC and a "mixed-blood" daughter of Alexander Kennedy. He was educated in the Red River Settlement and briefly worked for the HBC, but eventually moved to Great Britain, attending King's College (Aberdeen), the University of Edinburgh, and the University of London. He was a headmaster at various schools in Great Britain, edited a magazine, and fought hard on behalf of his Métis countrymen, whom he regarded as being under the tyranny of the HBC. See J.M. Bumsted, *Dictionary of Manitoba Biography* (Winnipeg: University of Manitoba Press, 1999), 119–20.

15 This petition, memorial, and considerable correspondence related to the question is found in "Hudson's Bay Company (Red River Settlement) Return to an Address of the Honourable the House of Commons, dated 9 February 1849; for Copies of any Memorials presented to the Colonial Office by Inhabitants of the Red River Settlement, complaining of the Government of the Hudson's Bay Company ..." in *British Parliamentary Papers – "Reports, Correspondence and Other Papers Relating to the Red River Settlement, the Hudson's Bay Company and other Affairs in Canada, 1849. Colonies. Canada* 18 (Shannon: Irish University Press, 1969).

16 Ibid., J.H. Pelly, "Report on the Memorial," 317–24. The various positions in this debate can be seen the Colonial Office correspondence noted above.

17 Ibid., J.H. Pelly to Earl Grey, 24 April 1847, 316–17.

18 Ibid., B. Hawes to A.K. Isbister, 23 June 1849, 409.

19 Alexander Christie to James Sinclair, Bapti Larocque, Thomas Logan and others, 5 September 1845, HBCA, D.5/15, fols. 139a–139b.

20 Ian MacLaren, in analysing exploration literature, has noted that journals and fieldnotes of these travellers were often edited and, in fact, rewritten by editors and ghost-writers for publication. See his "Exploration/ Travel Literature and the Evolution of the Author," *International Journal of Canadian Studies / Revue internationale d'études canadiennes* 5 (Spring 1992); I.S. MacLaren, "Creating Travel Literature: The Case of Paul Kane," *Papers of the Bibliographic Society of Canada* 27 (1988).

21 These groups were neither, strictly speaking, French or English Métis. The French Métis included descendants of Montreal Scots such as Cuthbert

Grant, and the English Métis included descendants of Highland Scots. This terminology (English Métis and French Métis) has been adopted for convenience. French Métis refers to French-speaking, Catholic Métis, and English Métis refers to English-speaking, Protestant Métis.

22 Ross Cox (1793–1853) was born in Dublin, Ireland, and was a clerk in John Jacob Astor's Pacific Fur Company. He was a member of the expedition that built Fort Astoria at the mouth of the Columbia River in 1811 and was present when it was surrendered to the North West Company in 1813. He then entered the service of that company and until 1817 was stationed west of the Rocky Mountains. Thereafter he returned to Ireland, travelling by way of Kamloops, the Athabasca Pass, and Fort Garry. His narrative was originally published in London in 1831.

23 Ross Cox, *Adventures on the Columbia River including The Narrative of a Residence of Six Years on the Western Side of the Rocky Mountains, among Various Tribes of Indians Hitherto Unknown: Together with A Journey Across the American Continent* (New York: J. & J. Harper, 1832). A slightly different version of this book had been published one year earlier in London.

24 Ibid., 309–10.

25 William H. Keating was a professor of mineralogy and chemistry at the University of Pennsylvania and a member of the American Philosophical Society. In 1823 he was invited to accompany a government-sponsored exploration of the American west led by Stephen H. Long. In 1824 he published a narrative of this expedition. Stephen H. Long was one of the initial group of United States topographical engineers who pioneered the mapping of the American west. As a leader of government-sponsored expeditions, Long was preceded in the west only by Merriweather Lewis, William Clark, and Zebulon Pike. He conducted several exploration expeditions between 1816 and 1823 and invited Keating to accompany him as secretary on the 1823 expedition.

26 William H. Keating, *Narrative of an Expedition to the Source of St Peter's River, Lake Winnipeek, Lake of the Woods, &c. &c. Performed in the Year 1823 by the Order of the Hon. J.C. Calhoun, Secretary of War. Under the Command of Stephen H. Long, Major U.S.T.E compiled from the notes of Major Long, Messrs Say, Keating, and Calhoun*, 2 vols (Philadelphia: H.C. Carey & I. Lea, 1824).

27 Ibid., 44.

28 Ibid., 44–6.

29 Pressures in the United Kingdom, the United States, and Canada to learn more about the western interior resulted in the dispatch of two important exploration expeditions in the 1857–60 period. The British party was led by Captain John Palliser and included geologist James Hector, botanical

collector Eugene Bourgeau, and magnetical observer Thomas Blakiston. The Canadian group was led first by George Gladman and then S.J. Dawson, a civil engineer, and H.Y. Hind, a geologist.

30 For this debate see George W. Stocking Jr, "The Persistence of Polygenist Thought in Post-Darwinian Anthropology," in George W. Stocking Jr., *Race, Culture, and Evolution: Essays in the History of Anthropology* (Chicago: University of Chicago Press, 1982).

31 For a spectrum of views on this question see Robert J.C. Young, *Colonial Desire: Hybridity in Theory, Culture and Race* (London: Routledge, 1995), 18.

32 A.P. Reid, "The Mixed or 'Halfbreed' Races of North-Western Canada," *Journal of the Anthropological Institute of Great Britain and Ireland*4 (1875): 46–7.

33 Henry Youle Hind, "Papers Relative to the Exploration of the Country Between Lake Superior and the Red River Settlement," Presented to both Houses of Parliament by Command of Her Majesty, June 1859. Published in *British Parliamentary Papers – Colonies: Canada* 22 (Shannon: Irish University Press, 1969), 548–9, 565–7.

34 Daniel Wilson, the foremost ethnologist writing on these subjects in Canada from the mid-1850s to the 1880s, was a personal friend of Paul Kane and was partly responsible for the appearance of his *Wanderings of an Artist*. He also reviewed Kane's work as well as the publications of Henry Y. Hind in the pages of the *Canadian Journal*.

35 Robert E. Bieder, "Scientific Attitudes towards Indian Mixed-Bloods in Early Nineteenth Century America," *Journal of Ethnic Studies* 8(2) (Summer 1980): 17. See also his *Science Encounters the Indian, 1820–1880: The Early Years of American Ethnology* (Norman: University of Oklahoma Press, 1986).

36 Bieder, "Scientific Attitudes," 18–19.

37 See Olive Dickason, "From 'One Nation' in the Northeast to 'New Nation' in the Northwest: A Look at the Emergence of the Métis," in *New Peoples*, 37–72.

38 Bieder, "Scientific Attitudes," 19–20.

39 William Stanton, *The Leopard's Spots: Scientific Attitudes Toward Race in America, 1815–1859* (Chicago: University of Chicago Press, 1960), 155.

40 J.C. Nott and George R. Gliddon, *Types of Mankind* (Philadelphia: Lippincott, Grambo, 1854).

41 Stanton, *The Leopard's Spots*, 193. As Stanton also points out, the most ardent supporters of slavery in the south were monogenists because of its biblical basis.

42 Bieder, "Scientific Attitudes," 21–2.

43 Ibid., 23–4.
44 Ibid., 26–7.
45 Ibid., 26.
46 Alice Kehoe argues that the work of Daniel Wilson was enormously influential in the creation of the discipline of prehistoric archaeology. See her *The Land of Prehistory: A Critical History of American Archaeology*, xiii. Bruce Trigger has argued that Wilson's *Prehistoric Man*, published in 1862, was not only the first anthropological survey of New World data, but also one of the most important works of anthropological synthesis produced in the nineteenth century. However, unlike Kehoe, he argues that Wilson's refusal to embrace Darwinian evolutionism made *Prehistoric Man* appear conservative and even old-fashioned by comparison with the Darwinian-inspired anthropology that was initially expressed in John Lubbock's *Pre-historic Times* published in 1865. From 1859 on, he argues, Wilson was a follower, not a leader. Because of his cautious attitude towards biological evolution, he seems to have been widely read by liberal Christians, who were troubled by Darwinian evolution but were willing to consider new ideas. Lubbock and others who accepted Darwin's ideas believed that, by adopting this position, Wilson had forfeited his place on the cutting edge of the scientific thought of his day. Trigger, however, does not dispute Wilson's significance in Canadian thought of the period. See his "*Prehistoric Man* and Daniel Wilson's Later Canadian Ethnology," in Ash et al., *Thinking with Both Hands: Sir Daniel Wilson in the Old World and the New*, ed. Elizabeth Hulse (Toronto: University of Toronto Press, 1999), 82, 92–4.
47 Trigger, "*Prehistoric Man* and Daniel Wilson's Later Canadian Ethnology," 82.
48 Daniel Wilson, "Displacement and Extinction Among the Primeval Races of Man," *Canadian Journal*, n.s., 1(1) (1856): 11–12.
49 Trigger, "*Prehistoric Man* and Daniel Wilson's Later Canadian Ethnology," 83.
50 The foregoing summary of *Prehistoric Man* borrows heavily from ibid., 87–90. For a more detailed analysis of Wilson's anthropological works see, B.E. McCardle, "The Life and Anthropological Works of Daniel Wilson, 1816–1892" (MA thesis, University of Toronto, 1980).
51 Daniel Wilson, "Hybridity and Absorption in Relation to the Red Indian Race," *Canadian Journal*, n.s. (July 1875). While this article was published in 1875, it represents only an elaboration of the ideas Wilson had worked out and written about in the 1860s.
52 Ibid., 441.
53 Ibid., 441–2.
54 Ibid., 444.
55 Ibid., 452, 450–1.

56 Ibid., 455–6
57 Ibid., 456–7.
58 Ibid., 459–63.
59 Between 1796 and 1815 the Indian Department had been administered by civil authorities; however, during the War of 1812 this arrangement had created internal dissension and control was shifted back to military authority in 1815; the changing military status of Indian allies was apparently not clear to legislators. See Robert J. Surtees, "Canadian Indian Policies," in *Handbook of North American Indians*, Vol. 4: *History of Indian-White Relations*, edited by Wilcomb E. Washburn (Smithsonian, 1988), 88; D.C. Scott, "Indian Affairs, 1840–1867," in *Canada and Its Provinces: A History of the Canadian People and Their Institutions*, Vol. 5 (Toronto: Printed by T. & A. Constable at the Edinburgh University Press for the Publishers' Association of Canada, 1913–1917); D.C. Scott, "Indian Affairs, 1867–1913," in *Canada and Its Provinces*, Vol. 7, 371–2.
60 Surtees, "Canadian Indian Policies," 88.
61 Between 1828 and 1858 there were six separate commissions that studied these problems. See John F. Leslie, *Commissions of Inquiry into Indian Affairs in the Canadas 1828–1858: Evolving a Corporate Memory for the Indian Department* (Ottawa: Indian Affairs and Northern Development, 1985).
62 "Report on the Affairs of the Indians of Canada," *Journals of the Legislative Assembly*, 8 Vict. 1844–45, Appendix EEE; "Report on the Affairs of the Indians in Canada; submitted to the Honorable the Legislative Assembly, for their information," Province of Canada, *Journals of the Legislative Assembly*, 11 Victoria A.1847, *Sessional Papers*, Appendix T.
63 "Report of the Special Commissioners Appointed on the 8th of September 1856 to Investigate Indian Affairs in Canada," *Journals of the Legislative Assembly*, 21 Vict. 1858, Appendix (No. 21).
64 John F. Leslie, *Commissions of Inquiry into Indian Affairs in the Canadas, 1828–1858*, 90.
65 "Report on the Affairs of the Indians in Canada," A.1847; see n62.
66 "An Act for the protection of the Indians in Upper Canada from imposition, and the property occupied or enjoyed by them from trespass and injury," *Statutes of the Province of Canada*, 13 & 14 Vict. c. 74; "An Act for the Better Protection of the Lands and Property of the Indians in Lower Canada," *Statutes of the Province of Canada*, 13 & 14 Vict., c. 42 .
67 *Statutes of the Province of Canada*, 13 & 14 Vict., c. 42, s. 5. The context for this legislation has been analysed in more detail in Ted Binnema, "Protecting Indian Lands by Defining Indian: 1850–76," *Journal of Canadian Studies / Revue d'études canadiennes* 48(2) (Spring 2014), 5–39.

68 "An Act to repeal in part and to amend an Act, entitled, An Act for the better protection of the Lands and Property of the Indians in Lower Canada," *Statutes of the Province of Canada*, 1851, c. 42.
69 *Statutes of Canada*, 1869, c. 6 [32–33 Vict.].
70 Ibid.
71 Ibid.
72 Letter of W.B. Robinson to Hon. Col. Bruce, 24 September 1850, in Alexander Morris, *The Treaties of Canada with The Indians of Manitoba and the North-West Territories including The Negotiations on which they were based* (Toronto: Belfords, Clarke, 1880), 19–20.
73 Ibid., 18.
74 "Report of the Special Commissioners appointed to investigate Indian Affairs in Canada (Messrs Pennefather, Talfourd, and Worthington) to Sir Edmund Head, April 1858, Province of Canada," *Journals of the Legislative Assembly. Sessional Papers 1858*, Appendix 21.
75 Jeremy Ravi Mumford, "Why Was Louis Riel, a United States Citizen, Hanged as a Canadian Traitor in 1885?" *Canadian Historical Review* 88(2) (June 2007): 237–62.
76 "Report of the Treaty Made with the Pembina Indians, at Pembina, by Alex. Ramsey, November 7, 1851," included in "The Report of the Commissioner of Indian Affairs," November 27, 1851. U.S. Congress, House Ex. Docs. No. 1st Session, 32nd Congress, Serial Set #636, page 285.
77 Mark Wyman, *The Wisconsin Frontier* (Bloomington: Indiana University Press, 1998), 165. See also Martha Harroun Foster, *We Know Who We Are: Métis Identity in a Montana Community* (Norman: University of Oklahoma Press, 2006), 43–50.
78 Treaties in the American west that had "half-breed" clauses included: the Chippewa Treaties of 1837, 1842, 1855, 1863, 1864; Kansa Treaty of 1825; Osage Treaty of 1825; Ottawa Treaty of 1836; Pawnee Treaty of 1857; Ponca Treaty of 1858; Sauk and Fox Treaties of 1830, 1836, Yankton Sioux Treaty of 1858, and the Winnebago Treaty of 1855. See Charles Kappler (ed.), *Indian Affairs: Laws and Treaties*, Vol. 2 (Washington, DC: Government Printing Office, 1904).
79 Article 3, Treaty With The Ponca, 1858, in Kappler, *Indian Affairs* 2: 772–5.
80 For an examination of this phenomenon in the Middle Missouri see Thorne, *The Many Hands of My Relations*, 141–4, 209–19.
81 The Minnesota Territorial Census of 1850 for Pembina County lists 1,105 individuals, almost all of whom were Métis, and 712 of whom had been born in British Territory. A few years after the census was taken, the Catholic priest G.A. Belcourt noted that thousands of Métis had emigrated

from the Red River Settlement to the United States and more would come and take the oath of allegiance if their rights were respected. Letter of G.A. Belcourt to Hon. G.W. Manypenny, Commissioner of Indian Affairs, November 20, 1854. Enclosure #24 in "The Report of the Commissioner of Indian Affairs," November 25, 1854. U.S. Congress, House Ex. Docs. No. 1, 2nd session, 33rd Congress, Serial Set #777, page 279.

82 "Report of the Treaty Made with the Pembina Indians, at Pembina, by Alex. Ramsey, November 7, 1851," included in "The Report of the Commissioner of Indian Affairs," November 27, 1851. U.S. Congress, House Ex. Docs. No. 1st Session, 32nd Congress, Serial Set #636, page 285.

83 Ibid.

84 Based on my analysis of the Minnesota Territorial Census of 1850 and the Red River Settlement Census of 1870. Many of those British-born Métis found in the Territorial Census of 1850 were enumerated in the Red River Settlement of 1870.

85 *Articles of a treaty made and concluded at the Old Crossing of Red Lake River, in the State of Minnesota, on the second day of October, in the year eighteen hundred and sixty-three, between the United States of America, by their commissioners, Alexander Ramsey and Ashley C. Morrill, agent for the Chippewa Indians, and the Red Lake and Pembina bands of Chippewas; by their chiefs, head-men, and warriors.* In Kappler, *Indian Affairs*, 2: 854–5. A year later this section was amended to read: "It is further agreed by the parties hereto, that, in lieu of the lands provided for the mixed-bloods by article eight of said treaty, concluded at the Old Crossing of Red Lake River, scrip shall be issued to such of said mixed-bloods as shall so elect, which shall entitle the holder to a like amount of land, and may be located upon any of the lands ceded by said treaty, but not elsewhere, and shall be accepted by said mixed-bloods in lieu of all future claims for annuities," ibid., 862.

86 Act 33 Victoria, c. 3, s. 31, assented to 12 May 1870.

87 See the journal of Father Ritchot. A microfilm copy of Richot's journal is in the Archives of Manitoba, MG 3, B14-1, no. 12 (M151). The French text was published by George F.G. Stanley as "Le Journal de l'abbé N.-J. Ritchot," *Revue d'histoire de l'Amérique française* 17 (1964): 537–64. The translated version used here is found in W.L. Morton (ed.), *Manitoba: The Birth of a Province* (Winnipeg: Manitoba Record Society, 1965), 140

88 *The New Nation*, 1 July 1870. This newspaper was reporting on Ritchot's speech of 24 June 1870 to the Legislative Assembly of Assiniboia. A translation of part of Ritchot's speech can be found in Thomas Flanagan, *Metis Lands in Manitoba* (Calgary: University of Calgary Press, 1991), 34.

89 House of Commons, *Debates*, 9 May 1870; repr. in Morton, *Manitoba*, 225.

90 Morton, *Manitoba*, 172.

91 Ibid., 204. See also House of Commons *Debates*, 9 May 1870, 1447. Speech of John A. Macdonald, 6 July 1885, Debates of the House of Commons of the Dominion of Canada, Third Session – Fifth Parliament, 48–49 Victoria 1885, 3113–14.

92 A.G. Archibald to Joseph Howe, 27 December 1870, LAC, RG 15, vol. 236, file 7220.

93 See Ian Hacking, "Making Up People," in *Reconstructing Individualism: Autonomy, Individuality, and the Self in Western Thought*, ed. Thomas C. Heller, Morton Sosna, and David E. Wellbery (Stanford: Stanford University Press, 1986), 222–36.

94 These sentiments and ideas can be found in all of the following works: Alexander Taché, *Sketch of the North-West of America by Mgr Taché, Bishop of St Boniface, 1868*, trans. Captain D.R. Cameron (Montreal, 1870); Alexandre Taché, *Histoire et origine des troubles du N.-Ouest: racontées sous serment par Sa Grandeur Mgr L'archevêque de St-Boniface* (1874); G. Dugast, *Histoire de l'Ouest canadien de 1822 à 1869: Époque des troubles* (Montreal: Librairie Beauchemin, 1906); A.G. Morice, *Dictionnaire historique des Canadiens et des Métis français de l'ouest* (Quebec: J.P. Garneau, 1908); A.G. Morice, *Histoire de l'église catholique dans l'ouest canadien, du Lac Supérieur au Pacifique (1659–1915)*, 4 vols (Winnipeg: Author, 1928); A.G. Morice, *A Critical History of the Red River Insurrection: After Official Documents and Non-Catholic Sources* (Winnipeg: Canadian Publishers, 1935); A.G. Morice, *La race métisse: étude critique en marge d'un livre récent* (Winnipeg: Author, 1938).

95 Auguste-Henri de Trémaudan, *Histoire de la nation métisse dans L'Ouest canadien* (Montreal: Éditions Albert Lévesque, 1935).

96 Morice, *La race métisse*, 10–11.

97 "Avertissement," in Trémaudan, *Histoire de la nation métisse*, 15–16. See also petition to incorporate L'Union nationale métisse Saint-Joseph du Manitoba, 1913. Centre du Patrimoine, Fonds Société historique métisse, Boîte 3.

98 See Carl Berger, *The Writing of Canadian History: Aspects of English Canadian Historical Writing since 1900*, 2nd ed. (Toronto: University of Toronto Press, 1986), 240–1.

99 George F.G. Stanley, *The Birth of Western Canada: A History of the Riel Rebellions* (London: Longmans, Green, 1936), 10.

100 A.S. Morton, "The New Nation: The Métis," *Transactions of the Royal Society of Canada*, Section II (1939).

101 A.S. Morton, *A History of the Canadian West to 1870–71* (London: Thomas Nelson, 1939).

102 See L.G. Thomas's introduction to the 2nd ed. of *A History of the Canadian West to 1870–71* (Toronto: University of Toronto Press, 1973), xxi–xxvii.

103 According to A.S. Morton, the argument went something like this: "that as the Indian population, depleted by smallpox and drawn off to the more distant posts for their livelihood, left the land vacant, the Métis inherited their vast domain through the mother's blood in their veins"; see Morton, "The New Nation."

104 Ibid.

105 This English-Canadian analysis of the Métis Nation placed a good deal of stress on the origins and growth of nationalism to explain the outbreak of the Riel Resistance of 1869 and the Riel Rebellion of 1885. This analysis, not surprisingly, did not portray the demise of the Métis Nation as a martyrdom, as Trémaudan had, but rather the futile resistance to the growth of the Canadian state.

106 Marcel Giraud, *Le Métis canadien: son rôle dans l'histoire des provinces de l'Ouest* (Paris: Institut d'ethnologie, 1945). All references are to the two-volume English-language edition translated by George Woodcock: *The Métis in the Canadian West* (Edmonton: University of Alberta Press, 1986).

107 Ibid., 408. The section that sets the stage, and describes the action and aftermath of the Battle of Seven Oaks encompasses more than 130 pages.

108 G.F.G. Stanley, "The Metis and the Conflict of Cultures in Western Canada," *Canadian Historical Review* 28(4) (December 1947); W.L. Morton, "The Canadian Metis," *The Beaver* (September 1950); E.E. Rich, "Colonial Empire," *Economic History Review*, n.s., 2(3) (1950).

109 Morton, *Manitoba: A History* (Toronto: University of Toronto Press, 1957), 51. All page numbers refer to the 2nd ed., published in 1967.

110 Ibid., 63. Like Giraud, W.L. Morton was unable to separate the racialized and ethno-national concepts of Métis identity.

111 Ibid.

112 Ibid., 121.

113 In his study of Cuthbert Grant published in 1963, W.L. Morton characterized the claim of Métis Nationalism as a NWC ruse. The Battle of Seven Oaks was, he said, the result of an accident that turned into a massacre, and its accidental nature formed the basis of the Métis reconciliation with the settlement after 1818. Margaret MacLeod and W.L. Morton, *Cuthbert Grant of Grantown: Warden of the Plains of Red River* (Toronto: McCelland & Stewart, 1963), 38–53. When this book was reissued in 1974, Morton had backtracked even further on the heroic stature of Cuthbert Grant, the erstwhile leader of the Métis Nation. By the 1970s, Morton had come to the conclusion that Grant had been used by the NWC to lead the Métis against the Selkirk

Colony and then used again by George Simpson to conciliate the Métis – not the behaviour of a national hero. Grant was also somewhat of a drunk, according to Morton, and neither Grant nor the Métis had performed any service in defending the Settlement from the Sioux and had probably incited Sioux retaliation against the Settlement by moving deep into Sioux territory to hunt the buffalo. Lastly, Morton committed heresy against the emerging orthodoxy he himself had helped to create by admitting that there was little evidence that Grant was ever revered as a folklore figure by the Métis. See Morton's introduction to the 1974 edition of *Cuthbert Grant of Grantown*.

114 Gerald Friesen, *The Canadian Prairies: A History* (Toronto: University of Toronto Press, 1984), 66.

115 Ibid., 75–7.

116 Ibid., 79–80.

117 Ibid., 117–18.

118 Albert Braz, *The False Traitor: Louis Riel in Canadian Culture* (Toronto: University of Toronto Press, 2003), 4–13.

119 Ibid.

2 Economic Ethnogenesis

1 As already noted in our introduction to this study, this economic focus does not deny the role of kinship in the formation of Métis identities, and we do deal with kinship where we think appropriate, but our focus here is on economic and instrumental ethnicity.

2 Pekka Hämäläinen, "Lost in Transition: Suffering, Survival, and Belonging in the Early Modern Atlantic World," *William and Mary Quarterly* 68(2) (April 2011): 223. This article was written in response to an article written by James Sidbury and Jorge Cañizares-Esguerra that argued for a more inclusive and integrated version of Atlantic ethnogenesis linking African, European, and Native Americans in pan-Atlantic processes. See their "Mapping Ethnogenesis in the Early Modern Atlantic," *William and Mary Quarterly* 68(2) (April 2011): 181–208.

3 For some of these dynamics see Colin G. Calloway, *One Vast Winter Count: The Native American West before Lewis and Clark* (Lincoln: University of Nebraska Press, 2003); Ted Binnema, "'With Tears, Shrieks, and Howlings of Despair': The Smallpox Epidemic of 1781–82," in *Alberta Formed / Alberta Transformed*, Vol. 1, ed. Michael Payne, Donald Wetherell, and Catherine Cavanaugh (Edmonton: University of Alberta Press, 2006), 110–31.

4 James Sweet, "The Quiet Violence of Ethnogenesis," *William and Mary Quarterly* 68(2) (April 2011): 212.

5 See Olive Dickason, "From 'One Nation' in the Northeast to 'New Nation' in the Northwest: A Look at the Emergence of the Métis," in *The New Peoples: Being and Becoming Métis in North America*, ed. Jacqueline Peterson and Jennifer S.H. Brown (Winnipeg: University of Manitoba Press, 1985), 19–36; see also Jennifer S.H. Brown, "The Métis: Genesis and Rebirth," in *Native People, Native Lands: Canadian Indians, Inuit and Métis* (Ottawa: Carleton University Press, 1991), 136–7.

6 Cornelius Jaenen, "Miscegenation in Eighteenth Century New France," in *New Dimensions in Ethnohistory: Papers of the Second Laurier Conference on Ethnohistory and Ethnology*, ed. Barry Gough and Laird Christie, Canadian Ethnology Service, Mercury Series Paper 120 (Ottawa: Museum of Civilization, 1991), 81.

7 John C. Kennedy, *People of the Bays and Headlands: Anthropological History and the Fate of Communities in the Unknown Labrador* (Toronto: University of Toronto Press), 41–4.

8 Ibid., 68–112.

9 John C. Kennedy, "The Changing Significance of Labrador Settler Ethnicity," *Canadian Ethnic Studies* 20(3) (1988); John C. Kennedy, "Aboriginal Organizations and Their Claims: The Case of Newfoundland and Labrador," *Canadian Ethnic Studies* 19(2) (1987).

10 See Peterson and Brown, *The New Peoples*.

11 A significant "mixed-blood" population also arose in the Pacific northwest, but the late date (1820s) when this population began to coalesce around fur trade posts in the Oregon Territory and the rapid influx of American settlers by the 1840s prevented the development of a distinctive Métis identity. One scholar has argued that a Métis culture and identity was emerging in the 1840s, but she argues that this was aborted by incoming American settlement in the Willamette Valley and the Métis exodus to the California goldfields in 1849; see Juliet Thelma Pollard, "The Making of the Metis in the Pacific Northwest – Fur Trade Children: Race, Class, and Gender" (PhD dissertation, University of British Columbia, 1990), xx. A more recent study is even more cautious, preferring to label the fur-trade community that arose in the Willamette as "French-Indian"; see Melinda M. Jetté, "Ordinary Lives: Three Generations of a French-Indian Family in Oregon, 1877–1931" (MA thesis, Laval University, 1996).

12 Brad Devin Edward Jarvis, "A Woman Much to be Respected: Madeleine Laframboise and the Redefinition of a Métis Identity" (MA thesis, Michigan State University, 1998), 1–11.

13 For a more detailed description of these marriage rites and the utility of these marriages see Sylvia van Kirk, *Many 'Tender Ties': Women in Fur-Trade Society, 1670–1870* (Winnipeg: Watson & Dwyer, 1980), 28–52.

14 A form of marriage in which a man has two or more wives at the same time.

15 Jennifer S.H. Brown, "Children of Early Fur Trades," in *Childhood and Family in Canadian History*, ed. Joy Parr (Toronto: McClelland & Stewart 1982), 44; Cornelius Jaenen, "Miscegenation in Eighteenth Century New France," 83.

16 See Jacqueline Peterson, "Prelude to Red River: A Social Portrait of the Great Lakes Métis," *Ethnohistory* 25 (Winter 1978): 41–67; Jacqueline Peterson, "Many Roads to Red River: Métis Genesis in the Great Lakes Region, 1680–1815," in Peterson and Brown, *The New Peoples*; and Jacqueline Peterson, "Ethnogenesis: Settlement and Growth of a 'New People' in the Great Lakes Region, 1702–1815," *American Indian Culture and Research Journal* 6(2) (1982): 23–64; Susan Sleeper-Smith, "Furs and Female Kin Networks: The World of Marie Madeleine Réaume L'archevêque Chevalier," in *New Faces of the Fur Trade: Selected Papers of the Seventh North American Fur Trade Conference, Halifax, Nova Scotia, 1995*, ed. Jo-Anne Fiske, Susan Sleeper-Smith, and William Wicken (East Lansing: Michigan State University Press, 1998), 53–72; Susan Sleeper-Smith, "Women, Kin, and Catholicism: New Perspectives on the Fur Trade," *Ethnohistory* 47(1) (Spring 2000): 423–52; Keith R. Widder, *Battle for the Soul: Métis Children Encounter Evangelical Protestants at Mackinaw Mission, 1823–1837* (East Lansing: Michigan State University Press, 1999).

17 Sleeper-Smith, "Women, Kin, and Catholicism," 424–31.

18 Widder, *Battle for the Soul*, 10–16.

19 For the years 1765–1818 the marriage registers for Ste Anne's Church at Michilimackinac show that 65 per cent of the Euro-American men married Indian (14 per cent) or Métis (51 per cent) women; see ibid., 3.

20 Peterson, "Many Roads to Red River, 41.

21 Jaenen, "Miscegenation in Eighteenth Century New France," 81.

22 Harriet Gorham, "Families of Mixed Descent in the Western Great Lakes Region," in *Native People, Native Lands: Canadian Indians, Inuit and Metis*, ed. Bruce Alden Cox (Ottawa: Carleton University Press, 1991), 40–2.

23 Ibid., 38, 48. Gorham does admit that the Great Lakes Métis appear to conform to the theoretical definition of an ethnic group on the basis of sharing certain objective criteria (common language, religion, style, dress, housing, and artistic expression), 39. In a slightly different vein, Susan Sleeper-Smith has warned that describing all mixed-ancestry descendants of traders who married Native women as Métis creates considerable confusion. At many smaller fur-trading posts in the Great Lakes, kinship more than ethnicity or nationality defined one's identity. See Susan Sleeper-Smith, *Indian Women and French Men: Rethinking Cultural Encounters in the Western Great Lakes* (Amherst: University of Massachusetts Press, 2001), 8, 52.

24 Chris Andersen, "*Moya 'Tipimsook* ('The People Who Aren't Their Own Bosses'): Racialization and the Misrecognition of 'Métis' in Upper Great Lakes Ethnohistory," *Ethnohistory* 58(1) (Winter 2011): 39. He writes that this ethnohistorical misrecognition "uncritically naturalized (and thus conceals) the relations of power through which historical colonial authorities sought to discipline the region's antecedent social relations by means of the imposition of a biological-cum-cultural differentiation between 'half-breeds' and 'Indians,'" 38–9.
25 Brown, "Children of Early Fur Trades," 49–52.
26 Widder, *Battle for the Soul*, 47–61.
27 See Tanis Thorne, *The Many Hands of My Relations: French and Indians on the Lower Missouri* (Columbia and London: University of Missouri Press, 1996), 6.
28 Ibid., 66–8.
29 Ibid., 77.
30 Ibid., 83–6.
31 Ibid., 66–8, 91, 115.
32 Ibid., 117–27.
33 Ibid., 135–75.
34 Ibid., 200–6.
35 Ibid., 208–44.
36 In the North West Company the term"bourgeois" was used as a respectful term of address to an officer in the fur trade. Miles Macdonell, the first governor of the colony of Assiniboia, noted that "free Canadians" and "half-breeds" and their children made a living by hunting the buffalo in all seasons: "These free Canadians were formerly in the service of the North-West company, and on becoming burthened with families and infirm, obtained permission to remain in the country on condition of giving all furs and provisions to the North-West company"; "A Sketch of the Conduct of the North-West Company towards Red River Settlement from September 1814 to June 1815 inclusive," Enclosure (2) in Sir G. Drummond's Letter of 6 December 1815, in "Papers Relative to the Red River Settlement, 1815–19," *British Parliamentary Papers. Colonies. Canada* 5 (Shannon: Irish University Press), 214.
37 The historian who has done the most to clarify the emergence of the Métis in the western interior is John E. Foster; see his "The Origins of the Mixed Bloods in the Canadian West," in *Essays on Western History*, ed. L.H. Thomas (Edmonton: University of Alberta Press, 1976), 69–80; "The Plains Metis," in *Native Peoples: The Canadian Experience*, ed. R. Bruce Morrison and C. Roderick Wilson (Toronto: McClelland & Stewart, 1986), 375–403; and "Wintering, the Outsider Male and Ethnogenesis of the Western Plains Métis," *Prairie Forum* 19 (Spring 1994): 1–13.

38 Foster, "Wintering," 7.

39 Ibid.

40 Hudson's Bay Company Archives, B.115/e/1, Lesser Slave Lake Report on District 1819–20. See also Trudy Nicks, "Native Responses to the Early Fur Trade at Lesser Slave Lake," in *Le Castor Fait Tout: Selected Papers of the Fifth North American Fur Trade Conference, 1985*, ed. Bruce Trigger, Toby Morantz, and Louise Dechêne (Montreal: Lake St Louis Historical Society, 1987), 278–310.

41 Of the approximately 700 applications for scrip (representing some 2000 claims) in the Treaty 8 area in 1899 and 1900, 40 per cent came from the Lesser Slave Lake District. See Gerhard J. Ens, "Taking Treaty 8 Scrip, 1899–1900: A Quantitative Portrait of Northern Alberta Metis Communities," in *Treaty 8 Revisited: Selected Papers on the 1899 Centennial Conference*, ed. Duff Crerar and Jaroslav Petryshyn. Special Issue of *Lobstick: An Interdisciplinary Journal* 1(1) (Winter 1999–2000): 229–58.

42 Charles Mair, *Through the Mackenzie Basin: An Account of the Signing of Treaty No. 8 and the Scrip Commission, 1899* (Edmonton: University of Alberta Press, 1999; reprint of 1908 ed.), 69–73.

43 Brown, "The Métis," 139.

44 Jennifer S.H. Brown, *Strangers in Blood: Fur Trade Company Families In Indian Country* (Vancouver: UBC Press, 1980), 60–4; van Kirk, *Many 'Tender Ties'*, 41–6.

45 Foster, "Origins of the Mixed Bloods," in *Essays on Western History*, 74–5.

46 Ibid., 75–6.

47 See Carol M. Judd, "Mixed Bloods of Moose Factory, 1730–1981: A Socio-Economic Study," in *American Indian Culture and Research Journal* 6(2) (1982): 65–88; Carol M. Judd, "Moose Factory Was Not Red River: A Comparison of Mixed Blood Experiences," in *Explorations in Canadian Economic History: Essays in Honour of Irene M. Spry*, ed. Duncan Cameron (Ottawa: University of Ottawa Press, 1985); John S. Long, "Treaty No. 9 and Fur Trade Company Families: North Eastern Ontario's Halfbreeds, Indians, Indians, Petitioners and Métis," in Peterson and Brown, *The New Peoples*, 137–62.

48 Marina Devine, "The First Northern Métis: An Overview of the Historical Context for the Emergence of the Earliest Métis in Canada's North," in *Picking up the Threads: Métis History in the Mackenzie Basin* (Ottawa: Métis Heritage Association of the Northwest Territories and Parks Canada – Canadian Heritage, 1998), 5–26.

49 Jennifer L. Bellman and Christopher C. Hanks, "Northern Métis and the Fur Trade," in *Picking up the Threads*, 29–30.

50 HBC post journals for this region date from the late eighteenth century through the nineteenth century.

51 CMS records for missions from the English River north through the Mackenzie and Yukon Rivers date from 1840s onwards.
52 The Oblate mission at Île-à-la-Crosse (Saint-Jean Baptiste) was one of the oldest Oblate missions in the region. It was established in 1846 by Father Alexandre-Antonin Taché. Eventually missions were also established across the north in the 1850s and 1860s. Oblate sources consulted include reports and correspondence from various missionaries published in *Missions de la Congrégation des Missionnaires oblats de Marie-Immaculée* (1862–1911).
53 Entry for 12 May 1837. Hudson's Bay Company Archives (HBCA), B.89/a/17B.
54 Entry for 17 November 1894. HBCA, B.89/a/37.
55 Journal of Robert Hunt, 15 July 1852. CMS records, C.1/O, Reel 15.
56 Lettre du R.P. Petitot au T.R.P. Superior Général, Notre Dame des Victoires, 30 December 1873, in *Missions de la Congrégation des Missionnaires oblats de Marie-Immaculée*, No. 48, December 1874, 486–7.
57 Bellman and Hanks, "Northern Métis and the Fur Trade," 32. A very different view is taken by Brenda Macdougall in her recent study of the Métis of northwestern Saskatchewan. She argues that Métis culture and identity in this region emerged from and was grounded in the Cree and Dene protocols of "*wahkootowin*" – an Aboriginal notion of family, land, home, and community transmitted to the Métis by their Native mothers and grandmothers; see *One of the Family: Metis Culture in Nineteenth-Century Northwestern Saskatchewan* (Vancouver: UBC Press, 2010).
58 Bellman and Hanks, "Northern Métis and the Fur Trade," 31–3.
59 "Remarks Regarding the HBC Posts in Upper English River District," by Wm. McMurray, 10 January 1873. Wm. McMurray (Green Lake) to Donald Smith, Fort Garry, 9 September 1873. HBCA, B.89/b/4, Île-à-la-Crosse Correspondence Book.
60 Bellman and Hanks, "Northern Métis and the Fur Trade," 61–2.
61 Samuel McKenzie (Ile-à-la-Crosse) to Chief Commissioner (Fort Garry) 1 June 1872. HBCA, B.89/b/4, Île-à-la-Crosse Correspondence Book.
62 Wm McMurray (Île-à-la Crosse) to Donald A. Smith (Fort Garry) 17 November 1873. Wm. McMurray to James A. Graham, 25 June 1874. Ibid.
63 Post Reports – Green Lake 1889–1892. HBCA, B.84/e/1–3.
64 Bellman and Hanks, "Northern Métis and the Fur Trade," 62.
65 Post Reports – Green Lake 1892–1894. HBCA, B.84/e/3–4. See also HBCA, B.89/d/275&282, Île-à-la-Crosse Account Books. Both the 1885 and 1887 accounts list approximately thirty freemen.
66 Post Reports – Green Lake 1900. HBCA, B.84/e/7.

67 The following short summary of the travel logistics of the fur trade has been compiled from the following sources: Gordon Charles Davidson, *The North West Company* (New York: Russell and Russell, 1916); H.A. Innis, *The Fur Trade in Canada*, rev. ed. (Toronto: University of Toronto Press, 1956); Eric Ross, *Beyond the River and the Bay* (Toronto: University of Toronto Press, 1970); Eric Morse, *Fur Trade Canoe Routes of Canada: Then and Now* (Toronto: University of Toronto Press, 1969); Michael Payne, *The Most Respectable Place in the Territory: Everyday Life in Hudson's Bay Company Service: York Factory, 1788–1870* (Ottawa: Canadian Parks Service, 1989); E.E. Rich, *Hudson's Bay Company, 1670–1870*, 2 vols (London: Hudson's Bay Record Society, 1958); Arthur S. Morton, *A History of the Canadian West to 1870–71* (London: Thomas Nelson & Sons); T. Smythe, "Thematic Study of the Fur Trade in the Canadian West, 1670–1870," Agenda Paper 1968–29 (Historic Sites and Monuments Board, St John's Newfoundland, 19–21 June 1968).

68 Smythe, "Thematic Study of the Fur Trade in the Canadian West, 40.

69 Ibid., 44.

70 By the 1830s all the La Loche Brigade tripmen were hired in the Red River Settlement. Philip Goldring, *Papers on the Labour System of the Hudson's Bay Company, 1821–1900*, Vol. 2. Parks Canada Manuscript Report No. 142 (Ottawa: Parks Canada, 1980), 145.

71 See A.A. Den Otter, "Transportation and Transformation: The Hudson's Bay Company, 1857–1885," *Great Plains Quarterly* 3(3) (Summer 1983): 171–85.

72 From the 1850s to the mid-1860s the Hudson's Bay Company sent from eight to sixteen boatloads of freight by way of the Portage La Loche Brigade. In 1867 the equivalent of four boatloads was sent overland by carts, and by 1871 this had risen to the equivalent of six boatloads; Goldring, *Papers on the Labour System of the Hudson's Bay Company*, 153–4.

73 Samuel Mckenzie (Île-à-la-Crosse) to Roderick McFarlane (Fort Chipewyan), 25 January 1872. HBCA, B.89/b/4, Île-à-la-Crosse Correspondence Book, fol. 7–7d.

74 "Batteaux" were not a single type of craft but a name applied to any rough-made vessel of modest size built inexpertly within a district for its own use. They often resembled smaller versions of the flat-bottomed York boats, but were more makeshift and seldom were used for more than two years. Goldring, *Papers on the Labour System of the Hudson's Bay Company*, 199–200.

75 By the 1870s some of the freight was sent by river steamboat from Lake Winnipeg to Fort Carlton; ibid., 155.

76 Ibid., 155–6. With the improvement of the road north of Edmonton to Athabasca Landing and the introduction of steamboat service on the

Athabasca River, the Portage La Loche route faded in importance. By the 1890s the route across Portage La Loche was seldom used by the HBC to supply the Athabasca and Mackenzie Districts. The route between Green Lake and Île-à-la-Crosse, however, remained in use to supply the English River District.

77 Pierre Laliberte, the son of a French Canadian and a "half-breed" woman named Belanger, was born at Fort Carlton in 1817 (see scrip application in 1887). He entered the HBC service in 1838 as a labourer and retired to the Red River Settlement in 1849. He re-entered service in 1851 in the capacity of steersman and was raised to the rank of postmaster in 1856 and clerk in 1862. He was in charge of Portage La Loche and the transport business there for eleven years. By the 1870s he was married and had a large family. See "Memoranda Regarding Officers in the Upper English River Dist.," Wm. McMurray, 10 January 1873. HBCA, B.89/b/4, Île-à-la-Crosse Correspondence Book, fol. 20.

78 Goldring, *Papers on the Labour System of the Hudson's Bay Company*, 150.

79 "Remarks Regarding the HBC Posts in Upper English River District," by Wm. McMurray, 10 January 1873. HBCA, B.89/b/4, Île-à-la-Crosse Correspondence Book, fols 18–18d.

80 Wm McMurray (Île-à-la-Crosse) to James Graham, 5 December 1874. HBCA, B.89/b/4, Île-à-la-Crosse Correspondence Book, fols 74d–75.

3 Fur Trade Wars

1 Lyle Dick, "The Seven Oaks Incident and the Construction of a Historical Tradition, 1816–1970," *Journal of the Canadian Historical Association*, n.s., 2 (1991).

2 Ibid.

3 A.S. Morton, *A History of the Canadian West to 1870-71* (Toronto: Thomas Nelson & Sons, 1939), 518–32; J.M. Bumsted, *Fur Trade Wars: The Founding of Western Canada* (Winnipeg: Great Plains Publications, 1999), 93–110.

4 For a general discussion of these trends see Timothy Ball, "Climatic Change, Droughts and the Social Impact: Central Canada, 1811–20, a Classic Example," and "The Year without Summer: Its Impact on the Fur Trade and History of Western Canada," both in *The Year without Summer: World Climate in 1816*, ed. C.R. Harington (Ottawa: Canadian Museum of Nature, 1992). Ball attributed these weather changes to the twenty-two-year cycle of Arctic or Polar atmospheric fronts. See his "Climatic Change, Droughts and the Social Impact," 188. While Ball is correct in identifying these macro changes, his argument on the effects of these crises is based on vague generalizations of what shorter summers, colder winters, and drought should result in – that is, that such weather conditions would have

diminished wildlife, reduced food supplies, changed buffalo migration patterns, caused starvation and hardship, and threatened the fur industry. From these generalizations he concludes that the harsh weather conditions of 1811 to 1820 and the uncertainties of the food supply made Indians see the fur trade as a threat to their traditional way of life and that the arrival of settlers in 1812 heightened tensions, as the Métis and Indians saw them as a threat to their way of life and usurpers of their land. Given these factors, it was not surprising that the Indians and Métis would attack the colony to drive the unwelcome settlers out of the country. Climate, he asserts, did not cause the Battle of Seven Oaks, but it acted as the catalyst for an already volatile situation. Absent from his account is any hint that the conflict between fur-trading companies contributed to the Battle of Seven Oaks.

5 My analysis of the provision trade in this period is based on the fur trade journals of Edmonton House, Carlton House, and Brandon House. I have extracted data on temperature, drought, fire, and plains provisions (buffalo availability and pemmican production) by year. Edmonton, Brandon, and Carlton were chosen because they provide evidence on all the provisioning districts of the northern plains: the Saskatchewan District, the Qu'Appelle District, and the Red River District.

6 Edmonton House journal, 6 January, 17 March, and 12 May 1811. HBCA, B.60/a/9, fols 4, 10, 12d.

7 Ibid., 18 October 1811. HBCA, B.60/a/10, fol. 4.

8 Ibid., 2 June 1812. HBCA, B.60/A/10, fol. 14d; 12 October 1812; 27 December 1812. HBCA, B.60/a/11, fols 2d, 5.

9 Ibid., 28 September 1813, 28 February 1814. HBCA, B.60/a/12, fols 2d, 10d.

10 Ibid., 17 February 1812. HBCA, B.60/a/10, fol. 12d.

11 Ibid., 2 June 2, 1812. HBCA, B.60/a/10.

12 Ibid., 21 May 1814. HBCA, B.60/a/12, fol. 15.

13 Carlton House journal, 28 December 1814, 15 January 1815. HBCA, B27/a/4, fols 6d, 8.

14 This is the last year journals exist for this post until the 1815–16 outfit.

15 Brandon House journal, 15 November 1811, 6 February 1812, 4 May 1812. HBCA, B.22/a/18b, fols 4d, 10d, 5d.

16 "General Report of Red River District by Peter Fidler, 1819 May," HBCA, B.22/e/1.

17 Edmonton House journal, 8 February 1814, HBCA, B.60/a/12, fol. 9–9d.

18 A copy of this proclamation can be found in *Report of the Proceedings connected with the disputes between the Earl of Selkirk and the North-West Company at the Assizes, held at York in Upper Canada, October, 1818* (Montreal: James Lane and Nahum Mower, 1819), 133–4.

19 This consisted of 96 bags of pemmican, 94 kegs of fat, and 865 pounds of dried meat. These provisions were seized at gun and bayonet point.
20 The NWC bourgeois negotiating this agreement was John Macdonald of Garth.
21 See Bumsted, *Fur Trade Wars*, 105.
22 The early Manitoba historian and Selkirk sympathizer, George Bryce, has argued that this speech was a forgery and was actually penned by a NWC trader; see *The Remarkable History of the Hudson's Bay Company including that of the French Traders of North-Western Canada and of the North-West, XY, and Astor Fur Companies* (London: Low, 1900), 247.
23 Speech of Grandes Oreilles, a great chief of the Chippewas, made 19 June 1814, addressed to Partners of the NWC. at Red River and reprinted in Samuel Hull Wilcocke [Edward Ellice & Simon McGillivray], *A Narrative of Occurances in the Indian Countries of North America, since the connexion of the Right Hon. The Earl of Selkirk with the Hudson's Bay Company, and his attempt to establish a colony on the Red River with a detailed account of His Lordship's military Expedition to, and subsequent proceedings at Fort William, in Upper Canada* (London: B. McMillan, 1817), Appendix XIII, 36.
24 The events of the spring and summer of 1815 at Red River can be followed in the Winnipeg Post journal of 1814–15, written by Peter Fidler. See HBCA, B.235/a/3.
25 These dynamics and the following course of events have been reconstructed from the evidence found in the HBC journals of Edmonton House, Carlton House, and Brandon House for the years 1814–16. For the events of the spring of 1816, I have relied on the eyewitness testimony of individuals produced by William Coltman in his investigation of the Battle of Seven Oaks and the testimony of eyewitnesses during the trials in Upper Canada. For the Coltman report and evidence see "Papers Relating to the Red River Settlement: viz Return to an Address from the Honourable House of Commons to His Royal Highness The Prince Regent, dated 24th June 1819 ... ," *British Parliamentary Papers. Colonies. Canada* 5 (Shannon: Irish University Press). For the testimony of witnesses during the trial see *Report of the Proceedings connected with the disputes between the Earl of Selkirk and the North-West Company*. Both sources also contain numerous supporting documents related to the events of 1815–16.
26 Brandon House journal, 30 July 1815. HBCA, B.22/1/19, fol. 2.
27 Ibid., 13 October 1815. HBCA, B.22/a/19, fol. 7d.
28 Ibid., 26 January 1816. HBCA, B.22/a/19, fol. 15d; Carlton House journals, 1815–17. HBCA, B.27/a/5–6. Edmonton House journals 1815–17. HBCA, B.60/a/15–17; Edmonton District Report 1815. HBCA, B.60/e/1. Even as Peter

Fidler noted a drought in the Red River District from 1816 to 1819, he also noted that despite the drought the buffalo were numerous in the district and indeed were teeming at the southern end of Lake Manitoba; "General Report of Red River District by Peter Fidler, 1819 May," HBCA, B.22/e/1; "General Report of the Manitoba District for 1820 by Peter Fidler," HBCA, B.51/e/1.

29 Edmonton House journal, 30 May 1816. HBCA, B.60/a/15, fol. 40d.

30 Ibid., 11 June 1816. HBCA, B.60/a/15, fol. 43–43d.

31 The records of this commission headed by W.B. Coltman can be found in, "Papers Relating to the Red River Settlement."

32 This interpretation emerges very clearly in Wilcocke, *A Narrative of Occurances in the Indian Countries of North America*, and Edward Ellice, *The communications of Mercator upon the contest between the Earl of Selkirk, and the Hudson's Bay Company, on one side, and the North West Company on the Other* (Montreal: W. Gray, 1817).

33 Since 1816, McGillivray had been at great pains to defend both himself and the North West Company from charges that they had been responsible for encouraging the Métis to attack the Red River Settlement. By asserting that the Métis were an independent tribe of Indians, McGillivray hoped to absolve himself and the North West Company of any blame for the killings. W.B. Coltman, the officer who headed the inquiry, noted that the Métis had been tutored by NWC officers to call themselves a nation of Indians. W.B. Coltman to Sir John Coape, 14 May 1818, in "Papers Relating to the Red River Settlement," 308, 314.

34 "Statement of Wm. McGillivray to W.B. Coltman, March 14, 1818," in "Papers Relating to the Red River Settlement," 318.

35 E.E. Rich, "Introduction," in *Colin Robertson's Correspondence Book, September 1817 to September 1822*, ed. E.E. Rich (Toronto: Champlain Society, 1939), lxviii–lxix.

36 *Statement Respecting the Earl of Selkirk's Settlement Upon the Red River in North America; Its Destructions in 1815 and 1816; and the Massacre of Governor Semple and his Party* (London: John Murray, 1817), 17–18.

37 Ibid., 71–4. Thomas Douglas, Earl of Selkirk, *The Memorial of Thomas Earl of Selkirk* (Montreal: Nahum Mower, 1819). Repr. in *The Collected Writings of Lord Selkirk, 1810–1820*. Vol. 2 in *The Writings and Papers of Thomas Douglas, Fifth Earl of Selkirk*, ed. J.M. Bumsted (Winnipeg: Manitoba Record Society, 1987), 113–14.

38 Edmonton House journal, 2 August 1816. HBCA, B.60/a/15, fol. 49d–50.

39 Brandon House journal, 1 June 1816. HBCA, B.22/a/19.

40 Ibid. Library and Archives of Canada (LAC), Selkirk Papers, MG 19, E1, D. McPherson to Selkirk, 4 September 1816, 2673.

41 "Statement of Wm. McGillivray to W.B. Coltman, March 14, 1818," in "Papers Relating to the Red River Settlement," 318.
42 W.B. Coltman, "A general Statement and Report relative to the Disturbance in the Indian Territories of British North America, by the undersigned Special Commissioner for inquiring into the Offences committed in the said Indian Territories, and the Circumstances attending to the Same," 30 June 1818, in "Papers Relating to the Red River Settlement," 372.
43 A record of the capitulation is recorded in Peter Fidler's journal of 1815 and is also found in the Selkirk Papers. LAC, MG 19, E1, 18514–16.
44 Bumsted, *Fur Trade Wars*, 150.
45 Miles Macdonell to Lord Selkirk, 17 July 1813. LAC, Selkirk Papers, MG19, E1, 790.
46 Ibid., 790–1. See also Donna G. Sutherland, *Peguis: A Noble Friend* (St Andrews, MB: Chief Peguis Heritage Park, 2003), 32–70.
47 Miles Macdonell to Selkirk, 16 March 1817. LAC, Selkirk Papers, MG 19, E1, 3238–48. Sutherland, *Peguis*, 32–70. Lucille Campey, *The Silver Chief: Lord Selkirk and the Scottish Pioneers of Belfast, Baldoon and Red River* (Toronto: Natural Heritage Books, 2003), 108.
48 The text of the treaty as well as the map accompanying it can be found in HBCA, E.8/1, Red River Settlement, Deeds and Agreements, 1811–36. The two-statute-miles distance was decided to approximate what could be seen by looking under the belly of a horse out on the prairie.
49 For various aspects of the treaty signing see LAC, Selkirk Papers, MG 19, E1, 17295–313. See also George Bryce, *Manitoba: Its Infancy, Growth, and Present Condition* (London: Sampson Low, Marston, Searle, & Rivington, 1882), 259.
50 See the censuses prepared by Peter Fidler in the Winnipeg Post journal, 1814–15. HBCA B.235/a/3, fols 32, 39d.
51 Pierre Falcon was born on 4 June 1793 at Elbow Fort in the Swan River District, the son of an NWC clerk, also named Pierre, and a Cree woman. At the age of five years he was taken back to Quebec by his father, where he was baptised in 1798 and received a rudimentary education. He returned to the west at the age of fifteen and entered the employ of the North West Company. In 1812 he married Marie Grant, the daughter of Cuthbert Grant, and eventually settled down in Grant's village of White Horse Plain (later the parish of St François Xavier) in the Red River Settlement. He lived there until his death in 1876. See Margaret Complin, "Pierre Falcon's 'Chanson de la Grenouillère,'" *Transactions of the Royal Society of Canada*, Section II (1939).
52 There are many variants of this song, and the one referred to here comes from J.J. Hargrave's *Red River*, published in 1871. According to Hargrave,

he took down the song from the dictation of Falcon, who was still alive at the time. Hargrave believed that the song had never appeared in print before; see *Red River* (Montreal: John Lovell, 1871), 488–9. For a fuller discussion of the various versions of the song and Falcon the author, see Margaret Arnett Macleod, *Songs of Old Manitoba* (Toronto: Ryerson Press, 1960), and "Bard of the Prairies," *The Beaver* (Spring 1956); Margaret Complin, "Pierre Falcon's 'Chanson de la Grenouillère'"); Bruce Peel, "Falcon, Pierre," in *Dictionary of Canadian Biography Online*; and *Pierre Falcon* (Winnipeg: Manitoba Culture, Heritage and Recreation, Historic Resources Branch, 1984).

53 For a longer analysis of the content of the song see: Kathy Durnin, "Mixed Messages: The Métis in Canadian Literature, 1816–2007" (PhD thesis, Comparative Literature, University of Alberta, 2008), 57–66.

54 Ibid., 66.

55 The song can be found in the Selkirk Papers, LAC, MG 19, E1, Reel C-99207–8).

56 J.A. Gilfillan, "A Trip through the Red River Valley in 1864," *North Dakota Historical Quarterly* 1(4) (July 1927).

57 Isaac Cowie, *The Company of Adventurers: A Narrative of Seven Years in the Service of the Hudson's Bay Company During 1857–1874 on the Great Buffalo Plains with Historical and Biographical Notes and Comments* (Toronto: William Briggs, 1913), 391.

58 H. De Lamothe, *Cinq mois chez les Français d'Amérique : voyage au Canada et à la rivière Rouge du Nord* (Paris: Librairie Hachette, 1879), 308–9.

59 Edmonton House journal, 2 September 1816. HBCA, B.60/a/15, fol. 54.

60 George Simpson to Colvile, 8 September 1821, 1116–16A; Simpson to Colvile, 31 May 1824, 1140–1. LAC, Selkirk Papers, MG 19, E1, Reel A27.

61 Winnipeg Post journal, 7 April 1827. HBCA, B. 235/a/8, fol. 22d.

62 Ibid.

63 George Simpson's Report on Districts, dated 20 June 1829. HBCA, D4/96, fols 13d–14.

64 Winnipeg Post journal, 7 April 1827. HBCA, B. 235/a/8, fol. 22d.

65 George Simpson's Report on Districts, dated 20 June 1829. HBCA, D4/96, fol. 14.

66 London Correspondence Inward from George Simpson, Letter of 10 August 1831. HBCA, A12/1, fol. 465d–466.

67 Ibid.

68 Letter from James Sinclair et al. to Alex Christie, Governor of Red River Settlement, 29 August 1845. HBCA, D5/15, fol. 139a. This letter was signed by twenty-three Métis.

69 Letter of Alex. Christie, Governor of Assiniboia, to Messrs James Sinclair, Bapti Larocque, Thomas Logan, and others, 5 September 1845. HBCA, D5/15, fols 139a–139b.
70 Alexander Kennedy Isbister was born at Cumberland House and was the son of an Orcadian clerk of the HBC and a mixed-blood daughter of Alexander Kennedy. He was educated in the Red River Settlement and briefly worked for the HBC, but eventually he moved to Great Britain, where he attended King's College (Aberdeen), the University of Edinburgh, and the University of London. He was a headmaster at various schools in Great Britain, edited a magazine, and fought hard on behalf of his Métis countrymen, whom he regarded as being under the tyranny of the HBC. See J.M. Bumsted, *Dictionary of Manitoba Biography* (Winnipeg: University of Manitoba Press, 1999), 119–20.
71 This petition, memorial, and considerable correspondence related to the question are found in "Hudson's Bay Company (Red River Settlement) Return to an Address of the Honourable the House of Commons, dated 9 February 1849; for Copies of any Memorials presented to the Colonial Office by Inhabitants of the Red River Settlement, complaining of the Government of the Hudson's Bay Company ..." In *British Parliamentary Papers – Reports, Correspondence and Other Papers Relating to the Red River Settlement, the Hudson's Bay Company and other Affairs in Canada, 1849. Colonies. Canada* 18 (Shannon: Irish University Press, 1969).
72 This petition, which was in French, was accompanied by 1,000 signatures attested to by William Dease, J. Baptiste Pyette, J. Louis Rielle, Charles Montigny, and Cuthbert M'Gillis. See ibid., 317–24.
73 Ibid., J.H. Pelly, "Report on the Memorial," 317–24.
74 Ibid., J.H. Pelly to Earl Grey, 24 April 1847, 316–17.
75 Ibid., A.K. Isbister's response to Pelly, 354–62.
76 Ibid., B. Hawes to A.K. Isbister, 23 June 1849, 409.

4 Louis Riel and the Religion of Métis Nationalism

1 Louis Riel, "Les Métis du Nord-Ouest," in *The Collected Writings of Louis Riel / Les Écrits complets de Louis Riel* (*CW*), Vol. 3, ed. Thomas Flanagan (Edmonton: University of Alberta Press, 1985), 278–94.
2 Ibid., 279–81.
3 Ibid., 281–3.
4 Ibid., 285.
5 Ibid., 274.
6 Albert Braz, *The False Traitor: Louis Riel in Canadian Culture* (Toronto: University of Toronto Press, 2003), 23–5.

7 This section on the Métis politics of 1869–70 borrows from an earlier article; see Gerhard Ens, "Prologue to the Red River Resistance: Pre-liminal Politics and the Triumph of Riel," *Journal of the Canadian Historical Association* 5(1) (1994): 111–23.

8 See Philippe Mailhot, "Ritchot's Resistance: Abbé Noël Joseph Ritchot and the Creation and Transformation of Manitoba" (PhD dissertation, University of Manitoba, 1986), 30.

9 Albert Braz contends that by 1868 Riel had begun to articulate an explicit Métis Nationalism, but it is not apparent in his actions, writings, or speeches of this period. See Braz, *The False Traitor*, 23–4.

10 Among other activities that were alarming the Métis, the Canadians were staking out land; they denounced the Americans, Fenians, and Métis in the colony; they ran up the Canadian flag; and they spoke of the Métis openly and contemptuously as cowards. William McTavish to W.G. Smith, 24 July 1869. HBCA, A.12/45, fol. 269–70. William McTavish to Joseph Howe, 14 May 1870, 2. HBCA, RG 1, Series 4/8.

11 Albert E. Dease Papers, State Historical Society of North Dakota, A26.

12 Two of William Hallet's sisters married French Métis and converted to Catholicism.

13 *Nor'Wester*, 24 July 1869.

14 While no minutes exist for this meeting, it can be reconstructed using the various accounts that do exist. See Dugast to Taché, 29 juillet 1869, T6695–6698. Centre du Patrimoine, Archives de la Société historique de Saint-Boniface ASHSB); William McTavish to W.G. Smith, 10 August 1868. HBCA, A12/45, fols 282–3; and "Ritchot's Narrative of the Resistance," vol. 1. Archives of Manitoba (AM).

15 This debate can be followed in the pages of the *Nor'Wester*. See "Native Title to Indian Lands," 14 February 1860; "Peguis Refuted," 28 February 1860; "The Land Question," 14 March 1860; "The Political Condition of the Country," 28 April 1860; "Peguis Vindicated," 28 April 1860; "The Peguis Land Controversy," 14 May 1860; "The Land Question," 14 June 1860; "The Halfbreed Meeting," 28 June 1860; "Paketay-Hoond on the Land Question," 28 June 1860; "The Land Controversy," 28 June 1860; "The Last Half-Breed Meeting," 28 September 1860.

16 "Indignation Meetings," *Nor'Wester*, 15 June 1861.

17 Mailhot, "Ritchot's Resistance," 30–1.

18 A.G. Morice, *History of the Catholic Church in Western Canada from Lake Superior to the Pacific (1659–1895)*, Vol. 2 (Toronto: Musson, 1910), 10.

19 Mailhot, "Ritchot's Resistance," 9–10.

20 Ritchot's Narrative of the Resistance, 16. AM.

21 Dugast to Taché, 29 juillet 1869. ASHSB, T6695.

22 Thomas Flanagan, *Louis 'David' Riel: 'Prophet of the New World,'* rev. ed. (Toronto: University of Toronto Press, 1996), 8.

23 Louis Riel, writing to the president of the Saint Jean-Baptiste Society of Montreal, 24 June 1874. Quoted in Thomas Flanagan, "The Political Thought of Louis Riel," in *Riel and the Métis: Riel Mini-Conference Papers,* ed. A.S. Lussier (Winnipeg: Pemmican, 1979), 140.

24 "Ritchot's Narrative of the Resistance."

25 Dugast to Taché, 29 juillet 1869. ASHSB, T6697.

26 "Report of the Select Committee on the Causes of the Difficulties in the North West Territories in 1869–70," Canada, Parliament, House of Commons, *Sessional Papers,* 1874, No. VII, App. 6, testimony of Noël-Joseph Ritchot, 20 April 1874.

27 Dugast to Taché, 31 août 1869. ASHSB, T6778–6780.

28 W. McTavish to W.G. Smith, 2 November 1869. HBCA, A12/45, fol. 313–14.

29 This sentiment is clearly visible in the letters written by Father Dugast to Taché in the ASHSB. See his letters of 14 août 1869, T6734–37; 24 août 1869, T6764–67; and 31 août 1869, T6778–80.

30 W. McTavish to Joseph Howe, 14 May 1870, 13, HBCA, RG 1, Series 4/8. The basis of this rumour had to do with McDougall's role in the Manitoulin Island Incident of 1862–63 in Canada. For an explanation of this incident and its bearing on McDougall's reputation among the Métis see Neil Edgar Allen Ronaghan, "The Archibald Administration in Manitoba, 1870–1872" (PhD dissertation, University of Manitoba, 1987), 61–85.

31 Dugast to Fr Joseph Grenier, 15 April 1905, Archives du Collège Sainte-Marie, Fonds-Immaculée-Conception. Quoted in W.L. Morton (ed.) *Alexander Begg's Red River Journal* (Toronto: Champlain Society, 1956), 51n. Morton quotes this letter only to dismiss it as inaccurate, citing as reasons that it was written thirty-five years after the fact, that Dugast possessed a flair for inaccuracy, and that he was a vain and garrulous man. A close reading of Dugast's correspondence written in 1869, along with "Ritchot's Narrative of the Resistance," suggests exactly the opposite.

32 See "Ritchot's Narrative of the Resistance." These events and Ritchot's influence on them are described in some detail in Mailhot, "Ritchot's Resistance," 31–9.

33 "Ritchot's Narrative of the Resistance," 1: 22–5.

34 See Gerhard J. Ens, *Homeland to Hinterland: The Changing Worlds of the Red River Metis in the Nineteenth Century* (Toronto: University of Toronto Press, 1996), chap. 6.

35 Many of the Métis who opposed Riel were later imprisoned by Riel, including: William Dease, Baptiste Charette, William Gaddy, William Hallet, and Gabriel Lafournaise. Hallet was kept in chains in an unheated room through the worst of the winter.

36 William McTavish to W.G. Smith, 11 December 1869. HBCA, A12/45, fols 328–9.

37 Flanagan, "The Political Thought of Louis Riel," 150–2. See also his "Political Theory of the Red River Resistance: The Declaration of December 8, 1869," *Canadian Journal of Political Science* 11(1) (March 1978): 153–64; and "The Case Against Métis Aboriginal Rights," *Canadian Public Policy* 9(3) (September 1983): 316–17.

38 Thomas Flanagan, "The Political Thought of Louis Riel," 139.

39 Debates in the Convention of Forty, Seventh Day, February 1, 1870. Reported in *New Nation*, 4 February, 1870. Throughout these debates and those that followed in the Debates of the Legislative Assembly of Assiniboia (also reported in *New Nation*) Riel makes it clear that the rights he desires for the Métis of Red River are the rights of British subjects.

40 Louis Riel, "La Métisse," in *CW*, Vol. 4, ed. Glen Campbell (Edmonton: University of Alberta Press, 1985), 88–9.

41 Louis Riel, "O Québec!" in *CW*, 4: 95–6.

42 George F.G. Stanley, *Louis Riel*, first published in 1963 (Toronto: McGraw-Hill Ryerson, 1985), 203.

43 Riel, "Autobiographical Notes," in *CW*, 3: 264.

44 Ibid., 261.

45 Ibid.

46 Braz, *The False Traitor*, 30. The best two detailed accounts of Riel's religious and political beliefs are Flanagan, *Louis 'David' Riel*, and Gilles Martel, *Le messianisme de Louis Riel* (Waterloo, ON: Canadian Corporation for Studies in Religion and Wilfrid Laurier University Press, 1984).

47 Quoted in Flanagan, *Louis 'David' Riel*, 61. Riel would later admit that Bourget had written to him several years later, telling Riel that he had never believed, and did not now believe, in the mission which Riel was convinced he had received from heaven. See Riel, "Carnet de meditations et de priers," in *CW*, Vol. 2, ed. Gilles Martel (Edmonton: University of Alberta Press, 1985), 353 (see entry for 1 June 1884).

48 Flanagan, *Louis 'David' Riel*, 61.

49 In 1876 he was committed to an asylum at Longue Point near Montreal under the diagnosis of "delusions of grandeur," and later that year was moved to another asylum at Beauport closer to Quebec. See ibid., 63–71.

50 Ibid., 81.

51 Ibid., 111–18. When Riel first came upon this idea he tried to enlist Ambroise Lépine, his former adjutant general from 1869–70, requesting a meeting to discuss his (Riel's) plans. While Lépine did travel to Montana to meet with Riel in 1879–80, he broke off his stay prior to meeting Riel and returned to St Boniface. He did this on the advice of Bishop Taché, who was worried about the potential for trouble in the Northwest. It is clear from Lépine's correspondence that he wanted no more to do with rebellion. Riel Papers, AM, MG 3 D1, #309 Lépine to Riel, 1879; #359 Father Barnabe to Riel, 1 February 1879; #368 Evelina Barnabe to Riel, 13 May 1879; #379 Lépine to Riel n.d.; #385 Lépine to Riel, 1 May 1880; #386 Lépine to Riel, 20 May 1880; MG 3 D2, File 14 – Lépine to Riel, 9 January 1880; Lépine to Riel, 9 March 1880. Lépine to Taché, 2 January 1880. ASHSB, T23082.

52 Flanagan, *Louis 'David' Riel*, 84–9.

53 Ibid., 90–1.

54 Riel, "Les Métis du Nord-Ouest," in *CW*, 3: 279.

55 Ibid., 3: 274.

56 Braz, *The False Traitor*, 31.

57 *The Queen vs. Louis Riel: Accused and convicted of the crime of high treason: Report of the trial at Regina: Appeal to the Court of Queen's Bench, Manitoba: Appeal to the Privy Council, England: Petition for medical examination of the convict; List of petitions for commutation of the sentence* (Ottawa: Printed by the Queen's Printer, 1886), 159.

58 Braz, *The False Traitor*, 33.

59 Morton, *The Queen vs. Louis Riel*, 312.

60 Flanagan, *Louis 'David' Riel*, 137–8.

61 Ibid., 138–51. Orangism or "*Orangisme*" (French) refers to the Orange Order, a Protestant fraternal organization dedicated to defending Protestant civil and religious rights. It was a dominant political force in Ontario through most of the nineteenth century and spread to the Canadian west with the arrival of the Wolseley Expedition in Manitoba in 1870. The Ontario members of this expedition were determined to avenge the death of Thomas Scott (a member of the Orange Order in Ontario), who had been executed on the orders of Louis Riel.

62 Braz, *The False Traitor*, 39.

63 Flanagan, *Louis 'David' Riel*, 151.

64 Riel, "Le peuple Métis-Canadien-français," in *CW*, 4: 319–25.

65 For an extended explication of the poem see Kathy Durnin, "Mixed Messages: The Métis in Canadian Literature, 1816–2007 (PhD thesis, Comparative Literature, University of Alberta, 2008), 70–81.

66 Flanagan, *Louis 'David' Riel*, 142.

67 Ibid., 151–8; Braz, *The False Traitor*, 33.
68 For Riel's writings in prison and his speeches during the trial see Riel, *CW*, Vol. 3; Morton, *The Queen v. Louis Riel*.
69 *Report of the Royal Commission on Aboriginal Peoples*, Vol. 4: *Perspectives and Realities – Section 5. Métis Perspectives – Subsection 2. The Métis Nation.* In *For Seven Generations: An Information Legacy of the Royal Commission on Aboriginal Peoples* (Ottawa: Libraxus CD-ROM, 1997).

5 L'Union nationale métisse Saint-Joseph

1 Martha Harroun Foster, *We Know Who We Are: Metis Identity in a Montana Community* (Norman: University of Oklahoma Press, 2006).
2 Benedict Anderson, *Imagined Communities: Reflections on the Origin and Spread of Nationalism* (London: Verso Books, 1991), 6.
3 Ernest Renan, quoted in David Lowenthal, *The Heritage Crusade and the Spoils of History* (Cambridge: Cambridge University Press, 1998), 130.
4 These effects or goals are precisely what David Lowenthal argues are the purposes of heritage as opposed to history. See ibid., chaps 5 and 6. It is not surprising that the translation of Trémaudan's *Histoire de la nation métisse* had the group-affirming title of *Hold High Your Heads*.
5 The first known Métis organization after 1870 was L'Union Saint-Alexandre, which was formed in 1871 and named after Father Taché. It was intended to unite the Métis after the events of 1869–70. Nothing is known of this organization other than the officers first elected. An earlier Union métisse de Saint-Joseph had been formed in September 1884 by Riel. In September 1884 Bishop Grandin travelled to St Laurent, in an attempt to repair a growing rift between the Métis and the Catholic clergy. At this time Grandin gave his blessing to a suggestion made by Riel to close the breach between the Métis and the Catholic Church. Riel suggested the formation of a national Métis association with St Joseph as its patron saint. Grandin approved this suggestion and authorized the celebration of the feast of the saint as a national holiday for the Métis people. His suggestion for this feast day was 24 July. As that day had already passed, it was decided to hold the feast day for 1884 on 24 September. On that day a special service was held to inaugurate the new society and Riel is reputed to have proclaimed, "Now we are established as a nation." George F.G. Stanley, *Louis Riel* (Toronto: Ryerson Press, 1963), 287–90. On the choice of St Joseph as the patron saint of the Métis by Riel and the choice of 24 July as the feast day, see Thomas Flanagan, *Louis 'David' Riel: 'Prophet of the New World'*, rev. ed. (Toronto: University of Toronto Press, 1996), 142. Flanagan argues that Riel's proposal

and date had symbolic dimensions that can only be appreciated in light of his entire doctrine. If John the Baptist (the patron saint of French Canadians) was the precursor of Christ, St Joseph was his earthly father and also bore the title "Patron of the Universal Church." The 24th of July came exactly one month after the feast day of St John the Baptist, the implication being that the Métis not only were a people distinct from the French Canadians, but had a mission that was higher than theirs. For reference to St Joseph as the patron saint of the Métis in Riel's writings see *The Collected Writings of Louis Riel / Les Écrits complets de Louis Riel,* Vol. 3, ed. Thomas Flanagan (Edmonton: University of Alberta Press, 1985), 103, 152, 262, 369, 501–2.

6 The founding members of the union were: Joseph St Germain (b. 1820), François Poitras (b. 1825), Joseph Riel (b. 1857 and brother of Louis Riel), Alfred Nault (b. 1854 and cousin of Riel), Benjamin Nault (b. 1832 and cousin of Riel), Pierre Lavallée, Jean-François Plouffe, François Marion, Martin Jérôme (b. 1850 and M.L.A.), Abraham Guay, Auguste Harrison (b. 1836 and cousin of Riel), Elzéar Lagimodière (b. 1830 and cousin of Riel), Joseph McMullen, Pierre St Germain (b. 1830), and Pierre Delorme (b. 1831 and member of Riel's Provisional Government in 1869). See Union nationale métisse Saint-Joseph du Manitoba, Archives de la Société Historique de Saint-Boniface (ASHSB), fonds 0285. Also see Camille Teillet, "Court historique de l'Union nationale métisse Saint-Joseph du Manitoba" (1953) at http://www.unionnationalemetisse.ca/court.html,accessed 17 February 2009.

7 Ibid.

8 Petition to Incorporate "L'Union nationale métisse St Joseph du Manitoba," 1913. ASHSB, fonds 0285, boite 3.

9 Translated from the French "Avertissement," Auguste-Henri de Trémaudan, *Histoire de la nation métisse dans l'Ouest canadien* (Montreal: Éditions Albert Lévesque, 1935), 15–16.

10 Minutes of Meeting 31 January, 1909. ASHSB, fonds 0285, boite 7. Ibid., 17.

11 "Constitution de L'Union Nationale Metisse St. Joseph de Manitoba 1910." ASHSB, fonds 0285.

12 Minutes of Meeting 31 January 1909. In particular, they had some disagreements with Father Morice's portrayal of Riel and the Métis. A.G. Morice, *Aux sources de l'histoire manitobaine* (Quebec: Impr. de la Compagnie de "L'Événement," 1907); *Dictionnaire historique des Canadiens et de Métis français de l'Ouest* (St Boniface: 1908); A.G. Morice, *History of the Catholic Church in Western Canada, from Lake Superior to the Pacific (1695–1895)* (Toronto: Musson, 1910).

13 "Constitution de L'Union Nationale Métisse St. Joseph de Manitoba 1910." Author's translation.

14 Ibid.
15 These clippings can be found in ASHSB, fonds 00449, boîtes 4, 5, 6, 7, and 10, La Sociéte historique métisse – Comité historique.
16 This debate can be found in the pages of the French-language newspaper *La Liberté* from December 1931 to the summer of 1932. The vehement response of the Historical Committee and the debate that ensued in the union can be found in ASHSB, fonds 00449, boîte 3, chemise 1; boîte 7, chemise 1; boîte 9, chemise 5.
17 In 1924 the *Winnipeg Free Press* noted that the Historical Committee of the union was planning an educational and propaganda campaign related to Riel and was planning to erect a statue of Riel. This clipping, found in the files of the committee's archives, gives the date of this article only as "25 M, 1924"; see boîte 7.
18 Samuel Nault to A.-H. de Trémaudan, 6 October 1924. ASHSB, fonds 00449, boîte 1, chemise 1.
19 Ibid.
20 Ibid. See advertisements for these celebrations, newspaper clippings, and invitations to dignitaries in ibid., boîtes 2, 3, and 7.
21 Ibid.
22 The last records of the of the Historical Committee deal with fund-raising efforts to publish the book during the Depression, correspondence to find a publisher, and the correspondence with the company that finally published the book at a cost to the committee of $750. The last correspondence is in 1938 and deals with the difficulties of raising money to translate the work into English. In 1943 the committee donated their research materials and books to the Provincial Library.
23 See their website: http://www.unionnationalemetisse.ca
24 "Avertissement," 15–28.
25 S.A. Nault to A.-H. de Trémaudan, 6 October 1924. ASHSB, fonds 00449, boîte 1, chemise 1.
26 Auguste-Henri de Trémaudan was born on 14 July 1874 in Sainte-Chrysostome, Quebec, to Auguste de Trémaudan and Jeanne Huet. Trémaudan's father and mother had immigrated to Quebec from France in 1871, where their son Auguste was born, though the family moved back to France around 1880. In 1893 the family moved again to Canada to help establish the colony of Montmartre in western Canada. Unsuited for farming because of his delicate health. Auguste studied at the Normal School in Regina, taught school, and worked as a clerk in a law office to familiarize himself with the law. In 1901 he married Madeleine Bastien in Montmartre, Saskatchewan, and they had three sons and two daughters. He practised law

in Manor, Saskatchewan, between 1902 and 1911 and then moved to The Pas, Manitoba. Here he established a newspaper and studied for the Manitoba Bar, to which he was admitted in 1913. He then moved to St Boniface, where he worked for the Winnipeg Trustee Company, wrote for a number of newspapers under the pseudonym Prosper Willaume, and also established a number of Liberal newspapers in which he promoted the policies of the federal Liberal Party and the defence of the French language. In 1924 Trémaudan moved to California because the milder climate was better for his failing health. It was here that he wrote, though never completed, *Histoire de la nation métisse*. He died in California on 29 October 1929. See Michel Verrette, "Trémaudan, Auguste-Henri de," in *Dictionary of Canadian Biography Online*.

27 See his *La Sang Français* (Winnipeg, 1919); *L'Invasion Fénienne* (Winnipeg, 1921); "Louis Riel and the Fenian Raid of 1871," *Canadian Historical Review* 4(2) (1923); "Louis Riel's Account of the Capture of Fort Garry, 1870," *Canadian Historical Review* 5(2) (1924); "Letter of Louis Riel and Ambroise Lépine to Lieutenant Governor Morris, January 3, 1873," *Canadian Historical Review* 7(2) (1926).

28 Trémaudan preferred to write in English and initially the committee wanted the manuscript in both languages to have a larger effect, but it was decided for reasons of cost and time to initially produce the book only in French so as to have an impact among the younger French Métis in the west.

29 See correspondence Between Samuel Nault and A.-H. de Trémaudan in ASHSB, fonds 00449, Société historique métisse, boîte 1, chemise 1. Nault to Trémaudan 6 October 1924; Nault to Trémaudan 30 November 1924, Nault to Trémaudan 14 December, 1925; Trémaudan to Nault 22 December 1925; Nault to Trémaudan 18 January 1926, Trémaudan to Nault 25 January 1926; Nault to Trémaudan 25th May 1926; Trémaudan to Nault 15 June 1926; Nault to Trémaudan 19 November 1926; Trémaudan to Nault 24 November 1926.

30 The purposes of heritage are clearly outlined in Lowenthal, *The Heritage Crusade and the Spoils of History*, 127–47. Lowenthal notes that the three principal modes of heritage revision are (1) updating the past, (2) highlighting and enhancing admirable aspects of the past, and (3) expunging what seems shameful or harmful (148).

31 "Avertissement," 15–28.

32 This is supported by both the extensive correspondence between Samuel Nault and Trémaudan between 1928 and 1929, and a comparison between Trémaudan's manuscript and the published book.

33 "Préface" to Trémaudan, *Histoire*, 9.

34 A.-H. Trémaudan to S.A. Nault, 25 April 1928. ASHSB, fonds 00449, Société historique métisse, boîte 1, chemise 1.

35 Ibid., Camille Teillet to Trémaudan, 25 February 1928.
36 Ibid., Trémaudan to Samuel Nault, 15 March 1928; 19 May 1928.
37 Ibid., Historical Committee to Trémaudan, 24 August 1928.
38 Ibid., Trémaudan to Nault, 9 September 1928.
39 Ibid., Nault to Trémaudan, 24 September 1928.
40 This new evidence was procured by sending Teillet and Charette to Batoche to collect sworn statements from surviving participants in the 1885 Rebellion.
41 Nault to Trémaudan, 26 October 1928. ASHSB, fonds Société historique métisse, boîte 1, chemise 1.
42 Nault to Trémaudan, 2 March 1929. Ibid.
43 This manuscript can be found in the records of the Historical Committee; ASHSB, fonds 00449, Société historique métisse, boîte 8, chemises 2–3. Even this very short reference to "insanity" was cut from the published book. The long discussion that Trémaudan retained in his manuscript of the $35,000 indemnity paid to Riel by the federal government to leave Canada after 1870 was taken out of the main text of the published book and put in a footnote, where it was substantially reworked, removing all notions of possible venality.
44 When Trémaudan died on 20 October 1929, the Historical Committee was faced with a sticky situation. Not only had their relations with the author soured significantly, but there were also disputes with his surviving family. The committee had to enlist the aid of Alexandre Desautels in California to retrieve the last manuscript and books they had lent to Trémaudan. Desautels was instructed to make sure he did not mention he was doing so for the committee. S.A. Nault to Alexandre Desautels, 30 October 1929.
45 Correspondence relating to the publication of the book can be found in ASHSB, fonds 00449, Société historique métisse, boîte 1, chemises 2–5.
46 The questions or charges they addressed in this appendix were as follows: (1) That the insurrection movement of the Métis in 1885 was senseless. (2) That Métis rights would have been accorded by the Canadian government as early as 4 March 1885. (3) That the decision to take up arms was made well before 1 March 1885. (4) That Riel forced the Métis to take up arms by using threats. (5) That Riel and the Métis took over the church in Batoche and desecrated it. (6) That Riel held the missionary fathers and sisters prisoners in the rectory at Batoche. (7) That Riel stirred up the Indians and that he was responsible for the Frog Lake Massacre. (8) That Riel (a) apostatized, (b) founded a new cult, and (c) compelled the Métis to abandon their faith. (9) That Riel was insane.
47 Although Trémaudan provided a bibliography, there are no footnotes to verify the various statements made.

48 For a discussion of the literary form and rhetorical strategy of the hagiographic epic see Alison Goddard Elliott, *Roads to Paradise: Reading the Lives of the Early Saints* (Hanover: Brown University Press, 1987), 1–41.
49 While the Métis descendants of British traders and explorers are acknowledged, it is to the French-Catholic Métis that Trémaudan turns to sketch their character.
50 A.G. Morice, *La race Métisse: étude critique en marge d'un livre récent* (Winnipeg: Author, 1938); see particularly 1–42.
51 Lowenthal, *The Heritage Crusade and the Spoils of History*, 132.
52 Marcel Giraud, *Le Métis canadien: son rôle dans l'histoire des provinces de l'Ouest*, 2 vols (Paris: Institut d'ethnologie, 1945); translated by George Woodcock as *The Métis in the Canadian West* (Edmonton: University of Alberta Press, 1986).
53 *Histoire de la nation métisse dans l'Ouest canadien* has been reprinted many times and in 1982 was published in translation as *Hold High Your Heads: History of the Métis Nation in Western Canada*.

6 The Manitoba Act and the Creation of a Métis Status

1 Ian Hacking, "Making Up People," in *Reconstructing Individualism: Autonomy, Individuality, and the Self in Western Thought*, ed. Thomas C. Heller, Morton Sosna, and David E. Wellbery (Stanford: Stanford University Press, 1986), 228.
2 Act 33 Victoria, c. 3, s. 31, assented to 12 May 1870.
3 The OIC of 3rd April 1873 declared that section 31 applied only to Métis children.
4 Métis scrip: literally provisional certificates entitling the bearer to a certain amount of federally owned and surveyed land in Manitoba and the Northwest Territories, was first issued to the Métis in Manitoba in 1876 and was extended to the Métis in the Northwest Territories in 1885.
5 See Hacking, "Making Up People," 222–36. See also Ian Hacking, "The Looping Effects of Human Kinds," in *Causal Cognition: A Multidisciplinary Debate*, ed. Dan Sperber, David Premack, and Ann James (Oxford: Clarendon Press, 1995), 351–83. Dipesh Chakrabarty, "Governmental Roots of Modern Ethnicity," in Dipesh Chakrabarty, *Habitations of Modernity: Essays in the Wake of Subaltern Studies* (Chicago: University of Chicago Press, 2002).
6 Hacking, "The Looping Effects of Human Kinds," 368–9.
7 *Debates* of the House of Commons, 2 May 1870; repr. in W.L. Morton (ed.), *Manitoba: The Birth of a Province* (Winnipeg: Manitoba Record Society, 1965), 172.
8 Ibid., 198.
9 Ibid., 199.

10 Ibid., 204.

11 A.G. Archibald to Joseph Howe, 27 December 1870. LAC, RG 15, vol. 236, file 7220.

12 Speech of John A. Macdonald, 6 July 1885, *Debates* of the House of Commons of the Dominion of Canada, Third Session – Fifth Parliament, 48–9 Victoria 1885, 3113–14.

13 For these debates see Thomas Flanagan, *Riel and the Rebellion: 1885 Reconsidered*, 2nd ed. (Toronto: University of Toronto Press, 2000). Thomas Flanagan, *Metis Lands in Manitoba* (Calgary: University of Calgary Press, 1991). Thomas Flanagan and Gerhard J. Ens, "Metis Land Grants in Manitoba: A Statistical Study," *Histoire Sociale / Social History* 27 (May 1994). Gerhard J. Ens, *Homeland to Hinterland: The Changing Worlds of the Red River Metis in the Nineteenth Century* (Toronto: University of Toronto Press, 1996). D.N. Sprague, "The Manitoba Land Question, 1870–1882," *Journal of Canadian Studies* 15(3) (1982): 79. D.N. Sprague, *Canada and the Métis, 1869–1885* (Waterloo, ON: Wilfrid Laurier University Press, 1988). P.R. Mailhot and D.N. Sprague, "Persistent Settlers: The Dispersal and Resettlement of the Red River Métis, 1870–1885," *Canadian Ethnic Studies*17 (1985). D.N. Sprague, "Dispossession vs. Accommodation in Plaintiff cs. Defendant Accounts of Métis Dispersal from Manitoba, 1870–1881," *Prairie Forum* 16(2) (Fall 1991). Ken Hatt, "The Northwest Scrip Commissions as Federal Policy – Some Initial Findings," in *Canadian Journal of Native Studies* 3(1) (1983). Ken Hatt, "The North-West Rebellion Scrip Commissions, 1885–1889," in *1885 and After: Native Society in Transition*, ed. F. Laurie Barron and James Waldram (Regina: University of Regina Press, 1986). Joe Sawchuk, Patricia Sawchuk, and Theresa Ferguson, *Metis Land Rights in Alberta: A Political History* (Métis Association of Alberta, 1981). In addition to these published books and papers see the various reports prepared for the Royal Commission on Aboriginal Peoples, including the following: J. Weinstein, "Metis Land Rights Research Project – Introduction"; Louise Mandell and E. Ann Gilmour, "Metis Land Rights in Canada"; D.N. Sprague, "An Administrative History of Metis Claims"; Joseph Eliot Magnet, "Metis Land Rights in Canada: Legal Issues"; Frank Tough and Leah Dorian, *"The Claims of the Half-breeds ... have been finally closed*: A Study of Treaty Ten and Treaty Five Adhesion Scrip"; and J. Weinstein, "Metis Land Rights Research Project – Conclusion." These reports can be found in the RCAP CD-ROM, *For Seven Generations: An Information Legacy of the Royal Commission on Aboriginal Peoples* (Ottawa: Libraxus CD-ROM, 1997.

14 See "The Proceedings in the Convention, February 3 to February 5, 1870," in Morton, *Manitoba: The Birth of a Province*, 5–24; the Second to Fourth "List of Rights," in ibid., 242–50. For a more detailed reconstruction of

the negotiations leading to the Manitoba Act see Flanagan, *Metis Lands in Manitoba*, 29–50.

15 A microfilm copy of Richot's journal is in the Archives of Manitoba (AM), MG 3, B14-1, no. 12 (M151). The French text was published by George F.G. Stanley as "Le Journal de l'abbé N.-J. Ritchot," *Revue d'histoire de l'Amérique française* 17 (1964): 537–64. The translated version used here is found in Morton, *Manitoba: The Birth of a Province*, 140.

16 *New Nation*, 1 July 1870. This newspaper was here reporting on Ritchot's speech of 24 June 1870 to the legislative assembly of Assiniboia. A translation of part of Ritchot's speech can be found in Flanagan, *Metis Lands in Manitoba*, 34.

17 House of Commons, *Debates*, 9 May 1870. Reprinted in Morton, *Manitoba: The Birth of a Province*, 225.

18 OIC of 3rd April 1873 declared that section 31 applied only to Métis children

19 OIC of 23rd March 1876; emphasis added.

20 Treaties in the American west that had "half-breed" clauses included the Chippewa Treaties of 1837, 1842, 1855, 1863, 1864; Kansa Treaty of 1825; Osage Treaty of 1825; Ottawa Treaty of 1836; Pawnee Treaty of 1857; Ponca Treaty of 1858; Sauk and Fox Treaties of 1830, 1836; Yankton Sioux Treaty of 1858; and the Winnebago Treaty of 1855. See Charles Kappler (ed.), *Indian Affairs: Laws and Treaties*, Vol. 2 (Washington, DC: Government Printing Office [GPO], 1904). See also "Half-breed Scrip, Chippewas of Lake Superior: the correspondence and action under the 7th clause of the 2d article of the treaty with the Chippewa Indians of Lake Superior and the Mississippi, concluded at La Pointe in the state of Wisconsin, September 30, 1854 ... including the report of the commission appointed by the Secretary of the Interior, April 21, 1871 ... and the report of the commission appointed July 15, 1872" (Washington, DC: GPO, 1874). CIHM/ICMH Microfiche series, no. 39318.

21 The Minnesota Territorial Census of 1850 for Pembina County lists 1,105 individuals, almost all of whom were Métis and 712 of whom had been born in the British territory. A few years after the census was taken, the Catholic priest G.A. Belcourt noted that thousands of Métis had emigrated from the Red River Settlement to the United States and more would come and take the oath of allegiance if their rights were respected. Letter of G.A. Belcourt to Hon. G.W. Manypenny, Commissioner of Indian Affairs, 20 November 1854. Enclosure #24 in "The Report of the Commissioner of Indian Affairs," 25 November 1854. U.S. Congress, House Ex. Docs. No. 1, 2nd session, 33rd Congress, Serial Set #777, p. 279.

22 Report of the Treaty Made with the Pembina Indians, at Pembina, by Alex. Ramsey, 7 November 1851, included in "The Report of the Commissioner

of Indian Affairs," November 27, 1851. U.S. Congress, House Ex. Docs., No. 2, 1st Session, 32nd Congress, Serial Set #636, page 285.

23 Ibid.

24 "Articles of a treaty made and concluded at the Old Crossing of Red Lake River, in the State of Minnesota, on the second day of October, in the year eighteen hundred and sixty-three, between the United States of America, by their commissioners, Alexander Ramsey and Ashley C. Morrill, agent for the Chippewa Indians, and the Red Lake and Pembina bands of Chippewas; by their chiefs, head-men, and warriors." In Kappler, *Indian Affairs*, 2: 854–5, 862.

25 A "power of attorney" is a legal instrument authorizing someone to act as another's attorney or agent.

26 Paul L.A.H. Chartrand, *Manitoba Métis Settlement Scheme of 1870* (Saskatoon: Native Law Centre, 1991), 228–9.

27 Adams Archibald to Joseph Howe, 27 December 1870. LAC, RG 15, vol. 236, file 7220.

28 Molyneux St John to Lt Gov. Archibald, 3 January 1871. AM, MG12, A1 #164a.

29 See appendices 1 and 2. See also A.A. Taché to Lt Gov. Morris, 14 January 1873. AM, MG 12, B2, #20.

30 OIC of 25th April 1871. LAC, RG 15, D-II-1, vol. 228, file 798. This OIC was confirmed by the Dominion Lands Act, SC 1872, c. 23.

31 OIC of 26th May 1871.

32 Allen Ronaghan, "The Confrontation at Rivière aux Ilets de Bois," *Prairie Forum* 14(1) (Spring 1989); Flanagan, *Metis Lands in Manitoba*, 68–9.

33 They included the parishes of St Boniface, St Vital, St Norbert, Ste Agathe, St Charles, St François Xavier, Baie St Paul, Ste Anne de la Pointe de Chène, and St Laurent. These notices appeared in the 8 June and 15 June editions of *Le Métis*. As Archibald later explained to the secretary of state, the Métis believed that Manitoba Act gave them first choice of the lands in Manitoba. As proof of this the Métis quoted a letter from George-Étienne Cartier to Ritchot and Scott dated 23 May 1879 during the negotiations leading to the Manitoba Act. This letter, however, which was printed in *Le Métis* on 15 June 1871, noted only that the 1.4-million-acre grant for the benefit of the families of the Métis residents of Manitoba would be of a nature that accorded with the desire of the Métis and would be granted in an effective and equitable manner. See Archibald to the Secretary of State, 17 June 1871. LAC, RG 15, D-II-1, vol. 230, file 167. The full text of Cartier's letter can be found in "Report of the Select Committee on the Causes of the Difficulties in the North-West Territories," *Journals of the House of Commons* (1874), vol. 8, Appendix 6, 74.

34 Lt Gov. Archibald to Joseph Royal et al., 9 June 1871, printed in *The Manitoban*, 17 June 1871. See also Archibald to the Secretary of State, 17 June 1871. LAC, RG 15, D-II-1, vol. 230, file 167.
35 These included the parishes of St James, Headingley, High Bluff, and Poplar Point. The publication of their choices appeared in *The Manitoban* on 24 June, 1 July, 8 July, 15 July, 22 July, 29 July, 12 August, 19 August, 26 August, 2 September, and 9 September 1871.
36 OIC of 15th April 1872. LAC, RG 15, D-II-1, vol. 228, file 1089.
37 Ibid.
38 S. Dennis to James Aikins (Sec. of State), 22 March, 2872. LAC, RG 15, D-II-1, vol. 227, file 635 (1872); A. Archibald to Sec of State, 27 July 1872. AM, MG 12, A1, DB4, #7.
39 A. Archibald to Sec of State, 27 July 1872. AM, MG 12, A1, DB4, #7.
40 Ibid.
41 Adams Archibald to Sec of State, 26 August 1872. AM, MG12, A1, DB4 #10.
42 Ibid.
43 Ibid. These parishes included Kildonan, St Paul, St Andrew's North and South, and St Peters.
44 At the time Morris was chief justice of the Manitoba Court of Queen's Bench. He was appointed lieutenant governor, replacing Adams Archibald on 2 December 1872.
45 Alexander Morris to the Sec. of State, 20 November 1872. AM, MG 12, A1, DB3 #114.
46 "The Half-Breed Grant," *The Manitoban*, 1 March 1873.
47 The reports of these meetings and the sentiments expressed were sent to Lieutenant Governor Morris and can be found in the Morris Papers in the Provincial Archives of Manitoba. MG 12, B1: Public Meeting held at Headingley, 7 January 1873 (#47); Public Meeting of the Inhabitants of the Parish of St Charles held 11 January 1873 (#55); Meeting of St François Xavier West, 12 January 1873 (#56); Meeting of St François East, 12 January 1873 (#57); Meeting of St Norbert, 12 January 1873 (#59); Meeting Held by People of St James, 14 January 1873 (#63); Meeting of Residents of St Boniface, 11 January 1873 (#66); Meeting of St Andrew's North and South, 10 May 1873 (#223); Meeting of St Paul, 5 June 1873 (#250).
48 For this sentiment see telegrams of J.C. Aikins to J.S. Dennis, 13 and 18 January 1873. AM, MG 12, B1, #62.
49 Report of the Commission Appointed to Enquire into the Nature and Extent of Rights of Common and Hay Privilege to Alexander Morris, 6 March 1873. AM, MG 12, B1, #129.

50 Public Notice of Commission for Settlement of Rights of Common and of Cutting Hay, sent in letter of A. Campbell, Minister of the Interior, to Lt Gov. Morris, 27 September 1873. AM, MG 12, B1, #502.
51 Lindsay Russell, Asst Surveyor General to Alexander Morris, 18 August 1873. AM, MG 12, B1, #399. These lands had been selected even before the OIC of 6th September 1873 because Morris had been forewarned that the OTM would be withdrawn by J.C. Aikins in June of that year. See J.C. Aikins to A. Morris, 23 June 1873. AM, MG 12, B1, #292.
52 Flanagan, *Metis Lands in Manitoba*, 77–8.
53 The rationale, process, and attendant delays are explained by Flanagan in ibid., 76–94.
54 Ibid., 82–4.
55 LAC, RG 15, D-II-8-a, vol. 1319.
56 Ibid.
57 Flanagan, *Metis Lands in Manitoba*, 84–6. For the process of moving from allocation to patent see pp. 85–90.
58 Ibid., 140. With many Metis having left the province prior to 1876, however, some scrip certificates took decades to deliver. The last known issue of Metis scrip in Manitoba is dated 3 April 1907.
59 Ibid., 146–8.
60 For the argument both that the Métis received the benefits due them and that these benefits amounted to a significant financial boon see: Flanagan, *Metis Lands in Manitoba*. Flanagan and Ens, "Metis Land Grants in Manitoba." For the obverse views see D.N. Sprague, "The Manitoba Land Question, 1870–1882," *Journal of Canadian Studies* 15(3) (1982), 79; D.N. Sprague, *Canada and the Métis*; Mailhot and Sprague, "Persistent Settlers. In 2007 Justice MacInnes of the Manitoba Queen's Bench ruled that the federal government had discharged its obligations to the Métis under ss. 31 and 32 of the Manitoba Act. The case is being appealed.
61 "Address to the Lieutenant-Governor, Alexander Morris, Public Meeting, 5th May, 1873." In "Papers and Correspondence in connection with Half-breed Claims and other matters relating to the North-West Territories," in Canada, *Sessional Papers*, vol. 13, Third Session of the Fifth Parliament, 48 Victoria 1885 (No. 116), 1.
62 Ryan's authorization to investigate Manitoba Métis claims in the Northwest Territories came by OIC of 14th June 1876.
63 Petition addressed to Lieutenant Governor of the Northwest Territories, from the "half-breeds of the parish of St Laurent" dated 1 February 1878, in "Papers and Correspondence in connection with Half-breed Claims and other matters relating to the North-West Territories," 28.

64 These petitions can be found in "Papers and Correspondence in connection with Half-breed Claims and other matters relating to the North-West Territories." The Prince Albert petition is on pp. 29–31, the St Albert petition on p. 25, the Manitoba Village, NWT, petition on pp. 41–2, the Edmonton petition on pages 42–4, and the Qu'Appelle Settlement petition on pp. 44–6.
65 Petition of "all half-breeds, living in the vicinity of Cypress Mountain" to The President and all the Honorable Members of the Privy Council of the Northwest Territories, in "Papers and Correspondence in connection with Half-breed Claims and other matters relating to the Northwest Territories," 32–5. This petition can also be found in LAC, RG 15, Series D-II-1, vol. 341, file 89435.
66 See "Resolutions passed at a largely attended public meeting, held in Prince Albert, N.W.T., 8th October, 1881," in "Papers and Correspondence in connection with Half-breed Claims and other matters relating to the Northwest Territories," 69–70. It should be noted that these petitions were not only concerned with scrip. They also often requested recognition and title to lands on which they lived, early survey of these lands, surveys in river-lots, and seed grain and implements to help them adjust to an agricultural economy.
67 For a summary of these petition and demands between 1880 and 1884 see *Debates* of the House of Commons of the Dominion of Canada, Third Session – Fifth Parliament, 48–9 Victoria 1885, 6 July, 3080–3.
68 House of Commons, *Debates*, 2 May 1870; repr. in Morton, *Manitoba: The Birth of a Province*, 172.
69 "Address of Alexander Morris to Augustine Brabant, Baptiste Davis, and others, half-breeds of the Lake Qu'Appelle and environs, dated Fort Qu'Appelle, 16th September 1874," in "Papers and Correspondence in connection with Half-breed Claims and other matters relating to the North-West Territories," 8.
70 David Mills, Minister of the Interior, to Lieutenant-Governor Laird, 18th March 1878, in "Papers and Correspondence in connection with Half-breed Claims and other matters relating to the North-West Territories," 26–7.
71 Speech of John A. Macdonald, 6 July 1885. See n12, 3113.
72 Ibid., 3114.
73 J.S. Dennis, "Memorandum on the Condition of the Half-breeds of the North-West Territories," 20 December 1878, in "Papers and Correspondence in connection with Half-breed Claims and other matters relating to the North-West Territories," 93–6.
74 Ibid.

75 Letter of Archbishop Taché to J.S. Dennis, 29 January 1879, in "Papers and Correspondence in connection with Half-breed Claims and other matters relating to the Northwest Territories," 84–8.
76 David Laird to J.S. Dennis, 13 March 1879; Hugh Richardson to J.S. Dennis, 1 December 1879; in "Papers and Correspondence in connection with Half-breed Claims and other matters relating to the North-West Territories," 81–2.
77 John A. Macdonald, reflecting the government view that the Manitoba scrip issue had been of little benefit to the Métis, noted in 1885 that "the claims of the half-breeds in Manitoba were bought up by speculators. It is an unfortunate thing for those poor people; but it is true that this grant of scrip and land to those poor people was a curse and not a blessing. The scrip was bought up; the lands were bought up by white speculators, and the consequences are apparent." Speech of John A. Macdonald, 6 July 1885. See n12, 3113–15.
78 "An Act to amend and consolidate the several Acts Respecting the Public Lands of the Dominion," 15 May 1879. *Statutes of Canada*, 42 Vict. (1879), c. 31, s. 125.
79 The report of the minister of the interior dated 15 February 1882 noted: "The condition of the half-breed population of the Territories, and the claims which have been preferred on their behalf to be dealt with somewhat similarly to those of the half-breeds of the Red River, have been receiving careful consideration, with a view to meeting them reasonably," quoted in *Debates* of the House of Commons of the Dominion of Canada, Third Session – Fifth Parliament, 48–9 Victoria, 1885, 3082. In 1883 the Dominion Lands Act was amended and subclause (e) of Clause 81 now provided that the Governor General in Council should have power "to satisfy any claims existing in connection with the extinguishment of the Indian title, preferred by halfbreeds resident in the North-West Territories, outside of the limits of Manitoba, previous to the fifteenth day of July, one thousand eight hundred and seventy, by granting land to such persons, to such extent and on such terms and conditions as may be deemed expedient."
80 Speech of John A. Macdonald, 6 July 1885. See n12, 3117–18.
81 OIC of 30th March 1885 (PC 688).

7 Extinguishing Rights and Inventing Catagories

1 J.A.J. McKenna, "Memorandum for the Minister," 27 September 1901. J.A.J. McKenna, "Memorandum for the Minister," 18 March 1903. LAC, RG 10, vol. 4006, file 241209-1.
2 Report on the negotiations leading to Treaty 10. Addressed to Frank Oliver, Superintendent General of Indian Affairs, 18 January 1907. Ibid.

3 Most of the questions and debates surrounding the issue of Métis scrip arise from the fact that it was rapidly sold to speculators, which has been interpreted as the loss of a potential land base for the Métis. In addition to these general questions there has been a good deal of debate about whether the federal government fairly administered the Métis scrip programs. The arguments that the government fraudulently administered these programs is summarized most explicitly in Joseph Eliot Magnet's research report for the Royal Commission on Aboriginal Peoples (RCAP). With regard to scrip in the Northwest Territories, Magnet argues as follows: (1) The scrip market was neither competitive nor free and the Métis did not receive a fair price; scrip therefore became irrelevant to the Métis, conferred no advantages on them, and the government should have known this. (2) The northern Métis were not allowed to locate their scrip where they lived, which meant that they could not sell directly to land purchasers and were forced to sell to scrip middlemen. (3) The government facilitated the sale of scrip and fraudulently administered this program. (4) Finally, the government breached its fiduciary responsibility to the Métis by unilaterally implementing a system that would leave the Métis without a land base or other benefits that Indians received. These are contentious issues, which would take a book-length study to unravel. Some of the secondary literature on these questions includes Joe Sawchuk, Patricia Sawchuk, and Theresa Ferguson, *Metis Land Rights in Alberta: A Political History* (Edmonton: Métis Association of Alberta, 1981); Ken Hatt, "The Northwest Scrip Commissions as Federal Policy – Some Initial Findings," in *Canadian Journal of Native Studies* 3(1) (1983); Ken Hatt, "The North-West Rebellion Scrip Commissions, 1885–1889," in *1885 and After: Native Society in Transition*, ed. F. Laurie Barron and James Waldram (Regina: University of Regina Press, 1986); Thomas Flanagan, "The Case against Métis Aboriginal Rights," *Canadian Public Policy* 9(3) (1983); Thomas Flanagan, "Comment on Ken Hatt, 'The North-West Rebellion Scrip Commissions, 1885–1889,'" in Barron and Waldram, *1885 and After*; Thomas Flanagan, "The History of Metis Aboriginal Rights: Politics, Principle, and Policy," *Canadian Journal of Law and Society* 5 (1990); Thomas Flanagan, *Metis Lands in Manitoba* (Calgary: University of Calgary Press, 1991); Thomas Flanagan, *Riel and the Rebellion: 1885 Reconsidered*. 2nd ed. (Toronto: University of Toronto Press, 2000); D.N. Sprague, "The Manitoba Land Question, 1870–1882," *Journal of Canadian Studies* 15:3 (1982); D.N. Sprague, *Canada and the Métis, 1869–1885* (Waterloo, ON: Wilfrid Laurier University Press, 1988). There are also book-length research reports prepared for RCAP. These can be found in the RCAP CD-ROM. *For Seven Generations: An Information Legacy of the Royal Commission on Aboriginal Peoples*, (Ottawa: Libraxus CD-ROM, 1997). These reports include

J. Weinstein, "Metis Land Rights Research Project – Introduction"; Louise Mandell and E. Ann Gilmour, "Metis Land Rights in Canada"; D.N. Sprague, "An Administrative History of Metis Claims"; Joseph Eliot Magnet, "Metis Land Rights in Canada: Legal Issues"; Frank Tough and Leah Dorian, "The claims of the Half-breeds … have been finally closed: A Study of Treaty Ten and Treaty Five Adhesion Scrip"; and J. Weinstein, "Metis Land Rights Research Project – Conclusion."

4 W.P.R. Street was first approached to head the commission in the second week of March. See W.P.R. Street, "The Commission of 1885 to the North-West Territories," ed. H.H. Langton, *Canadian Historical Review* 25(1) (March 1944): 41.

5 Ibid., 45.

6 OIC of 30th March 1885 (PC 688).

7 The description "half-breed head of family resident in the Northwest Territories previous to the 15th day of July 1870" was held to mean "half-breed mothers" equally with "half-breed fathers," or both as the case may be, and all children of a "half-breed head" or "half-breed heads" of family as described above, would be entitled, whether male or female. A.M. Burgess (DMI) to W.P.R. Street, 30 March 1885. LAC, RG 15, D-II-1, vol. 574, file 175917.

8 Ibid. In view of the exceptional conditions of the country previous to the 15th day of July 1870, the illegitimate children of a "half-breed head of family" were allowed to participate in the grant, and orphan children of "half-breed heads of families," the latter having died previous to the 15th day of July 1870, should also be entitled to participate, provided such children were resident in the Northwest Territories previous to the 15th day of July 1870. Children of "half-breed heads of families," resident in the Northwest Territories previous to the 15th day of July 1870, but who were themselves absent from the North West Territories at the said time, and who might not have returned to the Territories were also to be allowed to participate. "Half-breed children" living in the territories previous to the 15th day of July 1870, but whose parents or families were resident elsewhere at the said period, would not be entitled to participate.

9 Ibid. For those Métis who had died after 15 July 1870, the commission, upon being presented with proof of the deceased's age and residence in the Northwest Territories previous to 1870, would also grant scrip to an heir making an application.

10 W.P.R. Street (Winnipeg) to D.L. MacPherson, Minister of the Interior, 5 April 1885. LAC, RG 15, D-II-1, vol. 574, file 175917.

11 Ibid., Telegram of D.L. MacPherson to W.P.R. Street, 6 April 1885.

12 Street, "The Commission of 1885 to the North-West Territories," 48–50.

13 Of the 167 scrip certificates issued to Métis children at Qu'Appelle only two were land scrip. Of the 1,142 Métis children eligible for scrip who appeared before the commission in 1885 only 236 chose land scrip. The rest chose money scrip. See OIC of 13th April 1886 (PC 657).
14 A.M Burgess, Deputy Minister of the Interior G.W. Burbidge, Deputy Minister of Justice, Ottawa, 11 May 1885; G.W. Burbidge, Ottawa, to Sec. Dept of Interior, 6 June 1885; A.M Burgess DMI to W.P.R. Street, Ottawa, 29 June 1885. LAC, RG 15, D-II-1, vol. 574, file 175917.
15 W.P.R. Street (Fort Qu'Appelle) to David MacPherson (Minister of the Interior) 13 April 1885. Ibid.
16 A.M. Burgess to W.P.R. Street, 29 April 1885. Ibid. In response to a question of whether the commissioners were allowed to deliver scrip certificates to persons properly authorized by the claimants by powers of attorney, the department replied that, if the commissioners were satisfied that delivering the certificates to a properly authorized attorney would insure that the certificates would get into the proper hands, they were empowered to deliver them. Street noted that at every location they were obliged to leave behind persons whose claims were properly proved, but who had designated others to pick up their scrip certificates. W.P.R. Street (Maple Creek) to A.M. Burgess, 5 May 1885, ibid. See also A.M. Burgess to Mr. Hall, 18 May 1885. John R. Hall (Secretary of the Department of the Interior) to W.P.R. Street, 19 May 1885. Ibid.
17 "Report of the North-West Half-Breed Commission of the work done by them during the Past Summer," in *Annual Report of the Department of the Interior for the Year 1885*, Canada, *Sessional Papers* (No. 8), 49 Victoria 1886.
18 OIC of 1st March 1886 (PC 309).
19 For these instructions see A.M. Burgess, Deputy Minister of the Interior, to Roger Goulet, 17 May 1886. LAC, RG 15, DII-1, vol. 501, file 140682.
20 Ibid.
21 Roger Goulet, "Report Respecting Claims by Half-Breeds," in *Annual Report of the Department of the Interior for the Year 1886*. Canada, *Sessional Papers* (No. 7), 50 Victoria 1887, 76. Note that Goulet included in his total of 1,164 applications allowed the scrip applications of 5 "original white settlers.
22 Ibid., 78.
23 OIC of 9th May 1887 (PC 898).
24 A.M. Burgess to L. Vankoughnet, 23 March 1887. LAC, RG 15, D-II-1, vol. 488, file 138133. T.P. Wadsworth, inspector of Indian agencies, would accompany Goulet with respect to granting discharges in the Treaty 6 area, and E. McColl, inspector of Indian agencies at Winnipeg would do the same in the Treaty 5 area. L. Vankoughnet to A.M. Burgess, 16 April 1887, ibid.

25 Report of Roger Goulet and N.O. Coté to A.M. Burgess (Grand Rapids), 13 August 1887. LAC, RG 15, D-II-1, vol. 501, file 140682.
26 OIC 14th December 1888.
27 Flanagan, "The History of Metis Aboriginal Rights, 80–1.
28 Ibid., 80.
29 A.M. Burgess to L. Vankoughnet, 17 March 1888. LAC, RG 10, vol. 3793, file 46,025-2.
30 *Annual Report of the Department of the Interior for the Year 1889*. Canada. *Sessional Papers* (No. 14), 53 Victoria 1890, xxix.
31 Quoted in N. Anick, *The Métis of the South Saskatchewan*, Manuscript Report Series No. 364 (Ottawa: Parks Canada, 1976), 602.
32 *Annual Report of the Department of the Interior for the Year 1889*.
33 Ibid.
34 OIC of 12th March 1892 (PC 630). From June 1889 until 1894, 1,197 claims were preferred, and of these 765 were allowed and scrip was issued amounting to $165,2000. N.-O. Coté, "Grants to Half-Breeds in the Province of Manitoba and the North-West Territories, Comprising the Provinces of Saskatchewan and Alberta in Extinguishment of the Indian Title, 1870–1925, and Grant of Scrip to Original White Settlers, 1874–1894," (1929) Department of the Interior. LAC, RG 15, D-II-1, vol. 227, file 0, pt 4, 8–9. The scrip process from 1885 to 1894 had also included 189 application made by persons who on 15 July 1870 were living outside those territories ceded by Indians. It was considered advisable to accept these claims, and by OIC of 18th March 1889 (PC 592) and subsequent Orders in Council, these claims were settled as if the applicants were residing within those territories ceded.
35 An earlier precedent, however, had been set when in November 1888 arrangements were made to conduct negotiations with Green Lake Indians for an adhesion to Treaty 6 (signed 11 February 1889), and it was also arranged that one of the two commissioners appointed to negotiate the adhesion should be empowered to investigate claims to Métis scrip in the region just surrendered.
36 For Canadian Indian policy related to Treaty 8 see Robert Surtees, "Canadian Indian Treaties," in *Handbook of North American Indians*, Vol. 4: *History of Indian-White Relations*, ed. Wilcomb Washburn (Washington, DC: Smithsonian Institution, 1988), 202–10; René Fumoleau, *As Long as This Land Shall Last: A History of Treaty 8 and Treaty 11: 1870–1939* (Toronto: McClelland & Stewart, 1975); Richard Daniels, "The Spirit and Terms of Treaty Eight," in *The Spirit of the Alberta Indian Treaties*, ed. Richard Price (Montreal: Institute for Research on Social Policy, 1979), 47–100; Dennis Madill, *Treaty Eight Research Report* (Ottawa: Treaty and Historical Research Centre, Indian and Northern

Affairs, 1986). For a government statement of these aims see "Annual Report of Indian Affairs, 1899," *Sessional Papers*, 1900, No. 14, xviii–xix.

37 In 1898 Forget was the Indian commissioner for Manitoba and the Northwest Territories. In late 1898 he was appointed lieutenant governor of the Northwest Territories.

38 Forget to McKenna, 16 April 1898. LAC, RG 10, vol. 3848, file 75236-1.

39 Forget to Secretary of Indian Affairs, 12 January 1898. Ibid.

40 OIC of 27th June 1898 (PC 1703).

41 Hall, "The Half-breed Claims Commission," 4.

42 J.A.J. McKenna to Clifford Sifton, 17 April 1899. LAC, RG 15, D-II-1, vol. 771, file 518158.

43 OIC of 6th May 1899 (PC 918).

44 Ibid.

45 Father A. Lacombe to David Laird, Chairman of the Indian Treaty Commission, 22 June 1899. LAC, RG 15 D-II-I, vol. 771, file 518158.

46 Minutes of Joint Meeting of Indian Treaty and Half-breed Commissioners, held at Lesser Slave Lake, Athabasca District, on June 22, 1899. Ibid.

47 Charles Mair, *Through the Mackenzie Basin: A Narrative of the Athabasca and Peace River Treaty Expedition of 1899* (Toronto: William Briggs, 1908), 25–7, 58.

48 OIC of 2nd March 1900 (PC 460).

49 See "Index to Athabasca Claims taken by Conroy in 1903, 1905, 1907 and other Claims taken by Conroy in 1908." LAC, RG 15, vol. 1512.

50 "Memo regarding Claims to Land and Scrip in Peace River Country, 3 July 1912." LAC, RG 15, D-II-1, vol. 782, file 555680.

51 Report of J.A.J. McKenna to Clifford Sifton, 16 March 1901. (The claim numbers disallowed were 262–3, 265–7, 300–5, 313–21, 369–81). Ibid., pt 1.

52 Report of James McCrae, 19 January 1901. Ibid.

53 Report of J.A.J. McKenna to Clifford Sifton, 16 March 1901. Ibid.

54 "Report of J.A.J. McKenna on the 64 Applications Made before Mr Conroy," 17 February 1903. Ibid. For the opinion of the various missionaries in the Whitefish Lake area see W.G. White to Minister of the Interior, 28 September 1908. LAC, RG 10, vol. 3979, file 156710-31. Archdeacon Geo. Holmes to J.A.J. McKenna, 20 December 1903. LAC, RG 15, D-II-1, vol. 782, file 555680, pt 1. George Holmes to Frank Oliver, Minister of the Interior, 31 March 1910. LAC, RG 15, D-II-1, vol. 782, file 555680, pt 2.

55 This was confirmed by OIC of 13th December 1909 (PC 2354).

56 Report of J.A.J. McKenna to Clifford Sifton, 16 March 1901. LAC, RG 15, D-II-1, vol. 782, file 555680, pt 1.

57 J.A.J. McKenna to Clifford Sifton, 31 May 1901. This report constitutes Annex "A" approved by OIC of 6th June 1901 (PC 1182).

58 OIC of 6th May 1899 (PC 918). This Order in Council was passed under the authority of the amended Dominion Lands Act of 62-63 Vict. (1899), c. 16, s. 4, which had granted unrestricted authority to cabinet to "grant lands in satisfaction of the claims of half-breeds arising out of the extinguishment of Indian title."
59 Ibid.
60 In 1905, after receiving petitions from American Métis charging that a scrip buyer by the name of R.C. Macdonald had defrauded them of their scrip, the government stopped the scrip process and appointed a judge to investigate the complaints. This investigation was held in the town of Killarney, Manitoba, on 25–28 July, 3–9 and 11August1905. In his final report Judge Myers noted that Macdonald and his employees were not guilty of practising any deceit, fraud, or misrepresentation, and that the charges were wholly unwarranted. This episode in the history of Northwest Métis scrip illuminates a number of significant aspects relating to both scrip buyers and government oversight of the process. When the government disallowed large numbers of scrip applications from Métis resident in the United States in 1900–1, it was the scrip buyers who agitated and eventually convinced the government that it had disallowed legitimate scrip claimants. The charges of scrip fraud against R.C. Macdonald (as scrip buyer) were initiated by rival scrip buyers who convinced the U.S. Métis to petition the government for an investigation. When the government became aware of the potential of large-scale fraud in the purchase of land scrip, it immediately halted the location and patenting of this type of scrip and initiated a judicial investigation. Only after Macdonald had been cleared of these charges were locations of this land scrip allowed to continue. For the charges, evidence, and reports on this episode see LAC, RG 15, D-II-1, vol. 970, file 30397A.
61 OIC of 2nd March 1900 (PC 438).
62 James Sutherland (Acting Minister of the Interior) to J.A.J. McKenna, 5 May 1900. LAC, RG 15, D-II-1, vol. 783, file 556321, pt 1.
63 James Smart to Clifford Sifton (Minister of the Interior), 30 July 1900. Ibid.
64 Memorandum Re- Claims to scrip of the Halfbreeds of the North-West Territories to T.W. Crothers from N.-O. Cote, 28 April 1913. Ibid., pt 3.
65 J.A.J. McKenna to Clifford Sifton, 20 May 1901. Ibid., pt 2.
66 Report of J.A.J. McKenna on reserved claims to Clifford Sifton, Minister of the Interior, 31 May 1901. Annex "A" to OIC of 6th June 1901 (PC 1182).
67 Ibid.
68 Final Report of the Saskatchewan Commission dated 29 March 1901. LAC, RG 15, D-II-1, vol. 825, file 616753. In his interim report dated 8 January 1901, N.-O. Coté provided slightly different figures, including 76 disallowed claims

and 138 reserved. Presumably, between January and the end of March a good number of the reserved claims were approved on further examination. See "Preliminary Report of Scrip Commission for the Saskatchewan District," 18 January 1901. LAC, RG 15, D-II-1, vol. 783, file 556321, pt 1. In this preliminary report Coté also noted the average price paid by scrip speculators: $90 for a $240 money scrip and $110 for a 240-acre land scrip.

69 OIC of 6th June 1901 (PC 1182).

70 These claims included money scrip of $55,563.66 and land scrip certificates totalling 296,564 acres. Of those disallowed McKenna drew particular attention to a group of Métis claimants who came to Killarney from the Turtle Mountain reservation in North Dakota to claim scrip. He disallowed or rejected all of them on preliminary examination on the basis that they were claims made by persons who were classed as United States Indians. See Report of J.A.J. McKenna of 12 March 1903. LAC, RG 15, D-II-1, vol. 783, file 556321, pt 2. It is interesting to note that although the Turtle Mountain Reservation had been laid out, Congress had not yet ratified the treaty and would not do so until 1905, by which time many of the Canadian Métis living on the reservation were excluded from treaty rolls.

71 Quoted in J.A.J. McKenna to Clifford Sifton (Minister of the Interior) 21 May 21 1901. LAC, RG 15, D-II-1, vol. 783, file 556321, pt 2. N.-O. Coté noted in 1903 that until 1903 in every case the department had declined to reopen any of the claims that had been rejected or disallowed by McKenna – even when subsequent documentation established the case. N.-O. Coté to James Smart (Deputy Minister of the Interior), 15 August 1903. Ibid.

72 McKenna reiterated his position to the minister of the interior in December of 1901: "In acting under my Commission I have laid down rules based on the principle that the Halfbreed right is mainly a Territorial right; that it arises from the possession of the soil in an aboriginal way; and that residence in the Territories up to the time of the action for the extinguishment of Halfbreed title (1885) is therefore essential to the admission of the claim." Ibid.

73 James Smart (Deputy Minister of the Interior) to N.-O. Coté, 11 July 1903. Ibid.

74 According to departmental memory, "preliminary examination" entailed a questioning of these Métis by a clerk or clerks employed by the commissioners, where in each instance the applicant represented himself to have his claim investigated, but who because of such examination was not permitted to appear before the commission. Memorandum of T.G. Rothwell (Law Clerk's Branch) to the Minister of the Interior, 16 February 1913. Ibid., pt 3.

75 N.-O Coté to James Smart, 13 July 1903. Memorandum of N.-O. Coté to Clifford Sifton, 7 March 1904. Ibid., pt 2.

76 Ewart had practised law in Toronto before moving to Winnipeg in 1882. In Manitoba he became involved in the Manitoba Schools Question on behalf of the Roman Catholic Minority, arguing the case before the Supreme Court and the Privy Council. As result of this and other experiences, he became an expert in constitutional law, moving to Ottawa and undertaking only cases before the highest courts on appeal. See Henry James Morgan (ed.), *The Canadian Men and Women of the Time: A Hand-Book of Canadian Biography of Living Characters*, 2nd ed. (Toronto: William Briggs, 1912), 381–2.
77 J.S. Ewart to Messrs. Enderton and Macdonald, 15 January, 1904. LAC, RG 15, D-II-1, vol. 783, file 556321, pt 2.
78 See Memorandum of N.-O. Coté to James Smart (Deputy Minister of the Interior) 11 July 1904; and Memorandum of N.-O. Coté to James Smart, 10 August 1904. Ibid.
79 OIC of 13 August 1904 (PC 1613).
80 Memorandum of N.O. Coté to Clifford Sifton (Minister of the Interior), 27 February 1905. LAC, RG 15, D-II-1, vol. 783, file 556321, pt 2.
81 Ibid.
82 Report of N.-O. Coté to Frank Oliver (Minister of the Interior) 23 May 1905. LAC, RG 15, D-II-1, vol. 783, file 556321, pt 2.
83 Flanagan, "The History of Metis Aboriginal Rights," 85–6.
84 J.A.J. McKenna to Clifford Sifton, 22 February 1901. LAC, RG 10, vol. 3033, file 235, 225, pt 1.
85 Ibid.
86 Report of J.A.J. McKenna to Clifford Sifton, 12 March 1903. LAC, RG 15, D-II-1, vol. 783, file 556321, pt 2.
87 Memorandum to Clifford Sifton, "Report on Treaty in Northern Ontario and Quebec," 17 August 1903. LAC, RG 10, vol. 3033, file 235, 225, pt 1.
88 See agreement between Frank Oliver, Superintendent General of Indian Affairs, and Francis Cochrane, Minister of Lands and Mines of Ontario. Ibid.
89 Treaty 9 commissioners included D.C. Scott and Samuel Stewart representing the federal government and Daniel George MacMartin representing Ontario.
90 See John S. Long, "Treaty No. 9 and Fur Trade Company Families: Northwestern Ontario's Halfbreeds, Indians, Petitioners and Métis," in *New Peoples: Being and Becoming Métis in North America*, ed. Jacqueline Peterson and Jennifer S.H. Brown (Winnipeg: University of Manitoba Press, 1965), 147–9.
91 Quoted in Long, "Treaty No. 9 and Fur Trade Company Families," 148. This petition can be found in LAC, RG 10, vol. 3093, file 289, 300.
92 Ibid., 149.
93 Ibid.

94 See Wilfrid Laurier to J.A.J. McKenna (Indian Affairs) 6 March 1902; Petition of Half-breeds of Île-à-la-Crosse [1902]. LAC, RG 10, vol. 4006, file 214, 209-1.
95 Memorandum of J.A.J. McKenna to Clifford Sifton (Minister of the Interior), 27 September 1902. Ibid.
96 Memorandum of J.A.J. McKenna to Clifford Sifton (Minister of the Interior) 18 March 1903. Ibid. The numbers of Indian and Métis in the unceded territory had been obtained from Bishop Pascal, who had reckoned only those of Cree/White ancestry as "half-breeds." However, there were many Chipewyans of mixed ancestry as well.
97 David Laird, Indian Commissioner, to Department of Indian Affairs, 29 April 1904. Ibid.
98 David Laird (Indian Commissioner) to Sec. Dept of Indian Affairs, 7 October 1905; memorandum of Frank Pedley (deputy Supt. General of Indian Affairs) to the Supt. General of Indian Affairs, 7 April 1906. Ibid.
99 OIC of 20th July 1906 (PC 1459). OIC of 20th July 1906 (PC 1497).
100 Final report of J.A.J. McKenna dated 15 March 1907. McKenna noted that of the 498 claims approved 271 had been for money scrip totalling $65,040, and 227 had been for land scrip totalling 54,480 acres. LAC, RG 15, D-II-1, vol. 991, file 1247280.
101 Ibid.
102 OIC of 6th April 1907.
103 OIC of 15th February 1908.
104 Secretary of Indian Affairs to Thomas Borthwick, 29 April 1907. LAC, RG 10, vol. 4006, file 214, 209-1.
105 Secretary of Indian Affairs to Sec. Department of Interior, 7 May 1908. LAC, RG 15, D-II-1, vol. 1016, file 1578625, pt 1.
106 N.-O. Coté to W.W. Cory (Deputy Minister of the Interior, 8 May 1908. J.A. Coté (Acting Deputy Minister of the Interior) to N.-O. Coté, 13 May 1908. Ibid.
107 Ibid., Instructions to John Semmens (Inspector of Indian Agencies) from Department of Interior, 26 May 1908.
108 These problems and charges are outlined best in Frank Tough and Leah Dorian, *"The claims of the Half-breeds have been fully closed."*
109 OIC of 19th May 1909 (PC 1060).
110 N.O. Coté to Frank Oliver (Minister of the Interior), 28 May 1909. LAC, RG 15, D-II-1, vol. 1016, file 1578625, pt 1.
111 Letter of P.G. Keyes (Sec. Dept of Interior) to John Semmens (Inspector of Indian Agencies), 16 July 1909. Ibid.
112 N.-O. Coté to Frank Oliver (Minister of Interior), 26 May 1911. Ibid.

113 OIC of 24th May 1911 (PC 1193).

114 This included 77 land scrip totalling 18,480 acres, and 9 money scrip totalling $2,160. N.-O. Coté, "Grants to Half-Breeds in the Province of Manitoba and the North-West Territories, Comprising the Provinces of Saskatchewan and Alberta in Extinguishment of the Indian Title, 1870–1925, and Grant of Scrip to Original White Settlers, 1874–1894" (1929). LAC, RG 15, D-II-1, vol. 227, file 0, pt 4, 15–17.

115 N.-O. Coté to Frank Oliver (Minister of Interior), 26 May 1911. LAC, RG 15, D-II-1, vol. 1016, file 1578625, pt 1.

116 OIC of 12th April 1921 (PC 1172).

117 See n114, 17–18.

118 Statutes of Canada, c. 25, s. 20 (assented to 4 June 1921).

119 See n114, n.p.

120 Memorandum of N.-O. Coté to T.W. Crothers (Deputy Minister of the Interior), 28 April 1913. LAC, RG 15, D-II-1, vol. 783, file 556321, pt 3.

8 Indian Treaty versus Métis Scrip

1 For a more detailed examination of this subject and the differences in American and British attitudes see Gerhard J. Ens, "Hybridity, Canadian Indian Policy, and the Construction and 'Extinguishment' of Metis Aboriginal Rights in the Nineteenth Century," in *Reconfiguration of Native North America: An Anthology of New Perspectives*, ed. John R. Wunder and Kurt E. Kinbacher (Lubbock: Texas Tech University Press, 2009), 236–51.

2 The Métis had been involved in negotiations of American treaties on the Great Lakes in the 1830s, and tribal leaders argued strenuously to obtain concessions for the Métis, who were often close relatives. Government negotiators saw it as part of the game necessary to get treaties signed. As in Canada, many of these treaties allowed those "half-breeds," who elected to reside among their tribal kin, the same rights and privileges of "full-bloods." Those Métis who rejected a tribal identity and assignment to a band were not officially party to these treaties, but were granted some concessions at the insistence of tribal leaders.

3 Robert J. Surtees, "Treaty Research Report: The Robinson Treaties (1850)," Treaty and Historical Research Centre, Indian and Northern Affairs, 1986; online at https://www.aadnc-aandc.gc.ca/DAM/DAM-INTER-HQ/STAGING/texte-text/trerob_1100100028975_eng.pdf. See also Alexander Morris, *The Treaties of Canada with the Indians of Manitoba and the North-West Territories* (Toronto: Belfords, Clarke & Co., 1880), 16–21.

4 See *Indian Treaties and Surrenders, from 1680 to 1890*, Vol. 1 (Ottawa: B. Chamberlin, 1891), 147–52.
5 Report of William Robinson dated 24 September 1850, repr. in Morris, *The Treaties of Canada with the Indians*, 20.
6 Surtees, "Treaty Research Report: The Robinson Treaties (1850)."
7 With reference to the Robinson Treaties, this position is detailed in E.B. Borron, "Report relative to Annuities payable to Indians in terms of the Robinson Treaties," 31 December 1892, and E.B. Borron, "Supplemental Report on the Right of Half Breeds to participate in the Benefits of the Robinson Treaties," 27 October 1894. Archives of Ontario (AO), F 1027-1-2, Irving Papers 27/32/8-1&2.
8 Morris, *The Treaties of Canada*, 16.
9 Alan Knight and Janet E. Chute, "In the Shadow of the Thumping Drum: The Sault Métis – The People In-between," in *Lines Drawn upon the Water: First Nations on the Great Lakes, Borders and Borderlands*, ed. Karl S. Hele (Waterloo, ON: Wilfrid Laurier University Press, 2008), 105–6. See also Statement of Alexis Biron to E.B. Borron, 27 May 1893, Interview of Joshue Biron by John Driver, 27 May 1893, and Statement of Peter Ahbahjigance. AO, F 1027-1-2, Irving Papers 27/32/9.
10 Knight and Chute, "In the Shadow of the Thumping Drum," 108. See also the letters of John Driver to E.B. Borron, 4 March and 5 June 1893. AO, F 1027-1-2, Irving Papers 27/32/9-10.
11 E.B. Borron to Sir Wm Irving, 11 February 1893. AO, F 1027-1-2, Irving Papers 27/32/8-(2).
12 Shortly after Confederation the province of Ontario had agreed to pay $88,000 to the federal government as an equivalent to the $4,400 yearly annuities paid to Indians by the Robinson Treaties. E.B. Borron to Oliver Mowat, 20 January 1892. AO, F 1027-1-2, Irving Papers 27/32/8-(2).
13 E.B. Borron's reports to the provincial government can be found in AO, F 1027-1-2, Irving Papers 27/32/8-(1-2).
14 According to the Pennefather Commission of 1858, it was generally understood, based on usage more than any legal authority, that "an Indian woman marrying a white loses her rights as a member of the tribe, and her children have no claim on the lands or moneys belonging to their mother's nation." See "Report of the Special Commissioners appointed to investigate Indian Affairs in Canada (Messrs Pennefather, Talfourd, and Worthington) to Sir Edmund Head, April 1858," Province of Canada, *Journals of the Legislative Assembly, Sessional Papers 1858*, App. 21.
15 "An Act for the gradual enfranchisement of Indians, the better management of Indian Affairs, and to extend the provisions of the Act 31st Victoria,

Chapter 42," *Statutes of Canada* 1869, c. 6, 32–33 Vict. Section 6 of this act stated: "Provided always that any Indian woman marrying any other than an Indian, shall cease to be an Indian within the meaning of this Act, nor shall the children issue of such marriage be considered as Indians within the meaning of this Act."

16 "An Act to amend and consolidate the laws respecting Indians," *Statutes of Canada* 1876, c. 18, 39 Vict.). Section 3.3.c stated: "Provided that any Indian woman marrying any other than an Indian or a non-treaty Indian shall cease to be an Indian in any respect within the meaning of this Act, except that she shall be entitled to share equally with the members of the band to which she formerly belonged, in the annual or semi-annual distribution of their annuities, interest moneys and rents; but this income may be commuted to her at any time at ten years' purchase with the consent of the band."

17 E.B. Borron to Aemelius Irving, 17 May 1895. AO, F 1027-1-2, Irving Papers 27/32/06.

18 Quoted in ibid.

19 This finding is in keeping with the argument made by Theodore Binnema that defining "Indians" in the period from the 1850s to the 1870s was aimed at protecting Indian land from encroachment and occurred at the urging of eastern, particularly Iroquois, bands. See Binnema, "Protecting Indian Lands by Defining Indian: 1850–76," *Journal of Canadian Studies / Revue d'Études canadiennes* 48(2) (Spring 2014): 5–39.

20 The Indian Act of 1876 (*Statutes of Canada* 1876, c. 18, s. 3.3.e, 39 Vict.), stated: "that no half-breed of a family (except the widow of an Indian, or a half-breed who has already been admitted into a treaty), shall, unless under very special circumstances, to be determined by the Superintendent-General or his agent, be accounted an Indian, or entitled to be admitted into any Indian treaty."

21 Wemyss Simpson to the Secretary of State for the Provinces, 3 November 1871, repr. in Morris, *Treaties of Canada*, 41.

22 Nicole St-Onge, *Saint-Laurent, Manitoba: Evolving Métis Identities, 1850–1914* (Regina: Canadian Plains Research Center, 2004),

23 Clint Evans, "A History of Metis Activities and Settlement in Manitoba's Southern Interlake Region, 1800-1881," Report prepared for Manitoba Conservation and the Constitutional Law Branch of Manitoba Justice, 14 March 2008.

24 Report by the Indian Commissioner, 30 October 1875. Annual Report Indian Affairs Year ended June 30, 1875, *Sessional Papers* (No. 9), 1876, 33.

25 *Indian Treaties and Surrenders from 1680 to 1890*, 1: 308–9.

26 Morris, *The Treaties of Canada* , 293–5; see also 186–7, 195, 222.

27 Letter of David Laird, Indian Commissioner of the North-West Territories, to the Minister of the Interior, 15 November 1878. LAC, RG 15, vol. 171, file HB64. At treaty payment time at Fort Walsh in 1876 Inspector J.M. Walsh of the NWMP received a petition from the Cree and Saulteaux Métis around Cypress Hills to be admitted into Treaty 4 to extinguish their land claims, to receive annuities, and to be treated in common with the Indians with the exception that they would have their own chief. They noted that they had lived from childhood on the plains and had adopted the customs of the Indians. LAC, RG 10, vol. 3637, file 7089.

28 A particularly interesting aspect of this problem is dealt with by Melanie Niemi-Bohun in "Colonial Categories and Familial Responses to Treaty and Metis Scrip Policy: The 'Edmonton and District Straggler,' 1870–88," *Canadian Historical Review* 90(1) (March 2009): 71–98. See also her "The Edmonton and District Stragglers: Gendered Strategies of Treaty and Scrip, 1876–1886" (MA thesis, University of Northern British Columbia, 2005).

29 Letter of David Laird, Indian Commissioner of the North-West Territories, to the Minister of the Interior, 15 November 1878. LAC, RG 15, vol. 171, file HB64.

30 In 1880 the Indian agent at Edmonton noted that "many half-breed men, who are now taking treaty would like to withdraw were they able to pay back the money they have already received; as they are not likely ever to get this much ahead, I think it would be better to do so without exacting the return of the money, than to continue paying them and their families year after year." Report of J.G. Stewart, Indian Agent, Edmonton, in "Annual Report of the Department of Indian Affairs for the year ending December 31, 1880," 87.

31 "Local," *Edmonton Bulletin*, 10 October 1885.

32 W.P.R. Street (Maple Creek) to A.M. Burgess, 5 May 1885. LAC, RG 15, D-II-1, vol. 574, file 175917.

33 Ibid. These declarations can be found in this file.

34 W.P.R. Street (Calgary) to A.M. Burgess, 8 May 1885. Ibid.

35 L. Vankoughnet to A.M. Burgess, 30 May 1885. LAC, RG 15, D-II-3, vol. 172, file HB 141.

36 OIC of 1st March 1886 (PC 309)

37 A.M. Burgess, Deputy Minister of the Interior, to Roger Goulet, 17 May 1886. Geo. Duck to A.M. Burgess, Winnipeg, 26 May 1886. LAC, RG 15, D-II-1, vol. 501, file 140682.

38 A.M. Burgess to Roger Goulet, 11 June 1886. Ibid.

39 This initial draft can be found in LAC, RG 10, vol. 3584, file 1130.

40 Reed's recommendations of 13 July went through three different iterations before they were actually approved as the basis of policy in late October of 1885. His initial sixteen recommendations were discussed with Edgar Dewdney and then both cut and amended before being sent to Ottawa. The revised memorandum dated 20 July 1885 was forwarded to Ottawa on 1 August 1885. See Hayter Reed, "Memorandum for the Honble the Indian Commissioner relative to the future management of Indians," dated 20 July 1885. LAC, RG 10, vol. 3710, file 19, 550–3. A copy of this memorandum is reproduced in Blair Stonechild and Bill Waiser, *Loyal till Death: Indians and the North-West Rebellion* (Calgary: Fifth House, 1997), 205–53. In Ottawa, Vankoughnet, wrote an extended commentary on the recommendations before forwarding them for a decision to John A. Macdonald, the superintendent general of Indian affairs. Macdonald's demurs and agreements are pencilled in the margins. L. Vankoughnet to John A. Macdonald dated 17 August 1885. LAC, RG 10, vol. 3710, file 19, 550–3. As he noted to Dewdney, the superintendent general had found much in Reed's memo that he approved of, but he doubted that all his suggestions could be given effect to. He requested that either he (Dewdney) or Reed come to Ottawa to settle policy and receive instructions. L. Vankoughnet to E. Dewdney, 22 September 1885. LAC, RG 10, vol. 3584, file 1130. These instructions, based on Reed's recommendations, were sent to Dewdney on 28 October 1885. L. Vankoughnet to E. Dewdney, 28 October 1885. LAC, RG 10, vol. 3710, file 19,550–3.

41 Along with this set of recommendations Reed also enclosed a listing of bands he considered loyal and those he considered to be implicated in the Rebellion. Of some eighty bands he lists, twenty-eight were considered rebellious. This enumeration of bands can be found both in LAC, RG 10, vol. 3584, file 1130, and in LAC, RG 10, vol. 3710, file 19, 550–3. The list is transcribed in Stonechild and Waiser, *Loyal till Death*, 254–60.

42 Heather Devine, *The People Who Own Themselves: Aboriginal Ethnogenesis in a Canadian Family, 1660–1900* (Calgary: University of Calgary Press, 2004), 170

43 H.H. Smith, Dominion Lands Commissioner, Winnipeg, to Minister of the Interior, 4 August 1885. LAC, RG 15, D-II-1, vol. 488, file 138133.

44 John R. Hall to L. Vankoughnet, Deputy Superintendent General, Indian Affairs, 21 August 1885. Ibid.

45 R. Sinclair (for Deputy of the Supt. General of Indian Affairs) to John R. Hall, 31 August 1885. Ibid.

46 A.M. Burgess to H.H. Smith, Commissioner of Dominion Lands, 8 April 1886. LAC, RG 15, D-II-1, vol. 488, file 138133.

47 A.M. Burgess to Vankoughnet 10 April 1886. Ibid.

48 Vankoughnet to A.M. Burgess, 12 April 1886. Ibid.

49 Report of Roger Goulet to A.M. Burgess, Calgary, 19 June 1886. Ibid.,
50 Hayter Reed (Asst Indian Commissioner of the NWT) to Supt. Gen. Indian Affairs, 26 July 1886. LAC, RG 15, D-II-1, vol. 488, file 138133.
51 Hayter Reed to Supt General of Indian Affairs, 28 August 1886. Ibid.
52 A.M. Burgess to Roger Goulet, 15 September 1886. Ibid.
53 Report of Roger Goulet to A.M. Burgess dated 4 August 1886, Edmonton. LAC, RG 15, D-II-1, vol. 501, file 140682.
54 Wadsworth's telegram is quoted in Telegram of Roger Goulet to A.M. Burgess, 12 July 1886. LAC, RG 15, D-II-1, vol. 488, file 138133.
55 The Indian commissioner elaborated on this point to the superintendent general of Indian affairs, noting that applications for withdrawal were being made at Peace Hills by persons who had always followed an Indian mode of life and had never been regarded as being anything but Indians. It had not been expected that they would ever claim to be anything else, nor had it been anticipated that the legislation enacted for half-breeds would extend to them. E. Dewdney (Indian Commissioner) to Superintendent General of Indian Affairs, 7 July 1886. LAC, RG 10, vol. 3724, file 24,303-2A.
56 Letter of T.P. Wadsworth (Inspector Indian Agency) to E. Dewdney (Commissioner)7 July 1886. LAC, RG 10, vol. 3724, file 24, 303-2A
57 E. Dewdney (Indian Commissioner) to Superintendent General of Indian Affairs, 7 July 1886. LAC, RG 10, vol. 3724, file 24,303-2A. For instructions to Wadsworth and the scrip commission see Telegram of Roger Goulet to A.M. Burgess, 12 July 1886; Hayter Reed to Supt Gen. Indian Affairs, 26 July 1886. LAC, RG 15, D-II-1, vol. 488, file 138133. Goulet's telegram to Burgess and Hayter Reed's letter to the superintendent general can also be found in LAC, RG 10, vol. 3724, file 24, 303-2A.
58 Goulet's telegram to A.M. Burgess, 12 July 1886. Ibid.
59 Hayter Reed to Supt Gen. Indian Affairs, 26 July 1886. Ibid.
60 Report of Roger Goulet to A.M. Burgess dated 4 August 1886, Edmonton. LAC, RG 15, D-II-1, vol. 501, file 140682.
61 Quoted in Hayter Reed to Supt Gen. Indian Affairs, 26 July 1886. LAC, RG 15, D-II-1, vol. 488, file 138133 and also in LAC, RG 10, vol. 3724, file 24,303-2A.
62 Quoted in ibid.
63 Those who were allowed to withdraw from treaty had to sign the following declaration. "I hereby forfeit all Indian rights, I agree to leave the reserve, to give up my house and all other improvements which I may have on the reserve without compensation, also any cattle or any implements received by me as an individual or as a member of the band. I hereby certify that the above was read and explained to the parties named herein." T.P Wadsworth

(Edmonton) to E. Dewdney (Indian Commissioner), 27 July 1886. LAC, RG 10, vol. 3724, file 24,303-2A.

64 Goulet noted that after his commission left Edmonton he had received 469 applications (28 at Victoria, 231 at Lac La Biche, 22 at Fort Pitt, 115 at Battleford, and 73 at Prince Albert). The greater portion of these claims had been preferred by half-breeds who had obtained their discharges from the Indian treaties. Progress Report of Roger Goulet to A.M. Burgess, Prince Albert, 5 October 1886. LAC, RG 15, D-II-1, vol. 501, file 140682.

65 Roger Goulet, "Report Respecting Claims by Half-Breeds," in Annual *Report of the Department of the Interior for the Year 1886*. Canada, *Sessional Papers* (No. 7), 50 Victoria 1887, 76.

66 Ibid., 78

67 Ibid..

68 OIC of 9th May 1887 (PC 898).

69 A.M. Burgess to L. Vankoughnet, 23 March 1887. LAC, RG 15, D-II-1, vol. 488, file 138133. It was decided that T.P. Wadsworth, inspector of Indian agencies, would accompany Goulet with respect to granting discharges in the Treaty 6 area, and E. McColl, inspector of Indian agencies at Winnipeg would do the same in the Treaty 5 area. L. Vankoughnet to A.M. Burgess, 16 April 1887. LAC, RG 15, D-II-1, vol. 488, file 138133.

70 Report of Roger Goulet and N.-O. Coté to A.M. Burgess (Grand Rapids), 13 August 1887. LAC, RG 15, D-II-1, vol. 501, file 140682.

71 *Annual Report of the Department of the Interior for the Year 1889*. Canada, *Sessional Papers* (No. 14), 53 Victoria 1890, xxix.

72 The best account of these dynamics can be found in Evans, "A History of Metis Activities and Settlement.".

73 Scrip applications for these families can be found in LAC, RG 15, Series D-II-8-c, vols 1335–71. Most of these individuals also had Ojibwa names.

74 Church Missionary Society (CMS) correspondence from Westbourne and Portage noted that the arrival of the fugitive Sioux from Minnesota, following the massacre there in 1862, ruined the hunting grounds around Portage and Westbourne, resulting in an exodus of Métis and Ojibwa from the area. See Henry George to Rev. Chapman, 1 January 1863. Henry George Annual Letter, 28 September 1867. CMS Archives, C.1/0 Original Letters, microfilm reel A88. See also A.C. Garrioch, *The Correction Line* (Winnipeg: Stovel, 1933), 215.

75 Most of these families noted on their scrip applications of 1887 that, while they had camped in Manitoba in the period up to July 1870 at places such as Westbourne, Totogan, and Portage, they had no permanent residences there and had lived most of the year in what was then the

North-West Territories outside the boundaries of what would become Manitoba in 1870.

76 Report of Molyneux St John, 22 October 1873 in Report of the Deputy Superintendent General of Indian Affairs. Annual Report of the Department of the Interior for the year ending June 30, 1874. Canada, *Sessional Papers* (No. 8), 1875. Report of the Indian Commissioner, October 1874. Annual Report of Indian Affairs year ending June 30, 1875. Canada, *Sessional Papers* (No. 9), 1876.

77 Alexander Morris to the Minister of the Interior, 2 August 1875. Archives of Manitoba (AM), MG 12 B1, Alexander Morris Papers, LG Collection, Letter Book H & I, Item 134; Alexander Morris to David Laird, 8 July 1876, and 19 January 1877. AM, MG 12 B2, Alexander Morris Papers, Ketcheson Collection, Items 180 & 220; J. Lestock Reid to Alexander Morris, 3 November 1876. AM, MG 12 B1, Alexander Morris Papers, PG Collection, Item 1372.

78 Annual Report of the Department of Indian Affairs for the Year ending 1883. Canada, *Sessional Papers*, 1884.

79 Roger Goulet to A.M. Burgess (telegram), 28 January 1887. Telegram of Roger Goulet to A.M. Burgess, 3 February 1887. See also LAC, RG 15, D-II-1, vol. 501, file 140682. Report of Roger Goulet to A.M. Burgess, 24 March 24, 1887. Ibid.

80 Roger Goulet to A.M. Burgess, 7 April 1887. LAC, RG 15, D-II-1, vol. 488, file 138133. See also F. Marcoux O.M.I. to Roger Goulet, 1 August 1889. Roger Goulet to A.M. Burgess, Deputy Minister of the Interior, 15 August 1889. LAC, RG 10, vol. 3828, file 60, 717.

81 C.P. Brown to Minister of the Interior, 18 February 1888. LAC, RG 15, D-II-1, vol. 488, file 138133.

82 Thomas White (Minister of the Interior) to C.P. Brown, February 25, 1888. Ibid.

83 See Petition of Sandy Bay Métis to the Minister of the Interior, dated 1890 and the letter forwarding the petition. Letter of the Commissioner to Edgar Dewdney, Minister of the Interior, 19 December 1890. LAC, RG 10, vol. 3828, file 60,717.

84 L. Vankoughnet to Edgar Dewdney, 8 January 1891. Ibid.

85 L. Vankoughnet to E. McColl, 16 January 1891. Ibid.

86 H. Martineau, Indian Agent for Sandy Bay to E. McColl, 17 April 1894; E. McColl, Inspector of Indian Affairs, Manitoba to Deputy Superintendant General of Indian Affairs, September 24, 1894. Ibid.

87 G.W. Burbidge (Deputy Minister of Justice) to L. Vankoughnet (Deputy Supt. General Indian Affairs), 3 October 1887. LAC, RG 10, vol. 11194, file 4 (Legal Opinions).

88 Indian Commissioner to Indian Agent, Edmonton Agency, 10 January 1889. LAC, RG 10, vol. 3595, file 1239, pt 12.
89 This statement is based on entries in the Edmonton House journals of 27 September 1826, 22 October 1826, 24 January 1827, and 25 March 1827. HBCA, B.60/a/24. See also George Simpson, *An Overland Journey Round the World during the Years 1841 and 1842* (Philadelphia: Lea and Blanchard, 1847), 70, 73.
90 Bobtail's (Alexis Piché) scrip application of 1886 notes this as his mother's name. See LAC, RG 15, D-II-8-c, vol. 1363. Bobtail's entry in the Baptismal Registers of Fort Edmonton gives his mother's name as O'Petaskewis and his father's name as Louis Piché. See Baptêmes et Mariages faits dans les Missions des Forts des Prairies, Anneé 1842. Provincial Archives of Alberta (PAA), Oblate Archives, 71.220/5213.
91 The Baptismal Registers of Fort Edmonton record five children of Louis Piché and O'Petaskewis, all baptized in 1842. They included Isabelle (age 2), Joseph (age 5), baptized on 7 August 1842; Louis (age 8), Jean-Baptiste (age 11), and Alexandre (age 13) baptized on 14 August 1842. See Baptêmes et Mariages faits dans les Missions des Forts des Prairies, Anneé 1842. PAA, Oblate Archives, 71.220/5213.
92 Gerald M. Hutchinson, "Introduction" to *The Rundle Journals, 1840–1848* (Calgary: Alberta Records Publications, Historical Society of Alberta and Glenbow-Alberta Institute, 1977), xxxvii–xxxiii.
93 See A. Philippot, "La Mission de Saint-Paul-des-Cris et les premières origins des Missions Indiennes de l'Alberta-Saskatchewan," 34. PAA, Oblate Archives, 71.220/7259. See also Constantine Scollen, "Notes biographiques," 33–4, 40–3. PAA, Oblate Archives, 71.220/7340. Bobtail was among those Plains Cree chiefs who visited Chief Factor Christie at Fort Edmonton in 1871 requesting that Lieutenant Governor Archibald consult with them. By the time Treaty 6 was being planned in 1875–76, it was understood that Bobtail and his band would have to be brought into treaty. See Letter of W.J. Christie, 13 April 1871 reprinted in Morris, *Treaties of Canada*, 170–1.
94 Ibid. See also Piché family scrip applications of 1886. LAC, RG 15, D-II-8-c.
95 Scrip applications of Bobtail and his family. LAC, RG 15, D-II-8-c.
96 Letter of George McDougall (Edmonton), dated 25 April and 28 May 1873 repr. in *Wesleyan Missionary Notices*, Canada Conference, n.s. 20 (August 1873): 310–11. Letter of P. Campbell, dated Victoria Mission, 8 January 1874, repr. in *Wesleyan Missionary Notices*, Canada Conference, n.s., 23 (May 1874): 363.
97 George McDougall to Lt Gov. A. Morris, 23 October 1875. LAC, RG 10, vol. 3624, file 5152. Reports and Memoranda of W.J. Christie to Alexander Morris, 10 and 12 October 1876. AM, Alexander Morris Papers, MG 12, B2, #1323.

98 David Laird to Minister of the Interior, 9 May 1878. LAC, RG 10, vol. 3655, file 9000.

99 Ibid.

100 This is based on an analysis of the annuity lists of the three bands at Bear Hills. See also Diary of J.C. Nelson D.L.S. 1885. LAC, RG 10, vol. 3831, file 63465. Typescript of S.B. Lucas Diary for 1886, Peace Hills Agency, 2 April 1886. Glenbow Archives, Lucas Family Fonds, M5986/2.

101 Report of James Stewart, Indian Agent Edmonton, 21 August 1880, in "Annual Report of the Department of Indian Affairs for the year ending 31 December 1880," 103–4. W. Anderson (Indian Agent Edmonton) to E. Dewdney (Commissioner), 19 September 1881. LAC, RG 10, vol. 3768, file 33501. Samuel B. Lucas, Peace Hills Farm to W. Anderson, Indian Agent, Edmonton, 8 February 1883. LAC, RG 10, vol. 3673, file 10, 986. Samuel Lucas (Indian Agent), Edmonton, to Indian Commissioner, 15 April 1885. LAC, RG 10, vol. 3600, file 1634. S.B. Lucas (Acting Agent Peace Hills Indian Agency) to the Indian Commissioner, 15 May 1885. LAC, RG 10, vol. 3710, file 19, 550–3. See also Gerhard J. Ens, "Gabriel Dumont, Big Bear, and the Indian Rebellion of 1885: The Case of the Peace Hills Reserves, 1884–1885," in *Histoires et identities métisses: homage à Gabriel Dumont / Métis Histories and Identities: A Tribute to Gabriel Dumont*, ed. Denis Gagnon, Denis Combet, and Lise Gaboury-Diallo (Winnipeg: Presses universitaires de Saint-Boniface, 2009), 25–38.

102 S.B. Lucas (Acting Agent Peace Hills Indian Agency) to the Indian Commissioner, 15 May 1885. LAC, RG 10, vol. 3710, file 19, 550–3.

103 Report of Indian Agent Saml. B. Lucas of Peace Hill Agency, 12 August 1886, in *Annual Report of the Department of Indian Affairs for the Year Ended 31st December 1886*. Canada, *Sessional Papers* (No. 6), 50 Victoria A.1887. See also *Edmonton Bulletin*, 24 October 1885 and 7 November 1885.

104 "Local," *Edmonton Bulletin*, 24 October 1884.

105 Family heads were allowed to apply for scrip for those of their children born prior to 1870 whether living or dead. They were also allowed to apply for deceased parents.

106 List of Bobtail Members taking Scrip, 1885–86. LAC, RG 10, vol. 4012, file 266,600. The list of 1885 scrip takers underestimates the exodus of treaty "half-breeds" from Bear Hills. There were numerous "Stragglers" not on the Peace Hills annuity lists but who were living at Bear Hills and who took scrip in 1885. "Edmonton Stragglers" taking scrip in 1885 and listing their address as Peace Hills or Bear Hills included Margaret Cayen (wife of Daniel Whitford), Marcelline Dion (wife of Gilbert Whitford), Cécile Durand, Louison Nippissing, Patrice Nippissing, and Isabelle Paquette.

107 "Report of Indian Agent Saml. B. Lucas of Peace Hill Agency, 12 August 1886," in *Annual Report of the Department of Indian Affairs for the Year Ended 31st December 1886*; see n103, 132–3. In July of 1885 the Indian commissioner of the Northwest Territories sent a circular to all Indian agents warning them to be sure to strike those withdrawing from treaty off annuity lists as they had no further claims on the government. E. Dewdney to Indian Agents, 20 July 1885. LAC, RG 10, vol. 3714, file 21, 233. Having withdrawn from treaty and taken scrip, these former band members became to all intents and purposes "whites" and as such could not be permitted to reside on the reserve. Deputy Supt General of Indian Affairs to John R. Hall, 21 August 1885. LAC, RG 15, D-II-1, vol. 488, file 138133.

108 entries for 25–6 June and 2 and 6 July 1886. Ibid.

109 List of Bobtail Members taking Scrip, 1885–86. LAC, RG 10, vol. 4012, file 266,600.

110 Pay Sheets for Bobtail's band 1886.

111 "Report of Indian Agent Saml. B. Lucas of Peace Hill Agency"; see n103. Letter of Sam Lucas, Indian Agent Peace Hills Agency to Indian Commissioner, 30 September 1886. LAC, RG 10, vol. 3772, file 35452. In this letter Lucas, somewhat inexplicably, also noted there were 101 individuals still remained on the reserve. This must have included at least some scrip takers who had not yet left the reserve.

112 Sam. Lucas to Indian Commissioner, 9 February 1887. LAC, RG 10, vol. 3600, file 1634.

113 Hayter Reed (Asst. Commissioner) to Supt General of Indian Affairs, 29 June 1887. LAC, RG 10, vol. 3724, File 24, 303–3.

114 Supt General to E. Dewdney (Indian Commissioner) 11 July 1887. Ibid.

115 E. Dewdney (Indian Commissioner) to Supt. General of Indian Affairs, 18 August 1887. Ibid.

116 Ibid.

117 Indian Commissioner to Indian Agent, Edmonton Agency, 10 January 1889. LAC, RG 10, vol. 3595, file 1239, pt 12.

118 T.P. Wadsworth to E. Dewdney, 30 September 1887. LAC, RG 10, Vol. 3785, File 41,783–5 [Doc. CR-86].

119 Indian Commissioner to Sam. Lucas, 14 September 1889; Memo of Hayter Reed to Indian Agent, Bear Hills, 18 November 1890. Ibid.

120 The best account of the formation of the Papaschase band and its dissolution is Clint Evans, "Report on the Origin and Dissolution of the Papaschase Band," prepared for the Department of Justice Canada, Edmonton Regional Office, 27 January 2004.

121 Richard Hardisty to Joseph Wrigley, 17 August 1885. HBCA, B.60/b/3, Edmonton Correspondence Book, 1878–1886, fol. 96. See also T. P. Wadsworth to Indian Commissioner Edgar Dewdney, 26 October 1885. LAC, RG 10, vol. 3717, file 22550-2. Scrip application of George Quinns alias Kwenis alias Gladu, sworn at Edmonton, 31 July 1886, and Scrip application of Edward Quinns alias Kwenis alias Gladu, sworn at St Albert, 28 July 1886. LAC, RG 15, D-II-8-c, vol. 1364. Scrip application of John Kwenis, alias Quinns, alias Gladu, alias Wood Pecker on behalf of his deceased child Catherine, declared at St Albert, 13 July 1886, and Scrip application of Chief Pass-Pass-Chase or John Kwenis (Quinns) alias Gladu as sole heir of his son Paul Kwenis, declared at St Albert, 13 July 1886. LAC, RG 15, D-II-8-c, vol. 1352.

122 Scrip application of John Quinns Gladu (Chief "Paspaschess"), sworn at Edmonton, 31 July 1886. LAC, RG 15, D-II-8-c, vol. 1349.

123 This can be determined from the scrip applications of those band members who left treaty, as they were required to state where they were living on 15 July 1870. These other locations mentioned included the Victoria Settlement, Saint-Paul-des-Cris, Lac La Biche, Saddle Lake, and Red Deer River.

124 Richard Hardisty to Joseph Wrigley, 17 August 1885. HBCA, B.60/b/3, Edmonton Correspondence Book, 1878–1886, fol. 96.

125 A similar dynamic occurred with Lapotac, who was asked by the Indian Department to form a band to include the remaining "stragglers" around Fort Edmonton who wanted to enter treaty but were not affiliated with any band. In return he was recognized as chief and received a reserve. This would become the Enoch band.

126 This can be seen in the annuity lists for the Papaschase band. See Treaty annuity paylists – Treaties 4, 6, and 7, 1877–1885. LAC, RG 10, vols 9412–18.

127 "Annual Report of the Department of Indian Affairs for the Year ended 31st December, 1883," *Sessional Papers* (No. 4), 1884, pt 1, 126. "Annual Report of the Department of Indian Affairs for the Year ended 31st December, 1884," *Sessional Papers* (No. 3), 1885, xlvii.

128 Treaty annuity pay lists – Treaties 4, 6, and 7, 1886. LAC, RG 10, vol. 9419.

129 Indian Agency Inspector Wadsworth to Indian Commissioner Dewdney, 7 July 1886; Telegram from Indian Commissioner Dewdney to Deputy Superintendent General Vankoughnet, 7 July 1886; Deputy Indian Commissioner H. Reed to the Superintendent General of Indian Affairs, 26 July 1886. LAC, RG 10, vol. 3724, file 24303-2A.

130 Telegram from R. Hardisty to Indian Commissioner Dewdney, 9 July 1886. LAC, RG 10, vol. 3595, file 1239, pt 12; Telegram from John Quinns to Sir John A. Macdonald, 15 July 1886. LAC, RG 10, vol. 3724, file 24303-2A.

131 Agent Anderson to the Indian Commissioner, 30 December 1886. LAC, RG 10, vol. 3773, file 36440; "Annual Report of the Department of Indian Affairs for Year ended 31 December 1887," *Sessional Papers* (No. 15), 1888, pt 1, 104; Treaty annuity paylists – Treaties 4, 6, and 7, 1887. LAC, RG 10, vol. 9420.
132 William de Balinhard to the Indian Commissioner, 15 November 1887. William De Balinhard to the Indian Commissioner, 30 March 1888. LAC, RG 10, vol. 3582, file 1023½.
133 Assistant Indian Commissioner to the Deputy Superintendent General, 30 August 1889; Assistant Commissioner Forget to Acting Agent A. E. Lake, 4 January 1894. Ibid.
134 James Brady, "The Wisdom of Papasschayo, A Cree Medicine Man." Glenbow Archives, James Brady Fonds, Series 3, M125-19.
135 J.A.J. McKenna to Clifford Sifton, 31 May 1901. This report constitutes Annex "A" approved by OIC of 6th June 1901 (PC 1182).

9 The United States / Canada Border

1 Richard Maxwell Brown, "Western Violence: Structure, Values, Myth," *Western Historical Quarterly* 24(1) (February 1993): 5–20.
2 The population of Red River in 1835 was 3,646; in 1849 – 5,391; in 1856 – 6,523; and in 1870 – 12,000.
3 By the 1830s buffalo robes were becoming increasingly important in the fur trade of the Missouri River. Beaver stocks had been depleted, and buffalo robes found lucrative markets in New York, Montreal, St Paul, and St Louis. These robes consisted of the skin of the buffalo with the hair left on and the hide tanned. Prime robes, those taken from November to February and in excellent shape, fetched good prices of up to $10–12/robe by the 1870s. The Métis responded to this new market by smuggling their furs and robes across the border to American traders. For a discussion of these roles see Gerhard J. Ens, *Homeland to Hinterland: The Changing Worlds of the Red River Metis in the Nineteenth Century* (Toronto: University of Toronto Press, 1996), 28–56, 72–92.
4 Letter of G.A. Belcourt, St Paul, 25 November 1845, printed in House of Representatives Executive Document, no. 51, 31st Congress, 1st sess., 44; repr. in *Collections of the State Historical Society of North Dakota*, Vol. 5 (1921), 134–54.
5 G.A. Belcourt to Bishop of Dubuque, 16 février 1850. *Ann. de la Prop. de la Foi*, 106–10.

6 For more detail on Métis wintering sites and the structures in these villages see Jack Elliot, "Hivernant Archaeology in the Cypress Hills" (MA thesis, University of Calgary, 1971); Stuart Baldwin, "Wintering Villages of the Metis Hivernants" in *The Metis and The Land in Alberta Land Claims Research Project, 1979–80*, ed. Métis Association of Alberta (Edmonton: Métis Association of Alberta, 1980); D. Grainger and B. Ross, "Petite Ville Site Survey, Saskatchewan," *Research Bulletin*, No. 143 (Ottawa: Parks Canada, 1989); H.M. Robinson, *The Great Fur Land or Sketches of Life in the Hudson's Bay Territory* (New York: G.P. Putnam's Sons, 1879); Mary Weekes, *The Last Buffalo Hunter* (New York: Thomas Nelson & Sons, 1939); Isaac Cowie, *The Company of Adventurers: A Narrative of Seven Years in the Service of the Hudson's Bay Company during 1867–1874* (Toronto: William Briggs, 1913).

7 Cowie, *The Company of Adventurers*, 349–50.

8 William Davis, a Métis buffalo hunter who was born in 1845 and lived at St Joseph until the 1860s, recorded almost yearly conflicts with the Sioux between 1848 and 1858. In addition to these minor skirmishes, there were major battles in 1848, 1851, and 1853. Historical Society of North Dakota Archives, William Davis Papers, A35, Notebooks 1–4. See also WPA, Historical Data Project, Rolette County, William Davis File. As late as 1854, G.A. Belcourt, the Catholic missionary at St Joseph, complained of annual Sioux attacks on their settlement and warned the United States government that, if the army did nothing to stop these depredations, the Métis would take things into their own hands. At a meeting held in 1854 the Métis "resolved that next summer, after the first hunting trip, a party of war, of about five thousand men, shall go up the Missouri a little below Fort Mandan, and there separating into two corps, one each side of the river, will come down the Missouri and put to death all living beings they will meet on their way." Letter of G.A. Belcourt to Hon. G.W. Manypenny, Commissioner of Indian Affairs, 20 November 1854, Encl. #24 in "The Report of the Commissioner of Indian Affairs," November 25, 1854. U.S. Congress, House Ex. Docs. No. 1, 2nd sess., 33rd Congress, Serial Set #777, 279.

9 The agreement established the Sheyenne River as the dividing line between the Dakota, Chippewa, and Métis. It was also agreed, however, that if the buffalo became scarce on either side, bands could cross this boundary for food. "Affidavit of Michael Gladue locating the dividing line between the Sioux Indians and the Turtle Mountain Chippewa Country as settled between them, 9 February 1892." Repr. in "Turtle Mountain Band of Chippewa Indians," U.S. Congress, Sen. Ex. Docs. no. 444, 56th Congress, 1st sess., 1900, 151–2.

10 David McCrady has noted quite correctly that at no time were all Métis at peace with all Sioux bands. For the ongoing nature of these Sioux/Métis

conflicts see David G. McCrady, "Living with Strangers: The Nineteenth-Century Sioux and the Canadian-American Borderlands" (PhD dissertation, University of Manitoba, 1998), 22–8, 48–57. See also his *Living with Strangers: The Nineteenth-Century Sioux and the Canadian-American Borderlands* (Lincoln: University of Nebraska Press, 2006).

11 The Minnesota Territorial Census of 1850 for Pembina County lists 1,105 individuals, almost all of whom were Métis and 712 of whom had been born in British territory. A few years after the census was taken, the Catholic priest G.A. Belcourt noted that thousands of Métis had emigrated from the Red River Settlement to the United States and more would come and take the oath of allegiance if their rights were respected. Letter of G.A. Belcourt to Hon. G.W. Manypenny, Commissioner of Indian Affairs, November 20, 1854. See n8, above.

12 Report of the Treaty Made with the Pembina Indians, at Pembina, by Alex. Ramsey, 7 November 1851, included in "The Report of the Commissioner of Indian Affairs," November 27, 1851. See n8 above, 285.

13 Ibid.

14 Based on my analysis of the Minnesota Territorial Census of 1850 and the Red River Settlement Census of 1870. Many of those British-born Métis found in the Minnesota Census of 1850 were enumerated in the Red River Census of 1870.

15 Report of Gen. Isaac J. Stevens in relation to the Indians on his route of exploration from the head of navigation of the Mississippi River to the Pacific Ocean, September 16, 1854. Encl. No.86 in "The Report of the Commissioner of Indian Affairs," November 25, 1854. U.S. Congress, House Ex. Docs. No. 1, 2nd sess., 33rd Congress, 1854–55, Serial Set #777, 401. Stevens was appointed governor and superintendent of Indian Affairs of Washington Territory in 1853, and was assigned to the duty of exploring a route for a railroad from the sources of the Mississippi to Puget Sound.

16 John C. Ewers, "Ethnological Report on the Chippewa Cree Tribe of the Rocky Boy Reservation and the Little Shell Band of Indians," in *Chippewa Indians VI*, American Indian Ethnohistory: North Central and Northeastern Indians, Report presented before the Indian Claims Commission, Docket No. 221-B (New York: Garland, 1974), 72–4.

17 By 1870 there was a 20 per cent duty on the importation of buffalo robes into the United States. With the border no longer open, the Métis from the Canadian side could trade solely with the HBC, as they were the only traders who had the ability and resources to ship their robes in bond through the United States to Montreal. For more analysis of the duty on furs and its impact on the Métis see Ens, *Homeland to Hinterland*, 149–56.

18 Eli Guardipee recalled that his and ten other families moved to the Milk River country in 1868. Eli Guardipee's story as told to John B. Ritch, 9/27/40, University of Montana Archive, Small Collections. Ben Kline, as part of Pierre Berger's Métis band from St Joseph, moved to Montana in the winter of 1865 by way of Turtle Mountain and Wood Mountain. Others in Berger's group included Vital Turcotte, Frank Ouellette, and the Kline family. See "Ben Kline: Sketch of Ben Kline's life gathered by Father Van den Broeck during many private conversations with his friend Ben," Montana Historical Society Archives, Small Collection #942.
19 Jean-Marie Lestanc to Taché, 3 mai 1872 (T10300-03), 31 mars 1873 (T11789-92), Archives de l'Archevêché de Saint-Boniface.
20 Journal of George M. Dawson, 22 June 1874; repr. as "The Journals of George M. Dawson," *Saskatchewan History* 21(1) (Winter 1968) 19.
21 Ibid.
22 Although the Métis had traded with the Sioux since at least the truce of the 1850s, this trade had escalated as both the Métis and the Sioux moved westward. By the 1870s there were reports that the Métis and Teton Sioux had formed an offensive and defensive alliance allowing both groups to hunt in Cree and Blackfoot territory. This concerned not only the U.S. Army but also the other Indian groups in the area. See "Report of Edward McKay on the State of Affairs in the Northwest," encl. in Letter of Pascal Breland to Lt Gov. Morris, 18 May 1873. Lt Gov. Morris Papers. Archives of Manitoba (AM), MG 12, B1, #164.
23 Letter of A.J. Simmons, U.S. Special Indian Agent, Milk River Agency, to Col. J.A. Viall, Superintendent of Indians for Montana, 15 October 1871, Fort Benton, MT. National Archives and Records Administration (NARA), M234, Letters Received by the Office of Indian Affairs, 1824–1881, Montana Superintendency, 1864–80, Reel 491.
24 J.A. Viall, Supt of Indians for Montana to Gen. John Gibbon, 18 October 1871; H.B. Freeman, Capt. 7th Infantry, Report on Expedition against Half Breed Camp in Milk River District, 6 November 1871, Fort Browning; A.J. Simmons to J.A. Viall, 6 November 1871, Fort Browning; J.A Viall to H.R. Clum, Acting Commissioner Indian Affairs, 16 November 1871, Helena, MT. NARA, M234, Reel 491, Letters Received by the Office of Indian Affairs, 1824–1881, Montana Superintendency, 1864–80.
25 For more extensive treatments of the borderland Métis see Michel Hogue, "Crossing the Line: The Plains Cree in the Canada-United States Borderlands, 1870-1900" (MA thesis, University of Calgary, 2002); Michel Hogue, "Between Race and Nation: The Plains Métis and the Canada-United States Border" (PhD dissertation, University of Wisconsin-Madison, 2009);

Katie Pollock, "From Borderlands to Bordered Lands: The Plains Metis and the 49th Parallel, 1869-1885" (MA thesis, University of Alberta, 2009).

26 Report of Capt. William to Acting Asst. Adj. General, District of Montana, Fort Benton, 16 February 1878. NARA, RG 94, M666, Reel 362, File 1652 AGO 1878, F/W 4976 AGO 1877. Report of Wm Bird, Indian Agent, Fort Peck Indian Agencies, Poplar River, MT, 3 October 1878. NARA, RG 94, M666, Reel 362, File 7740 AGO 1878, F/W 4976 AGO 1877. Report of Guido Ilges, October 11, 1878. NARA, RG 94, M666, Reel 362, File 8215 AGO 1878, F/W/ 4976 AGO 1877.

27 Major Ilges, Camp 5 Miles below Fort Browning North of Milk River to Acting Asst Adjt General, Fort Shaw, MT, 22 October 1878. Major Ilges to Acting Asst Adjt General, Fort Shaw, 4 November 1878. NARA, RG 94, File 8215 AGO 1878, F/W/ 4976 AGO 1877, M666, Reel 362.

28 Report of Guido Ilges, October 11, 1878. See n26, above.

29 Report of the Deputy Superintendent-General of Indian Affairs, 1879. Canada, *Sessional Papers* (No. 4), 43 Victoria 1880, 88.

30 These movements can be traced in the following files: NARA, RG 94, Files 5698 AGO 1881, F/W 4163 AGO 1876; File 6381 AGO 1881, F/W/ 4163 AGO 1776; File 6095 AGO 1881, F/W 4163 AGO 1876; File 6099 AGO 1881, F/W 4163 AGO 1876; File 563 AGO 1882, F/W/ 4163 AGO 1876. All on M666 Reel 291.

31 Brief on Indian Incursions across the Northwest Boundary, File 1051 AGO 1882, F/W 4163 AGO 1876, M666, Reel 291.

32 Report of Jacob Kline to R. Bates, Fort Assiniboine, April 4, 1882. NARA, RG 94, M689, Reel 93, File 2892 AGO 1882, F/W/ 1540 AGO 1882.

33 Even on entering treaty and tribal politics, many of these families and individuals retained a sense of their Métis roots and identity. See David H. Dinwoodie, "Crossing Borders: Metis Movements on Montana's Flathead Frontier," paper presented at the Northern Great Plains History Conference, Brandon, Manitoba, 1995.

34 See the interviews some of these Métis in Historical Society of North Dakota Archives, WPA Historical Data Project, Rolette County. See also Gerhard J. Ens, "After the Buffalo: The Reformation of the Turtle Mountain Métis Community, 1879-1905," in *New Faces of the Fur Trade: Selected Papers of the Seventh North American Fur Trade Conference, Halifax, Nova Scotia, 1995*, ed. Jo-Anne Fiske, Susan Sleeper Smith, and William Wicken (East Lansing: Michigan State University Press, 1998), 139-51.

35 When the first Métis scrip was issued in Manitoba in the 1870s, Dominion land was valued at $1 an acre, so that a $160 scrip certificate would give the bearer the same amount of land as a 160-acre scrip certificate.

As the value of land increased, however, money scrip was good for a correspondingly smaller amount of land. An Order in Council of 30th March 1885 gave a commission the power to extinguish the claims of the Métis who had been living in the British northwest on 15 July 1870. Allotments were to be in money scrip worth $160 for Métis heads of family and $240 for children of Métis heads of family. A few weeks later another Order in Council allowed Métis children to take land scrip for 240 acres if they so desired.

36 Both Verne Dusenberry and Joseph Kinsey Howard have described these Métis communities in relation to the buffalo economy, and Dusenberry described the plight of these "dispossessed métis," but neither has attempted to explain why these Métis stayed in Montana after the Buffalo disappeared. See Joseph Kinsey Howard, *Strange Empire: A Narrative of the Northwest* (New York: William Morrow, 1952); Verne Dusenberry, "Waiting for a Day that Never Comes: The Dispossessed Métis of Montana," *Montana: The Magazine of Western History* 6 (1958).

37 Robert Bell to Morris, 17 October 1873. AM, MG 12 B1, Lt Gov. Morris Papers, #524.

38 One of the groups he met was led by Pierre Berger, who would eventually found the Métis settlement at Lewistown.

39 "Report of Edward McKay on the State of Affairs in the Northwest," encl. in Letter of Pascal Breland to Alexander Morris, 18 May 1873. AM, Morris Papers #164.

40 "Memorandum of a Conversation with Mr Edmund Mckay, formerly of the Hudson's Bay Company's service, and a man said, on good authority, to be thoroughly reliable and respectable." Encl. in a letter of Wm Thornton Urquhart to Judge McKegney, 19 May 1873. AM, Morris Papers, #165.

41 Bishop Grandin to David Laird, Minister of the Interior, 5 April 1875. Library and Archives Canada (LAC), RG 10, vol. 3622, file 4953. The letter was written in French and translated by the Department of the Interior. Grandin noted that of the 700 Métis established at St Albert 300 had relocated to Buffalo Lake.

42 James Kipp, a Blackfoot Métis who was trading out of Carrol at the time, claimed that Riel tried to enlist him to the cause, but that he refused. "James Kipp," by James Willard Schultz in the Montana Historical Society Archives, Small Collection, #936. For Riel's plans see also George F.G. Stanley, *Louis Riel* (Toronto: Ryerson Press, 1963), 322; John Peter Turner, *The North-West Mounted Police, 1873-1893* (Ottawa: King's Printer, 1950), 410. Eveline Barnabe to Louis Riel, 13 May 1879. AM, Louis Riel Papers, #368.

43 Lépine to Taché, 2 janvier 1880 (T23082). Archives de l'Archevêché de Saint-Boniface.

44 Lépine to Riel, 1 janvier 1880. AM, MG 3 D2, File 14, Riel Papers. Also see Lépine to Riel, 9 mars 1880; Lépine to Riel 1 mai 1880 (#385); Lépine to Riel, late December 1879, #379.

45 Howard, *Strange Empire*, 338-53.

46 1880 Census of Choteau County, Marriage Records of Fergus County, Valley County, and Sheridan County. *Teton County: A History* (Choteau: Teton County Historical Committee, 1988). *Fred Nault: Montana Metis* (Rocky Boy School, Rocky Boy's Reservation, 1977). Metis Cultural Recovery Inc., Interviews with Métis Descendants.

47 In 1899 Canada changed its scrip regulations and allowed those Métis born in the Canadian northwest between 1870 and 1885 to apply for scrip. Many Métis living in Montana fit the category and travelled to Canada to apply for this scrip. In 1900 and 1901 the scrip commissions took applications from 225 living Métis (parents were also allowed to apply for deceased children) who had been born in the Canadian northwest and had subsequently moved to Montana. Many applications were rejected on the grounds that these Métis were no longer living in Canada, but in 1904 an Order in Council restored their right to take scrip while living in the United States. These applications do not account for the parents of the applicants (who would have taken scrip earlier) or for those Métis who had been born in Montana or Dakota Territory, but they do give some indication of where the Plains Métis settled in Montana. This information has been summarized in figure 9.8. These scrip applications can be found in LAC, Department of Interior Records, RG 15, vols 1372-86.

48 This hivernant band headed by Pierre Berger included his brothers, Vital Turcotte, Frank Ouellette, Alex Wilkie, Antoine Fleury, Ben Kline, and some Lafontaines and Fayants and their families.

49 Mrs Clemence Gourneau Berger, "Metis Come to Judith Basin," in *The Métis Centennial Publication, 1879-1979*, ed. Bill Thackeray (Lewistown, MT: Central Montana Publication Co.), 13-16. Elizabeth Swan, "A Brief History of the first Catholic Pioneers of Lewistown," in *The Heritage Book of Central Montana*, ed. Dabbie Deal and Lorette McDonald (1976).

50 Ibid.

51 Ewers, "Ethnological Report on the Chippewa Cree Tribe of the Rocky Boy Reservation and the Little Shell Band of Indians," 97. *Fred Nault*, 97.

52 *Teton County*, 14-15. Interviews of the descendants of the Teton and Dupuyer Métis Communities, Metis Cultural Recovery Inc., Choteau, MT.

53 Ewers, "Ethnological Report on the Chippewa Cree Tribe of the Rocky Boy Reservation and the Little Shell Band of Indians," 97. *Fred Nault*, 105-7.

54 For more on the Montana Métis and the scrip issue see Hogue, "Between Race and Nation," 312-69.

55 Martha Harroun Foster, *We Know Who We Are: Métis Identities in a Montana Community* (Norman: University of Oklahoma Press, 2006).
56 Heather Devine, *The People Who Own Themselves: Aboriginal Ethnogenesis in a Canadian Family, 1660-1900* (Calgary: University of Calgary Press, 2004).
57 Brenda Macdougall, *One of the Family: Metis Culture in Nineteenth-Century Northwestern Saskatchewan* (Vancouver: UBC Press, 2010).
58 Foster, *We Know Who We Are*, 220.

10 St Paul des Métis Colony

1 As noted in previous chapters the political rationale of the Métis scrip programs was to extinguish Métis claims to "Indian title."
2 By the 1890s hunting and fishing regulations banned the hunting of ducks and partridges during the spring, banned fishing between October and December, and instated fishing licences in open season. See Library and Archives Canada (LAC), RG 18, A1, vol. 20, #330; NWMP Files, Comptroller's Office Correspondence. Anderson to Secretary of the Department of the Interior, 30 April 1890. See also Joe Sawchuk, Patricia Sawchuk, and Theresa Ferguson, *Metis Land Rights in Alberta: A Political History* (Edmonton: Métis Association of Alberta, 1981), 162.
3 Malcolm Norris to James Brady, 17 March 1934. Glenbow Archives, James Brady Fonds. Series 3, Correspondence 1933-1967, M-125-21.
4 John A. Macdonald, reflecting the government view that the Manitoba scrip issue had been of little benefit to the Métis, noted in 1885 that "the claims of the half-breeds in Manitoba were bought up by speculators. It was an unfortunate thing for those poor people; but it is true that this grant of scrip and land to those poor people was a curse and not a blessing. The scrip was bought up; the lands were bought up by white speculators, and the consequences are apparent." Speech of John A. Macdonald, 6 July 1885, *Debates* of the House of Commons of the Dominion of Canada, Third Session of the Fifth Parliament, 48–49 Victoria 1885, 3113.
5 "An Act to amend and consolidate the several Acts Respecting the Public Lands of the Dominion," 15 May 1879, *Statutes of Canada*, 42 Vict. (1879), c. 31, s. 125.
6 A.M. Burgess to T. Mayne Daly (Minister of the Interior), 12 December 1895. Various drafts of this letter can be found in LAC, RG 15, D-II-1, vol. 708, file 360530, pt 1. It is also attached to Order in Council (OIC) of 28th December 1895 as Annex "A" (PC 3723).
7 This plan, entitled "A Philanthropic Plan to Redeem the Half-Breeds of Manitoba and the North-West Territories," can be found in LAC,

RG 15, D-II-1, vol. 708, file 360530, pt 1. It is also attached to OIC of 28th December 1895 as Annex "B" (PC 3723).

8 Albert Lacombe, "Memoirs on the Half-Breeds of Manitoba and the Territories of the Canadian North West" (1901), 4–8.

9 A case can also be made that the colony did not fail, as when it was opened to settlement in 1909 about sixty Métis families did receive title to land in the former colony. In the eyes of the government and Church, however, opening the colony to non-Métis settlement in 1909 was seen as a failure of the experiment.

10 OIC of 28th December 1895 (PC 3723). The best secondary sources on the history of St Paul des Métis are Eméric O. Drouin, *Joyau dans la Plaine: Saint-Paul, Alberta* (Quebec: Paul Nicole, 1968); Stanley, "Alberta's Half-breed Reserve Saint-Paul-des-Métis; Sawchuk, Sawchuk, and Ferguson, *Métis Land Rights in Alberta*; John Fontaine, "St Paul des Métis, 1896 to 1909 – The Dual Roles of the Missionary Oblates of Mary Immaculate" (MA Project Paper, Department of History and Classics, University of Alberta, 2009).

11 A.M. Burgess to T. Mayne Daly, Minister of the Interior, 12 December, 1895. This letter forms Annex "A" of OIC of 28th December (PC 3723).

12 Ibid. See also Albert Lacombe to A.M. Burgess, 27 June 1895. LAC, RG 15, D-II-1, vol. 708, file 360530, pt 1.

13 A.M. Burgess to T. Mayne Daly, Minister of the Interior, 12 December, 1895; see n11.

14 Albert Lacombe to A.M. Burgess, 27 June 1895; see n12.

15 A.M. Burgess to T. Mayne Daly, Minister of the Interior, 12 December, 1895; see n11.

16 *Edmonton Herald*, 10 October 1896.

17 The Métis population of St Paul des Métis is hard to calculate accurately in its first years. Various other accounts put the number of families there at the end of 1896 at thirty. See Drouin, *Joyau dans la Plaine*, 149–50. Most sources agree, however, that by the end of 1897 there were only thirty-two Métis families in the colony. The numbers used here come from Father Lacombe's Report on the Colony in 1898. LAC, RG 15, D-II-1, vol. 708, file 360530, pt 1.

18 Ibid.

19 Drouin, *Joyau dans la Plaine*, 149–50.

20 These applications would have been from those Métis born between 1870 and 1885 who were not eligible for the 1885–86 scrip issue (fifty-two applications).

21 This information can been gleaned from scrip applications found in LAC, RG 15, D-II-8-c.

22 See J.P. Stan Hambly (ed.), *The Battle River County: An Historical Sketch of Duhamel and District* (New Norway: Duhamel Historical Society, 1974), 9–18.

23 Drouin, *Joyau dans la Plaine*, 150–1, 202–3.
24 A.A. Ruttan to Secretary of the Department of the Interior, 19 January 1899. LAC, RG 15, D-II-1, vol. 708, file 360530, pt 1.
25 Ibid.
26 This correspondence is summarized in Drouin, *Joyau dans la Plaine*, 115–18, 154,
27 Ibid., 115–20.
28 Thérien's refusal to grant credit opened the door to other merchants in the colony who also traded furs and sold liquor, such as Lawrence Garneau.
29 Drouin, *Joyau dans la Plaine*, 206.
30 Letter of Thérien to Lacombe, 19 September 1904 and Thérien to Legal, 17 April 19905 quoted in Drouin, *Joyau dans la Plaine*, 201.
31 Petition to Clifford Sifton from Thérien and four settlers 1901. LAC, RG 15, D-II-1, vol. 708, file 360530, pt 1.
32 J.A. Smart to J.I. Tarte, 13 April 1901. LAC, RG 15, D-II-1, vol. 708, file 360530, pt 1.
33 Shortly after the fire Thérien took a rest leave from managing the colony.
34 Adéodat Thérien, "St Paul – Notes historiques," Provincial Archives of Alberta (PAA), acc. no. 71.220, ile 5738, box 132.
35 The land around the reserve was opened to homesteading in 1906.
36 This debate can be followed in correspondence that was sent to the Department of the Interior between 1904 to 1906. See LAC, RG 15, D-II-1, vol. 708, file 360530, pt 1.
37 John Fontaine, "St Paul des Métis, 1896 to 1909 – the Dual Roles of the Missionary Oblates of Mary Immaculate" (MA project paper, Department of History and Classics, University of Alberta, 2009), 22.
38 Adéodat Thérien, "St. Paul – Notes historiques." PAA, Acc. No. 71,220, File 5738, Box 132. See also John Fontaine, 21. The financial problems of the colony are also detailed in Drouin, *Joyau dans la Plaine*.
39 Adéodat Thérien, "St. Paul – Historique de la paroisse, 1930," 19–20. PAA, acc. no. 71,220, file 5739, box 132. See also Fontaine, "St Paul des Métis," 39.
40 Thérien to Oliver, 19 June 1908. LAC, RG 15, D-II-1, vol. 708, file 360530, pt 2.
41 OIC of 13th August 1908 (PC 1800).
42 This was estimated at $68,000. See memo of 9 June 1908. LAC, RG 15, D-II-1, vol. 708, file 360530, pt 2.
43 Sections 8 and 9 and parts of Sections 4 and 5, lying north of Upper Therien Lake, Township 58, Range 9 west of the fourth meridian.
44 Samuel Maber to Minister of the Interior, 22 January 1909. LAC, RG 15, D-II-1, vol. 708, file 360530, pt 2. Later, in April of 1909, Maber increased the number of claims allowed to sixty-five and the number of disallowed

claims to twenty-one. Samuel Maber to Frank Oliver, 12 April 1909. LAC, RG 15, D-II-1, vol. 708, file 360530, pt 2. These grants were confirmed by a later OIC.

45 The OIC confirming the grants to the Métis and Oblates was signed only on 2 June 1909. It stipulated that in cases where Métis had settled on school lands their grant was to be disposed of by granting a quarter-section elsewhere in the reserve. It also noted that the Oblates could choose some alternative lands to make up their four-section grant, given that some of it was affected by the claims of Métis occupants. See OIC of 2nd June 1909 (PC 1246).

46 Fontaine, "St Paul des Métis," 44–8.

11 Political Mobilization in Alberta

1 Evidence of J.M. Dechene, 7 March 1935, 411, *Reports, evidence, etc. re: The Report of the Royal Commission on the Condition of the Halfbreed Population of the Province of Alberta, 1935–36*. Provincial Archives of Alberta (PAA), 70.340.

2 Joe Sawchuk, Patricia Sawchuk, and Theresa Ferguson, *Metis Land Rights in Alberta: A Political History* (Edmonton: Métis Association of Alberta, 1981), 187. Murray Dobbin, *One-And-A-Half Men: The Story of Jim Brady and Malcolm Norris* (Vancouver: New Star Books, 1981), 59.

3 Letter dated 10 September 1940, from J. Dion to F.J. Buck describing the early history of the Métis Association. Glenbow Archives (GA), Joseph Dion Fonds, Series 2, M-331-11.

4 Joe Dion to R.G. Reid, Memorandum of April 1932, *Reports, evidence, etc.* PAA, 70.340, 106–8. Sawchuk, Sawchuk, and Ferguson, *Metis Land Rights in Alberta*, 188.

5 Department of Lands and Mines Questionnaire summary, 148–248, *Reports, evidence, etc.* Sawchuk, Sawchuk, and Ferguson, *Metis Land Rights in Alberta*.

6 Dobbin, *One-And-A-Half Men*, 59.

7 "The Presidents Message," n.d. (probably 1933). GA, Joseph Dion Fonds, Series 2, M-331-11.

8 Minutes of inaugural meeting of L'Association des Métis d'Alberta et des Territoires du Nord-Ouest, December 28, 1932. Ibid., M-331-12.

9 Although most references are to the "Big Four" (e.g., Dobbin, *One-And-A-Half Men*, 64), I often heard references to the "Big Five" when I was with the Métis Association of Alberta in 1979–81, the fifth member of the group being Felix Calihoo.

10 These biographical sketches of the leaders are based on the following sources: Judith Hill, "The Ewing Commission, 1935: A Case Study in Metis-government Relations" (unpublished history honours essay, University of

Alberta, 1977); Dobbin, *One-And-A-Half Men*; F.K. Hatt, "Ethnic Discourse in Alberta: Land and the Metis in the Ewing Commission," *Canadian Ethnic Studies* 17 (1985):64–79. Sawchuk, Sawchuk, and Ferguson, *Metis Land Rights in Alberta*.

11 Hill, "The Ewing Commission," 23–4.
12 Dobbin, *One-And-A-Half Men*; Hatt, "Ethnic Discourse in Alberta."
13 Dobbin, *One-And-A-Half Men*, 64.
14 Hill, "The Ewing Commission"; Dobbin, *One-And-A-Half Men;* Hatt, "Ethnic Discourse in Alberta"; Sawchuk, Sawchuk, and Ferguson, *Metis Land Rights in Alberta*.
15 Hill, "The Ewing Commission," 23–5.
16 Dobbin, *One-And-A-Half Men*; Hatt, "Ethnic Discourse in Alberta."
17 Ibid.
18 Dobbin, *One-And-A-Half Men*, 66.
19 The following thirty-one councillors from twenty-six districts were named at the 1932 convention: Fishing Lake, Charles Delome; Winterburn, A.N. Norwest; Athabaska, George White; Beaver River, George Ward; Wolf Lake, Joe Louie; Lac La Biche and surrounding district, Augustin Ladoucer, John E. Huppie, T.F. Laboucane, Julien Cardinal, Innes Gairdner (alternate); Lac La Nonne, Maurice L'Hirondelle; Lac Ste Anne, J.G. Belcourt; Onoway, T.H. Noris; Wabumun, James Savard; LeGoff, James McFeeters; Cold Lake, John Cardinal (alternate); Beaver Crossing, Dieudonne Collins; Vermillion, J.B. Whitefish and Adelard Laboucane; St Paul, Norbert Beauregard and Felix Calihoo; Edson, J. Myles Lee; Peace River, Louis Calliou; Bonnyville, Michel Cardinal; Conklin, Joseph Cardinal; Rivière Qui Barre, H.A. White; Villeneuve, Joseph Hodgson; Hobbema, William Calder; St Albert, Henry Cunningham; Morinville, T.D. Cunningham; Slave Lake, Samuel Cunningham; Edmonton, M.F. Norris. "President's Message." GA, Joseph Dion Fonds, Series 2, M-331-11.
20 Dobbin, *One-And-A-Half Men*, 61.
21 Adrian Hope, interview with the author and P. Sawchuk, Edmonton, 9 March 1981.
22 Besides the version prepared by Brady, see also By laws of the Métis Association of Alberta, 1940. GA, Joseph Dion Fonds, Series 2, M-331-11; Article 2 states: "Active members consist of Metis, Non Treaty Indians or any person of mixed White and Indian blood." The document states the intention of registering under the Societies Act of 1924, but apparently this did not happen.
23 Joe Sawchuk, "The Metis, Non-Status Indians and the New Aboriginality: Government Influence on Native Political Alliances and Identity," in *Readings*

in Aboriginal Studies, Vol. 2: *Identities and State Structures*, ed. Joe Sawchuk (Brandon: Bearpaw Press, 1992); revision of an article that originally appeared in *Canadian Ethnic Studies* 17(2) (1985): 135–46.

24 Joe Dion to R.G. Reid, 1933, 78, *Reports, evidence, etc.* PAA, 70.340.
25 Joe Dion to Jim Brady, 4 October 1934. GA, James Brady Fonds, Series 4, M-125-27.
26 Ibid.
27 Joe Dion to R.G. Reid, 1933, 78; emphasis added; *Reports, evidence, etc.* PAA, 70.340.
28 Norris to Brady, 4 September 1933. GA, James Brady Fonds, Series 4, M-125-27.
29 Norris to Brady, 4 September 1934. Ibid., Series 3, M-125-21.
30 Ibid.
31 Norris to Brady, 29 December 1934. Ibid.
32 Norris to Brady 17 March 1934. Ibid.
33 Brady to Tompkins, 6 March 1934. Ibid., M-125-23.
34 Dobbin, *One-And-A-Half Men*, 61.
35 Minutes of Métis Association meeting, 28 December 1932; forwarded to R.G. Reid, Royal Half-Breed Commission, Premiers Papers. PAA.
36 *Reports, evidence, etc.*, 381–98. PAA, 70.340.
37 Ibid.
38 Norris to Brady, 5 February 1939. GA, James Brady Fonds, Series 3, M-125-21.
39 Calihoo to Brady, 30 July 1945. Ibid., Series 4, M-125-26.
40 Much of following section is based on Sawchuk, Sawchuk, and Ferguson, *Metis Land Rights in Alberta*, 190-200.
41 O.C. 1095/34, 323–4, *Reports, evidence, etc.* PAA, 70.340.
42 The commission held meetings at High Prairie, Lac La Biche, Good Fish Lake, Grande Cache, Chipewyan, Athabaska, Groff, Frog Lake, Marlboro, and Edmonton. *Report of the Royal Commission on the Condition of the Halfbreed Population of the Province of Alberta*, Sessional Paper No. 72, 1936.
43 *Reports, evidence, etc.*, 478–81; emphasis in original. PAA, 70.340.
44 *Reports, evidence, etc.*, 381–98. PAA, 70.340.
45 Sawchuk, "The Metis, Non-Status Indians and the New Aboriginality."
46 Ibid.
47 *Reports, evidence, etc.*, 512 (Brady testimony on 28 February 1935); 428 (Dechene testimony of 7 March 1935). PAA, 70.340.
48 Brady testimony. Ibid.
49 Dobbin, *One-And-A-Half Men*, 91.
50 "Metis society is divided into gradations at various stages of development. The agricultural and the nomadic. The fairly well to do and the exploited

and if we forget this basic division and neglect the contradictions between the agricultural and the nomadic, this means we neglect the fundamental fact. I don't deny the existence of intermediate strata who join either one aide or other as the forces of economic pressure determine, or who occupy a neutral position. If we neglect the fundamental struggle between these two basic types that means we ignore facts. This struggle between two worlds is taking place within the whole range of Metis thinking. Its outcome is decisive to the next stage of Metis development." "Politics in the Métis Association," October 1942. GA, James Brady Fonds, Series 5, M-125.

51 Hatt, "Ethnic Discourse in Alberta," 71.

52 Dobbin, *One-And-A-Half Men*, 91.

53 Ibid.

54 Hatt, "Ethnic Discourse in Alberta," 71–2

55 Falkener Testimony on 7 March 1935, 424, *Reports, evidence, etc*. PAA, 70.340.

56 Ewing Comments on 25 February 1935, 442. Ibid.

57 Proceedings of 28 February 1935, 490. Ibid.

58 Memorandum Relative to the Half-Breed Situation, submitted at Lac La Biche, Alberta, on the 19th day of August, 1935 by Dr Quesnel, Doctor of Medicine, 759. Ibid.

59 Proceedings of 25 February 1935, 438. Ibid.,

60 Dr Harold Orr to Dr Bow, 23 February 1935, 644. Ibid.,

61 Hill, "The Ewing Commission," 58.

62 Proceedings of 1 March 1935, 672–4, *Reports, evidence, etc*. PAA, 70.340.

63 Evidence of Bishop Breynat, April 1935, 543. Ibid.

64 Malcolm Norris testimony on 25 February 1935, 444. Ibid.

65 Dion testimony on 28 February 1936, 511. Ibid.

66 Hatt, "Ethnic Discourse in Alberta," 76–7.

67 "Report of the Royal Commission Appointed to Investigate the Conditions of the Half-Breed Population in Alberta." Sessional Paper 1936–72.

68 Ibid., 6.

69 Ibid., 10.

70 Ibid., 9.

71 Ibid., 13.

72 Ibid., 12–13.

73 Ibid.

74 Adrian Hope, interview with the author and P. Sawchuk, Edmonton, 9 March 1981.

75 At this time, a "legal" definition of Métis has not been clearly delineated, although some definitions have been suggested in various court cases on both the federal and the provincial level. Although the Constitution Act

recognized the Métis as one of Canada's Aboriginal peoples, no attempt has been made by the federal government to develop an official definition of Métis. What definitions there are have been worked out by the Métis political organizations and court cases. While the Federal Court in 2013 found that Métis and non-status Indians are indeed "Indians" under the 1867 Constitution Act and are the direct responsibility of Ottawa, what constituted a Métis was still not clearly defined (see chapter 15 of this volume).

76 This definition is an anomaly in Canada, where "blood" quantum has never been part of any other state definition of aboriginality. The definition had long been resented by the Métis, who rejected the idea of quantifying Native ancestry as a criteria for Métis identity. As Elmer Ghostkeeper has pointed out, "a literal interpretation of the Act's definition would exclude even Louis Riel from membership in a Metis Settlement Association." Elmer Ghostkeeper and Federation of Métis Settlements, *Metism: A Canadian Identity* (Edmonton: Alberta Federation of Métis Settlements, 1982), 31. Despite the opposition to this definition, it remained on the books for a surprisingly long time, until the 1990 Métis Settlements Act redefined Metis as "a person of aboriginal ancestry who identifies with Metis history and culture."

77 Sawchuk, Sawchuk, and Ferguson, *Metis Land Rights in Alberta*, 200.

78 Dobbin, *One-And-A-Half Men*," 118–19.

79 Background Paper No. 6, "The Metis Betterment Act: History and Current Status." Policy and Planning Branch, Native Affairs Secretariat, Province of Alberta, March 1985.

12 The Liberals, the CCF, and the Métis of Saskatchewan

1 Elizabeth Furniss, "Challenging the Myth of Indigenous Peoples' 'Last Stand' in Canada and Australia: Public Discourse and the Conditions of Silence," in *Rethinking Settler Colonialism: History and Memory in Australia, Canada, Aoteraroa New Zealand, and South Africa*, ed. Annie E. Coombes (Manchester: Manchester University Press, 2006), 172–92.

2 Murray Dobbin, "Metis Struggles of the Twentieth Century: The Saskatchewan Metis Society – 1935–1950. Part 1: Early Beginnings," *New Breed* (August 1978): 17. Hereafter referred to as Dobbin 1978 Part 1.

3 Ibid.

4 Ibid., 18.

5 Ibid.

6 Murray Dobbin, "Metis Struggles of the Twentieth Century: The Saskatchewan Metis Society – 1935–1950. Part 2: The Land Issues:

Whitemen's Advice and Government Deceit," *New Breed* (September 1978), 12. Hereafter referred to as Dobbin 1978 Part 2.

7 Dobbin 1978 Part 1, 18.

8 Dobbin 1978 Part 2, 12.

9 Despite the unpopularity of that opinion among the Métis, Hamilton's original assessment may not have been far off the mark. Although extensive research into this very issue was carried out by both the Alberta and Saskatchewan Métis associations as part of a Canada-wide research program into Métis land claims undertaken from 1978 to 1980, neither provincial organization was able to amass enough evidence to convince the federal government that the Métis still possessed Aboriginal title to the Northwest Territories (both Alberta and Saskatchewan were part of the Northwest Territories at the time of the scrip issues). Both organizations took the position that the large amounts of scrip fraud that had taken place during the dissemination of scrip negated the government's claim that the Métis's Aboriginal title had been extinguished. They also offered convincing evidence that the Métis had not benefited from the program to any appreciable amount, and that the Métis had not been consulted properly about what sort of compensation would have been appropriate. However, none of these arguments was sufficient to convince the federal government that the Métis's Aboriginal claims were still outstanding. Nevertheless, Dobbin suggests that there were some important issues missing from Hamilton's original 1939 research that may have weakened the SMS's original application. Apparently, Hamilton neglected to mention that the Dominion government had already recognized an Aboriginal claim for the Métis, or that the Manitoba Act and the Dominion Land Acts specifically mentioned "Indian title" with regard to the Métis.

10 Dobbin 1978 Part 2, 12.

11 F. Laurie Barron, *Walking in Indian Moccasins: The Native Policies of Tommy Douglas and the CCF* (Vancouver: UBC Press, 1997), 56.

12 Dobbin 1978 Part 2, 13.

13 Murray Dobbin, "Metis Struggles of the Twentieth Century: The Saskatchewan Metis Society – 1935–1950. Part 3: "Political Interference and Internal Divisions" *New Breed* (October 1978): 15. Hereafter referred to as Dobbin 1978 Part 3.

14 Ibid., 13.

15 Ibid., 12.

16 Ibid., 12, 13.

17 Interview with Wilma Moore by Murray Dobbin, n.d., Saskatchewan Sound Archives Program, http://ourspace.uregina.ca/handle/10294/1416.

18 Dobbin 1978 Part 3, 13.
19 Ibid., 14.
20 Moore interview.
21 Barron, *Walking in Indian Moccasins*; Murray Dobbin, "Prairie Colonialism: The CCF in Northern Saskatchewan, 1944–1964," *Studies in Political Economy* 16 (1985); David Quiring, *CCF Colonialism in Northern Saskatchewan: Battling Parish Priests, Bootleggers and Fur Sharks* (Vancouver: UBC Press, 2004).
22 Murray Dobbin, "Metis Struggles of the Twentieth Century: The Saskatchewan Metis Society – 1935–1950. Part 4: The Saskatchewan Metis Society –The Final Chapters, 1944–1949," *New Breed* (November–December 1978): 11. Hereafter referred to as Dobbin 1978 Part 4.
23 Ibid.
24 Ibid.; Barron, *Walking in Indian Moccasins*, 38, n51.
25 Conference of the Metis of Saskatchewan Proceedings, 30 July 1946 (hereafter referred to as the Métis Conference, 1946). SK Archives. The details of the organization of the conference come from Douglas's circular invitation letter, 18 July 1946, included in the Proceedings.
26 Shumiatcher, Morris Cyril (1917– 2004), *Encyclopedia of Saskatchewan*, http://esask.uregina.ca/entry/shumiatcher_morris_cyril_1917-_2004.html.
27 Métis Conference, 1946, 4.
28 Ibid., 14.
29 Ibid., 4–5.
30 Ibid., 62.
31 Ibid., 65.
32 Ibid., 67–8.
33 Dobbin 1978 Part 4, 13.
34 Métis Conference, 1946, 34.
35 Ibid., 51.
36 Ibid., 53; emphasis added.
37 Ibid.
38 Barron, *Walking in Indian Moccasins*, 39.
39 Ibid., 48.
40 This narrative of the genesis of the Métis colonies in Saskatchewan is taken from F. Laurie Barron, "The CCF and the Development of Metis Colonies in Southern Saskatchewan during the Premiership of T.C. Douglas, 1944–1961," *Canadian Journal of Native Studies* 10(2) (1990): 244–52.
41 Under a previous arrangement with the Patterson government, the Oblates had operated a farm about a mile north of Lebret for the purpose of employing and training Métis labourers. See ibid., 252.
42 Ibid.

43 Métis Conference, 1946, 35.
44 Barron, *Walking in Indian Moccasins*, 49.
45 O.W. Valleau, Métis Conference, 1946, 54.
46 Ibid., 53.
47 Barron, *Walking in Indian Moccasins*, 51.
48 Métis Conference, 1946, 52.
49 Ibid.
50 Barron, *Walking in Indian Moccasins*, 56.
51 Ibid., 57.
52 Ibid.,140.
53 Helen Buckley, *Trapping and Fishing in the Economy of Northern Saskatchewan*. Report No. 3: *Economic and Social Survey of Northern Saskatchewan* (Saskatoon: Research Division, Center for Community Studies, University of Saskatchewan, 1962).
54 Barron, *Walking in Indian Moccasins*, 144.
55 Quiring, *CCF Colonialism in Northern Saskatchewan*, 41.
56 In Frank's terms, underdeveloped is a condition fundamentally different from undeveloped, and is a direct result of colonization, of being a dependent state or satellite (or periphery) to a dominant state or metropolis, or core. "*Un*developed" simply means that existing economic resources in a geographic area are not being used. *Under*development refers to a situation in which resources are being used, but in a way that benefits the dominant state or metropolis, not the poorer state or satellites in which the resources are found. In other words, under colonialism, the local or peripheral economies are restructured to meet the needs of the core country or metropolis. Frank's thesis, developed for the Latin American scenario, is most famously explicated in his article "The Development of Underdevelopment," *Monthly Review Press* 18 (1966).
57 Murray Dobbin, "Prairie Colonialism: The CCF in Northern Saskatchewan, 1944–1964," *Studies in Political Economy* 16 (1985): 19–20.
58 Ibid., 25.
59 Barron, *Walking in Indian Moccasins*, 204.
60 Quiring, *CCF Colonialism*, xv.
61 Buckley, *Trapping and Fishing in the Economy of Northern Saskatchewan*, 3.
62 V.F. Valentine, "Some Problems of the Metis of Northern Saskatchewan," *Canadian Journal of Economics and Political Science* 20(1) (1954): 90.
63 ibid
64 V.F. Valentine and R.G. Young, "The Situation of the Metis of Northern Saskatchewan in Relation to His Physical and Social Development," *Canadian Geographer* 4 (1954): 50.

65 Buckley, *Trapping and Fishing in the Northern Economy of Northern Saskatchewan*, 17.
66 Ibid.
67 Valentine, "Some Problems of the Metis of Northern Saskatchewan," 95.
68 Valentine and Young, "The Situation of the Metis of Northern Saskatchewan ," 50.
69 Ibid., 54.
70 V.F. Valentine. *The Metis of Northern Saskatchewan* (Regina: Department of Natural Resources, 25 May 1955), 32.
71 Ibid., 33.
72 Valentine and Young, "The Situation of the Metis of Northern Saskatchewan," 54.
73 Ibid., 3.
74 Quiring, *CCF Colonialism*, 41.
75 Dobbin, "Prairie Colonialism," 32.
76 Valentine and Young, "The Situation of the Metis of Northern Saskatchewan," 50; Buckley, *Trapping and Fishing in the Northern Economy of Northern Saskatchewan*.
77 Barron, *Walking in Indian Moccasins*, 152.
78 Murray Dobbin, *The One-and-a-Half Men* (Vancouver: New Star Books, 1981).
79 Dobbin, "Prairie Colonialism," 14.
80 Ibid., 30.
81 Valentine, "Some Problems of the Metis of Northern Saskatchewan," 90.
82 Buckley, *Trapping and Fishing in the Northern Economy of Northern Saskatchewan*, 1–2.
83 Ibid.
84 Ibid., 23.
85 Valentine, *The Metis of Northern Saskatchewan*, 34.
86 Ibid.
87 Ibid., 35.

13 Social Science and the Métis

1 Ian Greene, "Lessons Learned from Two Decades of Program Evaluation in Canada," Deitmar Braunig and Peter Eichorn (eds), *Evaluation and Accounting Standards in Public Management* (Baden-Baden: Nomos Verlagsgesellschaft, 2002), 44–53.
2 Alexander M. Ervin and Lorne Holyoak, "Applied Anthropology in Canada: Historical Foundations, Contemporary Practice, and Policy Potentials," *NAPA Bulletin* 25 (2006): 134–55; Edward J. Hedican, *Applied Anthropology*

in Canada: Understanding Aboriginal Issues, 2nd ed. (Toronto: University of Toronto Press, 2008). Some significant milestones would include the volume *The North American Indian Today*, ed. C.T. Loran and T.F. McIlwraith (Toronto: University of Toronto Press, 1943), in which the authors urged government officials to "plan the broad outlines of an Indian policy for Canada," and the "Hawthorne Report" (H. Hawthorn et al., *A Survey of the Contemporary Indians of Canada: Economic, Political, and Educational Needs and Policies, Parts I and II* (Ottawa: Indian Affairs Branch, 1966–67). Another important event was the work initiated by the James Bay Hydroelectric Project, announced by the Quebec government in the early 1970s, which triggered a large research project under the leadership of Richard Salisbury of McGill University (R. Salisbury et al., *Development and James Bay: Socio-economic Implications of the Hydro-electric Project* (Montreal and Kingston: McGill-Queen's University Press, 1972). This project, which involved many graduate students, was set up to support the Cree in the James Bay area, providing research that would help them to demonstrate that the hydro project would produce significant negative impacts on their territory and way of life. McGill's research and involvement in the negotiations were an important factor in the development of the James Bay Agreement of 1975. Another well-known example of policy analysis is provided by the Mackenzie Valley Pipeline Inquiry of the Northwest Territories, headed by Thomas Berger, chief justice of the British Columbia Supreme Court. The Berger Inquiry was set up to examine the impact of a proposed gas pipeline from the Mackenzie Delta to southern Alberta on Dene, Athapaskan, and Métis social and economic life.

3 There were scores of reports on the Métis that were commissioned by the provincial governments in the period 1950–70, as well as one or two "pure" social science enquiries. Those that are considered here include W.F. Boek and J.K. Boek, *Appendix I: The People of Indian Ancestry in Greater Winnipeg*. Vol. 2 of *The People of Indian Ancestry in Manitoba: A Social and Economic Study. Under the direction of Jean H. Lagasse.* (Winnipeg: Department of Agriculture and Immigration, 1959), 9; Helen Buckley, *Trapping and Fishing in the Economy of Northern Saskatchewan* (Saskatoon: Saskatoon Research Division, Centre for Community Studies, University Of Saskatchewan, 1962); Helen Buckley, J.E.M. Kew, John B. Hawley, *The Indians and Metis of Northern Saskatchewan: A Report on Economic and Social Development* (Saskatoon: Centre For Community Studies, 1963; B.Y. Card, G.K. Hirabayashi, and C.L. French, *The Métis in Alberta Society: With Special Reference to Social, Economic and Cultural Factors Associated with Persistently High Tuberculosis Incidence* (Edmonton: University of Alberta Press, 1963); CASW, *The Metis in Manitoba: A Study by the Manitoba Branch, Canadian Association of Social Workers*. (Winnipeg:

Provincial Council of Women, 1954); Arthur K. Davis (ed.) and Vernon C. Serl and Philip T. Spaulding (asst eds), *A Northern Dilemma* Vol. 1: *Reference Papers* (Bellingham, WA: Western Washington University, 1967); Arthur K. Davis, *A Northern Dilemma*, Vol. 2: *Edging into the Mainstream: Urban Indians in Saskatchewan* (Calgary: Arthur K. Davis, 1965); Fred K. Hatt, *Metis of the Lac la Biche Area: Community Opportunity Assessment* [Research director: Charles W. Hobart, Alberta] (Edmonton: Human Resources Research and Development, Executive Council, Government of Alberta, 1967); Fred K. Hatt, "The Response to Directed Social Change on an Alberta Metis Colony" (PhD diss., University of Alberta, 1969); Walter Hlady, "Power Structure in a Metis Community," manuscript (Saskatoon: Centre for Community Studies, University of Saskatchewan, 1960); Walter M. Hlady and B. Ralph Poston, App. II: *The People of Indian Ancestry in Rural Manitoba*. Vol. 3 of *The People of Indian Ancestry in Manitoba: A Social and Economic Study. Under the Direction of Jean H. Lagasse* (Winnipeg: Department of Agriculture and Immigration, 1959); J.E. Michael Kew, *Cumberland House in 1960* (Saskatoon: Saskatoon Research Division, Centre for Community Studies, University Of Saskatchewan, 1962); Knill, William D., and Arthur K. Davis. "Provincial Education in Northern Saskatchewan: Progress and Bog Down, 1944–1962," in *A Northern Dilemma*, 1: 170–337; Jean H. Lagasse, *The People of Indian Ancestry in Manitoba: A Social and Economic Study. Under the direction of Jean H. Lagasse* (Winnipeg: Department of Agriculture and Immigration, 1959); Richard Slobodin, *Metis of the Mackenzie District* (Ottawa: Canadian Research Centre for Anthropology, Saint Paul University, 1966); Philip Taft Spaulding, "The Social Integration of a Northern Community: White Mythology and Metis Reality," in *A Northern Dilemma*, Vol. 1; Spaulding, "The Metis of Île-à-la-Crosse" (PhD diss., University of Washington, 1970); V.F. Valentine, *A Social Anthropological Study of the Metis Population of Northwestern Saskatchewan – Preliminary Report* (Regina: Saskatchewan Department of Natural Resources, 12 September 1953); V.F. Valentine, "Some Problems of the Metis of Northern Saskatchewan," *Canadian Journal of Economics and Political Science* 20(1) (1954); V.F. Valentine, *The Metis of Northern Saskatchewan* (Regina: Saskatchewan Department of Natural Resources, 1955); V.F. Valentine and R.G. Young. "The Situation of the Métis of Northern Saskatchewan in Relation to His Physical and Social Development," *Canadian Geographer* 4 (1954); Peter M. Worsley, H.L. Buckley, and A.K. Davis, *Economic and Social Survey of Northern Saskatchewan*, Interim Report No. 1 (Saskatoon: Research Division, Centre for Community Studies, University of Saskatchewan, 1961).

4 Joe Sawchuk, *The Metis of Manitoba: Reformulation of an Ethnic Identity* (Toronto: Peter Martin, 1978)

5 Jean Baudrillard, *Simulations*, trans. Paul Foss, Paul Patton, and Philip Beitchman (New York: Semiotest(e), 1983.)
6 Ultimately this boils down to *power*, controlling the world by naming it, which explains much of the objection to anthropological discourse in the first place.
7 James Clifford, "Partial Truths," In *Writing Culture: The Poetics and Politics of Ethnography*, ed. James Clifford and George E. Marcus (Berkeley, Los Angeles, London: University of California Press, 1986), 1–26.
8 CASW, *The Metis in Manitoba*, 1.
9 Worsley, Buckley, and Davis, *Economic and Social Survey of Northern Saskatchewan*, 5; emphasis added.
10 Card, Hirabayashi, and French, *The Métis in Alberta Society*, iii; emphasis added.
11 Spaulding, "The Social Integration of a Northern Community, 91.
12 Hartmut Lutz, *Contemporary Challenges: Conversations with Canadian Native Authors. Interviews Conducted by Hartmut Lutz* (Saskatoon: Fifth House, 1991), 191.
13 Maria Campbell, *Halfbreed* (Toronto: McClelland & Stewart, 1973), 13
14 Ibid., 26.
15 Hlady and Poston, App. II: *The People of Indian Ancestry in Rural Manitoba*, 8.
16 Ibid
17 Ibid.
18 Slobodin, *Metis of the Mackenzie District*, 151.
19 Interview with Sharon Gardiner, Hay River, NWT, July 1996.
20 Hatt, *Metis of the Lac la Biche Area*, 4
21 One of the more unlikely uses of the term occurred when an association in Morehead, Kentucky, adopted the term in the early 1970s. "Metis Group Organized in Kentucky," *Winnipeg Tribune*, 4 October 1972.
22 Chris Andersen, *"Métis": Race, Recognition, and the Struggle for Indigenous Peoplehood* (Vancouver, UBC Press, 2014), chap. 5)..
23 CASW, *The Metis in Manitoba*, 1; emphasis added.
24 Buckley, *Trapping and Fishing in the Economy of Northern Saskatchewan*; Buckley, Kew, Hawley, *The Indians and Metis of Northern Saskatchewan*; Kew, *Cumberland House in 1960*; Worsley, Buckley, and Davis, *Economic and Social Survey of Northern Saskatchewan*.
25 Kew, *Cumberland House in 1960*, 112.
26 Valentine, *The Metis of Northern Saskatchewan*, 2.
27 Ibid., 10.
28 Ibid., 8–9.
29 Boek and Boek, App. I: *The People of Indian Ancestry in Greater Winnipeg*, 9; emphasis added.

30 Ibid., 3.
31 Hlady and Poston, *Appendix II: The People of Indian Ancestry in Rural Manitoba*, 4.
32 Card, Hirabayashi, and French, *The Metis in Alberta Society.*
33 For example, Raoul Narroll,"Ethnic Unit Classification," *Current Anthropology* 5(4) (1964): 289–312.
34 Card, Hirabayashi, and French, *The Metis in Alberta Society*, 186.
35 Campbell, *Halfbreed*, 95–6.
36 Card, Hirabayashi, and French, *The Metis in Alberta Society*, 186.
37 Worsley, Buckley, and Davis. *Economic and Social Survey of Northern Saskatchewan*, 5; emphasis added.
38 Card, Hirabayashi, and French, *The Metis in Alberta Society*, 186.
39 Fredrik Barth, ed., *Ethnic Groups and Boundaries: The Social Organization of Culture Difference* (Boston: Little, Brown, 1969).
40 Slobodin, *Metis of the Mackenzie District.*
41 "Politics in the Metis Association," October 1942. GA, James Brady Fonds, Series 5, M-125. See also chapter 11 in this volume.
42 Slobodin, *Metis of the Mackenzie District*, 14
43 Ibid., 14
44 Ibid., 12.
45 Ibid., 30.
46 Ibid., 158
47 Spaulding, "The Social Integration of a Northern Community; Spaulding, "The Metis of Île-à-la-Crosse."
48 Davis et al, *A Northern Dilemma*, 2: 358.
49 Ibid., 357.
50 Ibid., 357.
51 Ibid., 412.
52 Fred K. Hatt, "The Canadian Métis: Recent Interpretations," *Canadian Ethnic Studies* 3(1) (1971): 4.
53 Hatt, *Metis of the Lac la Biche Area*; Hatt, "The Response to Directed Social Change."
54 The Métis Betterment Act, R.S.A., 1952, c. 329, S.1 (Edmonton: Government of the Province of Alberta).
55 Hatt, *Metis of the Lac la Biche Area*, 1–5.
56 Ibid., 3.
57 Ibid., 2.
58 Personal communication, 1978.
59 Hatt, *Metis of the Lac la Biche Area*, 3.
60 Ibid., 3.

61 Ibid., 4.
62 Ibid., 4.
63 Campbell, *Halfbreed*, 26.
64 Vern Serl, "Preface," *A Northern Dilemma*, Vol. 1.
65 Lagasse, *The People of Indian Ancestry in Manitoba*, 1.
66 Valentine, *A Social Anthropological Study*.
67 Valentine, "Some Problems of the Metis of Northern Saskatchewan," 90. In the four Métis communities in which Valentine was working (Portage La Loche, Buffalo Narrows, Île-à-la-Crosse, and Beauval) the results of the June 1952 provincial election yielded 65 votes for the CCF and 569 votes for the Liberals.
68 Kew, *Cumberland House in 1960*.
69 Murray Dobbin, "Prairie Colonialism: The CCF in Northern Saskatchewan, 1944–1964," *Studies in Political Economy* 16 (1985): 13–14.
70 Campbell, *Halfbreed*, 64–5.
71 Valentine, *A Social Anthropological Study*.
72 Valentine, "Some Problems of the Metis of Northern Saskatchewan," 91–2
73 Ibid., 93.
74 Valentine, Ibid., 95
75 Campbell, *Halfbreed*, 54–5, 63.
76 Valentine, *The Metis of Northern Saskatchewan*, 18
77 Ibid.
78 Spaulding, "The Social Integration of a Northern Community"; "The Metis of Île-à-la-Crosse."
79 Hlady, "Power Structure in a Metis Community."
80 Valentine, *The Metis of Northern Saskatchewan*, 19.
81 Ibid., 20
82 Christine Van der Mark, *In Due Season: A Novel* (Toronto: Oxford University Press, 1947; repr. with a new introduction by Dorothy Livesay and an afterword by Dorothy Wise (Vancouver: New Star Books, 1979).
83 Valentine, *The Metis of Northern Saskatchewan*, 20
84 Ibid..
85 Ibid., 23
86 Ibid., 22
87 Campbell, *Halfbreed*, 63.
88 Valentine, *The Metis of Northern Saskatchewan*, 24.
89 Ibid.
90 Ibid., 36.
91 Ibid., 33.
92 Ibid., 36.

93 Dobbin, *Prairie Colonialism*, 17
94 Kew, *Cumberland House in 1960*; Worsley, Buckley, and Davis, *Economic and Social Survey of Northern Saskatchewan*; Buckley, *Trapping and Fishing in the Economy of Northern Saskatchewan*; Buckley, Kew, and Hawley, *The Indians and Metis of Northern Saskatchewan*; Davis et al., *A Northern Dilemma*, Vols 1 and 2.
95 Davis et al., *A Northern Dilemma*, 2: 357.
96 Ibid., 351–2.
97 Spaulding, "The Social Integration of a Northern Community"; "The Metis of Île-à-la-Crosse."
98 Spaulding, "The Social Integration of a Northern Community," 93–4.
99 Spaulding, "The Metis of Île-à-la-Crosse," 126.
100 Ibid., 16.
101 Ibid., 82.
102 John J. Honigmann, "Social Disintegration in Five Northern Canadian Communities," *Canadian Review of Sociology and Anthropology* 2(4) (1965): 199–214.
103 Spaulding, "The Social Integration of a Northern Community"; "The Metis of Ile-à-la-Crosse," 98–9.
104 Spaulding, "The Metis of Île-à-la-Crosse," 99–100.
105 Ibid., 110.
106 Ibid., 115–16.
107 Ibid., 82.
108 Hatt, *Metis of the Lac la Biche Area*, i
109 Card, Hirabayashi, and French, *The Metis in Alberta Society*.
110 Ibid., iii
111 Ibid., 313.
112 Ibid.
113 Ibid., 375–84.
114 Ibid., 383.
115 Hatt, "The Canadian Metis."
116 Robert K. Merton, "Social Structure and Anomie," *American Sociological Review* 3 (1938): 672–82.
117 Card, Hirabayashi, and French, *The Metis in Alberta Society*, 383; emphasis in original.
118 Ibid., 400; emphasis added.
119 Lagasse, *The People of Indian Ancestry in Manitoba*; Boek and Boek, *Appendix I: The People of Indian Ancestry in Greater Winnipeg*; Hlady and Poston, *Appendix II: The People of Indian Ancestry in Rural Manitoba*.
120 Lagasse, *The People of Indian Ancestry in Manitoba*, 57; emphasis added.

121 Worsley, Buckley, and Davis, *Economic and Social Survey of Northern Saskatchewan*, 2
122 Cecil L. French, "Social Class and Motivation," in *The Metis in Alberta Society: With Special Reference to Social, Economic and Cultural Factors Associated with Persistently High Tuberculosis Incidence*, ed. B.Y. Card et al. (Edmonton: University of Alberta, 1963), 128.
123 Ibid.
124 Arthur K. Davis, "Canadian Society and History as Hinterland versus Metropolis," in *Canadian Society: Pluralism, Change and Conflict*, ed. R. Ossenberg (Scarborough, Prentice-Hall, 1971), 6–32; Davis, *A Northern Dilemma*, Vols 1 and 2.
125 Davis et al., *A Northern Dilemma*, 2: 352.
126 Ibid., 2: 529.

14 A Renewed Political Awareness

1 The name of the Native Council of Canada's newspaper in the 1970s and 1980s was called *The Forgotten People*; see also Harry Daniels (ed.), *The Forgotten People: Metis and Non-status Indian Land Claims* (Ottawa: Native Council of Canada, 1979); D. Bruce Sealey and Antoine S. Lussier, *The Métis: Canada's Forgotten People* (Winnipeg: Pemmican, 1975).
2 "Remark Angers Metis," *Winnipeg Free Press*, 6 November 1970.
3 Some early Métis leaders saw themselves more as a nation in the European sense – a national minority rather than one with Aboriginal rights – but that sentiment is rarely expressed by Métis leaders today.
4 One exception was Howard Adams, who was president of the Métis Society of Saskatchewan for a short time, but who left the political field to pursue a career in academia.
5 See Joe Sawchuk, *The Dynamics of Native Politics* (Saskatoon: Purich, 1998), 72–91, for a study of how government funding controlled and regulated Metis political activity in the MAA.
6 Sally M. Weaver, "Towards a Comparison of National Political Organizations of Indigenous Peoples: Australia, Canada and Norway" (manuscript, Lecture Series at the Institute of Social Sciences, University of Tromsø, Tromsø, Norway, 19–20 October 1983), 44.
7 Sawchuk, *The Dynamics of Native Politics*, 58–9.
8 T.C. Pocklington, *The Government and Politics of the Alberta Metis Settlements* (Regina: Canadian Plains Research Center, University of Regina, 1991), 101–2

9 Murray Dobbin, "Metis Struggles of the Twentieth Century: The Saskatchewan Métis Society – 1935–1950. Part 1: Early Beginnings," *New Breed* (August 1978): 17.

10 Murray Dobbin, "Métis Struggles of the Twentieth Century: The Saskatchewan Métis Society – 1935–1950. Part 3: Political Interference and Internal Divisions," *New Breed* (October 1978): 15.

11 Ibid.

12 Its own website, which posts a history of L'Union nationale métisse Saint-Joseph du Manitoba in point form, lists almost no activities for the association between 1957 and 1976, http://www.unionnationalemetisse.ca/histoire.html.

13 James N. Kerri, *The Human Element in Housing: An Evaluation of the Manitoba Remote Housing Program*, (Winnipeg: Manitoba Métis Federation, 1971), 2.

14 Neil Louttit, "Housing Plea By Metis," *Winnipeg Free Press*, Thursday, 19 October 1967.

15 Neil Louttit, "Indian Workshop Begins Saturday," *Winnipeg Free Press*, Friday, 13 October 1967.

16 Interview with Stan Fulham by Doug Racine, recorded at St Lazare, MB, 17 July 1995.

17 Neil Louttit, "Indian-Metis Program Discussed: New Organization May Not Include Metis Faction," *Winnipeg Free Press*, Monday, 16 October 1967; "Metis, Indians Split Unanimous: Two Groups But One Goal," *Winnipeg Free Press*, Tuesday, 17 October 1967

18 Stan Fulham, interview, 1995.

19 Ibid..

20 I first began working among Métis communities in January of 1970, when I was in Churchill, Manitoba, interviewing the Métis and Cree community of River Flats as part of a team of interviewers investigating the attitudes of townspeople towards medical services provided there. That summer, on a separate and independent research project, I visited several Métis communities, including St Laurent, Grand Rapids, The Pas, and Big Eddy. In the summer of 1971, I began working for the MMF as a researcher on their Remote Housing Evaluation Project. In the course of that research, I visited several other communities in the northern and southern regions of the province, including Duck Bay, Camperville, Amaranth, Eddystone, and Bacon Ridge. In all of these communities, I was working closely with members of the MMF locals, usually the chairman or vice-chairman.

21 Stan Fulham, interview, 1995.

22 Ibid.

15 Reformulated Identities

1 Fredrik Barth, ed., *Ethnic Groups and Boundaries: The Social Organization of Culture Difference* (Boston: Little, Brown, 1969).

2 Murray Dobbin, *One-and-a-Half Men: The Story of Jim Brady and Malcolm Norris* (Vancouver: New Star Books, 1981), 61.

3 By-laws of the Metis Association of Alberta, 1940. GA, Joseph Dion Fonds, Series 2, M-331-11.This particular version expresses "a desire" to be constituted under the regulations of the Alberta Societies Act of 1924, although it is not clear whether the Métis Association was ever actually registered under the 1924 act. In an interview with Adrian Hope conducted by the author and Patricia Sawchuk, recorded in Edmonton on 9 March 1981, Hope claimed that the MAA was never formally registered until he had it done in the 1960s. That version of the constitution, which was ratified under the Societies Act of 1961, is almost identical to the 1940 constitution, including the references to the "Red Race" and the brotherhood of all North American Native peoples cited in fn4.

4 The objectives of the 1940 constitution state in part: "(a) … although Metis and Indians [are] of diverse Nations they are 'ONE RACE' 'THE RED RACE OF THE AMERICAN CONTINENT.'" A second objective is "(b) … to acknowledge in all science the mysteries of the Great Spirit – God and his dominance over all things."

5 Some of the communities visited included St Laurent, Churchill, Grand Rapids, The Pas, Big Eddy, Duck Bay, Camperville, Amaranth, Eddystone, and Bacon Ridge.

6 Minutes of MMF workshop for the executive, 3 October 1969, Marlborough Hotel, Winnipeg, Manitoba.

7 Joe Sawchuk, *The Metis of Manitoba: Reformulation of an Ethnic Identity* (Toronto: Peter Martin, 1978), 48.

8 MAA constitution as passed by extraordinary resolution at the 49th Annual Assembly of the Métis Association of Alberta, Athabasca, Alberta, 13 August 1977; emphasis added.

9 Elmer Ghostkeeper and Federation of Metis Settlements, *Metism: A Canadian Identity* (Edmonton: Alberta Federation of Métis Settlements, 1982), 31.

10 "MAA to have local voting," AMMSA (Aboriginal Multi-Media Society of Alberta), 24 August 1984.

11 Ibid.

12 Catherine E. Bell, "Who Are the Métis in Section 35(2)?" *Alberta Law Review* 29(2) (1991): 351–81.

13 "'Metis' means an Aboriginal person who self-identifies as Metis, who is distinct from Indian and Inuit, and:

> is a descendant of those Metis who received or were entitled to receive land grants and/or Scrip under the provision of the Manitoba Act, 1870 or the Dominion Lands Act, as enacted from time to time; or a person of Aboriginal descent who is accepted by the Metis Nation and/or Metis Community(Amended Dec. 13/97). Any Metis who is a member of a duly registered Local is a member of the Metis Nation of Saskatchewan" (constitution of the Métis Nation of Saskatchewan).

14 Patty Fuller, "Mayhem among the Metis: The Metis Nation of Alberta Faces Membership-fixing and Corruption Charges," *Alberta Report*, 21(2) (1993):16.
15 Jean Teillet, "MNC Definition of 'Métis' submitted by the Métis Rights Panel," manuscript, draft for discussion, Métis National Council, 12 September 1999.
16 Ibid.
17 "Report to the Royal Commission on Aboriginal Peoples: Consolidation of the Métis Nation," *Métis Nation* (Newsletter of the MNC) 2(2) (1993): 6–7.
18 Métis National Council website, http://www.metisnation.ca/mna.html, accessed 2001.
19 Chris Andersen, "*Moya 'Tipimsook* ('The People Who Aren't Their Own Bosses'): Racialization and the Misrecognition of 'Métis' in Upper Great Lakes Ethnohistory," *Ethnohistory* 58(1) (Winter 2011): 37–63.
20 Congress of Aboriginal Peoples website, http://www.abo-peoples.org/cap-constituency/, accessed 2015.
21 Fuller, "Mayhem among the Metis."
22 In a letter dated 17 February 1994 from Harry W. Daniels, former president, Native Council of Canada, to Kirby Lethbridge, president of the Labrador Métis Association, concerning the application of section 35 of the Constitution Act, 1982 to Métis people who are not part of the Métis Nation, Mr Daniels stated: "In response to your question 'What did the term "Metis" mean when inserted into the Constitution of Canada?' I am providing the following for your information … With specific reference to the term 'Metis' it was understood at the time that it (Metis) included the member organizations and their constituents who self-identified as a Metis person … It was also understood that the term Metis was not tied to any particular geographic area, keeping in mind that Aboriginal people from coast to coast identified with the term Metis as their way of relating to the world." Royal Commission on Aboriginal Peoples (RCAP), *Report of the Royal Commission on Aboriginal Peoples*, 5 vols (Ottawa: Government of Canada, 1996), Vol. 4, chap. 5, 2, Appendix 5F; Correspondence Concerning the Metis of Labrador.

23 RCAP, *Report of the Royal Commission on Aboriginal Peoples*, Vol. 4, chap. 5, 2.
24 Ibid., 1.3.
25 Ibid.
26 John C. Kennedy, "The Changing Significance of Labrador Settler Identity," *Canadian Ethnic Studies* 20(3) (1988): 94.
27 Interview with Yvon Dumont, by Doug Racine and Joe Sawchuk, at the residence of the lieutenant governor of Manitoba, Winnipeg, 11 September 1995.
28 John C. Kennedy, *Peoples of the Bays and Headlands* (Toronto: University of Toronto Press, 1995), 230–1.
29 John C. Kennedy, "Métis," Newfoundland and Labrador Heritage website, http://www.heritage.nf.ca/aboriginal/metis.html, accessed April 2011.
30 Kennedy, *Peoples of the Bays and Headlands*, 230–1.
31 Ibid.
32 http://www.cbc.ca/news/canada/newfoundland-labrador/labrador-s-m%C3%A9tis-nation-adopts-new-name-1.927252, accessed December 2014.
33 For an in-depth analysis of the process by which the Labrador group first adopted the term "Métis," and later dropped it in favour of "Southern Inuit," (from the viewpoint of a Métis nationalist who is opposed to the idea of any group not linked to the historic Red River population appropriating the name "Métis") see Chris Andersen, *"Métis": Race, Recognition, and the Struggle for Indigenous Peoplehood* (Vancouver, UBC Press, 2014), chap. 5.
34 Andersen, *"Moya 'Tipimsook,"* 37–63; see also Andersen,*"Métis."*
35 Nothing in this discussion (or any other discussion in this volume) should be taken to suggest that the authors are of the opinion that the attempt of the MNC to limit the term "Métis" to those linked to the historic Red River population is somehow "unfair" or that claiming such an exclusive right either results in the denial of other Métis groups' rights or suggests that one group is somehow more legitimate than another. However, this suggestion has been made by other scholars; see, for example, Karl Hele, "Manipulating Identity: The Sault Borderlands Métis and Colonial Intervention," in *The Long Journey of a Forgotten People: Métis Identities and Family Histories*, ed. David McNab and Ute Lischke (Waterloo, ON: Wilfrid Laurier University Press, 2007), 181n2, quoted in Andersen, *"Moya 'Tipimsook,"* 46.
36 Joane Nagel, *American Indian Ethnic Renewal: Red Power and the Resurgence of Identity and Culture* (Oxford: Oxford University Press, 1997), 28.
37 The complications regarding Métis identity arising from these acts and the subsequent policy on scrip through the 1880s and 1890s, including aspects such as the revisions to the Indian Act, which dealt with the interchangeability of scrip and treaty status, are covered in chapter 9.

38 Section 91(24) of the Constitution Act, 1867 made "Indians and lands reserved for Indians" a federal responsibility. For years, the federal government insisted that "Indian" as specified in this act referred not to all aboriginal people in Canada, but only to that segment of the aboriginal population recognized as Indian by the various Indian acts. However, there are good arguments to suggest that both Métis and non-status Indians could also be considered "Indians" under the Constitution Act, 1867. In 1939 (*Re Eskimos, 5 C.N.L.C. 123 (S.C.C.)*) the Supreme Court ruled that Inuit were to be considered "Indians" under the Constitution Act, 1867, and were therefore the responsibility of the federal government (though not included in the Indian Act). *Daniels v. Canada,* 2013FC6 (2013) (see below) specifically deals with this issue.

39 *Official Report of the Debates of the House of Commons*, 6 July 1885, 3113.

40 The chain of events that led to the inclusion of the Métis (and the exclusion of non-status Indians) as one of the three recognized groups of Aboriginal peoples in Canada is a fascinating story with many ironic undertones, not the least of which is the role that Métis and/or non-status leaders such as Jim Sinclair and Harry Daniels played in the inclusion of one and the exclusion of the other. While parts of this story have been discussed here, limited space prohibits the full discussion this subject deserves. The best treatment, and one conducted by a first-hand observer, is found in John Weinstein's essential *Quiet Revolution West: The Rebirth of Métis Nationalism* (Calgary: Fifth House, 2007).

41 Kenneth M. Lysyk, "The Rights and Freedoms of the Aboriginal Peoples of Canada," in *The Canadian Charter of Rights and Freedoms: Commentary*, ed. Walter S. Tarnopolsky and Gerard A. Beaudoin (Toronto: Carswell, 1982). See also letter dated 17 February 1994 from Harry W. Daniels, in n22.

42 Douglas E. Sanders, "Aboriginal Peoples and the Constitution," *Alberta Law Review* 19 (1981): 420.

43 Joe Sawchuk, "The Metis, Non-Status Indians and the New Aboriginality: Government Influence on Native Political Alliances and Identity," in *Readings in Aboriginal Studies*, Vol. 2: *Identities and State Structures*, ed. Joe Sawchuk (Brandon: Bearpaw Press, 1992); revision of an article originally published in *Canadian Ethnic Studies* 17(2) (1985): 135–46.

44 Native Council of Canada (NCC), *Native People and the Constitution of Canada: The Report of the Metis and Non-Status Indian Constitutional Review Commission, Commissioner: H.W. Daniels* (Ottawa: Mutual Press, 1981), 96.

45 Ibid., 85.

46 Ibid.

47 Ibid., 8.

48 James Tully, *Strange Multiplicity: Constitutionalism in an Age of Diversity* (Cambridge: Cambridge University Press, 1995), 11–12.

49 "Indians to Petition the Queen on Constitution," *Globe and Mail*, 2 July 1979; "Indians Still Seek Talks with the Queen," *Winnipeg Free Press*, 3 July 1979; "Indian Goal Attracts High Level Support," *Winnipeg Free Press*, 6 July 1979.
50 Website of the Federal Interlocutor for Métis and Non-Status Indians, http://www.pco-bcp.gc.ca/interloc/default.asp?Language=E&Page=Home, Government of Canada, 2004.
51 R.S.A.1938, c.M-14.
52 R.S.A.1940, c.M-14.
53 Ghostkeeper, *Metism*, 31.
54 Metis Settlements Act, R.S.A. 1990, c. M-14.
55 Fuller, "Mayhem among the Metis."
56 *Manitoba Metis Federation v. Attorney-General of Canada* (sub nom. *Dumont v. A.-G. Canada)*, [1988] 3 C.N.R. 39 (Man.C.A.). O'Sullivan, Huband, Philip, Twaddle and Lyon JJA., 17 June 1988.
57 Ibid.
58 Ibid.
59 *R. v. McPherson*, [1994] 2 C.N.L.R. 137 (Man Q.B.). Schulman J. 19 January 1994.
60 *R. v. Blais* [1996] M.J. No. 391 (Man. Prov. Ct.).
61 Shin Imai, "Metis Rights," handout at a conference on Aboriginal law at Osgoode Hall Law School, Toronto, November 1997.
62 The Métis Nation Accord, *Report of the Royal Commission on Aboriginal Peoples*, Vol. 4, s.5, Appendix 5D.
63 *R. v. Powley* (2000) O.J. No. 99; *R. v. Powley* (1999) C.N.L.R. 153; *R. v. Powley* (2003) SCC 43.
64 Ibid.
65 *R.v.Powley* 2003 [para.10]; emphasis added.
66 *R. v. Powley*, 2003 SCC 43.
67 *Globe and Mail*, 23 September 2003.
68 Andersen, "*Moya 'Tipimsook*," 49.
69 Ibid., 50.
70 *Daniels v. Canada*, 2013 FC6 (2013) [para 619].
71 Ibid. [paras 130, 117].
72 Joe Friesen, "Defining Who Is Indian: A Confusing Question of Identity and Belonging," *Globe and Mail*, 11 January 2013.
73 "In *Powley*, above, the Supreme Court did not attempt to define the outer limits of "Métis" but it did provide a method for finding who a Métis is for purposes of s 35. *Aside from the sine qua non of mixed aboriginal and non-aboriginal ancestry*, a Métis is a person who (a) has some ancestral family connection (not necessarily genetic); (b) identifies himself or herself as Métis; and (c) is

accepted by the Métis community or a locally organized community branch, chapter or council of a Métis association or organization with which that person wishes to be associated," *Daniels v. Canada*, 2013 FC 6 (2013) [para 127]; emphasis added.

74 Ibid. [para 32].

75 Chris Purdy, "Could Metis Membership Applications Spike after Federal Court Ruling?" Canadian Press, 9 January 2013.

76 *Daniels v. Canada*, 2013 FC6 (2013) [para 126].

77 *Daniels v. Canada*, 2014 FCA 101.

78 Ibid. [para 3]

79 Ibid. [para 74].

80 Ibid. [para 78, 79].

81 Ibid. [para 88].

82 Ibid. [Para 96].

83 Ibid. [Para 99].

84 http://www.scc-csc.gc.ca/case-dossier/info/sum-som-eng.aspx?cas=35945, accessed 11/12/2014

85 J.H. Lagasse, *The People of Indian Ancestry in Manitoba* (Winnipeg: Department of Agriculture and Immigration, 1959), 56.

86 V.F. Valentine, *The Metis of Northern Saskatchewan* (Regina: Saskatchewan Department of Natural Resources, 1955), 18.

87 Christine Van der Mark, *In Due Season: A Novel* (Toronto: Oxford University Press, 1947; repr. with a new introduction by Dorothy Livesay and an afterword by Dorothy Wise (Vancouver: New Star Books, 1979).

88 This should not be taken to mean that Mr Sinclair's contributions were unrecognized by the Métis; the Métis National Council made Mr Sinclair a member of the Order of the Métis Nation, in recognition of his services to the Métis Nation; http://www.metisnation.ca/index.php/who-are-the-metis/order-of-the-metis-nation/jim-sinclair, accessed 14 December 2014.

89 Interview with Stan Fulham by Doug Racine. Recorded at St Lazare, Manitoba, 17 July 1995.

90 Ibid.

91 Canada-Aboriginal Peoples Roundtable, Government of Canada Conference Centre, Ottawa, 19 April 2004.

16 The Métis of Ontario

1 Taped interview with Mike McGuire, president of OMAA, 17 June 1997, Thunder Bay.

2 Clem Chartier, president of the MNC, *Sudbury Star*, 15 July 2004.

3 Carolyn Harrington, "Sault First Capitol," *Dimensions. Special Editions* 8(3) (1980): 8–9; A.J. Ray, "An Economic History of the Robinson Treaties Area Before 1860," unpublished report, 17 March 1998.
4 http://www.omaa.org/, downloaded 02 July 2013.
5 A third Métis organization in Ontario that should be mentioned is the Red Sky Métis Independent Nation. This organization represents "status Métis" – Métis who were included in treaties and still retain and maintain treaty status, but also wish to commemorate their Métis heritage and culture. Red Sky represents the descendants of eighty-four half-breeds who were included in the Robinson Superior Treaty of 1850. It is primarily a cultural organization, rather than a politically motivated one, and is local, rather than provincial, representing an area around Lake Nipigon.
6 *R. v. Powley* (2000) O.J. No. 99; *R. v. Powley* (1999) C.N.L.R. 153; *R. v. Powley* (2003) SCC 43. This case is discussed in more detail in chapter 15.
7 It did define a Métis community as: "a group of Métis with a distinctive collective identity, living together in the same geographical area and sharing a common way of life," and indicated that there could be more than one group of people who identify as "Métis." "We would not purport to enumerate the various Métis peoples that may exist." *R. v. Powley* (2003) [para. 12]. Nothing in the court's discussion of what comprises a Métis community required a demonstration of a link to Red River or the historic Metis Nation, or any other "larger Métis people that extends over a wider area such as the Upper Great Lakes." Ibid.
8 Interview with Mike McGuire.
9 Ibid.
10 Ibid.
11 Paddy McGuire, "Ontario Founder Paddy McGuire Outlines History," *Dimensions. Special Editions* 8(4) (1980): 4.
12 Interview with Mike McGuire.
13 "Mr Paddy McGuire," *Dimensions. Special Editions* 8(5) (1980): 12–15); emphasis added.
14 Interview with Mike McGuire.
15 Paddy McGuire, "Ontario Founder Paddy McGuire Outlines History."
16 Interview with Mike McGuire.
17 "Special Status: A 'Native Solution'" *Dimensions, Special Editions* 8(4) (1980).
18 "Mr Paddy McGuire"; emphasis added.
19 This "racialized" definition of Métis is at odds with the way many Métis are defining themselves today. See Chris Andersen, *"Métis": Race,*

Recognition, and the Struggle for Indigenous Peoplehood (Vancouver: UBC Press. 2014).

20 "Mr Paddy McGuire," 12–15.
21 OMAA website, http://www.omaa.org., accessed 2001.
22 Ibid.
23 *Métis: The Voice of the Métis Nation of Ontario* 1(1) (n.d., c. 1994).
24 Métis Nation of Ontario website, http://www.metisnation.org, accessed 2001.
25 OMNSIA, "Special Status Committee Hearings," *Dimensions. Special Editions* 8(4) (1980).
26 OMNSIA, "Interim Report of the Special Status Committee Meeting on June 16, 1980 to the Ontario Cabinet Committee," *Dimensions. Special Editions* 8(4) (1980).
27 "Testimony of Mike McGuire, OMNSIA Special Status Committee Hearings."
28 "Testimony of Robert Chilton, OMNSIA Special Status Committee Hearings."
29 "Testimony of Agnes Lidstone, OMNSIA Special Status Committee Hearings."
30 "Testimony of Solomon McGuire, OMNSIA Special Status Committee Hearings."
31 Ibid.
32 "Testimony of Jerry Guimond, OMNSIA Special Status Committee Hearings."
33 "Testimony of Paddy McGuire, OMNSIA Special Status Committee Hearings."
34 As of 1981, the proposed sections of the Canadian Constitution and Charter pertaining to Native people were as follows (note that these are *not* in their final form, but as they were proposed and debated at the time of the OMNSIA meeting):

Native Sections of The Constitution Act, 1981

Part I - Canadian Charter of Rights and Freedoms

General

25. The guarantee in this Charter of certain rights and freedoms shall not be construed so as to abrogate or derogate from any aboriginal, treaty or other rights or freedoms that pertain to the aboriginal peoples of Canada including

(a) any rights or freedoms that have been recognized by the Royal Proclamation of October 7, 1763; and

(b) any rights or freedoms that may be acquired by the aboriginal peoples of Canada by way of land claims settlement.

Part II – Rights of the Aboriginal Peoples of Canada

33. (1) The aboriginal and treaty rights of the aboriginal peoples of Canada are hereby recognized and affirmed.

(2) In this Act, "aboriginal peoples of Canada" includes the Indian, Inuit and Métis peoples of Canada.

Part IV – Constitutional Conferences

(2) A conference convened under subsection (1) shall have included in its agenda an item respecting constitutional matters that directly affect the aboriginal peoples of Canada, including the definition and identification of the rights of those peoples to be included in the Constitution of Canada, and the Prime Minister of Canada shall invite representatives of those peoples to participate in the discussions on that item.

35 *Dimensions. Special Editions* 9(3) (1981) is the workbook for the delegates to OMNSIA's Grand Assembly (July 1981), where the proposed constitutional amendments were discussed. It gave several background papers on several of the issues that were to be debated at the meeting. It also included a questionnaire that elicited opinions on many of the issues of concern, including Métis and non-status identity. *Dimensions. Special Editions* 9(4) (1981) is the report of the assembly. Most of the formal proceedings are presented in 9(4), including transcriptions of the main presentations, plus questions and answers.
36 OMNSIA Constitutional Commission of Inquiry, *Dimensions. Special Editions* 9(4) (1981).
37 Ibid., 41–2.
38 Sullivan McGuire, "Lake Nipigon Submission, OMNSIA Constitutional Commission of Inquiry," *Dimensions. Special Editions* 9(4) (1981).
39 The questionnaire is included in *Dimensions. Special Editions* 9(3) and the preliminary results are published in *Dimensions. Special Editions* 9(4).
40 Evelyn Peters, Mark Rosenberg, and Greg Halseth, *The Ontario Métis: Characteristics and Identity*, Native Issues No. 4 (Winnipeg: Institute of Urban Studies, University of Winnipeg, 1991).
41 Ibid., 11.
42 *Dimensions. Special Editions* 9(3) (1981): 53.
43 Peters, Rosenberg, and Halseth, *The Ontario Métis*, 13.
44 OMNSIA Constitutional Commission of Inquiry, *Dimensions. Special Editions* 9(4) (1981): 48.
45 Peters, Rosenberg, and Halseth, *The Ontario Métis*, 37.
46 Ibid.
47 Ibid., 53, 55.
48 Ibid., 55.
49 Ibid.; emphasis added.
50 Ibid.
51 "Commission of Inquiry Report," *Dimensions. Special Editions* 9(4) (1981): 48
52 *Dimensions* 4(5) (1976): 21

53 OMAA website, http://www.omaa.org, accessed 2001.
54 Interview with Mike McGuire.
55 Ibid.
56 Ibid.
57 "Métis Receive Sundance Song," press release, MNO, 9 August 2004.
58 Duke Redbird, *We Are Metis: A Metis View of the Development of a Native Canadian People* (Willowdale, ON : OMNSIA, 1980), 2–3.
59 Ibid., 50.
60 MNO website, http://www.metisnation.org/inon-statusIndiandeMNO/registry.html, accessed 2001; emphasis added.
61 Ray, "Economic History of the Robinson Treaties Area"; Harrington, "Sault First Capitol," 8–9.
62 Ibid.
63 "Métis Receive Sundance Song."
64 Interview with Mike McGuire.
65 MNO website.
66 Ibid.
67 Jean Teillet, "Draft for discussion – MNC Definition of 'Métis' submitted by the Métis Rights Panel – 09/12/99," manuscript, Métis National Council.
68 Ibid.
69 OMAA website, http://www.omaa.org, accessed 2001.
70 MNO website.
71 Ibid.
72 "Lakehead Deal Follows Ruling Favouring Métis Hunters in Sault," *Sault Star*, 8 July 2004, A10.
73 *Sudbury Star*, 15 July 2004, A9.
74 *What Is the MNO Registry?* MNO website.
75 Although no official description of the MNO's definition of an *Ontario* Métis Homeland is offered on its website or in other promotional literature, the president of the MNO, Tony Belcourt, did offer this unofficial definition in a radio interview: "Primarily the water routes along the Ottawa River Valley, for example, north to James Bay, that water route system from Mattawa across Nipissing, the fringe, around the shores of Lake Huron, northern Lake Superior and then out west through the Rainy River district"; as stated in the broadcast *Morning North* (Hr2) (CBCS-FM), Sudbury, 12 July 2004.
76 *Sault Star*, 8 July 2004.
77 *Sudbury Star*, 15 July 2004. One of the "individuals who (may) have joined" was Steve Powley himself.
78 Interview with Mike McGuire.

79 As of this writing, there still exists a strain between the MNO and the rest of the constituent members of MNC over the definition of Métis and the historic Métis Nation Homeland. Many within the prairie Métis organizations still maintain that Ontario is excluded from this definition, and the MNO is objecting to the MNC's adoption of the historic Métis Nation Homeland as a defining feature of the Métis Nation.

17 Organizational Politics, Land Claims

1 "Let's All Join Now," *Dene Nation Newsletter*, August/September 1982, 19.
2 Delegate Jim Allard, speaking at the Fourth Annual Assembly of the Métis Association of the Northwest Territories, *Minutes*, Fourth Annual Assembly, Métis Association of the Northwest Territories, 14–16 October 1976, Fort Providence, NWT (Métis Association of the NWT, 1976), 37.
3 Bill Enge, president of the North Slave Métis Alliance, speaking at the 9 February 2005 meeting of the Standing Senate Committee on Aboriginal Peoples reviewing the Tlicho land claim and self-government agreement, http://www.parl.gc.ca/38/1/parlbus/commbus/senate/Com-e/abor-e/04evc-e.htm?Language=E&Parl=38&Ses=1&comm_id=1, accessed 2009.
4 The dual nature of Métis identity in the NWT has been noted as early as 1960 by Richard Slobodin. He identified the two groups as "Red River Metis" and "Northern Metis," respectively. These terms are not in common usage in the NWT; they were developed by Slobodin as a shorthand way of discussing both populations in his analysis. Slobodin, *Metis of the Mackenzie District* (Ottawa: Canadian Research Centre for Anthropology, 1966), 14.
5 "Metis Now Included in Dene Constitution," *Dene Nation Newsletter*, August/September 1982, 9.
6 Ibid.
7 According to the Mackenzie Valley Resource Management Act, the Mackenzie Valley includes all of the Northwest Territories, with the exception of the Inuvialuit Settlement Region, and the Wood Buffalo National Park.
8 Michael Asch, "Dene Nation," *Canadian Encyclopedia*, http://www.thecanadianencyclopedia.ca/en/article/dene-nation/, accessed 2014.
9 The small number of Métis in the Yukon has made it difficult for them to organize effectively. As of 2009, neither the federal nor the Yukon territorial government would recognize the Yukon Métis Nation Society as the official representatives of the territory's Métis, even though the organization has been in existence for twenty years (CBC *News*, 22 January 2009). As a result, Métis living in the Yukon have been unable to procure official recognition as a distinct Aboriginal group from the territory and do

not enjoy the Aboriginal rights and benefits that accrue to the Métis in the Northwest Territories.

10 http://www12.statcan.gc.ca/census-recensement/2006/as-sa/97-558/table/t13-eng.cfm.

11 Slobodin, *Metis of the Mackenzie District*. Slobodin's work is one of the earliest studies of Métis in Canada based on fieldwork and personal interviews (from 1938 to 1963), and it remains the most useful discussion of Métis identity in the NWT as it was developing in the early part of the twentieth century.

12 James N. Kerri, *Utilization of a Native People's Voluntary Association as a Channel of Communication: The Case of COPE in Inuvik, NWT* (Winnipeg: Department of Manpower and Immigration, Prairie Region, October 1970).

13 John David Hamilton, *Arctic Revolution: Social Change in the Northwest Territories, 1935–1994* (Toronto: Dundurn Press, 1994), 137.

14 Interview with Charles Overvold, past president of the Métis Association of the NWT, 22 July, Yellowknife, NWT. This interview and all others quoted in this chapter were done in the NWT by research assistant Alan Bork in July of 1996.

15 Accounts of where this organization actually started and who was its first president vary. Hamilton, *Arctic Revolution* (131) claims that the NWT Indian Brotherhood was formed in Yellowknife. Mona Jacob was interim president until displaced by Roy Daniels four months later. Kerry Abel claims the sixteen chiefs met in Fort Smith in October 1969, with James Wah Shee as first president. Abel, *Drum Songs: Glimpses of Dene History*, 2nd ed. (McGill-Queen's University Press, 2005), 246.

16 Interview with Charles Overvold.

17 Asch, "Dene Nation."

18 Dene History, http://www.denenation.com/history.html, accessed 2014.

19 In this discussion, for simplicity, I will usually refer to the organization simply as the Métis Association (or MANWT).

20 Dene Nation and Métis Association of the NWT, *Public Government for the People of the North* (Yellowknife: Dene Nation and Métis Association of the NWT, 1982). Michael Asch, *Home and Native Land: Aboriginal Rights and the Canadian Constitution* (Toronto: Methuen, 1984), 96–9.

21 This local group, which first organized under the title the South Slave Lake Tribal Council, eventually took on a new name – the Northwest Territory Métis Nation – a name that indicates it was at least purporting to represent the Métis of the NWT, although in fact it represents only the communities of Hay River, Fort Resolution, Fort Smith, and Yellowknife.

22 "Metis Leaders Want Morin to Quit," CBC *News*, Tuesday, 8 February 2000.

23 "Metis Nation Calls It Quits," CBC *News*, Tuesday, 6March 2001.

24 "Metis Nation's Death 'Positive': Morin," CBC *News*, Wednesday, 7 March 2001.

25 Highlights: Sahtu Dene and Métis Comprehensive Land Claim Agreement, https://www.aadnc-aandc.gc.ca/eng/1100100031147/1100100031164, accessed 2015.

26 http://www.daair.gov.nt.ca/_live/pages/wpPages/Dehcho.aspx.

27 The NSMA represents Métis in Bechoko, Wati, Wekwatii, Gametii, Yellowknife, Dettah, Ndilo, Lutselke, and Resolution communities, http://www.atns.net.au/agreement.asp?EntityID=1867http://www.atns.net.au/agreement.asp?EntityID=1867.

28 Meeting of the Standing Senate Committee on Aboriginal Peoples, 9 February 2005 (see n3 above).

29 *Tlicho Agreement – Highlights*, https://www.aadnc-aandc.gc.ca/eng/1100100025022/1100100025024.

30 To date, NSMA has been unsuccessful in pursuing this claim. In February of 2013, the NSMA was informed by the federal department of Aboriginal Affairs and Northern Development (AANDC) that the organization "has not provided sufficient evidence to establish the existence of an ancestrally-based, present-day Métis community in the North Slave area with links to a historic Métis community in that area." Meagan Wohlberg, "North Slave Métis Denied Land Claim: Feds Say North Slave Métis Alliance Not 'Distinct, Rights-holding' Aboriginal Government," *Northern Journal*, 22 April 2013, http://norj.ca/2013/04/north-slave-metis-denied-land-claim/.

31 Interview with George Kurszewski, 26 July 1996, Fort Smith, NWT.

32 Trent University Archives, http://www.trentu.ca/admin/library/archives/77-018.htm

33 Peter A. Cumming and Neil H. Mickenberg (eds), *Native Rights in Canada*, 2nd ed. (Toronto: Indian-Eskimo Association of Canada, 1972).

34 Interview with Rick Hardy, past president, Métis Nation, NWT, 19 July 1996, Yellowknife, NWT.

35 See Joe Sawchuk, *The Dynamics of Native Politics: The Alberta Metis Experience* (Saskatoon: Purich, 1998) for a discussion of the role of CYC in the Métis Association of Alberta. Both Hamilton, *Arctic Revolution*, and Abel, *Drum Songs*, offer detailed discussions of the role of CYC in Native organizations in the NWT.

36 Interview with Charles Overvold.

37 Hamilton, *Arctic Revolution*, 136.

38 Ibid., 144.

39 Interview with Rick Hardy.

40 Interview with George Kurszewski.

41 Several books were published about the Berger Inquiry. See, for example, Mel Watkins (ed.), *Dene Nation, the Colony Within* (Toronto: University of Toronto Press, 1977) and Martin O'Malley, *The Past and Future Land: An Account of the Berger Inquiry into the Mackenzie Valley Pipeline* (Toronto: Peter Martin, 1976). One can search these volumes in vain for any pro-pipeline sentiments by Native people. George Kurszewski is quoted in Watkins, but by that time he had left the Métis Association because he was opposed to the pipeline.
42 Interview with Gary Bohnet, president, Metis Nation of the Northwest Territories.
43 Interview with George Kurszewski.
44 Interview with Charles Overvold.
45 A reasonable assumption, although, as I have pointed out elsewhere (Sawchuk, *Dynamics of Native Politics*), the structure of the MAA and other provincial organizations was heavily influenced by provincial statutes that dictated the basic formation of associations, requiring a president, a board of directors, an annual assembly, and so on.
46 Interview with Rick Hardy.
47 Slobodin, *Metis of the Mackenzie District*, 12.
48 Ibid.
49 Ibid.
50 Ibid., 151
51 Interview with Rick Hardy.
52 *Minutes*, Third Annual Assembly, Métis Association of the Northwest Territories, 29–31 August 1975, Fort Norman, NWT; Delegate Rene Mercredi, 49
53 Ibid.
54 Ibid., 50.
55 Ibid.; Tapwe Chretien, 51.
56 Ibid; emphasis added
57 *Minutes*, Fourth Annual Assembly, Métis Association of the Northwest Territories, 14–16 October 1976, Fort Providence, NWT, 143.
58 Ibid., 71.
59 Ibid.
60 Ibid.; Rene Lamothe, 110.
61 Ibid.; Charles Overvold, 71.
62 Ibid.; Bill Lafferty, 66–7.
63 Ibid.
64 Ibid.; Jim Allard, 146.
65 Ibid.; Charles Overvold, 71.
66 Ibid.; moved by Jim Allard, 148.

67 Joanne Overvold (ed.), *Our Metis Heritage ... A Portrayal* (Yellowknife: Métis Association of NWT, 1976).
68 *Minutes*, Third Annual Assembly, Métis Association of the NWT; Bob Overvold, 32.
69 "Heritage Editor Resigns"; "Joanne's Letter of Resignation," *The Metis*, (Newsletter of Métis Association of the NWT), 1977; Interview with Joanne Barnaby Hay River, NWT.
70 Interview with Joanne Barnaby.
71 Ibid.
72 Ibid.
73 Interview with George Kurszewski.
74 Interview with Rick Hardy.
75 According to Hamilton, Erasmus's mother was a Dog Rib and his father was a Cree Métis from outside the NWT. Hamilton, *Arctic Revolution*, 148
76 "Metis Now Included in Dene Nation." *Dene Nation Newsletter*, August/ September 1982, 9.
77 Ibid.
78 *Minutes*, Fourth Annual Assembly, Appendix; statement by Rick Hardy, president of MANWT, pp 114–116.
79 The motion read in part: "WHEREAS some members of the Metis Association of the Northwest Territories have been urging the formation of one Dene organization to represent all Dene people of the N.W.T.; WHEREAS the Metis Association and the Indian Brotherhood of the Northwest Territories are working co-operatively on a land claims settlement for all Dene of the Northwest Territories; WHEREAS it is desirous and the best interests of the present members of the Metis Association to join together with members of the Indian Brotherhood of the Northwest Territories to form one Dene organization, i.e., Dene Nation; THEREFORE BE IT RESOLVED that: (1) the Metis Association of the N.W.T. surrender its Certificate of Incorporation to the Registrar of Societies and take all necessary steps to dissolve the Society. (2) the Metis Association of the N.W.T. undertake with the co-operation of the Indian Brotherhood of the N.W.T. to take all necessary steps to incorporate a new Dene organization in which all persons of Indian descent can be members." *Minutes*, Fourth Annual Assembly, Appendix.
80 The Métis Association of The Northwest Territories press release, 25 June 1976.
81 *Minutes*, Fourth Annual Assembly, Appendix; statement by Rich Hardy, president of MANWT.
82 Interview with George Kurszewski.
83 *Minutes*, Fourth Annual Assembly, Appendix; statement by Rick Hardy.

84 Correspondence from IBNWT [chiefs and board of directors of IB] to MANWT, 5 September 1976, *Minutes*, Fourth Annual Assembly, Appendix.
85 *Minutes*, Fourth Annual Assembly; motion by Joe Mercredi, 36
86 Ibid.; Joe Mercredi, 40.
87 *Metis Newsletter*, Métis Association of the NWT, 4 November 1981, 20; emphasis added.
88 The Dene Declaration was a resolution passed unanimously by the delegates to the Second Annual Joint Assembly of the Indian Brotherhood of the NWT and the Métis Association in July 1975, at Fort Simpson, NWT.
89 Ibid.
90 Abel, *Drum Songs*, 254–5; "Wah-shee and the Left: A Tale of the Territories," *Saint John's Edmonton Report*, 23 May 1977; Hamilton, *Arctic Revolution*, 139. Hamilton cites Caroline Wah Shee, wife of James Wah Shee, to the effect that "she knew for a fact" that Puxley and some of the other advisors had written the Dene Declaration, and he goes on to state that Puxley "didn't quite deny writing at least one draft." Hamilton also suggests Julius Nyerere's Tanzanian Declaration of Independence as one possible source of inspiration for the Dene Declaration. However, the actual authorship is to some degree irrelevant, as it clearly represented the views of the Dene leadership and was accepted by the members of the Brotherhood and many members of the Métis Association. As Hamilton also points out, Erasmus himself was familiar with writers like Saul Alinski, the AIM movement, and so on.
91 Dene Declaration, 1975.
92 *Minutes*, Fourth Annual Assembly, Appendix; statement by Rich Hardy.
93 *Minutes*, Third Annual Assembly; Tapwe Chretien, 78.
94 Ibid., 79.
95 Ibid., Appendix B: Day 2: 30 August 1975. The press release is as follows: "1 September 1975: The Metis Association of the Northwest Territories unanimously endorsed the Dene Declaration of Rights as passed at the Second Joint Metis Association – Indian Brotherhood General Assembly held in Fort Simpson in July. The Metis Association met in Fort Norman for its Third Annual General Assembly and discussed the progress being made towards Land Claims. It was pointed out in the Assembly that the Press has confused the Dene Declaration of Rights with an unofficial working paper being circulated to communities for discussion. The Fort Simpson General Assembly and the Fort Norman Metis Assembly did not take any official position on the working paper which was printed in the News of the North. It was felt, however, that the working paper prepared by field workers, community leaders and resource staff, was useful for its intended purpose of encouraging community discussion on the kind of future the

Dene will choose for themselves. The Dene Declaration, as endorsed by the Metis Association in support of the position taken at the Fort Simpson Assembly is as follows: ADOPTED in principle at Fort Simpson, NWT at the Second Dene General Assembly, July 19, 1975."

96 *Minutes*, Fourth Annual Assembly, 129.

97 Ibid., 64

98 "It was moved by Jim Evans that the Metis Association of the N.W.T. totally reject the Dene Declaration and also the Dene statement of principles that are to be presented to the government of Canada on or about the first of November 1976. Be it further resolved that the Metis Association adopt the following policy: that if any party presented involved in land claims in the Mackenzie valley continues to use the Dene Declaration as the basis of the claim, that the Metis Association will begin immediately to develop a claim that is more in line with the thinking of the people of the Mackenzie Valley. Seconded by Joe Mercredi. Motion Carried (vote count: 3 abstentions, 3 against, 34 in favour)." Ibid., 141.

99 Ibid.

100 *Highlights of the Sahtu Dene and Metis Comprehensive Land Claim Agreement*, https://www.aadnc-aandc.gc.ca/eng/1100100031179/1100100031184, accessed 2015.

101 North Slave Métis Alliance, "Strong Like Two People: North Slave Metis History" in Barkwell et al. (eds) *Metis Legacy* (Winnipeg: Pemmican, 2001).

102 http://www.greatcanadianlakes.com/northwest/slave/cul_page3.htm.

103 http://www.dehchofirstnations.com/members/fort_simpson_metis.htm; emphasis added.

104 Ibid.

105 Stephanie Iribacher-Fox and the Fort Providence Métis Council, *Since 1921: The Relationship between Dehcho Metis and Canada* (Fort Providence: Fort Providence Métis Council, 2007).

106 Ibid.

107 http://www.nwtmetisnation.ca/ssfa.pdf.

108 Métis Declaration of Rights, passed unanimously by Resolution at the Northwest Territory Métis Nation Special Assembly, Hay River, NWT, 24 July 2000, http://www.nwtmetisnation.ca/declaration.html; accessed 4 August 2009.

109 Ibid.

110 Ibid.

111 Samantha Stokell, "Fort Smith Woman Designs New Metis Sash," *Slave River Journal*, 4 November 2009.

112 Métis Declaration of Rights.

18 Ethnic Symbolism

1 E.J. Hobsbawm and T.O. Ranger (eds), *The Invention of Tradition* (Cambridge and New York: Cambridge University Press, 1983).
2 Jocelyn Linnekin, "Defining Tradition: Variations on the Hawaiian Identity," *American Ethnologist* 10 (1983): 241–52; Richard Handler and Jocelyn Linnekin, "Tradition, Genuine or Spurious," *Journal of American Folklore* 97 (1984): 273–90; Roger M. Keesing, "Creating the Past: Custom and Identity in the Contemporary Pacific," *Contemporary Pacific* 1(1–2)(1989): 19–42; F. Allan Hanson, "The Making of the Maori: Culture Invention and Its Logic," *American Anthropologist* 91(1989): 890–902.
3 Jocelyn Linnekin, "Cultural Invention and the Dilemma of Authenticity," *American Anthropologist* 93(1991): 446–9.
4 For example, much has been written on the "invented traditions" of the Maori of New Zealand; see Hanson, "The Making of the Maori"; M.P.K. Sorrensen, *Maori Origins and Migrations: The Genesis of Some Pakeha Myths* (Auckland: Auckland University Press, 1979); Ruth Brown, "Maori Spirituality as Pakeha Construct," *Meanjin* 48(2) (1989). The charge is not only that aspects of Maori culture such as their elaborately carved meeting houses, the immigration canoes of the Great Fleet, and the spiritual belief in the supreme being, Io, are "inventions" being used to support the contemporary movement known as Maoritanga, but that these basic elements of Maori culture were originally created by non-Maori; see Armando E. Janetta, *An Introduction to the Politics of Dialogism and Difference in Métis Literature* (Augsburg: Wissner, 2001), 58. One of the most controversial essays was Hanson's "The Making of the Maori," which engendered a heated debate both in the academy and in the popular press, generating headlines such as "US Expert Says Maori Culture Invented" and "Anthropology Seen as Father of Maori Lore"; see Joane Nagel, *American Indian Ethnic Renewal: Red Power and the Resurgence of Identity and Culture* (Oxford: Oxford University press, 1996), 67–8.
5 Keesing, "Creating the Past," 19.
6 Linneken, "Cultural Invention and the Dilemma of Authenticity," 447.
7 E. Hobsbawm, "Introduction: Inventing Traditions," in Hobsbawm and Ranger, *The Invention of Tradition* , 14.
8 Many contemporary Métis challenge the characterization of themselves and their culture as primarily hybrid. For the most comprehensive articulation of this point of view, see Chris Andersen, *"Métis": Race, Recognition, and the Struggle for Indigenous Peoplehood* (Vancouver/Toronto: UBC Press, 2014).

9 Jean Teillet, Draft for Discussion – MNC Definition of "Métis" submitted by the Métis Rights Panel – 9 December 1999, Métis National Council.
10 Hanson, "The Making of the Maori."
11 Taped interview with Angus Spence by Joe Sawchuk, Winnipeg, 1971.
12 Dolores T. Poelzer and Irene Poelzer, *In Our Own Words: Northern Saskatchewan Métis Women Speak Out* (Saskatoon: Lindenblatt & Hamonic, 1986).
13 Ibid., 4.
14 Albert Memmi, *The Colonizer and the Colonized* (Boston: Beacon Press, 1965).
15 Keesing, "Creating the Past," 25.
16 Antonio Gramsci, *Selections from the Prison Notebooks of Antonio Gramsci* (New York: International Publishers, 1971).
17 This can easily be seen in the structure and function of Canada's Native political organizations, including the status, non-status, Métis, and Inuit associations, which are forced to take on structures and jurisdictional constraints dictated by Canadian society and its jurisprudence system.
18 For example, strains between the Métis Association of Alberta and the Indian Association of Alberta made it very difficult for the research departments within the two organizations to pool resources on areas of common concern in 1979–80.
19 *Saskatoon Star Phoenix*, news roundup, 25 June 2004.
20 A 1999 Angus Reid poll, undertaken for Ralph Goodale, the Federal Interlocutor for Métis and non-status Indians, indicated that most Canadians supported clearing the name of Louis Riel. Sixty-five per cent of people surveyed backed the idea of a bill to exonerate Riel and declare him a Father of Confederation. Twenty-eight per cent opposed the move, and seven per cent were undecided (Jim Bronskill, "'Treasonous' Riel Becoming a Hero: Most Canadians Would Exonerate Hanged Métis Leader," *Southam News*, 30 March 1999).
21 Albert Braz, *The False Traitor: Louis Riel in Canadian Culture* (Toronto: University of Toronto Press, 2003), 3–4.
22 Dan Gardner, "MPs Should Study History, Not Remake It Through Law," *Ottawa Citizen*, 11 May 1999. See also Stephen Smith, "Riel Still a Traitor, Professor Insists," *Ottawa Citizen*, 7 January 1998; Jack Aubry, "'You Can't Change History': Riel's Old Enemy, the Orange Lodge, Joins Attack on Rebel's Exoneration, *Ottawa Citizen*, 15 May 1998; Andrew Coyne, "The Forest from the Treason," *National Post*, 14 April 1999.
23 John Robson, "The Perils of Trying to Get History 'Right,'" *National Post*, 11 January 1999.
24 An excerpt from the audio-visual presentation "What Does Riel Mean to Me?" published on the MNO website, summer 2004.

25 Keesing, "Creating the Past,"19.
26 Métis Jason Madden, speaking on the MNO website, "What Does Riel Mean to Me?" summer 2004.
27 A complete listing of the bills regarding Louis Riel introduced in both houses is neither necessary nor practical for our purposes. Here are but a few, beginning in 1983. An Act to Pardon Louis David Riel was tabled in the House of Commons on 23 September 1983 and 14 March 1984 by MP William Yurko. A bill to revoke the conviction of Louis David Riel was tabled by Les Benjamin, member for Regina-Lumsden on 28 June 1984 and 13 December 1984. On 28 November 1985, the deputy prime minister sought posthumous pardon for Louis David Riel. Another bill to revoke the conviction of Louis David Riel was introduced on 16 September 1987 by the member for Kamloops. A notice of motion to recognize Louis Riel as a Father of Confederation was tabled on 13 October 1989 by Mr Skelly, member for Comox-Alberni. In 1992, Joe Clark, as constitutional minister, introduced a resolution that asked the House of Commons to recognize "the unique and historic role of Louis Riel as a founder of Manitoba and his contribution in the development of Confederation." Proposed legislation to exonerate Louis Riel was introduced by Bloc Québécois MP Suzanne Tremblay in March 1995 and December 1996. A private member's bill which vacated Riel's conviction in accordance with the Criminal Records Act and recognized him as a Father of Confederation was introduced in April 1997 by MP Ron Duhamel. In 1998, two Liberal backbenchers; Winnipeg South MP Reg Alcock and Bourassa MP Denis Coderre (later to become federal Interlocutor for the Métis under Prime Minister Paul Martin's administration in 2004) introduced yet another bill to exonerate Louis Riel, despite the fact that the cabinet was simultaneously considering similar legislation. The cabinet proposition was backed by Ralph Goodale, Interlocutor for the Métis, and Ron Duhamel, who was now secretary of state. Alcock and Coderre's proposed Act stated in its preamble that Riel was "wrongfully tried, convicted and executed for high treason by the Government of Canada on November 16, 1885," and that the Métis, under the leadership of Riel and Gabriel Dumont, were defending their homes during the Northwest Rebellion in Saskatchewan. The bill also set aside 15 July as Louis Riel Day. The bill, now known as the Louis Riel Act, was never passed. It was reworked and introduced to the Senate in 2001 by Métis Liberal Senator Thelma Chalifoux. It also recognized the Métis sash as the "recognized symbol" of the Métis. The bill was simultaneously sponsored in the Commons by Rick Laliberte, Liberal MP for Churchill River, Saskatchewan. This bill and the others that preceded it were vigorously opposed by many MPs, but despite continual opposition, it resurfaced in

2004, when Denis Coderre, now Privy Council president and Interlocutor for the Métis, once again indicated that it was "time to rethink" Riel's contentious place in Canadian history. This time, he was joined by Prime Minister Paul Martin, who indicated that there was great interest in the Liberal caucus in having "a tangible recognition of Louis Riel's contributions to the Métis Nation and to Canada as a whole" (Canadian Press, 2004). However, there was still opposition from within the cabinet and on the floor of the House.

28 Jean Teillet, Riel Day Speech delivered at Queen's Park, Toronto, Ontario, 16 November 2002. Métis Nation of Ontario website, http://Métisnation.org/, accessed 2002. Jean Teillet is the great-grandniece of Louis Riel, a political activist, and a lawyer best known for defending Métis hunting rights in *R. v. Powley*.
29 "Métis Rights: A Call to Action." Métis National Council, Ramada Marlborough Hotel, Winnipeg, , 3–4 April 1998.
30 Aubry, "Backbenchers Push for Riel Bill."
31 Jean Teillet, quoted in Gloria Galloway, "Métis Council Opposes Bill Reversing Riel's Conviction. 'Forgive Means Forget': Pardon would imply guilt, great-niece of hanged leader says," *National Post*, 29 March 1999.
32 Ibid.
33 Jack Aubry, "'Whitey Stole All the Land,' Métis Senator Complains," *National Post*, 26 February 2002.
34 Gerald Morin, leader of the Métis National Council, quoted in Aubrey, "Backbenchers Push for Riel Bill"; Jean Teillet, quoted in Galloway, "Métis Council Opposes Bill"; David Chartrand, President of the Manitoba Métis Federation, quoted in "Métis Leader Calls for Riel Inquiry: The President of the Manitoba Métis Federation Wants an Inquiry into What Went Wrong in the Trial of Louis Riel Nearly 120 Years Ago," CBC *News*, Winnipeg, 20 April 2004, http://www.cbc.ca/news/.
35 Jean Teillet, quoted in Galloway, "Métis Council Opposes Bill Reversing Riel's Conviction."
36 Aubry, "'Whitey Stole All the Land,' Métis Senator Complains."
37 Jack Aubry, "137 MPs in Favour of Bill that Exonerates Louis Riel: Act Will Be Fast-tracked: Members of All Five Parties Want to Call Métis Leader Father of Confederation," *Ottawa Citizen*, 12 April 1999; Galloway, "Métis Council Opposes Bill Reversing Riel's Conviction."
38 Galloway, "Métis Council Opposes Bill Reversing Riel's Conviction."
39 Sherry Farrell Racette, "Métis Man or Canadian Icon: Who Owns Louis Riel?" in *Rielisms*, ed. John Boyle et al. (Winnipeg: Winnipeg Art Gallery, 2001), 42–53.

40 Dominion Institute website, http://www.dominion.ca/, accessed 2004. This organization no longer exists under the name Dominion Institute, having merged with the Historica Foundation of Canada in 2009. It is now known as Historica Canada and bills itself as "the largest independent organization devoted to enhancing awareness of Canadian history and citizenship," https://www.historicacanada.ca/content/history, accessed 2015.

41 "Métis Nation Condemns 'Retrial' of Louis Riel by CBC," MNO press release, 22 August 2002,

42 Ibid.

43 For a description of the research project and its findings, see Joe Sawchuk, Patricia Sawchuk, and Theresa Ferguson, *Métis Land Rights in Alberta: A Political History* (Edmonton: Métis Association of Alberta, 1981).

44 See, for example, *Manitoba Métis Federation Inc. v. A.-G Canada* (sub nom. *Dumont v. A.-G Canada*) [1988] 3 C.N.L.R. 39 (Man. CA); *Manitoba Métis Federation Inc. v. A.-G. Canada*, [1990] 2 C.N.L.R. 19 (S.C.C.).

45 Taped interview with Yvon Dumont, lieutenant governor of Manitoba, 11 September 1995, by Doug Racine and Joe Sawchuk, in Winnipeg, MB, at the residence of the lieutenant governor.

46 The "historic Métis Homeland" is defined as "that area of land in west central North America used and occupied as the traditional territory of the Métis or Half-Breeds as they were then known," and is part of the definition of Métis as adopted at the Métis National Council's 18th Annual General Assembly, Edmonton, AB, 27–28 September 2002.

47 Keesing, "Creating the Past," 25–6

48 Ibid., 29.

49 *Winnipeg Sun*, 2 July 2004.

50 http://missoulian.com/news/local/skc-teacher-puts-student-master-together-to-pass-on-craft/article_79be7c1c-4a18-5214-804d-d0f96e700eaf.html, accessed 2015.

51 Omer C. Stewart, "Cart-using Indians of the American Plains," in *Men and Cultures: Selected Papers of the 5th International Congress of Anthropological and Ethnological Sciences*, ed. Anthony F.C. Wallace (Philadelphia: University of Pennsylvania Press, 1960), 351–5.

52 The publishers of *The Métis of Manitoba: Reformulation of an Ethnic Identity* (Joe Sawchuk [Toronto: Peter Martin, 1978]) insisted on a picture of nineteenth-century Métis, complete with a Red River cart, on the cover of the volume, despite the fact that the subject of the book was the twentieth-century reconstitution of Métis identity.

53 The information in this section is based on the RCAP Report 1997, *Ceremonies and Symbols*, Vol. 1, pt 3, chap. 15.8); Darren R. Préfontaine and Karon L. Shmon, "The Sash," in *The Virtual Museum of Métis History and Culture* (Regina: Gabriel Dumont Institute, 2003), http://www.Métismuseum.ca/media/document.php/00741.pdf; and the various websites of the Métis National Council, the Métis Nation of Ontario, the Manitoba Métis Federation, and the Métis National Youth Advisory Council.
54 Métis Nation of Ontario website, http://www.Métisnation.org/, accessed 2004; emphasis added.
55 Préfontaine and Shmon, "The Sash."
56 Ibid.
57 RCAP Report 1997, *Ceremonies and Symbols*, Vol. 1, pt 3, chap. 15.8.
58 "The Métis Sash," MMF website, http://www.mmf.mb.ca/index.php?option=com_content&view=article&id=92&Itemid=60, accessed 2004
59 Ibid.
60 Samantha Stokell, "Fort Smith Woman Designs New Métis Sash," *Slave River Journal*, 4 November 2009.
61 http://www.glinx.com/~metis/sash.html, accessed 2004.
62 Calvin Racette, *Flags of the Métis* (Regina: Gabriel Dumont Institute, 1987), 6.
63 For example, Métis fiddling and jigging have been made part of the regular school curriculum in Caslan elementary and junior high schools, a community about 150 kilometres northeast of Edmonton, Alberta; "Fiddling Around in Class Is Just Fine: Métis Students Getting Turned on Learning Their Culture," *Edmonton Journal*, 4 January 2004.
64 http://www.metisnation.ca/ARTS/hist_who.html(2004).
65 Keesing, "Creating the Past," 35.

Conclusion

1 John L. and Jean Comaroff, *ETHNICITY, INC.* (Chicago: University of Chicago Press, 2009), 82.
2 *Manitoba Métis Federation Inc. v. Canada (Attorney General)* (2013 SCC 14, Case Number 33880).
3 Comaroff and Comaroff, *ETHNICITY, INC.*
4 For example, the San of the Kalahari recently have begun complaining about "fake Bushmen" after certain plants growing in their territory showed commercial potential; the Bafokeng (a South African people made wealthy by platinum) are voicing concern about the influx of outsiders, and many Native American tribes have excised whole families from tribal membership when casino profits come into existence. Ibid., 143.

5 For a discussion of how this racial definition in the *Powley* decision has exerted a discernible force in the field of Métis studies, see Chris Andersen, "*Moya 'Tipimsook* ('The People Who Aren't Their Own Bosses'): Racialization and the Misrecognition of 'Métis' in Upper Great Lakes Ethnohistory," *Ethnohistory* 58(1) (Winter 2011): 49–52.

6 *Daniels v. Canada*, FC6 (2013) [para 117].

7 Ibid., [para 130].

8 Chris Andersen, "Settling for Community? Juridicial Visions of Historical Métis Collectivity in and after R. v. Powley," in *Contours of a People: Métis Family, Mobility and History*, ed. Nicole St Onge et al. (Norman: University of Oklahoma Press, 2012), 393

9 Comaroff and Comaroff, *ETHNICITY, INC.*, 1.

10 Ibid., 19.

11 Ibid., 15.

Bibliography

PRIMARY SOURCES

Archival Collections

Archives of Ontario (AO)
  Irving Papers
Archives of the State Historical Society of North Dakota
  Albert E. Dease Papers
  William Davis Papers
  WPA Historical Data Project, Rolette County
Archives de la Société historique de Saint-Boniface (ASHSB)
  Fonds Provencher
  Fonds Taché
  Fonds de la Société historique métisses
Glenbow Archives
  Lucas Family Fonds
  James Brady Fonds
  Joseph Dion Fonds
  Métis Association of Alberta fonds
Hudson's Bay Company Archives
  Edmonton House Journals, Correspondence, and District Reports, 1795–1900
  Île-à-la-Crosse Journals and Correspondence, 1805–1910
  Green Lake Post reports, 1889–92.
  Carlton House journals, 1795–1834
  Brandon House journals and district reports, 1795–1830
  Winnipeg Post journals, 1797–1830

Correspondence Inward, 1818–70
Correspondence Outward – George Simpson, 1821–60
Library and Archives of Canada (LAC)
Church Missionary Society (CMS) Records, North American Missions
Records of the Department of the Interior (RG 15)
Records of Indian Affairs (RG 10)
Selkirk Papers (MG 19 E1)
Métis Association of the Northwest Territories
Minutes, Third Annual Assembly, Métis Association of the Northwest Territories, 29–31 August 1975, Fort Norman, NWT
Minutes, Fourth Annual Assembly, Métis Association of the Northwest Territories, 14–16 October 1976, Fort Providence, NWT
Métis Cultural Recovery Inc., Choteau, MT
Interviews with Metis descendants. Teton and Dupuyer Metis Communities, Metis
National Archives and Records Administration – United States (NARA)
Letters Received by the Office of Indian Affairs, 1824–81, Montana Superintendency
Letters Received by the Office of the Adjutant General (Main Series), 1871–80
Letters Received by the Office of the Adjutant General (Main Series), 1881–89
Provincial Archives of Alberta (PAA)
Reports, evidence, etc. re: The Report of the Royal Commission on the Condition of the Halfbreed Population of the Province of Alberta, 1935–36.
Oblate Archives
Baptêmes et Mariages
A. Philippot, "La Mission de Saint-Paul-des-Cris"
Constantine Scollen, "Notes biographiques"
Adéodat Thérien, "St Paul – Notes historiques"
Adéodat Thérien, "St Paul – Historique de la paroisse, 1930"
Archives of Manitoba (AM)
Adams Archibald Papers
Alexander Morris Papers
Louis Riel Collection
Papers of J.N. Ritchot
Parish Lot Files
Saskatchewan Archives
Conference of the Métis of Saskatchewan Proceedings, 30 July 1946,

Interview with Wilma Moore by Murray Dobbin, n.d., Saskatchewan Sound Archives Program, http://ourspace.uregina.ca/handle/10294/1416

Published Primary Sources

Alberta. "Report of the Royal Commission Appointed to Investigate the Conditions of the Half-Breed Population in Alberta." *Sessional Paper 1936–72*.

Amos, A. *Report of Trials in the Courts of Canada Relative to the Destruction of The Earl of Selkirk's Settlement on the Red River with Observations*. London: John Murray, 1820.

Belcourt, G.A., to Hon. G.W. Manypenny, Commissioner of Indian Affairs, November 20, 1854. Enclosure #24 in *The Report of the Commissioner of Indian Affairs*, November 25, 1854. U.S. Congress, House Ex. Docs. No. 1, 2nd sess., 33rd Congress, Serial Set #777.

Belcourt, G.A., to Bishop of Dubuque, 16 février 1850. *Annales de la propagation de la foi pour la province de Québec.*

Bumsted, J.M. (ed.) *Writings and Papers of Thomas Douglas, Fifth Earl of Selkirk.* Vol. 2: *The Collected Writing of Lord Selkirk, 1810–1820*. Winnipeg: Manitoba Record Society, 1987.

Canada. *Annual Reports of the Department of Indian Affairs*, 1874–1900.

Canada. Federal Court. *Daniels v. Canada*, "Reasons for Judgement." 2013 FC6. Accesssed online at http://reports.fja-cmf.gc.ca/eng/2013/2013fc6.html.

Canada. Parliament, House of Commons, *Sessional Papers*, 1874. No. VII. *Report of the Select Committee on the Causes of the Difficulties in the North West Territories in 1869–70.*

Canada. *The Queen vs. Louis Riel: Accused and convicted of the crime of high treason: Report of the trial at Regina: Appeal to the Court of Queen's Bench, Manitoba: Appeal to the Privy Council, England: Petition for medical examination of the convict; List of petitions for commutation of the sentence*. Ottawa: Queen's Printer, 1886.

Cox, Ross. *Adventures on the Columbia River including The Narrative of a Residence of Six Year on the Western Side of the Rocky Mountains, among Various Tribes of Indians Hitherto Unknown: Together with A Journey Across the American Continent*. New York: J. & J. Harper, 1832.

Dawson, George M. "The Journals of George M. Dawson." Repr. in *Saskatchewan History* 21(1) (Winter 1968).

Goulet, Roger. "Report of Half-Breed Commission," dated 1 May, 1889. In *Annual Report of the Department of the Interior for the Year 1889*. Canada. *Sessional Papers* (No. 14) 53 Victoria 1890.

Goulet, Roger. "Report Respecting Claims by Half-Breeds." In *Annual Report of the Department of the Interior for the Year 1886*. Canada. *Sessional Papers* (No. 7) 50 Victoria, 1887, 76.

Goulet, Roger, and N.O. Coté. "North-West Half-Breed Claims Commission," dated 10 January 1888, in *Annual Report of the Department of the Interior for the Year 1887*. Canada. *Sessional Papers* (No. 14) 51 Victoria, 1887.

Hawthorn, H., et al. *A Survey of the Contemporary Indians of Canada: Economic, Political, and Educational Needs and Policies.* Parts I and II. Ottawa: Indian Affairs Branch, 1966–7.

Hind, Henry Youle. "Papers Relative to the Exploration of the Country Between Lake Superior and the Red River Settlement." Presented to both Houses of Parliament by Command of Her Majesty, June 1859. *British Parliamentary Papers. Colonies. Canada* 22. Shannon: Irish University Press, 1969.

Kappler, Charles Kappler (ed.). *Indian Affairs: Laws and Treaties*. 2 vols. Washington, DC: Government Printing Office, 1904.

Keating, William H. *Narrative of an Expedition to the Source of St Peter's River, Lake Winnipeek, Lake of the Woods, &c. &c. Performed in the Year 1823 by the Order of the Hon. J.C. Calhoun, Secretary of War. Under the Command of Stephen H. Long, Major U.S.T.E compiled from the notes of Major Long, Messrs Say, Keating, and Calhoun*. 2 vols. Philadelphia: H.C. Carey & I. Lea, 1824.

Lacombe, Albert. *Memoirs on the Half-Breeds of Manitoba and the Territories of the Canadian North West*. 1901.

Loran, C.T., and T.F. McIlwraith (eds) *The North American Indian Today.* Toronto: University of Toronto Press, 1943.

Missions de la Congrégation des missionnaires oblats de Marie Immaculée. Paris: Typographie A. Hennuyer, 1862–1900.

Morton, W.L. (ed.) *Alexander Begg's Red River Journal.* Toronto: Champlain Society, 1956.

Morton, W.L. (ed.). *Manitoba: The Birth of a Province.* Winnipeg: Manitoba Record Society, 1965.

Ontario Métis Aboriginal Association (OMAA). *The Woodland Métis Tribe.* http://www.omaa.org/. Downloaded 02/07/2013.

Ontario Métis and Non-Status Indian Association (OMNSIA). "Special Status Committee Hearings." *Dimensions. Special Editions* 8(4) (August/September 1980).

Ontario Métis and Non-Status Indian Association (OMNSIA). "Constitutional Commission of Inquiry." *Dimensions. Special Editions* 9(4) (September/October 1981).

"Papers and Correspondence in Connection with Half-breed Claims and Other Matters Relating to the North-West Territories." Canada. *Sessional*

Papers, Vol. 13, Third Session of the Fifth Parliament, 48 Victoria, 1885 (No. 116).

"Papers Relating to the Red River Settlement: viz. Return to an Address from the Honourable House of Commons to His Royal Highness The Prince Regent, dated 24th June 1819 ..." *British Parliamentary Papers. Colonies. Canada* 5. Shannon: Irish University Press, 1969.

"The Report of the Commissioner of Indian Affairs." November 25, 1854. U.S. Congress, House Ex. Docs. No. 1, 2nd Sess., 33rd Congress, Serial Set #777.

"The Report of the Commissioner of Indian Affairs." November 27, 1851. U.S. Congress, House Ex. Docs. No. 2, 1st Session, 32nd Congress, Serial Set #636,

"Report of the North-West Half-Breed Commission of the work done by them during the past summer." *Annual Report of the Department of the Interior for the Year 1885*. Canada. *Sessional Papers* (No. 8), 49 Victoria, 1886.

Report of the Proceedings connected with the disputes between the Earl of Selkirk and the North-West Company at the Assizes, held at York in Upper Canada, October, 1818. Montreal: Printed by James Lane and Nahum Mower, 1819.

"Report of the Special Commissioners Appointed on the 8th of September 1856 to Investigate Indian Affairs in Canada." *Journals of the Legislative Assembly*, 21 Victoria. 1858, Appendix (No. 21).

"Report of the Special Commissioners Appointed to Investigate Indian Affairs in Canada (Messrs Pennefather, Talfourd, and Worthington) to Sir Edmund Head, April 1858, Province of Canada." *Journals of the Legislative Assembly. Sessional Papers* 1858, Appendix 21.

"Report of the Treaty Made with the Pembina Indians, at Pembina, by Alex. Ramsey." November 7, 1851. Included in *The Report of the Commissioner of Indian Affairs*. November 27, 1851. U.S. Congress, House Ex. Docs. No. 2, 1st Sess., 32nd Congress, Serial Set #636.

"Report on the Affairs of the Indians of Canada," *Journals of the Legislative Assembly*, 8 Victoria, 1844–45, Appendix EEE.

"Report on the Affairs of the Indians in Canada; submitted to the Honorable the Legislative Assembly, for their information." Province of Canada. *Journals of the Legislative Assembly*, 11 Victoria, A.1847. *Sessional Papers*, Appendix T.

"Reports, Correspondence and Other Papers Relating to the Red River Settlement, the Hudson's Bay Company and other Affairs in Canada, 1849." *British Parliamentary Papers. Colonies. Canada* 18. Shannon: Irish University Press, 1969.

Selkirk, Lord. *Statement Respecting the Earl of Selkirk's Settlement Upon the Red River in North America; Its Destructions in 1815 and 1816; and the Massacre of Governor Semple and his Party*. London: John Murray, 1817.

"Turtle Mountain Band of Chippewa Indians." U.S. Congress, Sen. Ex. Docs. No. 444, 56th Cong., 1st sess., 1900, 151–2.
Wesleyan Missionary Notices. Canada Conference. New Series.
Wilcocke, Samuel Hull (Edward Ellice, Simon McGillivray). *A Narrative of Occurances in the Indian Countries of North America, since the connexion of the Right Hon. The Earl of Selkirk with the Hudson's Bay Company, and his attempt to establish a colony on the Red River with a detailed account of His Lordship's military Expedition to, and subsequent proceedings at Fort William, in Upper Canada.* London: B. McMillan, 1817.

Interviews

Angus Spence by Joe Sawchuk, Winnipeg, 1971
Adrian Hope by Joe Sawchuk and Pat Sawchuk, Edmonton, 9 March 1981
Wayne McKenzie, by Joe Sawchuk, Regina, August 1988
Cliff LaRoque, by Joe Sawchuk, Regina, August 1988
Don Ross, by Joe Sawchuk, Regina, August 1988
Jim Sinclair, by Joe Sawchuk, Regina, August 1988
Murray Hamilton, by Joe Sawchuk, Regina, August 1988
Mederic McDougal, by Joe Sawchuk and Murray Hamilton, Regina, August 1988
Joe Amyotte, by Joe Sawchuk, Regina, August 1988
Fortunat (Ferdinand) Guiboche, by Joe Sawchuk, Winnipeg, October 1988
Sharron Johnstone, by Joe Sawchuk, Edson, Alberta, February 1989
Dan Martel, by Joe Sawchuk. Edmonton, February 1989
Joanne Daniels, by Joe Sawchuk, Edmonton, February 1989
Sam Sinclair, by Joe Sawchuk, Edmonton, February 1989
Jim Durocher, by Joe Sawchuk, Regina, May 1989
Norval Desjarlais by Doug Racine, Grand Rapids, MB, 2 August 1995
Stan Fulham by Doug Racine, St Lazare, MB, 17 July 1995
Ed Head by Doug Racine, Winnipeg, July 1995
Dolly Fleury by Doug Racine and Joe Sawchuk, Dauphin, MB, June 1995.
Ernie Blais by Doug Racine and Joe Sawchuk, Winnipeg, MB, June 1995
John Lavallee by Doug Racine and Joe Sawchuk, St Ambroise, MB, June 1995
George Fleury by Doug Racine and Joe Sawchuk, Minnedosa, MB, June 1995
René Houle by Doug Racine and Joe Sawchuk, June 1995
Ron Erickson by Doug Racine and Joe Sawchuk, 12 June 1995
Yvon Dumont by Doug Racine and Joe Sawchuk, Winnipeg, MB, 11 September 1995
Daryl LaRose by Allan Bork, North Battleford, SK, 5 June 1996

Nora Ritchie by Allan Bork, Saskatoon, SK, 10 June 1996
Allan Morin by Allan Bork, Saskatoon, SK, 12 June 1996
Lorna Docken by Allan Bork, Saskatoon, SK, 13 June 1996
Stan Durocher by Allan Bork, La Ronge, SK, 20 June 1996
Vital Morin by Allan Bork, Île-à-la-Crosse, SK,25 June 1996
Armand Murray by Allan Bork, La Loch, SK, 25 June 1996
Louis Morin by Allan Bork, Turnor Lake, SK, 25 June 1996
Bertha Ouellette by Allan Bork, Meadow Lake, SK, 26 June 1996
Edward King by Allan Bork, Meadow Lake, SK, 26 June 1996
John Dorion by Allan Bork, Prince Albert, SK, 3 July 1996
Darlene McKay by Allan Bork, Prince Albert, SK, 3 July 1996
Janice Henry by Allan Bork, Prince Albert, SK, 3 July 1996
Ryan C. Calder by Allan Bork, Archerville, SK, 4 July 1996
Geri Vanwyck by Allan Bork, Balcarres, SK, 4 July 1996
Gloria Shmyr by Allan Bork, Melfort, SK, 4 July 1996
Clifford Larocque by Allan Bork, Regina, SK, 5 July 1996
George Pritchard by Allan Bork, Willowfield, SK, 10 July 1996
Leo Amyotte by Allan Bork, Kindersley, SK, 13 July 1996
Richard I. Hardy by Allan Bork, Yellowknife, NWT, 19 July 1996
James Bourque by Allan Bork, Yellowknife, NWT, 20 July 1996
Gary Bohnet by Allan Bork, Yellowknife, NWT, 22 July 1996
Charles Overvold by Allan Bork, Yellowknife, NWT, 22 July 1996
Ernie Daniels by Allan Bork, Hay River, NWT, 25 July 1996
Michael McLeod by Allan Bork, Fort Providence, NWT, 25 July 1996
Albert J. Lafferty by Allan Bork, Fort Providence, NWT, 26 July 1996
Richard C. Lafferty by Allan Bork, Fort Providence, NWT, 26 July 1996
George Kurszewski by Allan Bork, Fort Smith, NWT, 26 July 1996
Joanne Barnaby by Allan Bork, Hay River Reserve, NWT, 25 July 1996
Sharon Gairdner by Allan Bork, Hay River, NWT, 25 July 1996
Joe Whitehead by Cathy Sewell, Cadotte Lake, AB, May 1996
Tina St Germain by Cathy Sewell, Paddle Pairie, AB, May 1996
Rita Nooskey by Cathy Sewell, Paddle Prairie, AB, 21 May 1996
Robert John Calliou by Cathy Sewell, Paddle Prairie, AB, 21 May 1996
Nora Calliou by Cathy Sewell, Paddle Prairie, AB, 21 May 1996
Gregory Calliou by Cathy Sewell, Paddle Prairie, AB, 21 May 1996
Earl Wilds by Cathy Sewell, Hine's Creek, AB, 23 May 1996
Mona Wilds by Cathy Sewell, Eureka River, AB, 23 May 1996
Alvena Strasbourg by Cathy Sewell, Edmonton, AB, 1 June 1996
Bertha Clark Jones by Cathy Sewell, Athabasca, AB, 9 June 1996
Jane Woodvein by Cathy Sewell, Edmonton, AB, 14 June 1996

Cliff Calliou by Cathy Sewell, Kelly Lake, BC, 24 June 1996
Isabel Calliou by Cathy Sewell, Kelly Lake, BC, 24 June 1996
D. Campbell by Cathy Sewell, Kelly Lake, BC, 24 June 1996
Caroline Campbell by Cathy Sewell, Kelly Lake, BC, 24 June 1996
Stan Sewell by Cathy Sewell, Valhalla Centre, AB, 27 June 1996
Albena E. Sewell by Cathy Sewell, Valhalla Centre, AB, 27 June 1996
Brenda, Blyan by Cathy Sewell, Edmonton, AB, 9 July 1996
Lena Poelstra by Cathy Sewell, Fort McMurray, AB, 15 July 1996
Gerald White by Cathy Sewell, Fort McMurray, AB, 15 July 1996
Christine Daniels by Cathy Sewell, Edmonton, AB, 22 July 1996
Florence Parenteau by Cathy Sewell, Fishing Lake, AB, 29 July 1996
Karen Collins by Cathy Sewell, Elizabeth Metis Settlement, AB, 30 July 1996
Madeline Heath, by Cathy Sewell, Grand Centre, AB, 30 July 1996
Audrey Poitras by Cathy Sewell, St. Paul, AB, 2 August 1996
Gordon Poitra by Cathy Sewell, St Paul, AB, 2 August 1996
Mike McGuire, Thunder Bay, ON, 17 June 1997

SECONDARY SOURCES

"Mr. Paddy McGuire," *Dimensions. Special Editions* 8(5).

"Wah-shee and the Left: A Tale of the Territories." *St John's Edmonton Report*. 23 May 1977.

Able, Kerry. *Drum Songs: Glimpses of Dene History*. 2nd ed. Montreal/Kingston: McGill-Queens University Press, 2005.

Andersen, Chris. "From Nation to Population: The Racialization of 'Métis' in the Canadian Census." *Nations and Nationalism* 14(2) (2008).

Andersen, Chris. *"Métis": Race, Recognition, and the Struggle for Indigenous Peoplehood*. Vancouver/Toronto: UBC Press, 2014.

Andersen, Chris. "*Moya 'Tipimsook* ('The People Who Aren't Their Own Bosses'): Racialization and the Misrecognition of 'Métis' in Upper Great Lakes Ethnohistory," *Ethnohistory* 58(1) (Winter 2011).

Andersen, Chris. "Settling for Community? Juridicial Visions of Historical Métis Collectivity in and after R. v. Powley." In *Contours of a People: Métis Family, Mobility and History*, ed. Nicole St Onge et al. Norman: University of Oklahoma Press, 2012.

Anderson, Benedict. *Imagined Communities: Reflections on the Origin and Spread of Nationalism*. London: Verso Books, 1991.

Anick, N. *The Métis of the South Saskatchewan*. Parks Canada Manuscript Report Series No. 364. Ottawa: Parks Canada, 1976.

Asch, Michael. "Dene Nation." In *The Canadian Encyclopedia*.

Asch, Michael. *Home and Native Land: Aboriginal Rights and the Canadian Constitution*. Toronto: Methuen, 1984.

Aubry, Jack. "'Whitey stole all the land,' Metis Senator Complains," *National Post*, 26 February 2002.

Aubry, Jack. "'You can't change history': Riel's Old Enemy: The Orange Lodge, Joins Attack on Rebel's Exoneration." *Ottawa Citizen*, 15 May 1998.

Baldwin, Stuart. "Wintering Villages of the Metis Hivernants." In *The Metis and The Land in Alberta Land Claims Research Project, 1979–80*, ed. Métis Association of Alberta. Edmonton: Métis Association of Alberta, 1980.

Ball, Timothy. "Climatic Change, Droughts and the Social Impact: Central Canada, 1811–20, a Classic Example." In *The Year without Summer: World Climate in 1816*, ed. C.R. Harington. Ottawa: Canadian Museum of Nature, 1992.

Ball, Timothy. "The Year without Summer: Its Impact on the Fur Trade and History of Western Canada." In *The Year without Summer: World Climate in 1816*, ed. C.R. Harington. Ottawa: Canadian Museum of Nature, 1992.

Barron, F. Laurie. "The CCF and the Development of Metis Colonies in Southern Saskatchewan during the Premiership of T.C. Douglas, 1944–1961." *Canadian Journal of Native Studies* 10(2) (1990).

Barron, F. Laurie. *Walking in Indian Moccasins: The Native Policies of Tommy Douglas and the CCF*. Vancouver: UBC Press, 1997.

Barth, Fredrik (ed.). *Ethnic Groups and Boundaries: The Social Organization of Culture Difference*. Boston, Little, Brown, 1969.

Baudrillard, Jean. *Simulations*. Translated by Paul Foss, Paul Patton, and Philip Beitchman. New York: Semiotest(e), 1983.

Bell, Catherine E. "Who Are the Metis in Section 35(2)?" *Alberta Law Review* 29(2) (1991).

Bellman, Jennifer, L. Bellman, and Christopher C. Hanks "Northern Métis and the Fur Trade." In *Picking up the Threads: Métis History in the Mackenzie Basin*. Ottawa: Métis Heritage Association of the Northwest Territories and Parks Canada – Canadian Heritage, 1998.

Berger, Carl. *The Writing of Canadian History: Aspects of English Canadian Historical Writing since 1900*. 2nd ed. Toronto: University of Toronto Press, 1986.

Berger, Mrs Clemence Gourneau. "Metis Come to Judith Basin." In *The Métis Centennial Publication, 1879–1979*, ed. Bill Thackeray. Lewistown, MT: Central Montana Publication Co.

Berger, T.R. *Northern Frontier, Northern Homeland: Report of the Mackenzie Valley Pipeline Inquiry*. 2 vols. Ottawa: Supply and Services Canada, 1977.

Bhabba, Homi. "DissemiNation: Time, Narrative, and the Margins of the Modern Nation." In *Nation and Narration*, ed. Homi Bhabha. London: Routledge, 1990.

Bhabba, Homi. "Introduction: Narrating the Nation." In *Nation and Narration*, ed. Homi Bhabha. London: Routledge, 1990.

Bieder, Robert E. *Science Encounters the Indian, 1820–1880: The Early Years of American Ethnology*. Norman: University of Oklahoma Press, 1986.

Bieder, Robert E. "Scientific Attitudes Towards Indian Mixed-Bloods in Early Nineteenth Century America." *Journal of Ethnic Studies* 8(2) (Summer 1980).

Binnema, Ted. "Protecting Indian Lands by Defining Indian: 1850–76." *Journal of Canadian Studies / Revue d'Études canadiennes* 48:2 (Spring 2014).

Binnema, Ted. "With Tears, Shrieks, and Howlings of Despair': The Smallpox Epidemic of 1781–82." In *Alberta Formed Alberta Transformed*. Vol. 1, ed. Michael Payne, Donald Wetherell, and Catherine Cavanaugh. Edmonton: University of Alberta Press, 2006.

Binnema, Theodore. *Common and Contested Ground: A Human and Environmental History of the Northwestern Plains*. Norman: University of Oklahoma Press, 2001.

Binnema, Theodore, and Kevin Hutchings. "The Emigrant and the Noble Savage: Sir Francis Bond Head's Romantic Approach to Aboriginal Policy in Upper Canada, 1836–1838." *Journal of Canadian Studies / Revue d'études canadiennes* 39(1) (Winter 2005).

Boek, W.F., and J.K. Boek. *Appendix I: The People of Indian Ancestry in Greater Winnipeg*. Vol. 2 of *The People of Indian Ancestry in Manitoba: A Social and Economic Study under the Direction of Jean H. Lagasse*. Winnipeg: Department of Agriculture and Immigration, 1959.

Brass, Paul. *Ethnicity and Nationalism*. London: Sage, 1991.

Braz, Albert. *The False Traitor: Louis Riel in Canadian Culture*. Toronto: University of Toronto Press, 2003.

Bronskill, Jim. "'Treasonous' Riel Becoming a Hero: Most Canadians Would Exonerate Hanged Metis Leader," *Southam News*, 30 March 1999.

Brown, Jennifer S.H. "Children of Early Fur Trades." In *Childhood and Family in Canadian History*, ed. Joy Parr. Toronto: McLelland & Stewart, 1982.

Brown, Jennifer S.H. "The Métis: Genesis and Rebirth." In *Native People, Native Lands: Canadian Indians, Inuit and Metis*. Ottawa: Carleton University Press, 1991.

Brown, Jennifer S.H. *Strangers in Blood: Fur Trade Company Families in Indian Country*. Vancouver: UBC Press, 1980.

Brown, Richard Maxwell. "Western Violence: Structure, Values, Myth." *Western Historical Quarterly* 24(1) (February 1993).

Brown, Ruth. "Maori Spirituality as Pakeha Construct." *Meanjin* 48(2) (1989).
Bryce, George. *Manitoba: Its Infancy, Growth, and Present Condition.* London: Sampson Low, Marston, Searle, & Rivington, 1882.
Bryce, George. *The Remarkable History of the Hudson's Bay Company including that of the French Traders of North-Western Canada and of the North-West, XY, and Astor Fur Companies.* London, 1900.
Buckley, Helen. *Trapping and Fishing in the Economy of Northern Saskatchewan.* Report No. 3. *Economic and Social Survey of Northern Saskatchewan.* Saskatoon: Research Division, Centre for Community Studies, University of Saskatchewan, 1962.
Buckley, Helen, J.E.M. Kew, and John B. Hawley. *The Indians and Metis of Northern Saskatchewan: A Report on Economic and Social Development.* Saskatoon: Centre for Community Studies, 1963.
Bumsted, J.M. *Dictionary of Manitoba Biography.* Winnipeg: University of Manitoba Press, 1999.
Bumsted, J.M. *Fur Trade Wars: The Founding of Western Canada.* Winnipeg: Great Plains, 1999.
Calloway, Colin G. *One Vast Winter Count: The Native American West before Lewis and Clark.* Lincoln: University of Nebraska Press, 2003.
Campbell, Maria. *Halfbreed.* Toronto: McClelland & Stewart, 1973.
Campey, Lucille. *The Silver Chief: Lord Selkirk and the Scottish Pioneers of Belfast, Baldoon and Red River.* Toronto: Natural Heritage Books, 2003.
Card, B.Y., G.K. Hirabayashi, and C.L. French. *The Métis in Alberta Society: With Special Reference to Social, Economic and Cultural Factors Associated with Persistently High Tuberculosis Incidence.* Edmonton: University of Alberta, 1963.
Canadian Association of Social Workers (CASW). *The Metis in Manitoba: A Study by the Manitoba Branch, Canadian Association of Social Workers.* Winnipeg: Provincial Council of Women, 1954.
Chakrabarty, Dipesh. "Governmental Roots of Modern Ethnicity." In *Habitations of Modernity: Essays in the Wake of Subaltern Studies.* Chicago: University of Chicago Press, 2002.
Chartrand, Paul L.A.H. *Manitoba Métis Settlement Scheme of 1870.* Saskatoon: Native Law Centre, 1991.
Clifford, James. "Partial Truths." In *Writing Culture: the Poetics and Politics of Ethnography,* ed. James Clifford and George E. Marcus. Berkeley, Los Angeles, London: University of California Press, 1986.
Cohen, Abner. *Custom and Politics in Urban Africa.* Berkeley: University of California Press, 1969.
Comaroff, John L., and Jean Comaroff. *ETHNICITY, INC.* Chicago: University of Chicago Press, 2009.

Complin, Margaret. "Pierre Falcon's 'Chanson de la Grenouillère'," *Transactions of the Royal Society of Canada*, Section II, (1939).

Cowie, Isaac. *The Company of Adventurers: A Narrative of Seven Years in the Service of the Hudson's Bay Company During 1857–1874 on the Great Buffalo Plains with Historical and Biographical Notes and Comments*. Toronto: William Briggs, 1913.

Coyne, Andrew. "The Forest from the Treason," *National Post*, 14 April 1999.

Cumming, Peter A., and Neil H. Mickenberg (eds). *Native Rights in Canada*. 2nd ed. Toronto: Indian-Eskimo Association of Canada, 1972.

Daniels, Harry (ed.) *The Forgotten People: Metis and Non-status Indian Land Claims*. Ottawa: Native Council of Canada, 1979.

Daniels, Richard. "The Spirit and Terms of Treaty Eight." In *The Spirit of the Alberta Indian Treaties*, ed. Richard Price. Montreal: Institute for Research on Social Policy, 1979.

Davidson, Gordon Charles. *The North West Company*. New York: Russell and Russell, 1916.

Davis, Arthur K. "Canadian Society and History as Hinterland versus Metropolis." In *Canadian Society: Pluralism, Change and Conflict*, ed. R. Ossenberg. Scarborough, ON: Prentice-Hall, 1971.

Davis, Arthur K. *A Northern Dilemma*. Vol. 2: *Edging Into Mainstream: Urban Indians in Saskatchewan*. Bellingham: Western Washington State College, 1965.

Davis, Arthur K., et al. *A Northern Dilemma*. Vol. 1: *Reference Papers*. Bellingham: Western Washington State College, 1967.

Den Otter, A.A. "Transportation and Transformation: The Hudson's Bay Company, 1857–1885." *Great Plains Quarterly* 3(3) (Summer 1983).

Dene Nation and Métis Association of the NWT. *Public Government for the People of the North*. Yellowknife, The Dene Nation and Métis Association of the NWT, 1982.

Devine, Heather. *The People Who Own Themselves: Aboriginal Ethnogenesis in a Canadian Family, 1660–1900*. Calgary: University of Calgary Press, 2004.

Devine, Marina. "The First Northern Métis: An Overview of the Historical Context for the Emergence of the Earliest Métis in Canada's North." In *Picking up the Threads: Métis History in the Mackenzie Basin*. Métis Heritage Association of the Northwest Territories and Parks Canada – Canadian Heritage, 1998.

Dick, Lyle. "The Seven Oaks Incident and the Construction of a Historical Tradition, 1816–1970." *Journal of the Canadian Historical Association*, n.s., 2 (1991).

Dickason, Olive. "From 'One Nation' in the Northeast to 'New Nation' in the Northwest: A Look at the Emergence of the Métis." In *The New Peoples: Being and Becoming Métis in North America*. Winnipeg: University of Manitoba Press, 1985.

Dinwoodie, David H. "Crossing Borders: Metis Movements on Montana's Flathead Frontier." Paper presented to the Northern Great Plains History Conference, Brandon, MB, 1995.

Dobbin, Murray. "Métis Struggles of the Twentieth Century: The Saskatchewan Métis Society – 1935–1950. Part 1: Early Beginnings." *New Breed*, August 1978.

Dobbin, Murray. "Métis Struggles of the Twentieth Century: The Saskatchewan Métis Society – 1935–1950. Part 2: The Land Issues: Whitemen's Advice and Government Deceit." *New Breed*, September 1978

Dobbin, Murray. "Métis Struggles of the Twentieth Century: The Saskatchewan Métis Society – 1935–1950. Part 3: Political Interference and Internal Divisions." *New Breed*, October 1978.

Dobbin, Murray. "Métis Struggles of the Twentieth Century: The Saskatchewan Métis Society – 1935–1950. Part 4: The Saskatchewan Métis Society – the Final Chapters, 1944–1949." *New Breed*, November–December 1978.

Dobbin, Murray. "Prairie Colonialism: The CCF in Northern Saskatchewan, 1944–1964." *Studies in Political Economy* 16 (1985).

Dobbin, Murray. *The One-And-A-Half Men: The Story of Jim Brady and Malcolm Norris – Metis Patriots of the Twentieth Century*. Vancouver: New Star Books, 1981.

Drouin, Eméric O. *Joyau dans la Plaine: Saint-Paul, Alberta*. Quebec: Paul Nicole, 1968.

Dugast, G. *Histoire de l'Ouest canadien de 1822 à 1869*. Montreal, 1906.

Durnin, Kathy. "Mixed Messages: The Métis in Canadian Literature, 1816–2007." PhD thesis, Comparative Literature, University of Alberta, 2008.

Dusenberry, Verne. "Waiting for a Day That Never Comes: The Dispossessed Métis of Montana." *Montana: The Magazine of Western History* 6 (1958).

Elliot, Jack. "Hivernant Archaeology in the Cypress Hills." MA thesis, University of Calgary, 1971.

Elliott, Alison Goddard. *Roads to Paradise: Reading the Lives of the Early Saints*. Hanover, RI: Brown University Press, 1987.

Ens, Gerhard J. "After the Buffalo: The Reformation of the Turtle Mountain Métis Community, 1879–1905." In *New Faces of the Fur Trade: Selected Papers of the Seventh North American Fur Trade Conference, Halifax, Nova Scotia, 1995*, ed. Jo-Anne Fiske, Susan Sleeper Smith, and William Wicken. East Lansing: Michigan State University Press, 1998.

Ens, Gerhard J. "Gabriel Dumont, Big Bear, and the Indian Rebellion of 1885: The Case of the Peace Hills Reserves, 1884–1885." In *Histoires et identities métisses: homage à Gabriel Dumont / Métis Histories and Identities: A Tribute to*

Gabriel Dumont, ed. Denis Gagnon, Denis Combet, and Lise Gaboury-Diallo. Winnipeg: Presses universitaires de Saint-Boniface, 2009.

Ens, Gerhard J. *Homeland to Hinterland: The Changing Worlds of the Red River Metis in the Nineteenth Century*. Toronto: University of Toronto Press, 1996.

Ens, Gerhard J. "Hybridity, Canadian Indian Policy, and the Construction and 'Extinguishment' of Metis Aboriginal Rights in the Nineteenth Century." In *Reconfiguration of Native North America: An Anthology of New Perspectives*, ed. John R. Wunder and Kurt E. Kinbacher. Lubbock: Texas Tech University Press, 2009.

Ens, Gerhard J. "Prologue to the Red River Resistance: Pre-liminal Politics and the Triumph of Riel." *Journal of the Canadian Historical Association*5(1) (1994).

Ens, Gerhard J. "Taking Treaty 8 Scrip, 1899–1900: A Quantitative Portrait of Northern Alberta Metis Communities." In *Treaty 8 Revisited: Selected Papers on the 1899 Centennial Conference*, ed. Duff Crerar and Jaroslav Petryshyn. Special Issue of *Lobstick: An Interdisciplinary Journal* 1(1) (Winter 1999–2000).

Ervin, Alexander M., and Lorne Holyyoak. "Applied Anthropology in Canada: Historical Foundations, Contemporary Practice, and Policy Potentials." *NAPA Bulletin* 25 (2006).

Evans, Clint. "A History of Metis Activities and Settlement in Manitoba's Southern Interlake Region, 1800–1881." Report prepared for Manitoba Conservation and the Constitutional Law Branch of Manitoba Justice, 14 March 2008.

Evans, Clint. *Report on the Origin and Dissolution of the Papaschase Band*. Edmonton: Department of Justice Canada, Edmonton Regional Office, 27 January 2004.

Ewers, John C. "Ethnological Report on the Chippewa Cree Tribe of the Rocky Boy Reservation and the Little Shell Band of Indians." In *Chippewa Indians VI (American Indian Ethnohistory: North Central and Northeastern Indians)*. Report presented before the Indian Claims Commission. Docket No. 221-B. New York: Garland, 1974.

Flanagan, Thomas. "The Case Against Métis Aboriginal Rights." *Canadian Public Policy* 9(3) (September 1983): 316–17.

Flanagan, Thomas. "Comment on Ken Hatt, The North-West Rebellion Scrip Commissions, 1885–1889." In *1885 and After: Native Society in Transition*, ed. F. Laurie Barron and James Waldram. Regina: University of Regina, 1986.

Flanagan, Thomas E. "The History of Metis Aboriginal Rights: Politics, Principle, and Policy." *Canadian Journal of Law and Society* 5 (1990).

Flanagan, Thomas. *Louis "David" Riel: "Prophet of the New World."* Toronto: University of Toronto Press, 1979. Rev. ed. 1996.

Flanagan, Thomas. *Metis Lands in Manitoba*. Calgary: University of Calgary Press, 1991.

Flanagan, Thomas. "Political Theory of the Red River Resistance: The Declaration of December 8, 1869." *Canadian Journal of Political Science* 11(1) (March 1978).

Flanagan, Thomas. "The Political Thought of Louis Riel." In *Riel and the Métis: Riel Mini-Conference Papers*, ed. A.S. Lussier. Winnipeg: Pemmican, 1979.

Flanagan, Thomas. *Riel and the Rebellion: 1885 Reconsidered*. 2nd ed.. Toronto: University of Toronto Press, 2000.

Flanagan, Thomas, and Gerhard J. Ens. "Metis Land Grants in Manitoba: A Statistical Study." *Histoire sociale / Social History* 27 (May 1994).

Fontaine, John. "St Paul des Métis, 1896 to 1909 – The Dual Roles of the Missionary Oblates of Mary Immaculate." MA project paper, Department of History and Classics, University of Alberta, 2009.

Foster, John. E. "The Métis: The People and the Term." *Prairie Forum* 3(1) (Spring 1978).

Foster, John E. "The Origins of the Mixed Bloods in the Canadian West." In *Essays on Western History: In Honour of Lewis Gwynne Thomas*. Edmonton: University of Alberta Press 1976.

Foster, John E. "The Plains Metis." In *Native Peoples: The Canadian Experience*, ed. R. Bruce Morrison and C. Roderick Wilson. 1st ed. Toronto: Oxford University Press, 1986.

Foster, John E. "Wintering, the Outsider Male and Ethnogenesis of the Western Plains Métis." *Prairie Forum* 19 (Spring 1994).

Foster, John E., and Gerhard J. Ens. "The Metis," *Encyclopaedia of World Cultures*. Vol. 1: *North America*, ed. Timothy J. O'Leary and David Levinson. Boston: G.K. Hall, 1991.

Foster, Martha Harroun. *We Know Who We Are: Métis Identity in a Montana Community*. Norman: University of Oklahoma Press, 2006.

Frank, Andre Gunder. "The Development of Underdevelopment." *Monthly Review Press* 18 (1966).

French, Cecil L. "Social Class and Motivation." In *The Métis in Alberta Society: with Special Reference to Social, Economic and Cultural Factors Associated with Persistently High Tuberculosis Incidence*, ed. B.Y. Card, G.K. Hirabayashi, C.L. French. Edmonton: University of Alberta Press, 1963.

Friesen, Gerald. *The Canadian Prairies: A History*. Toronto: University of Toronto Press, 1984.

Friesen, Joe. "Defining Who Is Indian: A Confusing Question of Identity and Belonging." *Globe and Mail*, 11 January 2013.

Fuller, Patty. "Mayhem among the Metis: The Metis Nation of Alberta Faces Membership-fixing and Corruption Charges." *Alberta Report* 21(2) (1993).

Fumoleau, René. *As Long as This Land Shall Last: A History of Treaty 8 and Treaty 11: 1870–1939.* Toronto: McClelland & Stewart, 1975.

Furniss, Elizabeth. "Challenging the Myth of Indigenous Peoples' 'Last Stand' in Canada and Australia: Public Discourse and the Conditions of Silence." In *Rethinking Settler Colonialism: History and Memory in Australia, Canada, Aoteraroa New Zealand, and South Africa*, ed. Annie E. Coombes. Manchester: Manchester University Press, 2006.

Galloway, Gloria. "Metis Council Opposes Bill Reversing Riel's Conviction: 'Forgive Means Forget': Pardon Would Imply Guilt, Great-niece of Hanged Leader says," *National Post*, 29 March 1999.

Gardner, Dan. "MPs Should Study History, Not Remake It through Law." *Ottawa Citizen*, 11 May 1999.

Garrioch, A.C. *The Correction Line.* Winnipeg: Stovel, 1933.

Gellner, Ernest. *Nations and Nationalism.* Oxford: Blackwell, 1983.

Ghostkeeper, Elmer, and Federation of Métis Settlements. *Metism: A Canadian Identity.* Edmonton: Alberta Federation of Métis Settlements, 1982.

Gilfillan, J.A. "A Trip Through the Red River Valley in 1864." *North Dakota Historical Quarterly* 1(4) (July 1927).

Giraud, Marcel. *Le Métis canadien: son rôle dans l'histoire des provinces de l'Ouest.* 2 vols. Paris: Institut d'ethnologie, 1945.

Giraud, Marcel. *The Métis in the Canadian West.* Translated by George Woodcock. Edmonton: University of Alberta Press, 1986.

Goldring, Philip. *Papers on the Labour System of the Hudson's Bay Company, 1821–1900.* Vol. 2. Parks Canada Manuscript Report No. 142. Ottawa: Parks Canada, 1980.

Gorham, Harriet. "Families of Mixed Descent in the Western Great Lakes Region." In *Native People, Native Lands: Canadian Indians, Inuit and Metis*, ed. Bruce Alden Cox. Ottawa: Carleton University Press, 1991.

Grainger, D., and B. Ross., "Petite Ville Site Survey, Saskatchewan." *Research Bulletin* No. 143. Ottawa: Parks Canada, 1989.

Greene, Ian. "Lessons Learned from Two Decades of Program Evaluation in Canada." In *Evaluation and Accounting Standards in Public Management*, ed. Deitmar Braunig and Peter Eichorn. Baden-Baden: Nomos Verlagsgesellschaft, 2002.

Hacking, Ian. "The Looping Effects of Human Kinds." In *Causal Cognition: A Multidisciplinary Debate*, ed. Dan Sperber, David Premack, and Ann James. Oxford: Clarendon Press, 1995.

Hacking, Ian. " Making Up People." In *Reconstructing Individualism: Autonomy, Individuality, and the Self in Western Thought*, ed. Thomas C. Heller, Morton Sosna, and David E. Wellbery. Stanford: Stanford University Press, 1986.

Hall, D.J. "The Half-Breed Claims Commission." *Alberta History* 25(2) (Spring 1977).

Hambly, J.P. Stan (ed.). *The Battle River County: An Historical Sketch of Duhamel and District.* New Norway, AB: Duhamel Historical Society, 1974

Hämäläinen, Pekka. "Lost in Transition: Suffering, Survival, and Belonging in the Early Modern Atlantic World," *William and Mary Quarterly* 68(2) (April 2011).

Hamilton, John David. *Arctic Revolution: Social Change in the Northwest Territories, 1935–1994.* Toronto: Dundurn Press, 1994.

Handler, Richard, and Jocelyn Linnekin. "Tradition, Genuine or Spurious." *Journal of American Folklore* 97 (1984).

Hanson, F. Allan. "The Making of the Maori: Culture Invention and Its Logic." *American Anthropologist* 91(1989).

Hargrave, J.J. *Red River.* London, 1871.

Harrington, Carolyn. "Sault First Capitol." *Dimensions. Special Editions* 8(3) (1980).

Hatt, Fred K. "The Canadian Métis: Recent Interpretations." *Canadian Ethnic Studies* 3(1) (1971).

Hatt, Ken "Ethnic Discourse in Alberta: Land and the Métis in the Ewing Commission." *Canadian Ethnic Studies* 17(2) (1985).

Hatt, Fred K. *Métis of the Lac la Biche Area. Community Opportunity Assessment.* Edmonton: Human Resources Research and Development, Executive Council, Government of Alberta, 1967.

Hatt, Ken. "The Northwest Scrip Commissions as Federal Policy – Some Initial Findings." In *Canadian Journal of Native Studies* 3(1) (1983).

Hatt, Ken. "The North-West Rebellion Scrip Commissions, 1885–1889." In *1885 and After: Native Society in Transition* , ed. F. Laurie Barron and James Waldram (Regina: Canadian Plains Research Center, University of Regina, 1986).

Hatt, Fred Kenneth. "The Response to Directed Social Change on an Alberta Metis Colony." PhD dissertation, University of Alberta, 1969.

Hedican, Edward J. *Applied Anthropology in Canada: Understanding Aboriginal Issues.* 2nd ed. Toronto: University of Toronto Press, 2008.

Hele, Karl. "Manipulating Identity: The Sault Borderlands Métis and Colonial Intervention." In *The Long Journey of a Forgotten People: Metis Identities and Family Histories*, ed. David McNab and Ute Lischke. Waterloo, ON: Wilfrid Laurier University Press, 2007.

Hill, Judith. "The Ewing Commission, 1935: A Case Study in Metis-Government Relations." Unpublished history honours essay, University of Alberta, 1977.

Hlady, Walter. *Power Structure in a Metis Community.* Saskatoon: Centre for Community Studies, University of Saskatchewan, 1960.

Hlady, Walter M., and B. Ralph Posten. *Appendix II : The People of Indian Ancestry in Rural Manitoba.* Vol. 3 of *The People of Indian Ancestry in Manitoba. A Social and Economic Study.* Under the direction of Jean H. Lagasse. Winnipeg: Department of Agriculture and Immigration, 1959.

Hobsbawm, E.J., and T.O. Ranger (eds). *The Invention of Tradition.* Cambridge and New York: Cambridge University Press, 1983.

Hogue, Michel. "Between Race and Nation: The Plains Métis and the Canada-United States Border." PhD dissertation, University of Wisconsin-Madison, 2009.

Hogue, Michel., "Crossing the Line: The Plains Cree in the Canada-United States Borderlands, 1870–1900." MA thesis, University of Calgary, 2002.

Honigmann, John J. "Social Disintegration in Five Northern Canadian Communities." *Canadian Review of Sociology and Anthropology* 2(4) (1965).

Howard, Joseph Kinsey. *Strange Empire: A Narrative of the Northwest.* New York: William Morrow, 1952.

Hutchinson, Gerald M. Introduction. *The Rundle Journals, 1840–1848.* Calgary: Alberta Records Publications, Historical Society of Alberta and Glenbow-Alberta Institute, 1977.

Hutchinson, John, and Anthony D. Smith (eds) Introduction. *Ethnicity.* Oxford: Oxford University Press, 1996.

Imai, Shin. "Metis Rights." Handout from a conference on Aboriginal law at Osgoode Hall Law School, Toronto, November 1997.

Indian Treaties and Surrenders from 1680 to 1890. Vols 1–3. Ottawa, 1891.

Innis, H.A. *The Fur Trade in Canada.* Rev. ed. Toronto: University of Toronto Press, 1956.

Iribacher-Fox, Stephanie, and the Fort Providence Métis Council. *Since 1921: The Relationship between Dehcho Metis and Canada.* Fort Providence: Fort Providence Métis Council, 2007.

Irwin, Robert. "'A Clear Intention to Effect Such a Modification': The *NRTA* and Treaty Hunting and Fishing Rights." *Native Studies Review* 13(2) (2000).

Irwin, Robert. "'The successful pursuance of that humane and generous policy': Treaty 8 and the Introduction of Indian Policy to the Peace-Athabasca Country." In *Treaty 8 Revisited: Selected Papers on the 1899 Centennial Conference,* ed. Duff Crerar and Jaroslav Petryshyn. Special Issue of *Lobstick: An Interdisciplinary Journal* 1(1) (Winter 1999–2000).

Jaenen, Cornelius. "Miscegenation in Eighteenth Century New France." In *New Dimensions in Ethnohistory: Papers of the Second Laurier Conference on Ethnohistory and Ethnology*, ed. Barry Gough and Laird Christie. Canadian Ethnology Service, Mercury Series Paper 120. Ottawa: Museum of Civilization, 1991.

Janetta, Armando E. *An Introduction to the Politics of Dialogism and Difference in Metis Literature*. Augsburg: Wissner, 2001.

Jarvis, Brad Devin Edward. "A 'Woman Much to be Respected': Madeleine Laframboise and the Redefinition of a Métis Identity." MA thesis, Michigan State University, 1998.

Jetté, Melinda M. "Ordinary Lives: Three Generations of a French-Indian Family in Oregon, 1877–1931." MA thesis, Laval University, 1996.

Judd, Carol M. "Mixed Bloods of Moose Factory, 1730–1981: A Socio-Economic Study." *American Indian Culture and Research Journal* 6(2) (1982).

Judd, Carol M. "Moose Factory Was Not Red River: A Comparison of Mixed Blood Experiences." In *Explorations in Canadian Economic History: Essays in Honour of Irene M. Spry*, ed. Duncan Cameron. Ottawa: University of Ottawa Press, 1985.

Keesing, Roger M. "Creating the Past: Custom and Identity in the Contemporary Pacific." *The Contemporary Pacific* 1(1–2) (1989).

Kennedy, John C. "Aboriginal Organizations and Their Claims: The Case of Newfoundland and Labrador." *Canadian Ethnic Studies* 19(2) (1987).

Kennedy, John C. "The Changing Significance of Labrador Settler Ethnicity," *Canadian Ethnic Studies* 20(3) 1988.

Kennedy, John C. "Métis." Newfoundland and Labrador Heritage website. http://www.heritage.nf.ca/aboriginal/metis.html. Accessed April 2011.

Kennedy, John C. *People of the Bays and Headlands: Anthropological History and the Fate of Communities in the Unknown Labrador*. Toronto: University of Toronto Press, 1995.

Kerri, James N. *The Human Element in Housing: An Evaluation of the Manitoba Remote Housing Program*. Winnipeg: Manitoba Métis Federation, 1971.

Kerri, James N. *Utilization of a Native People's Voluntary Association as a Channel of Communication: The Case of COPE in Inuvik, NWT*. Winnipeg: Department of Manpower and Immigration, Prairie Region, October 1970.

Knight, Alan, and Janet E. Chute. "In the Shadow of the Thumping Drum: The Sault Métis – The People In-between." In *Lines Drawn upon the Water: First Nations on the Great Lakes, Borders and Borderlands*, ed. Karl S. Hele. Waterloo: Wilfrid Laurier University Press, 2008.

Knill, William D., and Arthur K. Davis. "Provincial Education in Northern Saskatchewan: Progress and Bog Down, 1944–1962." In *A Northern Dilemma*.

Vol. 1: *Reference Papers*. Ed. Arthur K. Davis et al. Bellingham: Western Washington State College, 1967.

Lamothe, H. De. *Cinq mois chez les Français d'Amérique: voyage au Canada et à la rivière Rouge du Nord*. Paris: Librairie Hachette, 1879.

Legasse, J.H. *The People of Indian Ancestry in Manitoba*. Winnipeg: Department of Agriculture and Immigration, 1959.

Leslie, John F. *Commissions of Inquiry into Indian Affairs in the Canadas, 1828–1858: Evolving a Corporate Memory for the Indian Department*. Ottawa: Indian Affairs and Northern Development, 1985.

Linnekin, Jocelyn. "Cultural Invention and the Dilemma of Authenticity." *American Anthropologist* 93(1991).

Linnekin, Jocelyn. "Defining Tradition: Variations on the Hawaiian Identity." *American Ethnologist* 10 (1983).

Long, John S. "Treaty No. 9 and Fur Trade Company Families: North Eastern Ontario's Halfbreeds, Indians, Indians, Petitioners and Métis." In the *New Peoples: Being and Becoming Métis in North America*, ed. Jacqueline Peterson and Jennifer S.H. Brown. Winnipeg: University of Manitoba Press, 1983.

Long, John S. *Treaty No. 9: Making the Agreement to Share the Land in Far Northern Ontario in 1905*. Montreal/Kingston: McGill-Queen's University Press, 2010.

Louttit, Neil. "Housing Plea By Metis." *Winnipeg Free Press*, 19 October 1967.

Louttit, Neil. "Indian-Metis Program Discussed: New Organization May Not Include Metis Faction." *Winnipeg Free Press*, 16 October1967.

Louttit, Neil. "Indian Workshop Begins Saturday." *Winnipeg Free Press*, 13 October 1967.

Louttit, Neil. "Metis, Indians Split. Unanimous: Two Groups But One Goal." *Winnipeg Free Press*, 17 October 1967.

Lowenthal, David. *The Heritage Crusade and the Spoils of History*. Cambridge: Cambridge University Press, 1998.

Lutz, Hartmut. *Contemporary Challenges: Conversations with Canadian Native Authors. Interviews Conducted by Hartmut Lutz*. Saskatoon: Fifth House, 1991.

Lysyk, Kenneth M. "The Rights and Freedoms of the Aboriginal Peoples of Canada." In *The Canadian Charter of Rights and Freedoms: Commentary*, ed. Walter S. Tarnopolsky and Gerard A. Beaudoin. Toronto: Carswell, 1982.

MacLaren, I.S. "Creating Travel Literature: The Case of Paul Kane." *Papers of the Bibliographic Society of Canada* 27 (1988).

MacLaren, I.S. "Exploration/Travel Literature and the Evolution of the Author." *International Journal of Canadian Studies / Revue internationale d'études canadiennes* 5 (Spring 1992).

MacLeod, Margaret Arnett. "Bard of the Prairies." *The Beaver* (Spring 1956).

MacLeod, Margaret Arnett. *Songs of Old Manitoba.* Toronto: Ryerson Press, 1960.

MacLeod, Margaret, and W.L. Morton. *Cuthbert Grant of Grantown: Warden of the Plains of Red River.* Toronto: McCelland & Stewart, 1963. Reprinted in the Carleton Library reprint series (no. 71) in 1974 with a new introduction by W.L. Morton.

Madill, Dennis. *Treaty Eight Research Report.* Ottawa: Treaty and Historical Research Centre, Indian and Northern Affairs, 1986.

Magnet, Joseph Eliot. "Metis Land Rights in Canada: Legal Issues." *For Seven Generations: An Information Legacy of the Royal Commission on Aboriginal Peoples.* Ottawa: Libraxus CD-ROM, 1997.

Mailhot, Philippe. "Ritchot's Resistance: Abbé Noël Joseph Ritchot and the Creation and Transformation of Manitoba." PhD dissertation, University of Manitoba, 1986.

Mailhot, P.R., and D.N. Sprague. "Persistent Settlers: The Dispersal and Resettlement of the Red River Metis, 1870–1885." *Canadian Ethnic Studies* 17 (1985).

Mair, Charles. *Through the Mackenzie Basin: An Account of the Signing of Treaty No. 8 and the Scrip Commission, 1899* . Edmonton: University of Alberta Press, 1999; reprint of 1908 edition.

Mandell, Louise, and E. Ann Gilmour. "Metis Land Rights in Canada." *For Seven Generations: An Information Legacy of the Royal Commission on Aboriginal Peoples.* Ottawa: Libraxus CD-ROM, 1997.

Martel, Gilles. *Le méssianisme de Louis Riel.* Waterloo, ON: Canadian Corporation for Studies in Religion and Wilfrid Laurier University Press, 1984.

McCardle, B.E. "The Life and Anthropological Works of Daniel Wilson, 1816–1892." MA thesis, University of Toronto, 1980.

McCrady, David G. "Living with Strangers: The Nineteenth-Century Sioux and the Canadian-American Borderlands." PhD dissertation, University of Manitoba, 1998.

McCrady, David. *Living with Strangers: The Nineteenth-Century Sioux and the Canadian-American Borderlands.* Lincoln: University of Nebraska Press, 2006.

McDougall, Brenda. "Whakootowin: Family and Cultural Identity in Northwestern Saskatchewan Metis Communities." *Canadian Historical Review* 87 (Sept 2006).

McDougall, Brenda. *One of the Family: Metis Culture in Nineteenth-Century Northwestern Saskatchewan.* Vancouver: UBC Press, 2010.

McGuire, Paddy. "Ontario Founder Paddy McGuire Outlines History." *Dimensions. Special Editions* 8(4) (August/September 1980).

Merton, Robert K. "Social Structure and Anomie." *American Sociological Review* 3 (1938).

Métis: The Voice of the Métis Nation of Ontario, n.d. (circa 1994), 1(1).

Morgan, Henry James. *The Canadian Men and Women of the Time: A Hand-book of Canadian Biography of Living Characters*. 2nd ed. Toronto: William Briggs, 1912.

Morice, A.G. *Aux sources de l'histoire manitobaine*. Quebec: Impr. de la Compagnie de L'Événement, 1907.

Morice, A.G. *A Critical History of the Red River Insurrection: After Official Documents and Non-Catholic Sources*. Winnipeg: Canadian Publishers, 1935.

Morice, A.G. *Dictionnaire historique des Canadiens et des Métis français de l'ouest*. Quebec: J.P. Garneau, 1908.

Morice, A.G. *Histoire de l'église catholique dans l'ouest canadien : du lac Supérieur au Pacifique (1659–1915)*. 4 vols. Winnipeg: Author, 1928.

Morice, A.G. *La race Métisse: étude critique en marge d'un livre récent*. Winnipeg: Author, 1938.

Morris, Alexander. *The Treaties of Canada with the Indians of Manitoba and the North-West Territories, Including the Negotiations on Which They Were Based*. Toronto: Belfords, Clarke, 1880.

Morton, A.S. "The New Nation: The Métis," *Transactions of the Royal Society of Canada*, Section II. Ottawa: RSC, 1939.

Morse, Eric. *Fur Trade Canoe Routes of Canada: Then and Now*. Toronto: University of Toronto Press, 1969.

Morton, Arthur S. *A History of the Canadian West to 1870–71*. London: Thomas Nelson, 1939.

Morton, Desmond (ed.). *The Queen v. Louis Riel*. Toronto: University of Toronto Press, 1974.

Morton, W.L. "The Canadian Metis." *The Beaver* (September 1950).

Morton, W.L. *Manitoba: A History*. Toronto: University of Toronto Press, 1957.

Mumford, Jeremy Ravi. "Why Was Louis Riel, a United States Citizen, Hanged as a Canadian Traitor in 1885?" *Canadian Historical Review* 88(2) (June 2007).

Nagel, Joane. *American Indian Ethnic Renewal: Red Power and the Resurgence of Identity and Culture*. Oxford: Oxford University Press, 1996.

Narroll, Raoul. "Ethnic Unit Classification." *Current Anthropology* 5(4) (1964).

Native Council of Canada (NCC). *Native People and the Constitution of Canada: The Report of the Metis and Non-Status Indian Constitutional Review Commission, Commissioner: H.W. Daniels*. Ottawa: Mutual Press, 1981.

Nault, Fred. *Fred Nault: Montana Metis, as told by himself*. Rocky Boy's Reservation, Montana: Chippewa-Cree Research, Rocky Boy School, 1977.

Nicks, Trudy. "Native Responses to the Early Fur Trade at Lesser Slave Lake." In *Le Castor Fait Tout: Selected Papers of the Fifth North American Fur Trade Conference, 1985*, ed. Bruce Trigger, Toby Morantz, and Louise Dechêne. Montreal: Lake St Louis Historical Society, 1987.

Niemi, Melanie. "The Edmonton and District Stragglers: Gendered Strategies of Treaty and Scrip, 1876–1886." MA thesis, University of Northern British Columbia, 2005.

Niemi-Bohun, Melanie. "Colonial Categories and Familial Responses to Treaty and Metis Scrip Policy: The 'Edmonton and District Straggler,' 1870–88." *Canadian Historical Review* 90(1) (March 2009).

North Slave Métis Alliance. "Strong Like Two People: North Slave Métis History." In *Métis Legacy: A Métis Historiography and Annotated Bibliography*, ed. Lawrence J. Barkwell, Leah Dorion, and Darren R. Préfontaine. Winnipeg: Pemmican, 2001.

Nott, J.C., and George R. Gliddon. *Types of Mankind*. Philadelphia: Lippincott, Grambo, 1854.

O'Malley, Martin. *The Past and Future Land: An Account of the Berger Inquiry into the Mackenzie Valley Pipeline*. Toronto: Peter Martin, 1976.

Payne, Michael. *The Most Respectable Place in the Territory: Everyday Life in Hudson's Bay Company Service: York Factory, 1788–1870*. Ottawa: Canadian Parks Service, 1989.

Peel, Bruce. "Falcon, Pierre." In *Dictionary of Canadian Biography Online*.

Peters, Evelyn, Mark Rosenberg, and Greg Halseth. *The Ontario Métis: Characteristics and Identity: Native Issues 4*. Winnipeg: Institute of Urban Studies, University of Winnipeg, 1991.

Peterson, Jacqueline. "Ethnogenesis: Settlement and Growth of a 'New People' in the Great Lakes Region, 1702–1815." *American Indian Culture and Research Journal* 6(2) (1982).

Peterson, Jacqueline. "Many Roads to Red River: Métis Genesis in the Great Lakes Region, 1680–1815." In Peterson and Brown, *The New Peoples*.

Peterson, Jacqueline. "Prelude to Red River: A Social Portrait of the Great Lakes Métis." *Ethnohistory* 25(1) (Winter 1978).

Peterson, Jacqueline, and Jennifer S.H. Brown (eds). *The New Peoples: Being and Becoming Métis in North America*. Winnipeg: University of Manitoba Press, 1985.

Pocklington, T.C. *The Government and Politics of the Alberta Metis Settlements*. Regina: Canadian Plains Research Center, University of Regina, 1991.

Poelzer, Dolores, and Irene Poelzer. *In Our Own Words: Northern Saskatchewan Metis Women Speak Out*. Saskatoon: Lindenblatt & Hamonic, 1986.

Policy and Planning Branch, Native Affairs Secretariat, Province of Alberta. "The Metis Betterment Act: History and Current Status." Background Paper No. 6. March 1985.

Pollard, Juliet Thelma. "The Making of the Metis in the Pacific Northwest – Fur Trade Children: Race, Class, and Gender." PhD dissertation, University of British Columbia, 1990.

Pollock, Katie. "From Borderlands to Bordered Lands: The Plains Metis and the 49th Parallel, 1869–1885." MA thesis, University of Alberta, 2009.

Préfontaine, Darren R., and Karon L. Shmon. "The Sash." *The Virtual Museum of Métis History and Culture*. Gabriel Dumont Institute. http://www.metismuseum.ca/media/document.php/00741.pdf.

Purdy, Chris. "Could Metis Membership Applications Spike after Federal Court Counting?" Canadian Press, 9 January 2013.

Quiring, David. *CCF Colonialism in Northern Saskatchewan: Battling Parish Priests, Bootleggers and Fur Sharks*. Vancouver: UBC Press, 2004.

Racette, Calvin. *Flags of the Métis*. Regina: Gabriel Dumont Institute, 1987.

Racette, Sherry Farrell. "Métis Man or Canadian Icon: Who Owns Louis Riel?" In *Rielisms*, ed. John Boyle, et. al. Winnipeg: Winnipeg Art Gallery, 2001.

Ray, A.J. *"An Economic History of the Robinson Treaties Area Before 1860."* 17 March 1998. Unpublished report.

Redbird, Duke. *We Are Metis: A Metis View of the Development of a Native Canadian People*. Willowdale, ON: Ontario Métis and Non-Status Indian Association, 1980.

Reid, A.P. "The Mixed or 'Halfbreed' Races of North-Western Canada." *Journal of the Anthropological Institute of Great Britain and Ireland* 4 (1875).

Report of the Royal Commission on Aboriginal Peoples. Vol. 1, Pt 3, chap. 15.8, "Ceremonies and Symbols." *For Seven Generations: An Information Legacy of the Royal Commission on Aboriginal Peoples*. Ottawa: Libraxus CD-ROM, 1997

Report of the Royal Commission on Aboriginal Peoples. Vol. 4: *Perspectives and Realities – 5. Metis Perspectives – 2. The Métis Nation*. In *For Seven Generations: An Information Legacy of the Royal Commission on Aboriginal Peoples*. Ottawa: Libraxus CD-ROM, 1997

Rich, E.E. (ed.). *Colin Robertson's Correspondence Book, September 1817 to September 1822*. Toronto: The Champlain Society, 1939.

Rich, E.E. "Colonial Empire." *Economic History Review*, n.s., 2(3) (1950).

Rich, E.E. *Hudson's Bay Company, 1670–1870*. 2 vols. London: Hudson's Bay Record Society, 1958.

Riel, Louis. *The Collected Writings of Louis Riel / Les Écrits complets de Louis Riel*, 5 vols. Gen. ed. George F. Stanley. Edmonton: University of Alberta Press, 1985.

Robinson, H.M. *The Great Fur Land or Sketches of Life in the Hudson's Bay Territory*. New York: G.P. Putnam's Sons, 1879.

Robson, John. "The Perils of Trying to Get History 'Right.'" *National Post*, 11 January 1999.

Ronaghan, Allen. "The Confrontation at Rivière aux Ilets de Bois." *Prairie Forum* 14(1) (Spring 1989).

Ronaghan, Neil Edgar Allen. "The Archibald Administration in Manitoba, 1870–1872." PhD dissertation, University of Manitoba, 1987.

Ross, Eric. *Beyond the River and the Bay*. Toronto: University of Toronto Press, 1970.

Royal Commission on Aboriginal Peoples (RCAP) *Report of the Royal Commission on Aboriginal Peoples*. 5 vols. Ottawa: Government of Canada, 1996.

Salisbury, R., et al. *Development and James Bay: Socio-economic Implications of the Hydro-electric Project*. Montreal: McGill University Press, 1972.

Sanders, Douglas E. "Aboriginal Peoples and the Constitution." *Alberta Law Review* 19 (1981).

Sawchuk, Joe. *The Dynamics of Native Politics: The Alberta Metis Experience*. Saskatoon: Purich, 1998.

Sawchuk, Joe. "The Metis, Non-Status Indians and the New Aboriginality: Government Influence on Native Political Alliances and Identity." In *Readings in Aboriginal Studies*. Vol. 2: *Identities and State Structures*, ed. Joe Sawchuk. Brandon: Bearpaw Press, 1992.

Sawchuk, Joe. *The Metis of Manitoba: Reformulation of an Ethnic Identity*. Toronto: Peter Martin, 1978.

Sawchuk, Joe, Patricia Sawchuk, and Theresa Ferguson. *Metis Land Rights in Alberta: A Political History*. Edmonton: Métis Association of Alberta, 1981.

Scott, D.C. "Indian Affairs 1840–1867." In *Canada and Its Provinces: A History of the Canadian People and Their Institutions*. Vol. 5. Toronto: Constable, at the Edinburgh University Press for the Publishers' Association of Canada, 1913.

Scott, D.C. "Indian Affairs, 1867–1913." In *Canada and Its Provinces*. Vol. 7. Toronto, 1913.

Sealey. D. Bruce, and Antoine S. Lussier. *The Metis: Canada's Forgotten People*. Winnipeg: Pemmican, 1981.

Sidbury, James, and Jorge Cañizares-Esguerra. "Mapping Ethnogenesis in the Early Modern Atlantic." *William and Mary Quarterly* 68(2) (April 2011), 181–208.

Simpson, George. *An Overland Journey Round the World during the Years 1841 and 1842*. Philadelphia: Lea and Blanchard, 1847.

Sleeper-Smith, Susan. "Furs and Female Kin Networks: The World of Marie Madeleine Réaume L'archevêque Chevalier." In *New Faces of the Fur Trade: Selected Papers of the Seventh North American Fur Trade Conference, Halifax, Nova Scotia, 1995*, ed. Jo-Anne Fiske, Susan Sleeper-Smith, and William Wicken. East Lansing: Michigan State University Press, 1998.

Sleeper-Smith, Susan. *Indian Women and French Men: Rethinking Cultural Encounters in the Western Great Lakes.* Amherst: University of Massachusetts Press, 2001.

Sleeper-Smith, Susan. "Women, Kin, and Catholicism: New Perspectives on the Fur Trade." *Ethnohistory* 47 (1) (Spring 2000).

Slobodin, Richard. *Metis of the Mackenzie District.* Ottawa: Canadian Research Centre for Anthropology, Saint-Paul University, 1966.

Smith, Anthony D. *The Nation in History: Historiographical Debates about Ethnicity and Nationalism*. Cambridge: Polity Press, 2000.

Smith, Stephen. "Riel Still a Traitor, Professor Insists." *Ottawa Citizen*, 7 January 1998.

Smythe, Terry. "Thematic Study of the Fur Trade in the Canadian West, 1670–1870." Agenda Paper 1968-29. Historic Sites and Monuments Board, St John's, NL, 19–21 June 1968.

Sorrensen, M.P.K. *Maori Origins and Migrations. The Genesis of Some Pakeha Myths*. Auckland: Auckland University Press, 1979.

Spaulding, Philip Taft. "The Metis of Île-à-la-Crosse." PhD dissertation, University of Washington, 1970.

Spaulding, Philip Taft. "The Social Integration of a Northern Community: White Mythology and Metis Reality." In *A Northern Dilemma:* Vol. 1: *Reference Papers*, ed. A.K. Davis. Bellingham: Western Washington State College, 1967.

Sprague, D.N. "An Administrative History of Metis Claims." *For Seven Generations: An Information Legacy of the Royal Commission on Aboriginal Peoples*. Ottawa: Libraxus CD-ROM, 1997.

Sprague, D.N. *Canada and the Metis, 1869–1885*. Waterloo, ON: Wilfrid Laurier University Press, 1988.

Sprague, D.N. "Dispossession vs. Accommodation in Plaintiff vs. Defendant Accounts of Métis Dispersal from Manitoba, 1870–1881." *Prairie Forum* 16(2) (Fall 1991).

Sprague, D.N. "The Manitoba Land Question, 1870–1882." *Journal of Canadian Studies* 15(3) (1982).

Stanley, George F.G. "Alberta's Half-breed Reserve Saint-Paul-des-Métis, 1896–1909." In *The Other Natives: Les Métis*. Vol. 2, ed. Antoine S. Lussier and D. Bruce Sealey. Winnipeg: Manitoba Métis Federation Press, 1978.

Stanley, George F.G. *The Birth of Western Canada: A History of the Riel Rebellions.* London: Longmans, Green, 1936.

Stanley, George F.G. *Louis Riel.* Toronto: Ryerson Press, 1963.

Stanley, G.F.G. "The Metis and the Conflict of Cultures in Western Canada." *Canadian Historical Review* 28(4) (December 1947).

Stanton, William. *The Leopard's Spots: Scientific Attitudes toward Race in America, 1815–59.* Chicago: University of Chicago Press, 1960.

Stocking, George W. "The Persistence of Polygenist Thought in Post-Darwinian Anthropology." In *Race, Culture, and Evolution: Essays in the History of Anthropology.* Chicago: University of Chicago Press, 1982.

Stokell, Samantha. "Fort Smith Woman Designs New Metis Sash," *Slave River Journal*, 4 November 2009.

Stonechild, Blair, and Bill Waiser. *Loyal till Death: Indians and the North-West Rebellion.* Calgary: Fifth House, 1997.

St-Onge, Nicole. *Saint-Laurent, Manitoba: Evolving Métis Identities, 1850–1914.* Regina: Canadian Plains Research Center, University of Regina, 2004.

St-Onge, Nicole. "Plains Métis: Contours of an Identity." *Australasian Canadian Studies* 27(1–2) (2009).

Street, W.P.R. "The Commission of 1885 to the North-West Territories." Edited by H.H. Langton. *Canadian Historical Review* 25(1) (March 1944).

Surtees, Robert. "Canadian Indian Treaties." In *Handbook of North American Indians.* Vol. 4: *History of Indian-White Relations*, ed. Wilcomb Washburn. Washington, DC: Smithsonian, 1988.

Surtees, Robert J. "Canadian Indian Policies." In *Handbook of North American Indians.* Vol. 4: *History of Indian-White Relations*, ed. Wilcomb E. Washburn. Washington, DC: Smithsonian, 1988.

Surtees, Robert J. "Treaty Research Report: The Robinson Treaties (1850)." Ottawa: Treaty and Historical Research Centre, Indian and Northern Affairs, 1986. Online at https://www.aadnc-aandc.gc.ca/DAM/DAM-INTER-HQ/STAGING/texte-text/trerob_1100100028975_eng.pdf.

Sutherland, Donna G. *Peguis: A Noble Friend.* St Andrews: Chief Peguis Heritage Park, 2003.

Swan, Elizabeth. "A Brief History of the First Catholic Pioneers of Lewistown." In *The Heritage Book of the Original Fergus County Area – The Heritage Book of Central Montana*, ed. Babbie Deal and Loretta McDonald. Lewiston: 1st Bank of Lewiston, 1976.

Sweet, James. "The Quiet Violence of Ethnogenesis." *William and Mary Quarterly* 68(2) (April 2011): 209–14.

Taché, Alexandre. *Histoire et origine des troubles du N.-Ouest: racontées sous serment par Sa Grandeur Mgr. L'archevêque de St-Boniface.* 1874.

Taché, Alexander. *Sketch of the North-West of America by Mgr. Taché, Bishop of St Boniface, 1868.* Translated by Captain D.R. Cameron. Montreal, 1870.

Taylor, Herbert C. "The Parameters of a Northern Dilemma." In *A Northern Dilemma.* Vol. 1: *Reference Papers,* ed. Arthur K. Davis, Vernon C. Serl, and Philip T. Spaulding. Bellingham: Western Washington State College, 1967.

Teillet, Jean. "MNC Definition of 'Metis' Submitted by the Metis Rights Panel." Manuscript. Draft for Discussion, Métis National Council, 12 September 1999.

Teton County: A History. Choteau: Teton County Historical Committee, 1988.

Thorne, Tanis C. *The Many Hands of My Relations: French and Indians on the Lower Missouri,* Columbia and London: University of Missouri Press, 1996.

Tough, Frank. *"As Their Natural Resources Fail": Native People and the Economic History of Northern Manitoba, 1870–1930.* Vancouver: UBC Press, 1996.

Tough, Frank, and Leah Dorian. "*the claims of the Half-breeds … have been finally closed:* A Study of Treaty Ten and Treaty Five Adhesion Scrip." *For Seven Generations: An Information Legacy of the Royal Commission on Aboriginal Peoples.* Ottawa: Libraxus CD-ROM, 1997.

Trémaudan, Auguste-Henri de. *Histoire de la nation métisse dans L'Ouest canadien.* Montreal: Éditions Albert Lévesque, 1935.

Trémaudan, Auguste-Henri de. *La Sang Français.* Winnipeg, 1919.

Trémaudan, Auguste-Henri de. "Letter of Louis Riel and Ambroise Lépine to Lieutenant Governor Morris, January 3, 1873." *Canadian Historical Review* 7(2) (1926).

Trémaudan, Auguste-Henri de. "Louis Riel and the Fenian Raid of 1871," *Canadian Historical Review* 4(2) (1923).

Trémaudan, Auguste-Henri de. "Louis Riel's Account of the Capture of Fort Garry, 1870." *Canadian Historical Review* 5(2) (1924).

Trigger, Bruce. "*Prehistoric Man* and Daniel Wilson's Later Canadian Ethnology." In Marinell Ash et al., *Thinking with Both Hands: Sir Daniel Wilson in the Old World and the New,* ed. Elizabeth Hulse. Toronto: University of Toronto Press, 1999.

Tully, James. *Strange Multiplicity: Constitutionalism in an Age of Diversity.* Cambridge: Cambridge University Press, 1995.

Turner, John Peter. *The North-West Mounted Police, 1873–1893.* Ottawa: King's Printer, 1950.

Valentine, V.F. *A Social Anthropological Study of the Metis Population of Northwestern Saskatchewan – Preliminary Report.* Regina: Saskatchewan Department of Natural Resources, 12 September 1953.

Valentine, V.F. "Some Problems of the Metis of Northern Saskatchewan." *Canadian Journal of Economics and Political Science* 20(1) (1954).

Valentine, V.F., and R.G. Young. "The Situation of the Métis of Northern Saskatchewan in Relation to His Physical and Social Development." *Canadian Geographer* 4 (1954).

Valentine, V.F. *The Métis of Northern Saskatchewan*. Ottawa: Department of Natural Resources. 1955.

Van der Mark, Christine. *In Due Season: A Novel*. Toronto: Oxford University Press, 1947.

Van Kirk, Sylvia. *Many Tender Ties: Women in Fur-Trade Society, 1670–1870*. Winnipeg: Watson & Dwyer, 1980.

Verrette, Michel. "Trémaudan, Auguste-Henri de." In *Dictionary of Canadian Biography Online*.

Watkins, Mel (ed.). *Dene Nation: The Colony Within*. Toronto, University of Toronto Press, 1977.

Weaver, Sally M. "Towards a Comparison of National Political Organizations of Indigenous Peoples: Australia, Canada and Norway." Manuscript. Lecture Series at the Institute of Social Sciences, University of Tromsø, Tromsø, Norway, 19–20 October 1983.

Weekes, Mary. *The Last Buffalo Hunter*. New York: Thomas Nelson, 1939

Weinstein, J. "Metis Land Rights Research Project – Conclusion." *For Seven Generations: An Information Legacy of the Royal Commission on Aboriginal Peoples*. Ottawa: Libraxus CD-ROM, 1997.

Weinstein, J. "Metis Land Rights Research Project – Introduction." *For Seven Generations: An Information Legacy of the Royal Commission on Aboriginal Peoples*. Ottawa: Libraxus CD-ROM, 1997.

Weinstein, John. *Quiet Revolution West: the Rebirth of Metis Nationalism*. Calgary: Fifth House, 2007.

Widder, Keith R. *Battle for the Soul: Métis Children Encounter Evangelical Protestants at Mackinaw Mission, 1823–1837*. East Lansing: Michigan State University Press, 1999.

Wilson, Daniel. "Displacement and Extinction Among the Primeval Races of Man," *Canadian Journal*, n.s., 1(1) (1856).

Wilson, Daniel. "Hybridity and Absorption in Relation to the Red Indian Race." *Canadian Journal*, n.s., 14(88) (July 1875).

Wohlberg,Meagan "North Slave Métis Denied Land Claim: Feds Say North Slave Métis Alliance Not 'Distinct, Rights-Holding' Aboriginal Government." *Northern Journal*, 22 April 2013. http://norj.ca/2013/04/north-slave-metis-denied-land-claim/.

Woodcock, George. *Gabriel Dumont: The Metis Chief and His Lost World*. Edmonton, AB: Hurtig, 1975.

Worsley, Peter M., H.L. Buckley, and A.K. Davis. *Economic and Social Survey of Northern Saskatchewan*. Interim Report No. 1. Saskatoon: Research Division, Centre for Community Studies, University of Saskatchewan, 1961.

Wyman, Mark. *The Wisconsin Frontier*. Bloomington: Indiana University Press, 1998.

Young, Robert J.C. *Colonial Desire: Hybridity in Theory, Culture and Race*. London: Routledge, 1995.

Index

www.ingramcontent.com/pod-product-compliance
Lightning Source LLC
LaVergne TN
LVHW020434080826
844660LV00033B/1283